COINAGE AND HISTORY OF THE ROMAN EMPIRE

COINAGE AND HISTORY OF THE ROMAN EMPIRE

C. 82 B.C. – A.D. 480

VOLUME I: HISTORY

David L. Vagi

CoinWorld

SIDNEY, OHIO

First Edition Published 1999 by
Amos Press, Inc.
P.O. Box 150
Sidney, Ohio 45365-0150

Published as two volumes:
Volume One: ISBN: 0-944945-29-5
Volume Two: ISBN: 0-944945-31-7
The Set: ISBN: 0-944945-32-5

Library of Congress Cataloging-in-publication data available

Permission to use illustrations was granted by the following companies: Classical Numismatic Group, Inc.; Leu Numismatik; Numismatic Fine Arts, Inc.; Numismatica Ars Classica; Sotheby's (New York and London); Münzen und Medaillen; Italo Vecchi, Ltd.; and Superior Galleries.

And by the following individuals: Rick Witschonke, David Hendin and the author.

Certain numismatic numbering systems are referenced by kind permission of British Museum Publications, Bibliothèque nationale de France, Cambridge University Press, The Danish National Museum, Dumbarton Oaks Research Library and Collection, David Hendin, and Spink and Son, Ltd.

Book design, typography and pre-press by Studio 31, Inc.

Printed in the U.S.A.

Dedicated in Living Memory
to
ESTHER IVANKA
1915–1996

Table of Contents

Acknowledgments and Credits

Were it practical to do so, this section would be as long as the book itself. After all, knowledge does not materialize from thin air. Thanks must first be given to the historians of antiquity, whose writings provide the basis of our knowledge, and to those who produced the coins which are the focus of this work. Every word in this book has a source, however remote, and even those portions which may come under the heading of 'original thought' are hardly original, for such ideas can only be developed in the context of existing knowledge. Now, to acknowledge some specific debts.

Contributions: Of the many people who contributed to this book, there are five to whom I am most deeply indebted. Foremost are Robert Hoge and Jim Wasserman, both of whom suffered with me since the start of this project. My mentor Robert Hoge, curator at the American Numismatic Association, reviewed every page of the text with selfless dedication. He searched for errors — large and small, conceptual and technical — and offered invaluable advice and encouragement. His considerable talents as a numismatist, historian, literary stylist and grammarian (in both English and Latin) were put to full use. The book's designer, James Wasserman, took on the project as if it were a personal jihad, not just another job. His eye for composition and his attention to detail have made this book appear magnificent even when its contents fall short. His dedication far exceeded any normal expectations, and all who find the book pleasant to the eye owe a hearty thanks to Jim. I am also deeply indebted to three other of my colleagues — Alan Walker, Curtis Clay and Victor England — each of whom made important contributions. Though their impacts cannot be fully appreciated without comparing the final product to early drafts which they reviewed, the reader may rest assured that without their help this would have been a significantly flawed work.

Thanks are also due to those who contributed in their areas of specialty: Rick Witschonke (the Imperatorial period), Matthew Kreuzer (the Julio-Claudians; and especially in helping advance the idea of Livilla on coinage), Kerry Wetterstrom (Roman Egypt), Lawrence Adams (Kingdom of the Bosporus) and Richard McAlee and Michel Prieur (Roman Antioch). I am also indebted to Herb Kreindler and Dennis Kroh, both of whom reviewed extensive portions of the book. For their help in a variety of matters I would like to thank Lawrence Adams, Marty Armstrong, James Beach, Simon Bendall, John Bergman, Harlan and Aaron Berk, Mike Bezayiff, Lucien Birkler, Jan Blamberg, Eldert Bontekoe, John Burnham,

Tom Cederlind, Greg Cole, Thomas Curtis, Ben Damsky, Kirk Davis, the Davisson's, Ralph DeMarco, Nick Economopoulos, Tom Eden, Rob and Tory Freeman, Eric Gold, Ira Goldberg, Dieter Gorny, Michael Harlan, David Hendin, Silvia Hurter, Stephen Huston, Bill Kalmbach, Jonathan Kern, Frank Kovacs, Matthew Kreuzer, Brian Kritt, Dennis and Desiree Kroh, Peter Lampinen, Hubert Lanz, John Lavender, Cathy Lorber, Constantin Marinescu, Eric McFadden, William Metcalf, David Michaels, David Miller, Barry Murphy, Wilhelm Müseler, John Pett, Rick and Kent Ponterio, Paul Rabin, Steve Rubinger, Roberto and Arturo Russo, Arnold Saslow, John Saunders, Wayne Sayles, David Sear, Fred Shore, Jon Subak, Richard Swan, Tom Tesoriero, David Tripp, John Twente, Italo Vecchi, Hans Voegtli, Edward Waddell, Bill Warden and Kerry Wetterstrom. Special thanks are due to all of the researchers who have produced auction catalogs with useful notations. To those who, in error, I have failed to thank, I offer my sincere apologies; rest assured that my gratitude is not diminished because of the oversight.

For the encouragement and practical advice that transformed this project from an idea into a going concern, I am indebted entirely to David Hendin, who freely shared his expertise in both publishing and numismatics. For initiating the process with Amos Press I thank Beth Deisher and Brad Reed, both of whom saw promise in my proposal. For carefully reviewing the text for syntactic errors I am indebted to Suellen Ruttkay and Bill Gibbs of Coin World and to Casey Corsa. Thanks are also due to Ann Marie Aldrich and Bill Corsa, whose patience and confidence — through understandably strained at times — were essential to the success of this project.

I am thankful beyond measure to Al, Marsha, Jean-Paul, Brian, Pratima, Jim, Mehrdad, VPJ and HCM for their constant mental support throughout this project. Equally important to the success of the project were all of the friends and relatives with whom I was in less-frequent communication. Without exception they offered encouragement when it was needed and were accepting of my unattentiveness. Finally, cheers to David Sear, whose immensely useful Roman Coins and Their Values has proven for more than three decades that a book of this kind is not only useful, but essential.

Valuations: For teaching me how to evaluate the quality and the market value of ancient coins I am principally indebted to Ira Goldberg. Were it not for the training I received from him, these values no doubt would be less useful. To assure a greater degree of consistency and accuracy, input on the values was solicited from several of my colleagues whose anonymity is preserved. All final decisions about the values were made independently by the author.

Illustrations: Without photographs, this work would be considerably less useful. Enough thanks cannot be given to Classical Numismatic Group, Inc., whose senior directors, Victor England and Eric McFadden allowed the use of illustrations from their auction catalogs. Additionally, the principals of CNG and of Freeman & Sear generously granted permission to use photographs from the catalogs of Numismatic Fine Arts, Inc. Equally important were the photographic contributions of my valued colleagues at Leu Numismatik (Zürich), Numismatica Ars Classica (Zürich), Sotheby's (New York and London), Münzen und Medaillen (Basel), Italo Vecchi, Ltd. (London) and Superior Galleries (Beverly Hills). Additional illustrations were provided by Rick Witschonke, Virginia Janssen, David Hendin and the author; line drawings were largely copied from antique books.

Sources

Many sources — primary and secondary — were used to gather information for this book. Some of the primary sources consulted were Tacitus' *Histories and Annals*, Suetonius' *De vita Caesarum* ('The Twelve Caesars'), the *Historia Augusta*, (seemingly by one author in the age of Theodosius or by several authors, collectively known as the *Scriptores Historiae Augustae*, during the ages of Diocletian and Constantine the Great), Cassius Dio's *Roman History* and Livy's *Ab urbe condita libri*. The works of other ancient historians and chroniclers, such as Aurelius Victor, Eusebius, Eutropius, Festus, Herodian, Lactantius, Zosimus, Ammianus Marcellinus, Saint Augustine, Saint Athanasius, Candidus, Joannes Antiochenus, Josephus, Malchus, Olympiodorus, Priscus, Zonoras, etc., were also invaluable. The secondary sources most frequently consulted were: Michael Crawford's *Roman Republican Coinage*, the 10 volumes of *The Roman Imperial Coinage* (various authors), *Roman Provincial Coinage*, Volume I (with supplement) by Burnett, Amandry and Ripollès, the *Catalog of Late Roman Coins in the Dumbarton Oaks Collection and in the Whittemore Collection* by Grierson and Mays, the 29 volumes of *A Catalog of the Greek Coins in the British Museum* (various authors), the *Oxford Classical Dictionary*, *The Magistrates of the Roman Republic* by T.R.S. Broughton, several works of Michael Grant (especially *The Roman Emperors*), Chris Scarre's *Chronicle of the Roman Emperors*, Clive Foss's *Roman Historical Coins*, Kenneth Harl's *Coinage in the Roman Economy*, John Melville Jones's *A Dictionary of Ancient Roman Coins*, and the *Atlas of the Roman World* by Cornell and Matthews. Hundreds of other books, articles and commentaries in auction catalogs were consulted, all of which have greatly enriched this work. A listing of many of these is provided in the bibliography.

Foreword

Everyone interested in the history and coinage of the ancient Romans will find many features to enjoy in the wonderfully comprehensive work undertaken by David Vagi. The capsule biographies of each coin-issuing individual are authoritative. Every biography has been designed to stand on its own in providing full and appropriate background information for putting the individual's place in history into perspective. Indeed, the author has not shied away from running the risk of redundancy in order to give the reader as complete as possible a presentation for each one, so that it can stand alone for those seeking data relating exclusively to a specific person. Information has been compiled from all sources, and from the best and most recent studies.

The other portions of this richly-crafted work are no less fully realized. Readers will find solid, up-to-date surveys of all numismatic aspects and will appreciate the care and skill devoted to every section of interest to collectors: interpretation, value, population, aesthetics . . .

This impressive tome has earned a prominent place on the shelf of anyone with an interest in Roman coinage. I know schools and libraries will find frequent use for it as well. Mr. Vagi is to be congratulated on a job well done.

Robert W. Hoge
Colorado Springs, Colorado
May, 1999

Author's Preface

The purpose of this book is two-fold: to provide numismatists with a study of Rome and its coinage which will enrich their avocation, and to afford historians the opportunity to appreciate the role of coinage in the Roman world. For these reasons, the story of Rome has been given a more prominent place than is usually found in numismatic references. After all, of what significance are coins without context?

The main reason people collect Roman coins is that they allow us, in some small way, to make a connection with a vanished world. This desire is no modern invention, for the ancients were also collectors of antiques. Pliny the Elder, in his *Historia Naturalis*, informs us that Rome's first emperor, Augustus, was a collector of antique and foreign coins. Two millenia later we can only imagine the silver decadrachms of Syracuse and the gold staters of Alexander the Great that he gave to friends as gifts.

At the other end of the spectrum we may shudder to think of the millions of ancient coins that have been unearthed over the centuries only to be melted for their bullion content. The reasons are manifold: sometimes possessing such 'antique' items is illegal; other times it is simply easier for the finder to reap his reward by converting coins into anonymous bricks of metal.

For all its inherent conflicts, a well-established collector market preserves ancient coins to a far-greater degree than it destroys them. Though much scholarship must be conducted after-the-fact, this is still preferable to having nothing at all to study. If ancient objects had no value above and beyond the intrinsic, the vast majority would end up in the melting pot, preventing any opportunity for study.

Thus, in an era when international legislation threatens the very foundation of collecting, collectors must remain focused on the true purpose of acquisition. These coins are not merely artifacts, or objects of value, but ambassadors of culture. After all, if Roman coins could only be seen in the pages of books or behind museum glass, would we be so motivated to learn about them? Or, for that matter, about the Roman Empire? Certainly not. The tangibility of such objects would escape us, and as a consequence, so might our fascination with their creation.

This book began as a modest project of perhaps 300 or 400 pages. As work progressed it became evident that a larger book would be required to tell the story of Rome and its coinage in any detail. As the level of research deepened, the page-count increased, deadlines were surpassed, and anticipations grew. The final deadline was an auspicious one: The Ides of March, 1999. Had I known in advance the amount of suffering required to bring this project to fruition — I must confess — I am not certain I would have penned the first word. But it was my intention from the outset to make a lasting contribution to a field which has provided me with countless hours of enjoyment. I hope that the final product was worth the herculian effort it required.

Over the years I have happily worked with ancient coins as a dealer, collector, cataloger, researcher, writer and consultant. As I intend to remain active in all of these areas, I invite serious enquiries regarding any of those capacities at the following address:

DAVID L. VAGI
P.O. Box 20155
Greeley Square Station
New York, NY 10001-0002

How to Use this Book

The book is divided into two volumes and is comprised of three main sections:

Volume I: History of the Roman Empire

- Biographies and historical introductions

Volume II: Coinage of the Roman Empire

- Part One: Numismatic Introduction
- Part Two: Catalog and Tables of Values

Biographies. The history of Rome from Sulla through the death of Julius Nepos is divided into 13 chapters based on individual epochs (with the three 'Separatist Empires' of the 3rd Century being discussed in a chapter of their own). The strictly chronological order of presentation changes with the death of Jovian in A.D. 364: the remainder of the Empire is discussed in two chapters, one for the Eastern and one for the Western Roman Empire. Within these separate chapters, the discussions follow the same chronological order as the earlier biographies.

A general introduction is given for each period. When necessary, the introduction is supplemented with an historical overview, family tree or a chronology table. The biographies are as comprehensive as possible within the practicial limitations of this work. Much of the latest scholarship has been incorporated, which sometimes alters the conclusions to which collectors have long been accustomed. The biographies have been written to stand alone, but they are most useful when read along with related biographies. The individual biographies are most often followed by sections entitled *Numismatic Notes*, which contain information about the subject's coins.

Numismatic Introduction. This section, which opens with a general introduction, is devoted to the coinage itself. Specialized sections on denominations, deities and personifications, determining the dates of coins, obverse types, reverse types, mints and mint marks, and how to determine market value follow. The last section (which includes a photo-grading guide) is vital for understanding how the values presented in the catalog apply to individual coins.

Coin Catalog: This final section is a listing of coins and their market values. For a detailed description, see the introduction in Volume II.

HISTORY OF THE ROMAN EMPIRE

Biographies

CHAPTER ONE

Collapse of the Republic (Imperatorial Period) c. 82–27 B.C.

During the six decades from the beginning of the Social War to the Battle of Actium, there occurred a gradual decay of Rome's traditional Republican form of government. The order of the old Republic — an elitist oligarchy — was replaced by the lawlessness of warlords who, when necessary, openly opposed the senate by force of arms. Men such as Sulla, Marius, Pompey, Caesar, Antony and Octavian all struggled for the top position in a government that was destined to become a virtual hereditary monarchy. What follows is a general framework of this turbulent era, which often is called the Imperatorial Period.

91–88 B.C. — The Social War. From 91–88 B.C., Italians were engaged in the "Social War," in which some non-Roman Italians — who had long been refused Roman citizenship — founded their own Italic senate and initiated hostilities against Rome. It was a traumatic time for the Romans. In the year 90 B.C. they struck more denarii than at any other time in the Republic. Furthermore, they raised more legions than at any other time except during the war against Hannibal. In 88 B.C., the allies even appealed to Mithradates VI of Pontus for military support, but received only some financial assistance. Eventually Rome earned a "victory" by conceding to their enemies' demands. All Italians were granted citizenship in 88 B.C., though the promise was not fully enacted until 70 B.C. In the aftermath of this war, Pompey Strabo, father of Pompey the Great, refused to disband his armies, and resisted the senate's attempt to disarm him forcibly. Along with equally lawless acts by Sulla, this set the stage for dozens of other men to act beyond the authority vested in them by the senate.

88–82 B.C. — The wars among Sulla, Marius and Mithradates VI. On the very heels of the Social War, a conflict of dire consequence arose in Asia Minor, where the Pontic king Mithradates VI opposed Roman rule with the aid of Greeks in Asia. The so-called "First Mithradatic War" began in 88 B.C. with an event that shocked the western world: Mithradates ordered the slaughter of all Romans living in Asia Minor. In a single night, 80,000 Romans were butchered. Though this should have caused Romans to unite, it instead created a division. The senate gave command of the war against Mithradates to Lucius Cornelius Sulla, but the people of

Rome opposed that decision, usurped the senate and instead gave the command to Marius. Thus, Sulla first waged war in Rome itself, ousted Marius and re-established the authority of the senate. He then went East to restore Asia in the name of Rome. Meanwhile, Marius and his supporters, Cinna and Carbo, returned to Rome and initiated a reign of terror :hat lasted until Sulla's return in 83/82 B.C. Meanwhile, Sulla was winning hard-fought victories over Mithradates in Greece, though rivalries with competing Republican generals Flaccus and Fimbria complicated matters. Finally, in 85 B.C., Sulla made peace with Mithradates at Dardanus. Thereafter he toured Greece and Asia, exacting revenge, seizing booty and establishing his own extraordinary authority.

82–79 B.C. — Sulla's Dictatorship. Sulla returned from the East in 83, and with the help of Crassus and Pompey the Great was able to defeat the remaining adherents to the Marian party (including the Samnites and the Lucans) at the Battle of the Colline Gate in 82 B.C., and subsequently in Spain. Thus began Sulla's dictatorship, and along with it the first Roman coinage that comes under the familiar term "Imperatorial." In the meantime Mithradates VI had renewed war against the Romans (83 to 81 B.C., the "Second Mithradatic War"). However, this time Sulla had Lucius Licinius Murena, the propraetor of Asia who had agitated Mithradates into action, conduct the war. During the three years Sulla exercised dictatorial powers, he fought to re-establish the authority of the senate, thus to return power to the privileged families. In the process many were executed, including some 90 senators and 2,600 equestrians. Sulla further restructured the terms of high political office, including the requirement that consuls and praetors must leave Rome and govern a province after their term ended. Sulla held his last consulship in 80 B.C.; he abdicated his dictatorship in 79 B.C. and retired, dying a year later.

82–67 B.C. — The Rise of Pompey. When Sulla returned from the East and ousted the Marians, an important command was given to Pompey the Great, who defeated armies of the Marian party in Sicily and North Africa. It was during these campaigns that he received both a triumph and the honorary title *Magnus* ("the Great"). Even after the abdication (79 B.C.) and subsequent death of Sulla, adherents to the Marian party remained active in Spain. Pompey spent 77 to 71 B.C. in Spain restoring senatorial authority in this important province. In 73 B.C. a devastating slave revolt erupted in Capua under the leadership of Spartacus, and it grew to such proportions that Rome itself was nearly sacked. The slave armies traveled the length of Italy twice, defeating every consular army sent against them. However, the slave army was defeated in Apulia in 72

B.C. by an army led by Crassus. This important victory had been earned by Crassus, but Pompey — seeking his share of glory — returned from Spain in 71 to stamp out the tattered remnants of the slave army. This angered Crassus, who not only had to share the credit of victory, but also the consulship of 70 with the upstart Pompey. Together they revoked many laws of Sulla (whom, ironically, they both had supported upon his return from the East in 83 B.C.), thus allowing common people to hold office.

67–60 B.C. — Pompey's glory. Once matters had been settled in Rome, Pompey next tackled two serious tasks. The first was piracy in the Mediterranean, against which he was given extraordinary authority (*imperium extraordinarium*) in 67 B.C. With great efficiency, Pompey eliminated piratical activity. He was next given command in the East against Mithradates, who had been waging a Third Mithradatic War since 74 B.C. Though previous generals had failed to crush Mithradates, Pompey was able to defeat the eastern monarch on the Euphrates and in 64 began to reorganize the entire eastern portion of Roman territories. Pontus, Cilicia and Syria became provinces and client kingdoms were established in Armenia, Cappadocia, Colchis, Galatia and Judaea. In the process, Pompey generously gave land to his own veterans, an overture that did not please the senate, which opposed it upon his return. However, for all Pompey gave away to his soldiers, he brought back to Rome an astounding amount of loot from the East, which enabled the Republic to become solvent for the first time in recent memory. Italy itself had not been without its crises in the meantime, for during the consulship of Cicero the conspiracy of Catiline had ended in bloodshed — some 3,000 of Catiline's supporters perished at Pistoria in 62 B.C.

60–53 B.C. — The First Triumvirate. Pompey, Crassus and Julius Caesar joined forces in 60 B.C., pooling a tremendous amount of wealth, influence and military prowess. This was a private pact without legal sanction but was remarkably effective in combating the senate and in establishing the supremacy of the generals. Through the arrangement, Caesar received a five-year appointment to Cisalpine Gaul, Illyricum and Gallia Narbonensis, allowing him to begin his famous campaigns in Gaul, which included a minor invasion of Britain and two crossings of the Rhine. Largely due to Caesar's mediation, the pact was renewed in 56 B.C. at the Conference of Luca, and in 55 B.C. Crassus and Pompey jointly held the consulship. The three then carved up the territories: Pompey taking Spain, Caesar retaining Gaul, and Crassus taking Syria, from which he launched his invasion of Parthia in 53 B.C. This campaign was a tremendous failure, and Crassus — the richest man in Rome — died during a retreat near Carrhae. The tattered remnants of the army were spared total destruction under the leadership of Cassius, then a quaestor, but later a tyrannicide and Imperator with his co-conspirator, Brutus.

53–49 B.C. — **Prelude to civil war.** With Crassus dead, Pompey and Caesar lost a powerful ally. Caesar, however, was building a stellar career with his victories in Gaul. It culminated with the defeat of Vercingetorix at Alesia in 52 B.C., and his conquest of Gaul was complete by 51 B.C. Meanwhile in Rome, the senate and Pompey had united, and were sharply opposed to the authority of Caesar. Aware of the danger he faced, Caesar (through Gaius Scribonius Curio Junior) proposed that he and Pompey both disband their armies. Though the senate passed the measure, it was vetoed by Marcellus (the husband of Octavia), who was consul. On January 7, 49 B.C., the senate (led by Pompey's father-in-law, Metellus Pius Scipio) issued a demand that Caesar, alone, disband his army and relinquish his Gallic command. Pompey was now given authority to defend the Republic against Caesar.

49–44 B.C. — **Civil war between the Pompeians and Caesar.** Caesar made his famous crossing of the Rubicon on January 10, 49 B.C., and took Italy with ease, for Pompey and many senators fled to Greece. Caesar secured Spain, and then pursued Pompey in Epirus, in northern Greece. On August 9, 48 B.C., Pompey was defeated in a pitched battle at Pharsalus. Some 20,000 of his men surrendered and Pompey fled to Egypt, where he was murdered upon landing. Pompey's cause, however, survived more than a dozen years under the leadership of his sons. Meanwhile, Caesar went to Egypt and found more trouble than he had anticipated. Ptolemy XIII had overthrown Cleopatra VII, and so Caesar set about restoring the queen. This he did, but with great difficulty, for he almost perished in the process. Next Caesar went to the Pontic region and defeated the rebel Pontic king Pharnaces II at Zela in a five-day campaign during the Spring of 47 B.C. (when he coined the phrase *Veni vidi vici*, "I came, I saw, I conquered"). Caesar returned to Italy, then battled still more Pompeians in North Africa (in the African War), which resulted in the suicide of Brutus' uncle Cato Uticensis at Utica, and Caesar's victory at Thapsus in April 46 B.C. Caesar returned to Rome late in July, and asked Cleopatra to join him. Romans were treated to the splendor of four successive triumphs being celebrated in September and October. Caesar was awarded a decade-long dictatorship. Early in 45 B.C., Caesar went to war against more Pompeians, and was victorious on March 17 at Munda, Spain, against the two sons of Pompey the Great: Pompey Junior (who was executed) and Sextus Pompey (who escaped). This was to be Caesar's last campaign.

44 B.C. — **The Murder of Caesar.** The senate now gave Caesar almost complete authority in Rome, including the title *dictator perpetuus* (dictator for life) on February 14, 44 B.C. Caesar now was preparing in earnest for an invasion of Parthia. Though Caesar subsequently rejected Marc Antony's offer of the royal diadem of a king three times, he was making arrangements to have a title to that effect outside of Italy. One month later, on the Ides (15th) of March, Caesar was murdered by a group of senatorial conspirators led by Brutus and Cassius. Subsequently, Marc Antony delivered Caesar's funeral eulogy on March 20, and in April presided at the Parilian games held in honor of Caesar's victory at Munda. Both events enraged the populace against the conspirators, who, in fear for their lives, fled to the East in August of that year. Though the senate abolished Caesar's dictatorship, it did not achieve its aim of reclaiming its authority in the long term.

44–43 B.C. — **Antony and Octavian Collide.** Nineteen-year-old Gaius Octavius (Octavian, later Augustus) was named heir to the political legacy and most of the fortune of his great-uncle (and adoptive father), Caesar. The beneficiary Octavian abandoned his studies in Greece and sped to Rome to collect his inheritance. He arrived in May or June of 44 B.C., and found Marc Antony (the most powerful ally of Caesar) to be confrontational. But Octavian proved formidable. After getting no satisfaction, Octavian invaded Rome with an army of Caesar's veterans in November 44 B.C., forcing Antony to leave for his proconsular duties in Gaul. But Antony first had to oust Decimus Brutus, who had been made governor of Gaul by Caesar. So Antony attacked, and besieged Decimus Brutus at Mutina. Meanwhile, the orator Cicero had emerged from retirement and began to defame Antony. The senate sent Octavian (now propraetor) and the two consuls, Pansa and Hirtius, to relieve Decimus Brutus, whom Antony had besieged at Mutina, in Cisapline Gaul. Though both consuls died, the senatorial army was victorious; Octavian was hailed Imperator and Decimus Brutus celebrated a triumph. Feeling their strength renewed, the senate granted extraordinary powers to Brutus and Cassius (in the East) and the naval commander Sextus Pompey (the surviving son of Pompey the Great) to command the fleet in the West. Meanwhile, Octavian felt left out, and so in May of 43 B.C., he occupied Rome militarily once again. By August he was able to force the senate to make him consul in place of Hirtius and Pansa, who had died, and to recognize officially his adoption by Caesar.

43–42 B.C. — **Triumvirs versus Republicans.** Having senatorial authority and an army, Octavian marched against Antony, but instead of fighting him, joined him in forming the Second Triumvirate on November 11, 43 B.C. The third member was Lepidus, the governor of Hither Spain and Gallia Narbonensis, who had fought on Antony's side at Mutina. By this political alliance, the trio ruled Rome and its territories for the next five years (through 38 B.C.). Unlike the First Triumvirate of Pompey, Caesar and Crassus, this was legally sanctioned (unwillingly) by a terrified senate as the *lex Titia: Triumviri rei publicae constituendae* (meaning "Triumvirs for the reorganization of the Republic"). Since the East was occupied by Brutus and Cassius, the three men divided the West among themselves, with Octavian getting the short-end, for his territories were occupied by enemies: the western islands (including Sicily) by Sextus Pompey and North Africa by Cornuficius. Thereafter the infamous Triumviral proscriptions began, which were spearheaded by Fulvia, Antony's ambitious wife. Some 130 senators and 2,000 equestrians were executed, with Cicero, the orator who had delivered his *Philippics* against the growing tyranny of Antony, being among the first to perish (in December 43 B.C.). In response, Brutus executed Gaius Antonius, a brother of Antony's who had been captured in Macedon. Also proscribed — rather foolishly — was Sextus Pompey, who subsequently used the fleet the senate had given him to blockade the coast of Italy. Octavian's commander, Salvidienus, was unable to defeat him. Meanwhile, the Triumvirs prepared for war against Brutus and Cassius. Antony and Octavian left Lepidus in charge in Italy, and led their armies east to Illyricum in preparation for war. Their supply lines (and route of retreat) were cut off by the Republican fleet commanded by Murcus and Ahenobarbus. Meanwhile, in the spring of 42 B.C., Brutus and Cassius campaigned successfully against the Lycians and Rhodians, and after meeting at Sardes in the summer, sailed for northern Greece. Two battles ensued at Philippi (at the beginning of October and on October 23). The Triumvirs, led by Antony and Octavian, were victorious over the Republicans, whose leaders, Brutus and Cassius, both committed suicide.

42–40 B.C. — The Division of Spoils. The memory of Julius Caesar was avenged, and the East — rebels and foreign enemies aside — now also belonged to the Triumvirs. Among these rebels were Sextus Pompey (and soon Murcus) in the West, Ahenobarbus in the Ionian Sea (soon allied with Antony) and Labienus, who defected to the Parthians. Antony went east and Octavian returned West. Late in 41 B.C., the Roman East was invaded by Labienus in concert with the Parthian prince Pacorus. All this occurred while Antony was in the East, but he was occupied with his new love interest, queen Cleopatra VII of Egypt, and soon had to sail West to resolve another crisis. During Antony's absence, the youngest brother of Antony, Lucius Antonius, and Antony's wife, Fulvia, began to harass Octavian. First they waged a verbal, then a military campaign against

Octavian known as the Perusine War (41–40 B.C.), which ended with the defeat of Lucius Antonius early in 40 B.C. Although both Lucius Antonius and Fulvia died of natural causes within months of the war's conclusion, civil war was imminent. However, it was averted when Antony and Octavian met at Brundisium in October 40 B.C. Here, they divided the Roman world: Antony received the East, Octavian received the lion's share of the West, while Lepidus was essentially limited to North Africa. Also in 40 B.C. both Antony and Octavian entered into political marriages, both destined to fail: Antony married Octavian's sister, Octavia, and Octavian married Scribonia, a relative of Sextus Pompey, who had a powerful fleet with which he controlled Sicily and Sardinia.

40–35 B.C. — Consolidation of Power. In addition to the marriage between Octavian and Scribonia, the Triumvirs made concessions to Sextus Pompey at the pact of Misenum in 39 B.C.: in return for grain shipments to Italy, the rebel admiral received Sicily, Sardinia, Corsica and even Achaea (Greece). Subsequently, in 38 B.C., Octavian broke the pact and attacked Sextus Pompey, but lost severely. The five-year Triumvirate pact expired late in 38 B.C., but was renewed at the Treaty of Tarentum, where Octavian traded many of his foot soldiers for 120 of Antony's war vessels. Now, Antony had enough soldiers for his planned invasion of Parthia, and Octavian could again challenge Sextus Pompey at sea. Thus, the next year, 36 B.C., was eventful. Antony's invasion of Parthia with some 100,000 soldiers failed miserably, due in large part to the treachery of Artavasdes II of Armenia. Antony withdrew with heavy losses (perhaps 40,000 casualties), and willingly received support from his mistress, Cleopatra VII. In the West, Octavian's campaign against Sextus Pompey had two results. First, it caused the downfall of the third Triumvir, Lepidus, who in August was unsuccessful in his treachery against Antony, and was expelled as a result. Second, Octavian's lieutenant, Agrippa, defeated Sextus Pompey at Naulochus in September, thus eliminating the tattered remnants of the Pompeian party (Sextus himself escaped to Asia Minor, where he was killed).

35–31 B.C. — Prelude to Actium. Now the Roman world was exclusively in the hands of Octavian and Antony. During the succeeding years, Antony went to great lengths to reorganize the Roman East into provinces and client kingdoms. With these reforms, and with Cleopatra VII as an ally, he was in firm control of Asia. However, his success was at the expense of Italian support, for Antony's orientalized life invited suspicion in the West, a situation which Octavian was only too willing to exploit. Antony and Octavian openly defamed each other, especially since the political marriages of 40 B.C. had ended or were in disrepair. Both Octavian and

Antony remained in their spheres of influence, rallying support for the civil war they knew would certainly come. The Triumviral pact expired at the end of 33 B.C. The two consuls of 32 B.C. were Ahenobarbus and Sosius, both of whom supported Antony. Octavian opposed their tenure by (yet again) occupying Rome with his legions and terrorizing the senate; both consuls and some 300 senators fled to the East for Antony's protection. In essence, war had been declared.

31–27 B.C. — Actium, and the foundation of the Empire. Now Octavian secured an oath of loyalty from citizens in Italy, declared war against Cleopatra VII (and cleverly, not against Antony), and set out for Greece, where he confronted Antony's 30 legions. However, Cleopatra's participation caused Plancus, Ahenobarbus and many others to desert to Octavian at the last moment, and Agrippa's naval blockade of Antony's camp took its toll. The Battle of Actium occurred on September 2, 31 B.C.; soon after, Antony and Cleopatra burst through the blockade and fled to Egypt. Antony's desperate effort to get four legions from Scarpus in Cyrene failed, and he committed suicide in 30 B.C., soon after landing in Alexandria. Cleopatra also committed suicide after a fruitless meeting with Octavian, who had come to collect her as a war trophy. Octavian subsequently made Egypt into a kind of Roman province which was declared his personal property. In 29 B.C., Octavian celebrated his triumph in Rome and disbanded many legions by settling 120,000 veterans with land grants. Octavian had achieved absolute power, and did not want to lose it in the same way Julius Caesar had nearly 15 years before. Thus, Octavian declared the restoration of the Republic by forfeiting most of his authority to the senate and the people on January 13, 27 B.C. He kept the consulship, the provinces of Spain, Gaul, Syria and Egypt, and the legions stationed therein. Three days later, the senate granted him the title *Augustus* (meaning "sacred" or "revered"), which was the name he came to be called for the remaining 41 years of his life. Thus began the Roman Empire, a political entity that would last more than 500 years in the West, and a thousand years beyond that in the East.

Note to the reader: The inclusion of minor historical figures in the biographies which follow has been limited to those who were both hailed Imperator and produced coinage.

THE IMPERATORIAL PERIOD

SULLA

DICTATOR, 82–79 B.C.

Lucius Cornelius Sulla, 138–78 B.C. The early life of Sulla is rather undistinguished, for he came from an obscure but apparently wealthy Patrician family and his only act of note was the arrest of Jugurtha in 107 B.C., when he was serving as a Quaestor under Marius. More than a decade later he attained a high administrative post in the East, propraetor of Cilicia, and in that capacity officiated at the first negotiations held between Rome and Parthia.

However, his career was launched during the Social War (91–89 B.C.), which earned him a reputation for vigorous military actions. He was the most successful commander in southern Italy, and as a result of his victories against the Samnites was made consul in 88 B.C., after the Social War had been resolved and all Italians were granted Roman citizenship. Just when Italy was on the verge of recovery, Rome was thrust into a new, distant crisis. King Mithradates VI of Pontus, in a single night, caused the slaughter of more than 80,000 Romans residing in Asia. A swift response was necessary, and the senate gave command against Mithradates to the consul and war-hero Sulla.

But the decision was reversed when the senate was usurped by adherents to Marius, a more experienced commander, who not surprisingly was given the command in place of Sulla. This came as a shock to Sulla, who was forced to flee. However, Sulla's legions — who had fought under him for two years — remained loyal. Enticed by the spoils of war and possible land allotments, they joined Sulla and marched on Rome itself. Now the tables had turned, and it was Sulla who chased Marius out of Rome, after which he re-established the authority of the senate.

After establishing his regime, Sulla headed East in 87 B.C. to conduct what is known as the First Mithradatic War (88–84 B.C.). Since Mithradates VI had also occupied Greece, Sulla concentrated his efforts there first, and by 86 B.C. was able to expel the Pontic king from Athens and the rest of Greece. Mithradates was now on the defensive and his defeat was within Sulla's grasp, but a schism in the Roman command prevented it. In 86 B.C. Sulla's command expired and the senate gave the new command to Lucius Valerius Flaccus (the *consul suffectus* who replaced Marius after his death in 86 B.C.), who headed East and began to fight the Pontic king with his own new command.

But when Flaccus' soldiers began to desert to Sulla, he quarreled with his own legate, Gaius Fimbria, who murdered Flaccus in Bithynia in 85 B.C. and took command. Fimbria nearly captured Mithradates VI in Asia, and in a moment of supreme selfishness, Sulla and Fimbria refused to cooperate (no doubt out of fear that the other would take credit for the victory), which allowed Mithradates the opportunity to escape. Sulla made a generous peace pact with Mithradates at Dardanus in 85 B.C., and then turned on Fimbria, who committed suicide.

Sulla next sought retribution from those cities in Asia and Greece that had betrayed Rome, and in the process established a great deal of authority, the likes of which had not been seen in the Greek East since the victories of Titus Quinctius Flamininus more than a century before. More importantly, perhaps, he collected a vast amount of war booty. This he put to immediate use during his invasion of Italy, for during his absence, Marius had forced his way into Rome shortly before his own death in 86 B.C. His supporters, first led by Cinna, then by Carbo, ruled cruelly thereafter.

When Sulla returned from the East, Marius' supporters were in control, but Sulla's new-found wealth and battle-hardened legions gave him the advantage. Upon landing at Brundisium in 83 B.C., Sulla was approached by many resourceful leaders who wished to join his campaign. Among them were Crassus, Metellus Pius and Pompey. The remaining members of the Marian Party were ousted as Sulla took Rome again (the Sibylline Books were burned in a resulting fire). Later, Sulla defended Rome from the Samnites at the Battle of the Colline Gate in 82 B.C. The remaining Marians fled to Spain, and were there defeated by Pompey, who had been sent by Sulla.

Thus, with Sulla's second invasion of Rome began his three-year dictatorship. In the meantime, Mithradates VI had renewed hostilities against Rome, initiating what is called the Second Mithradatic War (83 to 81 B.C.). Sulla entrusted the war to Lucius Licinius Murena, the propraetor of Asia whose careless actions had caused the Pontic king to rise up again. In 81 B.C., after victory was secured in the East, Sulla held a magnificent triumph in Rome.

During his dictatorship, Sulla fought to re-establish the authority of the senate in Rome and, in essence, to return power to the wealthy families (for the legislation of Marius had counteracted this traditional arrangement). Enacting his reforms was accomplished through strict measures, and in the process Sulla executed some 90 senators and 2,600 equestrians. Other landmark political reforms were introduced, including the requirement that consuls and praetors leave Rome to govern a province after their terms ended.

While battling Mithradates, Sulla had sacked much of Greece to pay his armies. One site victimized was Olympia, and so Sulla transferred the

Olympic Games to Rome, where they were held in 80 B.C., the year in which he held his second and last consulship. Sulla reluctantly forfeited his dictatorship in 79 B.C. and died of disease a year later after he had retired to his estates in Campania.

NUMISMATIC NOTE: The gilded equestrian statue awarded to Sulla for his victories against Mithradates VI is depicted on his coinage by the moneyer A. Manlius in 80 B.C. After the reign of Sulla, no standard bronzes were struck in the Republic until the time of Julius Caesar.

FLACCUS

IMPERATOR, 83-82 B.C.

Gaius Valerius Flaccus, lifespan unknown. Flaccus, a member of the distinguished *Valeria* gens, which is well-represented on Republican coinage, served as *praetor urbanus* (city prefect of Rome) in 96 B.C., consul in 93 B.C. with M. Herennius, and c. 85–81 B.C. served as proconsul in Gaul, notably during the consulships of L. Cornelius Scipio and C. Norbanus (83 B.C.). Of these three high appointments, it is his appointment in Gaul (by which time he had been hailed Imperator) for which he struck coins.

Sulla enlisted the services of Flaccus in the war he had begun to wage in Spain against the rebel Quintus, and as a result Flaccus later succeeded T. Didius as proconsul in Spain. Didius had ruled so cruelly that the Celtiberians revolted against him at Belgida, trapped all of the senators in their meeting house, and burned it to the ground while they were inside. Flaccus took Belgida by surprise, and executed all who had participated in the burning. In 81 B.C. Flaccus earned a triumph for his Gallic and Spanish campaigns. (See the biographies of Metellus Pius and Pompey the Great for details on Sertorius' revolt.)

Flaccus was the brother of the Lucius Valerius Flaccus who replaced Marius in 86 B.C. as *consul suffectus*, and who subsequently was chosen to replace Sulla as commander in the war against Mithradates VI of Pontus. Regrettably for Lucius Valerius Flaccus, he was murdered by his own lieutennant Fimbria while marching through Bithynia in 85 B.C., some two or three years before his brother Gaius Valerius Flaccus, the Imperator, struck his coinage in Gaul.

Flaccus appears also to have been the nephew of the Lucius Valerius Flaccus who struck coins as moneyer in 108 or 107 B.C., and who was consul in 100 B.C. That Flaccus borrowed the obverse type of a bust of Victory directly from the earlier coins of his uncle serves to confirm their close blood relationship.

NUMISMATIC NOTE: Flaccus' denarii of Massalia are a military issue. The obverse shows the bust of victory, and the reverse a legionary eagle between two standards, both of which bear a plaque with a single letter. At the left is an H, meaning *hastati*, and at the right a P, meaning *principes*. The *hastati* were the spear-bearers on the front-line of the Roman battle formation, and the *principes* held the secondary position directly behind them. This was a well-controlled coinage, as Crawford lists 41 different control marks, noting that each is represented by a single die. It is worth noting that the 'legionary eagle and standards' reverse created by Flaccus inspired a later issue of Gnaeus Nerius in 49 B.C. and served as the protoype for Marc Antony's prodigious issue of 'legionary denarii' half a century later. Flaccus' type was included in the restoration series of the emperor Trajan (A.D. 98–117).

METELLUS PIUS

IMPERATOR, 81 B.C.

ADOPTIVE FATHER OF METELLUS PIUS SCIPIO

Quintus Caecilius Metellus Pius, d. c. 63 B.C. Metellus Pius came to prominence during the Social War, during which he served as praetor (89 B.C.) and legate. He earned his surname Pius in 99 B.C. for his effort to recall from exile his homonymous father, surnamed Numidicus, who was instrumental in the defeat of Jugurtha.

Metellus Pius was called to Rome to oppose Marius, but left without finding success in his venture. Subsequently, he established himself as an independent power in North Africa until 84 B.C., when he was ousted by Gaius Fabius Hadrianus. In the following year he joined forces with Sulla, who had just returned victoriously from the First Mithradatic War. Metellus Pius gained distinction as Sulla's best general, and shared the consulship with him in 80 B.C.

Thereafter, he gained a proconsular command in Farther Spain where he campaigned from 79 to 71 B.C. against the rebel Quintus Sertorius, who had been a loose cannon in Spain and North Africa ever since he was proscribed by Sulla in 83 B.C. Sertorius had established his own senate, by which he ruled Spain. Sertorius relied upon local royalty as his base of power, but also allied himself with outsiders who opposed the senate in Rome; these included pirates, and even the Pontic king Mithradates VI, with whom Sertorius made an ineffective pact in 76 or 75 B.C.

Metellus Pius was greatly boosted in his floundering campaign against Sertorius by reinforcements led by Pompey the Great. But even together they were unable to defeat Sertorius easily or quickly. Indeed, they essentially wore him down until in 72 B.C., at the end of his resources, Sertorius was murdered. While campaigning in Spain, Metellus Pius had several places named in his honor. In 71 B.C., about the time the slave revolt of Spartacus was quelled, Metellus Pius celebrated his hard-earned Triumph, and afterward served as *Pontifex Maximus* from 81 to 63 B.C., after which Julius Caesar took over.

NUMISMATIC NOTE: Though Metellus Pius' fame is largely derived from his later campaigns in Spain against Sertorius, the coinage in his name was struck at a North Italian mint in 81 B.C. while he fought for Sulla against leaders of the Marian Party, such as Carrinas, Norbanus and Carbo. The obverse type of Pietas alludes to his surname Pius, and the reverse type of the elephant recalls the accomplishment of his ancestor Lucius Caecilius Metellus, who in 251 B.C. captured an army of Carthaginian elephants at Panormus.

CRASSUS

MEMBER OF THE FIRST TRIUMVIRATE, 60–53 B.C.

Marcus Licinius Crassus, c. 115/112–53 B.C. A man of immense wealth, and in the opinion of Cicero the most accomplished orator of his day, Crassus engaged in a remarkable career in which he opposed Marius, Sulla, Pompey the Great and Julius Caesar for leadership in the crumbling Republic.

Born into an influential aristocratic family, Crassus was introduced to the dangers of partisan politics when his father perished in 87 B.C. during the massacres of Marius. As a result, Crassus fled to Spain, where he was able to raise a formidable private army by 85 B.C., about the time he reached his 30th year. He offered his army to Sulla, who returned to Italy in 83 B.C. after achieving peace with Mithradates VI of Pontus.

Thus, Crassus became involved in the triumphant return of Sulla, and re-established himself in a position of great power in Rome. Crassus was especially avaricious, and focused principally on seizing the wealth of those adherents to the Marian party who were condemned in the proscriptions of Sulla. Throughout the 70s B.C. Crassus' fortunes and political status rose, though he was considerably jealous of the meteoric rise of Pompey, who late in the 70s earned the title Magnus (meaning "the Great"), for his victories over Marian remnants in Spain and North Africa.

Crassus had political clout and vast wealth, but he desired military honor beyond what little he had earned as commander of Sulla's right wing at the Battle of the Colline Gate in 82 B.C. Thus, when a slave revolt broke out in southern Italy under the leadership of Spartacus, it proved too good an opportunity for Crassus to miss. The first two armies Rome sent against Spartacus were led by the consuls, both of whom were roundly defeated.

Spartacus' army had now attracted fugitives, bandits and slaves of every description, including Thracian, German and Celtic renegades, and numbered 90,000 or more at its height. Spartacus' original idea of marching the length of Italy and crossing the Alps to freedom, was abandoned when his massive army decided instead to continue plundering Italy, and so the army traveled all the way back to the "toe" of Italy, defeating every Roman army sent against it.

Crassus gained the proconsular command in 72 B.C. and led six legions against Spartacus. His legions ended the revolt by crushing the rebels in Lucania, and for this he earned a minor triumph (*ovatio*) in 71 B.C. However, much of Crassus' glory was stolen at the last moment by Pompey, who returned from his campaigns against the Marians in Spain and "mopped up" the remnants of Spartacus' army. As a result, Crassus not only had to share his military glory with the upstart Pompey, but also the consulship of 70 B.C.

The next decade, from about 69 to 59 B.C., was one of limited success for Crassus. His political aim of forcing the elite to share authority with the common man was strongly opposed, but he was none-the-less able to revoke many of Sulla's laws. The one realm in which Crassus joined the elite (optimates) was in their opposition to the growing power of Pompey, who was in the East putting an end to piracy and defeating Mithradates VI (who had risen against Rome a third time). Though Pompey's gains were staggering, he was giving much of it freely to his veterans, which angered the senators.

The major crisis in Italy during Pompey's absence was the conspiracy of Lucius Sergius Catilina, a man who, like Crassus, enriched himself during Sulla's conscriptions of 82 B.C. His radical agenda was repeatedly thwarted by conservatives, and so, upon being denied the consulship of 62 B.C., he headed a minor revolution backed by the rural poor. The orator Cicero, then consul, easily crushed the revolt, which he subsequently exploited by magnifying its importance as a "conspiracy" against the state. Pompey returned to Rome late in 62 B.C., after the ordeal had come to an end.

The last seven years of Crassus' life were quite eventful. By about 65 B.C., Crassus had gained a new ally in Julius Caesar, a man in his late 30s who had remarkable talent as a politician, and who held similar anti-elitist views on government. Most importantly, Caesar was heavily in debt — a problem Crassus was able to help him resolve. With Crassus' patronage, Caesar rose considerably in office, and in 59 B.C. was elected consul.

Indeed, it was Caesar who convinced Crassus to join forces with his enemy Pompey, who had returned from the East laden with booty and fame.

Thus, the First Triumvirate, an unofficial pact which tied the resources and destinies of Crassus, Pompey and Caesar, was founded in 60 B.C., after Caesar had won his election to the consulship for the year following. From this arrangement, Caesar received a five-year proconsular command in Gaul, and thus began his famous campaigns.

Largely due to the negotiating skills of Caesar, the Triumviral pact was renewed in 56 B.C. at the Conference of Luca, thus ending the threat that Pompey would lend his credibility and resources to the cause of the *optimates*. The three men carved up the Roman world by attaining five-year proconsular commands: Crassus in Syria, Pompey in Spain and Caesar in Gaul. Meanwhile, in 55 B.C., Crassus became consul for a second time, an honor that he shared with Pompey.

Despite all of his success and influence, Crassus knew he lacked an essential ingredient: military distinction. The reputations of both Pompey and Caesar had grown from their achievements at the head of armies, and Crassus had done little. Even his signal victory over Spartacus was overlooked, for Pompey had robbed him of the glory he deserved. As such, Crassus went to Syria with the idea in mind of waging war against the Parthians — a relatively new foe through whom he could win the distinction he so desperately desired.

But this venture was not to be a success. Indeed, it ranked among the most shameful defeats in Roman history. With difficulty, Crassus raised an army, and set out for Syria late in 55 B.C., taking with him Cassius, one of the future assassins of Caesar. In the following year Crassus advanced into western Mesopotamia, and in 53 had marched deeply into Parthian territory. However, Crassus' eagerness for victory outstripped his skill as a general, and he was easily outmaneuvered by the commander Surenas (acting for king Orodes II), who hemmed him in and steadily killed off his legionnaires with volleys of arrows.

In the disorganized retreat, Crassus was killed by treachery. A great many soldiers died, and even more importantly for the wounded Roman pride, the legionary eagles (military standards) were captured. The recovery of these eagles was later of great importance to Octavian (Augustus), who extensively celebrated the fact on his own coinage. Thus ended the considerable, but hollow career of Crassus, who, for all his wealth, patrons and friends, failed to achieve the true power he desired.

NUMISMATIC NOTE: The only coinage attributable to Crassus are Syrian tetradrachms bearing the immobilized types of the Philip Philadelphus and Crassus' monogram and Syrian bronzes dated to the 12th and 13th year of the Pompeian Era. Additionally, a reference to his Parthian campaign may be found on denarii struck by his son, Publius Licinius Crassus, the moneyer of c. 55 B.C. The reverse of the son's denarii (Cr. 430/1) show Roma standing next to a horse, presumably a reference to the 1,000 Gallic horsemen the son brought to the campaign, or perhaps to a defeated Parthian cavalry. Crassus' son accompanied his father on the campaign, and died leading a cavalry engagement.

POMPEY THE GREAT

MEMBER OF THE FIRST TRIUMVIRATE, 60–53 B.C.

FATHER OF POMPEY JUNIOR AND SEXTUS POMPEY
HUSBAND OF JULIA (D. OF JULIUS CAESAR)
SON-IN-LAW OF METELLUS PIUS SCIPIO AND JULIUS CAESAR

Gnaeus Pompeius "Magnus," 106–48 B.C. Few Romans generals were as talented as Pompey, who earned his surname Magnus ("the Great") at the age of 23 while campaigning in North Africa. It was his struggle with Julius Caesar and Crassus that defined Roman rulership during the post-Sullan age, and set the stage for the civil wars that led to the foundation of the Empire.

Pompey the Great was the son of Pompeius Strabo, a man who, along with Sulla, ushered in the era of warlords that caused the half-century collapse of the Republic. Strabo had won important victories in the Social War, but afterwards refused to disband the large army he had built from his *clientela*. The senate was unable to force Strabo to give up his command, and so, when Strabo died in 87 B.C., the army passed into the hands of his son, Pompey the Great, who had fought at his father's side in the Social War.

Thus, the return of Sulla from his campaigns against Mithradates VI in the East spelled a great opportunity for Pompey the Great, who had a large army anxiously awaiting a cause. Sulla intended to oust the Marian Party, which had assumed control in Rome during his absence. Sulla was glad to have Pompey as an ally and together they waged war on Rome, finally earning a signal victory in 82 B.C. at the Battle of the Colline Gate. Italy now belonged to Sulla, and Pompey had shared prominently in the victory.

However, many Marians had fled to Sicily and North Africa, where they planned to continue their struggle. Since Sulla had plenty to take care of in Italy, he made Pompey a propraetor and empowered him to hunt down the renegade Marians, which he did with exceptional cruelty. Since

Pompey's wars were against Romans, the only popular part of his campaign occurred in North Africa, where he defeated Gnaeus Domitius, who had allied himself with the Numidian usurper Iarbal.

Pompey returned to Rome in 81 B.C., and extorted a triumph from Sulla who, as dictator, was busy re-establishing senatorial authority and revoking the populist laws of Marius. For good measure, the 25-year-old Pompey was given the honorific cognomen *Magnus* ("the Great"), by which he is best known to history.

After holding the consulship in 80 B.C., Sulla grudgingly retired from his dictatorship in 79 B.C., and died in the year following. With the great liberator and dictator gone, Marcus Aemilius Lepidus (the consul of 78 B.C. and an ally of Pompey) supported in Etruria a revolt, which his own propaganda had provoked. The senate entrusted Pompey and Lepidus' co-consul Catulus with the task of restoring order, which they did by 77 B.C.

Having learned well from his father's example, Pompey refused the senate's order to disband the army he had assembled to defeat Lepidus, and from a position of great strength he was able to extort a command in Spain. There, Metellus Pius had been waging war since 79 B.C. against the rebel Quintus Sertorius (who had established his own "Spanish Empire" after he was proscribed by Sulla in 83 B.C.). Pompey arrived in 76 or 75 B.C., and he and Metellus finally defeated Sertorius in 72 B.C.

Meanwhile in Italy, a massive slave revolt (called the Servile War) had erupted in Capua in 73 B.C. under the leadership of a Thracian gladiator named Spartacus. The slave army was invincible as it traveled the length of Italy twice, ravaging the countryside and defeating one consular army after another. However, the tide turned in 72 B.C., when one of Pompey's foremost opponents in Rome, Marcus Licinius Crassus, defeated Spartacus' army in Apulia. Sensing a great opportunity, Pompey led his armies from Spain to southern Italy in 71 B.C., just in time to mop up the shattered remnants of Spartacus' army.

In doing so, Pompey robbed Crassus of the glory he, alone, justly deserved. Crassus was only granted a minor triumph (*ovatio*), and Pompey took liberal credit for victories in Spain and Italy, even though in both cases he was not the principal commander. Crassus, who had always been envious of the upstart Pompey, was now justifiably angry at him, especially since he had to share the consulship of 70 with Pompey. However, the two men cooperated more than might have been expected, revoking many of Sulla's elitist laws. The legislative tide had once again turned in favor of the common man.

As remarkable as Pompey's accomplishments had been thus far, the future held even greater glory. In 67 B.C., Pompey gained a command to combat the piracy which had become so rampant in the Mediterranean. He was remarkably successful in this endeavor, finishing off the pirates within three months. In 66 B.C. he was given a command against the Pontic king Mithradates VI, who had been waging his third war against Rome since 74 B.C.

Pompey immediately put Mithradates on the run, defeating him repeatedly. The Pontic king became so unpopular with his war-weary subjects that his son, Pharnaces II, staged a revolt and Mithradates committed suicide in 63 B.C. With the Third Mithradatic War over, Pompey set about securing Roman interests in the East and reorganizing the territories. Much to the dismay of the senate, he did this without its approval, and even without its consultation, for in the process he was establishing a power base for his future ventures.

Behaving with the audacity of a Hellenistic monarch, Pompey transformed Pontus, Cilicia and Syria into provinces, and made client kingdoms of Armenia, Cappadocia, Colchis, Galatia and Judaea. Pompey was especially generous to his veterans, whom he richly rewarded with land grants. Despite selfish actions, Pompey still returned to Rome with enough war booty that the Republic became solvent for the first time in about three decades. At long last, Rome and her vast territories were at peace, and economic prosperity had returned.

During Pompey's absence in the East, Crassus had made every effort to defame him, for he was now more envious than ever. For all his wealth and influence, Crassus lacked the military glory of Pompey, and in this era of warlords, battle glory was an essential ingredient for those who desired supreme authority. To make matters worse, the wealth Pompey had personally amassed in the East now outstripped even that of Crassus.

But the two men were destined to unite, for they had a common enemy in the senate. Thus, when the senate opposed Pompey's arrangements in the East after-the-fact, these two old enemies came to terms. In 60 B.C. an anti-*optimates* coalition known as the First Triumvirate was born, which included Pompey, Crassus and a new man on the political front named Julius Caesar. Caesar had recently come to prominence under the patronage of Crassus, and had been elected to the consulship of 59 B.C. To seal the deal, Pompey married Julia, the daughter of Julius Caesar by his first wife Cornelia.

Though the First Triumvirate was a private pact without legal sanction from the senate, it proved to be remarkably effective. Caesar pushed Pompey's legislation through the senate, and in return earned a remarkable five-year appointment in Gaul.

However, the senate and the *optimates* tried to lure Pompey to their cause in hopes he would abandon Crassus and Caesar. Thus, in 56 B.C. Caesar called for a conference at Luca, at which the Triumvirate was renewed. Crassus and Pompey were elected to the consulship of 55 B.C., and by the *Lex Trebonia* were given virtually unlimited authority. The

Triumvirs established their territories: Pompey took Spain (which he ruled by proxy), Caesar retained Gaul, and Crassus chose Syria, from which he planned to invade Parthia.

If Crassus conducted the Parthian war successfully, he would gain the military glory he needed to round out his wealth and political clout. However, Crassus led his legions into an ambush near Carrhae in 53 B.C., and was defeated so shamefully that even in modern times it is considered one of the worst defeats suffered by the Romans. With the death of Crassus in 53 B.C., and the death in 54 B.C. of Pompey's wife Julia (who was equally devoted to her father, Caesar), the two remaining Triumvirs were destined to collide.

Caesar was winning important victories in Gaul, which he popularized in Rome by sending back his memoirs of the campaigns. Caesar's conquest was complete by 51 B.C., for in 52 B.C. he had defeated a Gallic confederation under the leadership of Vercingetorix. In Italy in the meantime, Pompey had become increasingly allied with the senate. He had been awarded a sole-consulship so he could restore order in Rome, which had suffered so greatly from gang warfare that even the senate house was burned in 52 B.C. The senate was anxious to have Pompey as an ally, for they feared the growing authority of Caesar.

If Caesar returned to Rome without his army, he would be at the mercy of Pompey and the senate, and no doubt would be charged with serious crimes. Caesar was now in a dangerous position. The threat was especially real, because Pompey was the sole-consul (in 52 B.C.), and was on good terms with the senate. Caesar thus proposed that he and Pompey simultaneously disband their armies. Though the senate had approved the measure, it was vetoed by the consul Gaius Claudius Marcellus. On January 7, 49 B.C. the senate demanded that Caesar (alone) disband his armies and forfeit his Gallic command. Caesar did not comply, and Pompey was thus given the task of defending Rome from Caesar.

Caesar wasted little time in invading Italy. Rome offered no serious resistance, as Pompey and many senators fled to Greece to mobilize their forces. Caesar first secured Spain, and then pursued Pompey in Greece, where his attempted naval blockade was easily thwarted. However, Pompey seems to have been pressured into engaging in a pitched battle at Pharsalus on August 9, 48 B.C., where he lost severely, and about 20,000 of his men surrendered.

Pompey fled from the battle, and is said to have even considered seeking asylum with the Parthian king Orodes II, with whom he recently had been in communication. Instead, Pompey proceeded to Egypt, where he was stabbed to death by courtiers of king Ptolemy XIII while disembarking on September 28.

NUMISMATIC NOTE: With the possible exception of provincial æs of Pompeiopolis (which bear no dates), no portrait coins of Pompey the Great were struck during his lifetime. Pompey struck only three issues of coinage. The first is an excessively rare aureus struck in 71 B.C. for his triumph of that year. The remaining two — denarii — were struck from 49-48 B.C., and must be associated with his preparation for war with Caesar. As such, they most likely were struck at (what seems to be) two different mints in Greece.

Pompey's portrait does, however, appear on many issues struck by his sons from 46 to 40 B.C., most of which are denarii. Though the majority of these were struck by Sextus Pompey, a series of now-rare denarii was also struck by Pompey Junior on which the style of the portrait is distinctly Hellenistic. Though Pompey's features are far from idealized on these coins, the large, upward gazing eyes and the crest of hair above his forehead are imitative of the style employed for Alexander the Great. Indeed, this is the only regular appearance of this style of portrait on a Roman coin until the reign of Constantine the Great (A.D. 307–337), when the Greek-inspired 'heavenward gaze' was again adopted.

On bronzes, Pompey's image occurs in the guise of the two-faced Janus on asses struck by Sextus Pompey. Portrait bronzes were also struck at Pompeiopolis, a self-named city that Pompey "founded" in Cilicia on the ruins of the antique city of Soli (which by then had been virtually abandoned) and repopulated it with the pirates he had defeated in his campaign of 67 B.C. The city's coins bearing his portrait (and dates based on an era beginning in 66 B.C.) were struck there well into Imperial times.

POMPEY JUNIOR

SON OF POMPEY THE GREAT AND MUCIA
BROTHER OF SEXTUS POMPEY

Gnaeus Pompeius (Junior), 79–45 B.C. As the eldest son of Pompey the Great, Pompey Junior was destined to be involved in his father's career. Unlike Sextus Pompey, his younger and more resourceful brother, Pompey Junior was considered by his contemporaries to be cruel and unintelligent.

His first action of note occurred in 49 B.C., when Pompey Junior took command of an Egyptian fleet and destroyed the transports that Julius Caesar had sent to support his armies at the Battle of Dyrrhachium. Early in the African War, he occupied the Balearic Islands and after the Pompeians were defeated by Caesar at Thapsus in April, 46 B.C., he went to Spain, where he linked up with his brother and the turncoat Titus Labienus.

The Pompeians chose Spain not only for its strategic importance, but also because it was in the midst of a revolt against Quintus Cassius, the man whom Caesar had left in charge since 49 B.C. In Spain, the brothers and Titus Labienus raised 13 legions and assumed control of the South of Spain. But their temporary rise to power ended when Caesar came to Spain to oust them. After some skirmishes, the Caesarean and Pompeian armies clashed at the Battle of Munda on March 17, 45 B.C. Though Sextus Pompey and many of his followers were able to flee, Titus Labienus died in battle and Pompey Junior was captured and executed.

NUMISMATIC NOTE: Much like his father, Pompey Junior died before the era of 'lifetime portraiture' on coinage had debuted at Rome, and so his bust only occurs on coinage struck posthumously. In Pompey Junior's case, however, there are only two such instances — a very rare denarius struck within months of his death, and a rare aureus struck by his brother in Sicily in 42 B.C., upon which his bust confronts that of his father on the reverse. Pompey Junior issued denarii with the portrait of his father (which are discussed above, under Pompey the Great).

SEXTUS POMPEY

SON OF POMPEY THE GREAT AND MUCIA
BROTHER OF POMPEY JUNIOR

Sextus Pompeius Magnus, 67–35 B.C. The legacy of Pompey the Great did not die when he was murdered in Egypt in 48 B.C., but was handed down to his two sons throughout the lifetime of Julius Caesar and nearly a decade beyond. The youngest of these sons, Sextus Pompey, was a remarkably resourceful naval commander whose life bears favorable comparison to that of the fugitive Greek king Demetrius Poliorcetes.

After the Battle of Pharsalus in the Summer of 48 B.C., Sextus Pompey accompanied his father to Lesbos, then to Egypt, and after the latter was murdered there, Sextus Pompey fled West to North Africa. Caesar pursued him there, and defeated him at the Battle of Thapsus in April 46 B.C. But Sextus Pompey escaped yet again, and found refuge with his older brother, Pompey Junior, in Spain.

While there, Sextus Pompey commanded the garrison of Corduba against Caesar at the Battle of Munda in March of 45 B.C. There, yet again, the Pompeians lost to the Caesareans. Though the defeat was decisive (and his elder brother Pompey Junior was captured and executed), Sextus Pompey escaped once more. He soon gathered an army, with which he harassed Carrinas and Pollio, the governors of Further Spain.

Following the murder of Julius Caesar in mid-March, 44 B.C., the political environment erupted. As soon as Antony left for his command in Cisalpine Gaul (late in 44 B.C.), Cicero went on the offensive. By February of 43 B.C., based on lobbying by Cicero and the future Triumvir Lepidus, Antony had been declared a public enemy, and the senate had given Sextus Pompey command of the Roman fleet (*Praefectus classis et orae maritimae*). However, opinion — once again — was quickly reversed; within months Antony was restored and Sextus Pompey was declared an enemy in the proscriptions.

Thus, Sextus Pompey's suspicion of the senate's resolve served him well, for he had temporarily based himself at Massalia. Sextus Pompey responded to his being named a public enemy by using his new fleet to rescue other fugitives of the Caesarean proscriptions, and to occupy Sicily. From that island base he began to blockade the western coast of Italy. This act brought reprisals from the Triumvirs, who in 42 B.C. sent Octavian's friend, the *legatus* Salvidienus, to oppose Sextus Pompey.

After some initial success near Rhegium, Salvidienus was severely defeated off the coast of Messana. Sextus Pompey assumed the fanciful title "son of Neptune" after this important victory, and began to receive refugees from the Republican defeat that had occurred at Philippi in October 42 B.C. Among those who joined his ranks were Murcus, a commander who initially was an asset but later fell out with Sextus Pompey and was murdered.

Since Sextus Pompey not only was popular in Rome, but seemingly was impossible to defeat, the Caesarean strategy shifted from warfare to diplomacy. In 40 B.C. Octavian married Scribonia, a relative of Sextus Pompey, and in the following year, with the pact of Misenum, Octavian and Antony agreed to give Sextus Pompey control over Sicily, Sardinia, Corsica and Achaea in exchange for his promise to supply grain to Italy.

This truce lasted until 38 B.C., when Octavian took command of the Roman fleet and waged war against Sextus Pompey, whom he branded a pirate chief. Though Octavian met only defeat in the first year, he bartered with Antony at the Treaty of Tarentum to get 120 new vessels, and renewed his efforts in 36 B.C.

The triumvir Lepidus, based in North Africa, joined the effort by landing 14 legions in Sicily. However, Lepidus proved to be of no help, for in August he used his legionary might to try to extort control of Sicily from Octavian, who resisted the offer and instead challenged him. Lepidus' legions defected, and he was expelled from the Triumvirate. Octavian was now able to focus on the naval campaign against Sextus Pompey, whom he defeated at the Battle of Naulochus in September 3, 36 B.C.

As was his custom, Sextus Pompey escaped yet again, but the legendary commander's luck ran out when he sailed to the East, hoping to establish a base in Asia Minor. By this point in time, Marc Antony was in control of the East, and Sextus Pompey was defeated in 35 B.C. by forces of Antony led by the general Ahenobarbus (who was Antony's governor of Bithynia at the time) and Plancus, after which he was executed by Marcus Titius.

NUMISMATIC NOTE: Since the main source of the Pompeian glory was its fleet, most issues show galleys, the sea god Neptune, or other objects related to naval exploits. The title awarded Sextus Pompey by the momentarily liberated senate early in 43 B.C., *Praefectus classis et orae maritimae*, (by which he was given command of the Roman fleet in the West), is proudly trumpeted in his coin inscriptions.

JULIUS CAESAR

MEMBER OF THE FIRST TRIUMVIRATE, 60–53 B.C.
DICTATOR FOR LIFE, 44 B.C.

GRANDUNCLE AND ADOPTIVE FATHER OF AUGUSTUS (OCTAVIAN)
HUSBAND OF CORNELIA, POMPEIA AND CALPURNIA
COMPANION OF SERVILIA (*m.* OF BRUTUS) AND QUEEN CLEOPATRA VII
FATHER OF JULIA (W. OF POMPEY THE GREAT) AND PTOLEMY XV (CALLED 'CAESARION')
SON-IN-LAW OF CINNA
FATHER-IN-LAW OF POMPEY THE GREAT

Gaius Julius Caesar, 100–44 B.C. Perhaps the most famous of all Romans, Julius Caesar hailed from a respectable, but not stellar, family of the gens *Julia*. He was nephew to the wife of the dictator Marius, and received a back-handed compliment from Marius' enemy, Sulla (dictator, 82–79 B.C.) when he commented that in Caesar he saw many Mariuses.

Julius Caesar came to prominence relatively late in life. Indeed, while serving as a quaestor in Spain in 69 B.C., Caesar gazed upon a monument to Alexander the Great, and was overcome with shame. While at age 31 Caesar had accomplished so little, Alexander had already conquered the world. In this same year, at the far end of the Mediterranean, his future lover Cleopatra VII was born.

His early career was a model of strict adherence to the *cursus honorum*, and as such was unremarkable. However, by 65 B.C., during his aedileship, he became an ally of the immensely wealthy Marcus Licinius Crassus. The reason for Caesar's association with Crassus was that he was heavily in debt, and Crassus had the means to solve his problem. Crassus, like Sulla before, recognized the many skills of Caesar and realized it would benefit him greatly to have Caesar as an ally.

Throughout his life, Caesar was married three times. His first wife, Cornelia (who died in 68 B.C.), was the daughter of Cinna, the famous henchman of Marius. Next, in 67 B.C., he married Pompeia, the granddaughter of Sulla, whom he divorced in 61 B.C. (for "Caesar's wife must be above suspicion"), and in 59 B.C. he married Calpurnia, the daughter of Piso Caesoninius (the consul of 58 B.C.), and remained married to her until his death, ignoring her warnings against attending the senate meeting at which he was murdered. Caesar was notorious for his many affairs, of which the two most serious were Servilia, the mother of his assassin Brutus, and queen Cleopatra VII of Egypt.

In 62 B.C., Caesar was implicated in the First Cataline Conspiracy, a movement backed by Crassus in which the rural poor were to rise up and murder the consuls (one of whom was Cicero). In truth there was little to the charges, but Cicero amplified the matter for his own political gain.

Later in that same year, another of Caesar's future allies, Pompey the Great, returned to Rome. Pompey and Crassus were sworn enemies. However, Pompey now had the upper hand, for he had rid the Mediterranean of pirates, defeated the Pontic king Mithradates VI, and reorganized the Roman east. In the process Pompey not only added to his already considerable military glory, but he had seized so much booty that he was now even wealthier than Crassus.

Caesar's involvement in politics, and especially in opposing the senate, continued to grow. After his governorship in Hispania Ulterior ('Farther Spain') ended in 60 B.C., Caesar waited outside Rome anticipating a triumph and asked of the senate that he be permitted to run for the consulate. When the senate refused, Caesar surrendered his anticipated triumph and allied himself with Crassus and Pompey. This informal pact, known as the First Triumvirate, was sealed by the marriage of Julius Caesar's daughter, Julia, to Pompey.

Not surprisingly, Caesar was now allowed to stand for election, and indeed won the consulship for 59 B.C. Pompey and Caesar worked together against the senate, with Caesar forcing through Pompey's legislation, and in return having his own minor provincial appointment transformed into the *Lex Vatinia*, by which Caesar was not only given a five-year proconsular command in Cisalpine Gaul, Illyricum and Gallia Narbonensis, but given command of four legions for that same period. So long an army command was exceptional in the Republic.

After finishing his consulship, Caesar remained outside Rome for the first 3 months of 58 B.C., until Cicero had been exiled and Cato had been sent to Cyprus. Caesar then departed to Gaul to begin what would be turned into a 9-year effort to pacify Gaul and to enlarge his own reputation. By conquering Gaul, Caesar hoped to conquer Rome itself. During his first term in Gaul, Caesar traveled widely, launching a minor invasion of Britain and twice crossing the Rhine. But the political front in Rome was equally treacherous, for the senate and the *optimates* were warming up to Pompey, and trying to lure him into abandoning Crassus and Caesar. So in 56 B.C., Caesar organized a conference at Luca, by which the Triumvirate was renewed. Crassus and Pompey jointly held the consulship in 55 B.C., and by the *Lex Trebonia* had been given virtually unlimited powers.

At the conference, the three men carved up the Roman territories through their five-year proconsular commands. Pompey received Spain, Caesar kept Gaul, and Crassus chose Syria, for he had a not-so-secret desire to invade Parthia, and in the process gain the military distinction he needed to complement his wealth. In 53 B.C., Crassus invaded Parthia, but his over-zealous nature caused him to fail on a monumental scale, and Crassus died a shameful death during the retreat near Carrhae.

It was during Caesar's second command in Gaul, beginning in 56 B.C., that he earned his most impressive victories. Each step of the way, Caesar made the most of his daring exploits by writing commentaries on them: the seven "books" of *De Bello Gallico*, (published in 52/1 B.C., either as one work or chapter-by-chapter) and the three of *De Bello Civili* (published posthumously). The writing was fresh and concise, remarkably free of rhetoric, and the subject matter was of great interest to the public. Between the distribution of his commentaries and the actions of his political henchmen, Caesar was as well represented as if he himself was in Rome.

Though Caesar's exploits could be discussed at great length, let it suffice to say that he did not begin his career as a general competently. Indeed, he barely escaped the consequences of serious tactical errors in his first few engagements. But Caesar was a fast learner, and soon he gained the upper hand on the Gauls. His conquest bears strong similarities to those of Alexander the Great in the East, for he was always far outnumbered while deep in enemy territory with weak or nonexistent supply lines. In most cases, Caesar made up his strategies on the spot.

Caesar's intuition and charisma as a commander of men gained him the undying loyalty of his soldiers. Though unlike Alexander he would not always lead from the front, he would rush to the front — at great personal risk — whenever a portion of his army was loosing ground. Caesar's personal appearance (apparently bare-headed and wearing an easily distinguished cloak) rallied his beaten-down and outnumbered soldiers time and time again to great victories.

His most ambitious campaign was the siege of Alesia, where the Gauls had put their differences aside to unite against Caesar. They hoped that through incredibly superior numbers they could destroy the Roman legions to the man. Leading the loose confederation of Gauls was Vercingetorix, a chieftain who had closely observed the ways of Roman warfare, making him especially dangerous.

Caesar had his own legions as well as some German cavalry units, but he could get no further supplies, for he was cut off. All told, his forces probably numbered less than 30,000. In Caesar's first engagement with Vercingetorix, he came into such great personal danger that the Gauls managed to strip him of his sword. But the Romans won the engagement. The Gauls had some 80,000 foot soldiers and a cavalry that was superior in number to the Romans and Germans combined. Realizing that large numbers of reinforcements were on their way, Vercingetorix withdrew to the hill-fort of Alesia, which Caesar began to besiege by establishing a perimeter siege wall nearly nine miles long on hilly terrain.

Caesar had only a fraction of the soldiers of the Gauls, and was constantly raided while building the fortifications. Furthermore, he did not have sufficient men to guard the lengthy wall and its 23 "forts." Caesar diverted a nearby river to fill the defensive trenches with water, and filled other trenches with sharpened sticks. The amount of earth moved and timber felled was astounding, but this was the Roman way: to win a war through strategy, hard manual labor and patience. A month passed, and Vercingetorix was running out of food and water.

But now the real trouble arrived. Caesar tells us that some 250,000 armed Gauls arrived to relieve the siege of Alesia — a force that alone was 10 times that which Caesar commanded. This meant that Caesar, in essence, was now the one being besieged, as if caught between a hammer and an anvil. Caesar quickly ordered the construction of a similar wall to defend their rear. Of similar construction, this wall was even longer, for it was the exterior ring of the existing fortifications.

Not only did the Romans have about 350,000 men to fight, but they were also prevented from gathering food, water, timber or other essentials. The fighting was incredibly fierce for many days: the Gauls were fighting in a last-ditch effort for their sovereignty, and the Romans were fighting for their very lives, and for Caesar. Each new attack presented a different problem, one to which Caesar had to respond to immediately. This meant re-forming cohorts, diverting his resources and reinforcing in person where his men needed him most. If there was any breach, his entire army would be destroyed. Finally, he drove off the relief army and starved Vercingetorix and his renegade army into capitulation.

Caesar's undying courage under the worst imaginable circumstances is almost beyond belief. Whereas most commanders would have withdrawn or surrendered, Caesar fought on, for he needed to achieve his goals. That his soldiers did not desert him is much to Caesar's credit. After Alesia, Caesar's men continued to fight in Gaul, finishing off the few remaining tasks, some of which were nearly as perilous.

Meanwhile in Rome, the rivalry between Pompey and Caesar was magnified. In 54 B.C., Julia, the wife of Pompey and the daughter of Caesar, died, and in 53 B.C., Crassus was killed. Now, there was little to bind the two, and the geographical separation did not help matters. The senate was becoming alarmed about the power Caesar was amassing (and especially his large and loyal army), and so once again it allied itself closely with Pompey. This time, there was no "Conference of Luca" at which they could settle their differences.

In 51 and 50 B.C., the conflict grew, for Caesar's five-year appointment in Gaul was coming to an end and his recent victory at Alesia had raised his popularity among the people of Rome to new heights. His legions were fiercely loyal to their commander. Caesar proposed that he and Pompey disband their armies simultaneously. The senate first approved this concept, which was then vetoed by the anti-Caesarian consuls. Instead, on January 1, 49 B.C., the senate demanded that Caesar alone disband his army before returning to Italy.

Realizing that he would be charged with crimes while at the mercy of Pompey and his army, Caesar refused the senate's demand. Meanwhile, the senate gave Pompey authority to defend the Republic from Caesar, and on January 10, Caesar crossed the Rubicon River with his legions. Though he was unable to prevent the flight of Pompey to Greece, he took Italy with the greatest of ease. Next, Caesar campaigned in Spain, where he defeated Pompey's lieutenants, Afranius and Petreius. In the meantime, his most trusted comrade-in-arms, Titus Labienus (the father of the Labienus who in 40 B.C. led the Parthian invasion of Syria), defected to Pompey.

Caesar's next move was against Pompey himself. Caesar crossed over to Greece to combat the forces Pompey had assembled in Epirus. On August 9, 48 B.C., Caesar defeated Pompey at the battle at Pharsalus, capturing some 20,000 of Pompey's men and sending Pompey in flight to Egypt. But there was no safety for Pompey there, for he was murdered by courtiers of King Ptolemy XIII while disembarking at Alexandria on September 28.

Pompey's head was then cut off and pickled, and we are told that when Caesar arrived four days later, the sight of Pompey's head caused him to shed tears. Despite their opposition, Caesar recognized Pompey as a great Roman, and felt his end was undignified. In any event, Caesar had come to Egypt not only to pursue Pompey, but also to collect on some very large loans made to the Lagid kings by Rabirius Postumus, loans which Caesar had underwritten. However, what Caesar imagined would be a short visit turned into an extended stay, and a very dangerous one at that, for it resulted in the so-called Alexandrian War of 47 B.C.

Caesar had arrived in the midst of an inter-palace rivalry between the siblings Ptolemy XIII and Cleopatra VII, who had jointly inherited the throne from their father in 51 B.C. Caesar immediately took command in Alexandria, and chose to support Cleopatra's bid for the throne. Her charm and courage had seduced Caesar, a seduction which was consummated in an amorous affair between the 52-year-old warlord and the 21-year-old queen.

The Alexandrian War did not involve a large number of soldiers, but it was very dangerous. On more than one occasion Caesar was nearly killed. However, in Caesar's most desperate hour, when all seemed certainly lost, he and his legionnaires were rescued by a small army led by Mithradates of Pergamum. On March 26, Ptolemy XIII fled, and was drowned in the Nile.

Cleopatra was now queen again, and in the Egyptian tradition, she married her 11-year-old brother, Ptolemy XIV and ordained him co-ruler. Caesar stayed on for a luxurious cruise on the Nile with his new lover, but soon left to solve other problems in Asia Minor.

In perhaps his most efficient war, Caesar defeated the rebel Pontic king Pharnaces II at Zela in a five-day campaign during the Spring of 47 B.C. It was at this time he uttered the famous phrase *Veni vidi vici* ("I came, I saw, I conquered"). For Caesar this was sweet revenge, as Pharnaces II had defeated his governor Calvinus at Nicopolis in the previous year. Thereafter, Caesar settled many other affairs in the East (with Cleopatra, in the meantime, giving birth to his son, Caesarion), and headed West.

Caesar arrived in Italy in July of 47 B.C. and stamped out a mutiny in Campania, after which he made his way to Rome in October and resigned his dictatorship. In December he departed for North Africa to battle more Pompeians in the so-called "African War." His campaigns were a success, and resulted in the suicide of Brutus' uncle Cato Uticensis at Utica, and a crushing victory in April of 46 B.C. at Thapsus, where the commander Metellus Pius Scipio committed suicide. Caesar returned to Rome on July 25th, having requested that Cleopatra join him there.

There was no end to the praise for Caesar. In addition to hailing Caesar dictator for the next decade, the senate awarded him four successive triumphs, for his victories in Gaul, Egypt, Pontus and North Africa. Cleopatra's entourage arrived later in the year, and she stayed with Caesar at his villa on the Tiber. Though Caesar was much beloved, the presence of Cleopatra, loose talk of Caesar's paternity of Caesarion, and the supposed idea of making Alexandria a "second capital" to Rome, were not well received by the conservative Romans.

However, Caesar still had more to accomplish. In November he set out for Spain, where he hoped to stamp out the remaining Pompeians, who were under the leadership of Pompey's two sons. On March 17, 45 B.C., Caesar won an extremely difficult, but monumental victory at Munda, resulting in the capture and execution of Pompey's eldest son, Pompey Junior. The victory was not complete, though, for the youngest son, Sextus Pompey, managed to escape. Though he would never again trouble Caesar, Sextus Pompey was a thorn in the side of Rome for the next decade.

Caesar returned to Rome yet again, to celebrate his Spanish triumph in October of 45 B.C. Now at the height of his power, he scarcely could have imagined that he had less than six months to live, though by this time the plot against his life may already have been formed. Meanwhile, the senate heaped more honors on the great conqueror. On February 14, 44 B.C., he was given the title *dictator perpetuus* (dictator for life). In the previous month he had placed his image on coinage. Both of these acts were unprecedented in the history of Rome, and were identical to the honors given to Greek kings of previous centuries.

Despite all that he had accomplished, Caesar still had visions of Alexander the Great in his mind — he wanted to conquer the rest of Asia as his hero had done nearly three centuries before. However, the Sibylline Books prophesied that only a king could conquer Parthia, and Caesar was a mere dictator.

Though no doubt the gestures were staged, Caesar's chief lieutenant, Marc Antony (who had run affairs in Rome during his absences in the last five years), offered him the golden laurel of a king on three occasions, which Caesar turned down each time. But it was known that he would ask the senate to give him the title of king (*rex*) for use when he was outside of Italy, though he would remain dictator in his own country. This, no doubt, would ensure success against Parthia.

About one month after Caesar had been hailed "dictator for life," he was murdered in an annex of the the Theater of Pompey on the *Campus Martius* (not the Senate House in the Forum, as is often reported) on the Ides (15th) of March, bringing his grandiose plans to a halt. The plot was well-concealed, and Caesar thus paid no heed to the warnings of his third-in-command, Lepidus, only the day before, to beware of a conspiracy. In all, about 60 vehemently Republican senators participated, and Caesar's body, riddled with stab wounds, fell lifeless at the base of a statue of

Pompey the Great. Leading the conspirators were Brutus and Cassius, two men in whom Caesar had invested much hope. Indeed, Caesar had recently appointed them to the two highest governmental posts in Rome.

Though the act of regicide was considered a noble one among Romans, it is important to remember that not only was a dictatorship at stake, but also the supremacy of the wealthy and high-born. As dictator, Caesar would have continued to introduce "lower born" men and provincials into the senate (which he had enlarged to 900 members) and into positions of power in his administration. To the aristocrats, this meant a reversal of the social order that had so greatly benefited them since Rome's foundation. Caesar's murder was equally an act of selfish practicality, as it was an act in defense of the Republic.

A period of great chaos followed, in which Cleopatra fled Rome with great haste, and Marc Antony maintained order, only later to have it challenged by Caesar's heir, young Octavian. The conspirators Brutus and Cassius left Rome almost immediately, and departed Italy for good in August.

The combination of Antony's stirring funeral eulogy, and the staging of the Parilia games in honor of Caesar's victory at Munda moved public opinion strongly in favor of Caesar. His bequest of 300 sestertii per citizen further endeared his memory to the Romans. When a comet appeared in the skies over Rome in July of 44 B.C., many were convinced that it embodied the soul of Caesar, for it occured during the public funerary games being held in Caesar's memory. Ever willing to exploit a political advantage, his heir Octavian placed comets upon the heads of Caesar's statues, and in that same year secured both the deification of Caesar and senatorial recognition of his status as Caesar's heir.

NUMISMATIC NOTE: In January 44 B.C., Caesar became the first living Roman to place his image on a coin *struck at Rome*, an action that shocked his contemporaries and which no doubt contributed to the urgency of his murder. With the exception of a very brief coinage struck by Flamininus in Greece 150 years before, this had never before occured on Roman coinage. Caesar's "lifetime" portrait occurs only on denarii, but after his death his portrait additionally occurs on gold and bronzes. Caesar's posthumous portrait coins were struck by his protégé, Marc Antony, by various moneyers who were sympathetic to the Caesarean cause, and by his adoptive son, Octavian. The fallen dictator is shown wearing a laurel wreath, and often also wearing a veil. Although a number of bronzes were struck with Caesar's portrait, only two gold pieces occur — a dual-portrait aureus of 43 B.C. struck by Octavian to advertise himself as Caesar's heir, and a restitution aureus struck by the emperor Trajan (A.D. 98–117), which features an unusual bare-headed portrait. These two aurei have portraits of very different styles, which has led some scholars to conclude that they are based on different sculptural prototypes.

PTOLEMY XV (CALLED 'CAESARION')

SON OF JULIUS CAESAR AND QUEEN CLEOPATRA VII

Ptolemy XV Caesar ('Caesarion'), 47–30 B.C. Born in Alexandria on June 23, 47 B.C., to Cleopatra VII, the last Greek queen of Egypt, Ptolemy XV (nicknamed "Caesarion") was reputedly the son of Julius Caesar. Whether or not this was factual, Caesarion probably would have succeeded his mother as the Roman-backed ruler of Egypt had Julius Caesar remained in power at Rome.

Cleopatra's association with Julius Caesar began shortly after the warlord defeated Pompey the Great at the Battle of Pharsalus on August 9, 48 B.C. Having lost this signal battle, Pompey fled to Egypt with Caesar in fast pursuit. Pompey was murdered at Pelusium on September 28 just as he was disembarking; Caesar arrived on October 2, and soon realized that his "visit" was going to become an extended stay, for Egypt had recently undergone its own court revolution, and Caesar had gotten more than he had bargained for.

Cleopatra had succeeded her father, Ptolemy XII Auletes, when he died in 51 B.C., for she was his oldest child. She shared her reign with her oldest brother, Ptolemy XIII, whom she married, for that was the custom in Egypt. However, Cleopatra was expelled by the courtiers of her brother not long after this, and she sought refuge in Syria.

Thus, after Pompey's defeat and murder, Cleopatra turned to the newly arrived Julius Caesar, a man whom she recognized as the undisputed ruler of the Roman world. She seduced him into her private life and into her struggle to regain the throne. It was during this tumultuous period, in the fall of 48 B.C., that Cleopatra and Caesar began an affair that may have resulted in the child Caesarion. The time-frame is tight, and in a best case scenario, Cleopatra would have been pregnant just short of nine months.

Caesar devoted himself to his Egyptian task (often called the Alexandrian War), though he achieved it only with great difficulty. Indeed, a part of the famous library went up in flames, and Caesar himself almost perished on more than one occasion. Late in March, 47 B.C., the tide turned against Ptolemy XIII, as Caesar was rescued by the perfectly timed arrival of an army led by Mithradates of Pergamum. Once Caesar's victory was complete, he arranged for his mistress Cleopatra to marry her 11-year-old brother, Ptolemy XIV, ordaining him as co-regent.

It was Caesar's intention that Caesarion would be heir to the Greek dynasty in Egypt, an important kingdom which Julius Caesar (unlike others in Rome) hoped to shore up rather than to destroy. Caesar had departed for Syria just weeks before Caesarion was born, and Cleopatra made the long journey to Rome in time for Caesar's great celebrations in September and October of 46 B.C. She resided with Caesar until his murder in March 44 B.C., after which she and her entourage made a hasty return to Egypt.

Upon returning to Alexandria, Cleopatra had her brother-husband Ptolemy XIV murdered and replaced him with her 4-year-old son Caesarion, whom she married and made co-regent of her kingdom. In the summer of 43 B.C., Cleopatra gained Roman recognition of Caesarion from Publius Cornelius Dolabella, the *consul suffectus* who had replaced Julius Caesar, and who subsequently gained the governorship of Syria. In exchange for this recognition, Cleopatra gave Dolabella the four Roman legions stationed in Egypt (which she was only too pleased to have an excuse to expel). However, Dolabella soon lost the legions to Cassius.

In succeeding years Cleopatra became ally and lover to Marc Antony, by whom she bore three more children, only one of whom (Cleopatra Selene, the first wife of king Juba II of Mauretania) appears on coins. Though Cleopatra's association with Antony was promising, it made her an enemy of young Octavian, Antony's rival in the West. When Antony lost to Octavian at the Battle of Actium in 31 B.C., Antony fled to Egypt. In the following year, both Antony and Cleopatra committed suicide, leaving Caesarion, then age 17, to the designs of Octavian, who promptly murdered him on August 29 of 30 B.C. With the boy's passing, the Lagid dynasty of Ptolemaic Egypt was rendered extinct.

NUMISMATIC NOTE: Coins depicting Caesarion as an infant in his mother's arms were struck on the island of Cyprus, which was an important naval station during the Hellenistic and early Imperial periods. It was captured in 48 B.C. by Julius Caesar and shortly thereafter conferred upon Egypt. Control of the island passed between Rome and Egypt several times in the succeeding years, until Octavian claimed it for Rome after the deaths of Marc Antony and Cleopatra in 30 B.C. A coin of Damascus formerly thought to depict Caesarion is now reattributed to the reign of the emperor Nero (A.D. 54–68), exactly one century later, based on a proper reading of its date.

METELLUS PIUS SCIPIO

IMPERATOR, 49(?) B.C.

FATHER-IN-LAW OF POMPEY THE GREAT

Quintus Caecilius Metellus Pius Scipio, d. 46 B.C. The career of Metellus Pius Scipio arose from the patronage of Pompey the Great, who two decades before had campaigned in Spain with Scipio's adoptive father, Metellus Pius (the consul of 80 B.C.). Though Scipio was descended of a noble family, he apparently inherited none of his ancestors' greatness, for he was detested by his contemporaries.

Scipio's political career was mere puppetry, and his military career was as brief as it was degrading. Pompey the Great had married Scipio's daughter shortly before he had become sole-consul in the abortive elections of 52 B.C. However, in the final months of 52 B.C., Pompey elected as his co-consul his new father-in-law, whom he also had just rescued from a bribery charge. But one hand washed the other, and Scipio spearheaded the "war" against Julius Caesar by introducing to the senate the legislation that demanded that Caesar disband his legions and relinquish his command in Gaul (January 7, 49 B.C.).

Caesar ignored the senate's demand, crossed the Rubicon on January 10, 49 B.C., and invaded Italy. Pompey and his allies were taken by storm, and had to flee to Greece. Shortly before this occurred, the senate had granted Scipio the governorship of Syria, for which he had immediately departed. When Scipio learned of Pompey's flight, he gathered two legions, apparently winning victories in the Amanus mountains, for which he was hailed Imperator. He then delivered the legions to his son-in-law in Thessaly (where he was confronted by Calvinus), apparently having refused a bribe from Caesar to defect.

At the Battle of Pharsalus (August 9, 48 B.C.), Scipio commanded Pompey's center. As the battle went in Caesar's favor, both Pompey and Scipio fled. Pompey went to Egypt, where he was murdered on September 28, as he was disembarking. Scipio headed to North Africa, where he took up supreme command of the Pompeian remnants that had gathered there, including Cato Uticensis and Sextus Pompey.

Caesar's subsequent travels to Egypt, Pontus and Italy allowed the Pompeians to re-group for yet another war. In 46 B.C. Caesar arrived in Africa, and the Pompeians were routed at Utica and at Thapsus (in April, 46 B.C.). The latter defeat was decisive, and was at the expense of Scipio, who committed suicide after it became clear all had been lost.

BRUTUS

IMPERATOR, 43–42 B.C.

CO-CONSPIRATOR OF CASSIUS
SON OF MARCUS JUNIUS BRUTUS AND SERVILIA
HUSBAND OF PORCIA AND CLAUDIA
NEPHEW OF CATO UTICENSIS
BROTHER-IN-LAW OF LEPIDUS AND CASSIUS

Marcus Junius Brutus (*adopted name* Quintus Caepio Brutus), 85 (or 79/8)–42 B.C. This amazing character has been judged by history in two different lights: as a champion of liberty who failed because of his virtues, or as a turncoat villain whom Dante placed in the lowest circle of Hell. He is best remembered by historians for his leading role in the assassination of Julius Caesar, and by numismatists for his remarkable "Ides of March" coinage that subsequently advertised that fact.

Brutus claimed descent from Lucius Junius Brutus, who in 509 B.C. is credited with expelling Tarquinius Superbus, the last of the kings to rule in Rome. This same Brutus subsequently served as the first consul of Rome's fledgling Republic, and put his own children to death for their involvement in a plot to restore the Tarquian kings. On his mother's side, Brutus claimed descent from Servilius Ahala, who in the 5th Century B.C. killed Spurius Maelius, who was threatening to overthrow the Republic and install himself as king.

Brutus was proud of his Republican ancestry, and thus depicted these two ancestors, Brutus (the ancient) and Ahala, on the coinage he struck as moneyer in 54 B.C. Indeed, the defense of the Republic, and the murder of kings, was the hallmark of Brutus' family.

A well-educated man belonging to the ruling elite of the Republic, Brutus counted among his close friends Atticus, Cassius, Cato Uticensis, Lepidus and Cicero, who declared Brutus to be "first among the younger generation," adding that he hoped he would soon be the "first man in the state." However, Brutus, like Seneca, was not entirely virtuous, despite his adherence to Stoicism. Indeed, early in his career he is known to have extorted 48 percent interest on loans to Greek cities in the East, even though 12 percent was the legal maximum.

Also among Brutus' friends was Julius Caesar, who viewed the young man as his protégé. Though Caesar engaged in many adulterous affairs with women, his most serious was with Brutus' mother, Servilia, who was deeply in love with Caesar. Indeed, we are told that Caesar may have believed that Brutus was his natural son, born of his affair with Servilia.

Despite all these connections, Caesar and Brutus had a complex relationship, and Caesar considered Brutus to be positively unsympathetic. Their first confrontation occurred when Brutus allied himself with Pompey the Great, and thus took up arms against Caesar. Considering that Pompey had killed Brutus' father in 77 B.C., this seemed an odd choice, but in terms of Republican causes, it was the noble choice. Even so, Caesar gave orders that Brutus was not to be harmed, and after the Battle of Pharsalus they reconciled, and Brutus was appointed as a legate in Cilicia.

Subsequently, in 46 B.C., Caesar appointed Brutus as proconsul of Cisalpine Gaul — an extremely important post, and one well beyond Brutus' qualifications. While serving in that capacity, Brutus remained loyal to Caesar, even though in the meantime the latter had defeated and killed his uncle, Cato Uticensis, in North Africa. Next, in 44 B.C., Caesar appointed Brutus and Cassius to the two top praetorships in Rome. Brutus, who held the top praetorship, the praetor urbanus, was also designated to share the consulship of 41 B.C. with Cassius, his brother-in-law and future co-conspirator.

Caesar was now the top man in Rome, and perhaps as early as September of 45 B.C., a conspiracy against his life had begun to form. By February 14 of 44 B.C., Caesar had achieved the unprecedented title "dictator for life." On February 15, 44 B.C. (and on two occasions thereafter), Caesar rejected Marc Antony's offer of the royal diadem of a king, only to subsequently try to persuade the senate to give him a royal title for his actions outside of Italy. Furthermore, he placed his image upon the coinage — something that had never before occurred at Rome. Despite the deep debt of gratitude that Brutus owed Caesar, such open acts of tyranny were intolerable, and so a plot which involved some 60 men finally materialized.

The secret was so well-kept that even Cicero was not privy. It is uncertain at which point Brutus became involved. Appian and Plutarch tell us that Cassius pressured Brutus into participating, whereas Dio Cassius suggests Brutus took the lead himself. In any event, Brutus' good character and ancestral legacy were an essential ingredient if the assassination was to be perceived as an act of clear conscience.

The assassination occurred at the senate meeting on the Ides of March (in March, the Ides falls on the 15th), 44 B.C. Caesar arrived late to the meeting, and the conspirators were terrified that Caesar had been warned; but he arrived none-the-less, and soon lay dead at the feet of a statue of his former nemesis, Pompey the Great.

What became clear after the fact is that this was no coup or junta, but rather an isolated act, to which there was no follow-up plan. Neither Lepidus nor Antony (who was co-consul with Caesar) were murdered, nor did the conspirators have gifts for the public. They did not have the support of the army, and had not even considered how they would calm Caesar's veterans. Cicero, perhaps in resentment for having been excluded from the plot, summarized it in six simple words in a letter to Atticus: "No plan. No thought. No method."

The murder of Caesar is often viewed as a noble act in the defense of a venerable institution. But what institution? The conspirators would have said the senate, and the right of the people to be ruled by a quasi-democratic form of government. Others, more accurately, would suggest it was in defense of what the senate represented to the wealthy and privileged — a guarantee that they would rule Rome. Caesar not only planned to keep supreme power himself, but he would have "polluted" the senate and top administrative and military posts with men of humble origins, allowing the common man to take a share in power. Thus, it was the preservation of status for the wealthy and aristocratic — not the liberation from tyranny — that was the heartfelt motive of the conspirators.

Brutus and Cassius occupied the Capitol after the murder, while Antony convinced the senate on March 18 to declare a general amnesty and also prevented Lepidus (whose troops had occupied the Forum) from taking military action. But these were not acts of generosity by Antony, for he did not want this great opportunity to slip by with a quick execution of the conspirators. Instead, he planned to use it as a springboard for the advancement of his own career.

Antony delivered an emotion-filled funeral oration for Caesar, and public sentiment turned against the conspirators. Seeing no safety in Rome, Brutus and Cassius left for calmer parts of Italy. They also ignored their menial senatorial appointments (Brutus was first given a grain commissionership in Asia, and subsequently the governorship of Crete). Indeed, they stayed in various cities along the western coast of Italy until they finally fled to the East in August of 44 B.C.

Cassius went adventuring along the coast of Asia Minor and Syria while Brutus went to Greece. There he gained the support of the governor of Macedon, and also the support of the senate, which granted him and Cassius proconsular commands, apparently late in February of 43 B.C. In March, Brutus captured Gaius Antonius, the brother of Marc Antony, and in the summer campaigned against the Bessi in Thrace, where he was hailed Imperator.

While Antony and Octavian crossed over to Illyricum, Brutus and Cassius met at Smyrna early in 42 B.C. and planned for the conflict by attacking the Rhodians and Lycians, both of whom had formidable fleets that could pose a threat to their rear. In the spring of 42 B.C. Cassius captured Rhodes, and Brutus ravaged Lycia with the help of his fleet commander Casca. Brutus and Cassius met at Sardes in the summer after their campaigns, and then departed to Greece to wage war against Antony and Octavian.

Meanwhile in Rome, the political climate had changed. Antony and Lepidus had joined forces with Octavian, and together they began to persecute the conspirators who remained in Italy. Among the first to fall was

Cicero, who, although not a conspirator, had openly opposed the tyranny of Antony and supported the Republican cause with his *Philippics*. In response, Brutus executed Antony's brother, Gaius Antonius, and became somewhat fatalistic about his role in history. In a letter to Atticus, he suggested there was no more noble a position than his own, for if victorious he would be the champion of the Republican cause, or he would be freed from slavery by his death.

In the late summer of 42 B.C., the opposing armies met at Philippi in northern Greece. Brutus and Cassius had agreed to a death pact in their campaign against Marc Antony and Octavian. It occurred in two battles in October, about three weeks apart. The first battle was won through some fast action by Brutus, but ended with the suicide of Cassius, who seemingly misinterpreted the outcome. The second began well for Brutus, who alone faced Antony and Octavian, but soon turned against him. His forces routed, Brutus sped away with a handful of close friends and committed suicide on October 23, thus fulfilling his pact with Cassius.

There are two versions concerning what happened to Brutus' body. Plutarch tells us that Antony gave it a respectful funeral and sent the ashes back to his mother in Rome. However, Suetonius and Dio Cassius suggest that Octavian — bent on revenge — sent Brutus' severed head via ship back to Rome so it could be thrown at the feet of Caesar's statue, but that it was thrown overboard by superstitious sailors *en route*.

NUMISMATIC NOTE: Brutus is best known to numismatists for his "Ides of March" denarii, which on the obverse bear his own portrait and on the reverse shows a liberty cap flanked by two daggers above the inscription EID. MAR. In the opinion of many numismatists, this is the most impressive of all Roman coins, for its reverse promotes the murder of Caesar as a selfless act in defense of the Republic, yet the obverse features Brutus' portrait in the same fashion as that of the dictator he had killed. So remarkable was this coin type that it was even described by the ancient historian Dio Cassius.

The other coins Brutus struck in gold and silver while preparing for war with Antony and Octavian usually feature the goddess Libertas (Liberty), military trophies, priestly implements or have naval references. The obverse design of aurei of the Thracian or Scythian king Koson are blatant copies of Brutus' coinage as moneyer, and some of them bear a monogram that almost certainly represents the name of Brutus. Therefore, they should be associated with Brutus' actions in Thrace, where he was hailed Imperator.

Brutus' portrait appears on three issues, and though they all seem to be derived from the same sculptural prototype, they differ in their treatment. Some are rather "Baroque" in appearance (the aurei of Servilius

Casca), others seemingly neo-Classical in their treatment (the aurei of Pedanius Costa). The EID MAR denarii of Plaetorius Cestianus offer two distinctly different busts: the so-called "plastic" type with softened features, and the "linear" type with strongly defined facial features.

A final mention is due the denarius of Lucius Servius Rufus, the moneyer of 41 B.C. who otherwise is unknown to history. The portrait on this issue is certainly that of Brutus, as it compares so favorably with the inscribed portrait issues Brutus himself struck. That there is no identifying inscription makes perfect sense, for it would have been too blatant an affront to the Triumvirs. However, it *was* struck at an opportune moment, for in 41 B.C. the partisans of Antony and Octavian were very much at war: Antony's brother, Lucius Antonius, had extorted permission from the senate to wage war on Octavian (resulting in the "Perusine War"); and Antony's wife, Fulvia, was doing her best to undermine Octavian, who had been saddled with the difficult task of settling 100,000 veterans. Amid all this chaos and infighting, a portrait of Brutus — representing the orderly Republic he had hoped to restore — is daring, but not out of place.

CASSIUS

IMPERATOR, 43–42 B.C.

CO-CONSPIRATOR AND BROTHER-IN-LAW OF BRUTUS
HUSBAND OF TERTULLA

Gaius Cassius Longinus, d. 42 B.C. From the start of his career, Cassius proved himself an able commander. When Crassus embarked for his invasion of Parthia in 53 B.C., Cassius was his quaestor. Indeed, it was Cassius who warned Crassus that his final advance was foolhardy, but Crassus did not listen, and forged on. In the engagement, both Crassus and his son were killed, and it was incumbent upon Cassius to rally the retreating armies.

Considering how severely shattered the Roman army had been, it is a testimony to Cassius' level head that he organized a successful retreat for what remained of the legions. Cassius — who reputedly was often sarcastic and ill-tempered, and certainly was a harsh disciplinarian — remained in Syria, and two years later, in 51 B.C., repelled the invasion led by the Parthian prince Pacorus I. For all he had done to protect Roman interests in the east, Cassius established a fine reputation quite early in his career.

In 49 B.C. he served as tribune, and commanded a Pompeian fleet in the Civil War of 49–48 B.C. However, he was not persecuted after Pompey's defeat at Pharsalus, but instead was pardoned by Caesar, who appointed him as one of his legates. Indeed, Cassius may even have accompanied Caesar on his lightning campaign against the Pontic king Pharnaces II.

Back in Italy in 44 B.C., Cassius was appointed *praetor peregrinus*, the second-highest command in the city of Rome; the highest office, *praetor urbanus*, was given to another protégé of Caesar, Marcus Junius Brutus. Not only were Brutus and Cassius political allies, but Cassius was married to one of Brutus' sisters, Tertulla. The two praetors were also designated to share the consulship of 41 B.C. Little could Caesar have known that these two young men whom he had supported, and indeed promoted to the two highest offices in Rome, would conspire against him.

After his return from the Battle of Munda, Caesar was hailed "dictator for life" by the senate on February 14, 44 B.C. Though he turned down the golden diadem thrice offered to him by Marc Antony, Caesar had made it clear that he would like to have that distinction bestowed upon him for the time when he was outside of Italy. Furthermore, in January he had placed his image on coinage — yet another unprecedented action. A conspiracy to murder Caesar, which appears to have been formed by Cassius, came to fruition on the Ides (15th) of March, 44 B.C., as a mob of 60 senatorial conspirators, including Brutus, stabbed Caesar to death in the Theater of Pompey.

Immediately after the murder, Cassius and Brutus occupied the Capitoline, while Antony, who had shared the consulship with Caesar, convinced the senate to declare a general amnesty and prevented Lepidus (whose troops had occupied the Forum) from taking military action. In the aftermath, Cassius and Brutus went to rural locations in Italy, and ignored their degrading senatorial appointments (Cassius was first given a grain commissionership in Sicily, to which he responded "Am I the man to accept an insult as if it was a favor?" and subsequently the governorship of Cyrenaica). Instead, he and Brutus stayed in cities along the western coast of Italy until they fled to the East in August of 44 B.C.

Cassius, having fled to Syria, was in familiar territory where his name still commanded respect, and so he seized Syria from the legitimate governor. Many others who either were involved in the conspiracy or who sympathized with the Republican cause, joined up with the refugee co-conspirators. Among those who offered their armies to Cassius were Marcius Crispus, Staius Murcus and Caecilius Bassus.

Cassius' ranks swelled by four additional legions from Publius Cornelius Dolabella, the treacherous *consul suffectus* who had replaced Caesar and subsequently gained the governorship of Syria. Dolabella confronted Cassius in the Summer of 43 B.C., but committed suicide after he was defeated by Cassius.

After the Battle of Mutina (at which Octavian defeated Lucius Antonius, the brother of Marc Antony), the senate gave Brutus and Cassius supreme authority in the eastern provinces. But after Octavian forcibly assumed power in Rome, the senate quickly reversed its decision and outlawed the renegade Republicans. Meanwhile, both rebels were campaigning in the East to gather resources and allies for the struggle against Antony and Octavian, who had since joined forces with Lepidus to found the Second Triumvirate.

Cassius met with Brutus at Smyrna early in 42 B.C., after which he subdued the island of Rhodes in the spring. In the summer he joined forces with Brutus (who in the meantime had ravaged Lycia) at Sardes in Lydia, and the two made their way to the northern Greece with their armies. Upon arriving in Thrace, they encountered the Triumviral armies headed by Antony and Octavian. The Republicans had the advantage, for not only were they better equipped, but one of the opposing generals, Octavian, was seriously ill. However, Brutus and Cassius had agreed to a suicide pact in the event they lost the battle, and it was this agreement, seemingly, that proved to be their undoing.

The armies clashed in two battles — the first, at the beginning of October, proving fatal for Cassius, the second, on October 23, proving fatal for Brutus. Though the first battle was won by some clever actions by Brutus, Cassius' camp was captured, and when he saw messengers approaching, he committed suicide. It is reported that he feared the worst, that Brutus had been defeated and that all hope was lost. And so, Cassius fulfilled his end of the suicide pact without wasting another moment.

This left Brutus in a bind, for now he had to lead both armies, and he was the lesser general in any case. The next battle occurred about three weeks later, and though it began in Brutus' favor, it ended with his defeat, after which he fulfilled his end of the suicide pact. One can only imagine how the course of the western world might have been altered had Brutus and Cassius emerged victorious, and Antony and Octavian (the future Augustus) had perished.

NUMISMATIC NOTE: Though Cassius did strike several issues of coinage, none of them bear his portrait. The two daggers on the reverse of Brutus' EID MAR denarius not only represent the act of regicide, but more specifically represent Brutus and Cassius as the principal conspirators. His most interesting issue is a denarius that shows a rose and a diadem, above which a crab holds an aplustre in its claws. His naval victory is represented by the aplustre, the location by the crab (the symbol of Cos, near where the signal battle occured) and the spoils of victory by the kingly diadem and the rose (the symbol of Rhodes).

CORNUFICIUS

IMPERATOR, 42 B.C.

Quintus Cornuficius (Cornificius), d. 42 B.C. Cornuficius ranked among the leading literati of the late Republic, and as a poet and orator was a friend of Cicero and Catullus. But his talents were not limited to the written and spoken word, for he was a capable governor and general. In 48 B.C., Julius Caesar appointed him propraetor of Illyricum, in which capacity he played an important part in defending his province from the Pompeians. Caesar subsequently rewarded him in 47 B.C. with the *augurship*, a permanent priestly office.

In 46 B.C. he was appointed to governorships in Syria and Cilicia, and subsequently was made governor of Africa Vetus in 44 B.C. Following the murder of Julius Caesar early in that year, Cornuficius refused to acknowledge the authority of the Triumvirs, and sided with the senate in the War of Mutina (43 B.C.). From his base in Africa, Cornuficius gave military support to Sextus Pompey and gave refuge to many who had been targeted in the Triumviral proscriptions.

In 42 B.C. Cornuficius was attacked by Titus Sextius, the governor of the adjacent province of Africa Nova, and though initially successful in his defense (for which he was hailed Imperator), he was defeated and killed near Utica late in 42 B.C. He should not be confused with Lucius Cornuficius, the friend of Augustus and consul of 35 B.C. who is best remembered for his unusual habit of riding an elephant in the streets of Rome.

NUMISMATIC NOTE: Although no portrait coins of Cornuficius were struck, he is represented as the standing figure being crowned by Juno Sospita on the reverse type he adopted. The coinage must date to 42 B.C., and it is one of the last issues that can be considered Republican in character. Cornuficius makes reference to his province of Africa, to his augurate and Imperatorship, and presumably to his Lanuvine origin (explaining his choice of Juno Sospita for a reverse type).

SALVIDIENUS

IMPERATOR, 42 B.C.

Quintus Salvidienus Rufus Salvus, d. 40 B.C. A boyhood friend of Octavian, Salvidienus was named a legate in 42 B.C. to protect Italy against Sextus Pompey, who had blockaded the Italian coast with the navy placed under his command. Initially, Salvidienus was successful in his task, defeating Sextus Pompey at Rhegium and being hailed Imperator. But shortly thereafter he was defeated off the coast of Messana, not far from his original victory; Octavian, we are told, observed the latter battle.

Thus, Rome's efforts to contain Sextus Pompey by force came to an end. In 39 B.C., at the pact of Misenum, the Triumvirs gave Sextus Pompey control of Sicily, Sardinia, Corsica and Achaea in exchange for his promise not to blockade grain shipments destined for Italy. (This arrangement lasted until 37 B.C., when Octavian took command of the fleet and waged war against Sextus Pompey.) In the meantime, Salvidienus joined Octavian in the "Perusine War" of 41–40 B.C. against Lucius Antonius, the youngest brother of Marc Antony. The Caesareans were victorious, though it required a cruel siege of Perusia (from which the name of the war is derived).

For his extraordinary service at Perusia, Octavian rewarded Salvidienus with the governorship of Gaul and designated him to be a consul in 39 B.C. But Octavian's fair-weather friend did not live long enough to enjoy the latter honor, for during a siege of Brundisium he engaged in a treasonous relationship with Marc Antony, who subsequently revealed the details of his correspondence to Octavian. In 40 B.C., Octavian had the senate declare Salvidienus a public enemy, upon which he seems to have committed suicide to avoid execution.

NUMISMATIC NOTE: No portrait coins of Salividienus are known, though he is mentioned by name on denarii of Octavian (Augustus) struck in 40 B.C. On that coinage, his upcoming consulship is noted.

CALVINUS

IMPERATOR, 39 B.C.

Gnaeus Domitius Calvinus, lifespan unknown. Calvinus began his political career as an outspoken opponent of the First Triumvirate, as a Tribune of the Plebs in 59 B.C. Although bribery was a normal part of attaining public office in the late Republic, Calvinus and his fellow candidate, Gaius Memmius, brought the concept to a new level of blatancy when, in the corrupt elections of 54 B.C., they bought the support of the incumbent consuls Ahenobarbus and Appius Claudius Pulcher. Though this fact was later revealed by Memmius, and Calvinus was not successful in his bid of 54 B.C., he did win election in July 53 B.C., and was consul for the rest of that year.

In achieving this, Calvinus demonstrated remarkable courage, and was the only candidate to withstand the threats and the very real aggressions of Caesar, Pompey and Crassus. However, in the civil war that later erupted, Calvinus was one of the few ex-consuls who supported Caesar. Calvinus fought for Caesar against Metellus Pius Scipio in Thessaly (just before Pharsalus), later against Pompey at Pharsalus, and later still against the Pontic king Pharnaces II (by whom he was defeated at Nicopolis in 48 B.C. while serving as governor of Asia).

Calvinus' promising career under Caesar (who planned on appointing him as Lepidus' replacement as *magister equitum*, "Master of Horse") was cut short by the dictator's murder in 44 B.C. He remained loyal to the Caesareans (Triumvirs), and though Antony and Octavian emerged victorious at Philippi, it was due in no measure to Calvinus who, early in 42 B.C., lost his entire fleet in the Adriatic to the Republican admirals Ahenobarbus and Murcus. Calvinus barely escaped the defeat by sailing to Brundisium, after which he apparently made his way back to Antony and Octavian's camp in time for the Battle of Philippi in October, 42 B.C.

Despite his embarrassments, Calvinus attained a second consulate in 40 B.C., after which, in 39 B.C., Octavian appointed him to a proconsulship in Spain. While serving in that capacity, he treated his soldiers with great severity, but won a triumph for his victories against the Cerretani, who had rebelled. Of the later history of Calvinus little is known, except that he held a priestly office in 20 B.C.

NUMISMATIC NOTE: Calvinus' Oscan-inspired denarii were struck for his campaign against the Cerretani in 39 B.C., and conspicuously make no mention of Octavian, who had appointed him proconsul. The priestly implements on the reverse refer to his status as *Pontifex*, granted c. 45 B.C.

MURCUS

IMPERATOR, C. 45–42 B.C.

Lucius Staius (Statius) Murcus, d. 39 B.C. During the civil war between Caesar and the Pompeians, Murcus served as a legate for Julius Caesar in Gaul and Africa from 48 to 46 B.C. In 44 B.C., he was appointed proconsul of Syria, where he was sent to restore order, for early in 46 B.C., Q. Caecilius Bassus (formerly a supporter of Pompey) had rebelled, causing the death of the governor Sextus Caesar (a young relative of Julius Caesar) and the defeat of the replacement governor L. Antistius Vetus. Murcus. With the help of Q. Marcius Crispus (proconsul in Bithynia and Pontus), Murcus captured the armies of Bassus at Apameia shortly after his arrival, and he was possibly hailed Imperator at this time.

After Caesar was murdered early in 44 B.C., Murcus supported Octavian, who had been named Caesar's heir. But he soon switched his allegiance to the Republican cause led by the renegades Brutus and Cassius. Thus, in July of 43 B.C., Murcus gave his Syrian legions to Cassius, who was campaigning in the region at the time. In gratitude, Cassius made Murcus commander of his fleet, and in the spring of 42 B.C. Murcus seems to have directed the siege of Rhodes.

Immediately thereafter, Murcus joined Brutus' admiral Ahenobarbus in the Adriatic, and together they defeated Calvinus, a Caesarean commander who was delivering soldiers and supplies to Antony and Octavian in Illyricum. As important a victory as this was (Ahenobarbus was hailed Imperator as a result), it did not prevent the defeat of Brutus and Cassius at Philippi in October of 42 B.C., after which Murcus continued to oppose the Triumvirs. Eventually, in 41 B.C., he joined the renegade Sextus Pompey in the western Mediterranean. Though warmly received at first, Murcus fell out of favor with Sextus Pompey and consequently was murdered at Syracuse in 39 B.C. Opinions vary about when and why Murcus was hailed Imperator in 45, 44, 43 or 42 B.C.

NUMISMATIC NOTE: Murcus' first coinage was tetradrachms of Antioch struck while he was in command in Syria. Later he struck denarii during his independent command from 42 to 41 B.C., after the Republican defeat at Philippi but before his joining up with Sextus Pompey.

AHENOBARBUS

IMPERATOR, 42 B.C.

Gnaeus Domitius Ahenobarbus, d. 31/30 B.C. Gnaeus Ahenobarbus was the son of Lucius Domitius Ahenobarbus (meaning "bronze beard"), a commander with strong connections in Gaul who was violently opposed to the First Triumvirate of Pompey, Caesar and Crassus, and who died at Pharsalus in 48 B.C. The most famous member of the *Domitii*, the emperor Nero (A.D. 54–68), was not to be born for nearly 70 years after Ahenobarbus' death.

Like his father, Gnaeus Ahenobarbus fought on the Pompeian side at Pharsalus, but was pardoned by Julius Caesar after the battle. Several months after Caesar was murdered, Ahenobarbus accompanied Brutus to Macedon in their flight from Italy. During the proscriptions of the Caesarians in 43 B.C., Ahenobarbus (perhaps unjustly) was named as a participant in the murder of Caesar. Thus, the early commitment he had made to the cause of Brutus and Cassius now became his only option.

Brutus put Ahenobarbus to good use as a commander of 50 ships in his fleet, and had him patrol the Adriatic, where he soon teamed up with

Murcus, one of Cassius' naval commanders. Early in 42 B.C. the two defeated the fleet of Caesarean commander Calvinus, who was in the process of delivering troops and supplies from Italy to Illyricum, where Antony and Octavian had already landed their armies. This action not only hindered the Caesarean war effort, but also made their return to Italy virtually impossible. It was for this naval engagement that Ahenobarbus was hailed Imperator.

After the defeat of Brutus and Cassius at Philippi in October, 42 B.C., Ahenobarbus remained a threat in the Ionian Sea, where he maintained his fleet until 40 B.C., when he allied himself with Marc Antony (then in the East) shortly before Antony became reconciled with Octavian at the Treaty of Brundisium in October of that year.

As an ally of Antony, Ahenobarbus was appointed governor of Bithynia and Pontus, and participated in the disastrous expedition Antony mounted against the Parthians in 36 B.C. He next served in the effort to eliminate Sextus Pompey, who in that same year had fled to the East after being severely defeated by Octavian near Sicily. The triumviral pact expired at the end of 33 B.C., and just as Ahenobarbus and Sosius (both of whom favored Antony) assumed their duties as the elected consuls of 32 B.C., hostilities came to a head between the supporters of Octavian and Antony. Ahenobarbus' and Sosius' efforts to censure Octavian were opposed by Octavian, who occupied Rome and marched into the Senate House with a complement of soldiers. Ahenobarbus, Sosius and some 300 senators fled Rome to the East to seek asylum with Antony at Ephesus. Civil war was now inevitable.

Though there was a privileged place for Ahenobarbus in the 30 legions gathered by Antony, he was opposed to the involvement of Cleopatra VII, the queen of Egypt whom Antony had taken as common-law wife. Already suffering from a deadly fever, Ahenobarbus defected to Octavian at the last moment before the Battle of Actium (September 2, 31 B.C.), and died of his illness either late in 31, or early in 30 B.C.

NUMISMATIC NOTE: Ahenobarbus struck coins on two occasions, though neither issue seems to bear his portrait. The first was in 41 B.C. as a renegade commander in the Ionian Sea following the Republican defeat at Philippi and before he joined the cause of Antony in 40 B.C. This issue includes an aureus and a denarius, both with portraits of different men — presumably his ancestors. Next, after joining Antony, he struck coins for the Triumvir that bore Antony's portrait on the obverse, and on the reverse featured his own name and a prow, an allusion to his own naval supremacy.

PLANCUS

IMPERATOR, 40 B.C.(?)

Lucius Munatius Plancus, d. after 22 B.C. Plancus enjoyed a long and varied career as a commander and politician during the late Republic and the early Principate. He began his career in 54 B.C. as a legate of Julius Caesar in Gaul (during the Gallic War) and in Africa (during the civil war).

From 46 to 45 B.C. he served as *praefectus urbi*, and from 44 to 43 B.C. was proconsul of Transalpine Gaul, where he founded colonies at Lugdunum and Augusta Rauricorum (near Basel, Switzerland) for veterans. During the course of the War of Mutina (43 B.C.), in which Decimus Brutus (who had issued coins as a moneyer five years before, *see Cr. 450 and 451*) fought Marc Antony, Plancus allied himself with Antony. As a reward for his service in that war, Plancus celebrated a triumph for his victories in Gaul and was named consul with Lepidus in 42 B.C.

Plancus next fought for Antony in the Perusine War of 41–40 B.C., and early in 40 B.C. was sent to Asia as proconsul, where he had to defend his territory from a Parthian invasion by the turncoat Quintus Labienus and the Parthian prince Pacorus I. Plancus was successful enough to be hailed Imperator (apparently for the second time), but later had to withdraw because of troop defections. Labienus now had free run, and only was defeated in 39 B.C. by another of Antony's commanders, Ventidius, who knew Plancus from their service in the Perusine War.

In 35 B.C., while governing Syria as a legate of Antony, Plancus acted with Ahenobarbus in capturing Sextus Pompey, who by then had run his course and was hoping to establish a new "Empire" in Asia. Though he had enjoyed a decade of service under Antony, in 32 B.C. Plancus switched his allegiance to Octavian because he objected to the participation of Cleopatra VII in the upcoming campaign at Actium. His defection was especially damaging to Antony, for he revealed the existence and contents of Antony's will (which favored Cleopatra, Egypt and the east). This gave Octavian the ammunition necessary to galvanize Italy in opposition to Antony.

Under Octavian Plancus enjoyed a fruitful career, and was noted for his associations with poets, including Horace. It was Plancus who proposed in 27 B.C. that Octavian be given the name Augustus. Though the date of his death is unknown, Plancus survived at least until 22 B.C., when he was censor. His magnificent tomb at Gaeta is inscribed with his accomplishments, and specifically mentions his having been consul, Censor, twice general of the army, a victor over the Rhaeti, and the builder of the Temple of Saturn.

NUMISMATIC NOTE: Munatius Plancus, the brother of Plautius Plancus (the moneyer who struck denarii in 47 B.C.; Cr. 453/1) struck coins on two occasions. The first was an issue of gold for Julius Caesar in 45 B.C. (while *praefectus urbi*), which included an entirely new denomination, the half-aureus (quinarius). The Caesar issue may have been a donative for the veterans of Munda. His final issue, aurei and denarii under Antony in 40 B.C., is associated with an issue of Ahenobarbus.

VENTIDIUS

IMPERATOR, 41 OR 39(?) B.C.

Publius Ventidius Bassus, c. 89–c. 38 B.C. The life of Ventidius was adventurous from birth, for he was born at the beseiged city of Asculum during the height of the Social War. Indeed, while still an infant he was captured and featured in the triumph of Pompeius Strabo, the cruel and avaricious consul (and father of Pompey the Great) who had directed the siege of Asculum.

Though Ventidius' origins may have been respectable, he subsequently had a difficult life, and seems to have earned a living either as an army contractor or as a muleteer (*mulio*), as he is often described (or perhaps slandered?). As such, it comes as no surprise that he gravitated toward the populist political movement of Julius Caesar, who saw great promise in him, and gave him sufficient support so that he became a member of the senate.

After his benefactor Caesar was murdered early in 44 B.C., Ventidius allied himself with Marc Antony. In 43 B.C. Ventidius became a praetor and raised three legions in his native Picenum, which he devoted to the defense of Antony following the latter's defeat at Mutina in 43 B.C. Later in that year, Ventidius was rewarded by being chosen to fill the consulship which had been made vacant by Octavian. Naturally, the meteoric rise of a man of such humble origins was resisted by the high-born senators.

Ventidius later returned to the field as a commander in Gaul, where in 41 B.C. he fought for Antony in the Perusine War. After Antony and Octavian had agreed to terms at Brundisium in October of 40 B.C., Venditius was sent to Asia as a proconsul to take over the duties of his comrade-in-arms Plancus, who had failed to repel the Parthian invasion led by the rebel Quintus Labienus and the Parthian prince Pacorus I.

In 39 and 38 B.C. Ventidius won successive victories against the invaders. In 39 he captured and killed Labienus in Cilicia, where he was victorious at Mount Taurus and at the Cilician Gates. For this Ventidius was hailed Imperator, after which, still in 39 B.C., he managed to drive Pacorus out of Syria and the Levant. When Pacorus renewed his assault in 38 B.C., Ventidius defeated and killed the Arsacid prince that same year at the Battle of Gindarus in Cyrrhestica.

But his accomplishments were tainted by rumor that he had taken bribes from Antiochus, the king of Commagene, who he was beseiging. Antony became concerned not only about the alleged improprieties, but also about the glory Ventidius was accumulating, and so he personally replaced him in about July of 38 B.C. Upon returning to Rome, Ventidius celebrated his Parthian triumph. This was the first of many Parthian triumphs to be celebrated in Rome over the next quarter-millenium, and was long-remembered by those who attended. He died shortly thereafter and was granted a public funeral.

NUMISMATIC NOTE: The excessively rare denarii of Ventidius, seemingly known from only two obverse and two reverse dies, were struck at an uncertain mint in the East in 39 B.C., and are to be associated with his campaigns against Labienus and Pacorus.

LABIENUS

IMPERATOR PARTHICUS, 40/39 B.C.

Quintus Labienus "Parthicus," d. 39 B.C. Quintus Labienus was son of Titus Labienus, the legate who Julius Caesar relied upon so heavily during his famous Gallic campaigns of 58–51 B.C. That his father abandoned Caesar to join Pompey's cause in 49 B.C. (and eventually died at Munda with remnants of the Pompeian Party) no doubt influenced his son to oppose the Caesareans, and later to traitorously defect to the Parthians rather than face the consequences of his wartime allegiances.

Labienus was sent to Parthia by Brutus and Cassius late in 43 or early in 42 B.C. to seek military support from king Orodes II (whose general Surenas had decimated the armies of Crassus in 53 B.C.) for their struggle with Antony and Octavian. But time ran short, and Labienus was unable to arrange any assistance before the battles of Philippi were fought in October 42 B.C., at which both Brutus and Cassius committed suicide. Labienus was consequently in a bind, for he was now unable to return to the West.

In the meantime, however, Labienus convinced Orodes II to invade Syria, and to allow himself to share the command with the king's own son, Pacorus I. Pacorus had invaded Syria more than a decade before, in 51

B.C., during the governorship of the famous orator Cicero (in nearby Cilicia). But that invasion had failed. Pacorus had been defeated by the future tyrannicide Cassius, who had remained in the East after surviving the debacle of Crassus in 53 B.C.

Together, Labienus and Pacorus invaded Syria. Some scholars place the invasion late in 41 B.C., but most agree it began early in 40 B.C., during Antony's absence. The invasion required some 20,000 horsemen, and was a success from the start. The first to be defeated was Antony's governor, Lucius Decidius Saxa, whose soldiers subsequently defected to Labienus. Saxa fled to Antioch, then to Cilicia, where he was captured and executed. The cities of Apamaea and Antioch quickly surrendered, after which the two leaders pursued separate attack routes — Labienus invading Asia Minor, and Pacorus invading Palestine and Phoenicia.

Labienus overran much of Asia Minor, and in the process was hailed Imperator. He was initially hindered by Antony's ally Plancus, but soon forced him to withdraw. Pacorus seized the coastal cities of Palestine and Phoenicia (except Tyre, which was notoriously difficult to take) and deposed the high priest John Hyrcanus II, replacing him with Mattathias Antigonus, who had by bribery invited the Parthian invasion of Jerusalem.

However, early in 39 B.C., a new legate of Antony's arrived, Publius Ventidius Bassus. Ventidius drove Labienus and Pacorus out of Roman territories with remarkable success. He first pursued Labienus, defeating him at Mount Taurus and at the Cilician Gates in 39 B.C., when the outlaw was captured and executed. Ventidius next drove the Parthians across the Euphrates, and when Pacorus invaded Syria yet again, in 38 B.C., he also was defeated and killed by Ventidius in battle at Gindarus in Cyrrhestica.

NUMISMATIC NOTE: The historical circumstance and engraving style of Labienus' aurei and denarii point to Antioch as the probable mint. Though they may have been struck early in 39 B.C., they most probably belong to the latter half of 40 B.C., before he and Pacorus pursued separate routes of conquest. Local tetradrachms and æs of Antioch dated to the period of his occupation may also be ascribed to Labienus.

SCARPUS

IMPERATOR, 31 B.C.(?)

GREAT-NEPHEW OF JULIUS CAESAR

Lucius Pinarius Scarpus, lifespan unknown. A member of the *Pinarii*, one of the oldest and noblest Roman families, Scarpus was also a great-nephew of Julius Caesar. Though it was another of Caesar's great-nephews,

Octavian, who received his political legacy (by being adopted as his son) and three-quarters of his wealth, Caesar bequeathed the remaining quarter to two other of his great-nephews, Quintus Pedius and Scarpus.

At first, Scarpus' allegiance was to Octavian, but after Philippi (October, 42 B.C.), he became more closely allied with Antony, who, in 31 B.C., placed him in command of four legions in Cyrenaica to defend Egypt from any invasion launched from the West. After Antony lost to Octavian at Actium (31 B.C.), he sought the support of Scarpus, who declined Antony and instead turned his legions over to the governor of Africa, Cornelius Gallus. Scarpus remained in high office in Cyrenaica until 27 B.C.

NUMISMATIC NOTE: Scarpus' issues of 31 B.C. are of considerable interest. First, they are struck at a significantly reduced weight (as such, they are possibly the only silver issues of the late Republic which were not struck to the normal weight standard); second, they are struck in the names of both Antony and Octavian. These two former allies were then formally at war during the period of Scarpus' coinage, and we must therefore assume that his coinage for Antony was struck shortly before the Battle of Actium, and that his coinage for Octavian was struck thereafter.

LEPIDUS

MEMBER OF THE SECOND TRIUMVIRATE, 43–36 B.C.

BROTHER-IN-LAW OF BRUTUS

Marcus Aemilius Lepidus, 90/89–13/12 B.C. The "third wheel" of political power in Rome during the Second Triumvirate, Lepidus hailed from a very important (but somewhat maligned) family that had been of consular status since 285 B.C. By far the most important of his ancestors were Marcus Aemilius Lepidus, consul in 187 and 175 B.C. This man's grandson held the consulship in 78 B.C., but died in exile for his strong support of Sulla. The family continued to be of importance long after the death of Lepidus the Triumvir, for he was married to Junia, a sister of Brutus, and by their offspring they were forebears of Nero (emperor, A.D. 54–68).

But equal fame was achieved by Marcus Lepidus, the Triumvir. Lepidus served as *praetor urbanus*, the highest post in Rome, in 49 B.C., and was appointed governor of Nearer Spain in 48 B.C. His remarkable career continued with the consulship in 46 B.C., followed by an appointment by Julius Caesar as his *magister equitum* (Master of Horse) from 46 to 44 B.C. Indeed, only one day before it occurred, it was Lepidus who warned Caesar to be wary of a plot against his life; but Caesar did not pay heed, and was murdered on March 15, 44 B.C.

As *magister equitum*, it was Lepidus who controlled the soldiers in Rome when Caesar was murdered, and had Marc Antony not restrained him, Lepidus no doubt would have executed the many conspirators. In the aftermath, Antony had named Lepidus *pontifex maximus*, and named him governor of Nearer Spain and Gallia Narbonensis. While serving in that capacity, Lepidus reconciled the senate with the Pompeian renegade Sextus Pompey, who was campaigning in Lepidus' territories.

Shortly thereafter, very late in 44 B.C., Antony left Rome to take possession of Gaul, but found the previous governor, Decimus Brutus, would not leave. And so began the war to forcibly remove Decimus Brutus, who soon was besieged at the city of Mutina, in Cisalpine Gaul. During the course of the war, Lepidus joined forces with Antony, for, at the urging of Cicero and Octavian, both men had been declared public enemies by the senate. Antony and Lepidus were defeated by a senatorial army led by Octavian and the two consuls, Pansa and Hirtius (both of whom were killed in the war), and retreated to exile in Gaul as Octavian and Decimus Brutus returned to Rome.

While this warfare was going on, the senate was temporarily in control and it began to dole out extraordinary powers to the Republican rebels Brutus, Cassius and Sextus Pompey. Octavian felt betrayed, and so, with his army, extorted the consulship and a command against Antony. But when Octavian confronted Antony, they agreed to join forces with Lepidus and formed the Second Triumvirate much like Caesar, Crassus and Pompey had done before. Lepidus got much of Gaul and Spain as his domain in this initial agreement.

Subsequently, the Triumvirs forced the senate to ratify their private pact, and the trio prepared for the war against Brutus and Cassius. In 42 B.C., Antony and Octavian departed for Greece, leaving Lepidus (consul, for a second time) to manage affairs in Italy. From the outset Lepidus was the least important member of the Triumvirate, and this only made it more obvious. After the Triumvirs were victorious at the battles of Philippi in October 42 B.C., they returned to restructure their arrangement. The loser was Lepidus, who was almost expelled for suspected collusion with Sextus Pompey, but later was allowed to rule in North Africa.

Although Lepidus supported Octavian in the Perusine War (41–40 B.C.), and subsequently in the war against Sextus Pompey in 36 B.C., he was denied the spoils of war, for Octavian had no intention of sharing. In the war against Sextus Pompey, Lepidus landed 14 legions in Sicily in August 36 B.C., ostensibly to engage the rebel's land forces while Octavian challenged him at sea. But before any such naval victory had been gained by Octavian, Lepidus demanded Sicily be added to his own North African territories. Octavian — no doubt feeling threatened and betrayed by the lack of cooperation — challenged the third Triumvir. Lepidus' legions swiftly deserted to Octavian, who subsequently humiliated Lepidus by stripping him of all authority except the title of *Pontifex Maximus*, which he held until his own death in 13 or 12 B.C.

NUMISMATIC NOTE: Lepidus first struck coinage in 61 B.C. as a moneyer. Three types are attributed to his term as moneyer, though some researchers believe that the two of them with the exceptional inscription SC were actually struck at later dates (in the 50s B.C.) under special commission from the senate. While in alliance with Octavian and Antony, Lepidus struck coins jointly with them. The issues with Antony have uninspiring designs, whereas those with Octavian (though not of great artistry) at least offer portraits of both men. The portrait of Lepidus occurs only once on provincials: on small bronzes of Ephesus on which he shares the canvas with Marc Antony and Octavian. There are three non-portrait provincial issues: two from Gaul that bear his name and were struck while he was governing there; and one series from Spain, presumably struck while he was governing Hither Spain, but with the added attraction that the city of issue (Celsa) was renamed *Colonia Lepida* in his honor. The city's name reverted to *Colonia Celsa* after Lepidus' downfall in 36 B.C.

MARC ANTONY (MARCUS ANTONIUS)

MEMBER OF THE SECOND TRIUMVIRATE, 43–33 B.C.

BROTHER OF GAIUS ANTONIUS AND LUCIUS ANTONIUS
HUSBAND OF FADIA, ANTONIA, FULVIA, OCTAVIA AND QUEEN CLEOPATRA VII
FATHER OF MARCUS ANTONIUS JUNIOR AND ANTONIA (*w.* OF NERO CLAUDIUS DRUSUS)

Marcus Antonius, c. 83/82–30 B.C. Another of the great and tragic figures of Roman history, Marc Antony was a commander of exceptional ability who, after what appears to have been a misspent youth, launched his career in politics and warfare under the guidance of Julius Caesar.

Antony was a natural soldier with a strong constitution that even the ravages of time and battle could not weaken. Furthermore, he had a generous, affable nature that endeared him to his soldiers, and only enriched his natural skills as a tactician. He was married four times to Roman women, and once to Cleopatra VII, the Greek queen of Egypt, and among the five women sired four boys and four girls.

The eldest of three sons of Marcus Antonius "Creticus" (so named for his ignominious death in 71 B.C., which resulted from battle against Cretan pirates), Antony's earliest position of note was as a cavalry commander for Aulus Gabinus in Palestine and Egypt from 57 to 55 B.C. After that assignment, Antony served his quaestorship of 52 B.C. in Gaul with Julius Caesar, who saw promise in him, for he soon gave Antony important responsibilities.

When civil war between Caesar and Pompey the Great was imminent in 49 B.C., Antony (then a tribune) defended Caesar in the pro-Pompey senate. When war broke out in 49 B.C., Antony fought at Caesar's side in Italy and Greece. After Caesar's victory at Pharsalus (August 9, 48 B.C.), at which Antony commanded the left wing, he returned to Italy as Caesar's *magister equitum*.

Thereafter, Antony became Caesar's top man in Rome, administering his affairs during his lengthy absences. From 48 to 44 B.C., Caesar returned only occasionally to Rome, for he was busy restoring Cleopatra VII to the throne of Egypt, defeating Pharnaces II of Pontus, settling Roman affairs in Asia Minor and Syria, as well as defeating the Pompeian remnants in North Africa and Spain.

In October of 45 B.C., Caesar returned to Rome, never to leave again. As reward for his loyal service, Antony was named Caesar's co-consul for 44 B.C. In grandiose (and perhaps staged) gestures, Antony thrice offered the golden diadem of a king to Caesar, who refused it each time. However, by this time Caesar had been granted the title "dictator for life" and had placed his image on coins, and so had already broken two of the most sacred Republican traditions.

Antony was helping Caesar prepare for the invasion of Parthia he so greatly desired. No doubt it came as a great shock to Antony when, on March 15, Caesar was murdered. Antony restrained Lepidus (another distinguished follower of Caesar, whose troops had occupied the Forum) from taking military action, and called for amnesty for the conspirators. Indeed, this was too great an opportunity for his own political ambitions to let it be solved by mob violence or decisive soldiering. Five days later, on March 20, Antony delivered a funeral eulogy for Caesar. This stirred the public against the conspirators, many of whom left Rome quickly, and fled Italy by mid-summer.

But Antony now had two new foes, a newly independent senate and 19-year-old Octavian, the heir to Caesar's political legacy and most of his fortune, who had abandoned his studies in Greece and arrived in Rome in

May or June of 44 B.C. to collect his inheritance. Antony immediately thwarted the efforts made by Octavian for recognition. But Octavian was resourceful, and managed to raise an army of Caesar's veterans, with which he occupied Rome in November, 44 B.C.

Because of Octavian's aggressive actions, Antony had to leave Rome, and so he headed to Gaul with the aim of assuming the proconsular duties he had recently awarded himself. But Gaul was staunchly defended by Decimus Brutus, who had been made proconsul of Gaul by Caesar, and so a war resulted in which Antony besieged Decimus Brutus at Mutina in Cisalpine Gaul. Joining Antony in his campaign was the governor Lepidus, who was second only to Antony within the Caesarean party.

Meanwhile, the orator Cicero had emerged from retirement to defame Antony, and the senate responded to his powerful words. Octavian (who had been named propraetor) and the two consuls, Pansa and Hirtius, were sent with an army to relieve Decimus Brutus. Though both consuls died in battle, the senatorial army was victorious. Decimus Brutus was allowed to celebrate a triumph, and Octavian was hailed Imperator.

Antony, meanwhile, exiled himself in Gaul until it was safe to emerge. In the aftermath, the senate granted extraordinary powers to Brutus and Cassius in the east, and gave command of the fleet in the west to Sextus Pompey. Octavian was given nothing, and so he used his military might to extort the consulship and a command to march against Antony, who since February of 43 B.C. had been declared a public enemy. But when he arrived, Octavian came to an agreement with Antony and Lepidus, and no fighting occurred.

A political alliance known as the Second Triumvirate was formed by Antony, Lepidus and Octavian on November 11 of 43 B.C., an alliance unwillingly ratified by the senate. By this arrangement, the trio would rule Rome and its territories for the next five years. Then followed the infamous proscriptions, spearheaded by Antony's wife, Fulvia, in which some 130 senators and 2,000 equestrians were executed (with Cicero being among the first).

In preparation for war against Brutus and Cassius, the two lead assassins of Julius Caesar who now controlled the eastern Roman territories, Antony and Octavian departed for Greece in the spring of 42 B.C., leaving Lepidus in charge in Italy. When the armies clashed several months later, in October, Antony and Octavian were victorious. Afterward, Antony went to the East and Octavian returned to the West.

While at Tarsus, Antony met Cleopatra VII, the queen of Egypt who formerly had been a lover of his mentor, Julius Caesar. Antony and Cleopatra, though not terribly compatible on a personal level, found they had political motives in common, and they wintered together in Egypt. Exactly at this time, a full-scale invasion of Syria was launched by the Parthians, led by the Republican renegade Labienus and the Parthian prince Pacorus. Many of the legions defected to Labienus, for he represented the Republican cause, and so the invasion was impossible to resist.

Despite the seriousness of the invasion, Antony had equally urgent business in the West, where his brother and Octavian had gone to war. Antony's brother, Lucius Antonius, had started a war against Octavian in 41 B.C., and was defeated in February of 40 B.C. after a cruel siege at Perusia (from which the "Perusine War" derives its name). Octavian's two main antagonists in the war, Lucius Antonius and Fulvia, the wife of Antony, died in the months following. Though their deaths did not directly result from the war, they still affected Antony, who had arrived from Egypt too late to alter the course of events.

Octavian and Antony met at Brundisium in October of 40 B.C. to settle their differences. It was a productive meeting, and the treaty held that Italy was common territory, Antony got the East, Octavian the West, and Lepidus was limited to Africa. To seal the pact, Antony, now a widower, married Octavian's sister, Octavia. In the meantime, Antony had sent his lieutenant Ventidius to restore order in Asia Minor, which he did with remarkable success from 39 to 38 B.C. Antony returned east in 39 B.C., after agreeing to the pact of Misenum, by which the problem of Sextus Pompey was temporarily resolved.

Antony again returned to the West in 37 B.C., when the five-year Triumvirate pact (then expiring), was renewed at Tarentum. The other productive result of the negotiations at Tarentum was that Octavian traded foot soldiers for war vessels — thus providing Antony with the legions he needed to launch his invasion of Parthia, and allowing Octavian once again to challenge the naval supremacy of Sextus Pompey, a renegade commander who controlled Sicily and other islands in the western Mediterranean.

Antony returned to the East immediately, where, later in the year, he married Cleopatra at Antioch, even though he was still married to Octavia. The marriage was not legally binding in Rome, but it indicated that Antony's long-term plans were in the East, where he intended to join the fortunes of Rome and Egypt.

The year 36 B.C. was eventful: in the West, Octavian ousted Lepidus from the Triumvirate, and defeated Sextus Pompey in a pitched naval battle off Sicily; in the East, Antony launched his Parthian invasion. Though Antony had some 100,000 soldiers, and an alliance with Artavasdes II of Armenia (which proved treacherous), his campaign was a complete disaster. He lost 35,000 or more of his soldiers, and after a disgraceful retreat, had to avail himself of the relief offered by Cleopatra. Antony later exacted his revenge on Armenia by annexing it in 34 B.C., and shamefully displaying Artavasdes II in his triumph in Alexandria.

Over the intervening years, tensions had grown between Antony and Octavian, now the sole masters of the Roman world. The Triumviral pact expired at the end of 33 B.C., after which (in 32) Ahenobarbus and Sosius (two staunch allies of Antony) took up their consulships. In an act of self-preservation, Octavian occupied Rome, terrifying the senate with his legions and causing the two consuls and about 300 senators to leave Italy and seek Antony's protection in the East. In 31 B.C., Octavian declared war against Cleopatra, which in essence was also a declaration against Antony.

The opposing forces of Antony and Octavian met near Actium on the west coast of Greece, where a battle would eventually be waged to determine which of the two men would rule the Roman world. Antony suffered last-minute defections by Plancus, Ahenobarbus and others, such as Asiatic kings, and found himself blockaded by Octavian's commander Agrippa. By early September, defections were increasing and Antony's supplies had run so low that he forced a pitched battle. His naval forces were quickly bested by Agrippa, and so he and Cleopatra broke through the blockade and sailed toward Egypt. What remained of his army and navy stayed to fight in his name, and were roundly defeated.

Cleopatra sailed directly for Egypt, while Antony stopped at Cyrene in an effort to get the four legions of his ally Scarpus, but this was in vain, for Scarpus had in the meantime changed his allegiance. So Antony, defeated yet again, made his way to Egypt to join Cleopatra. Antony committed suicide in 30 B.C., shortly before Octavian arrived. Cleopatra waited, but after realizing Octavian had nothing but hostile intentions, she too committed suicide, robbing Octavian of a fine trophy for his triumph.

NUMISMATIC NOTE: If one thing can be said of Marc Antony's considerable coinage, it is that he was willing to share his glory. Indeed, his famous "legionary denarii" were a fitting testimony to the legions that supported his cause. Furthermore, he allowed Ahenobarbus to strike highly personalized issues under his auspices, and he struck coins bearing the portrait of his third wife, Fulvia. But more interesting still is Antony's fondness for dual-portrait issues, which he struck bearing his own image paired with the busts of Julius Caesar, Octavian, Lepidus, Octavia, Lucius Antonius, Marcus Antonius Junior and Cleopatra VII. It is also worth noting that Antony was the second living Roman to place his image on coins struck at Rome. He did this in 44 B.C., very shortly after Caesar's murder. On this type (the only one struck in 44 B.C. for Antony), he is shown veiled and wears a short beard — the former indicated his priestly duties, and the latter, which he continued to wear until after Brutus and Cassius were defeated, was a sign of mourning for his fallen mentor.

GAIUS ANTONIUS

Brother of Marc Antony and Lucius Antonius
Uncle of Marcus Antonius Junior
Brother-in-law of Fulvia and Octavia

Gaius Antonius, d. 42 B.C. The second son of Marcus Antonius "Creticus," Gaius Antonius was the younger brother of Marc Antony and the older brother of Lucius Antonius. His career began as a legate of Julius Caesar in 49 B.C., during which he was blockaded by the Pompeian fleet on the island of Curicta, and subsequently taken prisoner. Caesar later appointed him *praetor urbanus* in 44 B.C.

After Caesar was murdered in March of 44 B.C., Gaius Antonius assumed the duties of *praetor urbanus*, the post which had been abandoned by Brutus. Later in 44 B.C., on November 28, Marc Antony was able to secure Gaius Antonius' appointment as governor of Macedon. This province was then occupied by the Republican renegade Brutus, who late in February seems to have been made governor of Macedon, Illyricum and Achaea by a then-independent senate. Gaius Antonius' efforts to oust Brutus failed, for the armies at Dyrrhachium and Apollonia deserted to Brutus, and poor Gaius Antonius was blockaded at Apollonia in March 43 B.C. Vigorous actions by Brutus and Marcus Tullius Cicero, the son of the orator Cicero who at age 17 had commanded a cavalry squadron at Pharsalus, caused Gaius Antonius to surrender.

Sometime after his capture, the senate revoked Gaius Antonius' status as governor, and the unfortunate brother of Marc Antony was executed by Brutus early in 42 B.C. The cause, it seems, was two-fold: firstly, as punishment for having tried to incite Brutus' troops to revolt, and secondly, in retribution for Marc Antony's proscription and execution of Cicero, the famous orator who had been a strong supporter of the cause of Brutus and Cassius.

Numismatic Note: Gaius Antonius had only one issue of coinage struck in his name, a denarius of 43 B.C. presumably struck at a mint that traveled with him to Illyricum. Regrettably, it does not bear his portrait.

LUCIUS ANTONIUS

BROTHER OF MARC ANTONY AND GAIUS ANTONIUS
UNCLE OF MARCUS ANTONIUS JUNIOR
BROTHER-IN-LAW OF FULVIA AND OCTAVIA

Lucius Antonius "Pietas," d. c. 40 B.C. The youngest of three brothers, Lucius Antonius began his career as a quaestor in Asia in 50 B.C., and six years later, in the final year of Julius Caesar's life, served as tribune, giving the dictator even more powers in appointing magistrates. After Julius Caesar's murder, Lucius' oldest brother, Marc Antony, became the unofficial leader of the Caesarean party. But Marc Antony was soon ousted by Caesar's grandnephew, Octavian, and thus had to leave Italy and take up the post he had been granted in Gaul. Lucius Antonius went with him as his legate (as the middle brother, Gaius Antonius, was sent to occupy Macedon), and together, at Mutina, they suffered a degrading loss to the senatorial army led by Octavian.

Through the influence of his brother, Lucius Antonius was elected consul in 41 B.C. Thus began his most noteworthy role in history, first as an antagonist, then as a military opponent of the Triumvir Octavian. Marc Antony had gone East to settle diplomatic matters and confiscate wealth, and Octavian had remained in the West to begin the unsavory task of seizing land from 18 cities so that it could be given to 100,000 veterans who were being discharged. Octavian's task was made more difficult by propaganda that was issued by Lucius Antonius and Fulvia, the wife of Marc Antony.

The verbal and political hostilities of 41 B.C. evolved into a military conflict when Lucius Antonius, by force of arms, gained permission to wage war on Octavian. The Triumvir Octavian responded with legions called in from Spain and with help from his friends Agrippa and Salvidienus (who subsequently was made governor of Gaul and consul designate). Lucius Antonius was besieged at Perusia (*mod.* Perugia), and the so-called "Perusine War" ended in February of 40 B.C. with his surrender. To distance him from the political scene in Rome, Octavian then appointed Lucius Antonius as a promagistrate in Spain, where he seems to have died not long thereafter.

Though a limited engagement, the Perusine War had serious consequences to the relationship between Marc Antony and Octavian. The two men met at Brundisium in October of 40 B.C. to settle their differences so that each could get on with the business of conquering their own enemies.

NUMISMATIC NOTE: The aurei and denarii honoring Lucius Antonius' consulship were struck at a mint moving in the East with his eldest brother,

Marc Antony. Thus, it is likely that Lucius Antonius never handled one of the coins bearing his own portrait. Two issues were struck, both of which bear Marc Antony's portrait on the obverse. One reverse type depicts Fortuna or Pietas and is inscribed PIETAS COS. The type is a direct reference to Lucius Antonius because Pietas was his cognomen and because he held the consulship in 41 B.C. The other reverse type features a fine portrait of Lucius Antonius (in which the family resemblance is obvious) accompanied by his name and title as consul. Of great interest is the fact that Marc Antony's series of 41 B.C. offers *equal* treatment to Octavian, thus virtually equating him to Lucius Antonius, even though Octavian was a Triumvir and Lucius Antonius was merely a consul.

FULVIA

THIRD WIFE OF MARC ANTONY
MOTHER OF MARCUS ANTONIUS JUNIOR
SISTER-IN-LAW OF GAIUS ANTONIUS AND LUCIUS ANTONIUS

Fulvia, d. 40 B.C. Of the four wives Marc Antony had, his third, Fulvia, was perhaps the most ambitious. She had a penchant for powerful men, and became active in the political intrigues of her husbands whenever the opportunity presented itself — taking the leading role when possible. She bore five children, two of whom, Marcus Antonius Junior and Iullus Antonius, were by Marc Antony.

Her first marriage was to Publius Clodius Pulcher, one of the most powerful Roman aristocrats in the 50s B.C. He was the most formidable opponent of the First Triumvirate, and indeed, it was his death in the gang violence he so actively promoted that caused the senate house to be set ablaze, thus leading to Pompey's reign as sole consul in 52 B.C.

She next married Gaius Scribonius Curio Junior, the son of the homonymous orator who helped Sulla besiege Athens, and who served as consul in 76 B.C. As for his son, Fulvia's second husband, he was a reckless but loyal lieutenant of Julius Caesar, fighting for him both in the political circles of Rome and on the battlefield. Indeed, it was Curio who made the proposal in 50 B.C. that Pompey and Caesar disarm simultaneously to prevent civil war. In the year following, Curio died fighting the Numidian king Juba I on behalf of Caesar.

Fulvia's subsequent life was no less turbulent. She married Marc Antony in 46 or 45 B.C., after he had established himself as the first man behind Julius Caesar. Ever active in politics, Fulvia is said to have found her true calling in 43 B.C. as the principal force behind the ruthless proscriptions issued by the Triumvirs (Caesareans).

She found another political cause in 41 B.C., the year her brother-in-law, Lucius Antonius, held the consulship. Since her husband was in the East settling political affairs and beginning an affair of the heart with the Egyptian queen Cleopatra VII, Fulvia and Lucius Antonius decided to advance his political standing by taking extreme actions of their own.

Much to her chagrin, the Triumvir Octavian had been given the thankless task of finding land upon which to settle some 100,000 veterans who were being discharged. This meant land had to be seized from 18 cities, providing Lucius Antonius and Fulvia a golden opportunity to discredit him. That Fulvia targeted Octavian comes as no surprise: not only was he the main political rival to her husband, but they had a long-standing feud from when a proposed marriage between Octavian and Claudia (Fulvia's daughter by Clodius, and thus Marc Antony's step-daughter) was called off because of quarreling between Octavian and Fulvia.

Lucius Antonius persuaded the senate to give him the necessary permission in 41 B.C. to wage war on Octavian, who in response brought in legions from Spain and called upon his friends Agrippa and Salvidienus for additional help. Lucius Antonius retreated to Perusia (modern-day Perugia), where he awaited the legions from Gaul who were loyal to his brother. However, the Gallic legions refused to move against Octavian unless the orders came directly from Marc Antony. The "Perusian War" ended in February of 40 B.C. with the surrender of Lucius Antonius, after which Fulvia fled to Greece, where she died later that year.

NUMISMATIC NOTE: Fulvia's portrait occurs in the guise of Victory, complete with wings, on silver quinarii from Gaul and on bronzes of Eumenia (in Phrygia), a city which was renamed Fulvia in her honor during the period of that coinage. Her regular bust also occurs on small bronzes of Tripolis, Syria.

MARCUS ANTONIUS JUNIOR

SON OF MARC ANTONY AND FULVIA
NEPHEW OF GAIUS ANTONIUS AND LUCIUS ANTONIUS

Marcus Antonius the Younger, c. 43–30 B.C. The eldest son of Marc Antony and his third wife, Fulvia (who died when he was about three years old), Marcus Antonius Junior was given the name "Antyllus" by the Greeks. In 37 B.C., as part of the agreements reached by Marc Antony and Octavian at the Treaty of Tarentum, the boy was betrothed to the only daughter of Octavian, Julia, who then was about 3 years old. Since the boy's father was at that time married to Octavian's sister, the betrothal added a further dimension to the dynastic ties.

Because of his youth, little can be said of the boy or his accomplishments. Shortly after his father was roundly defeated at Actium in September of 31 B.C., Marc Antony had his son assume the *toga virilis* in the event the tide of events would miraculously change. According to Suetonius, after the downfall of his father and of Cleopatra VII early in 30 B.C., Marcus Antonius Junior, then about 13 years old, took refuge near an image of the god Julius (Caesar). Despite his pleas for mercy from Octavian, he was nonetheless executed on April 30, 30 B.C.

Marcus had a younger brother named Iullus Antonius who survived the aftermath of Actium, and was able to live a fuller, though no less tragic life. Iullus married Marcella, the niece of Augustus, in 21 B.C. By her he had a son of his own, named Lucius. Iullus was elected consul in 10 B.C., and seems to have been proconsul in Asia thereafter. Later he was convicted of adultery with Julia, the daughter of Augustus, and after this he committed suicide.

OCTAVIA

FOURTH WIFE OF MARC ANTONY
SISTER OF AUGUSTUS (OCTAVIAN)
GRAND-NIECE OF JULIUS CAESAR
MOTHER OF MARCELLUS (HEIR OF AUGUSTUS) AND ANTONIA (W. OF NERO CLAUDIUS DRUSUS)
MOTHER-IN-LAW OF AHENOBARBUS, AGRIPPA, JULIA, NERO CLAUDIUS DRUSUS
AUNT OF JULIA
GRANDMOTHER OF GERMANICUS, CLAUDIUS AND LIVILLA
GREAT-GRANDMOTHER OF NERO CAESAR, DRUSUS CAESAR, CALIGULA, AGRIPPINA JUNIOR, DRUSILLA, JULIA LIVILLA, CLAUDIA OCTAVIA, CLAUDIA ANTONIA, BRITANNICUS, LIVIA JULIA, TIBERIUS GEMELLUS AND GERMANICUS GEMELLUS
GREAT-GREAT-GRANDMOTHER OF NERO

Octavia (Minor), d. 11 B.C. Octavia, the elder sister of Octavian, was the only daughter of the nobleman Gaius Octavius and his wife Atia, who was a niece of Julius Caesar. While under any circumstance Octavia would have been an important woman in society, she was destined for greatness because of the accomplishments of her great-uncle Julius Caesar and her brother Octavian (Augustus).

Because her family connections were so complex and important, her biography reads somewhat like a laundry list of relatives. What should not be lost in all of this is the strength of her personality. Octavia was dearly loved by the Romans, who admired her humanity and her undying loyalty, even to those who betrayed her.

Octavia's first husband was Gaius Claudius Marcellus, by whom she had two daughters and one son. Her son, named Marcus Claudius Marcellus (see his biography in chapter 2), became an heir-apparent of his uncle Octavian (who by then was called Augustus). One of the daughters from this marriage, Marcella, was married to Octavian's lieutenant Agrippa.

The year 23 B.C. was one tragic for both Octavia and Marcella, for Octavia's eldest son, Marcellus, died, a blow from which his mother did not soon recover. It was equally difficult for Marcella, who not only lost her only sibling, but who two years later lost her husband, Agrippa, because he was forced to marry Octavian's daughter, Julia (who, ironically, had only been compelled to marry Agrippa because she been widowed by the death of Marcellus).

In the same year that her first husband died, 40 B.C., Octavia entered into a politically motivated marriage with the Triumvir Marc Antony, who had been married three times before and was her brother's unwilling political colleague. Octavia spent the winters from 39 to 37 B.C. with Antony in Athens, and was instrumental in bringing about the Treaty of Tarentum in 37 B.C., through which the Triumvirate was renewed. Antony's subsequent ill-treatment of Octavia contributed greatly to his discredit in the West.

The treaty itself had no beneficial effect for Octavia. Immediately after the treaty had been signed, Antony married Cleopatra VII in Antioch. Even when in 35 B.C. Octavia traveled to Greece laden with troops and supplies, Antony forbade her to proceed beyond Athens, and sent her back to Italy. In 32 B.C. (by which time Antony and Octavian were sworn enemies) their separation became a divorce.

Octavia had two daughters by Antony, both of whom were named Antonia, and thus are often distinguished by the appellations Major and Minor (older and younger). The elder Antonia, born in 39 B.C., married Lucius Domitius Ahenobarbus, from whom the emperor Nero (A.D. 54–68) was descended. The younger Antonia, born in 36 B.C., was the future wife of Nero Claudius Drusus (the younger son of Livia and the brother of Tiberius), by whom she had Germanicus, Claudius and Livilla.

Octavia was loyal both to Octavian and Antony, and often undertook grave responsibilities to aid them in their endeavors. She seems to have loved Antony dearly, for even after he had forbidden her to visit him in 36 B.C., she rejected her brother's advice of 35 B.C. to leave him. Even after Antony divorced her in 32, Octavia became a willing parent to the three step-children (Alexander, Ptolemy and Cleopatra Selene, the future wife of Juba II) whom Antony and Cleopatra had sired.

NOTE: Octavia is often referred to as Octavia Minor, because she had an older half-sister from her father's previous wife, Ancharia, who also was named Octavia (Major). Thus, Octavia Minor (whose biography is presented above) was a full sister of Octavian, whereas Octavia Major was a half-sister. Since Octavia Major did not figure prominently in Roman history, there is little reason to make the distinction in this book, and so Octavian's sister is simply referred to as Octavia.

NUMISMATIC NOTE: Octavia's portraits on coinage occur in all three metals, though only the silver is commonly found. The gold is represented by two Imperial portrait aurei: one of 40 B.C. which must celebrate her marriage to Antony, and another of 38 B.C., when they lived together for the summer in Athens. Her silver coinage, with the possible exception of a quinarius of Gaul, is exclusively eastern cistophori (three-denarius coins): one shows her bust jugate with Antony; the other places her small bust above a cista on the reverse. The bronze is all of provincial manufacture, and with the exception of a small bronze of Ephesus, is limited to the "fleet coinage" series of Antony. The most interesting type in this series occurs on the 3-as piece (tressis), which shows the busts of Antony and Octavian jugate on the left, confronting Octavia's bust on the right.

CLEOPATRA VII

QUEEN OF EGYPT, 51–30 B.C.

DAUGHTER OF PTOLEMY XII AULETES
COMPANION OF JULIUS CAESAR
FIFTH WIFE OF MARC ANTONY
MOTHER OF PTOLEMY XV (CALLED 'CAESARION'), CLEOPATRA SELENE, ETC.
SISTER OF PTOLEMY XIII, PTOLEMY XIV, BERENICE IV AND ARSINOË IV

Cleopatra VII, 69–30 B.C. When Ptolemy XII Auletes ("the flute-player") died in the spring of 51 B.C., the throne of Egypt was inherited by his 18-year-old daughter, Cleopatra VII, and her eldest brother, Ptolemy XIII, then about 12 years old. Cleopatra proved not only to be the last of the Macedonian (Lagid) rulers of Egypt, but also one of the most remarkable people in the history of the western world.

Cleopatra was perhaps Rome's most dangerous foe after Hannibal, for she nearly conquered Rome twice — not by force of arms, but by the subtle art of seduction. She was a woman of remarkable courage, skill and intelligence, and was naturally gifted in business and politics. She was an excellent mathematician and was fluent in nine languages, Latin not being one of them. Her charm and ability cast a spell on two of Rome's legendary warlords, Julius Caesar and Marc Antony, which resulted in the survival of Egypt as a sovereign kingdom during the most turbulent period of Roman history.

Throughout Cleopatra's lifetime the political environment in Rome was unstable, so she tried to ally herself with the men she thought would be most willing to allow Egypt to keep its autonomy. She is said to have greatly admired Caesar, whom she considered her intellectual equal. However, she was constantly frustrated by Antony's vulgarity, emotional instability and apparent lack of intelligence.

Cleopatra, who believed herself to be the New Isis, and was fluent in the local language, was deeply respectful of Egyptian culture. Consequently, this Macedonian queen was popular among her subjects throughout Egypt, but was disliked by much of the population of Alexandria. As such, it is truly remarkable that she was able to manage affairs in Egypt while at the same time adeptly handling the Romans.

About the time Cleopatra became queen, in 51 B.C., a serious drought began in Egypt that was to last for two years. In 50 B.C., at the height of this natural disaster, Cleopatra went to war with her brother-husband, Ptolemy XIII, with whom she shared power. By 48 B.C. at the latest, Cleopatra was expelled from Egypt, and with her sister Arsinoë IV, took refuge in Syria, a region that in the previous year had suffered from a Parthian invasion.

Times were equally tumultuous in the West, for the two most powerful warlords of Rome had declared war on each other in 49 B.C. Their dispute reached its climax on August 9, 48 B.C., when Julius Caesar defeated Pompey the Great at the Battle of Pharsalus in Greece. After the battle, Pompey fled to Egypt where, on September 28, the ministers of Ptolemy XIII murdered him as he was disembarking.

The victorious Julius Caesar was in direct pursuit of Pompey, and landed in Alexandria a few days later, on October 2, 48 B.C. With king Ptolemy XIII on the frontier preparing to fight his sister Cleopatra, Caesar took control of the palace, only later to receive the two quarrelsome siblings as his audience. Caesar was unimpressed by Ptolemy XIII and was captivated by Cleopatra, who had had the audacity to be smuggled into the meeting by being concealed in a rolled up carpet.

Thus began Caesar's effort to restore Cleopatra to the throne, which resulted in a small but exceptionally dangerous conflict known as the "Alexandrian War." Caesar soon found this to be treacherous work, and in February of 47 B.C. he even had to abandon his purple cloak and swim to safety. But there was also a romantic aspect amid all the danger, for the 52-

year-old Caesar had taken the 21-year-old Cleopatra as his lover, with the affair seemingly resulting in the conception of a child.

The turning point in the war occurred on March 26, when Caesar and his legionnaires were rescued by forces led by Mithradates of Pergamum. His arrival was a godsend, and sent Ptolemy XIII into flight, during which the king drowned in the Nile. Caesar then installed Cleopatra on the throne, after which she married her 11-year-old brother, Ptolemy XIV, to maintain the Ptolemaic tradition. Having accomplished his task, Caesar and Cleopatra cruised the Nile for a few weeks, after which Caesar left to campaign against the Pontic king, Pharnaces II, and subsequently to settle various affairs in Syria and Asia Minor, North Africa and Spain.

In the meantime, Cleopatra remained in Egypt. On June 23, 47 B.C., she gave birth to Caesarion (Ptolemy XV), the boy who, we are told, was sired by Caesar. After Caesar returned to Rome late in July of 46 B.C., he summoned Cleopatra to join him. She and her entourage arrived in Rome in time to enjoy the celebrations in September and October of the four successive triumphs and the decade-long dictatorship Caesar had been awarded. Cleopatra stayed in Caesar's villa on the Tiber

Cleopatra's visit was a most unusual affair for the conservative Roman aristocracy, who found the whole affair to be exotic in the extreme. Cleopatra's demeanor, though stately, rubbed many the wrong way. The fact that she stayed in Caesar's villa on the Tiber, with her young brother-husband in company (not to mention the fact that she had borne Caesar a child), was sufficient to keep Rome buzzing with gossip for the entirety of Cleopatra's year-and-a-half stay.

Not surprisingly, Cleopatra departed Rome swiftly after Caesar was murdered in March, 44 B.C., and returned directly to Egypt. Upon landing, she promptly had her younger brother, Ptolemy XIV, murdered, so she could replace him as co-regent with her own 4-year-old son Caesarion, who she married in the Ptolemaic custom. Furthermore, Cleopatra's sister and potential rival, Arsinoë IV, was removed from Alexandrian politics, for Marc Antony, the top lieutenant of Caesar, appointed her regent of Cyprus in 44 B.C.

At long last, Cleopatra gained full control of her kingdom, and did not even have to concern herself with the needs of the Romans, who were occupied with their own political problems. The struggle between Republicans and Caesareans was settled at the Battle of Philippi in 42 B.C., at which the Caesareans emerged victorious, though a number of Republicans and Pomepeians remained renegades from Parthia in the east to Spain in the West.

In 41 B.C., Marc Antony met with Cleopatra in Tarsus. The two, no doubt, had dined together many times in the company of Caesar during the queen's residence in Rome. Though they were not very compatible personally, they shared political ambition, and one of the first things they agreed to do, for both of their best interests, was to execute Cleopatra's sister Arsinoë IV, who had been ruling Cyprus. Cleopatra lost a bitter enemy, Antony had one less loose end to contend with, and Rome recovered the strategically important island.

Antony determined to winter with Cleopatra in Egypt, and thus began the queen's second great affair with a noble Roman. During the course of his stay at Tarsus and Alexandria, Cleopatra was impregnated, which resulted in twins in 40 B.C. While Antony was in Egypt, a massive invasion of Syria was led by the Parthian prince Pacorus I, who was aided by the renegade commander Labienus. The invasion was devastating, and most of Asia Minor, Syria and the Levant were occupied through 39 B.C.

Despite the seriousness of the invasion, and the enjoyment of his stay in Egypt, Antony had equally urgent business in the West, where his brother, Lucius Antonius, and Octavian had gone to war (the "Perusine War," ending in February 40 B.C.). Antony left Egypt, perhaps promising to come back soon, but in fact not returning or even seeing Cleopatra for the next four years.

Antony arrived in Italy after the hostilities had ended, and met with Octavian at Brundisium in October of 40 B.C. to settle their differences. One result was that Antony's lieutenant Ventidius was sent to oust Pacorus and Labienus from Asia, which he did with remarkable success in 39 and 38 B.C. Antony went east in 39 B.C., spending the winter of 38 to 37 B.C. in Athens with his new wife, Octavia (the sister of Octavian), and returned to the West in the spring of 37 B.C., where he renewed the Triumviral pact at Tarentum. Immediately after, Antony returned to the East, where, later in 37 B.C., he married Cleopatra at Antioch (despite the fact he was still married to Octavia). Though this marriage was not legally binding in Rome, it was a signal event by which Antony and Cleopatra hoped to join the fortunes of Rome and Egypt both at the present and, especially, in the future, after Octavian was eliminated.

In the next year, 36 B.C., Cleopatra gave birth to her third child by Antony, who had already embarked on his invasion of Parthia. The campaign was a complete disaster, ending in a disgraceful retreat and the need to ask for the help of Cleopatra in restoring his large, tattered army. It was at this point that Antony cut off all relations with Octavia, forbidding her even to visit him.

In the spring of 34 B.C., Antony led a vengeful invasion of Armenia, whose king, Artavasdes II, had switched his allegiance to the Parthians during the invasion of 36 B.C., triggering the disaster that followed. Upon returning to Alexandria, Antony celebrated his Armenian triumph. In this same year, Cleopatra made her famous "Donations of Alexandria," by which she allocated large parts of the East to her children. This alarmed the Romans, for it appeared as though Antony was allowing Cleopatra to give away Roman territory. Since Sextus Pompey and Lepidus had been eliminated, Antony's only rival was Octavian. Antony's poor treatment of Octavia, and his open cooperation with Cleopatra made a bad impression in the West and gave Octavian the ammunition he needed to discredit his rival. The Triumviral pact, which expired at the end of 33 B.C., was not renewed.

Cleopatra was firmly allied with Antony as they prepared for war. While this had its advantages, it also offended many soldiers and good commanders, who consequently defected to Octavian. Antony and Cleopatra spent the winter of 32 to 31 B.C. in Athens, preparing for the inevitable conflict. In 31 B.C., Octavian forcibly caused the consuls and senators loyal to Antony to flee to Greece, after which he formally declared war on Cleopatra.

The armies and navies of Antony and Octavian confronted near Actium on the west coast of Greece, and Octavian's commander, Agrippa, blockaded the camp of Antony and Octavian. The blockade was taking its toll by early September, so Antony and Cleopatra burst through and fled to Egypt with their separate fleets. Although Antony's army and navy stayed to fight Octavian, they were roundly defeated. In a virtual repeat of Pharsalus 17 years before, Octavian pursued his vanquished foes to Egypt.

Though Cleopatra sailed directly for Egypt, Antony first visited Cyrene in hopes of gathering the four legions he had left under the command of his ally Scarpus, but this was in vain, for Scarpus could no longer be counted among his supporters. After returning to Egypt, Antony committed suicide in 30 B.C. shortly before Octavian landed.

Though her husband had lost his Empire and his life, Cleopatra, who was nearing 40 years old, did not give up hope. Indeed, she waited for Octavian to arrive, hoping to work out a new arrangement (and allegedly trying ineffectively to seduce him). But she realized that Octavian had only hostile intentions toward her, her family and toward her kingdom, which he turned into a province, and in the future declared to be the personal property of the emperor.

In her final act of chicanery, Cleopatra managed to commit suicide by the bite of an asp. Suetonius tells us that Octavian was so anxious to have Cleopatra as a trophy in his triumph that he enlisted Psyllian snake-charmers to suck the poison from her wound, but the effort failed. Octavian subsequently murdered Caesarion, Cleopatra's child by Julius Caesar, though her three children by Antony were allowed to live under the care of their step-mother, Octavia.

NUMISMATIC NOTE: Cleopatra's coinage was varied both in location of mint and in typology. Her earliest coins were billon tetradrachms of the standard Ptolemaic design that had been used for more than two centuries (bust of Ptolemy I/eagle standing); however, her coins were generally distinguished by a low silver content and a headdress of Isis before the eagle's legs on the reverse. Her most remarkable coins bear her easily recognizable but often unflattering portrait, which sometimes is paired with the bust of Marc Antony.

CHAPTER TWO

The Julio-Claudians
27 B.C. – A.D. 68

With the deaths of Marc Antony and Cleopatra in 30 B.C., Rome entered a new phase of its history known as the Empire. Although for all practical purposes the Republic had stopped functioning more than a decade before, most of its traditional, if decaying institutions remained. The task at hand for Octavian (later known as Augustus) was simple in purpose but complex in execution, for he intended to make a slow transition from a Republic to a dictatorship. This required a series of careful measures in the legal, social and military systems that would retain the façade of Republican virtue, but in fact secure his absolute authority.

This transition took several decades to achieve, and the coinage clearly reflects his progress. From the initial issues bearing the names of the moneyers, the great Augustus ended his principate with issues that bore no one's name but his own. Even though he was advanced in age, his image itself was youthful and idealized. (This alone was a remarkable transition from the Republican concept of harsh realism in portraiture.) Many volumes have been written on the achievements of Augustus, and so only a brief treatment is given here, and in his biography.

For nearly a century we find Rome under the autocratic rulership of the *Julian* and *Claudian* families. With the childless marriage of Augustus to Livia, these two powerful families joined fortunes, and came to be known as the Julio-Claudians.

The Julians came into prominence with the impressive political career of Julius Caesar, who achieved the unparalleled office of "dictator for life" in 44 B.C., but was murdered soon thereafter. In Caesar's will, he had named his grand-nephew Octavian as sole heir of his political legacy, and most of his fortune. It required nearly 15 years of civil war after Caesar's death before Rome was united, and this occurred only after Augustus gained the upper hand on his ally-turned-foe, Marc Antony.

The Julio-Claudians comprise the first half of Suetonius' "Twelve Caesars." Though of great interest to most students of Roman history, the interrelations of this dynasty are the most complex in the history of the Empire. But what appears at first to be a hopelessly complex web of associations is easily separated into several components. Once this is done, the whole array becomes approachable, and the enjoyment of collecting Julio-Claudian coins is greatly enhanced. What follows is a general outline of the dynasty.

The Julio-Claudians

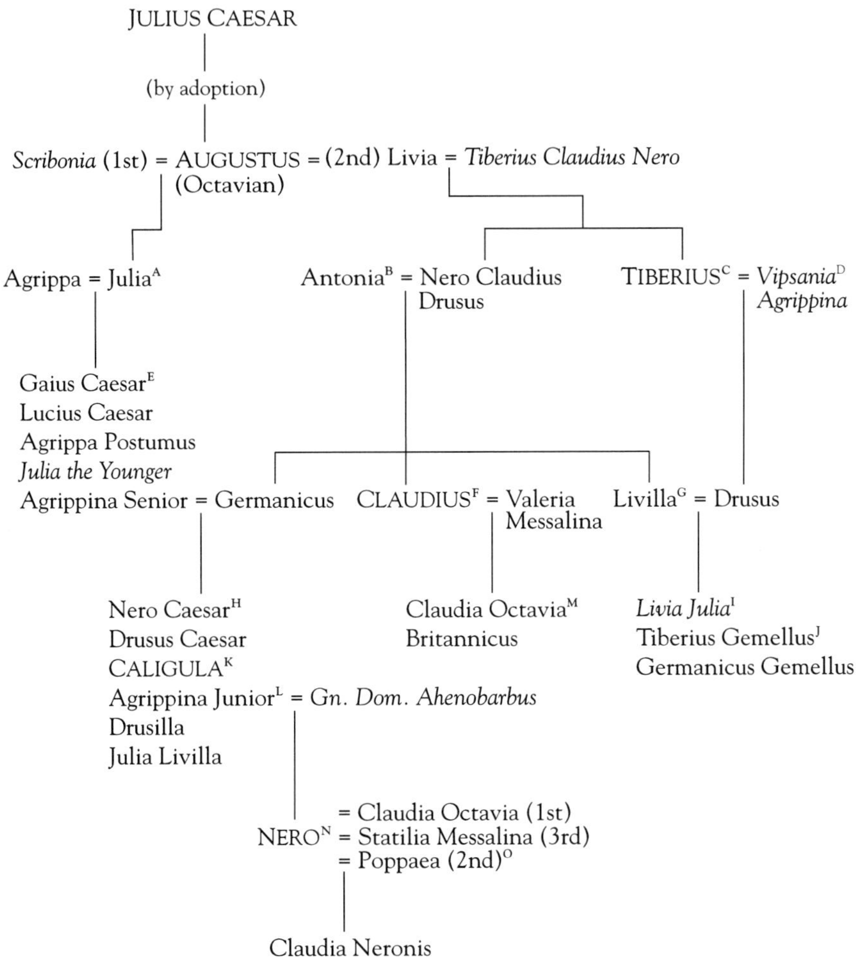

A. Earlier married to Marcellus; later to Tiberius.
B. Daughter of Octavia and Marc Antony (thus, niece of Augustus & half-sister of Marcellus).
C. Later married to Julia.
D. Daughter of Agrippa. Later wed Asinius Gallus.
E. First husband of Livilla.
F. First married to Aelia Paetina (by whom he had Claudia Antonia); later to Agrippina Junior.
G. Earlier married to Gaius Caesar; lover of Sejanus.
H. Husband of Livia Julia.
I. Wife of Nero Caesar; later betrothed to Sejanus.
J. He and his brother possibly sired by Sejanus.
K. Husband of Caesonia, father of Drusilla Minor.
L. Later married to Claudius.
M. Married to Nero.
N. Remote possibility he was sired by Claudius.
O. Earlier married to Otho (emperor, A.D. 69).

Note: Names in CAPITALS are of emperors or dictators; names in *italics* are of people not found on coinage.

- **Augustus (Octavian) comes to power in 44 B.C.** when the will of Julius Caesar is read, and it is revealed that he is heir to both his great-uncle's personal fortune and political legacy.

- **The dynastic foundations are set when Augustus marries Livia in 38 B.C.** Both of them had children from previous marriages, but in more than half a century of marriage they had none together. Therefore, different branches of the family existed along bloodlines, which was to be a source of great rivalry. Three principal branches existed: **the first** (I) was of Augustus' blood, **the second** (II) was of Livia's blood, and **the third** (III, IIIa and IIIb), through three later marriages, was of the mixed blood from Augustus, Livia and Marc Antony. These branches are described later.

- **With so many potential heirs to the throne**, conflicts occurred between the family branches. Regrettably, even inter-branch marriages did not reduce hostilities. **First**, Livia *may have* eliminated some of the heirs favored by her husband, Augustus (though that has not been proven to the satisfaction of many historians). **Second**, the emperor Tiberius tried to clear the path for his own son and grandsons by exterminating Germanicus and his sons, all of whom were the descendants of his long-since-deceased brother, Nero Claudius Drusus. **Third**, and much later, Agrippina Junior cleared the path for her own son, Nero, by murdering her uncle-husband, Claudius, and his son, Britannicus.

The three main family branches are:

- **Branch I: Augustus' direct descendants**. No male heirs of this branch survived. The initial rivalry was between the brothers-in-law Marcellus (Augustus' nephew) and Agrippa (Augustus' chief lieutenant). Shortly after Marcellus died in 23 B.C., Agrippa married his widow, Julia, who was Augustus' only daughter, and thus was uncontested heir-apparent until his own death in 12 B.C. Augustus next looked to his grandchildren, whom Agrippa Julia had produced from 20–12 B.C. They included three sons (Gaius Caesar, Lucius Caesar and Agrippa Postumus) and two daughters (Julia the Younger [for whom no coins were struck] and Agrippina Senior). All the boys and the eldest girl, however, died or were banished during a six-year period (A.D. 2–8). Only Agrippina Senior survived this traumatic period, and her marriage to Germanicus (a second cousin who headed Branch III) resulted in six children who lived past childhood (Gaius Caesar, Lucius Caesar, Caligula, Agrippina Junior, Drusilla and Julia Livilla), four of whom were important in future politics. But after having survived the destruction of her original family,

Agrippina Senior witnessed the systematic massacre of her husband and children under the regime of Livia's eldest son, Tiberius (the head of branch II), who as a result succeeded Augustus in 14. Despite her great suffering, it is Agrippina Senior who principally kept Augustus' blood flowing in the later Julio-Claudians.

- **Branch II: Tiberius' direct descendants.** This branch was headed by Tiberius, the older brother of Nero Claudius Drusus and one of two sons of Livia from her first marriage. Except in the grandchildren (who were born of Livilla, the daughter of Augustus' niece), no blood of Augustus flowed in this branch. Tiberius had one son, Drusus, by his wife, Vipsania Agrippina, a daughter of Agrippa. Through his son, Tiberius had at least one grandchild, Livia Julia, and two others, Tiberius Gemellus and Germanicus Gemellus, who were officially attributed to Drusus, but were likely sired by Tiberius' praetorian prefect, Sejanus. When Tiberius became emperor in 14, he tried to destroy the family of his long-since-deceased brother, Nero Claudius Drusus, for their line was rich with the blood of Augustus, and thus the people and senate favored them over his own offspring. Leading this rival branch was Tiberius' popular nephew, Germanicus. Though several fine members of Germanicus' family (including Germanicus himself) perished, the sinister designs of Tiberius were unsuccessful, for Tiberius' own son (Drusus) predeceased him and in 37 he was succeeded by Germanicus' youngest son, Caligula.

- **Branch III: Nero Claudius Drusus' direct descendants.** This was the most successful branch, despite the very early death of its founder in 9 B.C. (some 23 years before Augustus himself died). It was founded by Nero Claudius Drusus (a son of Livia, and the younger brother of Tiberius) and Antonia (the daughter of Marc Antony and Augustus' sister, Octavia). Unlike Tiberius' branch, this one was of very mixed blood, including that of Augustus, Livia and Marc Antony. Nero Claudius Drusus and Antonia had two sons, Claudius and Germanicus, and a daughter, Livilla. During their generation the branch splits into two sub-branches (IIIa and IIIb), headed by the sons, which (genetically, at least) developed separately. The daughter, Livilla, had marriages in both branch I and branch II.

- **Branch IIIa: Germanicus' direct descendants.** This sub-branch was headed by Germanicus, and was rich with Augustus' blood. Not only was his maternal grandmother, Octavia, a sister of Augustus, but his wife (Agrippina Senior) was Augustus' granddaughter. Despite suffering much loss at the hands of Tiberius and his prefect, Sejanus, three important children of Germanicus survived. The first was a son, Gaius (called

Caligula), who ruled cruelly from 37–41 and was murdered. The second was a daughter, Agrippina Junior, who became the mother of the third important offspring, the future emperor Nero (54–68), who, like his uncle Caligula, ruled cruelly and was murdered. With Nero's death, so ended the Julio-Claudian dynasty.

- **Branch IIIb: Claudius' direct descendants**. Since Claudius was born sickly, he was put aside early in life, and hopes resided with his highly popular brother, Germanicus. This obscurity spared Claudius fatal consequences in the "war" between the families headed by Tiberius and Germanicus. In the meantime, Claudius' marriages produced three children, of whom only a son, Britannicus, figured as a potential heir. When his demented young nephew Caligula was murdered in 41, Claudius was hailed emperor by the praetorian guards who wished to preserve their power, and recognized Claudius as not only a legitimate candidate, but one who they could dominate. Later, Claudius married one of his nieces, Caligula's sister Agrippina Junior, who also had a son from a previous marriage (Nero). Though they produced no children together in marriage, some have speculated that Claudius had sired Nero before they were wed. During Claudius' principate (41–54) only two legitimate male Julio-Claudian heirs remained: Britannicus and Nero, representing the two sub-branches of Germanicus' family. This spelled disaster for Claudius and his son, Britannicus, both of whom were murdered by Agrippina Senior and Nero so the latter could reign uncontested. Thus, Claudius' sub-branch ends.

AUGUSTUS 27 B.C. – A.D. 14

As Octavian: Member of the Second Triumvirate, 43–33 B.C.
As Octavian: Imperator, 31–27 B.C.
As Augustus: 27 B.C. – A.D. 14

Grand-nephew and adopted son of Julius Caesar
Husband of Scribonia and Livia
Father of Julia (by Scribonia)
Brother of Octavia
Brother-in-law of Marc Antony
Father-in-law of Marcellus, Agrippa and Tiberius
Adoptive father of Tiberius and Nero Claudius Drusus
Uncle of Antonia
Grand-uncle of Germanicus, Claudius and Livilla
Grandfather of Gaius Caesar, Lucius Caesar, Agrippa Postumus, Julia the Younger and Agrippina Senior
Great-grandfather of Nero Caesar, Drusus Caesar, Caligula, Agrippina Junior, Drusilla and Julia Livilla
Great-great-grandfather of Nero

Potential Heirs of Augustus

Marcellus	23 B.C.	Murdered(?)
Agrippa	12 B.C.	Died
Nero Claudius Drusus	9 B.C.	Died
Lucius Caesar	A.D. 2	Died
Gaius Caesar	A.D. 4	Died
Agrippa Postumus	A.D. 7	Banished
Asinius Gallus	—	Failed
Tiberius	A.D. 14	Succeeded

Caesar Augustus (earlier Gaius Octavius, modified subsequently), 63 B.C. – A.D. 14. Augustus was the son of Atia (a niece of Julius Caesar) and of Gaius Octavius, an aspiring *novus homo* ("new man"), who died young in 59 B.C. without achieving the nobility he desired. However, his two children by his second wife, Atia, would serve his memory well. They were Octavia, the future wife of Marc Antony, and Octavian, who came to be known as Augustus, and was the first "emperor" of Rome.

On balance, Augustus was a simple man who tackled enormous tasks in a pragmatic manner. As such, his accomplishments were both real and lasting. In his desire to achieve absolute power, Augustus demonstrated remarkable patience as he slowly and methodically accumulated titles and privileges, and restructured legal procedures to his advantage. Quietly, almost invisibly, he transformed a Republic into a constitutional hereditary monarchy.

His life was remarkable, and he enjoyed the company of great men, such as Virgil, Horace, Livy and Ovid. During his 57 years in power, he is said to have found Rome brick and left it marble. From this statement can be divined both a literal and a figurative truth which allows us, 2,000 years later, to reckon the greatness of his accomplishment.

NOTE TO THE READER: In his own biography, Augustus is referred to as Octavian during the period in which he used that name (63–27 B.C.), and as Augustus from 27 B.C. onward. However, in other biographies in this book in which he is mentioned, the name Octavian is used only in the Imperatorial Period (chapter 1), and the name Augustus is used for the Imperial Period (chapter 2 and beyond). This has been adopted for the sake of simplicity.

AS OCTAVIAN (63–27 B.C.)

Octavian was only 4 years old when his father died, and so he was raised by his mother. Julius Caesar took an interest in helping his fatherless great-nephew, and personally introduced him into society. While a teenager, Octavian was appointed *Pontifex* and *Praefectus Urbi* in 47 B.C., and in 46 he accompanied Caesar at his military triumph in Rome. In the following year, Octavian campaigned in Spain with Caesar, and subsequently went to Apollonia in northern Greece, where he was to finish his studies.

But on the 15th (Ides) of March, 44 B.C., Julius Caesar was murdered, and soon after Octavian learned that his great-uncle had adopted him as his son, and by doing so had named him heir to his political legacy. According to Suetonius, Octavian received three-fourths of Caesar's fortune (with the remaining one-fourth being divided between two other of Caesar's grandnephews, Quintus Pedius and Pinarius Scarpus).Though not yet 20 years old, and frail of constitution, Octavian sensed the calling of destiny and abandoned his studies (against the advice of his mother and other family members). He and his friend Marcus Agrippa traveled back to Rome, arriving in May or June of 44 B.C., whereupon he changed his name to Gaius Julius Caesar and launched his career in politics.

Octavian found Marc Antony (a former ally of Caesar, and the theoretical head of the Caesarean Party) to be confrontational, for Octavian was a threat to the career Antony had built. Indeed, Antony had good reason to fear, for Octavian proved himself to be a bold and resourceful politician from the start. Octavian allied himself with moderate Republicans, catered to Caesar's loyal veterans, and convinced the orator Cicero to emerge from retirement and take up his cause against Antony.

At this point, the political tide had turned strongly against Antony, who offered stubborn resistance, but still had to flee Rome. Octavian himself was getting resistance from the senate, which realized its peril and offered support to Brutus and Cassius (who had fled for their lives in 44 B.C.) by granting them great authority in Greece and Asia.

In 43 B.C., Octavian was given command with the two consuls, Hirtius and Pansa, and confronted the renegade armies of Antony in northern Italy at Mutina, where Antony was defeated by this senate-backed army. Though the victory belonged to the senate, both consuls were killed in the battle. Octavian (with the support of Caesar's veterans and Cicero) was named a replacement for one of the consuls, even though he was well below the requisite age. In this same year, Octavian's status as heir of Caesar was ratified by the senate, and his mother died, leaving him parentless.

Late in 43 B.C., laden with his new powers, Octavian marched against Antony, who in the meantime had allied himself with another Caesarean, Lepidus. But instead of fighting Antony and Lepidus, Octavian achieved a truce with his two rivals on November 27. This was a wise move by Octavian, who realized his power in Rome had only come through brute force, and had no guarantee of longevity. The three formed what is known as the Second Triumvirate, a legally sanctioned political alliance by which the trio would rule Rome and its territories for the next five years. In the pact, Octavian received control of Africa, Sicily and Sardinia.

On New Year's day, 42 B.C., Julius Caesar was declared a god, and Octavian thus became *divi filius* (son of a god). In the meantime, the Republican renegades Brutus and Cassius had been ravaging Greece and Asia, and had amassed a considerable war chest and a large, well-equipped army. It was only a matter of time before these "Republican" forces would engage whatever armies the Caesareans could assemble. The Republicans needed to win to justify their murder of Caesar, and the Caesareans needed to avenge Julius Caesar's death.

Antony and Octavian left Lepidus in command in Italy, and led their armies east to confront Brutus and Cassius. The armies of the Caesareans (Triumvirs) and the Republicans met in northern Greece, near Philippi, and engaged in two pitched battles. Octavian was so ill that he had to be carried about the battlefield on a litter, and thus he had to rely on the healthier and more experienced Antony to carry the day against the Republicans. In October of 42 B.C., these battles occurred at Philippi about three weeks apart. Cassius committed suicide after the first battle, and Brutus did the same after having lost the second.

The memory of Julius Caesar was avenged, and Rome awaited the triumphant return of Octavian and Antony. This marked a new era in the Roman world, and each of the Triumvirs thus tried to strengthen his own position. Also, the three carved up the Roman world. Antony headed to the east while Octavian and Lepidus remained in the West. In the following year, 41 B.C., Octavian came into conflict with Lucius Antonius, the youngest brother of Marc Antony, and defeated him in what is called the "Perusine War." Octavian wisely spared the life of Lucius Antonius, so as not to antagonize Marc Antony.

In 40 B.C., Octavian married Scribonia, a relative of Sextus Pompey, the youngest son of the long-deceased warlord Pompey the Great. After the murder of Julius Caesar (who in 48 B.C. had defeated Pompey the Great), Sextus Pompey had re-activated his ambitions, and had been given by order of the senate command of a powerful fleet which he used to gain control of Sicily and Sardinia.

Though Octavian's marriage to Scribonia had a political motive, it also resulted in a daughter named Julia, who was to be the only child Octavian fathered. In the same year, 40 B.C., Octavian also came to an agreement with Antony known as the Treaty of Brundisium, by which Antony married Octavian's only sister, Octavia. Though the marriage was received well by the public (who hoped it might prevent civil war), it was a private failure.

Two years later Octavian divorced Scribonia, not only because it was politically expedient, but also because (as Suetonius reports) he ". . . could not bear the way she nagged . . ." Octavian replaced Scribonia with an aristocratic lady named Livia, who proved to be his final wife. This marriage was based principally upon love and, though childless, endured 52 years. They seemed perfect companions though, admittedly, Livia frequently had to turn a blind eye to Octavian's extramarital affairs (which, we are told, were numerous).

The five-year Triumviral pact expired in 37 B.C., and Octavia (the sister to one Triumvir, and wife to another) was instrumental in organizing the Treaty of Tarentum, at which their pact was renewed. Only one year later, in 36 B.C., the complicated situation in the West was greatly simplified when Octavian's general Agrippa defeated Sextus Pompey in a pitched naval battle off the coast of Sicily.

Not only did this remove Sextus Pompey, the last member of the Pompeiian party, but during the campaign the least charismatic Triumvir, Lepidus (who had control of Africa), came into conflict with Octavian. In that same year, Lepidus was thus stripped of all honors except that of *pontifex maximus* (high priest). The Roman world was now exclusively in the hands of Octavian and Antony, who parceled it between themselves. Octavian received the West, and Antony took command in the wealthier East.

With the geographical separation came also a political division between Octavian and Antony. Octavian focused on restoring peace in Italy, where his support grew enormously. From 35 to 33 B.C. he was mainly occupied with wars in Illyria and Dalmatia, which gave Italy greater security on its eastern front. His building projects, headed by his lieutenant Agrippa, only added to Octavian's popularity. In the meantime,

Antony became more estranged to the Italians. His recalcitrant treatment of his wife, Octavia (Octavian's sister), in favor of the Egyptian queen Cleopatra VII, only worsened public opinion. Furthermore, Octavian fiendishly revealed the contents of Antony's will, which left no doubt that his tastes had become thoroughly Orientalized.

Even though public opinion in Italy was moving in Octavian's favor, when the Triumviral pact (and Octavian's consulship) expired at the end of 33 B.C., the incoming consuls (of 32 B.C.) were Ahenobarbus and Sosius, both of whom strongly supported Antony. Octavian thus occupied Rome with his soldiers and terrified the senators: the two consuls and some 300 senators fled to Ephesus to seek Antony's protection. The Triumviral Pact was not renewed, amounting to a declaration of war.

In 31 B.C., Italy and the western provinces submitted to Octavian, who assumed the consulship and officially declared war against Cleopatra VII, with the dual purpose of also eliminating Antony. The war came to a head in the spring of 31 B.C., when the armies and navies of the two warlords settled about five miles apart near the mouth of the Gulf of Ambracia on the western shore of Greece. Octavian's trusted naval commander, Agrippa, blockaded Antony's forces, and took his toll by the end of summer. Antony and Cleopatra VII burst through Agrippa's blockade and headed for Egypt, leaving the main parts of their army and navy to stay and fight.

The epochal battle occurred on September 2 at Actium. It was a massive engagement that filled the mouth of the gulf so thickly with warships that it has often been described as a virtual land war at sea. Agrippa proved to be the better admiral, and Antony's fleet, abandoned by its leader, capitulated. A few days later, Antony's land forces also surrendered, and one of the great victories in Western history was complete.

After having made their journey to Egypt, Antony and Cleopatra committed suicide separately in 30 B.C. rather than be taken to Rome to adorn Octavian's triumphal procession. As the new ruler of the Mediterranean, Octavian annexed Egypt (which had been a client kingdom) as his own private territory and executed the boy Caesarion, who Cleopatra claimed had been sired by Julius Caesar.

In 29 B.C., Octavian celebrated his triumph in Rome, and the doors of the Temple of Janus were formally closed. This was a rare occurrence, for they were only closed when Rome was at peace. Octavian subsequently was hailed Imperator by the senate, but instead of being a title, it was adopted as his praenomen. Octavian began the lengthy process of disbanding his many legions by settling veterans with land grants.

Now, came the artful part of Octavian's career, for after having achieved absolute power, he did not want to lose it in the same manner as Julius Caesar had nearly 15 years before. Thus began his mission to retain his absolute authority without having it appear so. Octavian declared the restoration of the Republic, and, on January 13, 27 B.C., forfeited most of his authority to the senate and the people of Rome.

He kept only his position as consul, and the provinces of Spain, Gaul, Syria and Egypt, complete with their legions. Three days later, the senate granted Octavian the title *Augustus* (meaning "sacred" or "revered"), which he chose in preference to that of *Romulus*. However, his true preference was *Princeps*, which meant "first citizen." Under succeeding emperors, *Augustus* came to mean the title of office of the emperor.

Note: For more details on this period, see the historical outline in the introductory section of Chapter 1.

As Augustus (27 B.C. – A.D. 14)

Although Augustus had achieved far more than one might have expected from the frail teenager of 43 B.C., his career as leader of Rome was just beginning. The five years following his being hailed Augustus were dangerous ones, in which Rome's new frontiers were secured or expanded. Augustus paid close attention to the submission and organization of Spain and Gaul, two of Rome's most important provinces.

In 23 B.C., Augustus resigned his decade-long possession of the consulship, but in its place the senate granted him for life the *tribuniciae potestas* ("power of the tribunate"). In this way Augustus attained perpetual veto power, and with this gesture the Republic formally came to an end. In that same year Marcellus, Augustus' only nephew and heir-apparent, died. Since Augustus had no son of his own, and was never in possession of good health (twice recently, in 25 and 23 B.C. he had been critically ill), his need for an heir seemed urgent.

Next in line was his lifelong friend and lieutenant, Agrippa, who two years later (21 B.C.) married Augustus' daughter, Julia (who recently had been widowed with the death of Marcellus). Only three years after that, in 18 B.C., Agrippa was granted a five-year co-regency with Augustus, which was renewed in 13 B.C. But the search for an heir who did not die prematurely proved to be Augustus' lifelong frustration. Indeed, he would lose no fewer than six prospects, only to be succeeded by Tiberius, the step-son whom he disliked.

Shortly before he began three years of travel in Sicily, Greece and Asia, Augustus turned down the senate's offer of becoming dictator. He introduced many pieces of legislation in 18 and 17 B.C. that supported traditional Roman family values. In the latter year, Augustus adopted his two eldest grandsons, Gaius Caesar and Lucius Caesar, and personally saw to their education in hope they might succeed him when they came of age.

From 15 to 13 B.C. Augustus focused on the western European provinces. He resided in Gaul and annexed Rhaetia and Noricum. One of his first actions in Gaul was to establish an Imperial mint at Lugdunum in 15 B.C., and, in a related measure, to reduce the senate's jurisdiction to the copper coinages only.

Two important deaths subsequently occurred. In 13 or 12 B.C., the long-since-demoted Triumvir Lepidus died. Since Lepidus had retained the title of *Pontifex Maximus*, it was now available and was given to Augustus, who became the head of the Roman religion. In 12 B.C., Augustus' heir-apparent and comrade-in-arms Agrippa died. Once again, Augustus had lost a promising heir, and his only daughter was widowed in the process. Now, Augustus was without a suitable heir should he die any time soon.

Having no other personal option (for his two grandsons were only 8 and 5 years old), Augustus brought into the Imperial fold his two stepsons, Tiberius and Nero Claudius Drusus, the sons of Livia by her previous marriage. With their promotion came an increase in Roman aggression in the unconquered lands bordering the Rhine and the Danube. Nero Claudius Drusus died just three years later, in 9 B.C., from an accidental fall off his horse.

Now Tiberius, who in 12 or 11 B.C. had been forced into an unhappy marriage with Augustus' daughter, Julia, was the only plausible heir in the event of an emergency. However, Augustus did not care for Tiberius, and viewed him simply as a regent for his two eldest grandsons, Gaius Caesar and Lucius Caesar. While this arrangement suited Augustus, it angered Tiberius, who realized that he was being used. Not only had he been forced to give up his blissful marriage to Vipsania Agrippina to enter into a hateful one with Augustus' daughter, but he now had to deal with the "spoiled" grandchildren of Augustus.

In the meantime, Tiberius' service to the Empire as its leading field general was being taken for granted by Augustus. The small measure of help Augustus offered in 6 B.C. — granting Tiberius the *tribuniciae potestas* for five years — rang hollow. Tiberius refused the title and "retired" to the island of Rhodes, where he stayed in self-exile for the next eight years. This left Augustus without a suitable heir who was of age.

In 2 B.C., after the most creative era of his principate had passed, the senate hailed Augustus *Pater Patriae*, meaning "father of his country." As flattering as this was, it had little effect on Augustus' spirit, for it occurred in the same year he banished his only daughter Julia on a charge of adultery, for she had engaged in many affairs while Tiberius was absent. Though heartbroken, Augustus had little choice in the matter, for about 15 years before he himself had introduced the legislation *(lex Iulia de adulteriis)* that made adultery a public crime.

Tiberius returned to Rome in the summer of A.D. 2 on the condition that he stay out of public affairs. Later in that same year, Augustus' second grandson, Lucius Caesar, died, and only two years after that (A.D. 4), his oldest grandson, Gaius Caesar, died. The only legitimate candidates for the succession were now the 46-year-old Tiberius and Augustus' remaining grandson, the recalcitrant 16-year-old Agrippa Postumus. Augustus formally adopted both of them in A.D. 4., but by A.D. 7 he had banished Agrippa Postumus, who would never return.

The years A.D. 6 to 9 were fraught with military crisis, which kept the heir-apparent Tiberius busy on the frontier. Augustus soon realized that his 28 legions (which were reduced from 60 at the height of his civil war with Antony) were insufficient. Indeed, when a revolt broke out in Pannonia, it required three years of Tiberius' full attention to suppress.

Just as Rome was emerging from this crisis on the Danube, the incompetent general Publius Quinctilius Varus lost three legions to a Germanic ambush in the Teutoburg forest. Now, Augustus had only 25 legions. This devastating blow sent Augustus into depression. For several months thereafter he occasionally banged his head against doors or walls and cried out "Quinctilius Varus, give me back my legions!" After having experienced these problems, Augustus postponed his plans to annex other European territories.

During the last five years of Augustus' reign, he resigned himself to the fact that Tiberius would succeed him. Even so, the aging emperor may have engaged in one last attempt to repair his relationship with Agrippa Postumus, whom he had exiled seven years previously. If this were true, it may have been what killed him, for Livia is said to have poisoned Augustus either to prevent such a meeting or in response to it having occurred.

Whatever the truth is, Augustus died at Nola on August 19, A.D. 14, just one month short of reaching his 76th year. Tiberius, who sped back from his journey to the Danubian front, arrived either while his adoptive father was on his deathbed or shortly after he died. Unpopular though he was, the 54-year-old Tiberius was hailed emperor. Except for the objection of the opportunist Asinius Gallus, there was no significant opposition or delay, for no one else was better qualified to succeed the great Augustus.

NUMISMATIC NOTE: Because of the various forms in which Augustus held power, and the great length of his political career (some 57 years), his is by far the most complex of all Roman coinages. As he shaped the political system from the crumbling Republic to the Principate (from *Imperium* to *Auctoritas*, as Michael Grant so appropriately described it in 1946), the character of his coinage changed. To simplify matters, his listings are divided according to the phase of his career in which they were struck. No serious attempt has been made to catalog all of his Imperatorial or Imperial coins, and relatively little attention has been paid to his 'provincial' coins, for he struck them at perhaps 150 mints. It should also be noted that the honorary coinage struck after his death was the largest of its kind in all Roman history.

JULIA

DAUGHTER OF AUGUSTUS (BY SCRIBONIA)
STEP-DAUGHTER OF LIVIA
WIFE OF MARCELLUS, AGRIPPA AND TIBERIUS
MOTHER-IN-LAW OF GERMANICUS
MOTHER OF GAIUS CAESAR, LUCIUS CAESAR, AGRIPPA POSTUMUS, JULIA THE YOUNGER AND AGRIPPINA SENIOR
GRANDMOTHER OF NERO CAESAR, DRUSUS CAESAR, CALIGULA, AGRIPPINA JUNIOR, DRUSILLA AND JULIA LIVILLA
GREAT-GRANDMOTHER OF NERO

Julia (*often called* Julia Major or Julia the Elder), 39 B.C. – A.D. 14. Famous for her kindness and sense of humor, Julia had little choice but to endure a tragic life. She was born to Augustus (Octavian) and his second wife, Scribonia, and because she proved to be Augustus' only natural child, she was important to her father's political career from the very outset. At the Treaty of Tarentum in 37 B.C., while only a small child, she was betrothed to Marc Antony's son Marcus Antonius Junior, who was only about 7 years old.

Because Marc Antonius Junior died in 30 B.C., Julia was wed to her 17-year-old cousin Marcellus in 25 B.C. Though this union cemented Marcellus' position as preferred eventual heir to Augustus' throne, it was not destined to last. Marcellus died in 23 B.C., apparently of natural causes, but perhaps on the orders of Livia. Augustus needed a new heir, and so he called upon his old comrade-in-arms, Agrippa, who all along had been the only serious rival to Marcellus. Julia was thus married to Agrippa in 21 B.C., even though he was some 25 years her senior and had been married several times before.

In 20 B.C. the couple produced a son, Gaius Caesar, and thereafter they had four more children: Julia the Younger in c. 19 B.C., Lucius Caesar in 17 B.C., Agrippina Senior in 14 B.C., and Agrippa Postumus in 12 B.C. No coins were struck for Julia the Younger, who (in A.D. 8), like her homonymous mother, was banished for rampant promiscuity (and apparently was kept alive until 28 by the support of her step-grandmother, Livia). Julia and Agrippa seemed to have gotten along well, and she accompanied her husband in the East from 16–13 B.C.

However, this fruitful marriage ended with Agrippa's tragic death in 12 B.C. Julia was now a widow, and Augustus had lost a second heir-apparent. Furthermore, he had no other immediate heir, as his grandsons were merely children. Thus began a very unhappy stage of Julia's life, as she was forced by Augustus and her stepmother Livia to marry yet again (in 12 or 11 B.C.), this time to Tiberius, Livia's eldest son. Tiberius was happily married to Vipsania Agrippina (a daughter of Agrippa, and the mother of Drusus) and did not want to divorce her so he could marry Julia, the widow of his ex-father-in-law. Political necessity, however, overshadowed personal desires; Tiberius would become the emergency heir, but in essence was perceived by Augustus as little more than the guardian of Augustus' eventual heirs, his eldest grandsons, Gaius Caesar and Lucius Caesar.

Tiberius and Julia proved to be completely incompatible, and the marriage was a failure. Tiberius spent as much time away from Rome on campaigns as possible, and in 6 B.C. exiled himself on the distant island of Rhodes while Julia remained in Rome. She engaged in affairs with many aristocratic men, including perhaps the poet Ovid, and Iullus Antonius, the youngest son of Marc Antony and Fulvia.

For her sexual escapades, Augustus reluctantly charged Julia with adultery in 2 B.C. and exiled her to the barren island of Pandataria, where she was accompanied by her mother, Scribonia. Suetonius tells us that this was perhaps the most tragic event in Augustus' life, and was far more hurtful even than the untimely deaths of his grandsons, Gaius and Lucius Caesars, or even the massacre of his legions under Varus in Germany.

While on Pandataria, Julia was forbidden to drink wine or indulge in any other luxury. Five years after she was banished, Julia was allowed to reside in somewhat greater comfort in Rhegium in southern Italy. Despite this upgrade in lifestyle, Julia still lived in virtually complete isolation for the next 11 years, during which time her three sons perished. According to Tacitus, Julia died of slow starvation in 14 sometime after her last son, Agrippa Postumus, was murdered (though some scholars suggest she actually died two years earlier). Julia's life was far from happy, and it seems the main cause of her suffering was the privileged position into which she was born.

NUMISMATIC NOTE: All coins depicting Julia were struck by her father, Augustus. Her Imperial issues are of interest, for one type is most unusual, and another is controversial. On the former (represented by two issues of denarii) Julia's bust is shown together with those of her two eldest sons, Gaius Caesar and Lucius Caesar. This format is interesting, but seldom yields detailed portraits. The controversial issue is a denarius from the same moneyer (C. Marius C. f. Tromentina) of 13 B.C., the year in which

Augustus renewed Agrippa's tribunician power and designated him as his successor. Several coins struck by the moneyers of 13 B.C. celebrate the foundation of an Augustan dynasty in which Julia and Agrippa represented the next generation, and their two sons Gaius and Lucius (for their other son, Agrippa Postumus, had not yet been born) were considered the eventual heirs. Indeed, it is in this remarkable series that 'Imperial' portrait coins are first struck for Agrippa, Julia, Gaius and Lucius. The historical context for the bust of Diana representing Julia is so strong that any doubts must be ascribed to overly cautious scholarship.

MARCELLUS

Nephew, son-in-law and intended heir of Augustus
Son of Octavia
First husband (and cousin) of Julia
Brother-in-law of Agrippa
Half-brother of Antonia

Marcus Claudius Marcellus, 42–23 B.C. Marcellus — just like the future emperor Tiberius — was born in the eventful year of 42 B.C., when his uncle, Augustus (Octavian), had joined forces with Marc Antony to defeat the Republican forces of Brutus and Cassius at Philippi.

Marcellus was the son of Augustus' sister, Octavia, by her first husband (the consul of 50 B.C.), after whom Marcellus was named. For political reasons, Octavia divorced Marcellus' father only two years after the boy was born so she could marry Marc Antony. This was a purely political marriage intended to bind Augustus and Antony, who had been allies since the murder of Julius Caesar in 44 B.C.

Since Augustus had no sons of his own, his nephew Marcellus was considered the foremost heir. Indeed, Augustus took a personal interest in his nephew's education in Spain, and originally betrothed him to a daughter of Sextus Pompeius. However, in 25 B.C. Augustus insisted instead that he wed Julia, the only child Augustus had fathered. Genetically this was a very close match (they were first cousins), and it is perhaps fortuitous that they did not have children.

After this marriage occurred, there remained no doubt that Marcellus was Augustus' preferred eventual heir, but since he was still only in his late teens, he was not yet a practical one. Marcellus' main rival was his brother-in-law Agrippa, the trusted lieutenant of Augustus. The two men often clashed — Agrippa because he believed his record of service should prevail, and the younger Marcellus because he was "family." Indeed, when Augustus fell seriously ill in 23 B.C., he gave his signet ring to Agrippa, not

Marcellus, for he felt his nephew was still too young for this responsibility at that point.

The likelihood that Marcellus would inherit the throne not only displeased Agrippa, but also Augustus' wife, Livia, who had two sons of her own (Tiberius and Nero Claudius Drusus). We can be justifiably suspicious that Marcellus' sudden death in 23 B.C. at age 19 was not natural, and was perhaps engineered by Livia. Although Agrippa perhaps had the most to gain from Marcellus' death, it would seem to be out of character for him to resort to such an underhanded act.

None-the-less, Agrippa became the leading heir to Augustus, a position which was greatly strengthened some two years later when he divorced Marcellus' sister, Marcella, and married his widow, Julia. Though Marcellus' death came as a shock to both Augustus and to the people of Rome, it proved to be the first in a long line of tragic and suspicious deaths of Augustus' intended successors.

NUMISMATIC NOTE: The coinage believed to portray Marcellus and Julia is rare and controversial. The most complicating factor is that there is no identifying inscription, and thus the attribution (even of the mint) is uncertain. However, since the coin belongs to the ninth consulship of Augustus (25 B.C.), it is likely that Marcellus and Julia are the subjects. Other authorities suggest the man's portrait is either Julius Caesar or Agrippa, and that the woman's portrait is Octavia, the mother of Marcellus. But in each of these alternate cases finding a proper context and a suitable partner in 25 B.C. is difficult, and so the attribution must tentatively remain with Marcellus and Julia.

AGRIPPA

SON-IN-LAW AND INTENDED SUCCESSOR OF AUGUSTUS
SECOND HUSBAND OF JULIA
BROTHER-IN-LAW OF MARCELLUS
FATHER-IN-LAW OF TIBERIUS
FATHER OF VIPSANIA AGRIPPINA, GAIUS CAESAR, LUCIUS CAESAR, AGRIPPA POSTUMUS, JULIA THE YOUNGER AND AGRIPPINA SENIOR
GRANDFATHER OF NERO CAESAR, DRUSUS CAESAR, CALIGULA, AGRIPPINA JUNIOR, DRUSILLA AND JULIA LIVILLA
GREAT-GRANDFATHER OF NERO

Marcus Vipsanius Agrippa, c. 63–12 B.C. The lieutenant and a chosen successor of Augustus, Agrippa was a close childhood friend of the first *princeps*, and was an ardent supporter of his until his own death in 12 B.C.

Although of relatively humble birth (he hailed from an equestrian family from Dalmatia), he was relied upon heavily by Augustus. When Augustus (Octavian) was recalled from his studies in Apollonia following the murder of his granduncle Julius Caesar in 44 B.C., it was Agrippa who accompanied him. He was an active commander in the Perusine War, governed Gaul, and later led an expedition across the Rhine. In 37 B.C. he served as consul in Rome and he twice received the tribunician power during his illustrious career.

Agrippa was the chief architect of Augustus' campaigns against Sextus Pompey, whom he defeated off the coast of Sicily in 36 B.C., thus stamping out the remnants of the Pompeian Party, and making it possible for Augustus to become the unrivaled commander of the Western Mediterranean. He also served with distinction in the Illyrian War of 35–33 B.C. But his greatest contribution to the building of Augustus' political career was yet to come. Indeed, it was Agrippa's genius as a naval commander to which Augustus owed his defeat of Marc Antony at the monumental Battle of Actium in 31 B.C.

Thereafter, Agrippa held additional consulships in 28 and 27 B.C. During the next few years, Agrippa had to contend with his brother-in-law Marcellus, who was Augustus' nephew and son-in-law. Because of Marcellus' blood connections to Augustus, the young man was intended to be Augustus' eventual heir. Not surprisingly, followers of Agrippa and Marcellus often clashed because both hoped to succeed Augustus, but each had different qualifications.

When Augustus fell seriously ill in 23 B.C., it was to Agrippa that he handed his signet ring, for Marcellus was only 19 years old and not ready for the responsibility of ruling an Empire. But the rivalry did not last for long, for Marcellus died prematurely in 23 B.C., perhaps as the result of a cunning murder.

After taking on a diplomatic mission in the East, Agrippa returned to Rome in 21 B.C., where he was compelled by Augustus to divorce his wife, Marcella (a daughter of Octavia, and niece of Augustus), and instead marry Augustus' only daughter, Julia. Together, Agrippa and Julia had five surviving children, four of whom appear on coins.

Agrippa spent the next two years pacifying parts of Spain and Gaul, and returned again to Rome in 18 B.C., whereupon he was given the *tribuniciae potestas* for a period of five years (which was renewed in 13 B.C.). His next important mission began in 16 B.C., when he spent three years in the East settling a variety of political and military problems and established veterans in colonies. After this, he returned in 13 B.C. to Pannonia, where his presence was instrumental in stamping out a potential revolt by frontier legions. Agrippa then returned to Rome, where he died a natural death in 12 B.C.

This came as a great shock to the nation, and to his long-time friend Augustus, who had chosen him as heir to the throne. Agrippa's career was remarkably eventful, but hardly as colorful as one might expect. Indeed, it reads like a laundry list of accomplishments, tireless service, and unquestioned loyalty to Augustus. No doubt, these character strengths must have concerned Livia, who was hopeful that one of her own two sons would succeed Augustus. It is worth noting that Agrippa's career was not entirely devoted to warfare, as he also held top governmental posts and supervised several massive building projects, including one that improved the water supply of the city of Rome. Among these was the Pantheon, one of the most enduring symbols of Rome, which much later in history was renovated by the emperor Hadrian.

NUMISMATIC NOTE: Agrippa's precious metal coinage was struck during two periods: 38 B.C. and 13–12 B.C. Most of Agrippa's provincial coinage occurred under Augustus, including the dual-portrait issues of Nemausus, which were struck in three phases, c. 27 B.C., c. 16–10 B.C. and c. 9–3 B.C. The most enigmatic issues of Agrippa, however, are the posthumous asses which are most often attributed to the reign of Caligula. Many scholars rightly believe the finest-style pieces were struck under Tiberius (14–37), and that the series continued through the reign of Caligula (37–41) and into the principate of Claudius (41–54). That they were struck by Caligula at all is enigmatic, as his disdain for Agrippa was well known. Suetonius relates: "Because of Agrippa's humble origin, Caligula loathed being described as his grandson, and would fly into a rage if anyone mentioned him, in speech or song . . .".

GAIUS CAESAR

SON OF AGRIPPA AND JULIA
GRANDSON AND INTENDED HEIR OF AUGUSTUS
FIRST HUSBAND OF LIVILLA
BROTHER OF LUCIUS CAESAR, AGRIPPA POSTUMUS, JULIA THE YOUNGER AND AGRIPPINA SENIOR

Gaius Caesar, 20 B.C. – A.D. 4. Gaius Caesar and his younger brother Lucius Caesar were adopted by their grandfather Augustus in 17 B.C., who personally saw to their education. After his father, Agrippa, died in 12 B.C., Gaius Caesar was hailed *princeps iuventutis*, as he and Lucius Caesar became the intended successors of Augustus.

But the brothers were spoiled and presumptuous about their future roles in government, so in 6 B.C. Augustus tried to teach them some humility by awarding Tiberius the tribunician power for five years. But Tiberius refused the honor since he was fed up with his marriage to Julia and was not anxious to be drawn into conflict with his stepsons Gaius and Lucius. Instead, Tiberius withdrew from public service and exiled himself on the distant island of Rhodes.

In the following year Gaius Caesar turned 15, upon which he was designated for the consulship of 1 B.C. and prematurely admitted to the senate. By all accounts, his public presentation was warmly received. Gaius Caesar's first and only wife was Livilla, the daughter of Nero Claudius Drusus and Antonia, whom he married in 1 B.C. Livilla is better known for her later marriage to Tiberius' son, Drusus, and for her adulterous affair with the praetorian prefect Sejanus. Though their marriage united the families of Augustus and Livia, it produced no children, and thus did not have the unifying effect their parents might have envisioned.

Gaius Caesar attained his first important mission in 1 B.C., when he was sent to the East to direct a campaign against Parthia, which had seized Armenia. Accompanying him as advisers were Sejanus, the future prefect of Tiberius, and Domitius Ahenobarbus, the grandfather of Nero. While in Syria, he celebrated his first consulate, and all seemed to be going well for the young heir to the throne, though the death of his younger brother, Lucius Caesar, in A.D. 2 must have come as a shock.

A similar fate, however, was awaiting Gaius Caesar, who near the end of the war in the East suffered a serious wound that eventually proved fatal (though some suggested Livia may have had a hand in his "natural" death). Gaius Caesar died at Limyra in Lycia in February of A.D. 4 while returning to Rome. His death was a shock not only to his adoptive grandfather, Augustus, but also to the people of Rome, who seem to have been fond of the young man. Once again — for the fourth time — Augustus had lost an heir to the throne.

LUCIUS CAESAR

Son of Agrippa and Julia
Grandson and intended heir of Augustus
Brother of Gaius Caesar, Agrippa Postumus, Julia the Younger and Agrippina Senior

Lucius Caesar, 17 B.C. – A.D. 2. The younger brother of Gaius Caesar, Lucius Caesar was cherished by his grandfather, the emperor Augustus. The brothers were jointly adopted by Augustus upon Lucius' birth in 17 B.C. After their father, Agrippa, died in 12 B.C., the brothers became the intended successors of Augustus, though as yet they were far too young for the task.

To remedy this, their mother, Julia, was married against her wishes to Tiberius, the eldest son of Livia, who at the time was married to her ex-husband's daughter. Tiberius was to act as guardian for the spoiled boys, but both the marriage and the guardianship proved too much for Tiberius to bear, and so he exiled himself to the island of Rhodes in 6 B.C. and left his new family to determine their own fates.

Lucius followed a similar path to that of his older brother, being presented publicly in 2 B.C., but he died of illness (though some suspected it came about on the orders of Livia) in A.D. 2 at Massalia, while *en route* to Spain to gain military experience. His death was a blow to Augustus, who not only valued Lucius Caesar as a grandson, but also as a potential heir.

AGRIPPA POSTUMUS

Son of Agrippa and Julia
Grandson and intended heir of Augustus
Brother of Gaius Caesar, Lucius Caesar, Julia the Younger and Agrippina Senior

Marcus Vipsanius Agrippa Postumus, 12 B.C. – A.D. 14. The third and youngest son of Agrippa and Julia, Agrippa Postumus was the last surviving male descendant of Augustus. He was born a few weeks after his father died, and as such he acquired the *agnomen* Postumus. However, Agrippa Postumus put a curious end to Augustus' familial heirs, for he did not possess the noble qualities of his two older brothers (spoiled though they were).

The ancient historians describe him as being physically tough, brutish, temperamental, stubborn, rebellious, seditious and depraved. Tacitus goes so far as to call him "a savage without either the years or the training needed for imperial responsibilities." Indeed, from the outset the young man was unable to deal with his older co-heir, Tiberius, who was adopted along with him by Augustus in A.D. 4.

Through the influence of Livia, Agrippa Postumus was sent to Surrentum by his grandfather, and in A.D. 7 was condemned by the senate to perpetual exile on the islands of Planasia, where he remained under guard for the next seven years.

Even the boy's death in 14 was an inauspicious event, and one for which several possibilities exist. It seems that his Augustus either secretly visited him a few months before his own death (where Tacitus tells us they had a "tearful display of affection") or was planning to do so. This aroused the suspicions of Livia, who feared Augustus would try to bring his natural grandson back into the Imperial fold. Since this would cost her own son, Tiberius, the inheritance he was so near to receiving, we are told that Livia poisoned Augustus before he embarked. If this were true, the grandson who had caused Augustus so much grief and pain in his lifetime proved also to be a cause of his death. Not surprisingly, after his grandfather's death in 14 Agrippa Postumus was murdered by a staff officer who took him by surprise.

Tiberius and Livia could now rest assured that no grandson of Augustus could threaten Tiberius' principate. It remains uncertain whether Agrippa Postumus' death was carried out on the orders of Augustus, Livia or Tiberius, though it seems most likely that Livia or Tiberius did it, for we are told by Tacitus that Tiberius blamed it on Augustus.

In one of the more colorful events in Julio-Claudian history, a man named Clemens, who had once been Agrippa Postumus' slave, sped to Planasia to rescue his former master and deliver him to the armies in Germany, but arrived too late. Tacitus tells us that the inventive Clemens stole Agrippa's ashes and went into hiding in Etruria until his hair and beard grew to sufficient length so that he could nearly pass as his former master. By now it was the year 16, and Clemens began to plant rumors of Agrippa's survival, which were eagerly accepted by those who sought an option to Tiberius.

We are told that many senators and members of Tiberius' household supported the impostor, who purported to have returned to claim his rightful inheritance. But Clemens' ruse did not last long after he emerged, for he was tricked by agents of Tiberius, who kidnapped him and interrogated him in the palace. After it became clear that Clemens would reveal no useful information, he was killed. And with this story, so ends the chapter of Augustus' last biological heir.

NUMISMATIC NOTE: Understandably few coins were struck for Agrippa Postumus. The few that exist were struck by Augustus in the provinces

ASINIUS GALLUS

POTENTIAL SUCCESSOR OF AUGUSTUS
SECOND HUSBAND OF VIPSANIA AGRIPPINA

Gaius Asinius Gallus, 41 B.C.–A.D. 33. The son of the distinguished orator and historian Gaius Asinius Pollio, Asinius Gallus was deeply involved with the affairs of state. Augustus characterized him as a man eager for supreme power, but unequal to the task.

The death of Augustus' lieutenant Agrippa in 12 B.C. was a loss on many levels, for not only was he a superb commander and the Imperial heir, but he was also Augustus' son-in-law, and the father of his grandchildren. Thus, Augustus' daughter, Julia, was now a widow — and far too important to remain unattached. Augustus' adopted son Tiberius was then happily married to Vipsania Agrippina (the daughter of Agrippa, and mother of Drusus), but was compelled by Augustus and Livia to divorce so he could enter a tragically unhappy marriage with the widowed Julia.

This chain of events spelled opportunity for Gallus, who married the freshly divorced Vipsania Agrippina. By marrying her, Gallus believed he had taken a step closer to the principate, but instead all he gained was the enmity of Augustus' eventual heir, Tiberius. Despite the apparent political advantages of the marriage, it seems the two were compatible, for she bore Gallus at least five sons.

Gallus had a distinguished career in government. It seems one of his earliest posts in government was the position of moneyer in about 16 B.C., after which he advanced through the *cursus honorum* at an accelerated pace under the patronage of Augustus. Gallus later served in the senate, was consul in 8 B.C., and then was governor of Syria from 6–5 B.C.

Though Gallus had been friendly with Augustus, his relationship with Tiberius was understandably poor, for not only was Gallus perceived as a competitor for the throne, but his sharp wit and opportunistic marriage to Tiberius' former wife earned him no gratitude. Tiberius' initial hatred for Gallus only grew when the latter made a fierce remark at the senate meeting in A.D. 14 where Tiberius was being confirmed emperor.

Gallus later fell victim to the political intrigues of Sejanus, and was accused by Tiberius of having had an adulterous affair with Agrippina Senior. Although Gallus had enjoyed a long and fruitful career, his downfall was rapid. He was imprisoned in 30 (one year after Agrippina Senior had suffered the same fate), and even after Sejanus was executed in 31, neither Agrippina nor Gallus emerged from their imprisonment, for Tiberius had no intention of freeing these two trouble-makers. Gallus died three years after his arrest without ever having received a trial.

NUMISMATIC NOTE: Gallus' coinage as governor of Syria was struck in 5 B.C., and there is no doubt that this portrait issue can be attributed to him. Though there is no record of his being a moneyer, Gallus appears also to have struck coins as one of Augustus' three moneyers who served in about 16 B.C. Though the approximately eight years between his serving as moneyer and becoming consul is less than the decade normally required, Gallus enjoyed such special patronage with Augustus that it would come as no surprise if his progress was more rapid than normal.

LIVIA

AUGUSTA, A.D. 14–29

WIFE OF AUGUSTUS
MOTHER OF TIBERIUS AND OF NERO CLAUDIUS DRUSUS
STEP-MOTHER OF JULIA
GRANDMOTHER OF GERMANICUS, CLAUDIUS, LIVILLA AND DRUSUS
GREAT-GRANDMOTHER OF NERO CAESAR, DRUSUS CAESAR, CALIGULA, AGRIPPINA JUNIOR, DRUSILLA, JULIA LIVILLA, BRITANNICUS, TIBERIUS GEMELLUS AND GERMANICUS GEMELLUS
GREAT-GREAT-GRANDMOTHER OF NERO

Julia Augusta (*earlier* Livia Drusilla), 58 B.C. – A.D. 29. The influence of Livia in the construction of the Empire cannot be underestimated, for she was the first matriarch of the Julio-Claudians, and one of the most trusted advisers of her second husband, Augustus (Octavian). Indeed, for Augustus' last 52 years, Livia was perhaps the most influential person in his life.

Before marrying Augustus she was married to Tiberius Claudius Nero, by whom she gave birth to the future emperor Tiberius, and to his younger brother, Nero Claudius Drusus. However, her husband had fought against Augustus in 40 B.C. and only returned to Italy when it was safe. In 38 B.C., while she was still pregnant with Nero Claudius Drusus, she divorced her first husband and married Augustus, who had been married three times before. This marriage was a successful political union based on what by all accounts was a genuine love and compatibility, but it produced no children.

Livia accompanied Augustus on many of his campaigns, and in his will she was adopted into the *Julii* family and given the lofty title of Augusta. She was the first lady to receive that title, and it was given sparingly until the principate of Domitian (81–96), after which it was granted to wives of the Augusti as a matter of formality.

Livia was legendary for her dignity and chastity, as well as for her tireless efforts to clear the path for her own son's accession. This required the banishment and murder of many people. Among her victims, it was rumored, were Gaius Caesar and Lucius Caesar and, even more likely, her own husband. Fearing that Augustus would try to bring his banished grandson Agrippa Postumus back into the Imperial fold (and thus cost her own son, Tiberius, the inheritance), she is said to have poisoned Augustus as a preventive measure. Livia may also be credited with ordering the subsequent murder of Agrippa Postumus to assure he would never pose a threat to Tiberius' principate. However, it should be noted that some historians consider these accusations of murder made against Livia to have been false.

After the death of Augustus in 14, Livia's life became far more difficult, as her son Tiberius eagerly shed her domineering influence. Even though she had inherited the name and title Julia Augusta from her deceased husband, Tiberius refused her any additional honors. What began as mere intolerance grew with the passage of time to become hatred, and she devoted her last few years to counteracting the intrigues of her son's praetorian prefect, Sejanus.

When Livia died in 29, Tiberius (who was then living in self-exile on Capri) did not attend her funeral, disregarded the instructions in her will, and forbade her deification. Her death was a great loss to the many who fought hard to limit the powers of Sejanus and Tiberius, and within months Agrippina Senior, Nero Caesar (and soon after, Drusus Caesar) were all banished or imprisoned. She was consecrated by her grandson Claudius in 42.

NUMISMATIC NOTE: Though Livia makes an impressive showing on provincial coinage during the reigns of her husband and son (and more modestly under Caligula, Claudius and Nero), there are markedly fewer dedicated to her in the Imperial series. This comes as somewhat of a surprise since she was Augustus' wife for 52 years and subsequently survived for 15 years into her son's principate. Indeed, there seems to be only one issue of Imperial coinage which offers a portrait bust of Rome's first Augusta — a dupondius struck grudgingly by her son in 22/3.

That the bust of Salus (health) on the dupondius represents Livia is a foregone conclusion. The supplemental inscription AVGVSTA is of great importance, for Livia was the only woman to hold the title Augusta at the time. Furthermore, its symbolism of a recovery from illness is shared with a sestertius from the same series depicting a carpentum, which certainly alludes to a *supplicatio* decreed by the senate for her recovery from illness. Tacitus (Annals 3.64) tells us that in the latter part of 22 Livia fell so seriously ill that Tiberius hastily return to Rome, adding that when Livia recovered the senate vote a *supplicatio* for her and decreed that great games *(ludi magni)* were to be held in honor of the Julian house. That the carpentum sestertius is inscribed IVLIAE AVGVST is additional evidence, for she was given both that name and that title in the will of Augustus. The other two dupondii in this series (inscribed IVSTITIA and PIETAS) are traditionally attributed to Livia, but in fact neither represents her. Of paramount importance is the fact that both lack the supplemental inscription AVGVSTA (which undoubtedly would have been added based on the precedent set by the Salus dupondius). Furthermore, there are a host of reasons why they are more applicable to others. See the discussions following the biographies of Livilla, Antonia and Agrippina Senior for further details.

It is worth noting that Livia was about 80 years old when the Salus dupondius was struck. That she appears to be pleasantly middle-aged is of no consequence, for it was standard since the reign of Augustus to falsify the youth of Imperial personages. The portrait on the Salus dupondius is identical to those on some provincial coins struck in Livia's honor, most notably a didrachm of Byzantium (RPC 1779) and a bronze of Oea (mod. Tripolis) in North Africa (RPC 835).

TIBERIUS A.D. 14–37

SON OF LIVIA
STEPSON, SON-IN-LAW AND HEIR OF AUGUSTUS
HUSBAND OF VIPSANIA AGRIPPINA AND JULIA
BROTHER OF NERO CLAUDIUS DRUSUS
FATHER OF DRUSUS (BY VIPSANIA AGRIPPINA)
SON-IN-LAW OF AGRIPPA
FATHER-IN-LAW OF LIVILLA
GRANDFATHER OF LIVIA JULIA, AND(?) OF TIBERIUS GEMELLUS AND GERMANICUS GEMELLUS
UNCLE AND ADOPTIVE FATHER OF GERMANICUS, CLAUDIUS AND LIVILLA
ADOPTIVE GRANDFATHER OF NERO CAESAR, DRUSUS CAESAR, CALIGULA, AGRIPPINA JUNIOR, DRUSILLA AND JULIA LIVILLA.

Potential Heirs of Tiberius		
Germanicus	A.D. 19	Murdered
Drusus	A.D. 23	Murdered
Nero Caesar	A.D. 30	Banished
Sejanus	A.D. 31	Executed
Drusus Caesar	A.D. 33	Starved
Tiberius Gemellus	A.D. 37	Executed
Caligula	—	Succeeded
Note: Two other potential heirs were Germanicus Gemellus (who died in childhood) and Claudius (who was never seriously considered by his uncle Tiberius).		

Tiberius Caesar Augustus (*earlier* Tiberius Claudius Nero), 42 B.C. – A.D. 37. Tiberius was the eldest of two sons born to Livia and Tiberius Claudius Nero, the head of the aristocratic *Claudii* family. His father was a strong believer in the Republic, and as such he took up arms against the Triumvirs in 40 B.C. After losing a battle he was forced to flee from the Triumvirs, and did not return to Italy until the following year. He suffered further injury when in 38 B.C. one of the Triumvirs, Octavian (Augustus), forced him to divorce Livia so that Octavian could take her as his own wife.

At the time Tiberius was 4 years old, and Livia was pregnant with his younger brother, Nero Claudius Drusus. Thus, while still a child, Tiberius was destined to play an important role in the politics of Rome. He was given his first important task in 20 B.C., when he led a campaign against the Parthians. Tiberius showed immediately that he had a flair for military leadership, and he recaptured the standards Crassus had lost 33 years before. Tiberius then tried his hand at governing Gaul in 16 B.C., and campaigned in the Alps in the following year with his brother. Tiberius then returned to Rome in 13 B.C. to assume his first consulship.

In the following year, 12 B.C., tragedy struck when the celebrated commander Agrippa died, for not only was he the husband of Augustus' only daughter, but he was also the emperor's foremost heir. Agrippa's death had dire personal consequences for Tiberius, who in 11 (or possibly 12) B.C. was forced to divorce his own beloved wife, Vipsania Agrippina. This was a doubly-cruel blow to Vipsania, who not only lost her loving husband, but who would now have to face life without her heroic father, Agrippa.

But it was not much better for Tiberius, who was forced to divorce his young, beautiful wife Vipsania (by whom he'd had a son, Drusus, who would be his future heir) so he could enter into an unhappy marriage with the widowed Julia. Tiberius spent most years of his marriage campaigning on the frontiers, as he could not tolerate Julia. During this period Tiberius was also the guardian of Gaius Caesar and Lucius Caesar, his new stepsons, who replaced their father as heirs-apparent.

Tragedy struck again in 9 B.C. when Tiberius' younger brother, Nero Claudius Drusus, died by accident. By 6 B.C. Tiberius found the political and social environment in Rome so unbearable that he moved to the island of Rhodes, where he isolated himself for eight years. Meanwhile in Rome, his wife, Julia, was engaging in embarrassing adulterous affairs, for which she was banished in 2 B.C. and was eventually killed 16 years later. Throughout Tiberius' self-exile his life seems to have been in danger, for the eldest heir-apparent, Gaius Caesar, did not want him back in Rome.

Tiberius returned in August of A.D. 2 on the condition that he not participate in public affairs. Shortly after Tiberius had returned, the younger heir, Lucius Caesar, died, and only two years after that, in A.D. 4, the oldest heir, Gaius Caesar, also died. Though the deaths of the boys must have come as a great relief to Tiberius (who was now 46 years old), it was traumatic for Augustus, whose options for an heir had narrowed considerably. Indeed, the only legitimate candidates were Tiberius and his remaining grandson, the temperamental 16-year-old Agrippa Postumus. So Augustus formally adopted both of them in A.D. 4., at which time Tiberius changed his name to Tiberius Julius Caesar and grudgingly adopted his nephew Germanicus as his son.

While Tiberius and Germanicus went off to fight in Pannonia and Germany, Agrippa Postumus continued to estrange his grandfather, never outgrowing his foul disposition. Three years later, in A.D. 7, Agrippa Postumus was banished, never to return. With renewed vigor, Tiberius spent most of his next eight years fighting in Germany and in the Balkans (during which the Roman general Varus lost his three legions to a Germanic ambush in the Teutoburg forest) and proved once again that he was a capable soldier and a competent leader.

He finally returned to Rome in October of A.D. 12, upon which he was granted supreme power along with Augustus, who was in his 75th year. In the summer of 14, Tiberius left Rome to head an army in the Balkans, but just when he arrived, he was instructed by Livia to return, presumably because she feared Agrippa Postumus would be named successor while Tiberius was absent. However, by the time Tiberius had returned, Augustus was either already dead or nearly so.

Despite the objections of Asinius Gallus (who we are told had long-aspired to the throne) and Tiberius' displays of false modesty, the senate hailed the 54-year-old Tiberius as the second emperor of Rome in August of the year 14, upon which he changed his name to Tiberius Caesar Augustus. The change of regime did not go over well with the public or with the army. The frontier legions showed signs of open mutiny and, to prevent a revolution, Tiberius sent his nephew Germanicus to Germany, and then his son, Drusus, to Pannonia to restore order.

After a rocky start, Tiberius' principate was launched by a fresh offensive deep into German territory, which Germanicus had the honor of leading. Though Germanicus' work was yet unfinished in 17, the new heir-apparent was recalled to Rome, where he celebrated a magnificent triumph. In the following year Tiberius shared the consulship with Germanicus, whom he then sent to Asia to settle a variety of urgent matters.

Tiberius perceived the great popularity of Germanicus as a threat — not only to his own regime, but also to the one he envisioned for his natural son, Drusus. Thus, Tiberius (it is believed) ordered his governor of Syria, Gnaeus Calpurnius Piso, to poison Germanicus when he returned to Antioch in 19. His widow, Agrippina Senior, and the people of Rome were outraged and demanded a trial. They received it in 20 and Tiberius found it politically expedient to abandon Piso, who was found guilty and killed himself.

Tiberius had narrowly escaped serious consequences, but in the process his goal was achieved, for now his son, Drusus, was clearly next in line to the throne. Thoughout all of the controversy Drusus had remained on the frontiers fighting, and in May of the year 20 he was recalled from Pannonia so he could jointly hold the consulship with his father, Tiberius.

Father and son were on good terms when he first arrived, but with the passage of time they grew apart. In the meantime, the praetorian prefect, Lucius Aelius Sejanus, had become increasingly important in Tiberius' regime, even though personally Tiberius did not care for him. Since Sejanus himself aspired to the throne, he was only too willing to poison Tiberius' mind against the other possible heirs, including his own son, Drusus, with whom Sejanus had come into public conflict on more than one occasion.

But Sejanus was as crafty as he was ambitious, and he had already seduced Drusus' wife, Livilla. Their adulterous affair moved from the lewd to the macabre when they conspired to murder Drusus so that they could later be wed and eventually claim the throne themselves. So Drusus was administered a slow-acting poison by his wife, the effects of which caused his death on September 14 of the year 23. The plot was so well concealed that it only became known when Sejanus' own wife revealed it prior to her own death eight years later.

Two years after Drusus' murder, Sejanus asked Tiberius for the widow Livilla's hand in marriage, but the request was denied because the prefect was not a senator, but merely an equestrian, and the match was not sufficiently dignified. As major a setback as this was, it did not cure Sejanus of his ambition, for he next determined to become emperor by default.

Tiberius was tiring of life in Rome and in 26 he left the capital. He first established residence in Campania, and in 27 settled permanently on the picturesque island of Capri in the Bay of Naples, never again returning to Rome. He left the day-to-day business of Roman politics in the hands of Sejanus, who had become de-facto ruler in the capital. Indeed, not only did he have the backing of Tiberius, but he also had an extensive network of spies and the might of the praetorian guards behind him.

In 29, Tiberius' 86-year-old mother, Livia, died. Their relationship had been cold for at least 15 years, and recently he had refused even to speak with her. Her estranged son, consumed by his debauched lifestyle on Capri, did not even come to Rome for her funeral. Furthermore, he refused her deification and ignored the instructions in her will. If Livia's death was pleasing to Tiberius, it was a windfall for Sejanus, who had long combated the forceful Augusta.

In that same year Sejanus renewed his attacks on the remaining obstacles in his rise to supreme power. In 29 and 30, three leading opponents — Agrippina Senior and her two eldest sons, Nero Caesar and Drusus Caesar — were imprisoned or banished after Sejanus charged them with a variety of offenses, including planning to overthrow Tiberius. Now, the only possible heirs other than Sejanus were Tiberius Gemellus (the grandson of Tiberius), Caligula (the youngest son of Germanicus) and Claudius (Tiberius' bookish and sickly nephew).

The Imperial partnership between Tiberius and Sejanus reached its apex in 31. In this single year Sejanus held the consulship with Tiberius (even though he was not of senatorial rank), and plotted to overthrow his regime. Details of Sejanus' plot, however, were discovered by Tiberius' sister-in-law Antonia, who had become the matriarch of the Julio-Claudians when Livia died in 29. Antonia informed Tiberius of the imminent coup – certainly not out of love for Tiberius (who probably had ordered the poisoning of her eldest son, Germanicus), but out of a desire to punish Sejanus, who had systematically targeted her grandchildren.

Five years of voluntary exile had not diminished Tiberius' survival instinct, and he arranged for Sejanus' arrest, execution and replacement all in one fell swoop. Sejanus' family and partisans were then hunted down with such speed and ferocity that it shocked contemporaries. There now remained six years in Tiberius' principate, which the ancient historians characterize as being increasingly filled with debauchery.

The emperor was residing at *Villa Jovis* (the villa of Jupiter) on the eastern summit of Capri. Here, Tiberius is said to have occupied himself with literature, mythology, language, astrology and unwholesome acts of violence and sexual perversion. We are told that condemned men were thrown to their deaths from the precipitous cliffs that flanked the villa, and that if they survived the fall, they were beaten to death below by men armed with oars and boat hooks. The aged emperor's sexual exploits are equally disturbing, and the future emperor Vitellius was numbered among the young male prostitutes, known as *spintriae*, who indulged the emperor's desires.

Residing with him on the island (and no doubt subjected to the cruelties of the environment) were Tiberius Gemellus and Caligula, both of whom were named Tiberius' heirs in 35. Caligula was older than his cousin by a decade, and certainly was the craftier of the two, for he had made his own plans for succession by securing the loyalty of the new praetorian prefect, Macro. While on a brief excursion to the mainland on March 16 of 37, the 77-year-old Tiberius died in his seaside villa at Misenum in Campania.

One version — which is not entirely unbelievable — is that Caligula had pulled Tiberius' signet ring from his finger before he was dead, and that the prefect, Macro, proceeded to smother the emperor with a pillow when he began to speak. In any event, the partnership of Caligula and Macro had at long last come to fruition, and the unfortunate Tiberius Gemellus was executed a few months later on a charge of treason, leaving Caligula unopposed as emperor.

Though the people called for Tiberius' desecration, his corpse was taken by armed escort to Rome where he was cremated by the soldiers, after which his ashes were placed in Augustus' mausoleum. Tiberius' frugality, Claudian arrogance and stiff personality caused him to be unpopular among the people, the senate, and oftentimes, the army. Indeed, it can rightly be said that he neither sought, nor received the love of his people. His reign was eventful only because of the dynastic intrigues and his regrettable association with Sejanus. Without these exceptional circumstances, his reign no doubt would have been a dull affair.

Curiously enough, the event of Tiberius' reign that has had the greatest impact on world history — the ministry and crucifixion of Jesus Christ — was no more than a minor event in the eyes of the emperor, who at the time was occupied indulging his pleasures on Capri.

NUMISMATIC NOTE: With Tiberius we find almost a complete reversal of the coinage policy of his predecessor, Augustus. Whereas Augustus' gold and silver offered an amazing variety of types, his æs coinage was mundane and utilitarian. Tiberius' precious metal coinage, in contrast, was dull and unimaginative, but his æs coinage is of great interest. Not only does it offer some memorable types, but it also established firmly the practice of honoring both predecessors and family members.

In the years 22 and 23 Tiberius struck a series of dated æs dedicated to family members who, in addition to himself, included his adoptive father Augustus (sestertius and as), his mother Livia (sestertius and 'Salus' dupondius), his son Drusus (as), his daughter-in-law Livilla ('Pietas' dupondius), his twin grandsons Tiberius Gemellus and Germanicus Gemellus (sestertius), and Agrippina Senior and/or Antonia ('Justitia' dupondius). Each of these types may be found in this catalog under the listings of the persons named.

This series is especially interesting because by 22/23, Tiberius was fond of none of these people, except Antonia (if she is even meant to be represented) and his twin grandsons (who were too young yet to have offended him or, perhaps, to have aroused his later suspicions that they were fathered by Sejanus). As such, the series is the perfect illustration of the propaganda value of coinage in the Empire, even if the messages promoted were not truthful.

When Tiberius ascended the throne, he sent his son Drusus and his nephew Germanicus to the Danube and Rhine, respectively, to prevent rebellion by the frontier legions. Since coins of Tiberius had not yet been produced, both Drusus and Germanicus countermarked existing bronzes with the abbreviated name of Tiberius. Also of note is that billon tetradrachms were first struck at Alexandria during Tiberius' reign for the first time since the regime of queen Cleopatra VII. Though they were further debased with the passage of time, the denomination served as the principal coin of the sealed Egyptian economy for nearly the next three centuries.

DRUSUS

SON AND INTENDED HEIR OF TIBERIUS
SECOND HUSBAND (AND COUSIN) OF LIVILLA
FATHER OF LIVIA JULIA AND(?) TIBERIUS GEMELLUS AND GERMANICUS GEMELLUS
COUSIN AND BROTHER-IN-LAW OF GERMANICUS AND CLAUDIUS
GRANDSON OF LIVIA AND AGRIPPA
FATHER-IN-LAW OF NERO CAESAR

Drusus Julius Caesar, (*often called* Drusus the Younger or Drusus Junior), 14/13 B.C. – A.D. 23. Drusus was the son of Tiberius and Vipsania Agrippina, the woman whom Tiberius was forced to divorce in 12 B.C. so he could marry Augustus' widowed daughter, Julia. As the only natural son of Tiberius, Drusus was from birth a potential heir to the throne.

Drusus' prospects as heir brightened in A.D. 2 when he was hailed *princeps iuventutis*, and further in A.D. 4, when his father was adopted by the emperor Augustus. Though Augustus was not fond of Tiberius, he evidently saw some promise in young Drusus. No doubt, Augustus had a hand in arranging the young man's marriage to Livilla, the sister of Germanicus, just as he had helped arrange his father's marriage to Julia. The marriage occurred shortly after A.D. 4, the year Livilla's previous husband, Gaius Caesar (Augustus' eldest grandson), had died from an injury he received fighting the Parthians.

This marriage bound together the two branches of Livia's family and served to cement Drusus' position as a legitimate heir. Drusus and Livilla soon had a daughter named Livia Julia for whom no coins were struck, but who in 20 or 22 (accounts vary) was wedded to Germanicus' eldest son, Nero Caesar. Drusus' prospects brightened further when Agrippa Postumus, the last grandson of Augustus, was banished in A.D. 7. This fortuitous event cleared the path for Tiberius and his son considerably.

Now only Germanicus and his three sons remained as rivals. Though slightly younger, Drusus was a contemporary of his popular cousin and adoptive brother, Germanicus. Tacitus informs us that not only were the two boys good friends, but that they did not allow their apparent rivalry to come between their friendship.

The most positive development of all for Drusus, however, occurred in 14, when Augustus died and the throne was passed on to his own father, Tiberius. Indeed, Drusus played an immediate and important role when he was sent to Pannonia to cure the frontier legions of their mutinous attitudes. Much like his cousin Germanicus (who had been sent to Germany to do likewise), Drusus won the army over with his strong personality and inspirational speeches.

In the year following his father's accession, Drusus held the consulship, and from 17 to 20 he commanded in Illyria, for which he celebrated a triumph. The year 19 was especially eventful, for his cousin (and adoptive brother) Germanicus was murdered in far-away Antioch by the Syrian governor, Gnaeus Calpurnius Piso. There was no doubt in the minds of the people that Piso had acted on orders of Tiberius.

Only a few weeks later (indeed, only a few days after news of Germanicus' death reached Rome) Drusus' wife Livilla gave birth to twin boys — Tiberius Gemellus and Germanicus Gemellus. With the birth of the twins (always an auspicious event to the Romans), Tiberius now had a dynasty of his own, complete with an able son and two grandsons. Now the path was clear for Drusus, who was much older than Germanicus' three sons. Indeed, what was a tragic year for Rome, was a glorious one for Tiberius.

But there was another contender for the throne — one not yet suspected by Tiberius — his praetorian prefect, Sejanus. Drusus was incensed at the power which Sejanus had amassed — power no doubt he felt entitled to as the emperor's only son and the leading Imperial commander in the field. He was also perceptive enough to see that Sejanus was looking after his own interests before those of his father. Thus, Sejanus and Drusus swiftly became mortal enemies, and it was not long before they clashed.

Time proved that Drusus was no match for Sejanus, who was not about to let Drusus interfere with his own grand scheme. In 21, Drusus held his second consulship and was given the *tribuniciae potestas*, and thus was a virtual co-ruler with his father. However, Sejanus had long been engaged in an adulterous affair with Drusus' wife, Livilla (indeed, he may have sired the twin boys), and together they plotted to remove Drusus from contention. Sejanus convinced Livilla to administer a slow-acting poison, from which Drusus died on September 14, 23. So ended the story of Drusus.

His father, Tiberius, we are told, was not particularly distressed, for with the passage of time he had become less and less fond of his son, whom we are told was vicious and of poor moral character. The young man apparently had a cruel streak and found great pleasure in killing. Indeed, the legionnaires had named the sharpest kind of sword, the *drusiani*, after him.

The secret of Drusus' death remained concealed for eight years, and was only revealed in 31 by Sejanus' wife, Apicata, as she cleared her conscience before her own execution. With the passing of Drusus, the field of likely candidates had narrowed to the two eldest sons of Germanicus, and they proved to be the next targets of Sejanus and Tiberius. As for the two other candidates: Caligula was only 11 years old, Tiberius' nephew Claudius was considered too sickly to be of consequence, and the twin grandsons of Tiberius were mere children.

NUMISMATIC NOTE: Drusus' lifetime Imperial coinage is limited to an as, a dupondius and a sestertius in the series produced by Tiberius in 22/23. Drusus himself is portrayed on the as, his wife Livilla is portrayed (in the guise of Pietas) on the dupondius, and the twin boys Tiberius Gemellus and Germanicus Gemellus are portrayed on the sestertius. Tiberius struck silver drachms (denarii) at Caesarea in Drusus' honor in 32/33 and 33/34. The central date of these two issues is 33, and since the tenth anniversary of Drusus' death occurred in that year, it no doubt was the reason for this otherwise inexplicable issue. This coinage is especially appropriate since only two years before, in 31, it was revealed that Drusus had been murdered by Livilla and Sejanus. After learning of this, Tiberius no doubt felt a measure of personal guilt for having invested enough trust and authority in Sejanus that he was able to murder Drusus with such ease.

LIVILLA

WIFE OF GAIUS CAESAR; WIFE AND COUSIN OF DRUSUS
MOTHER OF TIBERIUS GEMELLUS, GERMANICUS GEMELLUS AND LIVIA JULIA
DAUGHTER OF NERO CLAUDIUS DRUSUS AND ANTONIA
SISTER OF GERMANICUS AND CLAUDIUS
GRANDDAUGHTER OF LIVIA, MARC ANTONY AND OCTAVIA
DAUGHTER-IN-LAW OF TIBERIUS, JULIA AND AGRIPPA
SISTER-IN-LAW OF AGRIPPINA SENIOR
AUNT OF NERO CAESAR, DRUSUS CAESAR, CALIGULA, AGRIPPINA JUNIOR, DRUSILLA, JULIA LIVILLA AND BRITANNICUS

Livia Julia (*often called* Livia or Julia Livilla the Elder), c. 13 B.C. – A.D. 31. Although little-discussed in numismatic circles, Livilla was an important lady during the principates of Augustus and Tiberius. As the only daughter of Nero Claudius Drusus and Antonia (and the sister of Germanicus and Claudius), she was a desirable bride.

The date of Livilla's birth is uncertain, though it must have occured sometime between 14 and 11 B.C. Her absence from the design on the Ara Pacis has led some researchers to surmise that she was born in 12 or 11 B.C., though most prefer 13 B.C.

Her first marriage, in 1 B.C., was to Gaius Caesar, the eldest grandson of Augustus, and the young man in whom he had the highest hopes for succession when he came of age. Indeed, this marriage not only cemented the families of Augustus and Livia, but it also secured Livilla's eventual position as empress. Livilla accompanied her husband on his mission in the East, traveling extensively while there, but she suffered a great blow in A.D. 4 when her husband died at age 24 from a wound he received in battle against the Parthians.

Livilla was now a young widow, and eligible for another political marriage. Her second and final marriage was to her only cousin, Drusus, the son of her uncle Tiberius. Augustus is said to have seen promise in Drusus, and no doubt both he and Livia were happy to arrange the marriage in hopes that it would unite the two branches of Livia's family. The marriage occurred shortly after A.D. 4, and soon resulted in a daughter named Livia Julia, for whom no coins were struck.

We hear little of Livilla until well into the principate of Tiberius, and what we are told is less than flattering. After what seems to have been an initial period of closeness, Livilla and Drusus eventually grew apart. This spelled great opportunity for Tiberius' prefect, Sejanus: not only did he find Livilla a worthy conquest (for he was notorious for his seduction of noble wives), but through her Sejanus perceived a method of removing Drusus from the succession. It is difficult to determine when their adulterous affair began, but it may have been early enough for him to have sired her twin boys, Tiberius Gemellus and Germanicus Gemellus, to whom Livilla gave birth in 19.

Indeed, at some point later, Tiberius became openly suspicious that Sejanus — not Drusus — was the twins' natural father, thus making them not his grandsons. But what followed was far worse, for Sejanus was able to convince Livilla to poison her husband, Drusus, so that he could marry her as soon as she became eligible. The plan was executed with great precision, and Drusus died of what seemed to be natural causes in 23.

Livilla was now a widow again, and in the year 25 Sejanus asked Tiberius' permission to marry her. But Tiberius denied the request, explaining that Sejanus' low birth made the match impossible. Despite this setback, the two apparently continued their amorous relationship for the next six years, during which Sejanus made every sinister effort to achieve his goal of becoming emperor.

In 31, everything Sejanus and Livilla had planned came together at once, and just as swiftly fell apart. The first problem occurred when Livilla learned that Tiberius had given Sejanus permission to marry her own daughter, Livia Julia. Though Sejanus defended the marriage as a mere formality, Livilla understandably did not want Sejanus to share beds with both mother and daughter. (Note: There is confusion among the ancient historians on this matter, and it may well be that Sejanus actually got permission to marry Livilla, not her daughter, Livia Julia.)

When Antonia (the mother of Germanicus) found a document revealing Sejanus' plot to overthrow Tiberius, she delivered it to him

LIVIA JULIA

Though there are no coins known for Livia Julia, the granddaughter of Tiberius and the daughter of Livilla and Drusus, her story is of great interest. She was born shortly after Livilla and Drusus were wed, and, unlike Tiberius Gemellus and Germanicus Gemellus (who may have been sired by Sejanus) there is no reason to doubt her parentage. At the very least Livia Julia was their half-sister.

She herself was wed to her cousin Nero Caesar (the eldest son of Germanicus), either in 20 or 22 (Tacitus suggests the former, but the latter seems equally likely). Just as with her parents' marriage, this union bound the two branches of Livia's family. It turned out to be a promising union for Livia Julia because shortly after they were wed, her father, Drusus, died, thus making Nero Caesar the leading heir to the throne. But her clear path to becoming empress lasted only a few years, for in 31 her husband was executed on the orders of Sejanus, the prefect of Tiberius who had been having an adulterous affair with her mother, Livilla, for more than a decade.

Historians are in some disagreement over what happened next. It seems as though Sejanus pursued Livia Julia as the perfect bride by whom he could further his personal ambitions. At the height of his power in 31, Sejanus seems to have gained Tiberius' permission to marry her. Since Livia Julia was the eldest descendant of Tiberius, she was a better marriage prospect than her mother, Livilla, with whom Sejanus was still adulterously involved. As if this weren't strange enough, it must be considered that Livia Julia was available for marriage only because Sejanus had executed her husband.

But fate quickly sorted out the loose ends. Both Sejanus and Livilla were executed in 31 for their various crimes, and the mother-daughter love triangle never came to fruition. Livia Julia survived the chaos, and later grew heavy and married a "mere knight from Tibur" named Gaius Rubellius Blandus, by whom she had a son named Rubellius Plautus. Since her son was Tiberius' great-grandson — and thus a potential rival to the throne — he was put to death by Nero in 62. Concerning the fate of Livia Julia, we are told by Tacitus that she was murdered on orders of Valeria Messalina, the third wife of Claudius, and thus predeceased her son by perhaps as much as two decades.

personally. The aging emperor had Sejanus arrested and executed. As part of Sejanus' downfall, a great many of his partisans and family were also arrested and executed. Among them was Sejanus' ex-wife, Apicata, who in the final hours of her life revealed that Sejanus and Livilla had conspired to poison Drusus. Her statement was confirmed through the interrogation of other sources, and as a result Livilla was executed in that same year.

NUMISMATIC NOTE: Livilla is represented on only one coin type — a dupondius of 22/23 issued by Tiberius in the name of his son, Drusus. However, this is not acknowledged in the standard references, such as RIC, BMC and Cohen. Though this correct identification was proposed late in the 19th Century, it was not adopted in Cohen's multi-volume treatise (which was revised and republished from 1880–1892), and as a result it has been largely overlooked.

Of the three dupondii which Tiberius struck in the 'family' bronzes of 22/23, the one which honors Livilla bears the bust of Pietas, the personification of duty toward the gods, the state, and the family. As such, Pietas was the ideal guise for the public image of Livilla. She was, after all, the wife of Drusus and the mother of Tiberius' twin grandsons. Equally strong evidence can be found with the reverse inscription, for it is the only one of the three dupondii which bears Drusus' name and titles (the other two name Tiberius). In the family æs series of 22/23, only three coins bear Drusus' name in the inscriptions: the as which portrays Drusus, the sestertius which honors the twin sons he allegedly sired, and the Pietas dupondius. The three coins make a family set: a sestertius for the children, a dupondius for the mother and an as for the father. As if more evidence were necessary we should also consider that these are the only three Imperial coins bearing the name of Drusus (and, as such, they all should be of relevance to Drusus and his family). Indeed, to conclude anything other than that it is Livilla who is meant to be honored by the Pietas dupondius is simply to ignore the overwhelming evidence at hand.

Ironically, this issue reflects the public image of Livilla as a devoted mother and wife, in reality she was neither. Not only did she conspire with her adulterous lover Sejanus to murder her husband, but it seems likely that her twin sons were sired by Sejanus. As such, the Pietas dupondius is one of the least-forthright issues of the Julio-Claudians. For details about the other two dupondii in the series, see the Numismatic Notes following the biographies of Livia, Antonia and Agrippina Senior.

TIBERIUS GEMELLUS

CAESAR, A.D. 35–37

SON OF LIVILLA AND DRUSUS *or* SEJANUS
BROTHER OF GERMANICUS GEMELLUS AND LIVIA JULIA
COUSIN OF NERO CAESAR, DRUSUS CAESAR, CALIGULA, AGRIPPINA JUNIOR, DRUSILLA, JULIA LIVILLA AND BRITANNICUS
GRANDSON OF ANTONIA, NERO CLAUDIUS DRUSUS, AND(?) TIBERIUS
GREAT-GRANDSON OF OCTAVIA AND MARC ANTONY AND(?) OF LIVIA AND AGRIPPA

Tiberius Julius Caesar Gemellus, A.D. 19–37. As Tiberius searched for an heir to replace his own son, Drusus, who died in 23, he initially adopted the two eldest sons of Germanicus, though no doubt he hoped one of his twin grandsons, Tiberius Gemellus and Germanicus Gemellus, would eventually succeed. Theoretically, both of these boys were in Tiberius' direct bloodline, and thus to him were preferable to the sons of Germanicus.

However, Tiberius suspected (and over time was convinced) that the twins were born of the adulterous affair between Livilla and Sejanus. Were this the case, they would have been of no closer relation to him than Germanicus' sons, and this uncertainty was always in the back of his mind. Suetonius tells that Tiberius "hated" Tiberius Gemellus for being born of adultery, and that as such, he likened himself to the Trojan hero Priam, who also had outlived his entire family.

During the last years of Tiberius' life on Capri, his options for a youthful heir had narrowed to Tiberius Gemellus and his grandnephew Caligula (the only surviving son of Germanicus, whom he had adopted as a grandson). Claudius, it seems, was still considered too sickly for the job. Tensions between Tiberius and Caligula grew on Capri, for Tiberius was aware of the latter's capacity for brutality. Indeed, the dying emperor feared for the life of Tiberius Gemellus, and Tacitus tells us that in the last few months of his life, a weeping Tiberius clasped the 18-year-old boy and said to Caligula: "You will kill him! And someone else will kill you!"

Since Tiberius had formally adopted Tiberius Gemellus and Caligula as co-heirs in 35, there must have been ample tension between the two young men as Tiberius' health declined. Indeed, Suetonius tells us that Tiberius spared their lives not out of personal affection, but rather due to the counsel of his chief astrologer. Even so, Caligula was not willing to leave his own fate to chance, and so he made a pact with the praetorian prefect Macro. When Tiberius died (some said with the assistance of Macro), Caligula was hailed emperor just as had been planned.

Caligula then adopted his younger cousin and hailed him *princeps iuventutis*. But this arrangement did not last, and in the same year Caligula executed Tiberius Gemellus on suspicion of taking a poison antidote, an act which constituted treason. But Suetonius informs us that the smell Caligula detected on Tiberius Gemellus' breath was not an antidote, but medicine for "a persistent cough which was getting worse."

NUMISMATIC NOTE: It would seem that only three provincial cities struck for Tiberius Gemellus, and coins depicting him are understandably rare. The earliest pieces are from Cyrene, for they show him with his father and his brother and must date prior to 23. Most likely these African issues are associated with the 'family' bronzes struck at Rome by Tiberius and Drusus from 22 to 23. Later in his life, when he was an heir-apparent to Tiberius, coins seem to have been struck in his honor at Corinth and at Philadelphia in Lydia sometime between 35 and 37.

GERMANICUS GEMELLUS

SON OF LIVILLA AND DRUSUS *or* SEJANUS
BROTHER OF TIBERIUS GEMELLUS AND LIVIA JULIA
COUSIN OF NERO CAESAR, DRUSUS CAESAR, CALIGULA, AGRIPPINA JUNIOR, DRUSILLA, JULIA LIVILLA AND BRITANNICUS
GRANDSON OF ANTONIA, NERO CLAUDIUS DRUSUS, AND(?) TIBERIUS
GREAT-GRANDSON OF OCTAVIA AND MARC ANTONY AND(?) OF LIVIA AND AGRIPPA

Germanicus Julius Caesar Gemellus, A.D. 19–23/24. Although ancient historical sources make appropriate references to his twin brother, Tiberius Gemellus (who survived into his 18th year and was named co-successor to Tiberius), they are understandably silent regarding Germanicus Gemellus, who died at age 5. Some authorities place his death in 23, the same year as his father died, others in 24. The word *gemellus* is an infrequently used form of the word *geminus*, which means 'twin.'

NUMISMATIC NOTE: The Imperial issue (a sestertius with the twins's heads upon crossed cornucopias), and most likely the provincial issues, portraying Germanicus Gemellus and Tiberius Gemellus were struck by Tiberius c. 22–23.

SEJANUS

Praetorian Prefect, A.D. 14–31
Potential successor of Tiberius

Companion of Livilla
Father(?) of Tiberius Gemellus and Germanicus Gemellus
Uncle of Claudia Antonia

Lucius Aelius Sejanus, d. A.D. 31. As the praetorian prefect of Tiberius, and his principal adviser from 23 to 31, Sejanus figures prominently in Julio-Claudian history. Indeed, when addressing the senate, Tiberius characterized Sejanus as "the partner of my labors."

Though Suetonius tells us that Tiberius did not like him personally, Sejanus was his main instrument in the destruction of Germanicus' family. He also served as the emperor's agent in Rome for the first five years Tiberius spent in self-exile on Capri. Though he was of distinguished parentage on his mother's side, and his father had been a very successful man, Sejanus belonged to an equestrian, not a senatorial family. Ironically, it was only because his ambitions were so high that he rightly could be accused of "low birth," a fact that Sejanus spent the best years of his life trying to overcome.

Sejanus entered into the service of Tiberius along with his own father, with whom he shared the duties of praetorian prefect in Rome. When his father was appointed prefect of Egypt, Sejanus became the sole commander of the guard. Relatively early in his career (in the year 20 according to Tacitus) Sejanus arranged to have his daughter betrothed to the eldest son of Claudius (a boy named Claudius Drusus, for whom no coins were struck). Unfortunately, the boy, who was almost of age, choked to death on a pear a few days later, robbing Sejanus of an Imperial marriage that might have changed the course of his sinister career. Even the marriage of his sister Aelia Paetina to Claudius (who was not emperor, or even an heir-apparent at that time) did not improve Sejanus' nobility.

As time passed, Tiberius trusted Sejanus with ever-increasing authority that gave him a free hand in eliminating the potential rivals to the throne. His first victim was Tiberius' own son, Drusus, with whom Sejanus often found himself in conflict. Sejanus seduced Drusus' wife, Livilla, and their adulterous affair took a foul twist when he compelled her to poison her husband. In the same year Sejanus took yet another step to increase his power when he convinced Tiberius to let him gather all nine praetorian cohorts (which traditionally were spread out among Rome and other Italian cities) and station them in a single barracks in Rome. This event was to have a great impact not only on Sejanus' authority, but also on the way Rome was ruled for the next 450 years.

Sejanus' most gruesome task, however, was to exterminate the sons of Germanicus, whom Tiberius increasingly feared as rivals to the throne. For Sejanus (who himself was aspiring to the throne), this was pleasurable work — the fewer claimants, the better his own chances. Although Sejanus was successful in almost all of his endeavors, he suffered a great setback in 25 when his request to wed the recently widowed Livilla (with whom he was still carrying on an affair) was denied by Tiberius due to his low birth. However, Sejanus quickly recovered from this blow and moved on to other tasks.

The first of these was convincing Tiberius to act upon his desire to leave Rome and live the rest of his life in isolation on the island of Capri. Tiberius first left to Campania in 26, but by 27 had established his residence on Capri and never again returned to Rome. Sejanus now had virtually supreme authority in Rome, and acted both as the eyes and ears of Tiberius. The year 29 also brought good news to Sejanus, for Tiberius' mother, Livia, died. This made his sinister work easier to conduct, and in 29 and 30 he was able to imprison or banished his three most potent enemies: Agrippina Senior and her two eldest sons, Nero Caesar and Drusus Caesar.

But all of these foul acts were merely leading up to the year 31, when Sejanus conspired to overthrow Tiberius himself. During that year not only was Sejanus named joint consul with Tiberius, but Tacitus informs us that he was also able to convince Tiberius to give him the hand of his granddaughter, Livia Julia, in marriage. While this marriage no doubt suited Sejanus, it brought a violent objection from Livilla, who would not stand by idly as her own lover of several years married her daughter. As if the family aspect of this were not disturbing enough, it must also be remembered that Livia Julia was now a widow only because Sejanus had recently arrested and executed her husband, Nero Caesar. (It is worth noting that the ancient sources are not entirely clear whether it was the mother or daughter to whom Sejanus was betrothed.)

Regardless, Suetonius tells us that Tiberius took this outrageous action only to placate Sejanus while his downfall was arranged. The house of cards built by Sejanus was now beginning to tumble, and he determined to usurp the throne before the opportunity passed him by. Amid of all this tragedy Antonia — now the matriarch of the Julio-Claudians — appears to have found a document revealing Sejanus' plot. No doubt with great pleasure, she informed her brother-in-law Tiberius of her discovery.

Tiberius reacted quickly and cunningly, offering Sejanus' job to an ambitious soldier named Naevius Sertorius Macro if he would arrest Sejanus. The arrest was made in the senate house, and according to Tacitus, Sejanus was executed on October 18 (after which Macro served as praetorian prefect from 31–38.). As a consequence, Sejanus' family and partisans were hunted down and executed with shocking ferocity, and the many statues of himself he had erected were destroyed.

During the turmoil of this counter-revolution, Sejanus' wife, Apicata, revealed that Sejanus and Livilla had conspired to poison Drusus. Thus, the doomed Apicata took satisfaction in causing the demise of Livilla, who had been mistress to her husband for several years. Perhaps the greatest unsolved mystery of Sejanus' legacy was whether or not he was the natural father of Livilla's twin sons, Tiberius Gemellus and Germanicus Gemellus. Though they were officially attributed to Livilla's husband, Drusus, ample suspicion existed, and we are told that even Tiberius was convinced Sejanus was their father.

NUMISMATIC NOTE: No portrait coins of Sejanus exist, although a provincial coinage of Bilbilis in Spain mentions him by name as the joint-consul of Tiberius in 31, the year to which the coins are dated. Some of Sejanus' Spanish bronzes were purposefully damaged, by which his memory was condemned for his crimes against the state.

NERO CLAUDIUS DRUSUS

SON OF LIVIA
STEPSON OF AUGUSTUS
BROTHER OF TIBERIUS
HUSBAND OF ANTONIA
FATHER OF GERMANICUS, CLAUDIUS AND LIVILLA
GRANDFATHER OF NERO CAESAR, DRUSUS CAESAR, CALIGULA, AGRIPPINA JUNIOR, DRUSILLA, JULIA LIVILLA, BRITANNICUS, LIVIA JULIA, TIBERIUS GEMELLUS AND GERMANICUS GEMELLUS
GREAT-GRANDFATHER OF NERO

Nero Claudius Drusus (*often called* Drusus the Elder or Drusus Senior), 38–9 B.C. Nero Claudius Drusus was the youngest son of Livia and Tiberius Claudius Nero, head of the *Claudii* family. His father took up arms against Marc Antony and Augustus (Octavian) in 40 B.C., and after losing a battle he fled and did not return to Italy until the following year.

In 38 B.C. Augustus forced Tiberius Claudius Nero to divorce Livia so Augustus could take her as his own wife. At the time this occurred Nero Claudius Drusus had been conceived, but not yet born. Thus, Nero Claudius Drusus was born into the family created by the marriage of Livia to Augustus, and into the Julio-Claudians. Augustus treated Nero Claudius

Drusus as if he was a natural son of his own, for he raised him in his own household and saw to his education.

In 18 or 16 B.C., Nero Claudius Drusus married Augustus' niece Antonia, a remarkable woman who was destined to outlive her husband by nearly half a century. Their brief marriage of about seven years was a success, and they had three children. The first was a son born in 15 B.C., who eventually was given the name Germanicus; the second was Livilla, a daughter born in about 13 B.C.; and the last was a sickly son named Claudius, born in 10 B.C. All three children were destined for important roles in the history of the Julio-Claudians, with the youngest son becoming emperor in 41.

The career of Nero Claudius Drusus was as exceptional as it was brief. In 15 B.C. he campaigned with Tiberius against the Raetians and Vindelicians, and three years later he dedicated the famous altar to Augustus at Lugdunum. He was considered by Augustus to be his most capable general, and so he entrusted him with the invasion of Germany in 12 B.C. He spent the next three years fighting a host of Germanic nations. During these campaigns he conducted geographic explorations which were of great use to future generals.

In 9 B.C. he held the consulship, but died unexpectedly at the age of 29. He broke one of his legs after being thrown from his horse, and was taken to the army's summer camp, where he survived in agony for a month, only to die of complications from the wound. Tiberius was devastated. He traveled from Rome to the army camp at great speed, and arrived shortly before his brother died. He then accompanied his brother's body back to Rome for the entire, arduous journey.

The news was taken badly by Augustus, who had known him since the moment he was born and had raised him as his own. The grief-stricken emperor later wrote a biography of Nero Claudius Drusus. But hardest hit of all was his wife, Antonia, who at age 27 was widowed, and refused ever to marry again.

Although Nero Claudius Drusus was refused a full triumph for his Germanic campaigns (the results of which were somewhat illusory), in his memory the senate awarded him and his descendants the surname Germanicus, which his eldest son adopted. Nero Claudius Drusus was popular among the people, the soldiers and the senate (for he is said to have harbored strong Republican sentiments), and his death caused a lengthy period of mourning.

NUMISMATIC NOTE: All of Nero Claudius Drusus' coins were struck by his son Claudius more than half a century after his death. Claudius was almost exactly 1 year old when his father died.

ANTONIA

AUGUSTA, A.D. 37 AND 41

WIFE OF NERO CLAUDIUS DRUSUS
DAUGHTER OF MARC ANTONY AND OCTAVIA
HALF-SISTER OF MARCELLUS
DAUGHTER-IN-LAW AND NIECE OF LIVIA
SISTER-IN-LAW OF TIBERIUS
NIECE OF AUGUSTUS
MOTHER OF GERMANICUS, CLAUDIUS AND LIVILLA
GRANDMOTHER OF NERO CAESAR, DRUSUS CAESAR, CALIGULA, AGRIPPINA JUNIOR, DRUSILLA, JULIA LIVILLA, BRITANNICUS, LIVIA JULIA, TIBERIUS GEMELLUS AND GERMANICUS GEMELLUS
GREAT-GRANDMOTHER OF NERO

Antonia, 36 B.C. – A.D. 37. Of distinguished parentage, Antonia was also fabulously wealthy, for she inherited vast land holdings in the East from her father, Marc Antony. Though she needed no further credentials, Antonia became even better connected within the Julio-Claudians when in 18 or 16 B.C. she married Nero Claudius Drusus, the youngest son of Livia.

Early in her life Antonia was occupied with building a family. Indeed it was ideal that she concentrated on that early in the marriage, for Nero Claudius Drusus was doomed to a premature, accidental death. Together they produced three children who played important roles in Julio-Claudian history. The first, a son who eventually took the name Germanicus, arrived in 15 B.C. Their next child, a daughter named Livilla born in about 13 B.C., was destined for a troubled life. Their last child, a son named Claudius, who was born in 10 B.C., was sickly from birth but outlasted his contemporaries to become emperor in 41.

After her husband's tragic death in 9 B.C., Antonia's life took on a new character, for her grief was unbounded. She refused to remarry, though she remained active in raising her three children and in seeing to her economic interests in the East. She was especially active during the principate of her brother-in-law Tiberius, during which she witnessed firsthand the banishment, murder or execution of two children, their spouses, and two of her grandsons. When her mother-in-law, Livia, died in 29, Antonia became the matriarch of the Imperial household, depleted though it was.

Her most noteworthy contribution later in life occurred in 31, when she discovered a document proving that the ambitious prefect Sejanus was planning to overthrow Tiberius. Indeed, it was Antonia who informed Tiberius, and she must have been satisfied to know that she was the instrument of Sejanus' downfall, for he personally had caused so much tragedy in her family. Antonia now had only two surviving male heirs — her youngest son, Claudius, and her youngest grandson, Caligula. Antonia had gone to great lengths to protect Caligula from Sejanus, and also to curb the boy's bad behavior.

When Tiberius died in March of 37, and Caligula emerged as sole emperor, Antonia tried to exert a moderating influence over her grandson. Historians tell us that Caligula initially honored his grandmother (then the only true 'matriarch' of the Julio-Claudians) with all the honors previously accorded Livia, which included the title of Augusta, the top role in the priesthood of Augustus, and the privileges of the Vestal Virgins.

Though doubts have been raised as to whether Antonia was hailed Augusta by Caligula, there seems little cause for confusion. An inscription from Corinth names both Antonia (as Augusta) and Tiberius Gemellus, and thus it must date to the first few weeks of Caligula's principate. However, it is possible that she did refuse the title as Suetonius proposes. Clearly, the title was not used extensively with Antonia's name until after it was reconferred on her posthumously in 41 by her surviving son, Claudius.

Caligula quickly came to resent Antonia's meddling, and is said to have either poisoned her or to have driven her to suicide less than two months after he had become emperor, for she died on May 1 at the respectable age of 72. We are also told that Caligula did not attend her funeral in person, but rather watched her pyre burn from the comfort of his dining room. If this version of history can be trusted (and that is far from certain), it ranks among the greatest acts of ingratitude imaginable considering how hard Antonia fought to protect him from Sejanus. Four years later, Antonia was given posthumous honors by Claudius, who succeeded his nephew Caligula.

Numismatic Note: Most of Antonia's coins — aurei, denarii, dupondii and provincial issues — were struck posthumously by her surviving son, Claudius, who ruled from 41–54. The few issues struck during Antonia's lifetime include provincial coins from the beginning of Caligula's reign (in 37), when Antonia was first awarded the title of Augusta, and, seemingly the issue of 'Justitia' dupondii struck by Tiberius in 22/23 (which are traditionally misattributed to Livia). As such, these dupondii are of some interest, because they are the only Imperial coins struck in honor of Antonia during her lifetime.

It seems unlikely that we have an actual portait of Antonia on these dupondii, for the features of Justitia are impersonal and idealized. This certainly is not the case with the other two dupondii in this series, which are rightly attributed to Livia (as Salus) and Livilla (as Pietas). Instead, what we have with Justitia is nothing more than the personification of justice herself.

In the most general sense this coin applies specifically to the trial of Gnaeus Calpurnius Piso for the murder of Germanicus. From that perspective it is applicable to three people: Tiberius, Antonia and Agrippina Senior. In the first case, Tiberius, this is certain not only because the coin was struck in his name, but also because he went to great lengths of "damage control" to distance himself from the controversy over Germanicus' murder, which he successfully pinned on Piso as an act of his design. In the latter two cases, Antonia and Agrippina Senior, we can rightly view the bust of Justitia as symbolic of both women. Each suffered greatly from the murder of Germanicus — Antonia for having lost her only promising son, and Agrippina Senior for having lost the husband to whom she was so devoted. The facial features of Justitia are non-specific enough that she could easily apply to either of these women without ruling out one or the other. In all of these respects it is a masterful piece of propaganda, for in one fell swoop it honored three people. For further discussion of the three dupondii in this series, see the *Nusmismatic Notes* for Livia, Livilla and Agrippina Senior.

GERMANICUS

Son of Nero Claudius Drusus and Antonia
Brother of Claudius and Livilla
Husband of Agrippina Senior
Father of Nero Caesar, Drusus Caesar, Caligula, Agrippina Junior, Drusilla and Julia Livilla
Adopted son of Tiberius
Son-in-law of Agrippa and Julia
Brother-in-law of Drusus
Grandson of Livia, Octavia and Marc Antony
Grandfather of Nero
Uncle posthumously of Britannicus, Livia Julia, Tiberius Gemellus and Germanicus Gemellus

Germanicus Julius Caesar, 15 B.C. – A.D. 19. The older brother of Claudius and one of the legendary heroes of Rome, Germanicus was murdered in the prime of his life and was revered ever after. Though he received his name from German victories achieved by his father (Nero Claudius Drusus), Germanicus himself fought against the Germans on more than one occasion.

The year A.D. 4 was an eventful one for Germanicus, and for Rome. Augustus' eldest grandson, Gaius Caesar, had just died, leaving him with only one grandson, the repugnant Agrippa Postumus. So, dynastic arrangements were reconfigured yet again. Augustus jointly adopted Agrippa Postumus and his step-son, Tiberius, as heirs-apparent, at which time Tiberius was compelled by Augustus to adopt his own nephew Germanicus.

Although Germanicus was still far down the ladder of succession, he figured prominently into Augustus' contingency plans. It was at this point that Tiberius and the 19-year-old Germanicus left to wage war in Pannonia and Germany. A year later, in A.D. 5, Germanicus' status as potential heir was confirmed when he married Agrippina Senior, a granddaughter of Augustus. Their marriage was remarkably fertile, as they had nine children, one of whom (Caligula) was destined to be an emperor.

Germanicus was named consul both in 12 and 18. On the strength of his character alone he prevented a rebellion by the Rhine legions in 14, upon the death of Augustus. However, Germanicus obtained his place in history during the next three years, when he campaigned in Germany. Much like his father's campaigns of a quarter century before, Germanicus' daring exploits made great press in the capital, but had only fleeting results.

Contributing to his popularity with the army was his visit to the battlefield in the Teutoburg forest where Varus had lost three legions in an ambush seven years before. Indeed, Tacitus tells us that avenging the defeat of Varus was the only purpose of the campaign. In concert with his German campaigns, Germanicus assembled a fleet of some 1,000 ships in 16, which he failed to use with much success.

None of this pleased Tiberius in Rome, who viewed it as being contrary to his personal interests. After all, Germanicus was spending vast sums of money to benefit his own public image. Being both fiscally conservative and concerned about the longevity of his own regime, Tiberius recalled Germanicus in 17. Upon arriving in Rome, Germanicus celebrated a magnificent triumph before the people, who seem to have adored him unconditionally.

In the meantime, the eastern portion of the Empire had become unstable. Political upheavals in Armenia, Cappadocia, Commagene, Syria and Judaea required prompt attention, and so Tiberius sent Germanicus on a mission to settle these complex affairs. Germanicus' charm and talent served him equally well in the Greek East, though he seems to have abused his authority when he entered the emperor's province of Egypt to relieve a sudden famine without first receiving written permission from Tiberius. When Germanicus returned to Antioch in 19, he died under mysterious circumstances. Though it was reported as a death by illness, all of Rome was certain he had been poisoned.

The grief of the Romans was unbounded, and we are told that they screamed for days, and painted on walls "Give us back Germanicus!" Though Tiberius had expected there to be public mourning, he could not have anticipated it would be so emotionally charged. Leading the cry for justice was Germanicus' widow, Agrippina Senior, who had been with Germanicus in Antioch and had carried his ashes back to Rome. Her protestations resulted in the recall of Gnaeus Calpurnius Piso (a nobleman whom Tiberius had installed as the governor of Syria at the same time he had sent Germanicus to the East) to Rome. In 20 Piso was tried for the murder by the senate, with the trial being presided over by Tiberius himself.

Tiberius was now in a difficult position, for almost certainly it was on his orders that Piso had poisoned Germanicus. But the emperor was a crafty politician, and he distanced himself from the trial, abandoning Piso in the process. Piso was found guilty for his actions, and as a result he committed suicide. His wife of the time, Plancina, who Tacitus tells us was spared only due to the intercession of Livia, was forced to commit suicide in 34, after both Livia and Agrippina Senior were dead.

NUMISMATIC NOTE: Though Tiberius did not honor his adopted son on Imperial coinage, he portrayed him extensively on provincial coinage (on which he often appears with his cousin Drusus). Germanicus did not appear on Imperial coinage until nearly two decades after his death, when he was honored by his only surviving son Caligula (37–41), and then by his brother Claudius (41–54).

AGRIPPINA SENIOR

WIFE OF GERMANICUS
DAUGHTER OF AGRIPPA AND JULIA
GRANDDAUGHTER OF AUGUSTUS
SISTER OF GAIUS CAESAR, LUCIUS CAESAR, AGRIPPA POSTUMUS AND JULIA THE YOUNGER
SISTER-IN-LAW OF CLAUDIUS AND LIVILLA
MOTHER OF NERO CAESAR, DRUSUS CAESAR, CALIGULA, AGRIPPINA JUNIOR, DRUSILLA AND JULIA LIVILLA
GRANDMOTHER OF NERO
DAUGHTER-IN-LAW OF ANTONIA
AUNT OF BRITANNICUS, LIVIA JULIA, TIBERIUS GEMELLUS AND GERMANICUS GEMELLUS

Vipsania Agrippina, 14 B.C. – A.D. 33. The daughter of the commander Agrippa and Julia (the only daughter of Augustus), Agrippina Senior was destined to lead a life of tragedy and misery. In A.D. 5 she was married to Germanicus, the eldest grandson of Livia. Their marriage not only resulted in nine children (six of whom survived to adulthood and appear on coinage), but also served to bind the families of Augustus and Livia.

Agrippina was remarkably devoted to her husband, and accompanied him on all of his military campaigns. Initially this was on the Rhine from 14 to 16, and later during his mission in the East from 18 to 19. When Germanicus was poisoned by the governor of Syria, Gnaeus Calpurnius

Piso, it spelled the ruin of Agrippina's life. Though she had no hard evidence, she knew, based on the circumstances and the nature of Piso himself that he had acted on orders of Tiberius.

After Agrippina bore Germanicus' ashes back to Rome, she became outspoken in her demand for justice. Tiberius and Sejanus did not react well to her protestations, for they only added fuel to a fire they had hoped would be extinguished without much fanfare. Thanks to her efforts, Piso was recalled in 20 to Rome, where he stood trial, was found guilty, and committed suicide in response to the verdict.

From 19 to 29 Agrippina Senior proved to be an outspoken critic of Tiberius and his vicious prefect, Sejanus. With the same political adeptness with which he had abandoned Piso during his murder trial, Tiberius struck a dupondius which alludes to the tireless efforts of Agrippina in seeking justice for her slain husband. However, this small measure of public acknowledgment did not reduce the personal desires of Tiberius and Sejanus to ruin Agrippina Senior once and for all.

The pair began to malign Agrippina's reputation at every possible occasion, and even accused her of having had an adulterous affair with Gaius Asinius Gallus, a sharp-tongued character who had himself aspired to the throne since the reign of Augustus. In 26 Agrippina was refused the right to remarry, which did little to better her relations with Tiberius. By the year 29, Sejanus and Tiberius had managed to defame Agrippina and her eldest son Nero Caesar enough that they were both arrested.

Agrippina's punishment was so severe that she lost an eye during a flogging she received from a centurion. In that same year the senate banished her to the island of Pandateria, where she starved to death four years later. While she was in exile, Sejanus himself was executed, bringing his reign of terror to an end. But this did her no good, for she was not released, her eldest son, Nero Caesar, died, and her second son, Drusus Caesar, was imprisoned only to die as well. Tacitus informs us Agrippina died on October 18 of 33, the same day on which Sejanus had been executed two years before. Agrippina Senior's memory was honored by her only surviving son, Caligula, who became emperor in 37 (indeed, the first act of his reign was to bring back to Rome the ashes of his mother and his two brothers) and later still by her brother-in-law Claudius.

NUMISMATIC NOTE: Agrippina Senior was represented on coinage with some frequency. However, during her tragic lifetime this probably occurred only once on Imperial coinage: on a dupondius issued by Tiberius dated to 22/3, which traditionally has been attributed to Livia. In this case Agrippina is represented by Justitia, the personification of justice. Of the three dupondii in the series, Justitia offers the least-human portrait. Both the Livia (Salus) and the Livilla (Pietas) issues have human portraits, but in the bust of Justitia we see little more than the personification herself, complete with the linear forehead and nose joined by an unbroken line.

Since the facial features are not very helpful, we must rely on the historical context. The two viable candidates are Germanicus' wife, Agrippina Senior, and his mother, Antonia, as his murder would have been a great loss to both of them, and the concept of justice would apply to both. Because Agrippina Senior was younger and more important to the dynasty, she is the one most likely identified here, however, Antonia was not combative with Tiberius during the justice-seeking process, and thus would have been a more likeable candidate for Tiberius to honor.

Considering the artists at the mint were more than capable of producing exacting images, the indistinct character of the Justitia bust must be assumed to have been purposeful. This almost leads one to conclude that it was meant to represent Agrippina Senior *and* Antonia simultaneously, and interchangeably. We can only be certain that it does commemorate the justice achieved on behalf of the murdered Germanicus, and that the portrait bust was not meant to represent Livia.

Agrippina Senior's posthumous issues were far more extensive than her single lifetime issue. Her last-surviving son Caligula struck a massive issue of aurei, denarii as a compliment to the dual-portrait coins he also struck for Germanicus and Divus Augustus. Caligula also struck sestertii portraying her, which a few years later were followed up with a similar issue by her brother-in-law Claudius (which themselves were restored some three decades later by the emperor Titus). It is no exaggeration to say that a height in Julio-Claudian coin artistry was achieved on her portrait sestertii. The first ones, struck by Caligula, are the finest, and those later struck by Claudius are nearly as masterful.

NERO CAESAR

Son of Germanicus and Agrippina Senior
Adopted grandson and possible heir of Tiberius
Husband (and cousin) of Livia Julia
Son-in-law of Drusus
Brother of Drusus Caesar, Caligula, Agrippina Junior, Drusilla and Julia Livilla
Nephew of Claudius and Livilla
Grandson of Agrippa, Julia, Nero Claudius Drusus and Antonia
Cousin of Britannicus, Tiberius Gemellus, Germanicus Gemellus and Livia Julia
Great-grandson of Augustus, Livia, Octavia and Marc Antony

Nero Julius Caesar, A.D. 7–30/31. Nero Caesar began his public life on favorable terms with the emperors Augustus and Tiberius, perhaps because he and his younger brother, Drusus Caesar, were not the immediate heirs to the throne.

In 20 or 22 (Tacitus suggests the earlier date, though the latter seems equally likely) Nero Caesar was married to Tiberius' own granddaughter Livia Julia, who had just come of marriage age. By this point in time the political scenario had changed, for the young man's father, Germanicus, had recently been murdered. Now the only more-suitable candidate that remained was Drusus, the son of Tiberius — and this was simply because he was older.

Thus, what had begun as an amicable relationship between Nero Caesar and Tiberius degenerated into a life-and-death struggle. With the passing of Germanicus, Nero Caesar and Drusus Caesar were now fatherless, and were targets for Tiberius and his prefect Sejanus, who wanted to be rid of them as badly as did Tiberius. When Tiberius' own son, Drusus, died four years later (in 23), the emperor had even more reason to fear the sons of Germanicus, for they were the only significant rivals to Tiberius' twin grandsons (who were then merely 4 years old).

When Nero Caesar married Tiberius' own granddaughter, Livia Julia, the young man had perhaps believed this would endear him to the emperor, or at the very least afford him a degree of protection. But this was not the case, for Livia Julia would routinely reveal their private conversations to her mother Livilla, who would then pass the information to her adulterous lover Sejanus.

Tiberius and Sejanus defamed Nero Caesar and Drusus Caesar at every opportunity. Sejanus was especially crafty, and persuaded Drusus Caesar that he would gain the throne if he turned against his older brother. When the boys' great-grandmother Livia died in 29, they lost what little protection she had afforded them. In that same year, Sejanus convinced the senate to declare both Nero Caesar and his mother, Agrippina Senior, public enemies and to arrest them.

Most likely in the following year, Nero Caesar was exiled to the Pontian Islands, where he died in 30 or 31 (authorities disagree). Though he may have been executed, Suetonius tells us that he was forced to commit suicide when an executioner displayed a hanging noose and the hooks by which his corpse would be dragged. He further tells us that his and his brother's bodies were chopped into so many pieces that ". . . great difficulty was later found in collecting them for burial." Even the right of a decent burial, it seems, was denied by Tiberius. It was not until six years later that he and Drusus Caesar were honored by their brother, Caligula, who erected statues and struck coins in their names after he became emperor.

NUMISMATIC NOTE: Coins honoring Nero Caesar and his younger brother Drusus Caesar were struck by their adoptive grandfather Tiberius, and by their surviving younger brother, Caligula.

DRUSUS CAESAR

SON OF GERMANICUS AND AGRIPPINA SENIOR
ADOPTED GRANDSON AND POSSIBLE HEIR OF TIBERIUS
BROTHER OF NERO CAESAR, CALIGULA, DRUSILLA AGRIPPINA JUNIOR, AND JULIA LIVILLA
NEPHEW OF CLAUDIUS AND LIVILLA
GRANDSON OF AGRIPPA, JULIA, NERO CLAUDIUS DRUSUS AND ANTONIA
COUSIN OF BRITANNICUS, TIBERIUS GEMELLUS, GERMANICUS GEMELLUS AND LIVIA JULIA
GREAT-GRANDSON OF AUGUSTUS, LIVIA, OCTAVIA AND MARC ANTONY

Drusus Julius Caesar, A.D. 8–33. Drusus Caesar faced a similar fate to that of his brother (see the preceding biography), at first enjoying Imperial favor, but eventually finding the team of Tiberius and Sejanus too powerful to withstand.

Before he had reached his 20th year, Drusus Caesar realized the peril of his situation and allied himself with Sejanus, who had promised him the throne if he conspired against his older brother, Nero Caesar. But even this treacherous effort failed to win over Sejanus, for he had no intention of giving to Drusus Caesar that which he himself desired. Indeed, no amount of cooperation with Sejanus and Tiberius could erase Drusus Caesar's blood lines. As long as he lived Drusus Caesar constituted a threat to Tiberius' hopes for his surviving grandchild, Tiberius Gemellus, and to Sejanus' private designs on the throne.

In the year 29 the terror reached a new level when the boy's great-grandmother, Livia, died. Sejanus recognized their vulnerability and went on the attack, using his extensive spy network with the full support of Tiberius (from Capri). Drusus Caesar's mother, Agrippina Senior, and his older brother, Nero Caesar, were both arrested in 29, and neither of them emerged from their subsequent banishments.

Young Drusus Caesar's day of reckoning was not far off, and in 30, it seems, he too was arrested by Sejanus on trumped-up charges. The senate promptly declared him a public enemy, and the unfortunate young man was imprisoned in the Palatine Dungeons (some authorities are silent on this matter, and others suggest this actually happened in 33).

Even when Sejanus was executed in 31, Drusus Caesar was not released by Tiberius, for he was still perceived as a threat. After perhaps three years of imprisonment, Drusus Caesar was starved so severely that he ate the fleece of his mattress, and soon died. Like his brother two years before, Drusus Caesar's corpse was reportedly chopped into such small pieces that they could not easily be collected for a burial which, in any case, he was refused by Tiberius. Four years later, he and the older brother whom he had betrayed were honored by their younger brother, Caligula, who had survived to become emperor.

Numismatic Note: Coins honoring Drusus Caesar and his older brother Nero Caesar were struck by their adoptive grandfather Tiberius, and by their surviving younger brother, Caligula.

GAIUS (called 'CALIGULA')
A.D. 37–41
Caesar, A.D. 35–37

Son of Germanicus and Agrippina Senior
Adopted grandson and heir of Tiberius
Husband of Caesonia
Father of Drusilla Minor
Brother of Nero Caesar, Drusus Caesar, Agrippina Junior, Drusilla and Julia Livilla
Nephew of Claudius and Livilla
Grandson of Agrippa, Julia, Nero Claudius Drusus and Antonia
Cousin of Britannicus, Tiberius Gemellus, Germanicus Gemellus and Livia Julia
Great-grandson of Augustus, Livia, Octavia and Marc Antony

Gaius Caesar Augustus Germanicus (*earlier* Gaius Julius Caesar Germanicus), A.D. 12–41. Of all the emperors of Rome, Caligula is the best known for his personal depravity and abuse of power. Much like reports made concerning the final years of Tiberius on Capri, however, specific episodes of Caligula's behavior may have been exaggerated by the ancient historians. Even so, his dementia cannot be underestimated.

Caligula had a very different view of the office of emperor than did his predecessors. He would settle for nothing less than full and unquestioned authority, and even made strides toward having himself worshipped as a god, as well as an emperor. He was blessed with a sharp mind and a natural talent for public speaking and theatrics. This combination of talent and mental illness made him a formidable opponent for those who were accustomed to a rational emperor.

It was impossible to predict how Caligula would react to a situation — with generosity, indifference or shocking cruelty. His relationship with the senate was even worse than Tiberius' had been, and when he appointed his horse to the senate it was not an act of lunacy, but rather a flamboyant condemnation of that institution. Likewise, when he collected seashells as evidence of having conquered Neptune, he tested the limits of his power by demanding a triumph from the senate.

Regrettably for the Roman state, Caligula had little or no formal training in administration, or in warfare. Thus, he failed miserably in these vital areas and, much like the most debauched of eastern Greek kings, he sought to wield his authority through fear rather than virtue. Caligula was addicted to nearly every form of sexual deviation, including incest, and took personal delight in his cruelties, especially if they involved degrading people who dared not resist.

Though it seems clear that Caligula suffered from a host of mental and physical illnesses, it is difficult to identify them exactly. He is said to have suffered from epilepsy as a child and later in life was able to sleep only about three hours per night. When he was just a small boy with his parents at military camps in Germany, he earned his nickname "Caligula" from the soldiers because of the military boots he wore (a regular boot was called a *caliga*; his nickname, *caligula*, is the diminutive form meaning "little boot").

If anything positive can be said of the young Caligula, it is that he was a survivor. His youth was haunted by the destruction of his family at the hands of Tiberius and Sejanus, which resulted in his father's murder when Caligula was only 7 years old, and the downfall of his mother and two brothers when he was in his late teens. These events must have unnerved the young man and contributed greatly to his future mental problems.

But the torture was just beginning for this future emperor, for he subsequently spent five years (from 32 to 37) on the island of Capri with Tiberius during the final, haunting years of that emperor's life. By this point in time, Tiberius had narrowed the succession to Caligula and Tiberius Gemellus (theoretically his grandson, but whom he suspected to have been sired by the former prefect Sejanus). Since Tiberius, in 35, had declared Tiberius Gemellus and Caligula co-heirs to the throne and to his personal fortune, no doubt there was tension between the two young men as Tiberius' health declined.

Caligula was seven years older than his cousin and was also the craftier of the two, for he had secured the loyalty of the praetorian prefect Macro to ensure that there would be no doubt about his succession. His association with Macro may have gone back to 31, when he and Tiberius enlisted the prefect's help in arresting Sejanus. In any event, we are told that Caligula was sleeping with Macro's wife, and that when Tiberius died on March 16, 37 (with the able assistance of Macro, some said), Caligula was hailed emperor with Macro's help.

He returned to Rome, was warmly received by the senate, the people and the army, and adopted the name Gaius Caesar Augustus Germanicus. Nearly all had tired of Tiberius' stingy and cruel regime, and with the accession of Caligula came the opportunity for renewal, and for leadership by the only surviving son of Germanicus. Caligula immediately adopted Tiberius Gemellus and hailed him *princeps iuventutis*, though at the same time he convinced the senate to alter Tiberius' will so that he received all of the wealth rather than sharing it with Tiberius Gemellus.

Caligula's grandmother Antonia — who was then the matriarch of the Julio-Claudians — made the fatal mistake of trying to restrain Caligula's aggressions. Though Caligula at first honored Antonia and hailed her as the new Augusta, he soon tired of her heavy-handed influence, and is said to have forced her death on May 1, less than two months after his accession. However, this was only one of several important occurrences in the early part of Caligula's reign, for in October of 37 the new emperor fell deathly ill. The episode was so serious that he named his beloved sister Drusilla heir to the Empire.

Though Caligula soon recovered physically, the near-death experience contributed to the decline of his mental state. His first two important acts after his recovery were the murders of Macro and Tiberius Gemellus early in 38. Caligula had already tired of Macro's strong influence as praetorian prefect in Rome, so he appointed him prefect of Egypt, but even at that, he forced him to commit suicide shortly before he was to set sail.

After first ridding himself of his meddlesome grandmother, Antonia, and his overbearing prefect, Macro, Caligula next removed his cousin Tiberius Gemellus, who was the only serious rival to the throne. The unfortunate young man was executed on suspicion of taking an antidote for poison — an act which constituted treason. But Suetonius informs us that the odor Caligula detected on his cousin's breath was no antidote, only cough medicine. The act was not opposed, for Tiberius had not been beloved, and his grandson thus did not enjoy the support of the army.

Caligula, quite to the contrary, had an illustrious pedigree: he was the son of Germanicus, the grandson of Agrippa and Nero Claudius Drusus, and the great-grandson of the Divine Augustus.

Shortly after these episodes occurred, Caligula was in for yet another terrible shock. His favorite sister, Drusilla, whom he is said to have loved both spiritually and physically, died on June 10, 38. His grief was unbounded, and he forced the public to mourn for an extended period of time. Furthermore, he gave her the distinct honor of becoming the first woman to be consecrated.

Within a few months, Caligula had recovered from the shock, and began to take out his aggressions on those whom he perceived as enemies. At the beginning of 39, Caligula reinstated the treason trials which had so marred Tiberius' principate, and which resulted in the deaths of many great men. The senate now had no doubt that Caligula was both cruel and unstable.

The emperor next traveled to Germany, where he launched a military campaign in imitation of his father and paternal grandfather. His expedition had no tangible result, other than the deaths of many other fine men. Among those killed for allegedly plotting against him were the general Gaetulicus and Marcus Aemilius Lepidus, the widower of Caligula's sister, Drusilla, who up until that point was one of the emperor's frequent bed companions, and perhaps his most likely heir.

Caligula did not stop with these crimes, for he soon banished his two remaining sisters, Agrippina Junior and Julia Livilla. After wintering at camps in Gaul and Germany, Caligula returned to Rome on August 31, 40, out of fear that the senate and the praetorian guards might be plotting against his life. This turned out to be one of Caligula's more rational fears, for three serious plots were formed, with the last one being successful.

His end came swiftly on January 24, 41, underneath the palace on the Palatine Hill: before his German bodyguards could come to his rescue, he had been stabbed to death by praetorians and senators. Also perishing in the ambush (or later that same day) were his fourth wife, Caesonia, and their baby daughter, Drusilla Minor. Caligula was temporarily buried in the Lamian gardens, but later his remains were moved to the Mausoleum of Augustus.

Numismatic Note: Perhaps the most interesting reverse type of Caligula's reign is that which depicts his three sisters standing in a row in the guises of Securitas, Concordia and Fortuna. Caligula, however, did not limit his honorary issues to the living, for he struck massive issues in the names of deceased members of his ill-fated family. Among those honored were his father Germanicus, his mother Agrippina Senior, his two brothers Nero Caesar and Drusus Caesar, his great-grandfather Augustus (the inscription

PRON (*pronepos*) means great-grandson), and ironically, it would seem, Agrippa, the grandfather who he despised for his low birth even though the Empire was built upon his military genius.

A sestertius which shows Caligula saluting the praetorian guards (to whom he gave a generous bonus upon his accession) is of particular interest. Not only is the boldness of the design unprecedented in the Empire, but, it also lacks the SC customarily placed on æs coinage. This coinage was no doubt unnerving to the senators who Caligula despised and mistrusted. For both of the reasons cited, we must conclude that Caligula took great pleasure in producing this issue, and that he saw to it personally.

A long-running controversy in Roman numismatics is when the striking of precious metal coins shifted from Lugdunum (which had been doing the lion's share of this since about 15 B.C.) back to Rome (which in the meantime had produced æs coinage). Sometime between the reigns of Tiberius (14–37) and Otho (69) the shift occured; some scholars prefer the first year of Caligla's reign (the view taken in RIC), whereas others — seemingly with a stronger case — prefer the year 64, late in the reign of Nero.

Surprisingly, Caligula was not subjected to the *damnatio memoriae* process by which ones memory was condemned for crimes against the state. However, the senate did order that his æs coinage be recalled and melted because it bore the SC, a state of affairs they found intolerable. Indeed, it is not uncommon to find æs of Caligula on which the portrait is purposefully damaged or the first C in the obverse inscription (the letter on his Imperial coins which represents his full name, Gaius) is chiseled off.

CAESONIA

FOURTH WIFE OF CALIGULA
MOTHER OF DRUSILLA MINOR

Milonia Caesonia, d. A.D. 41. Not surprisingly, Caesonia began her association with her future husband, Caligula, as a mistress. He had been married three times before: in 33, to Junia Claudia; in 37, to Livia Orestilla; and in 38, to Lollia Paulina, making Caesonia his fourth. Caesonia was older than Caligula, and had three children from a previous marriage. We are told not only that she was promiscuous, but that Caligula adored her, although he would not marry her until she bore him a child. So on the day Drusilla Minor was born (or perhaps a month earlier) late in the summer of 39, they were wed. Despite his reprehensible conduct in other aspects of life, Caligula does appear to have been devoted to his last wife and daughter. Caesonia and Drusilla Minor were both murdered on January 24, 41 by the soldier Julius Lupus, either at the same time or shortly after Caligula was killed in an ambush beneath the palace on the Palatine Hill.

NUMISMATIC NOTE: Caesonia's portrait seems to appear only once — on a rare bronze issued in 40/41 by the Judaean king Herod Agrippa I. The bust of Salus (health) on æs struck at Carthago Nova (nos. 563–4) by Caligula is often misattributed as a representation of Caesonia. In fact, it was struck before they were wed, and it more likely is an allusion to Antonia, whose health was failing as she neared the end of her life. Since there is no relation between Caesonia and these relatively common Spanish bronzes, obtaining a portrait of Caesonia is a difficult task.

DRUSILLA MINOR

DAUGHTER OF CALIGULA AND CAESONIA
GRANDDAUGHTER OF GERMANICUS AND AGRIPPINA SENIOR
GREAT-GRANDDAUGHTER OF AGRIPPA, JULIA, NERO CLAUDIUS DRUSUS AND ANTONIA

Julia Drusilla (*often called* Julia Livilla the Younger), A.D. 39–41. Little is known of Drusilla Minor, the daughter of Caligula and his fourth wife, Caesonia. The infant was honored with the same name as her father's beloved sister, Drusilla, who had died only about one year before. Since Caesonia was so promiscuous, Caligula was not entirely certain of his paternity of Drusilla Minor. But Suetonius tells us his initial doubts were dispelled when he observed her trying to scratch the eyes and faces of her little playmates. Drusilla Minor was murdered on January 24, 41, along with her mother at the time (or later in the same day) that Caligula was assassinated in a corridor beneath the palace on the Palatine Hill. Her end was as swift as it was brutal, for a praetorian guardsman crushed her head against a wall.

NUMISMATIC NOTE: No portrait coins are known of Drusilla Minor. She makes only one appearance on coinage — as a standing figure on a coin struck by the Judaean king Herod Agrippa I. Agrippa I was raised at the Imperial household in Rome from the age of 6, and was a close friend of Caligula, Caesonia, and Claudius. Although she is shown as a more mature figure on Agrippa's coin, she is identified by the accompanying inscription ΘΥΓΑΤΡΙ, meaning "daughter." Unfortunately for collectors, this rare coin is also in great demand for its importance to Herodian specialists. (*Note:*

Because this coin also has a portrait of her mother Caesonia — and it is also her only coin — the catalog listings of mother and daughter are combined).

DRUSILLA

Daughter of Germanicus and Agrippina Senior
Sister of Nero Caesar, Drusus Caesar, Caligula, Agrippina Junior and Julia Livilla
Niece of Claudius and Livilla
Granddaughter of Agrippa, Julia, Nero Claudius Drusus and Antonia
Cousin of Britannicus, Tiberius Gemellus, Germanicus Gemellus and Livia Julia
Great-granddaughter of Augustus, Livia, Octavia and Marc Antony

Julia Drusilla, A.D. 16–38. The second daughter born to Germanicus and Agrippina Senior, Drusilla was the favorite sister of Caligula, her older brother by four years. Their relationship was incestuous, and Caligula was caught by his grandmother Antonia when he first seduced Drusilla before she was of age. Despite their being siblings, and married, they allegedly continued their unnatural relationship into adulthood.

Drusilla's first husband, Lucius Cassius Longinus, the consul of 30, was selected for her in 33 by her adoptive grandfather, Tiberius. But this was not to the liking of Caligula, who took her from him and treated her as his lawfully married wife. Drusilla's next marriage was to Marcus Aemilius Lepidus, a descendant of the Triumvir Lepidus. He was deeply involved with the Imperial family, and is said to have had sexual relations not only with his wife Drusilla, but also with Caligula and his two sisters-in-law, Julia Livilla and Agrippina Junior. But his eventful life came to an end in 39, when he and the general Gaetulicus were executed by Caligula for allegedly conspiring to murder him.

When Caligula fell deathly ill late in 37 — just a few months after his accession — he named Drusilla as heir to the Empire. But Caligula soon recovered, only to suffer the loss of his beloved sister in the summer of the following year. Drusilla died on June 10, 38, when she was only 22 years of age.

Perhaps nothing could have injured Caligula more than Drusilla's death, and in response he deified her. This was an unprecedented act, for even Livia had not yet been deified. Accompanying the deification was a mandatory period of public mourning throughout the Empire, during which it was a capital offense to laugh, to bathe, or even to dine with one's relatives. Drusilla's widower, Lepidus (who until his wife's death was considered to be Caligula's most likely successor), was executed in the following year, allegedly for conspiring against the emperor's life.

NUMISMATIC NOTE: Drusilla appears on a few Imperial and provincial coinages, usually with her sisters. In the latter case, when she is shown as a standing figure, she is given the attributes of Concordia. All of these coins were struck during the reign of her brother, Caligula — some while she was alive, others after she died and had been deified.

JULIA LIVILLA

DAUGHTER OF GERMANICUS AND AGRIPPINA SENIOR
SISTER OF NERO CAESAR, DRUSUS CAESAR, CALIGULA, AGRIPPINA JUNIOR AND DRUSILLA
NIECE OF CLAUDIUS AND LIVILLA
GRANDDAUGHTER OF AGRIPPA, JULIA, NERO CLAUDIUS DRUSUS AND ANTONIA
COUSIN OF BRITANNICUS, TIBERIUS GEMELLUS, GERMANICUS GEMELLUS AND LIVIA JULIA
GREAT-GRANDDAUGHTER OF AUGUSTUS, LIVIA, OCTAVIA AND MARC ANTONY

Julia Livilla (the Younger), A.D. 17/18–42. Although Caligula cherished Drusilla, he was not overly fond of his youngest sister, Julia Livilla.

She was the last child of Germanicus and Agrippina Senior, and Tacitus tells us she was born on the island of Lesbos shortly after her parents landed there early in the year 18. The date of her birth, however, is not certainly known. Though Tacitus suggests she was born in 18, Suetonius tells us the three sisters were born in "successive years," which would place Julia Livilla's birth in 17 since Agrippina Junior was born in 15 and Drusilla in 16.

As soon as Julia Livilla came of age (in 33), her adoptive grandfather, the emperor Tiberius, married her to Marcus Vinicius, a man remembered for his mild character and elaborate oratorical style. Although Caligula is said to have slept with Julia Livilla on occasion, he did not care much for her, and instead drew greater pleasure from making her available for his friends to sleep with.

When her elder sister, Drusilla, died in mid-38, Julia Livilla's life took a turn for the worse. Late in 39, when the widower Aemilius Lepidus was tried and convicted of plotting against the emperor's life, both Julia Livilla and her eldest sister, Agrippina Junior, were also implicated. As a result of the trial, the sisters were exiled to the Pontian Islands late in the year. Slightly more than a year later, their despotic brother was murdered, and the sisters' fates rested in the hands of his successor, their uncle Claudius.

He promptly recalled both young women in 41, and though he eventually married Agrippina Junior, he was not impressed with the behavior of Julia Livilla. She was quickly returned to her exile after being accused of having an adulterous affair with Seneca, the man who would tutor her sister's son Nero. In the following year (42), Julia Livilla was executed on charges that Tacitus tells us not only were unsubstantiated, but against which she was not given the opportunity to defend herself.

NUMISMATIC NOTE: Julia Livilla appears on very few Imperial and provincial coins, and her portrait bust occurs only on provincial coinage — once, or perhaps twice. All coins which honor her were struck by her brother, Caligula, sometime between 37 and 39. She is most often shown with her two sisters, and when shown standing she is given the attributes of Fortuna. Some researchers believe her portrait occurs on an issue attributed in this and in other catalogs to Julia (the daughter of Augustus) and her eldest son, Gaius Caesar. Though it might actually represent Julia Livilla and Gaius ('Caligula'), it seems better placed as an Augustan issue.

CLAUDIUS A.D. 41–54

SON OF NERO CLAUDIUS DRUSUS AND ANTONIA
BROTHER OF GERMANICUS AND LIVILLA
HUSBAND OF PLAUTIA URGULANILLA, AELIA PAETINA, VALERIA MESSALINA AND AGRIPPINA JUNIOR
FATHER OF BRITANNICUS, CLAUDIA OCTAVIA AND CLAUDIA ANTONIA
GRANDUNCLE AND ADOPTIVE STEP-FATHER OF NERO
NEPHEW OF TIBERIUS
GRANDSON OF LIVIA, MARC ANTONY AND OCTAVIA
UNCLE OF NERO CAESAR, DRUSUS CAESAR, CALIGULA, AGRIPPINA JUNIOR, DRUSILLA, JULIA LIVILLA, TIBERIUS GEMELLUS, GERMANICUS GEMELLUS AND LIVIA JULIA
BROTHER-IN-LAW OF GAIUS CAESAR, DRUSUS AND AGRIPPINA SENIOR

Tiberius Claudius Caesar Augustus Germanicus (*earlier* Tiberius Claudius Drusus), 10 B.C. – A.D. 54. Although the appearance of being sickly would be a disadvantage in the lives of most Romans, it proved to be an effective defense in the treacherous world of the Julio-Claudians. Because of the physical effects of his childhood diseases, which included a speech defect, Claudius survived the virtual extinction of his branch of the family either by being considered a nonentity, or by being kept around as the butt of jokes. Despite his physical ailments, Claudius was far from incapable, and his intelligence served him both in his private life, and as emperor.

He was born at the provincial city of Lugdunum (in Gaul) on the very day that the great altar of that city was dedicated. He was a well-connected child, being the grandson of Marc Antony and Livia, the son of Nero Claudius Drusus and Antonia, and the brother of Germanicus and Livilla.

In his youth he was tutored by the historians Livy and Pollio, and gained a thorough knowledge of Roman and related history. The subject proved to be of great interest to him, and he penned books on the history of the Carthaginians, the principate of Augustus, the game of dicing, and he even wrote an autobiography (which was not well-received). Regrettably, none of these works survive.

He also spent a great deal of his time amusing himself by attending games, gambling, womanizing and drinking. His family life was understandably poor, with even his own mother, Antonia, describing him uncharitably as "a monster of a man." Indeed, Claudius did have a cruel streak, for he is said to have enjoyed watching the faces of gladiators as they died. Later in his life, he seems to have become an alcoholic, a debilitation which no doubt contributed to his being dominated by his last wife, Agrippina Junior, and their adviser Pallas.

He fared poorly in his six arranged marriages, only four of which actually materialized. He was first betrothed to a noblewoman, Aemilia Lepida, but it did not occur once her parents fell out of favor. His second match was to Livia Medullina, who died on the very day they were to be wed.

His first marriage was to Plautia Urgulanilla, whom he divorced c. 24 for adultery and on the suspicion that she attempted to murder him. Of the two children from the marriage, the first, a boy, choked to death on a pear, and the second, a daughter, was believed to have been sired by his freedman Boter, and as such was denied. Claudius next married Aelia Paetina, by whom he had a daughter named Claudia Antonia. But he divorced her after the fall of Sejanus in 31, and engaged in a long-term affair with a concubine Calpurnia. Next, in 39, he married the debauched 14-year-old Valeria Messalina. Together they had a daughter named Claudia Octavia, and a son originally named Germanicus, but who later was named Britannicus after his father's victory in Britain.

The marriage with Valeria Messalina ended in extraordinary disgrace (*see* her biography), and so she was executed. His final marriage, in 50, was to his niece, Agrippina Junior. This union not only resulted in his own murder four years later, but also in the murder of his only son, Britannicus. Indeed, Tacitus tells us that Claudius believed it was his destiny first to suffer, and finally to punish the infamy of his wives.

During the first 47 years of his life, Claudius remained in the background of Julio-Claudian politics. Augustus entrusted him with only one augurate, and his uncle Tiberius invested no authority in him. Though

Claudius was not immune to drink and various entertainments, he seems to have led a quiet, scholarly life as crimes of every description were committed all around him.

Despite the anonymity of his early life, Claudius was brought forward in 37 by his sadistic nephew Caligula, who made him consul and heaped responsibilities upon him. No doubt Caligula was aware that his uncle was brighter than most imagined, but also, Caligula enjoyed having him around as a butt of his jokes.

When Caligula was murdered by the praetorians on January 24, 41, Claudius feared for his own life. No doubt, he considered the possibility that the praetorians (which had risen to great power a couple of decades earlier under Sejanus) would kill him as well. If they had wished to extinguish the remaining Julio-Claudian males, it would have been an easy task, for only Claudius and two small boys, Nero (age 4) and Britannicus (age 1) remained candidates.

The 50-year-old Claudius was discovered cowering behind a curtain in the palace, and was conducted to the camp of the praetorians, who declared their support for him at the same time that the senate was debating the possibility of restoring the Republic.

On this surprising turn of events, the historian Tacitus wrote: "The more I think about history, ancient or modern, the more ironical all human affairs seem. In public opinion, expectation, and esteem no one appeared a less likely candidate for the throne than the man for whom destiny was secretly reserving it."

Clearly, the praetorian guards selected Claudius because they believed he could be easily controlled. Though Claudius had no military distinction in his past, he was the brother of Germanicus and son of Nero Claudius Drusus, both of whom were heroes to soldiers. Claudius began his principate by paying a bonus of 15,000 sestertii (150 aurei) to each of the praetorians, which no doubt helped in crushing the senate-backed revolt of Scribonianus in Dalmatia in 42. He furthered his reputation with the army by personally taking part in the invasion of Britain in 43.

The major consequence of aligning himself so closely with the praetorians (as his uncle Tiberius had done) was that he earned the enmity of the senate, which would haunt him throughout his principate. Indeed, much of the "bad press" he received may be attributed to the poor relationship he had with the senate, and thus with the *literati* of the Empire. Claudius was a careful administrator who demanded that senators take their responsibilities seriously, a request which did not endear him to that august body.

In addition to the army, Claudius also relied heavily on his wives, freedmen and friends. This earned him even greater indignation from the senate, which now had another element with which they had to contend for authority. Foremost among his freedmen was Narcissus; even the father of the future emperor Vitellius numbered among his friend-advisers. However, Claudius receives the worst condemnation for his deep reliance on the counsel of his wives, all of whom had agendas of their own.

He was a strict ruler who executed at least 35 senators and 300 knights. For this practice Claudius was much maligned both in his lifetime and thereafter (notably by Seneca and Nero), but there were at least six serious attempts on his life, and he may have over-reacted out of fear.

Despite his stringent security measures and often violent retributions, Claudius was, on balance, a thoughtful and careful emperor who applied common sense to his legislation. He was traditional in his views, and vigorously supported the laws, values and religion of Rome, while at the same time being open-minded enough to see the Empire as something much larger than Italy itself, for he encouraged vacant seats on the senate to be filled with candidates from Roman Gaul.

His military conquests and building projects (both being categories by which emperors are often measured) were considerable. He added Britain, the provinces of Mauretania and Thrace to the Empire, completed two massive aqueducts, and in 42 began construction of a new port at Ostia that would be completed by Nero.

Though Claudius had always relied on the army and his closest advisers, there is ample evidence that he was firmly in control for the first eight years of his principate. However, when he wed his niece Agrippina Junior in 49, he came to be greatly influenced by his new wife and her ally, the freedman Pallas. Agrippina Junior went to great lengths to purge the palace of Claudius' supporters, and in turn replaced them with men loyal to her.

In the meantime, over a three-year period, Agrippina had convinced Claudius to heap honors upon her own son, Nero, to such a degree that he was honored far more than Claudius' own son, Britannicus. Having carefully constructed the scenario by which Nero would succeed Claudius uncontested, Agrippina was free on the evening of October 12, 54, to feed her 64-year-old husband a dish of poisoned mushrooms, which he devoured without suspicion. The first dose apparently did not take, and a second was required. So Agrippina had his doctor administer a second one, which proved fatal in the early hours of October 13.

Agrippina's plan was executed without a hitch, and her son Nero was hailed emperor without hesitation. Britannicus was soon poisoned, and thus removed as a rival. As successfully as Agrippina had achieved her ambition, she found her son less than willing to share authority with his domineering mother, and she spent the last five years of her life struggling to maintain her authority and her life.

NUMISMATIC NOTES: The accession of Claudius was secured by the praetorian guards, who escorted him within their walls shortly after the murder of Caligula. In recognition of their inital and continued support, Claudius issued aurei and denarii depicting the praetorian camp with its circuit wall inscribed IMPER(ator) RECEPT(us), as well as a second type bearing the inscription PRAETOR(ianus) RECEPT(us) and showing him greeting a soldier. His æs coinage is also of considerable interest, though it does not honor the praetorian. It is clear on stylistic grounds that Claudius struck much of his early æs coinage at auxiliary mints in Spain, Gaul and the Balkans. It is also of some interest that after coining æs so heavily up through about 45, production ceased, and no significant issues of Imperial sestertii, dupondii or asses were struck for about two decades, when Nero began sometime between 62 and 64. In addition to striking coins in his own name, Claudius also issued Imperial commemoratives for Augustus, Livia, Antonia, Nero Claudius Drusus, Germanicus and Agrippina Senior.

Perhaps the most interesting issue of Claudius, however, is a quadrans (or semis) which might mark his 50th year (his age upon accession). It depicts on its reverse the altar of Lugdunum, and since Claudius was born in Lugdunum on the very day the great altar was dedicated, this is a compelling conclusion to draw. However, von Kaenel (*Münzprägung und Münzbildnis des Claudius*, AMuGS 9, Berlin, 1986) opts for 44/45 instead. Chronology aside, the coin's greatest impact is on the theory of the location of the Imperial mint for precious metal coins from the reigns of Tiberius through Otho. This innocuous little coin cannot be separated on any stylistic ground from Claudius' precious metal issues, and its Lugdunese iconography is thus an important indicator that Claudius was still striking precious metal coins in Lugdunum. The 'shift' from Lugdunum to Rome, therefore, must have occured after Claudius stopped striking coins (seemingly in 44/45 for æs and in 51/52 for precious metals). The two possibilities are the production hiatus between Claudius and Nero, or later in the reign of Nero. The latter prospect is now heavily favored, with Claudius' altar quadrans being only one part of a larger body of evidence.

CLAUDIA ANTONIA

Daughter of Claudius (by Aelia Paetina)
Half-sister of Claudia Octavia and Britannicus
Niece of Sejanus
Step-sister of Nero

Claudia Antonia, A.D. 27–66. Of Claudia Antonia, the daughter of Claudius by his second wife, Aelia Paetina, not much is known except that she enjoyed a good reputation and endured a tragic life. Even though her father's earlier marriage to Urgulanilla had produced two children, Claudia Antonia was destined to be Claudius' longest surviving child.

Claudius' first child was a boy named Claudius Drusus, who met an inauspicious death in the year 20, just a few days after he had been betrothed to a daughter of Tiberius' prefect, Sejanus. Suetonius reports: "[Claudius] lost Drusus just before he came of age, choked by a pear which he had playfully thrown up and caught in his open mouth. . . ." To the satisfaction of those who suffered the loss of the boy (among whom would have been Claudia Antonia), the murderous pear tree was uprooted. Claudius' second child by Urgulanilla was a daughter apparently sired by Claudius' freedman Boter, and so she was denied.

Of Claudia Antonia's mother, Aelia Paetina, the sister of Sejanus, we know little except that she had married Claudius by the year 28, and was abandoned by him after three years of marriage so he could engage in an affair with his concubine Calpurnia, and subsequently enter into a disastrous marriage with Valeria Messalina in 38. For Claudia Antonia, her father's marriage to Messalina meant she acquired two younger step-siblings, a boy, Britannicus, and a girl, Claudia Octavia.

Following the disgraceful end to his marriage to Valeria Messalina, Claudius considered re-marrying Aelia Paetina, but instead chose his niece Agrippina Junior, whom he had recalled from exile. With this fourth and final marriage, Claudia Antonia gained three more step-brothers. Two of them, named Pompeius and Sulla, were soon executed, and the remaining boy, later known as Nero, was destined to marry his adoptive sister Claudia Octavia and to become emperor.

The remaining five years of her father Claudius' life were eventful, and Claudia Antonia no doubt observed the manipulation of her father by her step-mother, Agrippina Junior. Claudia Antonia survived the transition of power from Claudius to Nero in 54, shortly after which she endured the murder of her step-brother, Britannicus, in 55.

Claudia Antonia had two husbands, both young noblemen of the highest birth. The first, Gnaeus Pompeius Magnus, whom she married in 41, was put to death by Claudius. The second, Faustus Cornelius Sulla Felix, who was characterized by Tacitus as stupid, timid and despicable, fell victim to Nero, who was convinced in 56 that he had participated in a plot against his life. Tacitus tells us, however, that there was no plot, and that the lies of an old palace slave condemned the innocent man to banishment.

Claudia Antonia suffered a similar fate at the hand of her step-brother Nero, who implicated her in Piso's failed murder plot of 65, and had her executed in the following year. Though some historians doubt its veracity, one explanation for her being targeted was her apparent refusal to marry Nero after he had killed his second wife Poppaea with a kick to the stomach.

NUMISMATIC NOTE: All coins portraying Claudia Antonia were struck by her father Claudius. In every case she shares the canvass with her half-sister, Octavia and/or her half-brother, Britannicus.

VALERIA MESSALINA

AUGUSTA, A.D. 41–48

THIRD WIFE OF CLAUDIUS
MOTHER OF BRITANNICUS AND CLAUDIA OCTAVIA
DAUGHTER-IN-LAW OF ANTONIA
STEPMOTHER OF CLAUDIA ANTONIA
GRANDDAUGHTER OF OCTAVIA

Valeria Messalina (*or* Messallina), c. A.D. 25–48. The dissolute third wife of Claudius, Valeria Messalina married him in 39, when she was only 14 years old. She soon bore him two children, Britannicus and Claudia Octavia. Upon marrying Claudius, and though quite young herself, she also became the adoptive mother of Claudia Antonia, whom Claudius had had by his earlier marriage to Aelia Paetina.

Valeria Messalina was not shy about her ambitions, and she was ruthless in her pursuit of them. Most shocking was her destruction of her female rivals, including two of Claudius' nieces, Livia Julia (the only daughter of Drusus and Livilla) and Julia Livilla (the youngest sister of Caligula). Not surprisingly, Valeria Messalina was instrumental in the persecution of Agrippina Junior, whose son, Nero, was the rival to her own son, Britannicus. Since Nero and Britannicus were the only important male heirs of the Julio-Claudians, the throne would go to one of the two boys after the death of Claudius.

Suetonius and Tacitus tell us that she tried to have young Nero strangled one night as he slept, but that the attempt was foiled when the would-be murderers were frightened by a snake that emerged from beneath the boy's pillow. Despite her less-than-virtuous demeanor, Valeria Messalina was made the head Vestal. This appointment was in particularly bad taste, for she was notoriously promiscuous.

Indeed, it was this element of her personality which caused the greatest scandal in the principate of Claudius. Valeria Messalina had become smitten by Gaius Silius, the consul-designate who was reputedly the best-looking young man in Rome. So uncontrollable were her passions for Silius that even though she was still the emperor's wife, she married her lover in 48 while Claudius was away in Ostia.

The couple either did not wish to hide their deed, or were unable to do so. When Claudius found out with the aid of his freedman Narcissus, he did not take the news well, and it was only due to his freedman's decisive actions that disaster was averted. Many historians believe the marriage may have been the first stage of a coup against Claudius, in which the newlyweds would install Britannicus as emperor.

Though Claudius had always had poor luck with wives, this was the most shocking and humiliating event of his life. In what most considered justifiable revenge, Silius was brought to the praetorian camp (where Claudius had been taken for safety) and was swiftly executed. Messalina was driven to suicide, after which her memory was damned.

Numismatic Note: All coins of Valeria Messalina were struck under Claudius. A didrachm from Caesarea shows the dynasty of Claudius headed by his third wife Valeria Messalina, who appears on the obverse. The reverse — a masterpiece of Julio-Claudian propaganda — shows the two children by Valeria Messalina (Claudia Octavia and Britannicus) holding hands, and Claudia Antonia, Claudius' daughter by his earlier wife, Aelia Paetina, standing alone. This general format was adopted for similar issues struck elsewhere, and in the cases where the busts only were shown, those of Claudia Octavia and Britannicus are confronted to indicate their shared parentage, and the bust of Claudia Antonia is shown at the right facing her half-siblings.

BRITANNICUS

SON OF CLAUDIUS AND VALERIA MESSALINA
BROTHER OF CLAUDIA OCTAVIA
HALF-BROTHER OF CLAUDIA ANTONIA
STEP-BROTHER OF NERO
COUSIN OF NERO CAESAR, DRUSUS CAESAR, CALIGULA, AGRIPPINA JUNIOR, DRUSILLA, TIBERIUS GEMELLUS, GERMANICUS GEMELLUS AND JULIA LIVILLA

Britannicus (*earlier* Tiberius Claudius Germanicus), A.D. 41–55. As the natural son of Claudius and one of only two male heirs to the Julio-Claudian family, Britannicus would seemingly be the successor to his father. But with the passage of time, Claudius' son was surpassed by his step-son, Nero, who not only would replace Claudius as emperor, but who also would murder Britannicus soon thereafter.

Britannicus, according to Suetonius, was born 22 days into the reign of his father (February, 41), who was then consul for the second time. Though the senate awarded him with the new name Britannicus in honor of his father's invasion of Britain in 43, his name at birth seems to have been Tiberius Claudius Germanicus. But even this is debated among historians, who also cite Tiberius Claudius Caesar as his birth name.

Suetonius tells us that Claudius would proudly pick up little Britannicus and show him to soldiers or to audiences at games, all of whom would echo his declaration: "Good luck to you, my boy!" The seemingly bright future of Britannicus, however, was darkened when his mother, Valeria Messalina, was disgraced and executed in 48. Britannicus was 7 years old at the time, and some suspected his mother had planned to overthrow her husband, and place Britannicus on the throne.

Especially damaging to his position was his father's marriage to Agrippina Junior, who had three sons of her own, including a boy who would be renamed Nero. Though Britannicus' two step-brothers, Pompeius and Sulla, were executed, Nero remained, and was rapidly promoted beyond Britannicus, who was three years his junior. At the time Nero was adopted by Claudius in 50, he was hailed *princeps iuventutis*, which made him guardian of Britannicus. Perhaps most damaging to Britannicus' future, however, was the marriage of his own sister Claudia Octavia to Nero in 53.

Even though Claudius began to doubt the suitability of Nero toward the end of his own reign, nothing was done to strengthen Britannicus' standing. By that point, Agrippina Junior had replaced the key tutors, advisers and guardsmen with men loyal to her, and so the boy could rely on no one.

Thus, when Claudius was murdered by his wife, Agrippina Junior, Britannicus was locked away with his sister, Claudia Octavia, and his half-sister, Claudia Antonia, so that Nero could be hailed emperor without dispute. This left Britannicus in dire straits, for he had no real authority, yet he remained a legitimate rival to Nero. It came as no shock when Britannicus was poisoned at a dinner on February 11, 55, only four months into Nero's reign. The scenario hardly differed from the removal of Tiberius Gemellus by Caligula a generation before.

Though the teenager's death was officially attributed to epilepsy, it was not seriously doubted that he had been murdered. One person who knew for sure was Britannicus' boyhood friend Titus (the future emperor), who had shared some of the fatal beverage and had suffered severely from the poison. Britannicus' sister, Claudia Octavia (who was then Nero's wife), witnessed the shocking affair, but was unable to help her brother as he violently perished a few feet away. Britannicus' body was cremated that evening and a quiet funeral was held the following day.

It is difficult to say whether he was poisoned by Nero or by Agrippina Junior. Agrippina, however, is said to have wanted to keep Britannicus around as a "backup" in the event Nero became too unruly, and so it would seem Nero gained on both ends. Subsequently, other rivals were eliminated, including Marcus Junius Silanus (who, like Nero, was a great-great-grandson of Augustus), and much later a rival named Rubellius Plautus, who was the great-grandson of Tiberius, and thus a great-great-grandson of both Livia and Agrippa.

Historians are at a loss to explain why Claudius allowed Britannicus to be victimized. Having personally witnessed so much murder and treachery within his family, Claudius easily could have predicted that the boy would not long survive after his own death. Perhaps his memories of the boy's mother, Messalina, were so painful to Claudius that he simply gave up on Britannicus.

Some believe the reason for his abandonment was that Nero was also his natural son, conceived long prior to his marriage to Agrippina Junior. Though this possibility sounds far-fetched, there are a number of anecdotes recorded by ancient historians that indicate this may have been a well-kept family secret. The very fact that Claudius put to death Agrippina's two other sons, Pompeius and Sulla, and spared Nero seems to lend credence to this theory. However, if this were a common rumor in the Imperial household, it does seem odd that the gossipy Suetonius did not mention it directly, for he did not shy away from rumor and innuendo.

NUMISMATIC NOTE: A considerable number of small bronzes were struck in the cities of Asia Minor for Britannicus. Most if not all of them were struck near the end of the reign of his father Claudius. Britannicus' most impressive issue is of 'sestertii' from an Imperial mint in the Balkans. Though it almost certainly belongs to the end of the reign of Claudius (as a companion to the sestertius of Agrippina Junior and the sestertii and dupondii of Nero as Caesar), some have theorized, rather fancifully, that it was struck a quarter-century later by the emperor Titus (who attended the banquet at which Britannicus was poisoned) as a memorial issue to his boyhood friend. In this context it would be associated with the many 'restored' æs struck by Titus. But Britannicus' coin differs from others in the series in two important ways: it was struck in the Balkans (not at Rome) and there was no prototype issue to restore. Despite the many different issues struck for Britannicus, overall his coins are quite rare, especially in comparison to those struck for Nero during the same period (50–54). Of specific interest is the lack of Imperial coinage for Britannicus (the 'Balkan sestertius' aside), especially in light of the fact that young Nero had aurei, denarii and cistophori struck for him. All of this numismatic evidence supports the historical record, and we must conclude that from the very outset Britannicus was not the favored heir.

AGRIPPINA JUNIOR

AUGUSTA, A.D. 50–59

WIFE (AND NIECE) OF CLAUDIUS
MOTHER OF NERO
DAUGHTER OF GERMANICUS AND AGRIPPINA SENIOR
SISTER OF NERO CAESAR, DRUSUS CAESAR, CALIGULA, DRUSILLA AND JULIA LIVILLA
NIECE OF CLAUDIUS AND LIVILLA
STEP-MOTHER (AND COUSIN) OF BRITANNICUS
GRANDDAUGHTER OF AGRIPPA, JULIA, NERO CLAUDIUS DRUSUS AND ANTONIA
COUSIN OF BRITANNICUS, TIBERIUS GEMELLUS, GERMANICUS GEMELLUS AND LIVIA JULIA
GREAT-GRANDDAUGHTER OF AUGUSTUS, LIVIA, OCTAVIA AND MARC ANTONY

Julia Agrippina (*often called* Agrippina the Younger or Agrippina Minor), A.D. 15–59. Born late in 15 at Ara Uborium, Agrippina Junior was the eldest daughter of Germanicus and Agrippina Senior. She was also the sister of Caligula, the mother of Nero, and the niece of Claudius, whom she would marry some 34 years later. As such, she had the unique distinction of having been the sister of one emperor, the wife of another, and the mother of yet another.

The chronology of Agrippina's life up until the time of her marriage to Claudius in 49 is vague. She was only 3 or 4 when her father, Germanicus, was murdered in Antioch. When Agrippina turned 13 (in 28), Tiberius betrothed her to Gnaeus Domitius Ahenobarbus, a reprehensible man by whom she bore the future emperor Nero.

During the next five years she not only suffered through a difficult marriage, and the sexual relationship with her brother Caligula, but she also witnessed the murder of her mother and two older brothers, Nero Caesar and Drusus Caesar. Indeed, Agrippina's life could hardly be described as pleasant. Perhaps her devotion to her future son (the one who would be named Nero) was so extreme because of the extraordinary circumstances of her early life.

Agrippina and her two younger sisters survived the reign of Tiberius, along with their adoring brother, Caligula, who succeed him as emperor. At the beginning of their brother's reign, the three sisters were honored (and continued to be seduced), and it was several months into Caligula's principate that Agrippina's famous son, Nero, was born.

But when Caligula's favorite sister, Drusilla, died in mid-38, Agrippina and Julia Livilla's relationship with their brother worsened. Late in 38, at Mainz, the sisters were implicated in the conspiracy of the general Gaeticus, and were subsequently exiled for about two years. During their exile, in the year 40, Agrippina's near-invalid husband Gnaeus Domitius Ahenobarbus, the father of Nero, died.

After their tyrannical brother Caligula was murdered in 41, Agrippina and Julia Livilla were recalled by their uncle Claudius, who had been hailed emperor in his place. Claudius quickly tired of Julia Livilla, who wasted no time in engaging in an embarrassing affair with the philosopher Seneca. Both Julia Livilla and Seneca were exiled in that same year, with the former being executed in 42.

Claudius decided to keep Agrippina around, as he was fond of her and she apparently had behaved acceptably. At some point after her return from exile, Agrippina married Marcus Junius Silanus, a former consul who had given his daughter to Caligula in marriage shortly before he ascended the throne (but the daughter, Junia Claudilla, died in childbirth). The sources are unclear about when Agrippina married Marcus Junius Silanus, though Tacitus assures us it was before she married Claudius.

With the passage of time, this marriage was dissolved, for Claudius, had grown unnaturally fond of her. Agrippina's love life was strange and incestuous, for she not only engaged in sexual relations with her brother, but she was now seducing her uncle. According to Suetonius: "She had a niece's privilege of kissing and caressing Claudius, and exercised it with a noticeable effect on his passions . . ."

Having observed the emperor's affections for Agrippina, the enormously wealthy freedman Pallas allied himself with Agrippina, and persuaded Claudius to seek special approval from the senate to marry his niece. On January 1, 49 (shortly after the execution of his former wife, Valeria Messalina), Claudius made Agrippina Junior his fourth and final wife.

The following year, 50, was eventful for the new family. Agrippina was hailed Augusta, and the new Roman settlement on the Rhine, *Colonia Agrippinensis*, was named in her honor. As for her son, Lucius Domitius Ahenobarbus, he was adopted by Claudius and was renamed Nero. Although Claudius adopted Nero, according to Suetonius he executed Agrippina's other two boys, who where named Pompeius and Sulla. The ancient sources (it seems) are unclear whether the latter two boys were Nero's brothers, or his step-brothers by Marcus Junius Silanus.

The adoption of Nero in 50 meant that Claudius' own son, Britannicus, had a legitimate competitor as heir. Indeed, it demonstrates how much influence Agrippina had over her husband, for she was able to convince him that it was in Britannicus' best interest that he have the older Nero as his guardian. It also demonstrates that she would stop at nothing to achieve her goals: we are told that when a soothsayer prophesied that if Nero became emperor, he would afterward kill his mother, Agrippina replied "Let him kill me, only let him rule!"

Some three years after Nero had been hailed *princeps iuventutis* (in 51), Agrippina arranged his marriage to Claudia Octavia, the daughter of Claudius from his earlier marriage with Valeria Messalina. Since Claudia Antonia was the sister of Britannicus, Nero was not only the boy's guardian, but also his brother-in-law. With each successive step, the noose was tightened around the neck of young Britannicus.

But time was equally desperate for Agrippina, for Nero was less than two months away from turning 17, and if she waited much longer she would lose all claims to regency over him when he ascended the throne. So, taking no chances, Agrippina served Claudius a dish of poisoned mushrooms at dinner on October 12, 54. A second dose of poison was required to finish off the 64-year-old emperor, who died in the early hours of the 13th.

During the first few months of Nero's principate, Agrippina's influence over her son was considerable. Nero seemed amenable to her authority, having chosen "best of mothers" as the watchword for his first day on the throne. She was aided by three important allies, the freedman Pallas (who was rumored to be her lover), the praetorian prefect Burrus, and Nero's tutor, Seneca. Although there seems little merit to the rumor, she was said to have seduced her son in an effort to increase her control over him.

Regardless of the tactics Agrippina employed, her heavy-handed manner soon wore thin. The next major event which Agrippina may have engineered was the poisoning of her son's main rival, Britannicus, at dinner on February 11, 55. With the death of Britannicus, Nero was unopposed by any serious rival, and consequently had no further use for his mother, whom he expelled from the palace later that year. The government was then placed in the hands of Seneca and Burrus, who also had turned against Agrippina.

Nero's mother survived another four years, though she was constantly on guard against murder attempts. Indeed, Nero found killing her no easy task, and it required that he invent an elaborate scheme. If we can trust Tacitus' account, he constructed a ship that was rigged to collapse upon her and then capsize. In March of 59, Nero thus invited his mother to dine with him at Baiae, after which she boarded the magnificent vessel in the Bay of Naples.

When the ship collapsed and sank, his 44-year-old mother survived the ordeal and swam ashore (during her banishment by Caligula, she had taken up sponge diving, and thus was a strong swimmer). She sought refuge in one of her villas at Baiae, where she was murdered either by soldiers or by the freedman Anicetus. Though few could condone Nero's matricidal act, even fewer appear to have mourned her passing.

NUMISMATIC NOTE: Agrippina Junior first appears on coins struck by her brother Caligula, when he reigned from 37 to 41. On these sestertii she is shown in the guise of Securitas standing beside her two sisters (who are depicted in the guises of Concordia and Fortuna). Her more impressive appearances, however, are as Augusta on coins struck from 50 to 54 (as the wife of Claudius), and from 54–55 (as regent for her son, who had succeeded Claudius as emperor).

NERO A.D. 54–68

CAESAR, A.D. 50–54 (UNDER CLAUDIUS)

SON OF AGRIPPINA JUNIOR (BY AHENOBARBUS)
HUSBAND OF CLAUDIA OCTAVIA, POPPAEA AND STATILIA MESSALINA
FATHER OF CLAUDIA NERONIS
ADOPTED SON, GRAND-NEPHEW, AND SUCCESSOR OF CLAUDIUS
STEP-BROTHER OF CLAUDIA ANTONIA, BRITANNICUS AND CLAUDIA OCTAVIA
NEPHEW OF CALIGULA
GRANDSON OF GERMANICUS AND AGRIPPINA SENIOR
GREAT-GRANDSON OF AGRIPPA, JULIA, NERO CLAUDIUS DRUSUS AND ANTONIA

Nero Claudius Caesar Augustus Germanicus (*earlier* Lucius Domitius Ahenobarbus), A.D. 37–68. One of the most infamous of the Roman emperors, Nero was born in December of 37, the son of Agrippina Junior and her loathsome first husband, Gnaeus Domitius Ahenobarbus, who had been consul under Tiberius in 32 and died when Nero was only 3 years old.

Fatherless and without an inheritance (for Caligula had seized his father's worldly possessions), Nero was raised by his mother, who herself was sent into exile by her brother Caligula from 39 to 41. She was recalled after his murder in 41, and eventually married her uncle, the emperor Claudius, on New Year's day, 49. The wedding greatly enhanced Nero's chances of eventually becoming emperor.

In that same year Nero also gained as a tutor the philosopher Seneca, whom his mother had convinced Claudius to recall from Corsica (where he had been in exile for eight years, allegedly for having had an adulterous affair with her youngest sister, Julia Livilla). In the following year, 50, Claudius adopted the boy, at which point he acquired the more familiar name, Nero. As a result of his adoption, Nero became guardian of his step-brother, Britannicus.

Britannicus was three years younger than Nero, and, even though he was the natural son of the reigning emperor, he was accorded lower status than his new step-brother. In 51 Nero was hailed *princeps iuventutis*, and the emperor's preference for him advanced further in 53 when he allowed Nero to marry his own (youngest) daughter Claudia Octavia, who also was the sister of Britannicus.

In addition to being older than Britannicus, Nero also had the advantage of being a grandson (rather than a nephew) of Germanicus — a legendary figure among both the people and the army. But all of this mattered little, for it was his mother, Agrippina Junior, who was taking the necessary steps to assure that he became emperor. In mid-October 54, Agrippina poisoned her husband Claudius and detained Britannicus so that Nero could ascend the throne uncontested.

During the first few months of Nero's reign, Agrippina's influence was considerable, for she had regency over him. But her heavy-handed manner soon displeased Nero. Upon the urging of his friend, the future emperor Otho, Nero expelled his mother from the Palace shortly after he (or Agrippina) poisoned his rival, Britannicus, at a dinner on February 11, 55.

The government was now firmly in the hands of Nero, who had just turned 18. Since he had ousted his mother, Nero sought advice and support from Seneca and Burrus, both of whom had adeptly turned against Agrippina at the right moment. Although it took a great deal of planning, Nero was able to murder his mother four years later, in March of 59.

A few dramatic episodes aside, the first five years of Nero's reign were productive and peaceful under the guidance of Seneca and Burrus. Nero even made grandiose promises to the senate of a return to the principles of his great-great-grandfather, the Divine Augustus. The succeeding years were less impressive, as Nero indulged his passions for Greek culture, drinking, singing, acting, musicianship, and sexual adventure. Meanwhile, he left the seemingly mundane aspects of governing an Empire to a succession of advisers.

From 60 to 63 there were two serious crises in the provinces. The first occurred in far-away Britain, where in 60 a revolt erupted under the Celtic queen Boudicca. Some 70,000 people (mostly Romans) were murdered in London, and still more elsewhere; the Roman reprisals were equally terrifying, claiming the lives of 80,000 or more. The revolt bore an uncanny resemblance to the attack of the Pontic king Mithradates VI on Roman citizens in Asia nearly 150 years before. Meanwhile, in Asia, the general Corbulo, with some difficulty, was able to wrest Armenia from the Parthians and install a puppet king.

The year 62 was eventful for Nero, as he was able to rid himself of three important members of his entourage: the praetorian prefect, Burrus, his tutor, Seneca, and his first wife, Claudia Octavia. Burrus died an apparent natural death (though some believe he was murdered), Seneca was encouraged to retire, and Claudia Octavia was divorced and executed. Nero swiftly replaced Claudia Octavia with his lover Poppaea, who was formerly the wife of his friend Otho (whom Nero had earlier removed by appointing him governor of Lusitania). Now nearing his 25th year, Nero had completely reconstructed his life and his regime.

For the remainder of his reign, Nero relied upon lower-born men or Greek and Oriental freedmen for his policies and for the maintenance of his government. In the meantime, he devoted an unconscionable amount of time to indulging his passions. His frequent stage performances as an actor, poet, singer and musician were not to the liking of the public. Not only was his talent considered marginal, but his public appearances were thought undignified.

Though Nero's new freedom pleased him immensely, the senate and the public soon tired of his antics, which they deemed more in line with a Greek king than a Roman emperor. Especially shocking was the Great Fire of 64, in which much of Rome burned to the ground. Nero, who was at the seaside town of Antium when it started (there seems little truth to the rumor that Nero "fiddled" while Rome burned), did much to relieve suffering during and after the blaze, and then placed blame squarely on the small Christian community in Rome. However, many believed Nero had the fire started so that he could clear the land necessary to build his famous "Golden House," which he had begun to construct on a more modest level a few years before.

So massive and expensive was this project that it seems inconceivable that Nero would build it even in the best of times. With all of its gardens it occupied more than 300 acres of the best land in Rome, stretching from the Circus Maximus to beyond the Baths of Trajan and consuming prime land of the Palatine, Caelian and Esquiline hills. It had an artificial lake, and a colossal statue of Nero some 120 feet tall that was housed in a vestibule so large it required a triple-colonnade a mile long. The palace was a miracle of engineering; the dining hall had a ceiling which perpetually revolved by power of water, and other ceilings were made of ivory, and were cleverly built so as to shower guests with perfume and flowers.

Not only did Nero's new palace prevent the original inhabitants from returning to rebuild, but it compounded the fiscal crisis Rome faced from the general rebuilding of the capital, and the expensive wars in Britain and Armenia. Thus, it comes as no great surprise that in the following year, 65, a plot against Nero's life was formed.

The coup was headed by a nobleman named Gaius Calpurnius Piso, who hoped to replace Nero as emperor. Though well-organized, it was exposed shortly before its target date in mid-April, and Nero's reprisals were harsh. In the same year, Nero kicked his pregnant wife, Poppaea, to death in a fit of rage. He subsequently married Statilia Messalina, a depraved and ambitious woman who proved to be his last wife.

Nero's next great venture was his "grand tour" of Greece in 67, where he competed in the Isthmian, Pythian, Olympic and Nemean Games. He had to bring forward the dates of the latter two Games so they could be held while he was in Greece, and, not surprisingly, the emperor won numerous contests against more qualified candidates. At the Olympic Games Nero won a chariot race even though he fell out of his chariot midway. During one of Nero's drawn-out performances, the future emperor Vespasian fell asleep, and was dismissed from the emperor's entourage.

The Greek excursion was not only indulgent, but also was incredibly expensive when the Imperial coffers were in no position to afford it. Were it not for Nero's policy of restriking silver coins in Egypt and Syria, the Empire certainly would have been bankrupt. The political consequences of his extravagence were enormous, and the ex-slave Helius (whom Nero had left in charge of the government in Rome during his absence), traveled to Greece to beg his immediate return. Grudgingly, Nero complied even though he had not fully availed himself of Greek hospitality.

Nero returned to Rome late in 67, and within a few months a revolt broke out in Gaul under Julius Vindex, the governor of Gallia Lugdunensis. Though Vindex was easily defeated in May, he had gained the allegiance of Galba, one of Nero's most capable generals, who commanded legions in Spain. A revolt was also sparked in North Africa under Clodius Macer, and the Rhine legions (which had defeated Vindex) refused to take further commands from Nero. With all of these sinister developments in the provinces, the emperor's support in Rome eroded quickly.

With the assistance of a freedman named Phaon, Nero fled to his villa a few miles outside Rome. But Phaon seems to have betrayed Nero, for it was only a few moments later that soldiers confronted the cowering emperor in a back room. On June 9, 68, the 30-year-old Nero died in what is best described as a combination suicide attempt and murder. His last words "Qualis artifex pereo" (though translated differently depending on the source) were to the effect: "What an artist the world is losing!"

NUMISMATIC NOTE: If anything truthfully can be said of Nero, it is that he paid close, personal attention to his coinage. Nero's artistic sense can clearly be seen on his coinage, which does not feature the austere portraits of his predacessors, but instead offers a highly individualized image. His penchant for music and the arts in general is demonstrated by the Imperial reverse type that shows him as Apollo playing a lyre. The fiscal crises which struck Rome beginning in about 62 had an impact on coinage, for some time between 62 and 64 Nero reintroduced æs coinages (struck at both Rome and Lugdunum), which had not been struck at the main Imperial mints for nearly two decades. Furthermore, the intrinsic value of his precious metal coinage was decreased — slightly in the first decade of his reign, and more precipitously in 64 when Nero reformed his coinage (from 54 to 64 his precious metal coins are dated, thereafter they are undated). The weight of the aureus was dropped by about 2% (to 45 per Roman pound) and the denarius by about 7% (to 96 per Roman pound).

The debasement strategy was employed to an extreme in the eastern provinces where unimagineable quantities of tetradrachms in Egypt and Syria were recalled and melted, only to be replaced just as rapidly with new coins with a lower silver content. This occured most dramatically at Alexandria in Egypt, where silver content fell from about 23% to about 15% (in 65/6) and the output was enormous. It has been suggested that the profits Nero accrued from the conversion at Alexandria was sufficient to fund the rebuilding of Rome.

Not surprisingly, the Alexandrian tetradrachms from Nero's regnal years 10 through 14 (63/4 to 67/8) are remarkably common. Erik Christiansen, in *The Roman Coins of Alexandria* (Denmark, 1988), notes that when he studied tetradrachms of Nero's regnal year 12, he identified 1019 different dies out of the 1032 coins he examined. Considering this was only one year (and was a limited sampling within that year), one quickly comes to realize how many new tetradrachms Nero struck. Indeed, Christiansen notes that fully one-third of the coins in each Alexandrian tetradrachm hoard found at the turn of the last century was Neronian, and that experts such as Giovanni Dattari sent thousands to the melting pot because the bullion was worth more than the coins themselves.

Back in Rome and Lugdunum, Nero paid as much attention to his Imperial æs coinage as he did to the precious metal issues. He sometimes indicated a dupondius with the marking II, an as with the marking I, and a semis with the letter S. Furthermore, he experimented with different alloy-denomination combinations. The sestertius and the dupondius had traditionally been struck in orichalcum (an golden-colored mixture of copper and zinc often called "brass"), whereas the as, semis and quadrans were struck in pure copper. Nero struck some of the smaller three denominations in orichalcum. The fact that orichalcum was more highly valued than copper is shown not only by the historical record, but also by the fact that the orichalcum asses, semisses and quadrantes are lighter than their copper counterparts, and consequently are noticeably smaller in diameter. Nero's motivations for this experiment remain a mystery. Indeed, only rarely was the same done by later emperors, such as Vespasian and Trajan and Hadrian. In every one of these later cases these coins weigh less (are considerably rarer) than the standard copper issues.

Yet another interesting (but unresolved) aspect of Nero's reign is the strong likelihood that precious metal coin production was shifted from Lugdunum to Rome either at the beginning of his principate or in about 64, when his 'post-reform' coinage was first struck. See the *Numismatic Note* of Caligula for details.

CLAUDIA OCTAVIA

AUGUSTA, A.D. 54–62

FIRST WIFE (AND FIRST COUSIN-ONCE-REMOVED) OF NERO
DAUGHTER OF CLAUDIUS AND VALERIA MESSALINA
SISTER OF BRITANNICUS
STEPSISTER OF CLAUDIA ANTONIA

Claudia Octavia, A.D. 40(?)–62. The youngest daughter of Claudius and his third wife, Valeria Messalina, Claudia Octavia died young after enduring a tragic life. Her date of birth is unknown, but certainly was before 41, shortly after which her brother Britannicus was born.

She was originally betrothed to Lucius Junius Silanus, a nobleman descended from Augustus who was in good favor with Claudius. But Silanus was discredited so that Claudia Octavia could be betrothed to Nero in 49 (for that match had dynastic importance: in that same year her father, the emperor Claudius, married his own niece Agrippina Junior, who happened to be the mother of her future husband, Nero).

Claudia Octavia and Nero were married in 53, apparently premature of the normally acceptable age of 15. But since they were first-cousins-once-removed, and their parents were niece and uncle, this was just one of several dubious aspects of their family relations. The families of Claudius and Germanicus were now linked by two marriages. Nero's marriage to Claudia Octavia was especially important, for he was already Claudius' adopted son, and in 51 was hailed *princeps iuventutis*. Thus, the marriage virtually guaranteed he would be Claudius' successor.

In the following year, 54, Nero became emperor after Claudius was poisoned. With her new husband being hailed emperor, Claudia Octavia was made Augusta, a title she held until her downfall eight years later. One can only imagine how she viewed this honor — perhaps reluctantly, as she had earned it only because her father had been murdered. Her anguish could only have been increased when she witnessed her only brother, Britannicus, die violently from poison at a banquet that she also attended.

In addition to witnessing the murder of her father and brother, the young bride was treated terribly by Nero, who tried to strangle her to death several times and openly engaged in adulterous relationships. After five years of sour marriage, Nero became enamored of Poppaea Sabina, who then was the wife of Nero's close friend, the future emperor Otho. In 58, Nero seduced Poppaea and sent Otho to Lusitania (mod. Portugal) so that he could have her to himself.

Nero's relationship with Poppaea continued until, in 62, he determined to get rid of Claudia Octavia so he could marry Poppaea. To achieve this, he claimed Claudia Octavia was sterile (which may well have been true), and that as such she could not perform the duties required of an empress. The divorce was quickly granted (in 62), and Claudia Octavia was sent to rural Campania to live under military guard.

But the ex-empress was very popular among the people, and when a rumor of her reinstatement was sparked, Nero decided to get rid of her by inventing charges of adultery and treason. Claudia Octavia, then perhaps 22 years old, was exiled to the island of Pandateria, where she was executed on June 9th of 62, after which we are told Nero's new wife, Poppaea, gloated over her severed head.

NUMISMATIC NOTE: Two categories of coinage were struck for Claudia Octavia. The earliest pieces depict her as the daughter of Claudius (on which she always appears with her step-sister, Claudia Antonia) and the later pieces as the wife of Nero.

POPPAEA

Augusta, A.D. 62–65

Second Wife of Nero (former wife of Otho)
Mother of Claudia Neronis

Poppaea Sabina, A.D. 31 (or before)–65. The second wife of Nero, Poppaea is described by the historian Tacitus as having possessed "every asset except goodness." She was a beautiful young woman with hair the color of amber, who was rumored to have bathed in the milk of asses.

Tacitus continues: "From her mother, the loveliest woman of her day, she inherited distinction and beauty. Her wealth, too, was equal to her birth. She was clever and pleasant to talk to. She seemed respectable. But her life was depraved . . . To her, married or bachelor bedfellows were alike. She was indifferent to her reputation — yet insensible to men's love, and herself unloving. Advantage dictated the bestowal of her favors."

Poppaea was the daughter of a homonymous mother (who was a daughter of Poppaeus Sabinus, the consul of A.D. 9) and T. Ollius (who died in 31), and originally was married to the praetorian prefect Rufrius Crispinus, by whom she bore a child. But she was seduced away from Crispinus by the future emperor Otho, an extravagant young man who was one of Nero's closest friends. This seduction was quickly transformed into marriage, after which Otho boasted to Nero about the particular charms of Poppaea. Tacitus speculates that Otho enticed Nero into taking a communal interest in Poppaea so that he would be tied closer to the princeps, but that Otho's plan backfired when Nero decided he wanted Poppaea to himself.

So in 58, Nero seduced Poppaea and sent Otho to govern Lusitania so as to distance him from Rome. For the next four years Nero continued to tolerate his politically important but personally unfulfilling marriage to Claudia Octavia, the daughter of the former emperor Claudius. Both Nero and Poppaea dissolved their existing marriages in 62, and 12 days later they were married. Nero's affection, however, was limited to Poppaea and their own family, for he murdered Rufrius Crispinus, her only son from her previous marriage.

In short order the royal couple produced a daughter of their own, Claudia Neronis, who was born at Antium, probably early in 63. Nero's joy was so great that the infant was hailed Augusta along with her mother. But the Imperial couple's good fortune ended when Claudia died four months later.

By 65 Poppaea had become pregnant again, and Nero could anticipate having a child to replace Claudia Neronis, and possibly an heir to the throne. However, in the summer of that year, after having been chastised for returning so late from the races, Nero delivered a swift kick to Poppaea's stomach that proved fatal for both mother and fetus. By all accounts, Nero loved Poppaea deeply and was anxiously awaiting the birth of their second child, which have led some to believe the kick was "misguided." After this grave national disaster, Nero promptly deified Poppaea as well as her unborn child.

Although Poppaea possessed certain enviable attributes, few mourned her death. The death of Poppaea marked the beginning of Nero's period of great cruelty, which would last three years before he was finally murdered.

NUMISMATIC NOTE: Poppaea is represented on provincial coinages struck by Nero in Egypt and other provinces. On Imperial coinage she seems to make one appearance, standing next to Nero on a reverse type inscribed AVGVSTVS AVGVSTA (though the empress may be Statilia Messalina).

CLAUDIA NERONIS

AUGUSTA, A.D. 63

DAUGHTER OF NERO AND POPPAEA

Claudia Neronis (*or* Claudia Augusta), A.D. 63. Little can be said of Claudia Neronis because of the brevity of her life. Tacitus reports that she was born at Antium, the same city at which Nero had been born 26 years earlier. She most likely was born early in 63, though some authorities suggest 64. Tacitus says Nero's joy for his new daughter "exceeded human measure" and the infant and her mother were both hailed Augusta. But the family's elation was not to last, as Claudia died at only 4 months of age. Grief stricken, Nero had her declared a goddess.

NUMISMATIC NOTE: Tacitus notes that upon the birth of Claudia Neronis, the senate decreed the construction of a temple of Fertility, presumably to be built at Antium, which also was to host circus games. This building may be the one depicted on the only coin that honors Claudia Neronis.

STATILIA MESSALINA

AUGUSTA, A.D. 66–68

THIRD WIFE OF NERO

Statilia Messalina (*or* Messallina), lifespan unknown. The third and final wife of Nero, Statilia Messalina was empress from 66–68. She was wealthy, well-bred, and was noted for her intelligence and beauty. Regrettably for her, she married Nero when he was at his most depraved.

Though Statilia Messalina's family was noble at the time of her marriage to Nero, its fame was recent, and due almost entirely to the achievements of T. Statilius Taurus, who was second only to Agrippa in his distinction as a commander of Augustus. She seems to have been a daughter of a later T. Statilius Taurus, who was consul in 44.

In 65 Nero had kicked to death his beloved wife, Poppaea, who was then pregnant with their second child (the first one having died at 4 months old). After this tragic event, Nero went into depression, which only worsened after he was refused marriage by Claudia Antonia, another daughter of his adoptive father Claudius, and a half-sister of his first wife. For refusing, Nero implicated Claudia Antonia in Piso's plot of 65, and in the next year put her to death. Meanwhile, Nero continued his search for a bride.

In that same year, he decided upon Statilia Messalina, who had been a lover of his. However, she had recently married the consul Julius Vestinus Atticus, a man who was politically opposed to the emperor. So Nero decided to remove Vestinus, but when it could not be proven that he had been privy to the murder plot of Piso, Nero had to resort to strong-arm tactics. He sent guards to collect him at his home high above the Forum, but Vestinus locked himself in a bedroom and committed suicide by opening his veins.

Although Nero was murdered in the Palace coup of 68, Statilia Messalina survived the revolution and the civil war that followed. She would have married the future emperor Otho (who previously had been the husband of Nero's second wife, Poppaea Sabina) had his death not prevented the union. Indeed, Suetonius tells us that of the two letters Otho wrote the night before he committed suicide, one of them was to Statilia Messalina.

NUMISMATIC NOTE: Though the empress portrayed standing next to Nero on his AVGVSTVS AVGVSTA coinage is thought by some to be Statilia Messalina, she is most likely Poppaea, Nero's second wife. Statilia Messalina is represented on a few provincial issues.

A.L.R.

CHAPTER THREE

The Civil War of A.D. 68–69

The Civil War of 68–69 was a watershed moment in Roman history for many reasons. First and foremost, it brought about the extinction of the Julio-Claudians, who had ruled Rome for nearly a century. Second, it reacquainted Romans with the brashness of warlords and the privations of civil war, which they had been spared for several generations.

Late in the reign of Nero, governors in Gaul, Spain and North Africa revolted. Though the rebellions in Gaul and North Africa were ineffective, Galba's revolt in Spain was a success, and played no small part in causing Nero to be deposed in June of 68. Though Galba was the first to be proclaimed, it was the general Vespasian who emerged victorious late in 69. Vespasian was a cautious man of respectable Italian ancestry who established the "Flavian" dynasty, which began on solid footing but ended in disgrace 27 years later.

Most shocking to the senate and praetorian guards in Rome was the realization that an emperor could be made outside the capital. A similar scenario had occurred in A.D. 14, when the Rhine and Danube legions rebelled against the fledgling regime of Tiberius, but the grievances of the soldiers were addressed by Germanicus and Drusus. This time Rome was not so fortunate, and the course of events demonstrated the great power of the frontier legions.

The civil war involved soldiers from almost every region of the Empire: Gaul, Spain, North Africa, the Balkans, Syria, Judaea and Egypt. The standards of rebellion were raised by both the common soldier and commander alike. Indeed, the murder of Galba and his replacement by Otho was made possible by the rank and file (of the praetorian guards in Rome), as was the rebellion of Vitellius, which was sparked by the German legionaries who were frustrated for not having been paid a bonus.

To the citizen, this was also a different kind of civil war from that which had previously occurred in Rome. A century before, when the civil war between Marc Antony and Octavian was raging, the citizens could find enough substance in the causes of the war to choose sides. However, by the end of this civil war (especially during the principate of Vitellius), it had become a surreal affair.

This was no war of ideology, but one of simple greed and anarchy within the ranks. The people were largely excluded, except when they were being victimized. As might be expected, the citizens of Rome displayed a "brutish indifference" to the outcome, for the candidates were not deemed worthy of being fought over, and the causes for the war were without substance.

Tacitus describes the atmosphere in haunting terms: "Close by the fighting stood the people of Rome, like the audience at a show, cheering and clapping this side or that in turns as if this were a mock battle in the arena. Whenever one side gave way, men would hide in shops or take refuge in some great house. They were then dragged out and killed at the instance of the mob, who gained most of the loot, for the soldiers were bent on bloodshed and massacre, and the booty fell to the crowd. The whole city presented a frightful caricature of its normal self: fighting and casualties at one point, baths and restaurants at another . . . all of the vices associated with a life of idleness and pleasure, all the dreadful deeds typical of a pitiless sack. These were so intimately linked that an observer would have thought Rome in the grip of a simultaneous orgy of violence and dissipation."

For numismatists, however, this period is among the most impressive in all Roman history. Not only was a remarkable series of "anonymous" coinage struck, but on the Imperial issues, portraiture underwent a revolution. Though the portraits of Galba and Vitellius display none of the austere dignity of the Julio-Claudian age, they gained in return a gritty realism. The images of these two men are seldom flattering, and the best examples were struck at the Rome mint. The coins they struck at mints in Gaul, Spain and North Africa are also of interest for their style of engraving, which is less realistic, and often is curious to the modern eye.

Introduction to the Civil War and its Participants

Person	**as Imperator**	**as Augustus**
Nero		(deposed and killed: June 9, 68)
Galba	April 2 – June 9, 68	June 9, 68 – January 15, 69
Otho		January 15 – April 16/17, 69
Vitellius	January 1/3 – April 19, 69	April 19 – December 20, 69
Vespasian		hailed by legions: July 1, 69 hailed by senate: December 21, 69

During the period 68 to 69, the title of Augustus was held by five men in quick succession. Troubles began in March of 68 with an uprising in Gaul led by a governor named Vindex, who quickly gained the support of the Spanish governor Galba. Almost simultaneously, a separate and short-lived revolt erupted in North Africa under the legate Clodius Macer. The reigning emperor, Nero, soon was deposed and forced to commit suicide, after which the senate confirmed Galba's claim on the throne.

After reigning seven months, Galba's regime collapsed under internal pressures, and he was replaced by Otho, the man who led the coup. But to complicate matters, only a few days earlier the German legions had proclaimed their governor, Vitellius, as a candidate for the throne. During the next three months Otho and Vitellius fought for supremacy; Otho as the sanctioned emperor and Vitellius as a rebel. In the end, Vitellius' larger armies were victorious, though their leader proved unsuitable for the position.

Within six weeks of Vitellius' accession, the frontier general Vespasian was proclaimed emperor by his soldiers in the East and set his own plan into motion. Vitellius' reign lasted merely eight months, and during the final stages of his contest with Vespasian, another revolt erupted in the northernmost part of Roman Germany under a Batavian named Julius Civilis. This revolt was different from the earlier ones, for Civilis had no designs on Rome itself; rather, he intended to free Gaul of Roman control. After Vespasian ousted Vitellius, he turned his attention to Civilis, and was able to crush the revolt late in 70.

Although the above-mentioned men were the most important leaders of the era, many other people were instrumental in the flow of events. The biographies of six of these men are given below as a supplement to biographies of the three emperors and three rebels who issued coins. The biographies of Nero and Vespasian, who caused and ended the civil war, appear, respectively, in chapters two and four.

Lucius Verginius Rufus: Formerly a consul in 63, Verginius Rufus belonged to an elite group of North Italians who held sway in the government of Rome. He became governor of Upper Germany in 67, and, unlike Fonteius Capito, the indecisive governor of Lower Germany who controlled four legions, he came to the defense of Nero with his own three legions and auxiliaries.

Though it seems Rufus tried to negotiate with Vindex at first, the soldiers caused hostilities to escalate, the result being the battle at Vesontio late in May 68. Rufus denied the request of his own soldiers that he assume the purple, but none-the-less was slow to offer his support to Galba. Thus, Galba was justifiably suspicious of this capable governor. Just after Galba arrived in Rome in October of 68, Rufus was pressed once again by his German legions to revolt, this time with the additional support of the Danubian legions. But once again, Rufus refused.

Galba acted quickly, removing Rufus from his post and replacing him with a feeble man named Hordeonius Flaccus. Rufus returned to Rome, where Galba showed his gratitude by allowing him to be charged with a crime. In the meantime, Fonteius Capito (the governor of Lower Germany) was murdered by one of his own soldiers, Fabius Valens, and was replaced by the future emperor Aulus Vitellius.

A revolt against Galba was formed by the seven legions and auxiliary units of the two Germanies, and as their leader they chose Vitellius, who had been in command for only about a month. After the downfall of Galba in January, 69, Verginius Rufus (then in Rome) became suffect consul under the new emperor Otho, who hoped that by associating Rufus with his fledgling regime, he might loosen Vitellius' grip on the German legions.

After the defeat and death of Otho the legions present at the First Battle of Bedriacum tried to compell Rufus — for the third time — to assume the purple. This time, however, the soldiers made it clear they were not willing to accept his humble refusal. Despite this threat, Rufus did refuse, and narrowly escaped murder by fleeing.

He survived long after the civil war ended, socializing in literary circles and even becoming guardian to Pliny the Younger, whose letters are famous. Later in his life Rufus would purposely cloud the matter of his support of Nero by defending his actions as resistance to a nationalistic movement in Gaul (which, indeed, Vindex's revolt was not). Rufus died soon after his third consulship (under Nerva in 97), with his funeral oration being delivered by none other than the historian Tacitus.

Gaius Nymphidius Sabinus: One of several men who had designs on the throne during the civil war, Nymphidius was raised from tribune to prefect in the praetorian guards by Nero in 65 for his role in suppressing the Pisonian conspiracy. He shared the post with Ofonius Tigellinus, who had been prefect since 62, and who much earlier in his career had been exiled for his adulterous affairs with Caligula's sisters. But Tigellinus was by then elderly and ill, and so was easily ousted by Nymphidius, who took sole command of the guard in 68.

Nymphidius conspired with the senate to overthrow Nero, and in the process offered a bribe of at least 7,000 denarii (280 aurei) per man to the guards who were personally protecting Nero. During Galba's march on Rome, Nymphidius lost support with the senate, and especially with the new emperor, who refused to honor the bribes the prefect had earlier promised. Nymphidius' fate was sealed when Galba replaced him as praetorian prefect with one of his own close friends, Cornelius Laco.

Thus, before Galba arrived in Rome, Nymphidius staged a coup. He claimed to have been an illegitimate son of Caligula in hopes this would establish him as a Julio-Claudian, and thus make him the most legitimate candidate. Considering the nature of this claim, Nymphidius was probably in his late 30s at the time. But his revolt failed quickly, and Nymphidius was killed either by agents of Galba or by guards who were angered because the payments he had promised them were not going to be paid.

Lucius Calpurnius Piso Frugi Licinianus: This unfortunate young nobleman came into the historical limelight during the most desperate hour of Galba's faltering regime. He was chosen by Galba as his successor on January 10, 69, and was killed with him in the Forum at Rome only five days later, being only 30 years old at the time. Piso was descended from Crassus and was a great-great-grandson of Sextus Pompey on his mother's side.

However, this illustrious lineage had brought the family nothing but ill-fortune under the Julio-Claudians. One of Piso's brothers was briefly married to Claudius' daughter Claudia Antonia, but was executed along with his parents in 46. The subsequent reign of Nero proved no better, for another of his brothers, Gaius Calpurnius Piso, was the architect of the "Pisonian Conspiracy" which failed against Nero in 65 (with the Piso under discussion being exiled as a result). Alone, orphaned and exiled, Piso was recalled by Galba, who apparently had long intended to bequeath him his name and property. However, Piso proved to be an unsatisfactory candidate to the soldiers, and his adoption served the opposite of the intended effect, and only expedited Galba's downfall.

Gaius Licinius Crassus Mucianus: Another accomplished soldier of his age, Mucianus distinguished himself during the reign of Nero as one of Corbulo's subordinates. He also served as a governor in Lycia-Pamphylia and in Syria, the province he held when Vespasian staged his revolt against Vitellius. (*Note:* Coins were struck bearing Mucianus' name while governing Syria under Galba.) By mid-July of 69, Mucianus had been convinced by Vespasian's eldest son, Titus, to pledge his support to Vespasian's cause.

While Vespasian marched into Alexandria to control the grain supply destined for Rome, Mucianus led 20,000 of his soldiers on a purposely slow march across Anatolia, up through the Balkans, and into northern Italy. Indeed, it was Mucianus' advance that provoked the Balkan commander Antonius Primus to launch his own invasion of Italy before Mucianus arrived. Mucianus' advance in the Balkans was slowed when he had to repel a Dacian incursion, but he continued thereafter and seems to have arrived in Rome only one day after Primus had entered the capital.

Though Primus had been given the insignia of a consul, Mucianus sent Primus' legions back to the Balkans and quickly wrested control from the upstart commander. Thereafter, Mucianus held Rome for Vespasian as his praetorian prefect, awaiting his arrival via Brundisium. He used the troops to quell further rebellions, which occasionally erupted in the city. It also seems likely that Mucianus was responsible for the execution of Vitellius' brother and son. A man of many accomplishments, Mucianus remained one of Vespasian's principal advisers, all the time profiting incredibly and reminding the emperor that he owed his office to him. Eventually he was supplanted by Titus c. 76.

Marcus Antonius Primus: A Gaul by birth and a partisan of Galba, Primus commanded Legio VII Gemina in Pannonia. In 69, shortly after the downfall of Galba, he won over the armies of Pannonia and Moesia with his eloquence and irrepressible drive. However, in his lust for glory he caused Rome great harm, opening the gateway for a Sarmatian invasion and the Gallic rebellion of Julius Civilis, both of which plagued the first year of Vespasian's principate.

Learning that the governor of Syria, Gaius Licinius Mucianus, was leading his legions on a slow march to Italy, Primus decided to act first, and with considerable bravery invaded Italy. With five legions under his command, some 30,000 men in total (we are told), he captured Aquileia and caused the defection of the fleet at Ravenna.

After numerous skirmishes, Primus won a major victory against the Vitellian armies on October 24 and 25 at the Second Battle of Bedriacum. Primus encountered the Vitellian armies at the ideal time, for their emperor had remained at Rome, and his generals were either ill or were behaving treacherously. In such a state, the Vitellian armies were demoralized, and fought poorly despite their larger numbers.

Tacitus offers us a haunting insight into the turning-point of the Second Battle of Bedriacum, which raged all day and into the night: "Neither side had the advantage until, in the middle of the night, the moon rose, displaying and deceiving the combatants. But the light favored the army of Primus, being behind them; on their side the shadows of horses and men were exaggerated, and the enemy spears fell short, though those who were hurling them imagined they were on target. But the Vitellians were brilliantly illuminated by the light shining full in their faces, and therefore without realizing it provided an easy mark for an enemy aiming from what were virtually concealed positions."

After his victory, Primus pursued the Vitellian soldiers to the nearby city of Cremona, where he captured them and then, in an act even more scurrilous than his earlier sack of Aquileia, allowed his Danubian soldiers to loot the city continuously from October 27 to 31. Next he made his way toward Rome, gaining the defection of soldiers sent against him on December 17 at Narnia, just outside the city. This caused chaos in Rome: street fighting broke out among rivals, Vitellius tried to abdicate but was dissuaded, and the city prefect Flavius Sabinus (the brother of Vespasian) was executed after being besieged in the temple of Capitoline Jupiter, which burned to the ground in the process.

Primus entered Rome on December 20 (or 21), received the insignia of a consul, and broke the Vitellian resistance. The terrified Vitellius was captured, tortured and executed. For one day Primus was in control in the capital, but he was outmaneuvered politically by Gaius Licinius Mucianus, who arrived the following day with his army after the long trek from Antioch. The daring adventurer Primus then retired to Tolosa, where he lived perhaps three more decades.

Flavius Sabinus: The only brother of Vespasian, Flavius Sabinus was a senator, and it was his status that enabled Vespasian to pursue a respectable career. Sabinus had served the Empire in numerous capacities, but throughout the civil war he was the prefect of Rome (*praetor urbnanus*), a post that he may have held for more than a decade prior.

Sabinus figured prominently into Otho's plan for survival, for that short-lived emperor kept Sabinus on good terms in hopes of gaining the support of Vespasian, who was then commanding the war in Judaea. Sabinus survived the collapse of Otho's regime in mid-April 69, and when the news of Otho's suicide reached Rome, Sabinus took the lead in gaining approval from the senate and praetorians for Vitellius, who was declared emperor on April 19. Not surprisingly, Sabinus continued to serve as prefect of Rome under Vitellius.

When Vespasian declared war against Vitellius, Sabinus was in a precarious position, which only worsened as the armies of Primus and Mucianus advanced on Rome. When Vitellius expressed his desire to abdicate after his armies defected at Narnia on December 17, it was the silver-tongued Sabinus who was able to negotiate the terms. However, Vitellius' German praetorians — some 16,000 strong — joined with the public mobs and brought an end to the negotiations.

To make matters worse, a group of German auxiliaries pursued Sabinus and his supporters (including his nephew Domitian, the youngest son of Vespasian), forcing them to take refuge on the Capitoline Hill. They settled in the temple of Capitoline Jupiter, and were withstanding the siege when the temple — the supreme symbol of Rome and its Empire — burned to the ground around them in broad daylight.

Despite all of the obscene events that had occurred during this civil war, Tacitus considered this to be of particular importance. Indeed, he called it ". . . the most lamentable and appalling disaster in the whole history of the Roman commonwealth." Though Domitian, who was only about three months shy of his 18th birthday at the time, escaped in disguise, Sabinus was captured and callously executed, either on the spot or after being delivered to Vitellius.

VINDEX

REBEL, A.D. 68

Gaius Julius Vindex, d. A.D. 68. Descended from the kings of Aquitania (southeastern Gaul), and himself a senator, Vindex was the son of a Roman senator who seems to have been selected by Claudius. At the time of his revolt against Nero, Vindex was governor of Gallia Lugdunensis in Transalpine Gaul, a wealthy province in which no legions were stationed.

His revolt began early in March of 68, and seems to have been sparked in self defense. Nero had become increasingly hostile toward provincial governors, and furthermore, seems to have fallen behind in the payments normally sent to Gaul.

Vindex enjoyed widespread support among the oppressed citizenry, whom he made swear an oath to the senate and people of Rome. According to one (perhaps optimistic) estimate, he was able to raise 100,000 local troops. Although the legionary colony of Lugdunum was the capital of Vindex's province, its citizens did not support the cause of Vindex. So he besieged that city swiftly and successfully. Meanwhile, Vienne, further down the Rhône in Gallia Narbonensis, offered its support.

In Rome, Nero was branding Vindex as a Gallic nationalist so as to rally support. But the fact of the matter is that Vindex had no intention of seceding from the Empire. Indeed, that course of action was rejected by a Gallic council which met at Durocortorum (mod. Reims, about 90 miles northeast of Paris).

Despite the success of his revolt, Vindex's provincial background assured that he was not qualified to become emperor. So he sought the support of Galba, the elderly governor of Hispania Tarraconensis, in Spain. On April 2, at Carthago Nova, Galba assumed the title Imperator and agreed to spearhead the cause of Vindex. In the process he denounced an appeal from the governor of Aquitania for help, seemingly against the revolt of Vindex.

In that same month, another revolt — equally pro-senatorial, it would seem — was launched by Clodius Macer, the propraetor of North Africa. Despite overtures made by Galba, Clodius Macer did not join their cause and continued to act independently.

Although Vindex had an immense army and had easily taken Lugdunum, he now had to reckon with the legions under the command of Verginius Rufus, the governor of Upper Germany, who remained loyal to Nero. In May of 68, Vindex and Rufus both led their armies to Vesontio (*mod.* Besançon), some 115 miles to the north-east of Lugdunum, where the two commanders apparently discussed options to battle. But the Rhine legions were anxious to fight, and may have forced a confrontation before negotiations were finished. In any event, Vindex's armies were roundly defeated by the seasoned legionaries. Vindex died at the battle, though it is uncertain whether he died in combat, by execution or by his own hand.

NUMISMATIC NOTE: Since neither the name nor the portrait of Vindex appears on coins, issues must be attributed to him based on their historical and geographical context. Opinions vary as to where his coinage was struck. Vienne seems the most likely location for the bulk of the issues, though Lugdunum or Nemausus may have contributed. A third Gallic mint, at Narbo, is suspected to have coined for his colleague Galba.

CLODIUS MACER

REBEL, A.D. 68

Lucius Clodius Macer, d. A.D. 68. Very few details are known about Clodius Macer, who was *legatus Augusti propraetore Africae* late in the reign of Nero, and staged a revolt that lasted perhaps six months. His grasp for power seems to have begun in April 68, at about the same time that Galba, in Spain, joined the cause of Vindex in Gaul. Just like Vindex and Galba, Macer was revolting against Nero, an emperor who was notorious for his ill-treatment of provincial governors.

Though his revolt undoubtedly began in Numidia, where he commanded the Legion III Augusta, it soon was headquartered in Carthage, the ancient capital of North Africa. Macer gained control of the fleet stationed at Carthage, and made use of its excellent seaport to control the North African grain supply that was destined for Rome.

Though Galba made overtures to Macer to join his revolt against Nero, Macer did not respond favorably, preferring to stay his course alone. The terms of Galba's offer are unknown, and so it is difficult to gauge why he refused. However, it would not be out of line to presume that Galba wanted him to take a subordinate role, and that on those grounds alone Macer opted for independence. Furthermore, Macer had supporters in Rome, not the least of whom was Calvia Crispinilla, whom Tacitus describes as ". . . the woman who had been Nero's tutor in vice."

Macer tried to increase his chance of survival by raising a new legion, which he called Legion I Macriana. The numismatic evidence indicates that he had some interest in Sicily, which was less than 150 miles from the shores of Carthage, and he either made an abortive attempt to occupy the island or simply made overtures to its citizens and soldiers. Macer was executed by the local Imperial procurator in October, 68, just after Galba reached Rome and was able to arrange his murder.

NUMISMATIC NOTE: All of Clodius Macer's coins — aurei and denarii — bear the inscription SC, something usually not encountered on precious metal coins. His types are patriotic and commemorative in nature. They allude to the two legions under his control, to his main base of Carthage, to Africa in general, and in some cases to the island of Sicily. Denarii of Galba that are of identical style (and have the SC) no doubt were struck after Macer's downfall in October by partisans of Galba who took command in Carthage.

Macer's portrait coinage occurs in two main varieties, the rarer having his name in the genitive case (MACRI) and the more common with it in the nominative case (MACER). In any event, fewer than 20 specimens of his portrait coins are currently known, making them among the rarest in the Roman series. They are supplemented by six non-portrait types. It is of some interest that Macer borrowed his two most prominent designs from Marc Antony's legionary denarii, utilizing both the obverse and reverse types. Researchers have noted it probably is no coincidence that Antony's prototypes were struck almost exactly a century before.

GALBA A.D. 68-69

IMPERATOR, A.D. 68

Servius Sulpicius Galba, 3 B.C.–A.D. 69. The first emperor of Rome to reign briefly, Galba's 7-month principate was spent largely in the provinces. Indeed, he spent only about 100 days in Rome as emperor. His harsh discipline, aggressive reforms, and parsimonious nature caused him to be disliked by soldier, senator and citizen. In an earlier age, when Romans were not so fickle and greedy, he might have been a success, but Galba lacked the political instinct to see he was on a path of self-destruction.

Galba hailed from noble families on both his mother's and father's sides. Throughout his career he enjoyed the support of Augustus, Tiberius, Caligula and Claudius, and especially of the first Augusta, Livia. Indeed, she had bequeathed him 500,000 aurei in her will, but it was nullified by her bitter son, Tiberius, who instead seized the funds for himself. Galba was married to Aemilia Lepida, a granddaughter of the triumvir Lepidus. Together they had two sons, whose names are not known.

Despite having been shorted the fortune in gold bequeathed by Livia, Galba was immensely wealthy. So laudable were his qualities, and so extensive were his wealth and family connections, that upon the death of Caligula in 41, Galba was spoken of as a possible successor. Though he remained a private citizen during the principates of Claudius and Nero, Galba's opportunity to become emperor occurred 27 years later.

He spent his early career as governor of Aquitania, then as consul in 33, followed by a military command in Upper Germany and, in 45, as a proconsul in Africa. He ended his regular career as the governor of Hispania Tarraconensis, in northern Spain. It was while he was serving in that capacity that the revolt of Vindex against Nero occurred early in March, 68. Although Vindex's revolt found immediate success in his own province of Gaul, it could not prevail until someone with the necessary credentials stepped up as Nero's replacement.

The 70-year-old Galba proved to be a man of considerable ambition, for on April 2, while at Carthago Nova on the south-eastern shore of Spain, he allied himself with Vindex and was hailed Imperator by his troops. In the same month, a revolt against Nero also broke out in North Africa under the leadership of Clodius Macer, the propraetor in command of Legion III Augusta in Numidia.

Though Galba and Clodius Macer each had only one legion under their command, each soon raised an additional legion and stayed the course of revolution. Macer had the additional benefit of a fleet and the potential to disrupt grain shipments to Rome. Though Galba attempted to gain his allegiance, Macer was unwilling to join his effort.

Just as the revolution under Galba and Vindex was taking shape, the latter was defeated north of Lugdunum at the end of May by German legions still loyal to Nero. Either at the end of May or in early June, Galba arrived at Clunia, a city in the center of Spain, and learned of Vindex's death. However, he also received a good omen from the local oracle, and thus was encouraged in his enterprise.

Meanwhile, in Rome, Nero's regime was faltering. His guards were sufficiently bribed (at nearly 300 aurei each) and abandoned him before he could make good his escape to Alexandria by ship. On June 9, Nero was deposed and condemned to death by flogging by the senate. Thus, he reluctantly took his own life on that day, and Galba was hailed emperor in his place, seemingly within 24 hours. No longer was Galba a self-proclaimed Imperator hoping to gain the approval of the senate, but was emperor.

About this time Galba was *en route* to Tarraco on the East coast of Spain and had been joined by the 33-year-old governor of Lusitania (*mod.* Portugal), Otho, a man who not only disdained Nero, but who also hoped to become Galba's adopted successor. Invigorated with the support of the senate and the praetorian guard in Rome, Galba and Otho departed Tarraco late in the summer of 68, and led their modest army on a march directly for Rome. Galba's status was confirmed by a deputation of the senate and the praetorian guard that met him in Narbo (*mod.* Narbonne) early in July.

Rome was far from stable during his approach, which required all of July and the first half of October. Galba, a man of stern temperament, sent word ahead that he had no intention of honoring the bribes promised by the praetorian prefect Nymphidius, by which he had secured the murder of Nero. Indeed, he replaced Nymphidius with Cornelius Laco, a candidate of his own choice. Nymphidius thus staged his own coup, but it failed quickly, and Nymphidius was killed.

In October of 68, Galba arrived in Rome, which by then had been purged of the revolutionary Nymphidius, but which still suffered from an anxious praetorian cohort, whose members feared they would be dismissed and reassigned to legions in the provinces. Though this did not happen, Galba dismissed the German bodyguards, disbanded a legion of marines, and ordered the Spanish legionaries that had accompanied him on his journey to remain outside Rome.

However, good news came from North Africa, where Galba's rival at Carthage, Clodius Macer, was assassinated by the local Imperial procurator. Not surprisingly, Galba's partisans in North Africa declared for him and even struck coins in his name that are identifiable by their style, which is identical to that of Macer.

Galba's reforms were a combination of repaying favors owed to his main supporters and genuine attempts to restore morality and dignity. One of his more practical actions occurred in November or December, when he removed Verginius Rufus from his command in Upper Germany, and installed Aulus Vitellius in Lower Germany. Though these made sense at the time (for Rufus was immensely popular, and Vitellius was a dullard), it soon backfired because the former was loyal and the latter was treacherous.

Galba's downfall in January of 69 was swift. On New Year's Day, the legions of Upper Germany refused to recognize Galba; and by the 3rd, the armies of both Upper and Lower Germany had switched allegiance to the newly appointed governor Vitellius, even though he had virtually no military experience and had held his post only a month. Sparking the revolt of the seven German legions, it seems, was the anger they harbored for having been shorted a reward due for their defeat of Vindex.

News of the defection traveled the more than 800 miles from Trier to Rome, and reached Galba by the 8th or the 9th of January. Galba's repressive regime was fast losing support, and so on January 10 he adopted Lucius Calpurnius Piso Frugi Licinianus as his son, hoping that the presence of an heir would demonstrate stability and hope for the future. His candidate was a most noble young man descended from both Crassus and Pompey the Great, but was not to the liking of the soldiers or the common man. Making matters worse, he was also a brother of the Piso who had plotted against Nero in 65.

Worse still, the praetorian guards were not satisfied with this stingy emperor. Even a "mere token act of generosity," Tacitus reports, would have won the praetorian over to his cause. But even this Galba did not offer. While Galba was taking a hard line on the army and finances, his associate Otho was rallying support among the legionaries and praetorian guards. Otho's efforts were intensified after he was not chosen by Galba as his adopted son.

Through his many acts of monetary generosity, Otho hoped he would be the beneficiary of any revolt against Galba. Indeed, he most certainly needed to be, for his "campaign of generosity" had bankrupted him. Otho made one final bribe of 15,000 denarii to each of 12 key men in the praetorian guard, which inaugurated the plot for Galba's overthrow. It was impeccably timed to coincide with the arrival of the news in Rome of Vitellius' revolt in Germany. This not only worked against Galba, but caused the praetorians to rally about their own candidate, Otho, in opposition to Vitellius, whose armies were advancing on Italy.

Tacitus gives a dramatic, and probably accurate, description of the few minutes preceding Galba's murder in the Forum on January 15: "By this time Galba was being carried hither and thither by the irregular impact of the surging multitude. Everywhere the public buildings and temples were crowded with a sea of faces. As far as the eye could see, the view was one of doom. Not a cry came from the mass of people. But their faces wore a frightened expression."

The praetorian guards loyal to Otho charged into the crowd on foot and on horseback with their weapons drawn, trampling all between them and the sedan of Galba. The guards in Galba's personal escort defected to the cause of Otho, after which the elderly emperor was dashed to the ground and hacked apart with swords. Thus was the inglorious end of Galba, who was decapitated and whose body was dragged through the streets on a hook and tossed into the Tiber.

The triumphant praetorians proceeded with Otho to the Senate House, where they displayed a variety of severed heads as proof of their foul deed. Terrified by the events in the Forum and by the revolt by Vitellius in Germany, the senate did not hesitate to vote Otho full powers.

Though Galba's reign lasted from June 68 through January, 69, most of that time had been consumed by his arduous march from Spain to Rome.

The principate of Galba, it can be rightly said, was both sad and pathetic: sad because the once-high level of morality of Romans was no more, and pathetic because Galba was unable to believe the evidence before his eyes. His attempts to rule in an honorable manner more typical of the Republican or the Augustan age was a terrible failure. He tried to reform rapidly and in the process showed no political judgment, and in that respect his brief principate resembles that of Pertinax nearly 125 years later.

NUMISMATIC NOTE: Galba's coinage is among the most complex and diverse in the entire Roman series. Not only did he strike as Imperator (which includes many of the anonymous "civil war coinages," notably including those on which his facial features are assimilated in the portrait of Divus Augustus), but he also struck as emperor. He coined in all three metals and at an uncertain number of mints in Spain, Gaul and North Africa, as well as in Rome itself. His bronzes alone were complicated enough to require treatment in a detailed monograph by Colin Kraay (*The Aes Coinage of Galba*, ANS Numismatic Notes and Monographs no. 133, New York, 1956).

Galba's reverse types are varied, and many of them are historical in content. Most of his coinage as Imperator is propagandistic in nature, alluding to the provinces, the restoration of Rome and of liberty, and to his victory itself. One of his most common types as Augustus celebrates Livia, with whom he was closely acquainted. From this, Galba hoped to validate his principate (he was, after all, the first non-Julio-Claudian emperor) by demonstrating his ties to the Julio-Claudians. Beginning with his reign, Caesar and Augustus (which were personal names under the Julio-Claudians) became Imperial titles indicating rank. Partisans of Galba struck denarii on his behalf at Carthage after the downfall of Clodius Macer which are distinguished not only by the crude style which can be observed on Macer's denarii, but also by the fact that SC occurs on the reverse. This is a highly unusual feature for Roman silver, but was standard for the issues of Macer. The SC occurs on no other precious metal coins of Galba except for those which stylistically are attributable to Carthage.

OTHO A.D. 69

Husband of Poppaea

Marcus Salvius Otho, A.D. 32-69. Hailing from an equestrian family of only recent renown, Otho holds the distinction of being the first emperor to have openly attained his office through the murder of his predecessor. Even if we believe the story of Caligula causing the suffocation of Tiberius, his act merely expedited an imminent, natural death. Such cannot be said of Otho.

Otho, who is described by Tacitus as an "extravagant young man," spent his youth in fashionable pursuits. He was renowned for his effeminacy and vanity, and was particular about his grooming. Suetonius tells us "he shaved every day, and since boyhood had always used a poultice of moist bread to prevent the growth of his beard." He is famous to numismatists for his well-made toupee, which appears as a luxuriant head of hair on his Imperial coin portraits.

He chose as one of his companions the beautiful and depraved Sabina Poppaea, a woman nearly his age who hailed from a wealthy family and was married to the praetorian prefect Rufrius Crispinus. But Poppaea regularly engaged in adulterous affairs, and one of her bed companions was Otho, who later became her husband.

Being close friends with the new emperor Nero, and wishing to attain greater prominence, Otho boasted to Nero about the charms of Poppaea. He seems to have invited Nero to share their bed, but his plan of Imperial seduction backfired when Nero decided he wanted Poppaea to himself, and in 58 appointed Otho the governor of Lusitania (mod. Portugal) so that he would be far from Rome. Otho remained at that post until 68, when the standards of revolt was raised against Nero almost simultaneously in Gaul, Spain and North Africa.

Otho was quick to join the revolt headed by Galba, the governor of the neighboring province of Hispania Tarraconensis. Not surprisingly, Otho had his eye on the principate from the very outset of his alliance with Galba. Initially he hoped to be named Galba's adoptive son, and thus successor. Since Galba was 70 years old, the wait may not have been too long.

However, it became clear to Otho that he would be passed up for this honor (which eventually was given to Lucius Calpurnius Piso Frugi Licinianus). It was fortunate that Otho had hedged his bet by currying support among the soldiers and the praetorian guards. Indeed, his liberal bribery (during a time when Galba was behaving stingily) was potent, but also drove him deeply into debt.

At the turn of the New Year, 69, the armies of Germany revolted against Galba, hailing Vitellius, the governor of Lower Germany, as their leader. News of this development probably reached Rome shortly before Galba adopted Piso as his heir on January 10.

Otho's final overture was a bribe of 15,000 denarii to each of 12 key men in the praetorian guard. Through this act, Otho assured their support in his plot to overthrow Galba. On January 15, the plan was put into action, and Galba was murdered callously in the Forum by the very praetorian guards who were supposed to protect him. The frightened senators had little choice but to hail Otho emperor.

Suetonius tells us that although Otho was probably aware of Vitellius' rebellion before he made his own attempt at the throne, he did not expect Vitellius to oppose his elevation. A series of negotiations and assassination attempts by both men were made subsequently but failed. It became clear that only more civil war would determine the outcome. Otho soon gained the support of the legions in Egypt, Africa, the Euphrates and the Danube, but they would not prove to be large enough or close enough to protect him from the legions advancing from Germany.

During Vitellius' march, the environment was far from calm in Rome, where the praetorian guards were drunk with their renewed power. Conflicts with other soldiers and the senate were commonplace, and Otho restored order by executing a few particularly troublesome "ringleaders" in the camp, and by paying an additional bonus of 1,250 denarii per man. He also appealed to the legions outside Rome by introducing a favorable reform of the policy on annual leave. Otho was exhibiting the practicality and political prowess Galba had lacked.

He further improved his odds of survival by keeping Flavius Sabinus as prefect of Rome and Verginius Rufus as consul. The first appointment was meant to placate Sabinus' brother, Vespasian, who was commanding the war in Judaea (and who consequently recognized Otho's principate, which he had not done for Galba), and the second was supposed to undermine Vitellius' credibility with the German legions, which had twice before beseached Verginius Rufus to lead their rebellions.

It must be remembered that Vitellius commanded seven legions and a great many auxiliaries, whereas Otho had only one legion, together with auxiliary infantry and cavalry hastily gathered locally. Some of the praetorian remained in Rome to keep order in the unruly capital, while Otho even raised an army of 2,000 gladiators to help in the effort. The three Balkan legions were expected, but most of the soldiers were still far from the point of action.

In February, Vitellius' armies had already advanced deep into Gaul on their long march to Italy. Vitellius had not gone with the vanguard of his army, but instead remained behind to raise more troops for the upcoming war. In the process Vitellius gained the allegiance of the soldiers in Gaul and Britain. The fact that he had a completely different foe than he had when he began his revolt against Galba mattered little to Vitellius, for recalling his legions would certainly have had dire consequences.

The German legions were led by Aulus Caecina Alienus and Fabius Valens. Caecina led his legions through the Alps, and Valens along a more southerly route, and though the latter experienced a near mutiny *en route*, both armies marched rapidly, and joined in Italy near Cremona, a city on the north bank of the Po River.

In mid- or late March, after a few skirmishes had already occurred in southern Gaul and Italy (and it was clear that he had no more time to waste), Otho left Rome to march north and take command of the war. He established his headquarters at Brixellum (mod. Brescello), some 30 miles (and on the opposite side of the Po River) from where the decisive battle would be fought.

The skirmishes continued until early in April, finding Otho in a difficult position. Before he had received the full strength of his Danubian legions (of which only the Vanguard had entered Italy), Otho forced a pitched battle just after Vitellius had been reinforced. Historians believe he did this out of fear that with the passage of time he would lose the support of his army, and would be left without even the opportunity to fight.

The engagement, known as the First Battle of Bedriacum, took place on April 14. Otho's armies were defeated. It was an exceptionally bloody affair in which as many as 40,000 men died. The description of the aftermath given by Tacitus is grim. Neither Vitellius nor Otho were present when the engagement took place, for Vitellius was still marching in Gaul and Otho was at his headquarters south of the Po.

When Otho's armies were defeated, the emperor was disheartened. Even news that the bulk of the Moesian legions had reached Aquileia and the urging of his commanders could not lift Otho's spirits. It is possible, as some have suggested, that he was unwilling to engage in more civil war, and instead chose to commit suicide, which he did approximately two days later, on April 16 or 17 (opinions vary).

After the fact, Verginius Rufus was once again enjoined by the soldiers to become their candidate for emperor. This demand may have been made by soldiers from both armies, since Vitellius was still in Gaul marching south when the battle was fought. But Rufus, under threat of death should he refuse, did just that, and made a narrow escape back to Rome. Three days later, on April 19, Vitellius was hailed emperor by the senate.

NUMISMATIC NOTE: The coinage of Otho's reign is considerably different from that of Galba. Not only did Otho strike only as Augustus, but he struck Imperial coins only at Rome. Thus, we find none of the curious provincial styles so commonly observed on the issues of Galba. The relative brevity of his reign — approximately three months — also assured that there was no noticeable evolution of style. Also, his reign establishes a *terminus ante quem* for the transfer of precious metal coin production from Lugdunum to Rome, since no coins could have been struck for Otho had the facilities still been located at Lugdunum.

Otho's Imperial coinage consists entirely of aurei and denarii, for he did not strike any Imperial bronzes. Considering the vast output of asses, dupondii and sestertii by Galba and Nero, Otho's decision to not strike bronzes is understandable. However, the impressive issues of Galba must have been a persistent and disconcerting reminder of the man he had overthrown.

The issues can be divided into two major groups, depending on whether the office of Pontifex Maximus is indicated. Since he received that title on March 9, coins bearing PONT MAX (as the reverse inscription) must be dated to the period March 9 through mid-April. It is worth noting that Otho is never shown wearing a laurel wreath on his Imperial coinage, thus allowing us to fully appreciate the curly locks of his wig.

VITELLIUS A.D. 69

IMPERATOR, A.D. 69

SON OF LUCIUS VITELLIUS
FATHER OF PETRONIANUS, VITELLIUS GERMANICUS AND VITELLIA

Aulus Vitellius, A.D. 15(?)–69. Few of Rome's emperors have been as unsuited for the demands of the office as Vitellius. What little importance he enjoyed in Rome before his principate was due entirely to the achievements of his father, the consul Lucius Vitellius. Indeed, even his rise to supreme power was due to his lack of redeeming qualities, combined with a quirk of fate.

The ancient biographers are quite hostile to Vitellius, and speak almost exclusively of his faults, which included a tendency to steal and embezzle when he held posts that allowed such opportunities. They also tell us much of his gluttony at the dinner table, suggesting he spent some nine million sestertii on banquets during his brief reign. At one such gathering, we are told, 2,000 fish and 7,000 birds were served to the guests.

Historians are uncertain when Vitellius was born, variously citing A.D. 12, 14 or 15. Suetonius tells us he was born only a month or two after Tiberius was hailed emperor in 14, but many historians prefer 15. Because his father was the most renowned politician in Rome, Vitellius enjoyed a decadent youth. However, the success of his equestrian family in recent decades was not without a price, for his father owed his success to his gilded tongue and his uncommon skill of flattery.

One consequence for his son, the future emperor Vitellius, was that during the better part of his teenage years he served in the troop of male prostitutes assembled by Tiberius for his enjoyment on Capri. While serving in that capacity, he earned the nickname *spintria*, meaning "sexual invert," or more accurately, a prostitute who practices sodomy. Suetonius tells us this nickname clung to him for the rest of his life.

Vitellius had inherited his father's skill for flattery, and was on friendly terms with Caligula, with whom he must have become acquainted on Capri. Later, Vitellius was crippled in one thigh when he was run down by a chariot driven by Caligula who, Suetonius tells us, admired Vitellius for his skills as a charioteer. Claudius admired Vitellius' skill in dice — an avocation that Claudius knew well, having himself penned a book on the subject. Claudius was especially favorable to Vitelius' family, for the father, Lucius Vitellius, received the highest possible honors, and the future emperor Vitellius and his brother (named Lucius Vitellius), served as co-consuls in 48.

After enjoying the favor of the previous three emperors, Vitellius had become quite addicted to vice and gluttony in the manner of those close to the Imperial household. As such, he became an admirer of Nero (whom he accompanied on his singing tours), who appointed him governor of Africa from 55 to 57.

After a relatively undistinguished career, Vitellius was appointed by Galba as governor of Lower Germany in November or December of 68. We are told he won this position not out of merit, but rather for his lack of it, for Galba did not want a man of substance in a position that could endanger his principate. However, fate intervened in a manner such that Galba's caution proved to be his undoing.

When Vitellius had been headquartered at his new post in Cologne about a month, the legions under his command revolted against Galba, for they felt spurned for not having received a bonus for their earlier defeat of Vindex. The soldiers acknowledged that Vitellius did not have great courage or military experience, but he was convenient, and he had endeared himself to even the lowliest of soldier by readily offering a hearty embrace.

News of this revolt was dispatched from Trier and soon arrived in Rome. This contributed to the sequence of events that caused the murder of Galba on January 15. Galba's successor, Otho, gained the allegiance of the legions in Egypt, Africa, the Euphrates and the Danube. However, Vitellius had his seven German legions, and they would prove sufficient to dislodge Otho. The fact that the circumstances of his soldiers's rebellion had changed (for the man against whom they rebelled, Galba, was dead) mattered little to the soldiers, and Vitellius had neither the courage nor the desire to bring his unlawful act to an end.

Vitellius sent the bulk of his army south under the joint command of Aulus Caecina Alienus and Fabius Valens, the flamboyant soldier who had gained his position by murdering his own commander Fonteius Capito, the feeble old man Galba had appointed governor of Upper Germany in place of Verginius Rufus. During this period a series of negotiations and assassination attempts were made by both rivals, and it became clear that more civil war would be required to determine the outcome.

In the meantime, Vitellius stayed behind to raise troops for the upcoming war, and managed to gain the support of legions in Gaul and Britain. Caecina and Valens led their legions across the Alps, the former via Switzerland, the latter through France. The two armies joined near Cremona on the north bank of the Po River

Since the two armies of Vitellius marched at such a rapid pace (seemingly in competition with each other to arrive first), Otho found himself in a difficult position. In late March and early April fighting between the Vitellians and Othonians occurred on numerous occasions in southern Gaul and in northern Italy. Meanwhile, Vitellius had only just made his way into northern Gaul as hostilities began to escalate.

On April 14, at Bedriacum, some 22 miles from the city of Cremona, Otho forced a pitched battle out of fear that his legions would defect before the bulk of his reinforcements arrived from the Balkans. As many as 40,000 soldiers were killed by their fellow Romans at Bedriacum, and Otho committed suicide two or three days later, leaving Vitellius the victor. In a repeat of earlier history, Verginius Rufus (who was then a consul under Otho) refused the purple for a third time. This time it angered the soldiers so greatly that he barely escaped with his life.

Three days after the battle, on April 19, Vitellius was hailed Augustus by the senate. He received the news while marching south through Gaul, and celebrated it when he arrived in Lugdunum. Some 40 days after the First Battle of Bedriacum, on or about May 24, Vitellius arrived at the battle site, and proudly showed it to the soldiers who had accompanied him on his march.

Vitellius was now at the head of an army of 60,000 men, which had attached to it several times as many camp followers. He next engaged in an undisciplined march along the eastern coast of Italy, which occupied the end of May, all of June and the first half of July. We are told that he stopped frequently to enjoy local hospitality, as if on vacation. Hostilities often broke out in the ranks, and disputes with locals were no less common.

Finally, Vitellius entered Rome in July and led a splendid legionary procession through the streets, which impressed the historian Tacitus, who tells us that Vitellius was formally presented title of Augustus by the senate on July 18. One of the new emperor's first acts was to replace the existing praetorian cohorts with men from his own German legions. In the process he increased the count from 12 cohorts to 16, and doubled the size of each cohort from 500 to 1,000 men.

Rivalry among the various legions, however, was to cause even more civil war. At the beginning of July, the general Vespasian (who had been conducting the war in Judaea since 67) was hailed emperor by the legions in Judaea and Alexandria; the Syrian legions did so by the middle of the month. The situation was becoming quite confused: just as Vitellius' German legions had found a rival in Galba's Spanish legion, so had the eastern armies with Vitellius' Germans.

The eastern legions were quickly joined in their cause by the three Moesian legions that had been summoned by Otho but had not arrived in time to fight on his behalf at the First Battle of Bedriacum. Not only did they have a common bond with the eastern legions, but they had pillaged Aquileia before returning to their bases in the Balkans, and understandably feared reprisal. So, under the leadership of the commander Marcus Antonius Primus, they declared for Vespasian.

The end was already in sight for Vitellius before he had entered Rome: simultaneously, armies in the East and in the Balkans were preparing to move against the new emperor. The "coup" in the East enjoyed the support of the prefect of Egypt, Tiberius Julius Alexander and of the Syrian governor Gaius Licinius Mucianus, who had been persuaded by Vespasian's eldest son, Titus, to commit his legions to the cause.

Though Vespasian had not formally recognized Galba's principate, he did so with Otho, and it seems he was proclaimed Augustus upon learning of the latter's death. Caught in the middle was Vespasian's brother, Flavius Sabinus (who had been confirmed as city prefect of Rome by Otho) and Vespasian's youngest son, Domitian, who, though also residing in Rome, was given the rank of Caesar.

Vespasian's plan was simple, and probably was intended to minimize further bloodshed. In August he left his son Titus to finish off the war in Judaea and he moved to Alexandria, where he could seize control of the grain shipments destined for Rome. At the same time, Mucianus led his 20,000 Syrian soldiers on a slow march across Asia and the Balkans to Italy. By the time Vespasian himself arrived, the Romans would most likely have ousted Vitellius, or at the very least would have been receptive to a liberating army.

Throwing a wrench into the works, however, was the Danubian commander Primus, who prepared his renegade armies for a preemptive invasion of Italy. By October Primus launched his offensive, clashing with Vitellius' generals in northern Italy. In the end, Vitellius' leaders proved too ill, incompetent or treacherous to defend Italy, and even the fleet at

Ravenna defected. A pitched battle occurred at Bedriacum, the site of Vitellius' earlier victory against Otho.

This time Vitellius' forces (for he was not at this battle either) were defeated on October 24 and 25, at what is known as the Second Battle of Bedriacum. The remaining Vitellian armies fled to nearby Cremona, where they were captured. Even though Cremona was an Italian town, and had surrendered without offering resistance, it was sacked continuously from October 27–31 by the Danubian soldiers.

Meanwhile in Rome, the atmosphere was understandably chaotic. Even the army Vitellius had sent to protect the Appenine passes had defected to Primus at Narnia on December 17. Upon learning this, rival factions in the capital engaged in fierce street fighting, and Vitellius approached the city prefect Sabinus with an offer to abdicate in exchange for the staggering sum of one million aurei.

Though the deal was acceptable to Sabinus, it enraged the praetorian guards and the mob in Rome, which demanded Vitellius retract his offer. They took matters into their own hands, beseiging Sabinus and his supporters on the Capitoline Hill, which was set ablaze during the fight, claiming even the inviolable temple of Capitoline Jupiter. Though young Domitian escaped, his uncle Sabinus was executed.

On December 20, the Danubian legions led by Primus entered Rome, ostensibly in the name of Vespasian, and Vitellius was captured and dragged through the streets in an especially humiliating fashion. After considerable torture, he was murdered in the Forum and his corpse tossed into the Tiber. The senate then hailed Vespasian emperor in place of Vitellius. Primus' soldiers plundered the city and massacred their opponents before the arrival of Mucianus and his Syrian legions on the following day.

NUMISMATIC NOTE: Coins were struck in the name of Vitellius at mints in Spain (probably Tarraco), Gaul (probably Lugdunum) and Rome. The first two began to strike while Vitellius was Imperator and opposed to Otho, who himself only used the Rome mint. As would be expected, Rome began to strike for Vitellius only after Otho was overthrown and Vitellius was hailed Augustus by the senate. Since Vitellius resumed coining bronzes at Rome, it perhaps comes as no surprise that some of Galba's reverse dies were used by Vitellius.

The titulature in Vitellius' coin inscriptions is useful for establishing an internal chronology for the Rome mint issues. The title Germanicus is shortened in three successive phases (GERMANICVS; GERMAN; and GERMA, GERM or GER), with the longer renderings being earlier in the sequence. Vitellius' provincial coinage is limited to rare emissions for the federation *(koinon)* of Macedon and Alexandria.

LUCIUS VITELLIUS

FATHER OF VITELLIUS
GRANDFATHER OF PETRONIANUS, VITELLIUS GERMANICUS AND VITELLIA

Lucius Vitellius, lifespan uncertain. Lucius Vitellius was one of four sons born to Publius Vitellius, a knight from Luceria (not Nuceria, as is often cited). His father had a successful career as a steward (procurator) of the emperor Augustus, which paved the way for his sons. The most famous of his sons was Lucius Vitellius, who is considered the most successful politician of the age.

Though during his lifetime Lucius Vitellius was hailed as a model of integrity, according to Tacitus he was held by later generations ". . . to be an example of the ignominy that goes with sycophancy." His career was advanced principally through his connection to the ruling house of Augustus, and by the reign of Claudius he had distinguished himself remarkably. The very fact that he was able to survive the tyranny of Caligula (for whom he instituted the practice of his worship as a god) and maintained good relations with Claudius — an emperor who perceived senators as adversaries — speaks volumes of his talents.

As a flatterer, Lucius Vitellius had no equal. He was especially careful to attend to the needs of the Imperial women, and seems to have pursued Antonia, the mother of Germanicus, Livilla and Claudius. Though some sources suggest he actually married Antonia, this is unlikely for other sources insist she refused to remarry after the death of Nero Claudius Drusus.

When entering the Imperial presence Lucius Vitellius would always uncover his head, avert his gaze, and prostrate himself. Suetonius also tells us he begged the indulgence of Messalina, the third wife of Claudius, to remove her shoes, after which he occasionally kissed them. Toward the end of his life and career, he was among the leading proponents of Claudius' final marriage to Agrippina Junior.

Suetonius tells us that his sole embarrassment — beyond the shameless flattery — was a scandalous affair he had with a freedwoman ". . . whose spittle he would actually mix with honey and use not just secretly or rarely, but every day, quite openly, as a lotion for his neck and throat."

Of Lucius Vitellius' three brothers, one was renowned for his luxurious manner of living, another for his talents as a gourmet, and a third for his friendship to Germanicus. This particular brother, Publius Vitellius, is credited by Suetonius with the arrest of Gnaeus Piso, who was later convicted of Germanicus' murder. However, his relationship with Germanicus cost him his own life, for in 32 he was forced to commit suicide by Tiberius, who implicated him in the coup planned by Sejanus.

Despite the fall of his brother Publius, Lucius Vitellius made great advances in the last few years of Tiberius' reign. His progress was due not only to his own gift for flattery, but also because he volunteered one of his two sons, Aulus Vitellius (the future emperor) for the troop of male prostitutes that served Tiberius during his self-exile on Capri.

His career was varied, for he led the Roman armies in Armenia in 18, held a consulship in 34 and served as Legate of Syria from 35 to 37, during which he deposed Pontius Pilate in Judaea. His last two consulships occurred during the reign of Claudius, in 43 and 47. During the first of these, he virtually ran the government on behalf of Claudius (who was leading the invasion of Britain), and during the latter, Claudius chose him as his colleague in the censorship. An attempt to prosecute Lucius Vitellius in 51 failed, and it is believed that he died shortly thereafter.

NUMISMATIC NOTE: All coins depicting Lucius Vitellius were struck by his son, the emperor Vitellius, and bear his son's portrait on the obverse. Three main reverse types were produced. Aurei and denarii show his portrait bust with an eagle-tipped scepter before, or depict Lucius Vitellius as a seated figure. Sestertii depicting him seated on a platform, greeting togate figures. With the exception of an issue of dual-portrait aurei from a Spanish mint, all the remaining coins seem to have been struck at Rome. It would seem likely that issues were also struck at the Gallic mint at which denarii depicting Vitellius' children were struck.

VITELLIUS GERMANICUS and VITELLIA

CHILDREN OF VITELLIUS
HALF-SIBLINGS OF PETRONIANUS
GRANDCHILDREN OF LUCIUS VITELLIUS

Vitellius Germanicus (d. A.D. 69/70), Vitellia (lifespan unknown). Of Vitellius' two children, Vitellius Germanicus and Vitellia, little is known. They were both born of the same mother, Galeria Fundana, who was Vitellius' second wife. The boy was supposedly 6 years old when his father became emperor, and according to Suetonius, ". . . had so bad a stammer that he could hardly force out a word." Nothing is heard of the girl until after her father's reign.

Vitellius was so far in debt at the time Galba appointed him governor of Lower Germany that in order to finance his journey he pawned the family jewelry and, after relocating his wife and children to an attic, rented out his villa. This, no doubt, was one of the reasons Galba appointed Vitellius, for he presumed he would be so preoccupied with gleaning money from every possible source (as he was well known for doing) that the prospect of staging a revolt would not cross his mind.

Vitellius left his family in Rome as he marched north to take up his new command. After Galba was overthrown and Vitellius himself had rebelled, his wife and children were treated well by the new emperor, Otho. When Otho died in mid-April 69, Vitellius was promptly recognized by the senate as the new emperor. His son was hurriedly taken to Lugdunum so he could be united with his father, who was still marching south from Germany. There the boy was shown to the legionaries as proof that a dynasty to replace the Julio-Claudians had been formed, and he was given the agnomen *Germanicus*.

But Vitellius' regime was short-lived, and as a result of his downfall his son was killed. While Suetonius suggests the boy perished with his father and his uncle, other sources indicate he was executed in 70 on orders of the praetorian prefect Licinius Mucianus. The girl was more fortunate, for she not only survived the civil war, but Suetonius tells us Vespasian arranged a marriage for her that proved to be a "splendid match," and provided her with a dowry and a wedding gown.

Vitellius also had another son, Petronianus, from his first wife, Petronia. The poor lad, who we are told had only one eye, died of poison long before his father ascended the throne. The poison was either voluntarily taken to cure his parricidal tendencies, or more likely, was administered by Vitellius. Suetonius makes his opinion on the matter clear: ". . . most people believed simply that Vitellius had done away with the boy."

NUMISMATIC NOTE: Though the coinage portraying Vitellius' children is generally thought to be limited to denarii and aurei, an Imperial as must be added to the tally. Though in a poor state of preservation, its style identifies it as a product of a mint in Spain. Most of the commemorative aurei and denarii of Vitellius' children were struck in Rome, although examples are known from mints in Spain and Gaul (presumably Tarraco and Lugdunum).

JULIUS CIVILIS

REBEL, A.D. 69-70

Gaius Julius Civilis, lifespan unknown. As the chief of the Batavians, a Germanic tribe that had been loosely allied with the Romans since the campaign of Nero Claudius Drusus in 12 B.C., Julius Civilis was also a Roman citizen. Civilis was lured into the civil war in the summer of 69 by Antonius Primus, who was preparing to lead his Danubian legions on an invasion of Italy. Primus encouraged Civilis to create a disturbance serious enough that Vitellius' remaining legions in Germany would be too occupied to march on Italy after his own invasion of Italy had taken place.

The request was echoed by Hordeonius Flaccus, the feeble appointee of Galba who had replaced Verginius Rufus, and was still governing from his base in Mainz (Moguntiacum). In this capacity Civilis launched a nationalist revolt in Gaul. He gathered eight cohorts of Batavian regulars, enlisted Germans from north of the Rhine, and was ready to strike.

All of his actions occurred within about a 300-mile stretch along the Rhine, roughly between Mainz and where the river empties into the North Sea. Since this was the northernmost part of Roman Gaul, it was quite far from Rome, but would prove fatal to Rome's ability to control its provinces if it was not contained.

Civilis' first move, an unexpected attack on the legionary camp at Vetera, was a failure, principally because Hordeonius was able to dispatch two legions which came to their aid. However, in the meantime Hordeonius was murdered by his own soldiers, and news had reached Germany of the Vitellian defeat at the Second Battle of Bedriacum on October 24 and 25.

By early 70, many Gallic tribes had joined Civilis' cause. Foremost among these were the Treviri under Julius Classicus and Julius Tutor (who, like Civilis, had been in the service of the emperors), and the Lingones under Julius Sabinus. Tacitus tells us that the burning of the temple of Capitoline Jupiter was especially significant to the "idle superstition of Druidism," as it signaled the imminent collapse of the Empire.

Civilis, with the assistance of Classicus, then engineered the assassination of Dillius Vocula, the legionary commander who had foiled his first attempt to take Castra Vetera. This murder was perpetrated at Novaesium (mod. Neuss), where Civilis effortlessly gained the surrender of the two legions stationed there. After executing the commanders, he forced the legionaries to take an oath to the new Gallic Empire, which may have been headquartered at Noviomagus (*mod.* Nijmegen, in The Netherlands).

This was a seemingly unprecedented event in Roman history, and one which demonstrated how little integrity remained in the German legions: they surrendered without a fight, allowed their commanders to be executed or imprisoned, and then swore allegiance to the *imperium Galliarum* which had been established by the enemy.

Civilis made a second attempt to take Castra Vetera, this time unmistakeably in the name of his Gallic separatist movement. He success at Novaesium must have stricken sufficient fear into the members of Legion XV Primigenia that they quickly surrendered, only to be massacred by the German auxiliaries. Later in his campaign Civilis captured a flotilla of 24 ships, and in concert with his foot soldiers and cavalry, destroyed all legionary fortifications along the Rhine as far south as Mainz.

Most all of this transpired just after Vespasian secured power in Rome. In 70, the new emperor sent Quintus Petillius Cerialis and Annius Gallus to end the Gallic revolt. Sharing the command in a junior capacity was the emperor's youngest son, Domitian, then aged 18. Cerialis and Domitian established themselves at Trier, after which they defeated Civilis at Rigodulum. A few minor setbacks then followed, but Civilis was finally defeated at Vetera, where the rebel was forced to surrender late in 70. Civilis' subsequent fate is unknown.

NUMISMATIC NOTE: The attribution of coinage to the revolt of Julius Civilis is based on several factors, including the assumption that he would require coinage to pay his soldiers. Determining which of the "anonymous" coinages of this period belong to Civilis is a more difficult matter. The authors of RIC attribute five extremely rare issues — four denarii and one aureus — to Civilis.

Of the greatest interest are denarii honoring Legio XV Primigenia, which Civilis captured at Castra Vetera and then allowed his soldiers to butcher. (The legion was cashiered in 70.) It is possible that Civilis struck coins with the name of the legion in order to trumpet his accomplishment. However, other authorities believe the issue was struck earlier in support of Vitellius, for the auxiliaries of this dishonored legion were important to his victory at the First Battle of Bedriacum. Alternatively, it could have been struck to honor the heroes of the legion and its great leader Verginius Rufus, who had defeated Vindex at the outset of the civil war. The end of the war against Civilis is celebrated on a rare sestertius of Vespasian inscribed SIGNIS RECEPTIS and depicting a flying Victory offering to Vespasian a legionary eagle (*aquila*) — presumably of the captured XV Primigenia.

CHAPTER FOUR

The Flavians
A.D. 69–96

The destructive Civil War of 68–69 ended with the rebellion and accession of Vespasian, a man of relatively humble origins who founded a dynasty of his own. This was an important consideration for any candidate to the throne (as Vespasian's predecessor, Vitellius, recognized). The Romans had lived for nearly a century under the ruling house of the Julio-Claudians. Heirs, if anything, meant stability.

Stable succession was one of the principal reasons Vespasian hailed his two sons as Caesars, and immediately struck coins portraying them as heirs to the throne. Further, Vespasian went to great lengths to demonstrate his ties with the Julio-Claudians, both literally and spiritually. He celebrated the glories of the Augustan age, which began at the Battle of Actium almost exactly a century before his own accession. The new emperor made full use of the propaganda value of coins by copying coin designs associated with Augustus and his descendants.

The dynasty that Vespasian founded was not terribly long-lived, but it did salvage Rome from its costly civil war and serve as a conduit between the decaying Julio-Claudian dynasty and "adoptive" emperors of the 2nd century. But it must be said that the Flavians were in some respects merely a compressed version of the Julio-Claudians, for the dynasty began on a high note and ended in disgrace.

The Flavian dynasty is neatly composed of the family lines established by two brothers, which developed separately in the first generation, but were tied together in the second generation by two marriages of second-cousins. No fewer than nine members of the Flavian family are represented on coinage, including a boy of Domitian's who died in infancy, and whose name is not recorded in the sources which have survived to the modern day.

The portraits on Flavian coins are usually well executed, though the degrees of realism or idealism vary depending on the minting facility and the period. Later in the reign of Domitian the portraits take on a much softer appearance, though not at the expense of their individualism or accuracy. The portraits of the Flavian women typically bear a striking resemblance to the emperors with whom they were associated, as was often the case in the long history of Roman coinage.

And finally, another of the great institutions of 1st Century Roman coinage, the mint at Lugdunum, ceased operation during the Flavian

The Flavians

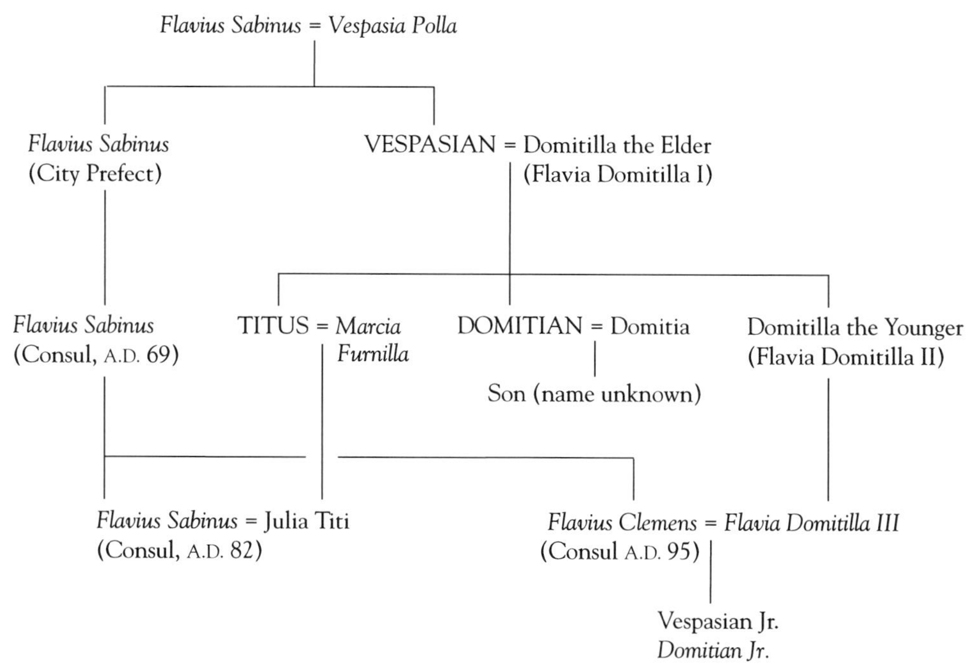

Note: Names in CAPITALS are of emperors; names in *italics* are of people not found on coinage.

dynasty, probably in about 79, but perhaps in 82. The mint at Rome had regained its role as the principal Imperial mint in the west either in 37, the first year of Caligula's reign, or more likely c. 64, during the reign of Nero (54–68).

VESPASIAN A.D. 69–79

A.D. 69–71: SOLE REIGN
(WITH TITUS AND DOMITIAN, AS CAESARS)
A.D. 71–79: SOLE REIGN
(WITH TITUS AS IMPERATOR;
DOMITIAN, AS CAESAR)

HUSBAND OF DOMITILLA THE ELDER
FATHER OF TITUS, DOMITIAN, AND DOMITILLA THE YOUNGER
FATHER-IN-LAW OF DOMITIA
GRANDFATHER OF JULIA TITI
GREAT-GRANDFATHER OF VESPASIAN JUNIOR

Titus Flavius Vespasianus, A.D. 9–79. With Vespasian we find a clean break from the Julio-Claudians and their revolutionary successors, for he was a simple man of modest family background. Indeed, the ancient historians speak principally of his humble lifestyle, his affability, and his sharp sense of humor as opposed to vices and moral bankruptcy, which is principally what we learn of the Julio-Claudians.

Vespasian was born at Reate, in Sabine country not far from Rome, with his father having been the first man in the family to amass a small fortune. This he did as a tax collector in Asia, and later as a banker in the Helvetian territory (mod. Switzerland). His mother's family was of equestrian rank, and Vespasian's maternal uncle entered the senate and held a praetorship.

Vespasian's brother, Flavius Sabinus, led a distinguished career, while the future emperor held somewhat undistinguished and predictable posts. He was military tribune in Thrace in 27, then quaestor on Crete and aedile in 38. Finally, he became praetor under Caligula in 40.

However, it was not until his family came to enjoy the patronage of Claudius' freedman, Narcissus, that his career took off. In 43 he gained command of Legio II Augusta in Claudius' invasion of Britain. In that campaign he was closely associated with the emperor and is said to have fought some 30 battles and taken 20 cities as he reduced most of the southern part of Britain and took the Isle of Wight. For all of this, Vespasian was awarded triumphal ornaments and two priesthoods, and later was renowned enough to hold the consulship in 51.

Thereafter he falls into relative obscurity, for he and his brother owed their prominence to Narcissus, and consequently came under the suspicion of Agrippina Junior, the wife of Claudius. Thus, it is not until later in the reign of Nero that we hear much of Vespasian again. In about 63 he was proconsul of Africa, but did not abuse his position for financial gain, and consequently was spared bankruptcy only by a loan from his brother. In 66 he was part of Nero's entourage, travelling with him on his tour of Greece. However, Vespasian offended Nero by falling asleep at one of his singing performances, and as a result was expelled from the emperor's entourage.

Since it was the habit of Nero to appoint governors and generals in the provinces who were of no extraordinary merit, he gave Vespasian command of three legions in 66, with which he was to direct the war in Judaea that is commonly known as the First Revolt or the Jewish War. In February of 67, Vespasian was appointed governor of Judaea. The future emperor conducted a difficult campaign, but by mid-68, when Nero was overthrown and replaced as emperor by Galba, he had pacified most of Judaea.

During the next year, from mid-68 to mid-69, Vespasian continued to direct the war in Judaea as the West became embroiled in civil war. Three successive emperors — Nero, Galba and Otho — fell in only 10 months. By mid-69 an unsavory character named Vitellius was in command, and Vespasian realized now was the time to act.

So, on July 1, presumably upon learning of Otho's defeat and suicide, his revolt began. Vespasian was hailed emperor by the legions in Alexandria under command of the prefect Tiberius Julius Alexander. Two days later, on July 3, Vespasian was hailed by his own legions in Judaea, and by mid-July (shortly before Vitellius entered Rome), he was also acclaimed by the legions in Syria, which were under the command of the governor, Gaius Licinius Mucianus. Though the senate did not officially recognize his principate until December 21, 69, Vespasian always considered July 1, when the soldiers hailed him emperor, to be his date of accession. This was a serious annoyance to the senate, but helped maintain his popularity with the soldiers.

Not only did Vespasian have excellent qualifications for the post, but he also had two sons as heirs, and a brother who was city prefect in Rome. Furthermore, there were many omens favorable to his accession, including one in which a dog brought a severed hand to his breakfast table, and another more ancient superstition that held that at about this time the rulers of the world would come from Judaea.

Vespasian based his revolt in Antioch and instructed Mucianus to lead 20,000 of his soldiers on a slow march to Italy. While in Antioch, Vespasian struck the first coins of his as-yet-unofficial reign. It was hoped that by the time Mucianus approached Rome, Vitellius would have been overthrown, or at the very least, would have lost popularity. Vespasian left his eldest son, Titus, in charge of the Judaean campaign (for Jerusalem had not yet been taken) so that he himself could move to Alexandria and take control of the grain supply, which was vital to Rome.

Meanwhile, legions in Spain and the Balkans supported Vespasian's claim. In the process, however, he did gain an unwanted ally in Marcus Antonius Primus, a commander who managed to gain control of several legions in Pannonia and Moesia. To give some legitimacy to what was little more than a personal adventure, Primus decided to act in the name of Vespasian. However, in his lust for glory, Primus created an opportunity for a Sarmatian invasion of Moesia, and sparked a nationalist rebellion in Gaul and Germany led by the Batavian prince Julius Civilis.

By October, Primus had invaded Italy with five legions and had outmaneuvered the Vitellian forces that had been left to defend northern Italy. After defeating the Vitellians decisively at the Second Battle of Bedriacum on October 24 and 25 of 69, Primus allowed his soldiers to plunder nearby Cremona for four successive days. Thereafter, Primus marched south to Rome, with the legions of Mucianus (who was delayed in Moesia repelling the Sarmatian invasion) not far behind.

Though Vitellius was still popular in the capital, his odds of survival diminished daily. They took a critical turn on December 17, when Primus met the Vitellian army at Narnia, some 40 miles outside Rome. Before a battle erupted, Primus convinced the Vitellians to defect, which left him a clear path to Rome. When news of the defection reached Rome, anarchy broke out in the streets and Vitellius approached the city prefect Flavius Sabinus (the brother of Vespasian) with an offer to abdicate.

Though acceptable to both men, the praetorian guards and the mob in Rome were incensed by the plan, and events in Rome moved violently and rapidly. Not only were Sabinus and many of his supporters besieged on the Capitoline Hill and killed, but Vitellius himself was brutally murdered shortly thereafter, on the 20th of December. Either on that day or the following, Primus and his Danubian legions entered Rome in the name of Vespasian. The plundering and massacre that ensued was halted only when the Syrian legions of Mucianus arrived the next day and ousted Primus.

While all these events were unfolding, Vespasian remained in Alexandria. Indeed, he stayed there for another six months or so awaiting the end of the Judaean war (then being directed by Titus), but it dragged on. Unable to wait any longer, Vespasian departed Egypt in the summer of 70 via ship to Italy. During this period, Mucianus continued to hold Rome for the emperor and reduced the size of the praetorian guard, which had been greatly enlarged by Vitellius.

The new emperor landed at the Italian port of Brundisium and made his way to Rome by land. While *en route*, the Judaean war ended (in September, though Masada held out until 73). Vespasian arrived in Rome in

October of 70, some 15 months after he had been hailed by his soldiers, and more than nine months after the senate had formally recognized his regime.

But even after Vespasian had secured power in Rome, he still had to contend with the nationalist revolt led by Julius Civilis in Gaul and Germany. The rebellion had been raging for about a year, and had cost Rome every legionary outpost north of Mainz. Vespasian appointed Quintus Petillius Cerialis as the new governor of Lower Germany, the province in which Civilis' revolt was based. Sharing command of an army with Annius Gallus and Vespasian's 18-year-old son, Domitian, Cerialis set out to crush Civilis. The operation was over quickly, and Gaul and the two Germanies were restored to Rome late in 70.

Everything was largely under control now, and the healing process could begin. Suetonius tells us that Vespasian estimated he would need 400,000,000 aurei to get the Empire back on solid footing. With such significant fiscal demands, he soon acquired a reputation for greed and stinginess — qualities that may have been inborn to his personality, but that were exacerbated by the financial crisis of the Empire. He raised money in every possible way, even charging entrance fees to public restrooms.

Vespasian shamelessly and openly sold pardons to convicted criminals, and took bribes from politicians and from those who desired posts in government. It is said that he purposely solicited bribes from the greediest applicants, knowing they would steal the most money, thus assuring there were would be more money for Vespasian to acquire when he charged them with extortion. Suetonius tells us this was so common a practice with Vespasian that these appointees were nicknamed "sponges" because he "... put them in to soak, only to squeeze them dry later." However, it must be said that through such extreme measures, Vespasian restored the fiscal health of the Empire. Furthermore, he was not stingy in how he spent the money, frequently spreading it among the most unfortunate.

Vespasian had a fairly static routine when in Rome. He rose early and worked hard, though he was certain to reserve sufficient time each day for pleasurable activities. He left much of the day-to-day operation of government to others; at first to Mucianus, but soon thereafter to his son, Titus. He may also be credited with introducing men of talent into important government posts, regardless of their family status.

Vespasian also added to the size of the Empire by annexing Commagene in 72, and later by annexing northern England and southern Scotland, and bringing order to Wales. Leading the British expeditions were Gnaeus Julius Agricola, the father-in-law of the historian Tacitus. Another famous governor who served under Vespasian was Marcus Ulpius Trajanus, the father of Trajan, the future emperor. He served with distinction in the

East, and dissuaded the Parthians from invading Syria when Vespasian refused to help them repel an invasion of their kingdom by the Alans.

Vespasian was responsible for much building in the West, including a new temple of Capitoline Jupiter, the temple of Peace in the Forum, and the Colosseum in Rome (the Amphitheatrum Flavium), which he began to build in 71 but which was incomplete at his death. Vespasian died of fever at a family villa in the Sabine country outside Rome on June 24, 79. Just as one might expect of this hardy man, he requested to be propped up on his feet just before he expired, for he believed that an emperor should die standing.

NUMISMATIC NOTE: The coinage of Vespasian begins with two series of coins struck in Judaea while he served as governor there under Nero. After his bid for the throne became official, Vespasian first struck coins at Antioch and Alexandria as he awaited the downfall of Vitellius in Rome. Throughout his principate Vespasian struck coins not only for himself, but also for his two sons, both of whom held the rank of Caesar

He struck a great many denarii and aurei in the East, principally at Antioch and Ephesus. The style of these pieces is remarkably fine, and they are easy to distinguish from the products of Rome and other western mints. Some of the coins attributed to Antioch, however, are better given to Alexandria, where Vespasian was in residence while awaiting the downfall of Vitellius. Two key diagnostics on these coins are the "scalloped" truncation of Vespasian's bust and the unusual letter G at the end of AVG, which appears more like a Sigma.

Since Vespasian emerged victorious from the civil war which began virtually on the centennial of the Battle of Actium, it comes as no surprise that many of his coin designs are inspired by Augustan prototypes. This had specific context because the civil war brought about the extinction of the Julio-Claudian dynasty, and Vespasian wanted to demonstrate some continuity for the dynasty he had established in its place. Also of interest are the denarii (or cistophori) that were countermarked during Vespasian's principate, probably at Ephesus in the 70s. These countermarks — usually applied to coins of older vintage — take the form of a sunken rectangle containing the raised letters IMP. VES (or similar), often in ligature.

DOMITILLA THE ELDER

Wife of Vespasian
Mother of Titus, Domitian, and Domitilla the Younger
Mother-in-law of Domitia
Grandmother of Julia Titi
Great-grandmother of Vespasian Junior

Flavia Domitilla (I), d. before A.D. 69. A woman of humble origins, Domitilla the Elder had only Latin citizenship at birth. Suetonius tells us she gained Roman citizenship only after her father, a quaestor's clerk from Ferentium, argued on her behalf before an arbitration board.

Though we have virtually no further details of her life or marriage, we do know that Domitilla married Vespasian in 39 or 40, and bore Vespasian two sons, Titus and Domitian, and a homonymous daughter. Coins were issued in the names of all three of these children. Both Domitilla and her daughter died sometime before Vespasian held a magistracy.

Prior to their marriage, Vespasian had as a mistress a freedwoman and secretary of Antonia named Caenis, and Domitilla was in a relationship with an African knight from Sabrata to whom she was possibly a slave, or "bond woman." According to Suetonius, when Domitilla died, Vespasian renewed his association with Caenis, ". . . who remained his wife in all but name even when he became emperor." After Caenis died, Vespasian continued to have relations with other mistresses on a daily basis.

Numismatic Note: Since Domitilla the Elder was not consecrated or hailed Augusta, it must be assumed that the aurei and denarii bearing the bust of a young woman identified as DIVA DOMITILLA AVGVSTA belong to her daughter, Domitilla the Younger (the sister of Titus and Domitian). As such, it would appear that there are no portrait coins of the wife of Vespasian, and that only the carpentum sestertii struck during the reign of Titus are attributable to her. The reverse inscriptions (which name the 8th consulship of Titus) date the coins to 80–81.

DOMITILLA THE YOUNGER

AUGUSTA: POSTHUMOUSLY

DAUGHTER OF VESPASIAN AND DOMITILLA THE ELDER
SISTER OF TITUS AND DOMITIAN
GRANDMOTHER OF VESPASIAN JUNIOR
AUNT (POSTHUMOUSLY) OF JULIA TITI

Flavia Domitilla (II), d. before A.D. 69. Like her mother, Domitilla the Younger died before Vespasian ascended the throne in 69. Unlike her mother, however, she was consecrated. Of this point we are certain, but it is of some interest that Domitilla the Younger also received the title of Augusta posthumously, for it accompanies the DIVA on her coin inscriptions. This escaped the attention of ancient sources such as Tacitus, Suetonius and Dio Cassius.

Little is known of Domitilla the Younger, except that she gave birth to at least one child, a daughter, who bore the same name as her mother and grandmother, and is thus called Domitilla III by historians. This youngest Domitilla married Flavius Clemens, who was one of two grandsons of Flavius Sabinus, the brother of Vespasian. Domitilla III and her husband had several children, one of whom was the unfortunate Vespasian Junior, who was adopted by and then murdered by Domitian.

NUMISMATIC NOTE: The attribution of coinage with the name Domitilla remains, unnecessarily, a point of confusion among numismatists. Most sources, including RIC, give all such coinage to Domitilla the Elder, the wife of Vespasian. Other sources, such as Cohen, apportion the carpentum sestertii to Domitilla the Younger. However, they are best attributed as follows: aurei and denarii inscribed DIVA DOMITILLA AVGVSTA belong to Domitilla the Younger, and the carpentum sestertii inscribed MEMORIAE DOMITILLAE (or simply DOMITILLA) belong to her mother, Domitilla the Elder.

Since the series of aurei and denarii herein attributed to Domitilla the Younger bear no reverse inscription that precisely dates them, they have traditionally been given to the reign of Titus, when the dated carpentum sestertii and the divi coinage of Vespasian were struck. However, metrological evidence argues for the reign of Domitian — specifically to c. 82 to 83, after his monetary reform of 82. (See I. Carradice, *Coinage and Finances in the Reign of Domitian*, A.D. 81–96, BARIS 178, Oxford, 1983, pp. 16–22.)

In addition to the metrological evidence, there are other aspects of the aurei and denarii that call for their association with Domitian's principate. Perhaps foremost is the fact that Domitian's facial features can be seen so clearly in Domitilla's portrait. This argument is especially valid when the coins of Julia Titi are taken in comparison, for her facial features are strongly assimilated with those of Titus. Also, it seems likely that Domitilla the Younger was hailed Augusta (posthumously) at the same time that Domitian's wife Domitia was given that title. Since Domitia seems to have been hailed in 82, and that date corresponds with the metrological and iconographical evidence already mentioned, the conclusion seems probable that these coins are best given to Domitilla the Younger.

TITUS A.D. 79–81

A.D. 69–71: CAESAR
(UNDER VESPASIAN, WITH DOMITIAN)
A.D. 71–79: IMPERATOR
(UNDER VESPASIAN; DOMITIAN, AS CAESAR)
A.D. 79–81: SOLE REIGN
(WITH DOMITIAN, AS CAESAR)

SON OF VESPASIAN AND DOMITILLA THE ELDER
BROTHER OF DOMITIAN AND DOMITILLA THE YOUNGER
FATHER OF JULIA TITI
GREAT-UNCLE OF VESPASIAN JUNIOR

Titus Flavius Vespasianus, A.D. 39–81. Though he was destined to rule only about 27 months, Titus was the ideal successor to his father, for the moral character of both men was well-suited for supreme power. His rave review by Suetonius as the "delight and darling of the human race," may have been well-deserved, but so generous a review is tempered by Dio Cassius, who queried whether he would have been judged in so positive a light had he ruled longer.

Because of the great favor his father and uncle enjoyed during the regime of Claudius (41–54), Titus was brought up at court along with the emperor's son, Britannicus, with whom he shared the same teachers and curriculum. They became very close friends, and Titus was seated near him at the fateful dinner at which Britannicus was poisoned. Having shared some of the poisoned wine from his friend's cup, Titus himself fell seriously ill as a result.

Suetonius relates a memorable story about the early life of Titus: ". . . when one day Claudius' freedman Narcissus called in a physiognomist to examine Britannicus' features and prophesy his future, he was told most emphatically that Britannicus would never succeed his father, whereas Titus (who happened to be present) would achieve that distinction."

Titus was given the same name as his father, but was called by his praenomen, Titus. He had two siblings, a sister named Flavia Domitilla

(Domitilla the Younger) who died while still a young woman, and a brother, Domitian, who was 12 years his junior. Titus was married twice, the first time to Arrecina Tertulla, the daughter of one of Caligula's praetorian prefects, and later to Marcia Furnilla. Both women bore him a daughter named Julia, though only the one from the second marriage (who is usually called Julia Titi), is represented on coinage.

The career of Titus was accelerated in his 27th year, when he joined his father in conducting the war in Judaea, of which the emperor Nero had given Vespasian command in 66. Though Titus assisted his father in military and diplomatic capacities throughout the campaign, he was given sole command after mid-69, when Vespasian became occupied with the details of his rebellion against Vitellius. At this time, both Titus and his younger brother, Domitian (who remained in Rome), were hailed Caesars by their father.

Titus finished the war in Judaea by taking Jerusalem late in 70, and consequently was hailed Imperator by his soldiers. Because of the suspicion aroused by the extreme loyalty of his soldiers, Titus sailed at once for Italy, arriving early in 71. Upon reaching Rome he surprised his father (who was not expecting him), saying "Here I am, father, here I am!" Together, he and his father celebrated the Judaean triumph, with young Domitian at their side.

Though both Titus and Domitian were named as heirs from the very outset of Vespasian's revolt, it was Titus in whom Vespasian had firmly placed his hopes for succession. Indeed, once Titus was in Rome, he took over command of the praetorian guards from Mucianus, the former governor of Syria who had held that post since he occupied Rome for Vespasian in December of 69.

During his tenure as Caesar and Imperator, collectively from 69 to 79, Titus was not very popular. Indeed, his considerable intellectual and physical attributes, as well as his pleasant singing voice, served as haunting reminders of the principate of Nero. Also adding to his unpopularity was his ruthless suppression of the two leaders of a plot against his father, and his love affair with the princess Berenice, whom he had met in Judaea. Berenice lived in Rome from about 75 to 79, and was only reluctantly sent away by Titus at the insistence of Vespasian, who died shortly thereafter, on June 23 of 79.

Titus succeeded his father smoothly, and his brief reign was marked with a host of accomplishments and some unfortunate natural disasters. The most significant of the latter was the eruption of Mount Vesuvius on August 24, 79. Much of the Bay of Naples was coated with its emissions, and the cities of Pompeii and Herculaneum were destroyed completely. A serious fire and outbreak of the plague also occurred in Rome in the following year. The fire was severe, causing the destruction of the newly rebuilt

Temple of Jupiter Capitolinus, the Temples of Isis and Serapis, and many other important structures.

One of the positive events was the completion and dedication of the Colosseum in Rome (the Amphitheatrum Flavium) in June of 80. It is estimated that 50,000 could be seated in the amphitheater, which ever since Titus' reign has been an enduring symbol of Rome.

The unpopularity Titus suffered prior to his accession was reversed during his principate. His relations with the senate were cordial, for he refused to put any of them to death or to confiscate property. Perhaps the most famous story of Titus concerns his generous spirit. We are told that at dinner one night he realized that he had done no good deed during that day, at which point he lamented, "Friends, I have lost a day."

While only about three months away from his 42nd birthday, Titus died on September 13, 81, of fever in the very same country home where his father had died slightly more than two years before. Though his relationship with Domitian was certainly strained, it is unlikely that Titus died of poison administered by Domitian, as is sometimes alleged.

For all the good Titus had done for the state and the people of Rome, he was not entirely guilt-free, for on his deathbed he is said to have uttered the words "I have made but one mistake." Historians have long debated what he meant by this, but to no avail. Perhaps it was his regret for having ended his relationship with the princess Berenice at the insistence of his father and public clamor. Alternatively, it may have involved his unfulfilling relationship with Domitian, or possibly the adulterous affair he was alleged to have had with his brother's wife, Domitia. The truth, regrettably, will never be known.

NUMISMATIC NOTE: Titus first had coins struck in his name by his father Vespasian, who did so both at Imperial mints and in the provinces from 69 to 79. Thereafter, Titus became emperor and struck coinages in his own name, but for a much briefer period, from 79 to 81. During his tenure Titus also struck coins in the name of his younger brother Domitian (who retained the rank of Caesar throughout), his daughter, and his deceased mother and father.

Also of interest is a series of 'restoration' coins Titus struck with the designs of various Julio-Claudian bronzes, all of which must have been familiar to the people. Not only was this series in line with Flavian dynastic propaganda, but it also testifies to the staying power of æs coinage in commerce, for the types honored would have been in circulation for 40 to 70 years. Titus honored ten different issuers with more than 60 varieties recorded; his brother continued the series, but on a more modest scale.

Titus' most famous issue, however, is his sestertius which depicts the colosseum and which commemorates its dedication in June of 80 — an event followed by 100 days of celebration. The colosseum sestertii are dated by the inscription COS VIII to the period January 1, 80 through his death in September, 81. Gold coins with the reddish "boscoreale" toning were essentially created during Titus' reign. The coins of this famous cache acquired their distinctive tone from centuries of burial in the ashes issued from Mount Vesuvius, which erupted in the summer of 79.

JULIA TITI

AUGUSTA, C. 79–90/91

DAUGHTER OF TITUS
NIECE OF DOMITIAN AND DOMITILLA THE YOUNGER
GRANDDAUGHTER OF VESPASIAN AND
DOMITILLA THE ELDER

Flavia Julia, A.D. 64/65–90/91. Julia Titi was born to Titus and his second wife, Marcia Furnilla, just before they divorced. She had an older half-sister, also named Julia, who was born to Titus' first wife, Arrecina Tertulla, and who is not represented on coinage. Shortly after the death of her grandfather Vespasian, and the accession of her father, Titus, Julia Titi was given the title of Augusta.

Her father had taken a strong personal interest in her marriage, for she figured prominently into the propagation of the fledgling dynasty. At first Titus tried to marry her to his younger brother, Domitian, but the latter was already married to Domitia and did not want to divorce. So, Titus arranged that she marry her second-cousin, Flavius Sabinus, one of two grandsons of Vespasian's brother (who also was named Flavius Sabinus).

This generation of the Flavian dynasty had two second-cousin marriages — one being the above-mentioned, another being between Flavius Clemens, the brother of the Flavius Sabinus, and Flavia Domitilla III, the homonymous granddaughter of Domitilla, the wife of Vespasian. This Domitilla, the third in the family line, was the first cousin of Julia Titi, and the mother of Vespasian Junior, the unfortunate lad who was half-heartedly adopted by Domitian.

Though already married to Flavius Sabinus, Julia Titi engaged in an illicit love-affair with her uncle, Domitian, the man who had refused to marry her the first time around. The affair had begun while Titus was still alive, but only came to public attention after Domitian divorced and exiled his own wife, Domitia, in c. 83. Thereafter, he openly lived with Julia Titi, behaving in all manners as if they were husband and wife.

In about 84, Domitian's attachment became so strong that he executed Julia Titi's husband, Flavius Sabinus, on the flimsy pretext that a herald had mistakenly declared him emperor instead of consul (the post to which he had been elected jointly with Domitian in 82). Julia died either in 90 or 91 while attempting to abort a child that presumably was fathered by Domitian. The emperor was devastated at her passing, and in 91 consecrated her. Suetonius tells us that after Domitian was murdered, his ashes were mixed with those of his beloved Julia Titi.

Numismatic Note: Though by no means common, the coinage issued in the name of Julia Titi is extensive and was struck over a long period. The first issues (limited to denarii and dupondii) occur under Titus, and celebrate her being hailed Augusta. Later issues were struck by Domitian, both during her lifetime and after her deification. The first issue under Domitian (c. 81 to 82) is of aurei featuring her bust paired with her deified father. Other issues of aurei, denarii and cistophori were struck in her name alone, perhaps as early as 81. Her consecration coinage under Domitian is limited to a rare, undated issue of aurei and two issues of sestertii dated to 90–91 and 92–94 based on their reverse inscriptions. Some provincial æs were also struck in her name.

Some of the coinage struck by Domitian for his wife, Domitia, and his common law wife, Julia Titi, feature peacocks as reverse types. Interestingly, the bird on Domitia's coinage is shown in profile with its tail feathers folded, whereas the bird on Julia Titi coins is shown facing, with its tail in splendor.

DOMITIAN A.D. 81–96

A.D. 69–71: Caesar
(under Vespasian, with Titus)
A.D. 71–79: Caesar
(under Vespasian; Titus as Imperator)
A.D. 79–81: Caesar (under Titus)
A.D. 81–96: Sole reign

Son of Vespasian and Domitilla the Elder
Brother of Titus and Domitilla the Younger
Husband of Domitia
Father of a deified son and a daughter, names unknown
Uncle of Julia Titi
Adoptive father and great-uncle of Vespasian Junior

Titus Flavius Domitianus, A.D. 51–96. As the last of Suetonius' famous "Twelve Caesars," Domitian occupies a precarious position in Roman history. Because of his autocratic, heavy-handed ways, he was despised by the senate, and because he increased salaries and led campaigns in person, he was loved by the army. His assassination comes as no surprise, for his regime, much like that of Commodus a century later, became increasingly despotic with the passage of time.

Domitian's upbringing was not as privileged as that of his brother, Titus, who was a dozen years his senior. While only 16 years old, Domitian got his first taste of the political and military chaos that accompanies civil war. The dangers became especially apparent when in mid-69 his father, Vespasian, was hailed emperor by the legions in the East (where he and Titus were leading the war in Judaea). Upon his father being elevated, Domitian and Titus were made Caesars. Considering Vespasian's revolt was in opposition to Vitellius — who was then in power at Rome — it was a far from secure situation for Domitian and his uncle, Flavius Sabinus, who was the city prefect of Rome.

It all came to a head in the middle of December 69, as the Danubian and Syrian legions loyal to Vespasian were advancing on Rome. Domitian and his uncle were attacked by unruly soldiers and withstood a siege in the temple of Capitoline Jupiter. Though his uncle was captured and executed, Domitian donned a disguise and fled to safety as the inviolable temple was burning to the ground. Within a day or two Vespasian had been recognized as emperor by the senate, and Domitian was out of immediate danger.

After his father arrived from the East in October of 70, Domitian was given a junior command in the campaign to end the nationalistic revolt of Julius Civilis in Gaul and Germany. The war was a quick success, and Domitian returned to Rome shortly before his brother, Titus, arrived from the east, himself having brought the war in Judaea to a conclusion. Together, in 71, the three men of the Flavian dynasty celebrated a magnificent triumph before crowds who no doubt welcomed the stability they represented to the war-torn Empire.

Throughout the next decade, however, Domitian played a minor role in government, even though the honors he received (including seven consulships) were considerable. It was clear to all that Titus was destined to inherit the throne from his father. When Vespasian died in 79, Titus was hailed emperor without opposition.

Domitian's relationship with his brother was not ideal, but certainly was not as bad as Suetonius would lead us to believe, for that historian suggests that Domitian ". . . never once stopped plotting, secretly or openly, against his brother." Most historians are equally quick to dismiss the rumors that Domitian either poisoned Titus, or took measures to expedite his death after he had fallen ill.

Even after Titus died late in 81 after ruling for 27 months, it was not entirely clear that Domitian was meant to succeed him. But we are told that Domitian took no chances, for he quickly covered the 40-plus miles from their family villa to Rome before his brother had yet died, and had the Praetorian Guards hail him emperor. As callous as this may appear, it no doubt was a practical necessity in the event any coups were in waiting. On the next day, September 14, Domitian was confirmed by the senate, and soon after had his brother (who was popular with the senate) consecrated.

Much like his brother and father, Domitian had inherited considerable talents. Even the hostile Suetonius tells us Domitian was an archer of the greatest skill, and that he was able to place an arrow between the spread fingers of a hand without error. He also inherited the work ethic and sense of responsibility that his father and brother had possessed, and which he used to better the government.

Domitian sometimes was too strict in enforcing the standards of conduct both in the government and in the private sector. In one of his more famous acts, Domitian executed four of the six Vestal Virgins: three for incest and one, the head Vestal, for her numerous love affairs. The head Vestal, named Cornilia, was buried alive, and her lovers were publicly beaten to death in the Forum. Such moral righteousness, however, demonstrates his hypocrisy, for Domitian's sex life was anything but pedestrian or moral.

Domitian married Domitia Longina while he was still in his late teens, and they remained married for about 13 years. However, he engaged in frequent affairs, and is said to have considered sex to be "bed wrestling." Most perverse, however, was his incestuous relationship with his niece, Julia Titi. After he divorced and exiled his wife in about 83, Domitian openly began to live with Julia Titi in the manner of husband and wife. Only her death in 90 or 91 from an attempted abortion ended the affair, and provided the opportunity for Domitia to re-enter the Imperial palace.

Even though Domitian left a surplus in the treasury after his death, he was not as capable as his father at managing finances, for he had to resort to heavy taxation, confiscations and debasement of the coinage to support his enterprises. Most troublesome was the fiscal drain caused by the army. But the soldiers were his strength both within and outside the Empire, so Domitian thought it best to spend his money on the army. In addition to other incentives, Domitian raised the annual pay of a legionnaire from 300 to 400 denarii.

His reign was relatively peaceful throughout the vast Empire, but was troubled by invasions along the Rhine and Danube. Though hardly a general of great repute, Domitian was the first emperor since Claudius to campaign in person while in office. During the course of his 16-year reign, Domitian led one campaign on the Rhine and three on the Danube.

The earliest campaign, in 83, was against a Germanic people called the Chatti, who lived on the far side of the Rhine. Two years later, a more serious war broke out on the Danubian front, where Romans battled Dacians led by the king Decebalus. The costly war raged from 85 to 88, only to be solved by diplomacy so that the Romans could fight the Quadi and Marcomanni on the Upper Danube. Later still, Domitian waged war against the Sarmatians on at least one occasion. The governor of Britain, Agricola, also made important progress during Domitian's reign by advancing into northern Scotland before he was recalled.

Late in 88 or early 89 a revolt was sparked by Lucius Antonius Saturninus, the governor of Upper Germany. However, it was unsuccessful because the Rhine thawed unexpectedly, and Saturninus was starved of the auxiliaries he had recruited in Germany. Left only with his two legions, which probably reconsidered their loyalty to Saturninus, the rebel was easily defeated by Lappius Maximus, the governor of Lower Germany. This was one of the few events that reflected poorly upon Domitian's command of the army.

The failed revolt of Saturninus proved to be a turning point in Domitian's reign, for with the passage of time, he became increasingly paranoid and severe. But, as Domitian so rightly observed: "no one believes in a conspiracy against the emperor until it has succeeded." The execution of senators increased and he came to rely upon spies, informants and the torture of suspects to gather the information he desired. By 93, his regime had become despotic, and few if any noblemen or senators felt secure in their person or their possessions.

In 95 his frequent executions touched too close to home, as he executed his second-cousin, Flavius Clemens, and banished the man's widow, Flavia Domitilla III, who was Domitian's own niece. In the same fell swoop, we may also presume he murdered or exiled the unfortunate couple's children, two of whom were Domitian's adopted heirs.

Now that not even those close to Domitian could feel secure, a successful coup was formed. The pattern of events which led to the coup, as well as its participants and its method of execution, bear an uncanny resemblance to those which caused the downfall of Commodus almost a century later. Among those leading the plot against Domitian were the leaders of the Praetorian Guards, certain freedmen and chamberlains, and Domitia, the wife whom he had recalled from exile about five years before.

Domitian's murder, which occurred about one month before his 45th birthday, was particularly gruesome. Having been relieved of the sword (or dagger) he always kept under his pillow, Domitian was set upon by the chamberlain Stephanus, who had been the steward of the recently exiled Flavia Domitilla III. Domitian was stabbed in the groin by Stephanus, and a fierce struggle ensued in which Domitian tried to gouge his attacker's eyes. But before Domitian could save himself, other conspirators burst into the room and hacked him to death.

Not surprisingly, the senate was overjoyed at the news and condemned his memory, though the army was angered at the passing of their benefactor. The circumstances permitted a momentary recovery of power by the senate, which elected an elderly senator named Nerva to fill the Imperial vacancy. However, the army soon came to its senses and Nerva was forced to adopt a military man, Trajan, as his son and intended successor.

Domitian's legacy is severely tainted by his declining years, and by an understandably hostile literary record written by members of the senatorial class. Though Domitian did not receive a dignified funeral, the nurse who cremated his body later returned to Rome and mixed his ashes with those of his beloved niece, Julia Titi.

NUMISMATIC NOTE: Much of Domitian's coinage was struck while he was Caesar — from 69 to 79 under his father Vespasian, and from 79 to 81 under his older brother Titus. Though his most common type as Augustus is that of Minerva standing, various interesting designs occur on gold, silver and base metal coinages, some showing elaborate scenes of sacrifice or architectural objects. Among his most interesting reverse types are those celebrating the Saecular Games of 88, which sometimes combine ritual with architecture. In addition to coinage struck in his own name, he also produced issues for his deceased sister, brother and son, and 'restored' æs coinages of six of his Julio-Claudian predacessors. Additionally, he struck a large coinage for his beloved niece/common law wife Julia Titi, and a single provincial issue for his would-be heir, Vespasian Junior. With the accession of Domitian we find a return to idealism in portraiture which had been so widely used in the Augustan age, but which had been abandoned during the civil war and its aftermath. Like Otho, Domitian was a wig-wearer, and his lush toupee is carefully modeled on the coinage.

DOMITIA

AUGUSTA, A.D. 82–96

WIFE OF DOMITIAN
MOTHER OF A DEIFIED SON AND A DAUGHTER, NAMES UNKNOWN
SISTER-IN-LAW OF TITUS AND DOMITILLA THE YOUNGER
DAUGHTER-IN-LAW OF VESPASIAN AND DOMITILLA THE ELDER

Domitia Longina, c. A.D. 50–55–c. 140. The daughter of Gnaeus Domitius Corbulo, the most renowned general of Nero (whose victories in the east were rewarded only with his execution in 66), Domitia was already married to a certain Lucius Lamia Aemilianus when she came to be pursued by Domitian. With his own father, Vespasian, now in supreme power,

Domitian was able to wrest Domitia from her husband. He initially took her as a mistress, then, in 70 (or later), as his wife.

The story of her association with Domitian is tragic, though it did not come to a crisis until after he became emperor. That Domitia was not a chaste woman is attested not only by her affair with the actor Paris that caused her to be exiled, but also by a great many other affairs, including one allegedly with her husband's brother, Titus. If this was true, Domitian may have viewed his own affair with Titus' daughter (which had begun long before Titus died) as a measure of reciprocation.

Despite their mutual fondness for extramarital affairs, they were compatible for the first decade or more of their marriage. Domitia bore two children, though exactly when they were born is disputed by historians — the girl may have been born in 73 and the boy in 74, or in 82 and 83, respectively. Since Domitia was hailed Augusta in 82, the latter seems more likely. Unfortunately for the Imperial couple, both the daughter and the son were short-lived.

Though the details are sketchy, it is known that Domitian divorced and exiled Domitia c. 83, about the time she probably gave birth to her ill-fated son. The reason Suetonius gives for this parting of the ways was that Domitia had become romantically involved with an actor named Paris, who, as a result, was murdered on orders of Domitian openly in the streets of Rome. (This Paris is not to be confused with the actor of the same name whom Nero murdered because he considered him to be a serious professional rival on the stage.)

In any event, after Domitia was exiled, Domitian became more public about the incestuous relationship he had already been engaged in with his niece, Julia Titi. The uncle-niece relationship was essentially a common law marriage, for they openly behaved as if husband and wife. The relationship lasted until 90 or 91 (opinions vary), when Julia Titi died during a botched abortion of a child whom Domitian presumably had sired.

Emotionally devastated and under public pressure, Domitian recalled Domitia from exile soon after Julia Titi's death and renewed his relationship with her. In the end, this proved to be a foolhardy move, for Domitia became involved in the plot of 96 in which her husband was murdered. Domitia — then a wealthy woman — survived her husband and lived in grand style to a ripe old age.

NUMISMATIC NOTE: The coinage issued jointly in the names of Domitian and Domitia seems to belong to the period 81–c. 83, whereas those which honor her alone belong both to this early period and to years after she returned from repudiation. See the *Numismatic Notes* for Julia Titi and "Son of Domitian" for other details which apply to Domitia's coinage.

DEIFIED SON OF DOMITIAN

SON OF DOMITIAN AND DOMITIA
GRANDSON OF VESPASIAN AND DOMITILLA THE ELDER
NEPHEW OF TITUS AND DOMITILLA THE YOUNGER

Name unknown, born c. A.D. 74 or 83. The infant boy portrayed on certain coins of Domitia, the wife of Domitian, died in infancy (or perhaps at two or three years old), and was consecrated. He is one of two children Domitia bore Domitian, a brother and sister, both of whom died young without their names being recorded in any source that survives. We can be certain, however, that this boy is not one and the same as Vespasian Junior, the great-nephew whom Domitian later adopted as his successor.

Exactly when the two children of Domitian and Domitia were born is disputed. The confusion derives from a passage in Suetonius, which reveals that Domitia ". . . had presented Domitian with a daughter during his second consulship and, in the following year, with a son." This could mean his second consulship, which began in 73 and continued into 75 (while he was still Caesar under Vespasian), or his second consulship as Augustus (Cos VIII), which occurred in 82.

Historians have interpreted Suetonius' passage both ways with equal frequency, and are still divided on the matter. However, considering Domitia was hailed Augusta in 82, the latter scenario may be more likely, as the wives of emperors were often hailed Augusta upon the occasion of giving birth (and that would be the year she gave birth to the girl).

Domitian seems to have divorced his wife and sent her into exile for her adulterous activities c. 83, about the time she would have given birth to the boy if the latter circumstance is the correct one. Thus, speculation is invited: did Domitian suspect the boy had been sired by one of Domitia's lovers (Paris, perhaps?), or did he believe that since Domitia had produced a viable heir to the throne it was practical to put her aside?

NUMISMATIC NOTE: The unnamed, deified boy makes his most remarkable appearance on aurei and denarii of Domitia, which portray him as young Jupiter, with raised arms, seated on a globe among the stars in the constellation of the Great Bear, surrounded by the inscription DIVVS CAESAR IMP DOMITIANI F. On rare occasions, this reverse type is mistakenly(?) muled with an obverse of Domitian. The boy is also represented on two other rare series of coins: denarii with the inscription PIETAS AVGVST showing him as a child standing before Domitia (who, in the guise of Pietas, is seated left) and on sestertii with a similar scene but with the inscriptions DIVI CAESAR MATRI or DIVI CAESARIS MATER.

VESPASIAN JUNIOR

Adopted son, and heir of Domitian
Grandson of Domitilla the Younger
Great-nephew of Titus and Domitian
Great-grandson of Vespasian and Domitilla the Elder
Nephew of Julia Titi

Titus Flavius Domitianus (Junior), d. A.D. 95/6(?). A considerable drawback to Domitian's principate was his lack of an heir. Thus, sometime prior to 95 (but certainly late in his reign), he adopted two of his great-nephews, and re-named them Vespasian and Domitian. Of the boys we know very little, except that they were tutored by the renowned rhetorician Quintillian, who counted Pliny the Younger among his pupils.

The boys were two of seven children born to Domitian's niece, Flavia Domitilla III and her husband (and second-cousin) Flavius Clemens, the grandson of Vespasian's brother, Flavius Sabinus, and the brother of Flavius Sabinus, the husband of Julia Titi. This particular Flavia Domitilla was the third generation of a family line of homonymous women: her mother was the sister of Titus and Domitian (listed as "Domitilla the Younger"), and her grandmother was Vespasian's wife (listed as "Domitilla the Elder").

Thus, the boys were of fine Imperial lineage, being great-grandsons of Vespasian's brother on the paternal side, and great-grandsons of Vespasian on the maternal side. It is worth noting that scholars disagree as to whether their father, Flavius Clemens, was the grandson or the son of Vespasian's brother. The confusion may be traced to the historian Eusebius, who, writing more than two centuries after the fact, refers to Flavia Domitilla III as Clemens' niece rather than his second cousin. Eusebius makes a further error by suggesting Clemens and wife were Christians, when they were more likely proselytes to Judaism.

Not only was Clemens an unsavory character (Suetonius describes him as being of "despicable idleness"), but he was also the only legitimate rival to the throne who was of age. So, in 95, the year in which Clemens was consul, Domitian leveled charges of atheism against him and Domitilla as well, executing Clemens and exiling his wife to Pandateria. Since we hear nothing of their boys, Vespasian Junior and Domitian Junior, after 96, we may presume they were killed or exiled as a result of the downfall of their parents.

Domitian took these violent measures against the family of Flavia Domitilla III to eliminate relatives-in-waiting for the throne. Though Domitian no doubt justified these treacherous measures as acts of self-defense, they only served to expedite his murder, which occurred in

September of the following year at the hands of Stefanus, the steward of Flavia Domitilla III.

NUMISMATIC NOTE: The identification of the Vespasian Junior on coins of Smyrna is secured by the obverse inscription OYECΠACIANOC NEΩTEPOC, which names the young man portrayed as 'the younger Vespasian.' The portrait is youthful and resembles no other Flavian male. As if more proof were necessary, some of these Smyrnian coins share reverse dies with issues of Domitian as Augustus, thus linking them to a period more than 15 years after Vespasian died. No coins are known which name or portray Domitian Junior.

Sometimes incorrectly attributed to Vespasian Junior are small bronzes struck at Aegae in Aeolis with the obverse inscription OYHCΠHCIANOC KAICAP, meaning 'Vespasian Caesar.' This curious issue features portraits of two radically different styles — one readily identifiable as Vespasian, and another inexplicably youthful. Despite the variant portraits and unusual inscription, the issue must be given to Vespasian himself, and probably to c. 69/70, at the beginning of his reign. Beyond the fact that we have no evidence of Domitian giving Vespasian Junior the title Caesar, we must also consider that all three members of the early dynasty — Vespasian, Titus and Domitian — are represented on that same series of coins. This circumstance alone takes the Aegae coinage out of context for the adopted Vespasian Junior, for it is at least 15 years too early, and in all likelihood about 25 years too early.

The strangely youthful bust of Vespasian would seem to have been produced upon the arrival in the East of news concerning Vitellius' overthrow, and thus it reflects little more than the die cutter's speculation as to Vespasian's appearance. When the official *imagios* arrived in the East shortly thereafter, the Vespasian portrait issue was continued, but now with an accurate image of the new emperor. In the same series at Aegae there are coins with the confronted busts of Titus and Domitian, with the former being laureate and the latter bare-headed. Since both sons were named Caesar upon Vespasian being hailed Augustus, they understandably were included in the issue of Aegae. The fact that Titus is laureate may easily be explained by the fact that he was Vespasian's heir apparent, and by the fact that he was then directing the war in Judaea, and was hailed Imperator by his soldiers after he took Jerusalem late in 70.

CHAPTER FIVE

The Adoptive Emperors and The Antonines A.D. 96–192

With the close of the chaotic 1st Century A.D., the Roman Empire entered a new phase of its history — one of prosperity that is often referred to as "the golden age" of the Empire. The wars and revolts that interrupted this peace (at least initially) occurred only infrequently, and seldom affected Rome itself. For more than eight decades the Empire was ruled by men chosen principally for their merit, and only marginally for their family ties. This was a marked contrast to the previous century, during which the Julio-Claudians and the Flavians treated the office of Augustus as a hereditary throne.

When Domitian's principate ended with his murder in 96, an elderly senator named Nerva was chosen as his replacement. In due course, he "adopted" a military man named Trajan, who took office immediately after Nerva's death. This set into motion a tradition which survived for decades.

Perhaps too much credit has been paid on this point, however, for none of the first four adoptive emperors (Nerva, Trajan, Hadrian and Antoninius Pius) appear to have had legitimate male heirs to whom they could pass the title of Augustus. Indeed, the first time in the 2nd Century that an emperor had a legitimate son (Marcus Aurelius and his son Commodus), the tradition was broken without hesitation. It has even been suggested that Aelius — Hadrian's first choice as successor — was his own illegitimate son. Considering Hadrian's frequent extramarital exploits, this would come as no surprise, and his adoption of Aelius might well have been a covert attempt to establish a hereditary monarchy. Though we should feel free to admire the fortitude and efficiency with which the adoptive emperors ruled the Empire, we should not place them on so high a pedestal as to believe they would not have appointed sons of their own had it been possible.

We should feel free to admire the wisdom and efficiency with which the "adoptive emperors" ruled Rome, but we should not place them on so high a pedestal as to believe they would not have appointed a son of their own had it been possible.

Once the laurel was passed to Trajan, a military man who wanted to conquer with the same fervor as his hero, Julius Caesar, Rome was once again poised for a significant expansion. When it became clear after the fact that Trajan had conquered too much territory to control, the reins were pulled back by Hadrian, who chose to concentrate his military might on frontier defenses rather than expansion. Hadrian traveled extensively, and devoted most of his attention, it seems, to the provinces. The reign of Antoninus Pius was relatively peaceful, and through a combination of good fortune and exportation of gold, he was able to maintain peace. Unlike his predecessor, Pius did not leave Italy in his 22 years on the throne, and worked hard to re-establish Italy as the most important "province" of the Empire.

But the security of Pius' era was shattered during the subsequent joint reign of Marcus Aurelius and Lucius Verus, as border wars erupted simultaneously in Europe and Asia. Most disconcerting was the increased strength of the Germanic nations that launched regular invasions across the Danube. Not only was this traumatic during Marcus Aurelius' reign, but it proved to be an even greater threat in the 3rd century. Indeed, almost the entirety of Marcus Aurelius' reign was spent fighting border wars. Like Trajan, Marcus Aurelius was an outstanding servant of the Empire, seeking to solve all problems at once. He fought tirelessly, and yet never lost his compassion for domestic matters that must have seemed trivial in comparison.

The steady decline in the fortunes of Rome that occurred during the principate of Marcus Aurelius were only compounded during the reign of Commodus, who had inherited the throne directly from his father. Commodus was not fond of frontier warfare, and preferred the more theatrical combat of gladiators and hunters. Thus, he spent most of his reign in Rome, leaving the frontier battles to his generals.

Commodus' degenerating state of mind and unbearable tyranny are well-known to all students of Roman history, and his consequent assassination came as a relief to the senate and the people. Only the chosen few in the army and private sector who benefited from his patronage did not applaud his passing.

This remarkable event forced Rome into a civil war during which five men claimed the throne in a single year. The war exhausted most of the energy and resources of the Empire until it was resolved in 197, and a great many Roman soldiers lost their lives in battles against their fellow Romans. Septimius Severus emerged as the victor, and with his Syrian wife founded a dynasty that survived more or less intact until 235, when yet a new age in Roman history began.

NERVA A.D. 96–98

ADOPTIVE FATHER OF TRAJAN

Marcus Cocceius Nerva, A.D. 30–96. After the downfall of Domitian, the senate elected a senator named Nerva as the new emperor. Although he probably was a distant relation of the Julio-Claudians, Nerva was elderly, unambitious and without children. As such, he seemed to be a perfectly harmless candidate for a state that had tired of despotic hereditary monarchs.

Nerva's father and grandfather were talented lawyers (the latter having lived on Capri with the emperor Tiberius) and Nerva's great-great-grand-father was a supporter of Marc Antony who was able to switch his allegiance to Octavian at the right moment. His career is a bit of a mystery, as he is not known to have held any military posts or provincial governorships, nor to have possessed any outstanding skills.

His most important asset may have been loyalty, for he found favor under Nero, and apparently was helpful in suppressing the conspiracy of Piso in 65. Nerva managed to survive the Civil War of 68–69 only to be honored with consulships under both Vespasian, in 71, and Domitian, in 90.

His 16-month reign was brief and unremarkable, though the purity of his intentions seemingly cannot be doubted. Though the much-improved relations between the senate and emperor might have been expected considering his career as a jurist, Nerva's efforts are still praiseworthy. The fact that his few accomplishments are loudly trumpeted on coinage and that he ruled at the beginning of a new era perhaps help to distort our view of his importance. None-the-less, his task was a difficult one, for he needed the support of the army (still fiercely loyal to the memory of Domitian) as well as the senate.

There were two plots against Nerva in 97, one among troops stationed on the Danube, and another by the praetorian guards. At one point the praetorians burst into the palace, pushing Nerva and his associates aside so they could hunt down two palace officials who had been instrumental in the murder of Domitian. In a humiliating gesture to maintain loyalty with the army, Nerva publicly thanked the praetorian mob for their lawless act of violence. His adoption of Trajan, the governor of Upper Germany, in September or October of 97 was not an act of Imperial foresight as much as a stop-gap measure to placate the army. Only about four months after Trajan had been adopted, the 63-year-old Nerva died of natural causes, possibly on January 25, 98.

NUMISMATIC NOTE: Though the bulk of Nerva's coinage is devoted to commonplace themes, such as the senate, the army, liberty of the people, and the like, he authorized a number of interesting types commemorating his charitable acts and popular legislation. These are among the most sought-after reverse types of the 1st Century. Commemorative *divi* coinages were struck after Nerva's death by his successor, Trajan, and some 150 years later by Trajan Decius.

TRAJAN A.D. 98–117

CAESAR: A.D. 97 (UNDER NERVA)
AUGUSTUS: A.D. 98–117

ADOPTED SON OF NERVA
SON OF TRAJAN PATER
HUSBAND OF PLOTINA
BROTHER OF MARCIANA
UNCLE OF MATIDIA
GRAND-UNCLE OF SABINA

Marcus Ulpius Traianus, c. A.D. 53–117. Born at Italica in southern Spain, Trajan belonged to the *Ulpii*, a family originally from Etruria which had become respectable only in the previous generation. Tall, well-built and dignified in appearance, Trajan pursued a career in the military in which he found much success.

After nearly two decades of distinguished service (perhaps half of which he spent in Syria, including while his father governed there) Trajan gained higher commands. Eventually he held a praetorship and commanded a legion. He became consul under Domitian in 91, ostensibly for his valor in that emperor's Germanic campaigns, and later was appointed governor of Upper Germany.

The emperor Nerva — who had replaced Domitian after a palace coup — was not in good standing with the army, and after surviving a second overthrow attempt, he adopted Trajan in September or October of 97 in hopes it would placate the army. Though it did little to serve Nerva (who died four months later) it offered a clear path of succession for Trajan, who in January of 98 became the first emperor of non-Italian origin. His reign of nearly 20 years was very productive, and his territorial gains — however ephemeral — represented the height of achievement in Roman history.

Upon becoming Augustus, Trajan remained in the provinces for more than a year, securing the Rhine and Danubian frontiers. He entered Rome in 99, and after holding games he initiated many building projects, he prepared for an invasion of Dacia, which he led personally in 101. He returned to Rome in 103 and celebrated a triumph. However, his victory was short-lived, for the Dacian king Decebalus rose again to massacre Roman garrisons in 105, causing Trajan to return. This time his invasion required the construction of the famous "Danube bridge," and the campaign resulted in Decebalus' death. The king's decapitated head, which was displayed in Rome, also makes appearances on Trajan's coins.

The eastern portion of the Empire was also growing, not through invasion, but through the annexation of Nabataea (the province of Arabia). The emperor returned to Rome in 107 and once again turned his attention to building projects, which included the *Aqua Traiana*, a massive aqueduct which brought water from Etruria to feed his new baths. He also constructed the *Via Traiana*, a road that linked Beneventum and Brundisium and provided an alternative route to the final leg of the *Via Appia*. His other important building projects were: a harbor at the mouth of the Tiber, a basilica, a magnificent forum and a column that recorded the Dacian campaign. Most of his important architectural projects (including an earlier restoration of the Circus Maximus) are commemorated on coins.

Trajan's final years were not spent supervising construction in Italy, but rather on the Parthian front. He departed for the East in October of 113, with the intention of destroying Parthia completely, so it could never again pose a threat to Romans. His successes in the East were enormous, but too ambitious to be long-lived. Among the spoils were Armenia and Upper Mesopotamia, and after sacking the Parthian capital of Ctesiphon, the emperor made an excursion to the Persian Gulf.

Amid all of this success there was a general uprising in different parts of Asia and Africa by Jews who were upset with their Roman overlords. Hardest hit were Cyrenaica, Egypt, Cyprus and Judaea, where the revolts caused much bloodshed and required a significant military response.

Meanwhile, revolts began to occur in his newly conquered territories, and Trajan soon realized how vulnerable his "gains" were. As such, he installed on the Parthian throne a puppet-king named Parthamaspates, who was the son of the Parthian king, in hopes he would rule that nation in the best interest of Rome. But this effort also proved ineffective.

Despite the problems in the East, the 64-year-old Trajan decided to march west when he heard of new problems in Europe, but he died of natural causes in Cilicia while *en route* early in August 117. While on his deathbed, Trajan is supposed to have named Hadrian as his heir, but this declaration may have been falsified after his death by his wife, Plotina, who was at his bedside.

Though Trajan is principally remembered for his military actions, he was also a kind and caring administrator who continued most of Nerva's charitable policies. His accomplishments as a builder are also of some consequence. Senators of his own day and far beyond considered Trajan to be perhaps the best emperor Rome had ever known, in many cases holding him in higher esteem than the great Augustus.

NUMISMATIC NOTE: The inscriptions on Trajan's sestertii, which tout his many accomplishments, are the longest on all Roman coinage. His coinage is of great interest for the many vivid reverse types as well as the "restoration" issues he struck in 107 to commemorate the millions of older, heavily worn denarii he recalled from circulation. Though all coins from that series are very rare, about fifty types were struck. Trajan also struck coinage in the name of relatives, including his father, Trajan Pater; his adoptive father, Nerva; his wife, Plotina; his sister Marciana, and his niece, Matidia.

TRAJAN PATER

FATHER OF TRAJAN AND MARCIANA
GRANDFATHER OF MATIDIA
GRANDUNCLE OF HADRIAN
FATHER-IN-LAW OF PLOTINA

Marcus Ulpius Traianus, died c. A.D. 100. A man of great accomplishment both in politics and war, *Ulpius* Trajanus was the first senatorial member of the Ulpii, a family originally from Tuder in Umbria, which more recently had settled in Baetica in southern Spain.

Trajan's father must have served with distinction under Nero, for he came to prominence during the Jewish War (the First Revolt) waged by Vespasian and Titus, in which he commanded the 10th Legion, and laid siege to Joppa. After he had reduced the city to its final resistance, he presented Titus with the honor of launching the final assault. When Vespasian returned to Italy and consolidated his power in Rome, he rewarded the elder Trajan with the high office of consul, presumably in 70.

Trajan Pater served as governor of Syria from 73 through 77, and was proconsul of all Asia from 79 to 80. During his tenure in the east he reorganized the frontier defenses and constructed two important roads. He earned triumphal insignia (ornamenta triumphalia) for his success against the Parthians in 75/6, who were incensed at Vespasian's refusal to help Vologases I repel an invasion of Parthian territory by the Alans.

Though the historians do not record the deification of Trajan Pater, the numismatic record offers clear evidence. Indeed it was his first-generation success which paved the path for his own son's rise to the highest office.

NUMISMATIC NOTE: On coinage struck during Trajan Pater's lifetime in Syria, he is mentioned only by name. On the coinage struck for Trajan Pater's consecration, he is shown bare-headed, thus distinguishing him as a private citizen rather than an emperor. The dating of the *divi* series is securely placed in 115 by Hill (*The Undated Coins of Rome*, A.D. *98–148*), though the authors of RIC had placed the silver in the years 112–114.

PLOTINA

AUGUSTA, C. A.D. 105–122(?)

WIFE OF TRAJAN
SISTER-IN-LAW OF MARCIANA
AUNT OF MATIDIA

Pompeia Plotina, c. A.D. 70–122(?). A modest and benevolent woman born at Nemausus in Gaul, Plotina married Trajan (who apparently was a relative) while he was still a soldier. She bore him no children and served her Empire by offering counsel to him on many occasions.

Plotina apparently lived in harmony with her sister-in-law, Marciana, who predeceased her by a decade or so. Though both women were offered the title of Augusta on Trajan's accession in 98, they apparently refused, and seem only to have accepted the honor in 105. Plotina seems to have been above reproach on all but perhaps one subject, the future emperor Hadrian. Accounts of her involvement with Hadrian vary, but it is certain that she took a personal interest in his career and was fond of him personally. Though probably nothing more than gossip, some believed she was in love with Hadrian. Indeed, it was at her insistence that Trajan reluctantly betrothed his grand-niece Sabina to Hadrian. The marriage was not a happy one, but it tied Hadrian ever closer to Trajan, and thus to the title of Augustus.

Plotina's final act on behalf of Hadrian — of which two accounts survive — occurred at the time of her own husband's death. The first suggests Plotina convinced her husband (while on his deathbed) to name Hadrian as his successor. The other version purports that when she was unable to convince Trajan to adopt Hadrian, she delayed the announcement of her husband's death for several days so she could forge documents proving it was Trajan's desire to be succeeded by Hadrian. Both Plotina and Hadrian were in the East when Trajan died in Cilicia (117), and she bore her husband's ashes back to Rome.

Authorities are in disagreement as to the year Plotina died, which is variously reported to have been 121, 122, 123 or 129. The year 122 seems most likely, but in any case, she died during the reign of her beneficiary Hadrian, who did not hesitate to consecrate her.

MARCIANA

AUGUSTA, C. A.D. 105–112/4(?)

SISTER OF TRAJAN
DAUGHTER OF TRAJAN PATER
MOTHER OF MATIDIA
GRANDMOTHER OF SABINA
SISTER-IN-LAW OF PLOTINA

Ulpia Marciana, d. A.D. 112/4(?). By all accounts, Marciana was a woman of high character, though very little is recorded of her deeds. Throughout her brother's reign she lived as a widow, for she had lost her husband, C. Matidius Patruinus, in the preceding years and did not remarry.

She was fortunate to enjoy a close friendship with her brother's wife, Plotina, and they spent a great deal of time together. The two were united in most of their actions, including their joint acceptance of the title of Augusta, which they refused in 98 but apparently accepted in 105. Like other women in Trajan's family, historians disagree about the date of her death. Some suggest she died in the same year she was hailed Augusta (105), but she more likely died in 112 or 114.

NUMISMATIC NOTE: The word *consecratio* makes its first appearance on the coinage of Marciana, and thereafter became the standard employed for issues of the *divae* and *divi* thereafter.

MATIDIA

AUGUSTA, A.D. 112/4(?)–119

DAUGHTER OF MARCIANA
NIECE OF TRAJAN
MOTHER OF SABINA
MOTHER-IN-LAW OF HADRIAN

Matidia, c. A.D. 68-119. As the daughter of Trajan's sister and the mother of Sabina (wife of the future emperor, Hadrian), Matidia was an important member of the Imperial court during the reign of her uncle Trajan. Having no offspring of his own, the emperor apparently cared for Matidia as if she was his own daughter.

We know regrettably little about Matidia's life, except that she received the title of Augusta when her mother died, and held it until her own death in 119. Determining when Matidia became Augusta is difficult, for opinions on the year of Marciana's death vary considerably among historians, who place it in 105, 112 or 114.

Matidia was married at least twice and had at least as many children. From one marriage she produced a daughter named Sabina, who was wed to the future emperor Hadrian. From another marriage Matidia gave birth to a daughter named Rupilia Faustina, whose grandson was the future emperor Marcus Aurelius. Matidia lived two years beyond her beloved uncle Trajan, and was consecrated by her son-in-law Hadrian, who delivered her funeral oration and built a temple for her in the Forum of Trajan.

NUMISMATIC NOTE: On the reverse of Matidia's lifetime aurei and denarii, she is shown with two children. One of these two girls must be Sabina, and the other is most commonly called Matidia the Younger.

HADRIAN A.D. 117–138

FIRST-COUSIN-ONCE-REMOVED AND ADOPTED SON OF TRAJAN
HUSBAND OF SABINA
ADOPTIVE FATHER OF AELIUS AND ANTONINUS PIUS
GRAND-NEPHEW OF TRAJAN PATER

Publius Aelius Hadrianus, A.D. 76–138. The character of Hadrian is difficult to assess, for there were many dimensions to his personality and his policies. He would act in an enlightened and responsible manner in some cases, and in others behave in a cruel and monstrous fashion one might more readily expect of Nero or Domitian. Thus, ancient and modern historians have judged him in very different lights.

Although probably born in Rome, Hadrian belonged to a family living in Italica in Spain, and was a blood relative of Trajan (Hadrian's grandfather was the brother of Trajan's father — indeed, had they not been a generation apart they would have been first cousins). Their close association can be traced back to Hadrian's childhood, when at the age of ten his own father died and he came under Trajan's care. Although often annoyed by Hadrian's youthful indiscretions, Trajan none-the-less was fond of him.

When Nerva died in 98, it is said that Hadrian (then about 22 years old) outran several other messengers so he could be the first to tell Trajan of his accession. Two years later, the existing family ties were strengthened when Hadrian married Trajan's grandniece, Sabina (whom he treated very poorly for the next 36 years). Under the guidance of Trajan, Hadrian made rapid progress in the army, rising from lower offices, such as staff officer, to higher ones, such as legionary commander and praetor.

In positions of great responsibility, Hadrian served the Empire well in the first and second Dacian wars. He later came to govern Lower Pannonia and to hold the consulship in 108. Throughout the principate of Trajan, Hadrian's greatest supporter was the emperor's wife, Plotina. Not only did she engineer his marriage to Sabina, but she arranged (either by persuasion or forgery) his succession after her own husband's death in 117. Power was transferred to Hadrian, who was then governing Syria and was designated to hold the consulship in the following year. Though many doubted the veracity of his adoption, it was not challenged.

The new emperor led his army to Europe where he settled the Danubian frontier. Initially, he quelled a few minor revolts in the provinces and conducted acts of generosity to the public in order to establish his principate firmly. He also wisely reversed the expansionist policies of Trajan, who had conquered more land than could be properly defended. He consolidated Trajan's gains by appointing client kings or by ceding territories that were vulnerable.

Hadrian's popularity with the senate suffered when he executed several ex-consuls suspected of conspiring against the throne, even though he had promised never to execute a senator. Throughout his reign, Hadrian was deeply involved in legal and administrative matters of government, and many of his reforms caused him to be despised by the senate.

Hadrian's reign was relatively uneventful in military terms, as Rome's enemies were quiet and Hadrian fortified the borders. Indeed, Hadrian ushered in an era of domestic security commonly called the *Pax Romana*. The one major exception was the Second Revolt in Judaea (132–135) led by Simon bar Kosiba, which grew out of the chaos experienced late in Trajan's reign and was sparked by some careless actions by the new emperor.

Hadrian is best known for his extensive travels throughout the Empire, which had many practical applications, but were also cultural excursions. His first trips (120–122) were to Gaul, Britain and Spain, then to Asia (123) and Greece (125), after which he returned via Sicily to Rome (127). He then resumed his travels (128–133), visiting Africa, Greece, Asia Minor, the Levant and Egypt, and finally returning to Italy, where he spent his remaining years.

Like many emperors, Hadrian was an accomplished builder. Three of his most famous projects were the 80-mile wall along the border of England and Scotland (known as Hadrian's Wall), the massive temple of Roma and Venus, and a complete reconstruction of Agrippa's century-old Pantheon, which was transformed into an architectural marvel. His most personal building project, however, was his magnificent villa at Tivoli — a

160-acre estate so grand it could rightly be compared with the Golden House of Nero.

The personal life of Hadrian was rife with pleasure, for he was a patron of the arts and a great lover of Greek culture (which in his adolescence earned him the nickname "Greekling"). He had many adulterous affairs with married women and young boys, the most notorious of the latter being with a Bithynian youth named Antinoüs, for whom he established a cult after the boy's tragic death on the Nile in 130.

The homosexual aspect of Hadrian's life may have inspired his choice of a handsome, and apparently gay man named Aelius as his first heir. Just as likely, however, is the possibility that Aelius was his own illegitimate son (as some had rumored), and that Hadrian was covertly establishing what he knew to be a hereditary monarchy. This possibility aside, Hadrian had no rightful children of his own, and his failing health required that in 136 he name an heir.

His first choice (as related above) was Aelius, who in a quirk of fate predeceased the emperor by about six months. Hadrian then adopted a 52-year-old aristocrat named Antoninus Pius on the condition that he in turn adopt both Aelius' son, Lucius Verus (then 7 years old), and a distant relative, Marcus Aurelius, a 17-year-old boy for whom Hadrian had great affection. After what was an enigmatic but productive reign of 20 years, the 62-year-old Hadrian died of natural causes on July 10, 138.

SABINA

Augusta, A.D. 128(?)–136

Wife of Hadrian
Daughter of Matidia

Vibia Sabina, d. A.D. 136. As the grand-niece of the emperor Trajan (who had no children of his own) Sabina was destined for a political marriage. Arranging her marriage was Plotina, the wife of Trajan and the confidant of Sabina's grandmother Marciana. It seems Trajan himself was not in favor of the marriage, but deferred to his wife, who was insistent. The wedding occurred in the year 100, and though Hadrian's position as heir to the throne was by no means guaranteed, this made it highly probable. Like so many political marriages, this one was not blissful, and not surprisingly produced no offspring.

Hadrian was a man composed equally of good and bad qualities, and the unfortunate Sabina was subjected almost exclusively to the latter. It also seems Hadrian's interests were too diverse to allow much affection for

Sabina. Even though she accompanied her husband on most if not all of his travels, Hadrian largely ignored her and pursued his many affairs with married women and young boys.

Despite his openly adulterous behavior, Hadrian did not approve of similar behavior by Sabina, and in 121 or 122 he dismissed two court officials with whom she had developed close relationships. The first was the praetorian prefect Septicius Clarus, and the second was the historian Suetonius, who as a result was barred thereafter from the imperial archives.

Sabina was granted the title of Augusta at some point during her husband's principate, and like most specific facts about the Augustae of the Adoptive emperors, it is unclear exactly when this occurred. Some historians suggest 117 or 120, while others prefer 128, the year that Hadrian accepted the title *pater patriae* (and most likely the true date). After what must have been an unhappy life and an unbearable marriage of 36 years, Sabina died in 136 or 137. Though she may have died from natural causes, it was widely rumored that Hadrian, realizing his own demise was not far off, either poisoned her or forced her to commit suicide.

NUMISMATIC NOTE: The coinage of Sabina bearing the inscription SABINA AVGVSTA HADRIANI AVG P P was not struck early in the reign of Antoninus Pius as is stated in RIC (the error was corrected in BMC).

AELIUS

CAESAR, A.D. 136–138 (UNDER HADRIAN)

ADOPTED SON AND INTENDED SUCCESSOR OF HADRIAN
FATHER OF LUCIUS VERUS

Lucius Aelius Verus (*earlier* Lucius Aurelius Ceionius Commodus Verus), d. A.D. 138. Descended from a distinguished Etruscan family, Aelius was a cultured and learned man with refined tastes, but with a fragile constitution and effeminate habits. It was the opinion of Gibbons that as a "gay and voluptuous nobleman" of "uncommon beauty," Aelius easily won the approval of Hadrian over several other candidates of more distinguished merit.

Others of the era preferred the idea that Aelius was an illegitimate child of Hadrian, and that his curious adoption occurred for that reason. After Aelius died, Hadrian made certain that Aelius' son Lucius Verus, figured into the long-term succession. This lends credence to the theory that Aelius was in fact the son of Hadrian, for in this measure he would have assured that his grandson would one day occupy the throne.

However, Aelius was not an unqualified provincial, as both his father and grandfather had attained the high office of consul. Though the details are incomplete, it would seem the combination of the emperor's own failing health and the death of his empress Sabina prompted Hadrian to adopt Aelius late in 136. Upon being adopted, the new Caesar changed his name to Lucius Aelius Verus and attended to the duties of his new appointment as governor of Pannonia.

Aelius held consulships in 136 and 137, but his first must have occupied a negligible amount of time as only coins of his second are known. Aelius energetically executed his duties in Pannonia, and near the end of 137 returned to Rome to make an address in honor of his benefactor Hadrian. But after reigning scarcely more than a year, he died of an acute illness on January 1, 138, the very day that he was to deliver his oration. The increasingly ill Hadrian was now without an heir, and so on February 25 he filled the Imperial vacancy by adopting Antoninus Pius, who succeeded him shortly thereafter.

ANTINOÜS

COMPANION OF HADRIAN

Antinoüs, d. A.D. 130. The peace and prosperity of Hadrian's principate allowed the emperor luxuries uncommon to the office, including his extensive, leisurely travels throughout the Empire. In addition to absorbing local culture, Hadrian also indulged his romantic inclinations, about which he composed many verses.

Hadrian is chastised by contemporaries for these frequent adulterous affairs, for — however unhappily — he was married to Sabina. His preference seems to have fallen upon married women and young boys. Foremost of his male love interests was the youth Antinoüs, a native of Claudiopolis in Bithynia whom he met when his travels brought him to that region.

The boy accompanied the emperor on his remaining travels, which soon brought the entourage to Egypt. Perhaps the most tragic event in the emperor's life occurred there in October 130, when Antinoüs drowned in the waters of the Nile under mysterious circumstances. Some said the drowning was an accident, whereas others believed it was a ritualistic suicide intended to cure the emperor's failing health. Indeed, the latter may offer the best explanation for the unprecedented 'honorary' coins struck in the boy's name.

Hadrian was grief-stricken and established a city named Antinoopolis (Sheikh Abade) near where the boy drowned. He also identified a new star in the heavens which he believed embodied Antinoüs' soul, and established a cult in the youth's honor.

NUMISMATIC NOTE: As part of the cult of Antinoüs, the Greeks built temples and created priesthoods to service them. Festivals and games were held in Antinoüs' honor, and fortunately for collectors, coins were also struck in numerous cities, often in connection with these events. No Imperial coins were struck in the name of Antinoüs, and the largest emissions occurred at the mint of Alexandria in Egypt.

ANTONINUS PIUS A.D. 138–161

CAESAR: A.D. 138 (UNDER HADRIAN)
AUGUSTUS: A.D. 138–161

ADOPTED SON AND SUCCESSOR OF HADRIAN
HUSBAND OF FAUSTINA SENIOR
FATHER OF FAUSTINA JUNIOR AND GALERIUS ANTONINUS
GRANDFATHER OF COMMODUS, ANNIUS VERUS, LUCILLA AND AURELIUS ANTONINUS
ADOPTIVE FATHER OF MARCUS AURELIUS AND LUCIUS VERUS

Titus Aelius Caesar Antoninus (*earlier* Titus Aurelius Fulvus Boionius Arrius Antoninus), A.D. 86–161. When Aelius died unexpectedly on New Year's Day of 138, it came as unwelcomed news to Hadrian, who was only too aware that his own days were numbered. The ailing emperor announced on January 24 that Antoninus Pius, a respectable senator whom he had relied upon as a close advisor, was his new successor. On February 25 Antoninus was invested with the rank of Caesar, which he held until Hadrian died on July 10.

The new emperor — age 52 when he took office in August — was uncommonly tall and hailed from a good family that originally came from Nemausus but had settled in Lanuvium. Not only had his grandfathers and his father been consuls in Rome, but Antoninus himself had served in that capacity in 130, and sometime between 133 and 136 was proconsul of Asia. Though he largely owed his succession to his marriage to Faustina Senior (an aunt of Marcus Aurelius), he proved to be an excellent choice. Antoninus earned his title "Pius" from the senate, who admired the tenacity with which he lobbied for the deification of Hadrian, whom the senate had grown to despise before his death.

Antoninus' reign was similar to Hadrian's in that the Empire enjoyed great prosperity, no effort was made to expand territories, and military conflicts were limited. Revolts of some consequence broke out twice in the north of Britain (where he built the Antonine Wall some 80 miles north of Hadrian's Wall), and once in Mauretania, each of which took considerable time and effort to quell. Lesser disturbances occurred along the Rhine and Danube as well as in Egypt and Judaea. Diplomacy at the end of Antoninus' reign prevented a conflict with Parthia, which otherwise had been silent since the reign of Trajan.

Antoninus was frugal in his expenditures, and we find his building programs are less extravagant than those of Trajan and Hadrian; indeed, when he died there were some 675 million denarii in the treasury. His personality was more balanced than that of his predecessor, as he was not prone to cruelty or arrogant dictatorship. He also differed from Hadrian in that his personal habits and preferences were more in line with traditional Roman culture, and he is not known to have left Italy in his more than two decades as emperor.

His solitary weakness, it seems, was women, and even in that he was not ostentatious. Thanks to his tact and diplomacy, relations with the senate improved greatly during his reign despite his opposition to sharing power with that institution. Indeed, Antoninus reserved the right to make all serious decisions after consulting with his own council. His beloved wife, Faustina Senior, died a young woman during the third year of his reign, and he honored her memory extensively.

In accordance with the wishes of Hadrian, Antoninus had adopted both Lucius Verus and Marcus Aurelius, whom he groomed as his successors. While the former was given few responsibilities, the latter was made Caesar in 139 and held that title for more than two decades before he became emperor. Antoninus Pius' principate was the height of the *Pax Romana*, during which the fruits of many centuries of Roman labor were enjoyed. Hardly a more ideal reign existed than his in which the 900th anniversary of Rome's foundation should be celebrated. This was the most important event of his reign, and was commemorated with a series of coins.

After a productive (if not extraordinary) reign of 22 years, the 74-year-old Antoninus died of natural causes at his palace in Etruria on March 7, 161. In accordance with the wishes of Hadrian, he was succeeded in an orderly manner by Marcus Aurelius and Lucius Verus.

FAUSTINA SENIOR

AUGUSTA, A.D. 138–140/1

WIFE OF ANTONINUS PIUS
MOTHER OF FAUSTINA JUNIOR AND GALERIUS ANTONINUS
AUNT OF MARCUS AURELIUS
GRANDMOTHER OF COMMODUS, ANNIUS VERUS, LUCILLA AND AURELIUS ANTONINUS

Annia Galeria Faustina, A.D. 98/105–140/1. Although only a distant in-law of Trajan, Faustina Senior was an aunt of Marcus Aurelius, one of two boys whom Hadrian designated to inherit the throne. Indeed, it was probably because of his marriage to Faustina Senior that Antoninus Pius was unexpectedly named the immediate successor to Hadrian, and thus the custodian of young Marcus Aurelius and Lucius Verus.

Her marriage to Antoninus Pius was congenial, though not without its problems. Faustina bore him four children, only one of whom, Faustina Junior (later the wife of Marcus Aurelius), survived to see her parents become emperor and empress. Faustina Senior was probably hailed Augusta late in 138, but she died in only the third year of her husband's reign, while she was still a young woman.

Of Faustina's character we have few insights, except that she was perhaps too frank, light-hearted and promiscuous for the demands of her office. In this respect she was the exact opposite of her sober husband, who executed his duties with tact, diplomacy and an unwavering devotion to duty.

Though Antoninus never remarried, he did indulge what may have been his only weakness by taking as a concubine a certain Galeria Lysistrate, who was formerly one of Faustina's slaves. Indeed, the slave-turned-mistress appears to have wielded great authority over the widowed emperor. Another important lady in the courts was Antoninus' sister-in-law Domitia Lucilla, who devoted herself to her son Marcus Aurelius, who for more than two decades was groomed as successor to the throne.

Despite the troublesome personality of Faustina Senior, it is clear that Antoninus Pius cared deeply for her. Regrettably, even the most fundamental details of Faustina's life are not certainly known. She may have been born in 98 or in 105, and is said to have been married to Antoninus in 110, but even this seems unlikely. Alas, even the date of her death seems uncertain, for it may have occurred in October or November of 140, or early in 141. The greatest monument dedicated to this empress is a massive temple dedicated in 141/2 and completed in about 150. It originally was dedicated just to Faustina Senior, but after the death of Antoninus in 161, Marcus Aurelius re-dedicated it to both husband and wife as the Temple *Divi Antonini et Divae Faustinae*. Today the impressive remains (which enclose the church of S. Lorenzo) still loom high above the ruins of the Forum in Rome.

NUMISMATIC NOTE: The majority of the coinage Antoninus Pius struck for Faustina Senior is commemorative, for she died early in his reign. As such, it is the most extensive of its kind ever struck for a empress.

GALERIUS ANTONINUS

SON OF ANTONINUS PIUS AND FAUSTINA SENIOR
BROTHER OF FAUSTINA JUNIOR

Marcus Galerius Aurelius Antoninus *or* Marcus Annius Galerius Antoninus, d. before A.D. 138. Little is known of this boy except that he was one of four children born to Faustina Senior and Antoninus Pius. His siblings included a brother, Marcus Aurelius Fulvius Antoninus, and two sisters, Aurelia Fadilla (who died before 134) and the future empress Faustina Junior.

Though the *Historia Augusta* reports that Antoninus Pius had two boys (whose names are known by inscriptions from the tomb of Hadrian preserved in Medieval times), Dio Cassius reports that Pius had no sons when he was adopted by Hadrian in 138. This scanty evidence leaves two options: that Galerius Antoninus died before Pius' accession, or that he was born between 138 and 140/1. Because the ancient biographers do not otherwise discuss the boy (and as an heir-apparent they certainly would have) we must side with the option that he died before his father's accession. Some early scholars, including Cohen, believed Galerius Antoninus survived well into his father's reign because of a 'mature' portrait on a coin that later was proven false.

NUMISMATIC NOTE: Galerius Antoninus is honored only on copper coins intended to circulate in the provinces (exactly where is unknown, though they often are found in the Balkans). His coinage was struck in two denominations, approximating the Imperial sestertius and dupondius (or as). Though they have Greek inscriptions, there are good stylistic reasons to believe the dies were cut and the coins struck in Rome, and later shipped to their destinations. They must have been struck after Faustina Senior's death, for she is *diva*. The lack of the title Caesar or the designation *divo* for the boy is no obstacle for his having died before 138, as in that case his family would not have been of Imperial rank during his lifetime and he would not have been eligible for those honors.

MARCUS AURELIUS
A.D. 161–180

CAESAR: A.D. 139–161
(UNDER ANTONINUS PIUS)
AUGUSTUS: A.D. 161-180
(A.D. 161–169: WITH LUCIUS VERUS)
(A.D. 169–177: SOLE REIGN)
(A.D. 177–180: WITH COMMODUS)

ADOPTED SON OF ANTONINUS PIUS AND HEIR OF HADRIAN
HUSBAND OF FAUSTINA JUNIOR
FATHER OF COMMODUS, ANNIUS VERUS, LUCILLA AND AURELIUS ANTONINUS
SON-IN-LAW OF ANTONINUS PIUS AND FAUSTINA SENIOR
FATHER-IN-LAW OF LUCIUS VERUS

Marcus Aelius Aurelius Verus (*earlier* Marcus Annius Verus), A.D. 121–180. Marcus Aurelius was the central figure of the Antonine dynasty, for not only was he directly descended from Trajan's father (fifth generation), but he was related through marriage to Antoninus Pius and Lucius Verus, and was the father of Commodus. Even more importantly though, he was the ultimate choice of Hadrian as heir to the throne.

During the 22 years Marcus Aurelius held the rank of Caesar under Antoninus Pius, he was cared for by his mother, the wealthy Domitia Lucilla, who was the sister-in-law of Antoninus Pius and Faustina Senior. She made certain that he studied under the finest tutors, and she devoted herself to clearing her son's path of succession of all obstacles. She no doubt was also involved in solving her son's early matrimonial complexities (see the biography of Faustina Junior for details).

The pivotal event of Marcus' reign as Caesar was his marriage to Faustina Junior in 145. Though a far from ideal union, it resulted in a dozen or more children. Marcus was awarded his first tribunician power in 146 and his wife was hailed Augusta, seemingly in 147. Through this sequence of events, Marcus became virtual co-ruler with Antoninus Pius.

When Antoninus Pius died in 161, Marcus collected the inheritance promised by Hadrian more than two decades before, and was hailed co-emperor along with his younger colleague Lucius Verus. In conjunction with this event, Marcus Aurelius betrothed his 12-year-old daughter Lucilla to his new co-emperor, who married her three years later.

Their joint reign started in crisis: the Parthians had broken their earlier peace treaty and had invaded Roman territories. Lucius Verus was sent east to lead the Roman counter-offensive, which was extraordinarily successful and ended with the sack of Ctesiphon and Seleucia. All told, Verus and his generals recovered Syria and Armenia, and conquered Mesopotamia and Media. Furthermore, in 166 they forced the Parthians to sue for an unfavorable peace.

The high spirits and acclamations that accompanied the victory, however, were soon tempered by the side effects. One consequence was an outbreak of plague, which the soldiers carried when returning to Europe. This decade-long epidemic almost completely depopulated some regions of the Empire and inflicted great harm on the city of Rome, which had not suffered an outbreak in centuries. The depleted European provinces were thus vulnerable to invasion by a host of Germans and Sarmatians. Most alarming were invasions by the Marcomanni and Quadi, who crossed the Alps and ravaged Italy itself. The joint emperors pressed hard and repelled the invasion over three seasons of brutal warfare.

At the conclusion of these border wars in 169, when the emperors were returning to Rome, Lucius Verus suffered a fatal stroke. Marcus Aurelius was now sole emperor, and his stay in Rome was brief, for renewed Germanic invasions required his presence on the frontiers, from which he did not return for six or eight years.

During the course of his wars, Marcus led his legions across the Danube and deep into German territory, where his army was spared destruction twice by miraculous events. His goal, it seems, was to force the borders back into mountainous regions and away from the rivers. He also allowed some of the invaders to settle within Roman territory — a strategy which was not unprecedented, but which received mixed commentary. Throughout it all, young Commodus was gaining valuable experience and Faustina Junior was honored for her personal devotion to her husband's campaigns.

In 175 the emperor's plans in Europe were cut short when he learned of a revolt in Syria by the governor Gaius Avidius Cassius. The general had led the Roman legions into Ctesiphon a decade before. Cassius revolted after being misinformed about the emperor's death. Delivering the misinformation, apparently, was Faustina Junior, who not only had amorous feelings for Cassius, but apparently believed her husband would not recover from a serious illness he had contracted while on campaign. Historians disagree on whether Marcus Aurelius proceeded directly to Syria or returned to Rome first, but in any event it seems Cassius was murdered within about 100 days after he rebelled.

Marcus Aurelius traveled to Asia, not only to assure his eastern legions that he was alive and still in command, but also to be certain the revolt was completely crushed. It was on this journey that Faustina Junior died of natural causes at a remote village in Cilicia.

After the eastern front was settled, Marcus Aurelius returned to Italy, barely surviving a shipwreck *en route*. Upon arriving in December of 176, he and his son Commodus celebrated their hard-earned German triumph. Despite being only fifteen years old, Commodus was permitted to hold his first consulship in 177. While in Rome he also married Crispina, and was raised to the rank of Augustus. Barring his own death, Commodus was now certain to succeed his father.

The two Augusti soon returned to the Danubian front to wage yet another grueling border war in which Marcus Aurelius hoped to achieve his original goals. However, after a reign of 19 years, Marcus Aurelius died of natural causes in camp on March 17 of 180, and was succeeded by his son Commodus.

Strong parallels can be drawn between Trajan and Marcus Aurelius, both of whom were constantly fighting on the frontiers, and both of whom won impressive victories over the Parthians and Germans. Furthermore, these two reigns serve as a frame for the relatively tranquil reigns of Hadrian and Antoninus Pius, during which the *Pax Romana* reached its apex. Marcus Aurelius is best known for the 12 books of personal observations and memoirs (his *Meditations*), which he composed in the last decade of his life.

Marcus' one weakness was his blind charity toward his own family: not only did he tolerate gross marital indiscretions (and even treachery) by his wife, but he bequeathed the Empire to his son, who must have demonstrated signs of the mental imbalances that marked his sole reign as one of the vilest in all of Roman history. But if we ignore the atrocious acts of his wife and son, and judge him solely for the actions of his own reign, it becomes clear that Marcus Aurelius was a skilled and dutiful emperor whose stoic demeanor would have achieved even greater form had the world been at peace while he reigned.

FAUSTINA JUNIOR

AUGUSTA, A.D. 147–175/6

WIFE OF MARCUS AURELIUS
DAUGHTER OF ANTONINUS PIUS AND FAUSTINA SENIOR
SISTER OF GALERIUS ANTONINUS
MOTHER OF COMMODUS, ANNIUS VERUS, LUCILLA AND AURELIUS ANTONINUS

Annia Galeria Faustina, d. A.D. 175/6. The early life of Faustina Junior might best be described as a game of matrimonial musical chairs.

She was originally betrothed to Lucius Verus, whereas her future husband, Marcus Aurelius, was originally betrothed to the daughter of Aelius. But the year 138 brought a complete dynastic restructuring, for both

Aelius and Hadrian died, and Antoninus Pius was named emperor on the condition that he adopt Marcus Aurelius and Lucius Verus. With such a complex situation having arisen, the earlier marriage plans were abandoned. Because of Lucius Verus' extreme youth, it was deemed that his older colleague Marcus Aurelius was better suited to marry Faustina Junior. Nearly two decades later (in 164) Lucius Verus was compensated for his loss of Faustina Junior when he married Faustina's second daughter, Lucilla. In any event, the new arrangement was made official in 145 when Marcus Aurelius married Faustina Junior.

Their first child arrived in 146 or 147 (opinions vary), and in the next 25 years she had 12 or 13 more, with only five or six surviving childhood. By 146 it was clear that Marcus Aurelius was heir to the throne, and Faustina Junior was hailed Augusta in the year following (though some scholars prefer 146). The Empire had been without an Augusta since her mother died in 140/1, and so Faustina Junior was given the title even though her husband was only Caesar at the time. Faustina Junior accompanied her husband on his many campaigns, and her devotion earned her the unprecedented title *Mater Castrorum* ("mother of the camps") in June of 174.

But it seems the apple did not fall far from the tree, for Faustina Junior inherited her mother's playful disposition and more. Rumors of her adulterous affairs were rampant, with it being generally known she had a penchant for sailors and gladiators. Another widely accepted rumor was that Commodus (her only son to survive childhood) was sired by one of her gladiator lovers rather than her husband.

More treacherous, however, was her last noteworthy act, which was to alert the governor of Syria, Gaius Avidius Cassius, of her husband's ill health. Perhaps believing Marcus Aurelius would not survive the illness, she may even have told Cassius that her husband was already dead. This news prompted Cassius to stage a revolt in 175 that lasted perhaps 100 days. When news reached the East that Marcus Aurelius was very much alive and in command, the usurper was murdered. It was believed that Faustina Junior had amorous feelings for Cassius, and that this was why she informed him of Marcus' presumed death.

Though the veracity of individual rumors cannot be confirmed, the sheer volume of these reports leads one to the unavoidable conclusion that her sexual and moral conduct was reprehensible. Nonetheless, Marcus Aurelius appears to have cared for her deeply, and he bore this burden with the same fortitude as the other problems of state.

When Faustina Junior died at a small mountainside village in Cilicia in 175 or 176, Marcus Aurelius honored her memory in many ways, including a vast posthumous coinage. Though most of Faustina's children died in infancy or childhood, two of them (Commodus and Lucilla) achieved Imperial rank. Though they may have been friendly during childhood, they came into conflict in 182. Lucilla (who formerly had held the rank of Augusta when her first husband Lucius Verus was alive) plotted to murder her brother, who was then sole emperor. When the plot failed, Commodus banished and executed his estranged sister. Only a decade later Commodus himself met an ignominious fate, which brought to a close the story of Faustina Junior's ill-fated brood.

NUMISMATIC NOTE: The children of Faustina Junior make frequent appearances on coins, but usually in indistinguishable form, either being held in Faustina's arms or standing at her side. In one instance six children are shown at once. In terms of specific depictions there are perhaps six: Lucilla and Commodus (on coinages in their own names), Aurelius Antoninus (appearing with Lucilla on the reverse of coins of Antoninus Pius dated to 148/9), Annius Verus (appearing on medallions with Commodus, and possibly on a provincial coinage), and two other children who appear on the reverse of sestertii of Antoninus Pius dated to 156/7. Unfortunately, the latter two cannot be certainly identified.

AURELIUS ANTONINUS

SON OF MARCUS AURELIUS AND FAUSTINA JUNIOR
BROTHER OF COMMODUS, ANNIUS VERUS AND LUCILLA
GRANDSON OF ANTONINUS PIUS AND FAUSTINA SENIOR

Titus Aurelius Antoninus, A.D. 149. Aurelius Antoninus, the most obscure of the Antonine children to appear on coinage, died in the same year he was born. He may have been the first boy born to the Imperial couple, and the fact that he had a twin sister, Lucilla (later to be the wife of the emperor Lucius Verus), was cause for celebration. Some authorities, however, suggest another of his brothers, Titus Aelius Aurelius, was the firstborn male, but in any case, he also died in infancy.

NUMISMATIC NOTE: During the reign of the childless Antoninus Pius, an issue of coinage (including aurei, sestertii and dupondii) was struck to celebrate the birth of Lucilla and Aurelius Antoninus. The cherubic busts of the boy and his twin sister are set upon crossed cornucopias, in the same manner as was done some 126 years before to honor Tiberius' grandchildren. The obverses of the issue depict Antoninus Pius (who was then Augustus) and are dated to his 12th tribunician renewal in 148/9. Since this corresponds with the year the twins were born, we can be certain Aurelius Antoninus and Lucilla are depicted. A similar issue of 'crossed cornucopias' sestertii was struck during Pius' 20th tribunician renewal in 156/7, but their identifications are not secure.

ANNIUS VERUS

Caesar, A.D. 166–169/70 (under Marcus Aurelius, with Commodus)

Son of Marcus Aurelius and Faustina Junior
Brother of Commodus, Lucilla and Aurelius Antoninus
Grandson of Antoninus Pius and Faustina Senior

Marcus Annius Verus, A.D. 163–169/70. The year 165 was tragic for Marcus Aurelius and Faustina Junior, for two of their boys died: their lastborn, Hadrianus, died shortly after he was born; and the twin of Commodus, Titus Aurelius Fulvus Antoninus. This left the Imperial couple with only two boys, Commodus (aged four or five) and Annius Verus (aged three). It was upon their shoulders that the hope for succession rested.

This brings us to the year 166, when Marcus Aurelius and Lucius Verus jointly celebrated a triumph over the Parthians, and Marcus Aurelius commemorated the 20th renewal of his tribunate. This was a watershed year, and was the perfect occasion for Marcus Aurelius to elevate his two young sons to the rank of Caesar. The ceremony took place on October 12, 166, and in some small way it must have lifted the spirits of the Romans who — amid all their glory — were suffering from renewed barbarian invasions and a crippling plague epidemic. Although Commodus survived into adulthood to become emperor, his younger brother (who bore his father's original name) died soon thereafter, either in 169 or 170.

Numismatic Note: Some early scholars, such as Cohen, believed the young male bust on a series of anonymous quadrantes (see nos. 1172–5) was that of Annius Verus. However, this view has been abandoned since the portraits (which occur in four distinct varieties) are better identified as the four seasons. Even the issue of Tarsus described in Annius Verus' listings section may not portray him. Some authorities argue that it is actually Marcus Aurelius and Lucius Verus who are portrayed as the adopted sons of Antoninus Pius. Regrettably, the inscription is of no help in clarifying this matter. Indeed, were it not for the commemorative medallions struck at Rome (a cast copy of which is illustrated above), the numismatic record of this young Caesar might have to be abandoned entirely.

LUCIUS VERUS A.D. 161–169

(Co-emperor of Marcus Aurelius)

Son of Aelius
Adopted son of Antoninus Pius and heir of Hadrian
Husband of Lucilla
Son-in-law of Marcus Aurelius

Lucius Aelius Aurelius Commodus (*earlier* Lucius Ceionius Commodus), c. A.D. 130–169. In the year 138 the 7-year-old boy who would come to be known as Lucius Verus was brought into the Imperial fold. In the previous year his destiny seemed clear: his father, Aelius, had been appointed as Hadrian's Caesar and intended successor. But Aelius died unexpectedly only a few months before Hadrian himself died. Even so, Hadrian made provisions for Aelius' son by requiring that his new heir, Antoninus Pius, adopt Lucius Verus (who may have been Hadrian's illegitimate grandson) as one of his successors.

During the next 22 years Verus was aware he was destined to be emperor, but apparently showed little desire to participate in government. Meanwhile, his co-heir, Marcus Aurelius, held the rank of Caesar and was heaped with titles and responsibilities. Verus' only significant posts were those of quaestor in 153, and of consul in 154 and 161.

Immediately after the death of Antoninus Pius in 161, Marcus Aurelius and Lucius Verus were appointed co-Augusti, though the lofty title of *Pontifex Maximus* was given only to Marcus. Not only was Marcus nine years Verus' senior, but the title was itself indivisible (and remained so until it was first shared in 238 by Pupienus and Balbinus). In that same year Verus was betrothed to Lucilla, the 12-year-old daughter of his Imperial colleague.

In the meantime, the peace which Antoninus Pius had negotiated with the Parthians late in his reign had collapsed, and Verus was sent to defend the eastern territories from a new invasion. Already Armenia had been captured and Syria was on the defensive.

Though historians dispute whether Lucius Verus spent most of his time in the East fighting or luxuriating (indeed, in 164 he went to Ephesus to marry Lucilla), he does seem to have been an excellent commander. But the Parthian's gains were short-lived, as Verus and his generals recovered Syria and Armenia, and occupied Mesopotamia and Media (which formerly had not been part of the Empire). Just as in Trajan's day, the Romans captured the capital city of Ctesiphon (165), and this time set it ablaze.

After Verus had forced the Parthians to sue for peace in 166 on terms highly favorable to the Romans, he returned to Rome later in the year to celebrate his triumph jointly with Marcus Aurelius. However, the Parthian victory had two serious side effects: the European provinces were vulnerable because so many soldiers had been withdrawn, and even worse, the returning soldiers brought the plague with them. This plague epidemic was very serious, and almost completely depopulated some regions of the Empire. Rome (which was already suffering from a food shortage) was hit especially hard and even a decade later was still suffering from this plague.

During the three years that followed the Parthian campaign (166–169), Marcus Aurelius and Lucius Verus were fully occupied fighting the Marcomanni and the Quadi. Though difficult, their effort was a success, and tragedy only struck when they were returning to Rome early in 169 to celebrate another triumph. The 38-year-old Verus died of a stroke (or epileptic fit) in northern Italy, at Altinum.

Although we cannot say Lucius Verus was a gifted leader or a man free of vices — for he was fond of hunting, wrestling and other sports — it would be equally unfair to malign him as an irresponsible lush who drank himself to death. Indeed what he lacked in talent and resolve he made up for with a strong sense of duty and loyalty to Marcus Aurelius. On balance he seems to have been more of an asset than a burden to his senior colleague, who was characteristically charitable toward him both in life and in *memoria.*

LUCILLA

AUGUSTA, A.D. 164–182/3

WIFE OF LUCIUS VERUS
DAUGHTER OF MARCUS AURELIUS AND FAUSTINA JUNIOR
SISTER OF COMMODUS, ANNIUS VERUS AND AURELIUS ANTONINUS
GRANDDAUGHTER OF ANTONINUS PIUS AND FAUSTINA SENIOR
SISTER-IN-LAW OF CRISPINA

Annia Aurelia Galeria Lucilla, A.D. 148/9–182/3. The second of six daughters born to Marcus Aurelius and Faustina Junior, Lucilla was the twin of Titus Aurelius Antoninus, who died in the year of his birth.

Lucilla was engaged to Lucius Verus when he was named co-emperor with her own father in 161. Lucilla was only 12 years old at the time of her betrothal to Verus, who was about 31 years old, so the wedding was delayed until Lucilla turned fifteen or sixteen. She remained in Italy as her future husband traveled to the eastern front and waged war against the Parthians, though in 164 Lucilla traveled to Ephesus where Verus took leave of the campaign to marry her.

Together they had at least one, and possibly three children, the fate(s) of whom are unknown. Considering the endless military demands on her husband, they were probably not able to spend much leisurely time together, and the fatal stroke he suffered while returning to Rome in 169 must have come as a shock to her. Lucilla's life took a turn for the worse thereafter.

The 20- or 21-year-old widow next entered into an unhappy marriage with an elderly senator named Tiberius Claudius Pompeianus, a native of Antioch who had twice been consul. The new marriage was carefully arranged by her father Marcus Aurelius, who sought a man of unquestioned loyalty (for Lucilla still bore the title of Augusta). Descended from two generations of adulterous empresses, Lucilla maintained the family tradition by engaging in frequent extramarital affairs.

Lucilla seems not to have gotten along with her sister-in-law Crispina, and was envious of the fact that Crispina also held the title of Augusta. Lucilla survived into the reign of her brother Commodus, but they too quarreled, and either in 182 or 183 she joined in a plot ot murder him. Her co-conspirators included an ex-consul and cousin named Marcus Ummidius Quadratus, one of her husband's nephews, Quintianus, and most likely her sister-in-law Crispina. The plot succeeded to the point that Quintianus was able to draw his dagger, but he was overpowered before he could strike Commodus down.

When Lucilla's role in the plot was exposed, Commodus exiled her to Capri, where she was soon executed. Since the conspiracy was hatched within the palace walls, it greatly unnerved Commodus, who thereafter viewed most senators and advisors as potential assassins.

NUMISMATIC NOTE: For an infant portrait of Lucilla celebrating her birth, see the listing of her twin, Titus Aurelius Antoninus (nos. 1574–6).

COMMODUS A.D. 177–192

CAESAR: A.D. 166–177
(UNDER MARCUS AURELIUS)
(A.D. 166–169/70: WITH ANNIUS VERUS)
(A.D. 169/70–177: ALONE)
AUGUSTUS: A.D. 177–192
(A.D. 177–180: WITH MARCUS AURELIUS)
(A.D. 180–192: SOLE REIGN)

SON OF MARCUS AURELIUS AND FAUSTINA JUNIOR
HUSBAND OF CRISPINA
BROTHER OF ANNIUS VERUS, LUCILLA AND AURELIUS ANTONINUS
GRANDSON OF ANTONINUS PIUS AND FAUSTINA SENIOR

Marcus Aurelius Commodus Antoninus (*earlier, and from* 191–2, Lucius Aelius Aurelius Commodus), A.D. 161–192. Born at Lanuvium about five months after his father became emperor, Commodus was the only boy of Marcus Aurelius and Faustina Junior to survive childhood. Although the practice of hereditary rulership had been abandoned since the age of the Flavians, the otherwise laudable Marcus Aurelius bestowed the title of Augustus on his son.

Commodus' career began in 166, when, as a 5- or 6-year-old, he was made Caesar along with his 3-year-old brother Annius Verus (who died about three years later). Commodus' training began in his early adolescence, when he accompanied his father on military campaigns on the Danubian frontier and the Near East.

The dynastic intentions of Marcus Aurelius came to fruition in 177 when Commodus, then 15, was raised from Caesar to the rank of Augustus, and entered into a tragic marriage with Crispina. Commodus held the title of Augustus jointly with his father for three years until the latter died in 180. Commodus quickly abandoned his father's expansionist policies and frontier wars by negotiating a quick treaty with the Marcomanni in which he forfeited territory and agreed to pay annual indemnities.

Commodus then returned to Rome to establish his new regime. Within a year or two the emperor had managed to alienate his sister Lucilla and his wife, Crispina, who overcame their personal differences to conspire in 182 or 183 to murder him. Though their plot failed, it greatly affected Commodus, who was unable to size up his silent enemies as easily as he could a barbarian army. It also made him wary of the senate, because at the moment the assassin drew his dagger and came forth he screamed: "See! This is what the senate has sent you!"

Probably in the year 183 he banished and executed both his sister (for her role in the plot) and his wife, whom he had divorced on a charge of adultery. The latter act was one of supreme irony, for Commodus was a rampant adulterer, and is said to have had a harem of 300 women and an equal number of men.

From the very beginning of his principate Commodus showed no interest in frontier warfare or the tedious details of government: he left these tasks to his generals, prefects and courtiers. Making matters worse, we are told that such appointments were not made rationally.

For the last dozen years of Commodus' reign, the Empire was almost entirely in the hands of his praetorian prefects, whom the emperor executed with the same enthusiasm that he appointed them. The first to exercise great authority was Perennis, who after "reigning" for five years (180–185) was murdered by his own soldiers on a false rumor that he planned to usurp the throne. Perhaps responsible for Perennis' downfall was his successor, Cleander, who was virtual ruler of Rome for the next five years (185–190). Cleander was only dethroned by an elaborate plot hatched by the official in charge of Rome's grain supply. By falsely creating a shortage and blaming it on the incompetence and greed of Cleander, so were sown the seeds of Cleander's demise.

We hear very little about military conflicts during Commodus' reign, perhaps because his best generals, Ulpius Marcellus, Septimius Severus, Pescennius Niger, Pertinax and Clodius Albinus, fought so efficiently that the emperor did not have to leave Rome. In the final analysis, however, this was a disadvantage to Commodus, for it allowed him to remain idle in Rome, where his mental illness grew daily. Had Commodus been personally involved in the border wars, his reign may not have taken on such a foul character.

His cruelties and excesses increased with the passage of time, and rivaled those of Nero, Domitian, Elagabalus and of Caligula, with whom he shared the same birthday. Toward the end of his reign a fire destroyed much of Rome, which Commodus decided to rename *Colonia Commodiana* in honor of himself. He was partial to Jupiter, Serapis, Isis and the hero Hercules, and had himself venerated as the living incarnation of the latter. The emperor took singular pleasure in public games and gladiatorial combat, in which he sometimes participated, remniscent of the stage indignities of Nero more than a century before.

The emperor's foul disposition and gladiatorial bent only served to validate for many Romans the rumor that he had been sired by one of the gladiators with whom his mother had consorted. Commodus was an excellent archer and could decapitate ostriches with arrows with crescent-shaped tips. He was in the habit of role-playing in every aspect of his life, and in his final years often appeared in public wearing the lion skin and carrying the club of Hercules — a guise he even dons on some coins struck in 192. The list of his offenses could fill several pages, and thus will be halted here with that in mind. Fortunately for historians, the veracity of such outrageous behaviors — which otherwise might be easily dismissed as hostile propaganda — is confirmed by some of the coins he struck.

Though Commodus had survived several murder plots in his 15-year reign, by the end of 192 his mental state had degenerated so greatly that not even his closest advisors felt secure. Fearing the degrading and possibly lethal actions Commodus would take on New Year's Day, 193, a plot was hastily formed by his chamberlain Eclectus, his concubine Marcia (who was Eclectus' wife), and the praetorian prefect Quintus Aemilius Laetus.

On New Year's eve of 192, Marcia administered poison to Commodus, who vomited in reaction. Fearful of discovery, the conspirators commanded an athlete named Narcissus to strangle the 31-year-old emperor. Commodus' death brought great joy to the senate, which had been living in mortal fear for more than a decade. Though his memory was initially erased (*damnatio memoriae*), only three years later Commodus was deified by the senate at the insistence of Septimius Severus, who had no choice but to honor Commodus so as to honor his own false claim of being the son of Marcus Aurelius.

CRISPINA

AUGUSTA, A.D. 177–182/3

WIFE OF COMMODUS
DAUGHTER-IN-LAW OF MARCUS AURELIUS AND FAUSTINA JUNIOR
SISTER-IN-LAW OF LUCILLA

Bruttia Crispina, d. A.D. 182/3. The daughter of Lucius Fulvius Bruttius Praesens, a nobleman who had campaigned with Marcus Aurelius against the Sarmatians, Crispina married the emperor's 15-year-old son, Commodus, in 177 or 178 (accounts vary). Contemporary historians tell us Crispina was an exceptionally beautiful young woman, a fact which is supported by some of her more flattering coin portraits.

For young Commodus, the year 177 was an important one: he celebrated a military triumph with his father, who then appointed him consul and raised him from Caesar to Augustus. The awarding of these public honors left no doubt that Commodus was the intended successor to his father. These events were also important for Crispina, who was hailed Augusta in place of her mother-in-law, Faustina Junior, who died a year or two before (though she shared the title with her sister-in-law Lucilla).

As her husband's megalomania and paranoia became more acute, the couple grew apart, and each pursued their own adulterous affairs. Though Crispina may have been quite active in this manner, she could hardly have compared with her husband, who is said to have had a harem of several hundred women and men.

Commodus eventually divorced Crispina on charges of adultery and banished her to the island of Capri, where she was later strangled to death. This almost certainly occurred in 182 or 183 (though some historians even suggest 188), and as such it seems likely that her falling out with Commodus was more closely related to the murder plot organized by Lucilla than to her infidelity.

CHAPTER SIX

Civil War and The Severan-Emesan Dynasty A.D. 193–235

The murder of Commodus on New Year's Eve, 193, brought to a conclusion the "golden age" of the Roman Empire, though in fact it had ceased to glitter more than two decades before. What followed was a disgraceful display of greed, power lust and vanity that lasted six months.

The first of the new emperors, Pertinax, was a man of good intentions who was murdered by corrupt men whose special interests he threatened. This was followed by the lowliest event in Roman history, the selling of the throne to the highest bidder, a man named Didius Julianus, who had little to recommend himself to the office. Indeed, even the money he had promised (for he was exceptionally wealthy) failed to materialize.

When Didius Julianus bought the throne, appeals went out to frontier generals to liberate Rome and restore its dignity. Three men responded — one in Britain, one in Syria and another in Pannonia. The latter, Septimius Severus, marched on Rome quickly, ousted Didius Julianus and replaced the corrupt praetorian guards with his own loyal Illyrian soldiers. He made quick enemies of senators, who prayed for their deliverance by the other two frontier generals, Clodius Albinus and Pescennius Niger.

Septimius Severus was equally capable as a politician and a soldier: he bought off one of his adversaries while he defeated the other. Then, when he was in a better position, he provoked his last opponent, Clodius Albinus, into a war that Severus won in a pitched battle in Gaul. After a costly and degrading civil war of slightly more than four years, the Empire was at peace, and a new ruling house, the Severan-Emesan dynasty, had been established.

This chapter is divided into two sections. The first, following this brief introduction, concerns the Civil War of 193–197, and the second, following another introduction, chronicles the dynasty founded by the North African emperor Septimius Severus and his Syrian wife, Julia Domna.

THE CIVIL WAR OF A.D. 193–197

PERTINAX A.D. 193

HUSBAND OF TITIANA
FATHER OF PERTINAX JUNIOR

Publius Helvius Pertinax, A.D. 126–193. Pertinax was a self-made man whose father, a freedman, had been a timber merchant. It would appear that he rose from his humble origins to the highest offices in the Empire through talent and dedication alone. His brief principate represented an opportunity for deliverance from the injustices of Commodus, but its quick failure only served to demonstrate how deeply ingrained corruption had become.

Though he is portrayed as a man of unimpeachable morality, Pertinax could not have been a complete stranger to corruption in the military and government, for he held the two highest posts in Rome when Commodus was at his most wicked. Indeed, it is better, perhaps, to believe he viewed his principate as a golden opportunity to become a benevolent dictator, and to restore the integrity that was then a thing of the past. But others were unwilling to live up to the high standards Pertinax applied to his own conduct, and it was naive that he should have expected to reform a corrupt nation overnight.

There can be little doubt that Pertinax was privy to the coup by which he gained the throne. To secure their positions, the conspirators spread rumors that Commodus had died of natural causes and that Pertinax had already been acclaimed Augustus. For this reason we may rightfully suspect Pertinax was hailed emperor on the evening of December 31, 192, rather than on New Year's Day 193. Pertinax embraced his fellow senators, whom he viewed as brothers who also had survived the tyranny of Commodus.

Pertinax began his career as a teacher, after which he embarked on a career in the military. In that capacity he served honorably in Parthia, Britain and Noricum. As a general under Commodus, he had suppressed two revolts in Africa in 190. He had also served as consul for the first time in 175, and as governor of Moesia Inferior, Dacia, Syria, Britain and Africa. At the time of Commodus' murder, he not only was serving out his second consulship, but also was the prefect of Rome.

Important tasks faced Pertinax, for the treasury was virtually empty and the systems of government were entirely corrupted. He immediately engaged in fiscal and legal reforms that by all accounts were sensible and equitable, and given enough time he might have restored the Empire to the glory it enjoyed under Marcus Aurelius and his predecessors. But his noble intentions alarmed those who had become accustomed to the benefits derived from their posts in the government and the army. Most of Pertinax's reforms were aimed at cutting out corruption that benefited the few, and better distributing the wealth of Rome to the common man. Simply put: Pertinax was changing too much too quickly, and at the expense of the people who could do him the greatest harm.

Two coups were hastily attempted. The first occurred on January 3, only two or three days after Pertinax had been hailed emperor, and the second in early March. Among those who led a plot against him was the consul Sosius Falco. Although the evidence against Falco was damning, Pertinax pled for the man's life, insisting his reign would not be stained with the blood of a senator.

The truest threat against Pertinax came from the praetorian guards, who felt slighted at the murder of Commodus and in not having a hand in the selection of his successor. On March 28 the praetorians revolted and stormed the palace, murdering the 66-year-old Pertinax after he had reigned only 86 days. They placed his decapitated head on a lance and paraded it in triumph before the citizens, who, it seems, understood their grave misfortune. The senate — realizing the seriousness of its loss — consecrated Pertinax, and Septimius Severus not only expelled the praetorians, but also adopted Pertinax's name along with that of the Antonines.

NUMISMATIC NOTE: Only Pertinax and Antoninus Pius depicted Ops, the personification of wealth, on their coinage. A denarius of considerable rarity features his most interesting reverse type: MENTI LAVDANDAE, which loosely translates as "praiseworthy good sense." The majority of Pertinax's coins were struck at Rome, although he did strike denarii of distinctive style at Alexandria. His portraiture is often magnificent, with his rare consecration coinage offering a particularly virile image.

TITIANA

AUGUSTA, A.D. 193

WIFE OF PERTINAX
MOTHER OF PERTINAX JUNIOR

Flavia Titiana, lifespan unknown. Little is known of the origins and fate of Titiana, the wife of the emperor Pertinax, except that she bore her husband a homonymous son who was accorded the rank of Caesar in 193, and a daughter whose name is not known.

In addition to the grief Titiana suffered from the disgraceful murder and desecration of her husband, she had still more to endure. Her own father, Flavius Sulpicianus, immediately proceeded to the camp of the praetorians in hopes of persuading them to hail him emperor in place of his murdered son-in-law. What began as a shameful exercise in flattery and bribery turned into a public auction in which Sulpicianus went head-to-head with Didius Julianus, who in the end offered the larger sum and was hailed emperor.

But the bad news was not over for Titiana, for her father was ousted from his position as city prefect (Sulpicianus had been appointed by Pertinax, who himself had to abandon the post so he could assume the duties of emperor). Although Sulpicianus survived the reign of Didius Julianus, he was executed by Septimius Severus in 197 for his support of Clodius Albinus. His daughter and grandson, it would seem, survived the civil war and were honored by the Severans.

NUMISMATIC NOTE: Most Alexandrian tetradrachms bearing on their obverse the bust of Titiana, and on their reverse the figure of Nike advancing, which have appeared in the marketplace in the last few decades are known counterfeits struck around the turn of the century (though the type itself is known and confirmed as genuine). Also suspect are bronzes of 27mm and 24mm listed by Dattari, which may be genuine but which require confirmation. Perhaps the only genuine issue that portrays Titiana is the dual-portrait piece now in the British Museum.

PERTINAX JUNIOR

CAESAR, A.D. 193

SON OF PERTINAX AND TITIANA

Publius Helvius Pertinax (Junior), d. A.D. 211/2. Bearing the same name as his father, Pertinax Junior was perhaps 5 to 10 years old when his father was hailed emperor. The *Historia Augusta* reports that the senate proclaimed the boy Caesar, but that his incorruptible father refused the offer, suggesting his son should be raised to that rank only when he had earned it.

Unlike his father, Pertinax Junior was not murdered by the praetorians; he survived nearly another 20 years. Septimius Severus was unbending in his devotion to the memory of Pertinax, and subsequently placed Pertinax Junior in charge of the sacerdotal (priestly) college. The young man also became a close friend of the emperor's youngest son, Geta. However, the latter association proved to be his undoing, for when Caracalla murdered Geta in 211 he initiated a general massacre of Geta's partisans, which included Pertinax Junior. Although the figure is probably exaggerated, the historian Cassius Dio tells us that perhaps 20,000 were killed in the fratricidal purge, ranging from the lowliest slave to men of high station.

Among those who fell with Pertinax Junior were Pompeianus (a grandson of Marcus Aurelius), Papinian (one of his father's distinguished colleagues, and the praetorian prefect), and Cornuficia (a granddaughter of Antoninus Pius and daughter of Marcus Aurelius). Though it is hardly a valid excuse for Caracalla's generally savage actions, it is perhaps understandable that the emperor perceived Pertinax Junior as a threat. Not only had he been a supporter of Geta, but he was also the son of Pertinax, a former emperor who was much beloved by the Romans.

NUMISMATIC NOTE: Coins depicting Pertinax Junior were struck only at Alexandria. They occur in two issues: one dedicated exclusively to the young prince (of which fewer than six specimens are known), and one bearing both his portrait and that of his mother (which is believed unique).

DIDIUS JULIANUS A.D. 193

HUSBAND OF MANLIA SCANTILLA
FATHER OF DIDIA CLARA

Marcus Didius Severus Julianus, c. A.D. 133/5–193. After the praetorian guards murdered Pertinax on March 28, 193, the capital was in chaos but the soldiers were in command. An immediate appeal was made by Flavius Sulpicianus, the father-in-law of Pertinax, that he should be made emperor. But Sulpicianus found competition from a senator named Didius Julianus, who was also one of the wealthiest men in Rome.

Julianus was born in Milan and raised in the household of Domitia Lucilla, the mother of Marcus Aurelius. He subsequently had an impressive career, governing several provinces and serving as consul with Pertinax almost a decade before. Caught up in the moment, Julianus began to bid against Sulpicianus for the chance to be hailed emperor. The bidding war continued until Julianus pledged the sum of 25,000 sestertii per guard, an offer that even Sulpicianus could not exceed. Before the day had ended, one emperor had been murdered and another had bought his throne.

Drunk with power and blinded by greed, the praetorians conducted Julianus in tight formation to the senate house, where the terrified senators had little choice but to hail him emperor. Even greater than the senate's fear was the rage of the people, who immediately sent deputations to frontier commanders, requesting that they march on Rome and deliver them from the tyranny of Didius Julianus and the praetorian guards. Since the leading generals of the day had all been comrades-in-arms with Pertinax, they were eager to avenge his murder and no doubt saw this as an ideal opportunity to seize the title of Augustus.

This was a rare opportunity, and three generals responded: Clodius Albinus, Septimius Severus and Pescennius Niger. Albinus and Niger were far from Rome, which gave the upper hand to Septimius Severus, who commanded three legions in nearby Pannonia. Severus rallied his men, promised a generous bonus, and marched on Rome at a furious pace. Events were moving at such an alarming rate that Julianus realized he was doomed. Though he resorted to every act of desperation (including sending assassins after Severus, and even offering to share power with him), it was to no avail, for Severus and his legions were nearing Rome.

To avoid bloodshed, Severus promised immunity to the whole of the praetorian guard if they turned over the few men who killed Pertinax. Fearful of the battle-hardened frontier legions, and still without the payment promised by Julianus, the praetorians agreed to Severus' terms and informed the senate of their change of heart. The senate promptly deified Pertinax, condemned Julianus, and declared Septimius Severus emperor. On the 1st or 2nd of June (opinions vary) Didius Julianus was captured and beheaded in the manner of a common criminal, thus bringing to a conclusion his brief and shameful reign.

NUMISMATIC NOTE: The name Severus, which only appears on some of Julianus' coin inscriptions, was probably added after some coins had already been struck without it. It has been suggested that the name was initially excluded in an oversight (for Severus was one of Julianus' names), or that it was added later to demonstrate the sincerity of Julianus' offer to share his throne with Septimius Severus, who was then advancing on Rome.

MANLIA SCANTILLA

AUGUSTA, A.D. 193

WIFE OF DIDIUS JULIANUS
MOTHER OF DIDIA CLARA

Manlia Scantilla, lifespan unknown. On the day the senate was forced to hail her husband Didius Julianus emperor, it also bestowed the rank of Augusta on Manlia Scantilla and Didia Clara, the new emperor's wife and daughter. Of the virtues Manlia Scantilla may have possessed, beauty, it seems, was not one of them. Indeed, the 19th Century historian S.W. Stevenson goes so far as to describe her as "the most deformed of women." She remains almost a complete mystery, and of her fate subsequent to being stripped of her title of Augusta, we have no details and can only conclude that she died in obscurity sometime thereafter.

DIDIA CLARA

AUGUSTA, A.D. 193

DAUGHTER OF DIDIUS JULIANUS AND MANLIA SCANTILLA

Didia Clara, born c. A.D. 153. In stark contrast to her mother, the daughter of Didius Julianus was a woman of considerable beauty. Indeed, the same historian who maligned her mother's countenance suggests Didia Clara was no less than "the most beautiful of the young women of her age."

Didia Clara was married to a cousin named Cornelius Repentinus, who was destined to be one of three men who held the job of prefect of Rome during the tumultuous 13-week period that followed the murder of Commodus. The office had originally been occupied by Pertinax, who upon being hailed emperor vacated it and appointed his father-in-law, Flavius Sulpicianus, to the post. Following Pertinax's murder, Didius Julianus ousted Sulpicianus (who had been Julianus' competitor at the "auction" held by the praetorian guards) and appointed his own son-in-law, Repentinus, in his place.

In addition to being hailed Augusta, having a father as emperor and a husband as city prefect, Didia Clara was also named beneficiary of her father's estate. But all of her fortune turned sour in a single day, either June 1 or 2 of 193, when her father was beheaded, she was stripped of her imperial title, and her inheritance was confiscated by the new emperor, Septimius Severus.

PESCENNIUS NIGER

A.D. 193–194

Gaius Pescennius Niger, c. A.D. 135/140–194. Of the three frontier generals who answered Rome's call for liberation from Didius Julianus, Pescennius Niger was the most legitimate candidate. Indeed, when a group of outraged citizens gathered in the Circus Maximus to draft a plea, it was to Niger that they sent their request.

Unfortunately for Niger, the command he had gained through the patronage of Narcissus (the athlete who strangled Commodus) was in Syria, and thus news did not reach him fast enough to react before Septimius Severus, who commanded legions in Pannonia, was able to march on Rome and depose Didius Julianus. While glad to be rid of Didius Julianus, the senators disliked Septimius Severus, and we are told they prayed for Niger's success even though they were forced to declare him a public enemy.

Niger hailed from an equestrian Italian family from Aquinum, a small city about half way between Rome and Pompeii. He rose to high office through a successful if unexceptional career in the army. He found his greatest achievements under Commodus, for whom he fought the Dacians, served as consul in 190, and finally as governor of Syria beginning in 191.

By all accounts he was a knowledgeable man with a great deal of integrity, but who was also ferocious, lustful and a strict disciplinarian. Though Niger had originally been hailed in opposition to Julianus, his new rival unquestionably was Septimius Severus. After Severus had consolidated his power in Rome and neutralized Clodius Albinus in the West by giving him the empty title of Caesar, he marched east in the summer of 193 to confront Niger.

Niger had consolidated his own authority in the East, and with nine legions under his banner marched toward the Bosporus to meet the armies of Severus. However, Severus' Illyrian soldiers easily routed the Syrian legions in successive engagements in Thrace (except at Byzantium), Cyzicus and Nicaea. By this time, perhaps February of 194, Egypt and some cities in Syria had switched allegiance to Severus.

The most important battle, however, occurred at Issus, in south-eastern Cilicia, where Alexander the Great had routed the Perisan king Darius some 500 years before. This was a critical defeat, and according to one source cost the lives of 20,000 of Niger's men. Now a fugitive, Niger fled south to his capital of Antioch, from which he apparently planned to flee to the Parthians for safety. However, Severus' general, Anullinus, captured and executed him, and sent his severed head to the delighted Severus.

The chronology of these events is inconsistently reported, and a summary is worth presenting. The time frame for Niger's being hailed emperor spans the period from late April to June 1 of 193; his defeat at Issus is variously reported as having occurred sometime in March, April or May of 194. Niger's subsequent fate is even more vague, as he may have been overtaken before reaching Antioch, captured soon after reaching the city, or he may have endured a siege of several months. Thus, his death occurred sometime between March and October of 194.

Severus remained in the East for a while, punishing the cities in Syria that had supported Niger to the end and dividing that region into two provinces, Coele-Syria and Phoenicia. Subsequently, he led a campaign against the Parthian vassals who had supported Niger's claim to the throne. In the process, Severus annexed most of Osroëne and parts of northern Mesopotamia, for which he was hailed *Parthicus Arabicus* and *Parthicus Adiabenicus*.

Numismatic Note: Like Otho some 125 years before, Pescennius Niger struck no Latin bronzes, only Latin silver and gold, and provincial coinages. Niger's Latin coinage (mostly from Antioch, although some from Caesarea in Cappadocia) is rife with misspellings, reverted letters and other technical imperfections. His portraits vary considerably in their treatment, and the planchets of his denarii are often irregular in shape. Because of their debased metal, the denarii typically have porous surfaces.

CLODIUS ALBINUS A.D. 195–197

Caesar: A.D. 193–195
(under Septimius Severus)
Augustus: A.D. 195–197
(against Septimius Severus)

Decimus Clodius Septimius Albinus, c. A.D. 140/150–197. Born into a distinguished family from Hadrumetum, about 75 miles south of Carthage, Clodius Albinus was a tall and portly man who pursued a career in the army. Although a North African like Septimius Severus, he was from a family of senatorial rank, and grew up in the lap of luxury. Little is known of his personality, except that he had a melancholy outlook and a foul sense of humor, but was brave in battle and harsh in his discipline.

He served admirably under Marcus Aurelius, who made him governor of Bithynia in 175, and later under Commodus, for whom he fought the Dacians and held many posts. He served as consul in 187, as governor of Lower Germany in 189, and finally as governor of Britain in 191. When the rapid succession of Commodus, Pertinax and Didius Julianus occurred early in 193, Albinus was one of three frontier generals to answer Rome's call for liberation. However, before Albinus made a concerted effort on his own account, his neutrality was purchased by Septimius Severus, who gave him the empty title of Caesar, designated him as his heir, and even had him add the name Septimius to his own. With Albinus placated and Rome secured, Severus devoted much of 193 and 194 to defeating Pescennius Niger in the East. Now only Severus and Albinus remained in positions of authority.

Upon Severus' triumphant return to Rome, his relationship with Albinus (with whom he shared the consulship that year) began to sour. The level of hostility reached a new height in 195, when Severus named his own sons, Caracalla and Geta, as his successors, and forced the senate to declare Albinus a public enemy. The news could hardly have come as a shock to Albinus, who moved into Gaul and was immediately hailed emperor by his own soldiers at Lugdunum in the fall of 195 (or early in 196, as other accounts would have it).

While Severus was busy passing laws in Rome, Albinus gained control or the allegiance of Spain and the Rhineland, though the Rhine legions withheld their loyalty. His original army of some 40,000 men quickly grew in size. It was not until January of 197 that Severus marched from Rome to meet his western foe. The two Roman armies met on February 19, 197, near Lugdunum. The historian Cassius Dio (who is prone to exaggeration) tells us each general commanded 150,000 men.

The battle was one of the largest in Roman history, and though Severus initially was thrown from his horse, a quick cavalry action permitted his escape and the battle continued. Eventually, Severus' Illyrian legions defeated the soldiers of Albinus, who is said to have fled the battle and committed suicide.

Severus is reported to have ridden his horse over the corpse of Albinus, which he decapitated so he could display the rebel's head in Rome. This may be an invention by pro-senatorial historians, but if it was true, it no doubt had a great effect in terrifying the senate. As a final insult to his adversary's memory, Severus is said to have executed Albinus' wife and children, and cast all of their corpses into the icy waters of the Rhône.

The legacy of Albinus is a difficult one to decipher, as he is usually depicted as the innocent victim of Severus' evil designs. One can only marvel at his naiveté in accepting Severus' hollow gesture of shared authority, and read on in shock as he failed to march on Rome during Severus' year-long absence in Syria. No doubt Albinus would have been warmly received by his friends in the senate who feared the day Severus returned from the East.

Alternatively, he may have doubted the strength of his position, and did not challenge Severus out of fear of certain failure. More likely, though, Albinus was probably awaiting the right moment to strike. Perhaps he believed it was a wiser policy to let Severus march all the way to Syria and exhaust his own legions fighting Niger. Indeed, had circumstances been slightly different, Severus would have been defeated by Niger, in which case Albinus would have been able to occupy Rome unopposed.

Clearly, it seems Albinus made an error in timing, for he did not go on the offensive until after Severus had returned to Rome and declared him a public enemy, at which point he had no choice but to engage in a costly civil war.

NUMISMATIC NOTE: Clodius Albinus' coinage falls into two distinct categories: the early issues struck at Rome while he was Caesar under

Septimius Severus, and the much scarcer coinage he struck at the capital of Lugdunum after he was proclaimed Augustus against Severus. The styles are completely different and the coinages can be distinguished with the greatest of ease, even when the inscriptions are indistinct.

Severan-Emesan Dynasty
A.D. 193–235

The 42 years between the acclamation of Septimius Severus in 193 and the murder of Severus Alexander in 235 is usually described as that of the "Severan Dynasty." Though this is an appropriate enough label, it is perhaps too simplistic, for the dynasty was composed of both North African (Severan) and Syrian (Emesan) members. Indeed, it was the Syrian side of the family that restored the dynasty after it was overthrown by the usurper Macrinus in 217.

Founding the dynasty was the North African general Septimius Severus and his Syrian-born wife, Julia Domna. Severus and his two sons, Caracalla and Geta, ruled the Empire for the first 24 years, from 193 to 217. The dynasty was restored by the family of Domna's sister, Julia Maesa, whose two grandsons, Elagabalus and Severus Alexander, collectively ruled nearly 17 years, from 218 to 235.

Although Rome had first been ruled by a foreign-born emperor almost a century earlier, when the Spaniard Trajan ascended the throne in 98, these were foreigners of a more exotic bent. The Punic and Syrian rulers contributed greatly to the introduction of foreign customs and religions in Rome. The Severans introduced the worship of numerous North African, Punic and Egyptian deities, whereas the Emesans imported the worship of the sun-god Heliogabal. Even the usurper Macrinus, who temporarily interrupted the dynasty, was a mere knight of Moorish extractions. Indeed, no true Roman occupied the throne during this period of history.

These eastern and Punic religions were to have profound effects, not only during the period of this dynasty, but also in the succeeding years. Most important, perhaps, was solar worship, which became popular with soldiers, especially in the form of Mithraism. Solar worship eventually served as the conduit by which Constantine the Great was able to adopt Christianity early in the 4th Century.

The fanaticism of eastern religion was quite different from the quiet, reverent form of worship to which the Romans were accustomed. Their form of paganism relied more on ritual and formula than actual belief, so the bizarre rituals introduced by Elagabalus (218–222) as the chief priest of the sun-cult of Heliogabal were quite a spectacle to the Romans.

Elagabalus combined his exotic rituals with a desecration of Roman institution by marrying a Vestal Virgin. Few could have imagined that the Imperial government would get that far out of hand, and it comes as no surprise that he was murdered.

The Severan-Emesan dynasty came to an end in 235, when the rather docile emperor Severus Alexander, still only 26 years old, was murdered near the Rhine. Executing him were mutinous soldiers who wanted someone who would courageously lead them into the forests of Germany, not someone who would instead negotiate peace with offerings of gold. His murder heralded a new era in Roman history in which warfare on the three fronts — the Rhine, the Danube and the Euphrates — was rampant, and no Imperial continuity was achieved until the formation of the Tetrarchy some 50 years later.

SEPTIMIUS SEVERUS
A.D. 193–211

AUGUSTUS: A.D. 193–211
(A.D. 193–198: SOLE REIGN;
195–198 CARACALLA AS CAESAR)
(A.D. 198–209: WITH CARACALLA;
GETA AS CAESAR)
(A.D. 209–211: WITH CARACALLA AND
GETA)

HUSBAND OF JULIA DOMNA
FATHER OF CARACALLA AND GETA
UNCLE OF JULIA SOAEMIAS AND JULIA MAMAEA
GREAT-UNCLE OF ELAGABALUS AND SEVERUS ALEXANDER
BROTHER-IN-LAW OF JULIA MAESA
FATHER-IN-LAW OF PLAUTILLA

Lucius Septimius Severus, A.D. 145/6–211 An intensely superstitious man, Septimius Severus hailed from a privileged and thoroughly Romanized family from the North African metropolis of Leptis Magna. He was a short, powerful man perfectly suited to the rigors of war, and ambitious enough to aspire to the throne.

On his father's side he was descended from the *Septimii*, who were of Punic origin, and on his mother's side from the *Fulvii*, who were of Italian descent. One of his grandfathers was the leading man in Leptis Magna during the principate of Trajan (98–117). Two of his family members were in the senate when he was born, and through this, Severus and his brother, Publius Septimius Severus, were themselves able to attain senatorial rank from the emperor Marcus Aurelius (161–180).

Severus and his brother pursued careers in the army, and Severus himself governed Gallia Lugdunensis from 185 to 187. During this time he married as his second wife, Julia Domna, a daughter of the chief priest of the Emesan sun-cult of Heliogabal. Together they had two sons, Caracalla in 188 and Geta in 189.

In 190 Severus held the consulship in Rome, and in the following year was appointed governor of Pannonia Superior. In that capacity he had command of three legions. He did not act upon the murder of Commodus on New Year's Eve of 192, but only 12 days after the praetorian guardsmen subsequently murdered the emperor Pertinax, Severus was hailed emperor by his soldiers at Carnuntum on April 9, 193 (the *Historia Augusta* gives the date as April 13, but this has been disproven by the "Dura Calendar").

He assumed the name of the slain Pertinax, and marched on Rome to claim the throne, which had been purchased by a wealthy senator named Didius Julianus at an informal auction held by the praetorian guardsmen on March 28. Not only did Severus earn the support of his three Pannonian legions, but he also gained approval from the remaining legions stationed on the Rhine and Danubian fronts, giving him 16 legions in all.

Severus had three opponents to his claim: Didius Julianus, then the emperor in Rome; Clodius Albinus, the governor of Britain; and Pescennius Niger, the governor of Syria. Despite all this opposition, Severus was in the best position, for he had the support of many legions, and was closer to Rome than either Albinus or Niger. Furthermore, Julianus had little more than the fickle praetorian guards to defend him.

Severus marched on Rome at so rapid a pace that all in Rome realized Julianus was doomed. Julianus' attempts to assassinate Severus failed, as did his subsequent offers to share his authority. In hopes of avoiding a massacre in Rome, Severus promised immunity to all the praetorian guardsmen if they would turn over the men who murdered Pertinax. The praetorians agreed to the terms, and the senate deified Pertinax, condemned Julianus and hailed Septimius Severus emperor in his place. On either the 1st or 2nd of June, 193, Julianus was captured and executed.

The senate soon came to despise Severus, and the now-humiliated praetorian could hardly have benefited from his presence. But both feared his frontier legions, and so had no choice but to support his claim to the throne. Meanwhile, the senate and the people vested much hope in Albinus and Niger, both of whom had been proclaimed emperor by their troops.

One of Severus' first actions was to trick the praetorian guards into assembling, unarmed, for an address. Once they were all present, his Illyrian soldiers rushed in, deposed them, and replaced them. In addition to replacing the treacherous praetorians with his loyal Illyrians, Severus also doubled the size of the praetorian cohorts from 500 to 1,000 men. Pay was increased from 300 denarii to 500 denarii, and other subsidies were added.

Though in reality these overtures barely kept pace with the reduction of the purity of the denarius (now at about 50 percent silver), Severus created a large, loyal army that could safeguard Rome while he conducted his upcoming campaign against Niger. His inherent distrust of senators and Italians was well served by their replacement with his Illyrian troops, savage and offensive though they seemed to the local population.

After he had consolidated his power in Rome, Severus bought peace with Albinus and the British legions by investing him with the rank of Caesar. This was a shallow, diversionary tactic that Albinus accepted, for he must have considered the combined legions of the Rhine and Danube too much to overcome at present. Now secure in the West, Severus turned his attention to Niger in the East, and led an army toward Asia in the summer of 193.

Niger, with nine legions under his command, marched to the Bosporus to confront Severus, only to be routed in successive engagements in Thrace, and at Cyzicus and Nicaea. By approximately February of 194, word had spread throughout Niger's Empire that Severus had gained the upper hand, and Egypt and some cities in Syria switched their allegiance to Severus. The critical defeat, however, occurred in the spring of 194 at Issus, in southeastern Cilicia, where perhaps 20,000 of Niger's men perished. Niger fled to Antioch in the South, where he then hoped to flee to the Parthian vassals who were his allies. However, he was captured and executed sometime between March and October of 194.

Severus remained in the East, exacting revenge on the cities in Syria and the Parthian vassals who had supported Niger. During these campaigns, Severus was hailed *Parthicus Arabicus* and *Parthicus Adiabenicus* for having annexed most of Osroëne and northern Mesopotamia. Severus then returned to Rome, more certain than ever that the astrologer he had consulted before he married Julia Domna was correct — that whomever she married would become a king.

Upon returning to Europe, Severus declared himself to be the son of Marcus Aurelius, and made clear his intentions toward Albinus when, in December of 195, he raised his own son, Caracalla, to the rank of Caesar. Thus, in one fell swoop, Albinus was replaced both as Caesar and as Severus' heir to the throne. Furthermore, Severus forced the senate to declare Albinus a public enemy. In response, Albinus moved into Gaul and was hailed emperor at Lugdunum in the fall of 195 or early in 196.

After about a year of preparations, the opposing Augusti met near Lugdunum on February 19, 197. In what was undoubtedly one of the largest battles in Roman history, Severus emerged victorious, causing Albinus to flee the battlefield and commit suicide.

With Severus now in supreme command, the senate braced itself for what it knew would be a difficult relationship with the emperor. Severus now took his family with him on his conquest of Parthia. The war was a great success, and when his legions occupied the Parthian capital of Ctesiphon on January 28, 198, they were ruthless. In addition to stripping the great city of all its portable wealth, they killed all the men and enslaved some 100,000 women and children.

Severus consequently hailed his 9-year-old son, Geta, Caesar, and raised his 10-year-old son Caracalla from Caesar to Augustus. Two attempts to take the city of Hatra failed, and the Imperial family traveled to Egypt. They remained there nearly a year, during which a visit to the tomb of Alexander the Great must have made a strong impression on young Caracalla, who later in his life became obsessed with the Greek king's legacy. Late in 200 the family departed Egypt.

Severus and his eldest son Caracalla assumed the consulship at Antioch on January 1, after which the royal family returned to Rome, arriving before the end of 202. Not long after their arrival, Caracalla was forced into a hateful marriage with Plautilla, the daughter of prefect Plautianus. The ceremony was magnificent, but if there was anyone Caracalla hated more than his new bride, it was her father, Plautianus. Even Domna objected to the union, but Severus paid no heed. Severus had made Plautianus, a possible kinsman from his home town of Leptis Magna, praetorian prefect in 197. The two were inseparable and he accompanied the emperor on all of his early campaigns. Plautianus was given authority over taxation and the grain supply, as well as other important functions of government. As a result, Plautianus became exceptionally wealthy, and by the time he convinced Severus to agree to the wedding, he was virtual co-ruler with Severus.

As might be expected, the great wealth and power achieved by Plautianus caused him to suffer from an inflated ego, and he may even have plotted to overthrow Severus and Caracalla. Plautianus was famous for erecting statues of himself not just in Rome, but throughout the Empire. In 205, all of the prefect's good fortune came to an end, when Severus' brother, Lucius Septimius Geta, offered damning words about Plautianus while he was on his own deathbed.

Caracalla was eager to strike while the iron was hot, and managed to coerce statements from praetorian guardsmen confirming the suspicion that Plautianus was plotting against Severus and Caracalla. Even Severus could not deny the combined impact of the opinions of his wife and eldest son, his deceased brother and a loyal praetorian guard. Severus called Plautianus to the palace on January 22, 205, where he did not contradict an order given by Caracalla to a nearby guard to execute Plautianus. Caracalla promptly divorced and banished Plautilla, and because Plautianus was subjected to *damnatio memoriae*, his statues were torn down and his inscriptions were erased.

Though this was a tragic event for Severus, to first discover that his closest ally was unfaithful and then to have him executed, it was a moment of triumph and relief for Caracalla and Domna. The populace in general rejoiced, for Plautianus had behaved arrogantly.

Before the downfall of Plautianus, Severus and his family made an expedition to North Africa, visiting his home town of Leptis Magna from late in 202 to some time in 203. While in the region, Severus led a campaign against the desert tribes beyond Tripolitana — something he may have wanted to do since childhood. Over the years, Severus lavished Leptis Magna with a great many building projects, much of which remain today to make that city one of the most impressive Roman ruins in existence.

In 203 the Severans returned to Italy, and in 205, Severus made his two sons share the consulship, hoping they would learn how to cooperate; instead, it served only to fuel their rivalry. The Imperial family spent the three years from 205 to 208 partly in Rome and in Campania. Severus and Domna were in for a difficult period as parents, for not only were Caracalla and Geta well into their teens, but both Plautianus and Severus' brother were now deceased, and so there were fewer in the household to prevent the siblings from clashing.

Severus gave his sons one last opportunity at sharing the consulship in 208, but again they proved to be unable to work together. At wit's end, Severus decided that a frontier military campaign would do his sons good, and so he organized just such an offensive against the Caledonians in the north of Britain.

The family arrived at Eburacum (*mod.* York) in the north of England in 209, and in the beginning, Severus had both of his sons fight on the front. This gave Severus the opportunity to raise his youngest son, Geta, to the rank of Augustus. Domna now occupied a unique niche in history, for she was simultaneously the wife of one emperor and the mother of two others.

During the remainder of the war, Severus became increasingly ill, and left Geta behind with his mother at camp headquarters while Caracalla led the campaign. Father and eldest son often quarreled and, to the many soldiers who witnessed the event, it even appeared as though Severus was about to be stabbed in the back by Caracalla. Warning shouts from the soldiers, we are told, foiled Caracalla's attempt. As Herodian reveals: "He regarded his father, who was suffering from a drawn-out illness and taking a long time to die, as a troublesome nuisance and tried to persuade his doctors and attendants to do him some mischief while they tended to the old man, so as to get rid of him sooner." However, Severus, in his mid-60s, survived that altercation and died a natural death on February 4, 211, at Eburacum. To his sons he gave a simple piece of advice: "Agree with each other, give money to the soldiers, and scorn all other men."

Peace was made with the Caledonians and the offensive abandoned so they could conduct Severus' body back to Rome. Caracalla was now the senior Augustus, but he shared authority with his brother and, to a certain degree, with Domna. Once the family arrived in Rome, they celebrated Severus' funeral and consecration, and placed his ashes in the Mausoleum of Hadrian.

Though they paid him honor in public, his sons ignored Severus' deathbed advice to settle their differences. Instead, within 10 months Geta had been murdered by Caracalla, who for the remainder of his life was haunted by dreams in which he was pursued by his deceased father and brother, brandishing their swords.

Numismatic Note: The silver coinage was significantly debased during Severus' reign. Though the denarius had regained some of its integrity during the brief reigns of Pertinax (at about 87 percent pure), it returned fast to approximately the 75 percent purity to which it had fallen during the reign of Commodus. During Severus' war with Pescennius Niger, the silver content of the denarius dropped precipitously to about 65 percent, and by the end of his reign had fallen to about 56 percent. His eldest son, Caracalla, let it fall to about 50 percent, where on average it stayed until the reign of Gordian III (238–244).

The coinage of the Severan-Emesan dynasty through 211 was truly the coinage of Septimius Severus, for the coins issued in the names of his sons (and to the degree possible, his wife) followed suit. The early period, through about 202, offers interesting dynastic issues showing the portraits of two or more family members. Sometimes their busts occur individually on opposite sides of the coin; at other times they are jugate, confronted, or facing. However, the most creative period in terms of reverse types was c. 201 to 206. Some of Severus' "better" reverse types include: temple and sacrifice scenes for the Saecular Games, the four seasons at play, a ship in the Circus Maximus surrounded by exotic animals, Dea Caelestis riding a lion bounding over gushing water, the arch of Septimius Severus and the Stadium of Domitian.

JULIA DOMNA

AUGUSTA, A.D. 193–217

WIFE OF SEPTIMIUS SEVERUS
MOTHER OF CARACALLA AND GETA
SISTER OF JULIA MAESA
AUNT OF JULIA SOAEMIAS AND JULIA MAMAEA
GREAT-AUNT OF ELAGABALUS AND SEVERUS ALEXANDER
MOTHER-IN-LAW OF PLAUTILLA

Julia Domna, c. A.D. 170–217. Of all the members of the Severan-Emesan dynasty, the one who probably deserves the highest accolades is Julia Domna, the empress who served her Empire, her family and her army with great dedication in spite of all the sinister events unfolding around her.

Perhaps her greatest contribution to Rome was her staunch opposition to the division of the Empire between her two sons. Had Caracalla and Geta been allowed to carve up the Empire between east and west, a horrific civil war could have resulted. Alternatively, the plan might have worked, and the division between East and West that was achieved by the emperors Valentinian I and Valens in 364 could have been effected much earlier.

Julia Domna was born in Syria, and was the only sister of Julia Maesa, both of whom were daughters of Julius Bassianus, the high priest of the Emesan cult of the sun-god Heliogabal. Theirs was one of the most prominent families in Syria, and one which became enormously wealthy through their leadership of the religious cult. While Domna was destined to help establish the Severan-Emesan dynasty in 193, Maesa was responsible for its resurrection in 218, after the downfall of Macrinus.

Though of Syrian origin, Domna traveled to the western Mediterranean as a young woman. It would seem that her hand in marriage was desirable, for her horoscope foretold that whomever she married would become king. Her choice was Lucius Septimius Severus, a man of North African extraction who already had been married once and was then governor of Gallia Lugdunensis. She married Severus in 187 and promptly gave birth to two sons, Caracalla in 188 and Geta in 189.

Domna was hailed Augusta in 193 when her husband was hailed emperor by the senate in Rome. She continued to feed her penchant for travel by accompanying her husband on most of his military campaigns. It was not since the era of Faustina Junior that an empress had traveled so widely with the army, so in 195 she was honored as Mother of the Camp (*Mater Castrorum*), a title that she retained over the next 22 years.

In addition to serving her family and Empire, Domna was a patron of the arts and literature. Her beauty was complimented by her intelligence and broad intellectual interests, which earned her the nickname "the philosopher." She kept company with the *literati* of her day, including the physician Galen, the lawyer Ulpian and the philosopher Philostratus, whose *Life of Apollonius* she seems to have inspired. Later in her life, she gained a reputation for adultery, and is even accused by the authors of the *Historia Augusta* of plotting against her husband.

Her two greatest sources of grief, no doubt, were the intense rivalry between her two sons and the dangerous authority of Plautianus, her husband's praetorian prefect. Plautianus was possibly a kinsman of Severus, and at the very least hailed from the same city. In total disregard for the contempt all his family members held for Plautianus, Severus gave him ever greater responsibilities. The hatred between Domna and the prefect was well known, as each felt free to berate the other in public.

When, in 202, Plautianus arranged for his daughter, Plautilla, to marry Domna's eldest son, Caracalla, it must have come as the shock of a lifetime. If anything, the event demonstrates that the true authority was wielded by Severus and Plautianus, for the vehement objections of Domna and Caracalla fell upon deaf ears. Geta, who intensely disliked his brother, no doubt supported the endeavor, for his brother was bound to suffer as a consequence.

It came as a great relief to Domna when, in January of 205, she learned that Plautianus had been executed on Caracalla's orders. Sitting in the room with Domna when the news arrived was her daughter-in-law, Plautilla, who reacted with terror rather than joy, for her fate was also sealed in the bargain. Caracalla promptly divorced her and banished her to the barren island of Lipari.

After Plautianus' death, Domna attempted to strengthen family ties and defuse the rivalry between her sons. But they were now in their teens and were becoming more difficult to control with each passing day. Even moving to rural Campania did not help matters. The joint-consulships the boys held in 205 and 208 only gave them more topics upon which to disagree.

Severus believed the only true solution was to give them a taste of frontier warfare so that their aggressions might be put to more productive use and so that they would be exposed to a harsher lifestyle. Early in the campaign, Geta was raised to Augustus, the same rank Caracalla and Severus held, and Domna was thus hailed *Mater Augustorum*. Domna remained at Eburacum (*mod.* York) with Geta while the offensive was led by Caracalla and Severus.

The campaign came to a grinding halt in February 211 when Severus died. Peace was made and the family returned to Rome to celebrate Severus' funeral and consecration. The senate hailed Domna *Mater Senatus* and *Mater Patriae* ("mother of the senate and of the fatherland"), titles unparalleled in Imperial history. In taking such titles, Domna was, perhaps, drawing a comparison between herself and the great mother-goddess *Magna Mater* (Cybele). However, grandiose titles did not help her defuse the competition between her sons, who had set up a barrier to divide the palace in Rome, and furthermore, intended to divide the Empire between themselves.

Domna knew this would result in a civil war and, at the very least, would diminish her authority over Imperial affairs. Thus, in her objection to the idea, she posed the observation: "You may divide the Empire, but you cannot divide your mother." Through methods that are not entirely clear, she was able to derail the idea before it gained acceptance.

But Domna would now have to deal with a tragedy far greater than the death of her husband or the marriage of Caracalla to Plautilla. Late in December of 211, Domna was tricked by Caracalla into inviting Geta to a private meeting, at which the three were to settle their differences through negotiation. Shortly after Geta arrived, however, Caracalla's guards burst into the room and murdered him, by some accounts while he lay in Domna's arms, begging her to save his life. It was a traumatic event and it is a great testament to Domna that she was able to overcome it and remain productive to both the Empire and to Caracalla.

Though she seems not to have accompanied Caracalla on his Germanic campaign, she did go to the East with him as he embarked on his Alexander-inspired conquest of Parthia. She remained in Antioch to monitor Imperial correspondences and oversee a great many other things. Being back in her native Syria and being in a position of great power (she even had her own praetorian guards) all appealed to Domna.

But her new-found happiness was shattered when she learned of Caracalla's murder in April 217. Indeed, realizing that she had no direct family left and that she would lose her authority and prestige, Domna contemplated suicide. But a message from Macrinus, who was attempting to distance himself from the murder of Caracalla, informed her that she was still Augusta, and so she chose to live on.

She remained in Syria, but being an essentially powerless Augusta did not appeal to her and she seems to have devoted her energies to stirring up a revolt against Macrinus, who seems to have consequently banished her to Rome. After bearing her son's ashes back to Rome and perhaps suffering the effects of cancer, Domna starved herself to death.

NUMISMATIC NOTE: The coinage of Julia Domna, though struck over a long period, is relatively uneventful in terms of its reverse types. The most noteworthy type that is truly her own is that commemorating, in 213, the dedication of the Temple of Vesta, which had burned in 191. She does, however, appear on a number of interesting dynastic issues commissioned by Septimius Severus. The most famous is that which depicts Severus on the obverse, and on the reverse Domna's facing head between the confronted heads of her two sons. Her issues belonging to the lifetime of Severus bear the obverse inscriptions IVLIA DOMNA AVG or IVLIA AVGVSTA, whereas those struck during the period after his death are inscribed IVLIA PIA FELIX AVG.

ANTONINUS (CALLED 'CARACALLA') A.D. 198–217

CAESAR: A.D. 195–198
(UNDER SEPTIMIUS SEVERUS)
AUGUSTUS: A.D. 198–217
(A.D. 198–209: WITH SEPTIMIUS SEVERUS)
(A.D. 209–211: WITH SEPTIMIUS SEVERUS AND GETA)
(A.D. 211: WITH GETA)
(A.D. 211–217: SOLE REIGN)

SON OF SEPTIMIUS SEVERUS AND JULIA DOMNA
BROTHER OF GETA
HUSBAND OF PLAUTILLA
NEPHEW OF JULIA MAESA
COUSIN OF JULIA SOAEMIAS AND JULIA MAMAEA

Marcus Aurelius Antoninus (*earlier* Lucius (Julius or Septimius) Bassianus, *nicknamed* Caracallus, commonly called Caracalla), A.D. 188–217. Born at Lugdunum while his father was governor of Gallia Lugdunensis, Caracalla was a docile, affable youth who changed with the passage of time. As he matured into his teens, his rivalry with his brother, Geta, intensified, and after he murdered his sibling late in 211, his mental and physical illnesses became quite serious, eventually causing his decline and murder.

Caracalla was appointed Caesar and *princeps iuventutis* in December 195 (often erroneously cited as 196), shortly after his father had defeated Pescennius Niger and settled affairs in Asia Minor. At this time he was also re-named Marcus Aurelius Antoninus, for his father was now claiming to be the son of the emperor Marcus Aurelius (161–180). Severus' main purpose in all this was to establish ties to the golden age of Rome and to make clear to Clodius Albinus that he was establishing his own dynasty — into which Albinus no longer figured. In 197 he became *Pontifex* and *Destinatus Imperator.*

After Clodius Albinus had been defeated in February of 197, Severus once again turned his attention to the East, taking his family with him on a conquest of Parthia. The offensive was a great success, and upon taking the Parthian capital of Ctesiphon on January 28, 198, the 10-year-old Caracalla was raised from Caesar to Augustus, while his 9-year-old brother, Geta, was hailed Caesar.

The family remained in Syria in 199, as Septimius failed on two occasions to capture the city of Hatra. Then they traveled to Egypt, entering that country before the year was out and remaining in Egypt for almost a full year, after which Caracalla aided his father, and on January 1, 202, Caracalla shared the consulship with his father in Antioch.

In that same year, his father celebrated his decennalia with lavish games, and Caracalla was forced into a hateful marriage with Plautilla, the daughter of the corrupt and arrogant praetorian prefect Plautianus. If anything positive could be said about the marriage, it was that the dowry was immense and the ceremony was as grand as Rome had ever seen.

However, Caracalla despised his new bride as much as he did his avaricious and treacherous father-in-law. Indeed, Caracalla and Plautilla may justifiably be compared with Drusus and Livilla, in the same way Severus and Plautianus equate to Tiberius and Sejanus. It was a re-run of palace politics that almost exactly duplicated the situation that existed about 175 years earlier. The situation was not a productive arrangement to anyone but Plautianus, who was profiting immensely from the trust and responsibility Severus had given him. Caracalla grew more hateful of his lot in life with each passing moment. By January 205, only a few days after he had been elected consul for a second time (this time sharing the honor with his brother), Caracalla arranged the murder of Plautianus, and subsequently divorced and banished his unwanted bride.

Caracalla spent the next three years in cosmopolitan Rome and rural Campania with his family, and it was during this period that his social excesses and his sibling rivalry grew to intolerable proportions. Caracalla and Geta were both in their teens now, and their father did not approve of the direction in which their energies were being spent, so he invented the need to personally take charge of a campaign against the Caledonians in what is modern Scotland.

After the two young heirs had shared the consulship again in 208, Severus prepared for the campaign that would be his last. In 208 the family departed Italy and arrived at Eburacum (*mod.* York), which served as a base for the campaign. Throughout most of the war, Geta and Julia Domna remained there, while Caracalla and Septimius led the legions.

Septimius was ill at the time, and so Caracalla assumed overall responsibility for the campaign. This led to some disagreements, and he became quarrelsome toward his father. At one point, the bickering became so heated that we are told Caracalla appeared ready to stab Severus in the back in full view of the army. However, a sword was not necessary to slay his father, for on February 4, 211, the emperor died of natural causes.

Caracalla made a peace with the Caledonians which was not entirely unfavorable to the Romans, but did require that the border be withdrawn to Hadrian's Wall. The three remaining family members returned to Rome bearing Septimius' corpse. Along the way the hatred and mistrust that had long been evident between the siblings grew to new proportions. Indeed, each was so concerned about being poisoned by the other that they did not dine or lodge together.

Their return to the capital began with a celebration of their father's funeral and consecration, but soon turned into a fratricidal war within the palace, which had to be physically divided to prevent their murdering one another. Their mother, Julia Domna, was at her wit's end, and it was only her strong objection that prevented the brothers from dividing the Empire between themselves along geographical lines, Geta in the East and Caracalla in the West.

With Geta gaining numerous and important allies to his cause, the brinksmanship being practiced by the brothers lasted only about 10 months from the day their father died. After an earlier plan to poison Geta was exposed, Caracalla convinced Domna to invite Geta to meet with him late in December, perhaps on the 26th. Together, he said, the three of them could work out their differences and put everything right again. But the laurel branch turned out to be a sword; Caracalla had his guards burst into the meeting room and slay Geta shortly after he had arrived.

All in Rome were shocked and many outraged, though few could have considered it a surprise. Caracalla hastened to the praetorian camp where he pled his case with the guardsmen, insisting he had killed Geta while defending his own life. The story was not convincing enough, so he offered a bonus of 2,500 denarii per man to gain loyalty and support. He furthermore increased the payments-in-kind made throughout the ranks of the army, and increased the salary of the legionnaire from 500 to as much as 750 denarii per year. Though he offered no money or payment-in-kind, Caracalla was able to convince the senate to support him as well.

The murder was bad enough, but what followed was difficult to accept, for Caracalla ordered a general massacre of Geta's partisans, and some 20,000 are said to have perished. Among those killed were the former Caesar, Pertinax Junior; Caracalla's former wife, Plautilla (who was in exile on the island of Lipari); and many others, from the lowliest friend or athlete to praetorian prefects and senators.

At last, Caracalla was sole emperor of Rome. The many promises he had made, however, were costly, and there was an urgent need to raise revenue. To this effect, Caracalla doubled the inheritance tax on estates, and in 212 he introduced a law, the *Constitutio Antoniniana*, which granted citizenship to virtually all free men in the Empire. This greatly increased his base of taxation, principally that on inherited estates and slaves. Hidden within this law was also a hint of Caracalla's infatuation with Alexander the Great, who likewise tried to integrate all the people he conquered.

In 213 the young emperor assumed his fourth and final consulship, but departed Rome early in the year to wage war against the Alemanni, a confederation of Germanic people who are first mentioned by ancient sources during this campaign. It is at this time that the emperor began to wear the *caracallus* (the hooded cloak from which his nickname, "Caracalla," is derived) and the wig of golden hair arranged in the German fashion.

Caracalla claimed a military victory, but he won more through subsidies, the regular payment of which kept the Germans pacified for another two decades. For all of this, he won the title Germanicus Maximus from the senate. In the following year, Caracalla defeated the Danubian Carpi and reorganized a number of provinces as he made preparations to conquer the non-Roman east.

Conquering Persia, be it under Parthian or Sasanian control, was a goal common to many emperors, and a disproportionate number of them died in their attempts. For Caracalla, however, this ideal took on a dimension far greater than simply adding to the holdings of Rome, for it also fed upon his desire to replicate the legendary accomplishments of Alexander the Great.

In 214 Caracalla attended the Pythian games at Philoppopolis, Thrace, where he was hailed "Alexander" (with the title appearing on the commemorative coins struck for the games). Indeed, that Caracalla envisioned himself as *Alexander novus* is not surprising, for Alexander was about 22 years old when he crossed the Hellespont and launched his Persian invasion. At the similar age of 26, Caracalla held an identical position — leader of the most powerful Empire in the Mediterranean world. Both men thought in terms that were larger than life, and both were driven by an insatiable (and perhaps slightly insane) desire to conquer the East.

Later in 214, Caracalla recruited a phalanx of 16,000 men, whom he had outfitted in the same fashion as would have been Alexander's soldiers nearly 550 years before. He recruited soldiers from Sparta, supposedly added elephants to his arsenal, and even chose commanders who had the same names as Alexander's own subordinates.

Caracalla next followed in Alexander's footsteps, visiting Troy and honoring it as did Alexander before him. The now-deranged emperor staged military exercises there to honor the heroes of the Trojan War. He himself played Achilles, and one of his closest friends, Festus, played the role of Patroclus. However, to fulfill the Homeric drama, it was necessary for the otherwise healthy Festus to die, which he did with immaculate timing. A grand funeral was held for this fallen (poisoned) comrade, anointing the upcoming war.

In addition to obvious mental illness, Caracalla was also suffering from physical ailments. One of his visits while in the East was to Pergamum, where he sought a cure at the shrine of Aesculapius. (He had previously visited a shrine of the Celtic healing god Apollo Grannus in Germany, and later sought relief at the Temple of Serapis in Alexandria.) In 214, the emperor wintered in Nicomedia, where he remained until early April of 215. He then embarked for Antioch, arriving there in May, 215 with eight legions and establishing his headquarters. His mother, Domna, remained there, coordinating many aspects of the campaign and monitoring the Imperial correspondence.

The emperor first campaigned unsuccessfully in Armenia, and then went to Alexandria, arriving in December of 215. Not surprisingly, he visited Alexander's tomb and sought cures for his illnesses while he wintered in that city of half a million people. During his stay, a great tragedy occurred that resulted in the slaughter of tens of thousands of unarmed Alexandrian citizens. What prompted the slaughter is not certainly known, but it may have been jeers directed at him for his impersonations of Alexander, his murder of Geta or the unfounded insinuation that he was having an affair with his mother. Regardless of the cause, Caracalla lured many of those who jeered him into a confined area (on false pretenses, just as he had done with Geta) and had them butchered to the man. The slaughter continued for several days in all quarters of the city, as his soldiers raped, robbed and murdered without cause, restraint or discretion. Caracalla and his soldiers remained in Alexandria until March or April of 216, when they departed for Antioch.

Caracalla could now focus on his much anticipated Parthian campaign. He began by humbly requesting to marry the daughter of the Parthian king, Artabanus. This overture was rejected, perhaps wisely. Enraged, Caracalla crossed the Euphrates and invaded Media. He spent the winter of 216 at Edessa, where he imprisoned the king of the Osroëne, Abgar, whom he also had lured to his court through trickery.

This was an ideal point in time for invading Parthia, since the kingdom had been divided between rival siblings, Artabanus IV and Vologases VI. Since the two Parthian brothers could not get along, they had divided their kingdom at some point after the death of their father, Vologases V. This sibling rivalry offers an uncanny historical parallel to the situation that had just been resolved in Rome. In any case, the dispute of the Parthian brothers was eventually resolved by the vassal king of

Persis, Artashir, who overthrew the Parthians within a decade of Caracalla's war.

Although the Parthians had been unprepared for Caracalla's earlier invasions, the kingdom was now ready to oppose his aggressions. However, while *en route* to Mesopotamia, the 29-year-old emperor was murdered near Carrhae on April 8, 217, as he stopped by the side of the road to relieve himself. Responsible for the coup was Caracalla's praetorian prefect and successor on the throne, Macrinus, who may have feared for his own life based on some correspondence he had read. Delivering the fatal sword thrust was a soldier named Martialis, who held a grudge against the emperor.

Caracalla's body was cremated and his ashes sent to his mother, Julia Domna, who was then residing in Antioch. Widowed and deprived of both of her sons, Domna was ordered by Macrinus (who had been hailed emperor) to accompany Caracalla's ashes back to Rome, where she later starved herself to death. Caracalla was deified *Divus Antoninus Magnus* either early in September (perhaps on the 1st) of 217 under Macrinus, or in 218 under Elagabalus.

NUMISMATIC NOTE: The early coinage of Caracalla, from c. 196 to 211, followed patterns established by his father. There are many interesting "dynastic" issues bearing two or more portraits, and a considerable number of interesting reverse types. During this period, Caracalla's portrait demonstrates his maturation from a small boy to a young man of 23; however, his most interesting coinage begins in 212, after he had murdered Geta. The portrait is now fully bearded and develops over the next five years into a baroque image, often with a menacing scowl.

In 215 (or toward the end of 214), Caracalla introduced the double-denarius, an entirely new coin that is usually mistakenly called an *antoninianus*, after Caracalla's given name. It was an inflationary coin: though presumably tariffed at two denarii (for it was 'radiate'), it only weighed as much as 1-1/2 denarii. Caracalla took another inflationary measure in 215, when he reduced the weight of his aureus by 10 percent. These were only part of his overall plan to increase revenue to pay for his massive army.

Other interesting types were struck to celebrate Severus' victories in Britain, and the rebuilding of the Circus Maximus in 213. Regrettably, the emperor's greatest architectural achievement, the *Thermae Antoninianae* (Baths of Caracalla), is not commemorated or depicted on coinage. Caracalla's commemorative coinage, inscribed DIVO ANTONINO MAGNO, was struck by Elagabalus or Macrinus, presumably at the same time as the issues that honor his mother, Julia Domna.

PLAUTILLA

AUGUSTA, A.D. 202–205

WIFE OF CARACALLA
DAUGHTER-IN-LAW OF SEPTIMIUS SEVERUS AND JULIA DOMNA
SISTER-IN-LAW OF GETA

Publia Fulvia Plautilla, d. A.D. 211/2. As the daughter of Gaius Fulvius Plautianus, a man who came from the same town as Septimius Severus and may have been his relative, Plautilla became a tool in her father's rise to power. Indeed, it was her father who, in 202, convinced Severus to allow Plautilla to marry the emperor's eldest son, Caracalla, even though neither bride nor groom desired the match.

The marriage was accompanied by great festivities, for Plautilla had been allotted an extraordinarily large dowry. Descriptions of the quality and quantity of items, and the splendor of the procession make it hard to imagine that a grander event had ever taken place. Upon being wed to Caracalla, Plautilla was hailed Augusta, a title that she held with her uninviting mother-in-law, Julia Domna, for three years.

Caracalla and Plautilla never got along, and their marriage was one of political necessity rather than love. They despised each other so greatly that they refused even to dine together. However, the stories of her loose sexual conduct are probably unfounded, and may be chalked up to Severan propaganda.

Plautianus had been made praetorian prefect in 197 and accompanied the emperor on all of his early campaigns. He was given ever-increasing authority over governmental functions, including the most important ones — taxation and the grain supply. Through these high offices, he became exceptionally wealthy and by the early 200s had become the virtual co-ruler of Septimius Severus. In addition to having his daughter marry the heir-apparent, Plautianus even held the consulship in 203.

During his rise to power, however, Plautianus had become too avaricious, and perhaps even planned to overthrow his benefactor. Whether or not the latter is true, he had alienated the emperor's wife, brother and eldest son (his own son-in-law, Caracalla), and in so doing had made some powerful enemies. With Severus, he seems only to have had one important quarrel, which resulted from his erecting statues of himself all over the Empire. More often than not, Plautianus' own statues were larger than those of the Imperial family; at other times he would include his own statues among those of the Severans.

A deathbed testimonial by Severus' brother, Lucius Septimius Geta, however, brought the matter of Plautianus' loyalty to a head. Caracalla, who was wholly unsatisfied with his marriage to the prefect's daughter and so deeply resented the man's authority, furthered matters by coercing statements from some praetorian guardsmen that Plautianus had asked them to murder Severus and Caracalla. Retribution was swift. Plautianus was called into the palace on January 22, 205, where on Caracalla's orders he was murdered by a guard as the two Augusti stood by watching.

Considering the way Plautianus gained and abused his power, alienated members of the Imperial family and perhaps even plotted against the emperor, it comes as no surprise that historians have drawn a parallel between him and Tiberius' more notorious prefect, Sejanus. It comes as no surprise that Plautianus was subjected to *damnatio memoriae*.

For Caracalla, the death of Plautianus was a welcome event. Not only did he remove the man whom he considered his main rival to the succession, but he also was able to divorce Plautilla. In this task, Caracalla wasted no time and immediately banished her to Lipari, a barren volcanic island situated just off the north-eastern shore of Sicily. Plautilla was put to death late in 211, after Caracalla had murdered Geta.

NUMISMATIC NOTE: This empress' coinage began in 202 with issues celebrating her marriage to Caracalla, and continued until her divorce three years later. One of Plautilla's otherwise pedestrian coin types, inscribed PIETAS AVGG (SC) and showing Pietas holding a scepter and child, suggests the Imperial couple had a child.

GETA A.D. 209–211

CAESAR: A.D. 198–209
(UNDER SEPTIMIUS SEVERUS AND CARACALLA)
AUGUSTUS: A.D. 209–211
(A.D. 109–211: WITH SEPTIMIUS SEVERUS AND CARACALLA)
(A.D. 211: WITH CARACALLA)

SON OF SEPTIMIUS SEVERUS AND JULIA DOMNA
BROTHER OF CARACALLA
BROTHER-IN-LAW OF PLAUTILLA
NEPHEW OF JULIA MAESA
COUSIN OF JULIA SOAEMIAS AND JULIA MAMAEA

Publius Septimius Geta (*earlier* Lucius Septimius Geta), A.D. 189–211. The short life of Geta is not remembered for any particular achievement, for he had little opportunity to accomplish anything positive. Instead, his energies were devoted to a destructive and competitive relationship with his elder brother, Caracalla. So intense was this fratricidal war that when their plan to divide the Empire between themselves was foiled by their mother, they determined that murder was the only viable alternative.

It is hard to explain why Caracalla, who was less than a year older than his brother, was promoted so rapidly while Geta was essentially left behind. Since we have no reason to doubt that the rivalry between the siblings was any less intense than the ancient authors have led us to believe, it may be that this was born of the inequality of the authority they were given by their father: Geta's bitterness for being denied, and Caracalla's, envy of any honor, no matter how small, that his brother received.

Geta was born at Milan in March of 189, and physically resembled his father. He never married, though no doubt there was ample opportunity. He was originally named Lucius after his father, but later, in 205, he assumed the name Publius after his uncle, who died that year.

As a boy, Geta traveled far and wide with his family. In 197 he traveled to the East, accompanied by his mother and brother, joining their father, who was preparing to launch a campaign against Parthia. The war was a success, and when the Romans captured the capital city of Ctesiphon on January 28, 198, Geta was hailed Caesar and *princeps iuventutis*. His brother, who had held the title of Caesar since December 195, was raised to the rank of Augustus. Thereafter, through 202, the family traveled throughout Asia and the Balkans, after which they visited their father's native province in North Africa from 203 to 204.

Upon returning to Rome, the boys' uncle died, and Caracalla arranged the murder of Plautianus. With these two members of the court now deceased, there was less of a buffer between the quarrelsome siblings. Considering that they were sharing the consulship of 205, their duties provided ample opportunity for them to disagree and take opposing views on all sorts of matters.

Both Caracalla and Geta were now in their teens, and began to indulge in the pleasures of life offered in cosmopolitan Rome and rural Campania. Dio Cassius relates: "They outraged women and abused boys, they embezzled money, and made gladiators and charioteers their favorite companions . . . if the one attached himself to a certain faction, the other would be sure to choose the opposite side." He continues his commentary, telling of how Caracalla broke one of his legs after falling from his chariot in a fierce race with Geta.

The brothers were again joint consuls in 208, after which their parents decided enough was enough. In the following year, 209, the family departed for Britain, where Septimius Severus had decided to wage war personally against the Caledonians. It was not necessary for the emperor himself to lead this campaign, but he believed it would be good experience for his sons, who at this stage of their lives were in dire need of discipline and diversion from the attractions of palace life.

Upon arriving, Geta participated in some of the battles, and was raised from Caesar to Augustus. Geta adopted the praenomen *Imperator* as a result, but in 210 abandoned it in favor of *Britannicus*. Throughout the rest of the campaign, Geta remained at the base camp of Eburacum (*mod.* York) with his mother, while Caracalla and Severus battled ever-further north on the Caledonian front.

On February 4, 211, Septimius Severus died at Eburacum, and Caracalla arranged peace with the Caledonians so the family could return to Rome with their father's corpse. Septimius' deathbed advice to his sons was, in essence, to get along with each other, pay heed to the soldiers, and to pay no heed to anyone else. On the journey home, Caracalla and Geta did not stay in the same locations or dine together, out of fear of being poisoned. Their joint reign lasted barely more than 10 months.

When they arrived at Rome the family celebrated Severus' consecration and funeral. Ignoring their father's advice on being civil to each other, the siblings physically divided the palace to prevent conflicts. They next determined that the best solution to their fighting was to divide the Empire, much as they had the palace: Geta would take Asia and Egypt, and Caracalla would take Europe and the rest of North Africa. But Domna prevented the plan, saying, "You may divide the Empire, but you cannot divide your mother."

Although Geta may have been the more likable of the two, he no doubt realized he was in a life-or-death struggle with his brother, and so he gathered a large following of partisans who were prepared to support his cause. While Caracalla had the marginal support of the praetorian guard, Geta sought alliances among the *literati* and the senate. The growing popularity of Geta must have alarmed Caracalla, who decided to act before being acted upon. He first planned to murder Geta at the Saturnalian festival held on December 17 of 211, but word of his plot leaked in advance, and Geta only redoubled his security. Caracalla then approached his mother, asking that she invite both him and Geta to a private meeting at which they could settle their differences. Ever hopeful, Domna agreed, and the meeting was set for late December, perhaps on the 26th.

Caracalla had set his trap, and Geta, who had not yet reached his 23rd birthday, was murdered by guards who burst into the room on Caracalla's orders. The story of his being butchered by Caracalla while in his mother's arms may well be true, but it does have a melodramatic twist that invites skepticism.

To safeguard himself, Caracalla went to the praetorian camp, where he claimed he had narrowly escaped Geta's attempt to murder him, and that he had resorted to killing his brother only in self defense. Though they probably did not believe Caracalla, the bribe and the pay raise he offered helped them muster the resolve to support his cause. Without the cash incentive, Caracalla pleaded the same case with the senate.

Geta's many supporters were now leaderless, and Caracalla ordered their slaughter to a man. We are told the victims numbered 20,000 and included everyone from casual friends and charioteers to governors, praetorian prefects and senators. The murders occurred in every sort of location, public or private. Though Geta was also subjected to *damnatio memoriae*, the authors of the *Historia Augusta* tell us his funeral was surprisingly elaborate.

Caracalla's behavior toward Geta is often viewed as evidence of his particular brand of evil, and his victim is likewise depicted as an innocent victim of a butcher. Clearly, neither extreme is truthful, and either of the young men was ready and willing to murder the other. In the end, perhaps Geta was the lesser of the two evils, but Dio Cassius tells us he was mean, stingy, brusque and gluttonous. Other histories, perhaps less reliable, such as that of Victor and the *Historia Augusta*, depict him as a mild-mannered youth who was courteous and mindful of his father's opinions.

The slaughter of so many of Geta's partisans, though a reprehensible act, no doubt was necessary if Caracalla was to survive the ordeal, as many powerful men and women were among those slaughtered. Had they not been eliminated, it would only have been a matter of time before they would have undermined Caracalla's regime or would have successfully attempted his murder.

Chronological Note: The death of Geta has traditionally been assigned to February of 212, but is better placed in December of 211, perhaps even on the 26th day. The date of 211 is now generally accepted by the academic community. The confusion derives from piecing together information from different ancient sources. The generally reliable Dio Cassius provides the age of Geta (230 months and 9 days), but offers no actual birth date, whereas the notoriously unreliable *Historia Augusta* suggests Geta was born in May of 189. When combined, these two pieces of information yield a date of death for Geta in February of 212.

However, other more reliable sources are available for determining Geta's date of birth. One of the Lives (or Passions) of the Martyrs dateable to 203 records that a particular Christian martyr died on the birthday of Geta, and another document (later in date, but probably accurate) indicates that that martyr died on March 7. This is confirmed by an additional Church source.

Thus, we must "back date" Geta's birth and murder by about three months. Supporting this view is what we are told of Caracalla's failed plan to murder Geta at the festival of the Saturnalia (held December 17). The numismatic evidence also supports this conclusion, for coins of Geta inscribed TR P IV are of great rarity, with only a handful known. Thus, if the renewal was on the traditional date of December 10, or was to occur on New Year's Day (in which case some coins were struck in anticipation), their rarity is understandable, assuming he died in December. However, if he had lived through February, their rarity would be difficult to explain.

NUMISMATIC NOTE: Much like his brother, Caracalla, the physical maturation of Geta is plainly shown on his coinage, which was struck during the last 13 years of his life. His earliest coins depict him as a 9-year-old boy, and his latest as a fully bearded 22-year-old. His portrait also figures into the many combinations of the "family" issues of the Severans meant to demonstrate the promise of the dynasty. Other important types celebrate his two consulships and his participation in the victories gained in Britain.

Though Geta's coins are quite common, a great many of them were melted or destroyed as part of the *damnatio memoriae* that followed his death. Evidence of this can best be observed on medallic bronzes from the provincial city of Stratonicea in Caria, upon which the name and portrait of Geta has been frequently "erased" with a chisel.

MACRINUS A.D. 217–218

AUGUSTUS: A.D. 217–218
(A.D. 217–218: SOLE REIGN)
(A.D. 218: WITH DIADUMENIAN)

FATHER OF DIADUMENIAN

Marcus Opellius Severus Macrinus (*earlier* Marcus Opellius Macrinus), c. A.D. 164/5–218. Born at Caesarea in Mauretania, Macrinus began his career as a lawyer and eventually rose to become one of two praetorian prefects under Caracalla. As such, he was involved in the murder of his benefactor, and three days after Caracalla's murder at Carrhae (in Mesopotamia) on April 8, 217, was hailed emperor in his place — assuring the soldiers that their beloved emperor had died a natural death.

Macrinus, who ruled only for about 14 months, was the first emperor not of senatorial rank (he was only a knight), and was also the first to hail from Mauretania. One of his first official acts was to add the name Severus to his own, and that of Antoninus to his son's, in hopes that it would demonstrate his ties to the previous dynasties. Despite Caracalla's unpopularity among the people, he had been extremely popular with the soldiers.

Macrinus took command of the war Caracalla had begun with the Parthians, but soon tired of the effort and sued for peace, offering the enemy large sums of money in exchange. This did not please the soldiers, and his questionable appointments of officials in Rome did little to ingratiate the senate and the general public. Even though Macrinus was very much in command, he was an easy target for a coup.

Just such a coup was raised by the remnants of the Severan-Emesan dynasty, the members of which had returned to Syria on Macrinus' orders after the murder of Caracalla. Leading the revolt were Julia Maesa (the sister of the former Augusta, Julia Domna), and one of her two daughters, Julia Soaemias. Together, they proposed Soaemias' 14-year-old son, Elagabalus, then the chief priest of their solar religious cult, as the candidate to replace Macrinus.

Macrinus was residing at Antioch with his soldiers when the revolt of Elagabalus arose on May 16, 218, at Emesa, the home of his family's hereditary priesthood. Macrinus sent his prefect, Ulpius Julianus, at the head of an army with orders to crush the rebellion at Emesa. In the meantime, Macrinus proceeded to nearby Apamaea, where he raised his son to the rank of Augustus and gave the praetorians a generous bonus.

Julianus' army was of divided opinion. Some of his loyal men began to enter the city after battering down gates, but they were ordered to withdraw for the evening. In the intervening hours, the camp was infiltrated by men from the Emesan army who spread the necessary rumors to undermine what little loyalty remained, and when the battle began in the morning the Antiochene soldiers soon turned against their officers, murdering them to a man, and defecting to the Emesan cause.

The severed head of Julianus (rather than that of Elagabalus, for which Macrinus had hoped) was delivered to the emperor at Apamaea. Macrinus apprised the senate in Rome of the happenings, and it offered support to Macrinus, for at the very least he did not represent two women and a teen-aged sun priest.

The two armies eventually clashed on June 8 about 20 miles outside Antioch, at the tiny village of Immae. Macrinus led his forces and Elagabalus' tutor, Gannys (a man of negligible military experience, if any), led the Emesan legions with Elagabalus, his mother and grandmother there to rally the men. The battle was hard-fought in the midday sun, and Macrinus himself fled to Antioch just as the tide of battle turned against him. His loyal praetorians were won over by Elagabalus, who promised them their jobs and their lives if they would defect. Since Macrinus had already fled, the offer seemed reasonable, and they accepted.

Thus, the victory belonged to the revolutionary army raised by the Syrian women. The 54-year-old Macrinus made good his own escape in disguise, and entrusted Diadumenian to loyal men who were to deliver him to Parthia. Macrinus made it all the way to Calchedon and only a contrary wind prevented him from crossing the Bosporus to European soil. But instead, he was captured and dragged back across Asia Minor. Since a self-inflicted injury prevented his being delivered to Antioch, the soldiers escorting him executed Macrinus some 75 miles from the Syrian border — but not before news reached him of the execution of his beloved son.

NUMISMATIC NOTE: Macrinus' coinage has two especially interesting aspects. The first concerns his portrait, which is sometimes shown with a long beard, and at other times with a cropped beard. Until not long ago some scholars believed this indicated the coins were struck at different mints, but it has been proven that all were struck at Rome. The second aspect of note are his coins with the inscription COS II. The confusion, as scholars can best determine, arose when the mint workers in Rome assumed Macrinus would consider the consulate that began on January 1, 218, to be his second (for he had already been in office for about eight months). However, that was contrary to Macrinus' wishes, and the orders must have reached Rome after the COS II coins had already begun to be struck. There was no official COS II because Macrinus did not reign into 219. So the fictional second consulship appears only on some coins struck in the early part of 218. Both of these aspects are discussed in detail by Curtis Clay in *The Roman Coinage of Macrinus and Diadumenian* (1979 Numismatische Zeitschrift, pp. 21–40).

DIADUMENIAN A.D. 218

CAESAR: A.D. 217–218 (UNDER MACRINUS)
AUGUSTUS: A.D. 218 (WITH MACRINUS)

SON OF MACRINUS

Marcus Opellius Antoninus Diadumenianus (*earlier* Marcus Opellius Diadumenianus), A.D. 208–218. Little is known of Diadumenian, though we have a good idea of his appearance, not only from his coin portraits, but also from the *Historia Augusta*, in which he is described as "... beautiful beyond all others, somewhat tall of stature, with golden hair, black eyes and an aquiline nose; his chin was wholly lovely in its modeling, his mouth designed for a kiss, and he was by nature strong and by training graceful."

Diadumenian was 8 years old when in April of 217 he was hailed Caesar and given the name Antoninus (after the slain emperor Caracalla) by the soldiers at Zeugma while he being escorted from Antioch to join his father in Mesopotamia.

In faraway Rome, the boy's ninth birthday was celebrated with chariot races on September 14, 217. It was during these celebrations, we are told, that the Colosseum (Flavian Amphitheater) was struck by lightning, the weapon of Jupiter, who happened to be the very god to whom the Romans were praying for delivery from the unworthy reign of Macrinus. The damage was so severe that it was not sufficiently repaired until early in the reign of Severus Alexander (222–235).

Despite his natural gifts and the great authority his father had attained, fate was not favorable to Diadumenian. When the armies of Elagabalus revolted at Emesa on May 16, Macrinus traveled to the praetorian fortress at Apamaea, where he raised his son (who apparently was there in residence) to the rank of Augustus. As an added incentive, we are told, he offered the praetorians a bonus of 20,000 sestertii each, paying one-fourth of the bounty on the spot and restoring certain other of their privileges.

Such measures restored the army's loyalty, but did not result in final victory, as the armies of Macrinus were defeated outside Antioch by those of Elagabalus on June 8, 218. After reigning as Caesar for 13 months, and as Augustus for less than one, Diadumenian's taste of supreme power came to an end. After the battle, Macrinus fled north toward the Bosporus, and entrusted Diadumenian to loyal men who were to deliver him to the Parthians for safe keeping. However, the boy was captured *en route* at Zeugma and executed sometime later in June.

NUMISMATIC NOTE: Though rarer than the coins of his father, many coins were struck for Diadumenian while Caesar. His Imperial coinage as Augustus — seemingly limited to denarii — is extremely rare, and until relatively recently was known by only one example. It is suggested by Curtis Clay (*The Roman Coinage of Macrinus and Diadumenian*, in the 1979 Numismatische Zeitschrift), that a large issue was struck, only to be melted down when news reached Rome of Macrinus' defeat. Some of Diadumenian's provincial coins, notably from Antioch, give Diadumenian the title Sebastos (Augustus).

JULIA MAESA

AUGUSTA, A.D. 218–224/5

SISTER OF JULIA DOMNA
SISTER-IN-LAW OF SEPTIMIUS SEVERUS
MOTHER OF JULIA SOAEMIAS AND JULIA MAMAEA
GRANDMOTHER OF ELAGABALUS AND SEVERUS ALEXANDER
AUNT OF CARACALLA AND GETA

Julia Maesa, d. A.D. 224/5. After the murder of Caracalla in 217, it must have seemed as though the Severan-Emesan dynasty had come to extinction. Had it not been for the wealth, prestige and desire of Julia Maesa, the sister of Julia Domna, that would have been the case. But after returning to her home in Emesa, Julia Maesa began to plot her family's return, and achieved her goal in short order.

Maesa had moved to Rome in about 193, accompanying her sister, Domna. Though she was as shrewd as her sister, Maesa did not have so broad an intellectual interest, a facet of Domna's personality that made her a more enduring figure in Roman history. Through her marriage to Julius Avitus, a wealthy and prominent Roman who governed Asia, Mesopotamia and Cyprus (and who had been consul in 209), Maesa gave birth to two daughters, Julia Soaemias and Julia Mamaea.

The Severan-Emesan dynasty thus divided along two family branches. The first to rule was the one founded by Julia Domna and Septimius Severus, who had two sons, Caracalla and Geta. The second was founded by Domna's sister, Julia Maesa, whose two grandsons, Elagabalus and Severus Alexander, represented the "renewed" dynasty beginning in 218. All told, the family produced five emperors and four empresses, not including the five women who married into the family and also were hailed Augusta.

Though Maesa was an important adviser and ally of her sister while she was empress, Maesa would not wield true power until after her nephew Caracalla had been murdered and her sister had died. Following these events, the new emperor, Macrinus, ordered Maesa and her family to return to Emesa, though at the same time he forced Julia Domna to remain in Rome, where she starved herself to death.

Upon returning to their home city, Maesa arranged for her eldest grandson, Elagabalus, to take over duties as chief priest of the sun-cult of the god Heliogabal. She soon discovered that the Roman soldiers stationed in their city were fond of the young priest, and from this observation were sewn the seeds of revolt. Maesa began to spread the rumor that her grandson was the illegitimate son of Caracalla, the recently slain emperor who commanded the loyalty of soldiers even after his death.

The revolt quietly gained momentum until on May 16, 218, after celestial portents (a solar eclipse and a comet), the soldiers hailed the 14-year-old Elagabalus emperor in opposition to the unpopular Macrinus, who had assumed office only after participating in Caracalla's murder. The fact that Maesa was one of the wealthiest women in the Roman Empire did much to motivate the soldiers, who were all too anxious to receive a generous bribe.

Although advanced in age, Maesa took the leading role in rallying the troops and staging the coup. An initial effort by Macrinus to crush the rebellion failed, ending with the soldiers defecting to the cause of the Emesan forces. On June 8, 218, the two armies met at Immae, about 20 miles outside Antioch, for a pitched battle to determine the outcome of the rebellion.

The battle was difficult and many soldiers (all of whom were Roman) died. If we believe the ancient sources, Maesa and her daughter, Julia Soaemias, and the future emperor Elagabalus were all present at the battle, riding in golden chariots. Though their soldiers began to retreat early in the battle when Macrinus' soldiers gained the upper hand, the three leaders apparently were able to convince them to renew the fight. However, the account is glorified and reads like fiction, which it most likely is.

In any case, the armies loyal to Elagabalus emerged victorious. The boy was hailed emperor, and his mother and grandmother were both hailed Augusta. Though Macrinus and his son, Diadumenian, escaped after the battle, both were eventually captured and executed. A handful of minor revolts occurred throughout Asia and Egypt, but they apparently were quelled without much difficulty.

The royal Emesan family, composed of Maesa, her two daughters and two grandsons, made their way to Rome, wintering in Nicomedia *en route* and only arriving in Rome in July of 219. Once there, Maesa continued to wield power over her grandson, arranging his first marriage to the noblewoman Julia Paula. We are even told that she demanded and was given a seat in the senate, a governing body that excluded women.

Despite her political prowess and best efforts to restrain young Elagabalus, the boy turned out to be uncontrollable. The marriages Maesa arranged for him failed miserably, and did nothing to reduce the severity of his offenses to the Roman people. Julia Soaemias, the boy's mother, was not much suited for the rigors and responsibilities of the office of Augusta. Indeed, her own contemptible behavior no doubt served as an inspiration for her son to behave irresponsibly.

Maesa soon acknowledged that Elagabalus was a liability too great to bear, and that if the dynasty she was re-founding was to survive, another would have to take his place. The only choice that remained was her other grandson, Severus Alexander, whom she was able to have appointed

Caesar in the summer of 221. This enraged Elagabalus, who tried to have his younger cousin assassinated, but failed each time.

In the end this jealousy proved to be the emperor's undoing; Alexander clearly had become the candidate of the army, which preferred the respectful boy to his ridiculous cousin. The praetorian guardsmen murdered the emperor and his mother in March 222 and in their place installed Severus Alexander as emperor, and the boy's mother, Julia Mamaea, as empress.

Though Maesa gained a more stable regime from this exchange, she lost much of her control, for Mamaea was both ambitious and talented. Maesa was slowly phased out of power as her daughter assumed greater responsibilities. After having rescued her own dynasty from certain collapse, Maesa died either in 224 or 225, and was consecrated by her reverent grandson, Severus Alexander.

JULIA SOAEMIAS

AUGUSTA, A.D. 218–222

MOTHER OF ELAGABALUS
DAUGHTER OF JULIA MAESA
MOTHER-IN-LAW OF JULIA PAULA, AQUILIA SEVERA AND ANNIA FAUSTINA
SISTER OF JULIA MAMAEA
NIECE OF JULIA DOMNA AND SEPTIMIUS SEVERUS
AUNT OF SEVERUS ALEXANDER
COUSIN OF CARACALLA AND GETA

Julia Soaemias Bassiana, d. A.D. 222. Of the four Syrian-born women who held the title Augusta in Rome, Julia Soaemias was the least capable. Like her profligate son Elagabalus, she preferred indulging herself in pleasure to taking on the responsibilities of her office.

Soaemias was the wife of Sextus Varius Marcellus, a man of high position and varied interests. In 204 she bore a son, the future emperor Elagabalus, who may well have been fathered by Marcellus, but considering Soaemias' adulterous record, this can hardly be confirmed. Her husband's duties required that he travel throughout the Empire with some frequency, and so Soaemias lived with a great deal of personal freedom.

Marcellus was an equestrian who embarked on a procuratorial career during the reign of Septimius Severus, for that emperor's wife, Julia Domna, was his wife's aunt. Marcellus was procurator in Britain at the time of Septimius Severus' fateful expedition there (208–211), and after Geta was murdered in 211, Marcellus was made praetorian prefect and prefect of Rome by Caracalla. Thereafter he was elected to the senate, and served later as governor of Numidia, where he seems to have died sometime before 217.

Of the four Emesan women who held the title Augusta, Soaemias was by far the most voluptuous and most promiscuous, engaging in numerous extramarital affairs. In this respect she was the opposite of her sister, Julia Mamaea. While living in Rome during the heyday of Severan-Emesan rule, her loose conduct may have been a source of embarrassment for her aunt and uncle, Septimius Severus and Julia Domna.

With the murder of Caracalla on April 8, 217, the Severan-Emesan dynasty came to a temporary end with the acclamation of the commander Macrinus. No doubt fearing for their safety, Soaemias and her immediate family members returned to Emesa under orders of the new emperor. There they engineered the elevation of Elagabalus on May 16, 218, partly by convincing the soldiers that he had been sired by Caracalla, whose memory was dear to the common legionary.

After its victory over Macrinus was complete, the entourage of the revived Severan-Emesan dynasty made its way slowly to Rome, spending the winter of 218 luxuriously at Nicomedia. Even though Soaemias now had true responsibilities as empress, her legendary promiscuity continued. One of her more noteworthy affairs was with Gannys, the tutor of Elagabalus, who had commanded the army that was victorious over the legions of Macrinus on the outskirts of Antioch. There seems to have been some discussion of his marrying Soaemias, and being appointed Caesar. Though the marriage never occurred, young Elagabalus seems to have been in favor of the prospect initially, but the man's condemnation of Elagabalus' aberrant sexual practices caused problems. At some point the two men drew swords (Gannys supposedly in self defense) and Gannys was slain by the emperor's guards.

Soaemias proved to be as irresponsible as an empress as she was in private life, and her lack of restraint in her own conduct no doubt proved to be a source of encouragement for her son's unusual behavior. Along with her son she was murdered on March 11, 222, by the praetorian guards, who had grown tired of his demands to remove Severus Alexander from power. Their beheaded, nude bodies were dragged through the streets like common criminals and tossed into the Tiber.

Numismatic Note: A common reverse type of Julia Soaemias depicts Venus Caelestis, the Roman equivalent of Dea Caelestis, the Carthaginian (Punic) goddess to whom her son wed the god Heliogabal in a ceremony that paralleled the emperor's own marriage to Annia Faustina in the summer of 221.

ANTONINUS (CALLED 'ELAGABALUS') A.D. 218–222

SON OF JULIA SOAEMIAS
HUSBAND OF JULIA PAULA, AQUILIA SEVERA AND ANNIA FAUSTINA
GRANDSON OF JULIA MAESA
NEPHEW OF JULIA MAMAEA
COUSIN OF SEVERUS ALEXANDER
SECOND-COUSIN OF CARACALLA AND GETA (REPUTEDLY THE NATURAL SON OF CARACALLA)
GREAT-NEPHEW OF SEPTIMIUS SEVERUS AND JULIA DOMNA

Marcus Aurelius Antoninus (*earlier* Varius Avitus Bassianus), A.D. 203/4–222. Perhaps the most bizarre of all Roman emperors was the one who was nicknamed Elagabalus, after the Syrian sun-god Heliogabal for when he had formerly been high priest. Considering the shocking nature of his activities — religious, social and sexual —— it is not the brevity of his reign which causes such amazement, but rather that it lasted so long.

Historians have not been charitable to Elagabalus. Edward Gibbon in the 18th Century characterized him as an emperor who ". . . abandoned himself to the grossest pleasures with ungoverned fury, and soon found disgust and satiety in the midst of his enjoyments." Taking it a step further was the 19th Century historian, S.W. Stevenson, who called Elagabalus ". . . the most cruel and infamous wretch that ever disgraced humanity and polluted a throne . . ."

Born in 204, Elagabalus was the son of Julia Soaemias and Sextus Varius Marcellus. His mother was a promiscuous and voluptuous woman, and his father (who died before he ascended the throne) was a man of immense wealth and authority who had been made praetorian prefect under Caracalla. His grandmother, Julia Maesa, was the sister of Julia Domna, the wife of Septimius Severus and mother of Caracalla and Geta.

Elagabalus and his family had been living in Rome when Caracalla was murdered in 217 and replaced by the prefect Macrinus — an event that effectively ended the Severan-Emesan dynasty founded in 193 by Septimius Severus. The family of three women and two boys returned to Emesa under orders of Macrinus. There, Elagabalus, the older of the two boys, assumed the office of high priest in the cult of the sun-god Elagabalus.

Indeed, Elagabalus was executing his solemn but festive duties when his grandmother, Julia Maesa, and mother, Julia Soaemias, gained the support of the Roman armies stationed at Emesa and caused a revolt against the unpopular Macrinus on May 16, 218. As their candidate for emperor, they chose the 14-year-old priest of Heliogabal.

In the young priest's favor were two celestial events: an eclipse of the sun that occurred one day in April and, only a few days later, a comet that streaked across the sky. Both were interpreted as portents — the first that the sun-god was displeased with Macrinus' reign, and the second, that a redeemer was at hand.

The propaganda war between Macrinus and Elagabalus to a large degree involved the slain emperor Caracalla. Macrinus had added Severus to his own name, and Antoninus (the name of Caracalla) to that of his son, Diadumenian, whereas Elagabalus was hailed as the illegitimate son and rightful heir to Caracalla. The armies faced a difficult decision, but the claims of Elagabalus seemed more probable, for he is said to have looked much like the former ruler.

Macrinus, who was at Antioch, responded by sending his prefect Ulpius Julianus to Emesa to restore order, while he traveled to the nearby fortress of Apamaea. There, he gave the praetorians a bonus and raised his own son from Caesar to Augustus. However, the soldiers whom Macrinus had sent to Emesa ended up revolting, slaughtering their own commanders and joining the cause of the young boy they presumed to be the son of Caracalla. Alarmed, the senate in Rome supported Macrinus, for they had tired of Severan rule long before and did not wish to see it return.

The two Roman armies clashed outside Antioch on June 8, 218, and in a hard-fought engagement, the armies of Emesa emerged victorious. Though both Macrinus and Diadumenian escaped — the former to the north, the latter to the east — both were overtaken and executed. Elagabalus was invested with the title of Augustus, while both his mother and grandmother were hailed Augusta.

Elagabalus and his family were now in power, and began a slow march toward Rome to take command. His principate was not met with universal acceptance, though. The citizens of Alexandria rioted, causing many deaths. Poorly planned revolts broke out among the Legio III Gallica, Legio IV Scythia and among the fleet stationed off the coast of Asia Minor. However, all were quelled, and the Imperial entourage was able to winter in Nicomedia. In the middle of May, 219, they resumed their journey — with the sacred stone of Emesa in tow — arriving in Rome in July.

Aside from his original victory over Macrinus and the few initial uprisings, Elagabalus' reign was uneventful in terms of military conflicts or provincial uprisings. Instead, everything of interest occurred in Rome. If we can believe even a portion of what the ancient historians have left us, Elagabalus did not miss a single opportunity to offend the Romans and their moral standards.

The ancient historians were extremely hostile toward his sexual practices, some of which (no doubt) must be taken with a grain of salt. He is accused of going in the night to taverns dressed in his transvestite fashion, where he ousted the prostitutes already there and monopolized the activities for the evening. Even in the Imperial palace he would stand nude in doorways, seducing passersby to his bed chamber. We are also told that he wished to have his genitals removed by surgery, and in exchange be given the anatomy of a female.

One thing that is clear about Elagabalus is that he preferred men to women. Indeed, there was only one "spouse" he did not divorce, the charioteer Hierocles, a blond Greek slave from Caria. Not only did Elagabalus behave in every respect as "wife" to Hierocles, but we are told that he relished being beaten by him, and would contrive opportunities of being caught in adulterous situations so that he could be guaranteed a beating in consequence.

His religious rituals were as shocking to traditional Roman values as was his personal conduct. Dio Cassius relates: "I will not describe the barbaric chants which Sardanapalus (the emperor), together with his mother and grandmother, chanted to Heliogabal (the god), or the secret sacrifices that he offered to him, slaying boys and using charms, in fact actually shutting up alive in the god's temple a lion, a monkey and a snake, and throwing in among them human genitals, and practicing other unholy rites, while he invariably wore innumerable amulets."

Also troubling were his marriages, of which there were at least three, and perhaps more than five. His first, in the summer of 219, was to Julia Paula, an aristocratic lady who was the daughter of the praetorian prefect Julius Paulus, and the first of Elagabalus' several wives. Though magnificent games were held, the marriage lasted barely more than a year, and they divorced late in 220.

Immediately thereafter, Elagabalus took the almost inconceivable step of marrying Aquilia Severa, a Vestal Virgin. As a member of the most solemn and holy of Roman religious institutions, she had taken a vow of celibacy and was forbidden to marry. But Elagabalus was the chief priest and chose to break that rule. To avoid more trouble than already was raised, the wedding was a low-key affair in which the sun-god Heliogabal represented was also married to the Roman goddess Vesta.

Though the young emperor seems to have cared for Aquilia Severa (indeed, she may have been the only woman for whom he cared), the marriage failed in the summer of 221, perhaps at the insistence of his grandmother, Maesa, who arranged his subsequent marriage to her friend Annia Faustina, a much older (she was 35 to 45 years old) noblewoman descended from the house of Marcus Aurelius.

Elagabalus also repudiated the parallel marriage of the gods Heliogabal and Vesta, for he came to consider Vesta an unsuitable consort for his own god. Instead, he re-married the god Heliogabal to Venus Caelestis (Dea Caelestis), a lunar fertility goddess of Punic origin. Along with the new marriages, Maesa also engineered the assassination of Annia Faustina's husband and raised Elagabalus' 13-year-old cousin, Severus Alexander, to the rank of Caesar on June 26, 221.

All of these changes failed to please the insatiable emperor, and within a few months (late in 221) he divorced Annia Faustina and returned immediately to Aquilia Severa. Maesa's effort to stabilize her wild grandson's regime had failed. Elagabalus and Aquilia Severa were married for a second time, though the celestial marriage between Heliogabal to Venus Caelestis remained unbroken. Aquilia Severa remained Elagabalus' wife until his murder less than six months later.

Especially troubling to Elagabalus was the rivalry of his popular cousin, Severus Alexander. Elagabalus' own mother, Soaemias, did not get along with her sister, Julia Mamaea, the mother of Severus Alexander, and thus the rivalry took on an internal dimension as well. Quietly overseeing the whole affair was the boys' grandmother, Maesa, who must have favored the mild-mannered Severus Alexander as a desirable option to the inflammatory Elagabalus.

The nine months between when Severus Alexander was hailed Caesar and when Elagabalus was murdered were treacherous ones for Mamaea and Alexander. The popularity the young heir enjoyed with the soldiers did bode well for his future, but also caused Elagabalus to try (unsuccessfully) on several occasions to have him assassinated.

Early in 222, Mamaea and Maesa convinced the praetorian guardsmen to murder Elagabalus and Soaemias. The event occurred on March 11, 222, after Elagabalus demanded that his cousin be stripped of his title, and the praetorians did not obey his order. Instead, they murdered Elagabalus and his mother, Soaemias. Their mutilated, nude bodies were dragged through the streets of Rome and finally thrown into the Tiber like common criminals. Two days later, on March 13, 222, Alexander was hailed emperor in his cousin's place, and his own mother, Mamaea, was hailed Augusta in place of her slain sister, Soaemias.

Numismatic Note: The portraits of Elagabalus evolve in a relatively short period from an idealized, youthful image to a rather sinister-looking individual with a "horn" protruding from his forehead, just above the laurel wreath. His first interesting types celebrate his victory over Macrinus (VICTOR ANTONINI AVG) and his relation, either as son or second-cousin, to Caracalla (DIVO ANTONINO MAGNO). Some authorities suggest the latter type was struck under his successor, Severus Alexander, for whom similar patrimonial claims had been made.

Several of his later reverse types allude to his particular religious bent (with inscriptions such as INVICTVS SACERDOS AVG, SACERD DEI SOLIS ELAGAB or SVMMVS SACERDOS AVG), but his most noteworthy type depicts the stone of Emesa (a conical meteorite), shaded below umbrellas, in a cart being drawn slowly by four horses. The stone is also featured alone, adorned with stars and an eagle, on extremely rare denarii, and is shown in temples or in carts on far more common provincial bronzes.

JULIA PAULA

AUGUSTA, A.D. 219–220

FIRST WIFE OF ELAGABALUS
DAUGHTER-IN-LAW OF JULIA SOAEMIAS

Julia Cornelia Paula, lifespan unknown. Hailing from one of the most aristocratic families in Rome, Julia Paula was the daughter of the praetorian prefect Julius Paulus, and the first of Elagabalus' several wives. The union was probably arranged by the shrewd Julia Maesa, and occurred in the summer of 219 shortly after the emperor arrived in Rome from Nicomedia in July.

Maesa no doubt viewed the marriage as a necessity for her 15-year-old Syrian grandson, who would thus be integrated into aristocratic Roman society. The age of Paula is unknown, with estimates ranging from that of a 12-year-old girl to a woman in her 30s.

The wedding ceremony was a grand event. Games and banquets were held, donatives were given to equestrians, senators and the army, and Julia Paula was hailed Augusta. At the games, the public witnessed the deaths of many gladiators, 51 tigers and an elephant. Despite the pomp and circumstance, the marriage was a quick failure and lasted barely more than a year. The couple was divorced late in 220, perhaps in September, with Elagabalus using the excuse that that Paula was somehow bodily unsuitable to be the wife of an emperor. Immediately thereafter, Elagabalus married Aquilia Severa.

NUMISMATIC NOTE: The fact that Julia Paula's marriage occurred, or at least was being promoted before August 28, 219, is proven by an extremely rare issue of Alexandrian tetradrachms dated "year 2" of Elagabalus' reign.

In addition to Alexandria, perhaps 30 provincial cities struck coins for the first wife of Elagabalus.

AQUILIA SEVERA

AUGUSTA, A.D. 220–221 & 221–222

VESTAL VIRGIN
SECOND AND FOURTH WIFE OF ELAGABALUS
DAUGHTER-IN-LAW OF JULIA SOAEMIAS

Julia Aquilia Severa, lifespan unknown. If Elagabalus' first marriage was a disaster, his second was an atrocity. Elagabalus married Aquilia Severa late in 220, seemingly within weeks of his divorce of Julia Paula. In this case, the marriage was not merely a social event, but a religious ritual and an affront to Roman divine law and ancestral custom.

Aquilia Severa was a Vestal Virgin, and a representative of the most sacred religious order in Rome. As such she was forbidden to marry, and had taken a 30-year vow of chastity (during which the first decade was devoted to learning the rituals of her office, the next ten to executing those duties, and the final decade to teaching their replacements). To become a Vestal was a great sacrifice on behalf of Rome, and the citizens recognized it as such.

But this did not deter Elagabalus, who at this point in his reign was shedding the influence of his grandmother. Furthermore, the emperor was also the chief priest (*pontifex maximus*) of the state religion, and could do as he pleased within that realm. The true strength of the Roman religion was in the observance of custom and ritual rather than in blind faith. Thus, the violation of revered custom was especially troubling to Romans. Sensing this, no doubt, Maesa insisted that the ceremony be modest, without games or festivals.

There were several divine associations with the marriage, and these alone may have been all that was necessary for Elagabalus to choose a Vestal as his second bride. Indeed, not only did he have notions that a divine child would result from the marriage of a high-priest of the god Heliogabal and a priestess of Vesta, but he also held a parallel ceremony in which his god Heliogabal married Vesta.

Probably during the course of this marriage, Elagabalus removed sacred religious objects from shrines and temples throughout Rome, and relocated them in his own new temple (the Elagaballium) on the Palatine Hill. Among the many important objects he removed from the Vestal temple were the Palladium, the shield of Numa Pompilius, and the Vestal fire itself.

The marriages of Elagabalus and Aquilia Severa and of the god Heliogabal and Vesta were as short-lived as they were unorthodox. Presumably at the insistence of his grandmother, Maesa (who was seeking some "damage control" in Elagabalus' faltering regime), the emperor divorced Aquilia Severa in the summer of 221, seemingly in June or July. He also repudiated the parallel marriage of the two gods, for regardless of his personal feelings toward his earthly bride, he came to consider Vesta an unsuitable companion for the god Heliogabal.

The marriage Maesa arranged in exchange was to the considerably more noble Annia Faustina. Along with this new marriage also came the raising of Elagabalus' young cousin, Severus Alexander, to the rank of Caesar, and a new celestial marriage in which the god Heliogabal was paired with Venus Caelestis (Dea Caelestis). But the earthly union failed within a few months, and the emperor divorced Annia Faustina in the later part of 221 so he could immediately return to Aquilia Severa, who seems to have been the only woman he desired. The couple were married for a second time, but this time around there was no celestial component, for Elagabalus did not see any good reason for his deity to divorce Venus Caelestis. Elagabalus and Aquilia Severa remained married until the emperor was murdered in 222.

ANNIA FAUSTINA

AUGUSTA, A.D. 221

THIRD WIFE OF ELAGABALUS
DAUGHTER-IN-LAW OF JULIA SOAEMIAS

Annia Aurelia Faustina, born c. A.D. 175 or c. 185. The shortest-wed of his three attested wives, and certainly the most noble, Annia Faustina represented a final, desperate measure by Elagabalus' grandmother to salvage the boy-emperor's faltering regime.

Of Annia Faustina's parentage there are several possibilities but no certainty, except that she was a patrician descended from Marcus Aurelius on both sides of her family. The strong friendship she shared with Maesa is testified to by the very act of her marrying Elagabalus: she was already married, and was between 35 and 45 years old — about twice the age of the teen-age Elagabalus.

Despite the difference of a generation, their apparent personal incompatibility and the fact that her husband, Pomponius Bassus, would have to be executed (on a seemingly trumped-up charge of treason), Annia Faustina was either ambitious enough or loyal enough to comply with Maesa's request.

Annia Faustina was married to Elagabalus in June or July of 221, and duly received the rank of Augusta, although she did not to adopt the name Julia as Elagabalus' previous wives had done. About the same time, the emperor's mild-mannered 13-year-old cousin, Severus Alexander, was raised to the rank of Caesar.

Not only might such a match have helped to restore some of the damage caused by the emperor's two earlier marriages, but it also rejuvenated the connection between the Severan-Emesans and the Antonines that Septimius Severus had gone to great lengths to falsify at the beginning of his principate nearly three decades before.

The wedding also had an exotic bent, for a parallel ceremony was held for the emperor's own deity, Heliogabal, whom he had divorced from Vesta (not considered a suitable consort for the Emesan sun-god in his opinion) when he separated from Aquilia Severa. This time, Elagabalus decided upon the Uranic goddess Dea Caelestis. This particular goddess was of Carthaginian (Punic) origin, and known to the Phoenicians as Astarte and to the Assyrians and Babylonians as Ishtar, but most commonly as Venus Caelestis or Juno Caelestis to the Romans. Symbolically, this worked on several levels, for not only was the god Heliogabal a solar deity and Dea Caelestis a lunar goddess, but the marriage also represented the union of the Syrian and the North African (Carthaginian, Punic) elements that comprised the Severan-Emesan dynasty. This was no mere coincidence, for Septimius Severus had established the worship of Dea Caelestis at Rome.

However, all of the obvious merits of this third earthly and second celestial marriage failed to have the stabilizing effect for which Maesa had hoped. It was only a few months before Elagabalus tired of Annia Faustina. The couple was divorced before the year 221 was out, and though the emperor maintained the celestial union of the god Heliogabal and Venus Caelestis, he immediately returned to his previous wife, the former Vestal Aquilia Severa.

NUMISMATIC NOTE: Although provincial coins of Annia Faustina are rare, they were struck at more than a dozen mints throughout Asia Minor and the Levant. The prolific mint of Alexandria employed some 15 different reverse types on her coinage. This demonstrates that a large coinage was planned for her, but that it was cut short by the brevity of her marriage.

JULIA MAMAEA

AUGUSTA, 222–235

MOTHER OF SEVERUS ALEXANDER
DAUGHTER OF JULIA MAESA
MOTHER-IN-LAW OF ORBIANA
SISTER OF JULIA SOAEMEIAS
NIECE OF JULIA DOMNA AND SEPTIMIUS SEVERUS
AUNT OF ELAGABALUS
COUSIN OF CARACALLA AND GETA

Julia Avita Mamaea, d. A.D. 235. The mother of the emperor Severus Alexander, Julia Mamaea was the last of the Severan-Emesan women to rule in Rome. From her second husband, the procurator Gessius Marcianus of Arca Caesarea in Syria, she had two sons, one of whom was the future emperor. Regrettably for historians, most of that which is recorded about her in the *Historia Augusta* must be regarded as pure fiction.

Mamaea's relations with the emperor Caracalla before his death in 217 were so frequent that it was not possible to disprove her claim that Severus Alexander was the illegitimate son of Caracalla. This was just as in the case of her sister, Julia Soaemias, and her own son, the emperor Elagabalus. However, unlike her promiscuous sister Soaemias (with whom she had a poor relationship), Mamaea was reserved in her sexual conduct, and so the possibility seems remote.

From 218 to 221, Mamaea could do little but stand aside and witness the foul conduct of her sister and nephew, who ranked among the most debauched of all emperors — in many respects outdoing even Caligula. But her moment to grasp power came in June of 221, when affairs had become so treacherous that the family matriarch, Julia Maesa, arranged for Elagabalus to adopt his younger cousin Alexander as Caesar.

The next nine months were terrifying, for Elagabalus could see the writing on the wall and he showed no modesty in his desire to have his cousin assassinated. If this had taken place, Mamaea certainly would also have been murdered, so she had much to gain in her opposition to Elagabalus. Indeed, a lethal family feud had begun.

Eventually, early in 222, Mamaea and her mother, Maesa, conspired with the praetorian guardsmen to have Elagabalus and Soaemias murdered. Thus, having rid Rome of her despotic nephew and contemptible sister, Mamaea had cut a clear path of succession for herself, for she intended to rule Rome through her pliant son. Mamaea was hailed Augusta when her son became emperor on March 13, 222. She remained the dominant person in the political affairs in Rome for the 13 years her son reigned.

The transition of power was peaceful at first, even welcomed, but it became explosive late in 223 or early in 224 when Mamaea's principal adviser, the lawyer and writer Ulpian (Domitius Ulpianus), seems to have caused the murder of the two praetorian prefects over whom he had authority. The enraged guardsmen were bent on revenge, and even though Ulpian took refuge with Mamaea and the emperor in the palace, the soldiers still slew him there after a bitter three-day struggle.

The composition of the ruling house changed further when in 224 or 225 Mamaea's mother, Maesa, died. Her now-vacant title of Augusta was taken up by the noblewoman Orbiana, whom Mamaea arranged for her son to marry in 225. However, after less than two years Mamaea dissolved the marriage because it was eroding her own influence with her son, and because the father-in-law, Sallustius (who seems to have been raised to the rank of Caesar), was conspiring against her with the praetorian guards.

From that point on, Mamaea did not allow her son to remarry, and she remained the only Augusta in the Empire. As such, she claimed the boastful title "Mother of the emperor, of the camp, of the senate and of the nation" (*Mater Augusti et castrorum et senatus et patriae*) and, later still, "Mother of the whole human race" (*Mater universi generis humani*). She gained a reputation for greed, and is said to have confiscated many properties and estates — a practice of which we are told her son strongly disapproved, but could do little to prevent.

Mamaea was popular in some circles, and despised in others. She had much to overcome, for the extravagances of Elagabalus were not only fresh in the minds of the Romans, but were also inextricably linked to the dynasty itself. Her domination of Severus Alexander wore thin among the soldiers as her son grew older, and many of the soldiers and senators resented being ruled by a woman, preferring a stronger emperor. For these reasons, there was an air of revolution in the Empire from the mid-220s.

In the end, it was Mamaea's strength of character and her son's lack of resolve that brought the Severan-Emesan dynasty to an end after four almost uninterrupted decades. After having returned from a mediocre Persian campaign, mother and son began to lead a campaign across the Rhine against the Alemanni. But in February or March of 235, the soldiers revolted and murdered Mamaea as she clutched to her breast her 26-year-old son, who all the while was cursing her for having caused his grave misfortunes.

SEVERUS ALEXANDER

A.D. 222–235

CAESAR: A.D. 221–222 (UNDER ELAGABALUS)

SON OF JULIA MAMAEA
HUSBAND OF ORBIANA
GRANDSON OF JULIA MAESA
NEPHEW OF JULIA SOAEMIAS
COUSIN OF ELAGABALUS
SECOND-COUSIN OF CARACALLA AND GETA
GREAT-NEPHEW OF SEPTIMIUS SEVERUS AND JULIA DOMNA

Marcus Aurelius Severus Alexander (often called Alexander Severus; *earlier* Gessius Bassianus Alexianus), A.D. 208/9–235. The reign of Severus Alexander, like that of Gordian III that followed him by three years, seems out of place in the militant 3rd Century. Not only did he dislike warfare, but he was completely overshadowed in his regime by other people — most notably his mother, Julia Mamaea. It could rightfully be said that the story of his principate is largely one of his domineering and ambitious mother.

Severus Alexander was born Gessius Bassianus Alexianus at Arca Caesarea, Phoenicia, and in 218 accompanied his cousin, Elagabalus, to Rome after the latter had been hailed emperor by the eastern legions. He was a virtual unknown in Rome during most of his cousin's depraved principate, but came to the forefront when he was hailed Caesar on June 26, 221, at which point the 13-year-old Alexianus had his name changed to Alexander.

The next nine months were treacherous times, as Elagabalus was becoming ever more unstable in his behavior and increasingly jealous and suspicious of his young cousin. Popular superstition held that the spirit of Alexander the Great was making its way from the East about this time, and when it "disappeared" after crossing the Bosporus, it was speculated that it might reappear in Rome in the guise of young Severus Alexander. This and many other factors swelled the popularity of the young Caesar and severely damaged the faltering regime of his cousin, who tried on more than one occasion to have the boy assassinated but was unable to find anyone who would take on the task.

Finally, in March of 222, Elagabalus could take no more. He demanded that Severus Alexander be stripped of his title and the praetorian guards refused. Instead, they turned on Elagabalus and his equally debauched mother, Julia Soaemias, and murdered them. Two days later, on March 13, 222, young Alexander was hailed the new emperor of Rome.

Since Alexander was only 13 or perhaps 14 years old, power was squarely in the hands of his mother, Mamaea, and his grandmother, Julia Maesa. His mother quickly took the leading role, ostensibly sharing power with a council of 16 senators, among them the historian Dio Cassius. Much else returned to normal, including the level of morality in the palace and the nature of religious practice in the capital. The sacred stone of Emesa was returned to Syria and the temple built by Elagabalus was re-dedicated to Jupiter Ultor. Still, the facts that the Empire was essentially run by a woman and that the senate had taken on a stronger leadership role caused a general atmosphere of hostility among the praetorians, who felt slighted. With the passage of time the schism became greater, to the extent that Dio Cassius had to leave Rome during his second consulship (in 229), for his safety could not be assured.

Late in the year 225, Mamaea arranged a marriage for her 16-year-old son with Barbia Orbiana, a noblewoman whose father, Seius Sallustius Varius Macrinus, seems to have been invested with the rank of Caesar on the occasion. About this same time, Severus Alexander's grandmother, Maesa, died.

Severus Alexander's marriage did not produce children, but seems to have been compatible so much as to threaten Mamaea's influence over her son. Furthermore, the new Caesar and father-in-law Sallustius was causing trouble with the already-disgruntled praetorian guards, perhaps trying to convince them to support his own desire to replace Severus Alexander, or at the very least to displace Mamaea.

Mamaea was unwilling to wait quietly as the praetorian guards took matters into their own hands. She dissolved her son's marriage in 227, banished Orbiana, and charged Sallustius with high treason, for he had by then taken some revolutionary measures. Severus Alexander did not have the fortitude to prevent the banishment of his wife or the subsequent execution of his former father-in-law in 227 or 228.

In the meantime, the venerable Parthian kingdom was overthrown during the period of 223–230 by a more aggressive nation of people led by King Ardashir. Known as the Sasanians (after Ardashir's grandfather, Sasan), this nation claimed to revive in the East the Achaemenid rule, which had been displaced by the arrival of Alexander the Great more than 550 years before. In reality, the ethnic aspect of the "revival" was not so clear-cut, but the Sasanians proved to be much more aggressive toward the Romans than had been the Parthian kings, who had witnessed the decline of their kingdom over the last few decades, being unable to prevent the Romans from sacking their own capital, Ctesiphon, three times. By contrast, the Sasanians were on the rise and showed every intent of expanding the current kingdom to the shores of the Aegean, as their distant ancestors had done.

In 230 news reached Rome that Ardashir had invaded Mesopotamia, had taken Nisibis and Carrhae, and was pushing into Syria. After negotiations failed to produce results, Alexander and his mother departed to the

East at the head of an army to make a second diplomatic effort backed with a show of force. This attempt also failed, especially since the Romans were occupied with putting down a revolt by the Legio II Trajana within their own ranks.

The Romans launched a costly three-pronged offensive in 232, which resulted in heavy losses on both sides. Unfortunately for the Romans, it was not executed with enough conviction to achieve any real success. However, it forced a stalemate, allowed the Romans to recover Mesopotamia and stopped Ardashir from advancing further during what little remained of Alexander's reign. The docile emperor, who had played a relatively nominal role in the whole affair, returned in the fall of 233 to Rome, where he was given a triumph and was hailed *Persicus Maximus*.

This mild success in the East and the consequent celebration in Rome represented only temporary jubilation, for trouble of a more serious nature erupted on the Rhine, where the Alemanni had invaded Roman territory. During the previous few years the European river-fronts had become dangerous, and not only would they prove to be the demise of Severus Alexander, but also a continual torment to the Romans over the next half century and beyond.

The legions that had been withdrawn from the Rhine and Danube fronts to fight the Sasanians were anxious to return and defend their homeland. After their brief stay in Rome, Severus Alexander and Mamaea headed their legions to the Rhine in 234, where the soldiers expressed a great desire to cross the river and take revenge against the Alemanni. To this effect, a pontoon bridge was constructed and the Romans went on the offensive. But after a quick Roman victory, Alexander, ever peaceful and cautious, attempted to buy peace until the rest of his legions had arrived from the East. Wise though this policy may have been, it only incensed his battle-hungry soldiers, who mutinied and gave their support to Julius Verus Maximinus (Maximinus I "Thrax"), an aggressive Thracian officer of monstrous proportions.

The 26-year-old emperor was murdered at Vicus Britannicus (a village not far from Mainz) in February or March 235, as he was being clutched by his mother — an event that brought to an end the Severan-Emesan Dynasty. The young emperor's memory was at first condemned by an intimidated senate, but he was later consecrated after a revolt was mounted against Maximinus in 238.

The author(s) of the *Historia Augusta* portrays the reign of the gentle Severus Alexander as a return to an earlier age when the senate had just authority. As such, he is styled a noble, gentle, ideal prince. Though he does seem to have been docile and his mother and grandmother did establish an advisory committee of 16 senators, it is doubtful the jealous and autocratic Mamaea allowed them much actual authority.

NUMISMATIC NOTE: The first coinage struck in Severus Alexander's name was during his nine-month tenure as Caesar under Elagabalus. Even though Severus Alexander abandoned the inflationary Antoninianus (double-denarius) introduced by Caracalla, his coinage was a far cry from that of the emperor Augustus nearly 250 years earlier: though his aureus was nearly comparable, his silver denarius had been reduced both in weight and purity, and thus contained only 40 percent of the silver content of an Augustan denarius. Despite the disproportionate suffering of the denarius, that coin retained its traditional exchange rates of 25 per aureus and one per 16 asses.

Three interesting architectural types were struck by Severus Alexander. The first celebrates the construction of the Nymphaeum, the second the re-dedication of Elagabalus' temple to Jupiter Ultor, and the third, on coins and medallions, commemorating the repair of the Colosseum (Flavian Amphitheater), which had suffered a lightning strike in 217. Equally interesting, and certainly more enigmatic, was a "reform" of c. 229 celebrated with dupondii inscribed RESTITVTOR MON (Alexander standing) and MON RESTITVTA (Moneta standing). The nature of this event is a mystery, though it may be a celebration of the effectiveness of Alexander's decision in 222 to abandon the inflationary double-denarius.

ORBIANA

AUGUSTA, A.D. 225–227

WIFE OF SEVERUS ALEXANDER
DAUGHTER-IN-LAW OF JULIA MAMAEA

Gneaea Seia Herennia Sallustia Barbia Orbiana, lifespan unknown. Late in 225, more than three years into his reign and at about the same time his grandmother died, Severus Alexander married an ill-fated young woman named Orbiana. Severus Alexander was about 16 years old at the time of his marriage, which proved not only to be short-lived and childless, but also his last. Little is known of Orbiana, including her age.

Orbiana hailed from a distinguished family and was the daughter of Seius Sallustius Varius Macrinus, a nobleman of senatorial rank. We are told that Sallustius was given the rank of Caesar after his daughter's marriage had taken place, but it is impossible to establish truth in the matter. Certainly, no coins confirm this.

Orbiana was selected for marriage by the emperor's mother, Julia Mamaea. It would seem that the match was too well-made; Alexander and

Orbiana got along well and perhaps even grew to love each other over the course of their brief marriage. To most mothers this would be a blessing, but the stakes in Imperial marriages were high, and to Mamaea, her son's fondness for his wife proved to be an obstacle rather than an asset.

Mamaea soon realized that Orbiana had a strong will of her own. This was intolerable for Julia Mamaea; not only was there now a second Augusta in the Imperial household (something that Herodian tells us Mamaea greatly disliked), but the new Augusta would not be cowed by her mother-in-law. No doubt, Mamaea's ability to control her obedient son was slowly being eroded by the intimacy he shared with Orbiana.

Adding fuel to the fire was the father-in-law, Sallustius, who could not have been blind to the machinations of Mamaea and seems to have stirred up trouble with the praetorian guards to further his own designs on the throne. When Mamaea dissolved her son's marriage in 227, dire consequence followed for Orbiana and her father, who seem to have taken refuge in the camp of the praetorians.

Since this was a clear act of rebellion, Sallustius was executed on charges of high treason and Orbiana was banished to North Africa. It is impossible to say whether the "plot" that set all of these acts into motion was real or was merely invented by Mamaea so she had a legitimate excuse to end the marriage. In any event, young Severus Alexander — then about 18 years old — could do little but stand aside as his domineering mother took matters into her own hands.

Numismatic Note: The dearth of literary evidence on Orbiana caused early historians and numismatists to speculate as to her identification. In error, they determined that she was the wife of Trajan Decius (249–251), and only changed consensus with the discovery of double-headed coins of Severus Alexander and Orbiana.

MINERVA

CHAPTER SEVEN

Crisis and Decline
A.D. 235–268

A tumultuous age began in 235 with the murder of Severus Alexander, the last of the Severans to rule Rome. The relatively docile youth was replaced by the militant giant, Maximinus I "Thrax" who, in an extreme sense, characterizes the era that followed and came to a close in 268, when Claudius II "Gothicus" put Rome on a road to recovery.

For the historian, this is perhaps the darkest in all Roman history. Beginning with the reign of Gordian III, we enter a period in which the written histories are not only sparse but often unreliable. No longer do we have a Suetonius, Tacitus, Herodian or Dio Cassius to guide us, but rather the summary accounts of the Christian writers of the 4th Century (which tend to be "revisionist"), and the highly unreliable biographies of the *Historia Augusta.* The bleakest period occurs from the accession of Philip the Arab in 244 to the capture of Valerian I in 260 when a sparse historical record is further complicated by an alarming number of men (18 of whom struck coins) who claimed the title of Augustus.

Though the fortunes of the Empire were gradually declining from the start of this period, the most serious slips occurred in the early 250s, when invasion and border warfare was incessant and was greatly outstripping the capacity of Rome to respond. Complicating matters was the host of new nomadic peoples by whom the Romans were confronted. Not only did they present problems of their own, but their arrival forced more established enemies out of their own lands and into Roman territory. As a result, defenses along the Danube and Rhine were breached almost yearly, often in a coordinated manner so as to spread thin the Roman armies.

In Asia Minor the situation was no better, because a particularly fierce and gifted man, Shapur I (241–272), became king of the Sasanians. He was as terrifying an enemy as Rome had ever known, and in military terms was as destructive as Hannibal or Mithridates VI. There hardly could have been a worse time in Roman history for an enemy of Shapur's ability to emerge, for he was not content with his own kingdom, but wanted to incorporate lands long-held by the Romans. His title alone, "King of Kings of Iran and non-Iran," said it all.

To make matters worse, the fickle frontier legions often hailed their own commanders emperor, forcing one civil war after another — all at a time when the Empire could least afford to squander its resources. Legions were withdrawn from the borders to support pretenders who marched on Rome. In the meantime, a fresh assault would be launched into the territories that were stripped of their armies. But the soldiers can hardly be blamed. Not only did such campaigns get them away from the cruelties of the front, but they usually meant that a donative was paid out. Moreover, the battles that occurred between two Roman armies were usually nominal or were avoided entirely by negotiation or treachery within the ranks.

The 250s, and especially the 260s, were a period of adjustment in the history of Rome, when it was forced to come to terms with the unpleasantness of its fate. Constant invasion caused frontier legions to revolt with some frequency, often demanding that their own commanders accept the purple. Since this often was equivalent to a death sentence, most did so reluctantly.

The year 260 was disastrous. In the West, Gallienus' youngest son, Saloninus, was executed; in the Balkans, the commander Regalianus revolted; in Asia Minor, Gallienus' father, Valerian I, was captured by the Persians, and in consequence a revolt was staged by Macrianus and Quietus in Antioch. Though Gallienus is much maligned by historians, he showed remarkable energy and dedication in trying to restore an Empire that was under siege on all fronts and several times from within. That his Empire did not completely collapse is remarkable.

Usually the revolts staged by Roman commanders were not successful, but the reign of Gallienus was ripe with opportunity for such men, and two major "breakaway states" or "separatist Empires" were founded. The first, in Gaul, was founded in 260 by the general Postumus, and the second, in Palmyra, was founded in about 261 by the leader Odaenathus. This powerful eastern monarch assumed the titles "Ruler of the Romans" and "Governor of the East." Earlier, breakaway attempts were made in Syria by Uranius Antoninus (253) and Macrianus and Quietus (260–261), but both were short-lived. Information on the first two of these "separatist Empires" may be found in chapter 8.

During this period, three unfathomable events occurred. In the summer of 251, the emperor Trajan Decius, his teenage son Herennius Etruscus, and most of their soldiers were killed in a Gothic ambush led by Kniva. They were the first Roman emperors ever to fall in battle against a foreign enemy. Even worse were two other "firsts" in Roman history, both of which occurred in 260. The 17-year-old emperor Saloninus was captured and executed at Cologne by the rebel Postumus, and the emperor Valerian I was captured by the Sasanian king Shapur I while attempting to negotiate a truce. Shapur subsequently mutilated the elderly ex-emperor, paraded him about using him as a footstool, and then putting his skinned and stuffed body on display. Both of the latter tragedies contributed to the establishment of separatist Empires.

The coinage suffered greatly during this period. The double-denarii of the late 230s and early 250s were reduced in purity from earlier times, but at 40 percent or more silver they were still readily recognizable as silver pieces. After the reign of Gordian III, the denarius becomes a great rarity. In the later 250s the currency began to slide so severely that, with the exception of denarii struck by the separatist Carausius, no true silver coin was struck again until Diocletian's reform of 294. Gold coinage did not suffer any significant reduction in purity, but it came to be struck with less frequency, and often at weights that were both inconsistent and low.

The aes coinage also suffered, with the as and dupondius gradually being abandoned and the sestertius coming to be struck on small, square planchets of reduced weight. Furthermore, orichalcum (brass), the more valuable copper alloy, was abandoned in favor of leaded bronze, regardless of denomination. A new denomination, the double-sestertius, was introduced by Trajan Decius (249–251), but failed to take hold, except during the reign of Postumus, the founder of the separatist Romano-Gallic Empire.

So poor were the final double-denarii of Gallienus that they have only the slightest trace of silver. There was no attempt to maintain the beauty of these coins: they are small, ragged and of poor artistry. Considering that Gallienus was a grand patron of the arts (and a devout Neo-Classicist), the pitiful decline in coinage is a very real reflection of the almost insurmountable difficulties he faced. The Romans established new mints to provide the vast quantities of coinage (however worthless) necessary. The most important of these new facilities were located at Milan, Siscia and Antioch.

Beginning with Claudius II Gothicus in 268, the period of decline comes to an end. Almost every emperor for the next 60 years was of Illyrian origin — this being a noticeable shift from the heavy concentration of African and Syrian emperors earlier in the century. About a generation after the accession of Claudius II, the Empire saw an even greater degree of organization and efficiency when Diocletian partitioned duties along geographic lines. This innovation certainly helped Rome's plight, but seldom resulted in true peace and prosperity, and never brought back the good fortune of the 2nd Century.

MAXIMINUS I 'THRAX'
A.D. 235–238

HUSBAND OF PAULINA
FATHER OF MAXIMUS

Gaius Julius Verus Maximinus, A.D. 172/3 or c. 182/3–238. A man of truly humble origin, Maximinus "Thrax" ("the Thracian") was supposedly born of a Gothic father and Alan mother, and was destined to be a Thracian herdsman had he not enlisted in an auxiliary unit of the Roman army. Indeed, Maximinus was the first man in history to rise from the ranks to the high office of emperor, and was also the first emperor who did not set foot in Rome during his reign.

Maximinus is best remembered for his great physical stature, legendary strength, paralyzing stare and voracious appetite — all of which seem to be exaggerated to some degree by the authors of the *Historia Augusta*, who say he was no less than eight and a half feet tall. In any case, Maximinus' physical attributes were remarkable, and they caused him to be recognized while wrestling at a competition in Thrace that was attended by the emperor Septimius Severus. The emperor was greatly impressed, and thus did his best to Romanize him, and even appointed him as a personal bodyguard.

Caracalla, who also valued Maximinus' skills and loyalty, raised him to the rank of Centurion, but the giant quit the army when Macrinus replaced the murdered Caracalla. He later was voted the power of a tribune under Elagabalus, though apparently he was offended by the youth's perverted advances. He remained aloof from military service until after the accession of Severus Alexander, who appointed him to high posts during the Mesopotamian and German campaigns of the 230s.

A long period of instability in the Empire began in March of 235, when Severus Alexander was murdered by mutinous soldiers in Germany. It seems the soldiers had earlier voted to hail Maximinus as his replacement. His rise to power set the stage for emperor-making in the next half century, during which so many low-born soldiers from the Danubian region claimed the purple. The senate found no comfort in this turn of events, but could do little to change matters.

Two coups were hastily formed and aborted during Maximinus' inaugural year. The first one was a plan to tear down a bridge over the Rhine after Maximinus had crossed it, thus stranding him. The second was formed by the corps of archers from Osrhoene, but it also failed. These attempts produced a level of bitterness and paranoia in Maximinus. One of his remedies was to dismiss high-ranking officers in the army and to replace them with his own hand-picked men.

After solidifying his authority, Maximinus set about pacifying Germany, which he attempted at great personal risk — in one case leading his army through chest-high water to fight. For his costly but impressive victory at the swamps in Württemberg in 235, the senate (which was sent a painting depicting the Herculean feat) reluctantly awarded him the title *Germanicus Maximus*. At this time, perhaps, Maximinus also raised his son, Maximus, to the rank of Caesar.

Maximinus next occupied his armies on the Danubian frontier, where he based himself in Sirmium and spent the next two years fighting Sarmatians and Dacians. To pay for these protracted campaigns, the peasant-emperor exacted his revenge on the wealthy and upper-classes by taxing them at an extraordinarily high rate, and by demanding payment in bullion or its equal. Even though the more humble classes felt the pinch of Maximinus' taxation, it was the upper-class and the senate which, in the spring of 238, acted upon their dissatisfaction by electing a council of 20 senators to organize the defense of Italy and by declaring Maximinus a public enemy. To back up their decree, the senate supported the revolt of the Gordiani in North Africa, which lasted only three weeks.

Maximinus led an invasion of Italy that he hoped would result in a visit to Rome as conqueror, and the opportunity to punish the noblemen within. In the meantime, the senate appointed two of their own members, Balbinus and Pupienus, to rule and defend Italy during the crisis. Luckily for the two bickering senators, Maximnus met resistance early on, and was unable to take the city of Aquileia, which resisted his advance. Indeed, the minimal actions taken by Pupienus to organize the defense of Italy were hardly necessary.

The Thracian's harsh discipline, incompetent subordinates, and disaffected army (which was facing possible starvation) proved to be his undoing. He and his son, Maximus, were assassinated by soldiers of Legion II Parthica after they were awakened from sleeping off a midday meal. The senate and the people of Rome must have been greatly relieved when the severed heads of the Maximinus and his son were delivered to the capital. The date of their murder is inconsistently reported as being sometime in April, on May 10, or on June 24 of 238.

NUMISMATIC NOTE: The earliest portraits of Maximinus I are mere adaptations of those of his predecessor, Severus Alexander. Though Maximinus had lived in Rome, his bold features and "jutting chin" apparently were not known to the die engravers. Later, the engravers adopted his true portrait, which appears on the vast majority of his coins.

PAULINA

WIFE OF MAXIMINUS I
MOTHER OF MAXIMUS

Caecilia Paulina, died c. A.D. 235 or before. Very little is known of Paulina, though her memory is consecrated on coinage struck during the reign of Maximinus I. It is an assumption — though a safe one — that she was the wife of Maximinus I rather than his mother, sister or other relation. Maximinus is said to have wed during the reign of Caracalla, and as a result fathered a son, Maximus. It seems almost certain that Paulina died before Maximinus became emperor because of the dating of some provincial bronzes.

NUMISMATIC NOTE: We can be certain that Paulina was associated with Maximinus I for she is portrayed on bronze coins of Anazarbus, Cilicia, which is dated to that reign. On the bronze in question, the date ΔNC indicates year 254 of the local Era of Anazarbus, which began in the fall of 19 B.C. Thus, the Era year 254 equates the date 235/6, just at the start of Maximinus I's reign. Also from Anazarbus emanated a bronze coinage in the name of Maximus, which bears the identical date. As if further evidence were needed, the portrait of Paulina is closely assimilated with those of Maximinus and Maximus.

MAXIMUS

CAESAR: A.D. 235/6–238
(UNDER MAXIMINUS I)

SON OF MAXIMINUS I AND PAULINA

Gaius Julius Verus Maximus, c. A.D. 216–238. The son of Maximinus I "Thrax," and presumably of Paulina, Maximus was raised in the manner of an aristocratic Roman, for his barbarian father had been in the service of the emperors for about two decades before he was born. It is not entirely certain when Maximus was raised to the rank of Caesar. It may have occurred in 235, when his father was hailed *Germanicus Maximus*, but it may also have occurred in 236. In either case, Maximus was about 20 years old at the time.

Though by all accounts Maximus was handsome and capable, he is said to have abandoned his responsibilities in favor of frivolous pursuits, and his arrogance soon caused him to be as intensely disliked as his father. No doubt he was not anxious to serve on the frontiers, for he was a cosmopolitan Roman on the verge of marrying Junia Fadilla, a descendant of Antoninus Pius (who no doubt was related to Fabia Orestilla, the wife of Gordian I). However, this wedding, which would have mixed the barbarian blood of Maximus with the noble blood of the Antonine House, never occurred. After serving at least two years at his father's side on the frontiers, Maximus was murdered along with his father outside of Aquileia, and his severed head was delivered to his beloved Rome.

GORDIAN I A.D. 238
(CO-EMPEROR WITH GORDIAN II)

FATHER OF GORDIAN II
GRANDFATHER OF GORDIAN III

Marcus Antonius Gordianus Sempronianus Romanus "Africanus," c. A.D. 157/59–238. Gordian I is said to have been descended from the Gracchi on his father's side, and from Trajan on the side of his mother. His first wife, Fabia Orestilla, was said to have been a great grand-daughter of Antoninus Pius. It is uncertain how much of this is true, and modern historians have expressed serious doubts about the nobility of Gordian's ancestry. What we can be certain of is that he was perhaps the wealthiest man in all the Empire. His vast estates constituted a small Empire in their own right, and his home in Rome was once owned by Pompey the Great.

The tales of his personal expenditures on public games seem almost beyond belief: he could spend staggering sums on a regular basis without concern that his wealth would be diminished, as his estates produced an enormous and steady flow of income. But his unimaginable resources did not seem to sour his disposition, for he is also said to have been a man of the greatest integrity. We know he was very fond of philosophy and literature, and that he penned 30 books of verse on the lives of Antoninus Pius and Marcus Aurelius. We are told he was especially fond of bathing and sleep, and did nothing to excess.

Later in his life he achieved high offices, including the consulship in Rome when he was in his 60s, and the governorship of Lower Britain. In 237 or 238, when Gordian was in about his 80th year and nearing the end of his career, he became governor of North Africa. Indeed, he probably hoped that the severe exactions of Maximinus (which especially targeted the wealthy) would end so he could live his remaining days in peace. This was not to be, however. Several local noblemen were levied fines so severe that they would cause their immediate ruin, and so they murdered the procurator rather than paying. Desperate for a leader who could both sympathize with their dilemma and assemble an army, these renegades implored the elder Gordian to accept the title of emperor. The elder Gordian, with some reluctance, agreed to take on the task and was made co-emperor along with his middle-age son. Thus, father and son were drawn into the conflict, presumably on March 19 or 22 of 238.

After entering Carthage and assuming the additional name *Africanus*, the two Gordians drafted a letter expressing their intent, which arrived at Rome within a few days. Along with the letter, the Gordiani sent one of their agents on a mission to assassinate the praetorian prefect Vitalianus, who was fiercely loyal to Maximinus and was an obstacle to the fledgling revolt. Vitalianus was killed, which no doubt helped the senate to muster its courage to confirm the request of the Gordiani. When news was posted in the Forum, the people rejoiced and there followed several days of riots during which informers, officials and tax collectors of Maximinus were slaughtered to the man.

Maximinus was at Sirmium when news of the rebellion reached him, and he immediately prepared to invade Italy. Meanwhile, the Gordiani committed a fatal error when they demanded the resignation of Capellianus, the governor of neighboring Numidia and a loathsome man with whom the Gordiani had a bitter legal dispute. Instead of surrendering, Capellianus marched on Carthage at the head of his legions. The younger Gordian left Carthage with a group of local militia and crudely armed citizens to oppose Capellian's advance. That the younger Gordian died in battle, and his father hanged himself we are certain, but accounts vary as to whether Gordian I committed suicide before or after news reached Carthage of the defeat. Both of these events are said to have occurred on April 12, ending a joint reign of only three weeks. For more details, see the biography of Gordian II, below.

CHRONOLOGICAL NOTE: It is of some interest that although most historians place this revolt in March and April of 238, at least one authority suggests it occurred in January. Indeed, many of the details of this revolt are probably different from what has come down to us in the *Historia Augusta*. Historians and numismatists are at a loss to explain how such a well-crafted and well-organized coinage could have been struck at Rome and at Alexandria under circumstances as urgent as those described above. A time-frame of three weeks (21 or 22 days) seems wholly insufficient for the quantity of coinage struck. Rather than a spontaneous revolt, the numismatic evidence suggests theirs was a coup planned in advance with key senators in Rome.

NUMISMATIC NOTE: Because the inscriptions on the coins of Gordian I and Gordian II are identical, the coins can only be distinguished by the characteristics of the portraits. The elder Gordian has a full head of hair, a thin face, beak nose and slightly recessed jaw. The younger Gordian has a receding hairline, a long, flat nose, a pronounced forehead, heavy jaw and jutting chin, and is fleshier in appearance.

GORDIAN II A.D. 238

(CO-EMPEROR WITH GORDIAN I)

SON OF GORDIAN I AND ORESTILLA
UNCLE OF GORDIAN III

Marcus Antonius Gordianus Sempronianus Romanus "Africanus," c. A.D. 191/92–238. The son of Gordian I and his first wife, Fabia Orestilla, the younger Gordian was praised by his contemporaries as kind-hearted, remarkably handsome, and in possession of an extraordinary memory. He was a skilled administrator who governed Achaea, served as Quaestor under Elagabalus, and as Prefect of Rome and consul under Severus Alexander. Later, he served as his father's deputy in North Africa.

Though he was his father's equal in administrative skill and learning (for he had a library of some 62,000 volumes), he did not possess his high level of integrity. He was a staggeringly wealthy middle-aged bachelor with many vices, foremost among them being women. The *Historia Augusta* tells us that ". . . he had 22 mistresses formally attached to him, from all of whom he had three or four children apiece."

Indeed, the most telling assessment of his personal legacy is also found in the *Historia Augusta* in which he is described as a man who wasted his considerable genius by giving himself over to pleasure. Furthermore, he was ". . . a man of huge size. . . . He had a craving for cold drinks and passed the summer with great difficulty unless he drank a great many of them."

As his father's deputy in the government of North Africa, the younger Gordian became co-emperor with his father at the request of local nobleman and with the consent of the senate in Rome. He was his father's titular equal, except that he did not share the high priesthood. When the Numidian governor, Capellianus, opposed the elevation of the Gordiani, it was the younger Gordian who assembled a large number of locals to prevent his advance on Carthage. Though the Carthaginian forces were far larger in number than the Numidian legionaries, they were an untrained, undisciplined mob consisting of inexperienced local militia and enthusiastic provincials armed with farm implements and knives.

When the two forces met, perhaps on April 12, the Carthaginians lost their composure at the mere sight of the Numidian cavalry, who were renowned for their ability to control their horses precisely and to launch their javelins with deadly accuracy. The "army" of Gordian II fled *en masse* before the battle had even begun. What followed was not so much a battle as a mass slaughter of Gordian's undisciplined forces, many of whom died of trampling by their own comrades. The slaughter was so complete that the body of Gordian II — who had reigned only about three weeks — could not be recognized after the fact. For more details, see the biography of Gordian I, above.

NUMISMATIC NOTE: Because the inscriptions on coins of both Gordians are identical, we must rely on the characteristics of the portraits when determining which Gordian is portrayed. The elder Gordian has a full head of hair, a thin face, beak nose and slightly recessed jaw. The younger Gordian has a receding hairline, a long, flat nose, a pronounced forehead, heavy jaw and jutting chin, and is fleshier in appearance.

PUPIENUS A.D. 238

(CO-EMPEROR WITH BALBINUS)

Marcus Clodius Pupienus Maximus, c. A.D. 164/74–238. With the death of the Gordiani in North Africa, the hopes of the senate were dashed, as they realized they had no choice but to defend themselves. Maximinus had begun his invasion of Italy and though he was not making rapid progress, the senators had no reason to expect mercy if he reached Rome.

The senate, which had met in the temple of Castor and Pollux to vote on its support of the Gordiani less than a month before, gathered in the temple of Jupiter Optimus Maximus on the Capitoline Hill to determine its own fate. It had already established a council of 20 members to see the Empire through the crisis, and at this point selected two members of that council, Balbinus and Pupienus, to take the leading positions as joint emperors.

This act was not only practical (one to manage government, the other to defend Italy from Maximinus' invasion) but was also symbolic: Rome traditionally had been ruled by two consuls. It is also of some importance that the two men shared their honors equally (although one man's name had to come before the other, and this proved to be a bone of contention for Balbinus, whose name came second). Even the chief priesthood, the *pontifex maximus*, was shared by the emperors. Although this had never before occurred with this indivisible office, the practice would appear again under future emperors.

Pupienus was perhaps a few years younger than his colleague and, according to Herodian, hailed from a distinguished Etruscan family (which is more likely than the "humble birth" the authors of the *Historia Augusta* report. Like Balbinus, Pupienus had twice been consul and held governorships in the provinces, and seems also to have been Prefect of Rome sometime in the 230s. The first problem the co-emperors encountered was that the people of Rome were opposed to the leadership of these two patricians. An angry mob demanded that a member of the Gordiani be included, for that family, though also noble, was popular with the poor. The senate thus bestowed the title of Caesar on Gordian III, the 13-year-old grandson of Gordian I, in an effort to placate the public and no doubt to gain access to the considerable wealth of the boy's family.

Balbinus saw to administrative matters, while Pupienus was charged with organizing the military defense of Italy. Pupienus and the council of 20 mobilized troops throughout the province and blockaded the roads around Aquileia, the city at which the army of Maximinus was bogged down in a tiresome siege. In addition to starving Maximinus of supplies, Pupienus was making covert efforts to undermine the loyalty of his soldiers, who in any case were not enthusiastic about waging war on their own people. It did not take long for a plot to hatch, and Pupienus did not even have to leave his headquarters at Ravenna before Maximinus and his son were murdered in their camp after being roused from a midday nap. Immediately, the army of Maximus wished to make peace with the Aquileans, who were wary of a possible ruse. So they first showed the people of Aquileia the severed heads of Maximinus and Maximus before they dispatched them to Pupienus at Ravenna, and subsequently to Balbinus in Rome. Pupienus then went to Aquileia to resolve the concerns of both parties. The armies of both sides disbanded without incident.

Pupienus returned to Rome to great acclaim as the savior of Italy, which did nothing but strain his already tense relationship with Balbinus, who pointed out at every opportunity that his colleague really had done nothing, and that Maximinus had defeated himself. To solve their differences, the two men had hatched a plan which involved their jointly leaving Rome on military campaigns: Pupienus against the Sasanians, and Balbinus against the Goths on the Lower Danube. However, the rivalry had become absurd and destructive, and proved to be their downfall. This spelled opportunity for the praetorians, who were not in favor of being ruled by men whom they did not choose. Riding a tide of public resentment, the praetorians burst into the palace and dragged both men into the streets. (In a stroke of bad timing, Pupienus' German bodyguards had been sent elsewhere, and could not come to their rescue.) After being dragged through the streets and mutilated, the two men were killed, to the relief of everyone but the senate. *For more details*, see the biography of Balbinus, below.

CHRONOLOGICAL NOTE: Most authorities agree that the revolt of the Gordiani ended late in April of 238, and that Pupienus and Balbinus were elected as co-emperors in that month (perhaps on the 22nd day). Using that time-frame, a reign of 98 or 99 days would place their murders at the very end of July (perhaps on the 29th day). However, the authors of RIC suggest they reigned from the beginning of April through the end of June, and at least one authority places the revolt of the Gordiani in January, and thus dates the rule of the co-emperors from early February through early May.

NUMISMATIC NOTE: The reverses of Pupienus and Balbinus are shared on all denominations except the double-denarius, upon which there is a common reverse design ("clasped hands"), but six different inscriptions. Each emperor used three of these inscriptions on his own double-denarii, and only on very rare occasions are they mistakenly "muled" with an obverse of the other colleague.

BALBINUS A.D. 238

(CO-EMPEROR WITH PUPIENUS)

Decimus (or Decius) Caelius Calvinus Balbinus, c. A.D. 178/65–238. When the revolt of the Gordiani failed in North Africa, the senate elected two of its own members, Pupienus and Balbinus, as their replacement emperors. Balbinus was a distinguished senator who had been consul in 203 and 213 and held several governorships in the provinces.

While Pupienus was initially in charge of the military defense of Italy, Balbinus was responsible for administrative matters and securing peace in Rome. This was no easy task for the elderly senator, who faced a riotous population, a frantic senate and, worst of all, a dissatisfied praetorian guard that felt slighted for not having been the instrument by which the new emperors were chosen. The schism between the senate and the praetorians was particularly strong, and resulted in violence when senators armed with daggers murdered some unarmed praetorians who had impetuously burst in on one of their meetings.

This incident was followed by an attack on the praetorian camp by two senators, Gallinicus and Maecenas, who led an angry mob of citizens and gladiators, hastily armed and driven to riot. The praetorians repelled the attacks and later went on the offensive themselves, causing a small civil war in Rome for several days. Amidst this chaos, Balbinus attempted to make peace, but to no avail, for he was universally viewed as a weak man with no real authority; he was even wounded when the public pelted him with bricks.

The praetorians were now besieged in their camp, and the citizens attempted to starve them of water. After suffering for a few days, the praetorians burst out of the camp and began to slaughter the citizens. Guerrilla-style warfare ensued and a considerable section of Rome was burned to the ground in the process. Considering the circumstances, it would have been difficult even for a popular emperor to keep the peace, but the unpopular Balbinus had no chance at all.

Once the military threat of Maximinus had ended, Pupienus returned, riding a tide of popularity that only exacerbated the rivalry between the Imperial colleagues. Clearly, Balbinus was the loser in the situation, for while he was barely able to keep Rome from self-destruction, Pupienus had "won" an important victory which spared Rome from certain invasion. The two men quarreled over many things — at first privately but then publicly, as their hostility grew. Their main bone of contention was which of the two rulers should be accorded the highest honor. Balbinus was upset that his colleague's name had come first in inscriptions from the very outset, even though he believed his own record and ancestry were more illustrious. He was also jealous of the popularity his colleague enjoyed for his easy victory over Maximinus, who had defeated himself. Pupienus could do little in return but call Balbinus a timid, obese, lazy Sybarite.

Balbinus was especially concerned about Pupienus' German bodyguards, who were both loyal and fearless. Understandably, Balbinus feared that he might be assassinated by them. The praetorians had their concerns, for they suspected Pupienus might try to replace them with Germans in the same way Septimius Severus had done with his Illyrians. Finally — after Balbinus and Pupienus had ruled scarcely three months — the praetorian guards decided to act before they were acted upon. They stormed the palace while the German guards were occupied elsewhere and dragged the two emperors into the street, where they were mutilated and killed. For more details, especially on the chronology of the reign, see the biography of Pupienus, above.

NUMISMATIC NOTE: The first silver coinage of Balbinus and Pupienus was exclusively of denarii, as that had been the only silver denomination struck for the previous 16 years (under Severus Alexander and Maximinus I). However, to stretch resources the co-emperors soon began to strike double-denarii, an inflationary coin introduced by Caracalla in 214 and which had been abandoned in 222.

GORDIAN III A.D. 238–244

CAESAR: A.D. 238
(UNDER BALBINUS AND PUPIENUS)
AUGUSTUS: A.D. 238–244

GRANDSON OF GORDIAN I
NEPHEW OF GORDIAN II
ADOPTED SUCCESSOR OF BALBINUS AND PUPIENUS
HUSBAND OF TRANQUILLINA

Marcus Antonius Gordianus "Pius," c. A.D. 225–244. Although orphaned as a child, Gordian III belonged to a prominent and exceptionally wealthy family, then headed by his grandfather, Gordian I. His mother was Maecia Faustina, a daughter of Gordian I and a sister of Gordian II. Although we have virtually no insight into the personality of Gordian III, we are told by the *Historia Augusta* that he was light-hearted, handsome, winning and ". . . was loved by the people, the senate and the soldiers as no prince had ever been before."

The joint emperors Balbinus and Pupienus raised young Gordian III to the rank of Caesar shortly after his grandfather and uncle perished in their failed North African revolt. For the two emperors it was a prudent move: not only did they fulfill the demands of the rioting populace, but they also placated the praetorian guards, who viewed young Gordian as their candidate. Additionally, the joint-emperors presumably gained access to his family's enormous wealth, from which it seems they hammered out a large coinage in less than 100 days. Among these coins were ones honoring the young Caesar, though they constituted only a very small portion of the output.

The chronology of this chaotic period is far from certain, although it seems the co-emperors reigned with Gordian as their Caesar until July of 238, when the two Augusti were murdered and Gordian III was hailed emperor in their place. Despite his youth (he was then about 13 years old), Gordian was probably the best candidate, for he was not mature enough to have an agenda of his own.

During this intense civil war, the enemies of Rome had become active. The Goths and the Carpi had crossed the Danube, and the Sasanians made advances in the East. Though his predecessors had planned to meet these challenges (Balbinus against the Goths and Pupienus against the Sasanians), their executions prevented any such action. The first three years of Gordian's reign were ostensibly under the guidance of the senate, though no doubt they were careful not to upset the praetorians or the army in the process. The Danubian frontier was managed through the presence of existing legions and the payment of subsidies.

Among Gordian's earliest tasks was the veneration of his deceased grandfather and uncle, which included the dismissal of the legion that caused their deaths under Capellianus. Although overtures like these, which earned Gordian the title "Pius," were commendable, in the latter case it opened North Africa to a new revolt in 240 (by the provincial governor Sabinianus) which had to be quelled by soldiers based in Mauretania.

In 241, the 16-year-old Gordian changed the complexion of his reign by appointing Timesitheus, a man of exceptional character and experience, as his commander of the praetorian guard. At the same time he strengthened his ties to Timesitheus by marrying his daughter, Tranquillina. But the "honeymoon" was over before it began, for the Sasanian king, Shapur I, had invaded Syria, requiring immediate attention from the emperor and his father-in-law. *En route* to Syria, Gordian and Timesitheus were delayed on the Danubian frontier, where they defeated the Carpi and re-established peace in the region.

Gordian's army was finally able to engage Shapur in the spring of 243. The Romans quickly gained the upper hand against the Persians, and were able not only to preserve Antioch, but to recover Nisibis, Hatra and Carrhae as Gordian's legions advanced deep into Mesopotamia with the goal of taking the capital, Ctesiphon. But the death of Timesitheus in the winter of 243 dampened the effort. The cause of Timesitheus' death is not certainly known; he either died of natural causes or was murdered by Philip the Arab, his rival in life and replacement in death.

Though Gordian could no longer rely upon the counsel of Timesitheus, he none-the-less led his army further against the Sasanians. It seems, however, that he did not lead aggressively enough to satisfy his soldiers, who no doubt wanted to sack the Sasanian capital and strip it of its legendary wealth. The death of Gordian III at Zaitha in February or March of 244 is a bit of a mystery, and is usually attributed to a coup by Philip I.

Philip told the senate that Gordian had died of natural causes, while Shapur reports that he died in battle against the Sasanians at Misikhe. Regardless of how Gordian — then 19 years old — actually died, it must have been a lonely, frightening affair. Gordian was without an adviser he could trust, and was at odds with the ambitious Philip, all the while trying to lead an army so far from the comforts of the Rome he had known as a child. We are told that Gordian, in a fit of desperation, offered to abdicate in place of Philip and take a subordinate role, such as that of Caesar, or even a lesser position, in exchange for his life.

NUMISMATIC NOTE: Gordian III was the last emperor to strike the denarius in quantity, and even in his reign it was being eclipsed by the double-denarius, which had been reintroduced by Pupienus and Balbinus. Denarii of subsequent emperors are extremely rare. Antioch, which had been safeguarded by Gordian's armies, now became a regular Imperial mint.

TRANQUILLINA

AUGUSTA, A.D. 241–244

WIFE OF GORDIAN III

Furia Sabinia Tranquillina, lifespan unknown. Tranquillina was the daughter of Gaius Furius Sabinius Aquila Timesitheus, a man of good conscience whom Gordian III appointed as the commander of the praetorian guard in 241. This was presumably before or upon the young emperor's marriage to Timesitheus' daughter in May of that year. We know regrettably little of Tranquillina, but are probably not out of line to assume she was perhaps 16, or of similar age to her husband. Except that she produced no children and accompanied Gordian and her father on their Sasanian campaign, details of the marriage are unknown. Though her father died of illness (or murder) in 243, Tranquillina remained married to Gordian until he died in 244. She appears to have survived him, but her subsequent fate is uncertain.

NUMISMATIC NOTE: The great rarity of Tranquillina's Imperial coinage is mysterious considering the great volume of coins struck in the name of her husband. Furthermore, under the Antonines and Severans there existed a tradition of striking large coinages in the name of empresses. Adding to this enigma is the fact that her provincial coinage is not terribly scarce. Some researchers suggest that her Imperial coins were recalled from circulation by Philip I, who is said to have despised her father, Timesitheus. However, this seems impractical and unlikely. A more probable theory is that her Imperial coinage was purposely small so as to avoid the appearance of a conflict of interest, considering that her father was the emperor's praetorian prefect and trusted adviser.

PHILIP I 'THE ARAB'
A.D. 244–249

AUGUSTUS: A.D. 244–249
(A.D. 244–247: SOLE REIGN)
(A.D. 247–249: WITH PHILIP II)

HUSBAND OF OTACILIA SEVERA
FATHER OF PHILIP II
SON OF JULIUS MARINUS

Marcus Julius Verus Philippus, c. A.D. 199/204–249. The specifics of Philip's origins are obscure, although we can be certain he was from the Hauran in Arabia Trachonitis, and most likely from the city which he later renamed Philippopolis. One source, Eusebius (4th Century), suggests he was the first Christian emperor, though his actions clearly point to the contrary.

If we believe the worst reports of the ancient historians, Philip's rise to the highest office was a cruel and calculated affair. He is said to have caused the murders of both the prefect Timesitheus and the emperor Gordian III. However, in even the most charitable version — where both deaths occurred naturally — Philip cannot be absolved of personal ambition, for he was an acknowledged enemy of Timesitheus, and he purposely roused the army against Gordian.

In any event, Philip replaced Timesitheus as praetorian prefect (joining his brother, Gaius Julius Priscus, the other praetorian prefect) and by the time of Gordian's death in February or March of 244, he was hailed as the next emperor. His first actions were to inform the senate of Gordian's death and negotiate a quick peace with Shapur I. Many found the treaty terms, which included an initial payment of 500,000 denarii (20,000 aurei), were disgraceful — especially considering the recent success of the Romans. However, Philip may have suspected that taking Ctesiphon would be no easy task, and instead settled for easy terms so he could safely go to Rome. Because of this "victory," Philip assumed the title Persicus maximus.

Philip quickly turned his attention to family affairs by placing his brother, Priscus, in charge of the eastern portion of the Empire *(rector Orientis)* and by appointing an in-law named Severianus governor of Moesia. He also deified his father, gave his 6- or 7-year-old son the rank of Caesar, and hailed his wife as Augusta. Philip acted hastily in all of these matters, for he did not wish to delay his long journey to Rome, where he was anxious to establish his authority with the senate.

Upon his arrival at Rome in July of 244, Philip was well-received by the senate. From 245 to 247, Philip was occupied on the Danubian frontier, repelling invasions by the Carpi and apparently fighting the Germans.

At the conclusion of the campaign in 247 he returned to Rome in triumph and raised his son to the rank of Augustus. In 248 the Imperial family celebrated the Saecular Games, which honored the 1,000th anniversary of the foundation of Rome. Though celebrations began on April 21, the magnificent games (which used exotic animals gathered by Gordian III for his anticipated Persian triumph) seem to have been held later in the year. For the people of Rome, this was a great event accompanied by a donative, which did much to raise their spirits.

Philip's glory was short-lived, for there was trouble once again on the Danube, where soldiers had hailed the commander Pacatian as their emperor. Although the rebellion was eventually stamped out, it proved to be an open invitation for Goths, Carpi and various Germans to invade Roman territories. As bad as this was, it was only one of four revolts that plagued the final year of Philip's rule. Ephemeral revolts by Silbannacus on the Rhine and Sponsianus on the Danube are proven by the numismatic evidence, but are not attested to in the historical record. The most serious revolt occurred in the East, where the cruelties of Philip's brother, Priscus, had enraged both citizen and soldier. The legions chose a certain Jotapian to lead their revolt, which proved difficult to quell, especially since Philip could not attend to it personally.

This series of usurpations shook Philip's confidence as a ruler, and he is even said to have tendered his resignation to the senate, only to be dissuaded by Decius, a senator and the prefect of Rome. But for Philip and his family, the worst was yet to come. Having lost his confidence, Philip appointed Decius to replace his in-law Severianus as commander-in-chief of Moesia and Pannonia. This was a foolhardy move since all of the rebellious legions in that region would now come under the command of a single man. Decius was successful in his mission to restore order to the region before the end of 248.

The inevitable occurred in about June of 249 when the soldiers promoted Decius as emperor. After some initial attempts at negotiation with Philip, Decius was urged to march on Rome. Philip left the capital to engage the approaching legions, which he encountered near Verona (another account suggests Beroea in Macedon) in September or October of 249. Though Philip had a larger army, he lost the battle and perished in the process, either while engaging the enemy or by treachery among his own soldiers.

NUMISMATIC NOTE: The main event Philip celebrated on his and his family's coinage was the millenniary celebration of Rome's foundation. Many of the coins struck for this important event depicted exotic animals that were featured in the games. One issue in particular, bearing the inscription AETERNITAS AVGG, features the elephant, an animal noted for its indelible memory and long lifespan. Particularly noteworthy was the reintroduction of the Æ drachm in Alexandria, Egypt, where the denomination had essentially been abandoned. The mint at Rome under Philip was organized into six *officinae*, which are often indicated on the double-denarii by Roman numerals or Greek letters that appear in the exergue or in the fields. The P M in the inscriptions on some of Philip's coins does not stand for the traditional *pontifex maximus*, but rather the title *Persicus maximus*, which he earned for his victory over the Sasanians.

OTACILIA SEVERA

AUGUSTA, A.D. 244–249

WIFE OF PHILIP I
MOTHER OF PHILIP II
DAUGHTER-IN-LAW (POSTHUMOUSLY?) OF JULIUS MARINUS

Marcia Otacilia Severa, d. A.D. 249(?). Very little is known of Otacilia Severa, an empress for whom a great quantity of coinage was struck. She seems to have married Philip about a decade before he became emperor, and gave birth to their only son, Philip Junior, in about 237. She may have been the daughter of a governor of Pannonia named Severus. Much as with her husband, later Christian writers speculated that Otacilia was a Christian, and that she sought penance from Saint Babylas, Bishop of Antioch, for her role in the murder of Gordian III. It is, of course, unlikely that this is true.

Upon her husband's accession in 244, Otacilia was given the title Augusta. She later was hailed *Mater Castrorum* ("mother of the camps") and *Mater Senatus et Patriae* ("mother of the senate and the country"). It is not known whether she spent most of the reign in Rome or accompanied her husband on his campaigns, but she almost certainly was in Rome at the time of her husband's defeat by Decius. Although it seems likely that she was executed by the praetorian guards, one source informs us that she survived the ordeal to pass the remainder of her days in retirement.

PHILIP II A.D. 247–249

CAESAR: A.D. 244–247 (UNDER PHILIP I)
AUGUSTUS: A.D. 247–249 (WITH PHILIP I)

SON OF PHILIP I AND OTACILIA SEVERA
GRANDSON OF JULIUS MARINUS

Marcus Julius Severus Philippus, c. A.D. 237–249. This young prince was destined for a short and eventful life, for at about age 7 he was raised to the rank of Caesar when his father was hailed emperor in February or March of 244. The child retained that rank while on the arduous journey from Mesopotamia to Rome, and during the more than two years of warfare against the Carpi and Germans on the Danube. At the conclusion of that campaign, Philip Junior — then in his 10th year — was raised to the rank of Augustus when Philip made his triumphant return to Rome in July or August of 247.

The sources differ in their telling of the boy's fate, though his death came as the result of his father's death in battle against Decius in September or October of 249. One version is that Philip Junior remained in Rome with his mother, and that he did his best to secure his own safety by administering bribes, perhaps surviving as late as November. But it is just as likely that he was at his father's side at Verona, and was either killed in battle or was captured and then taken to Rome, where he was executed by the praetorian guards.

JULIUS MARINUS

FATHER OF PHILIP I
GRANDFATHER OF PHILIP II

Julius Marinus, d. before A.D. 244. The father of Philip I, Julius Marinus was an Arab chieftain (*Sheik*) from Trachonitis who also apparently held the rank of a Roman knight. Beyond this, nothing is known with certainty except that he was deified by his son.

Upon the accession of Philip in 244, the name of what presumably was his home town (located about 12 miles from Bostra, the capital of Roman Arabia) was changed to Philippopolis. Furthermore, the town was accorded the status of a Roman *colonia*, and Philip erected there a temple dedicated to the deified Marinus and, seemingly, another relative (his mother?), for the seated Roma on Philippopolitan coins holds two small figures. Portions of this temple bearing inscriptions naming Philip and his family members were discovered at the archaeological site.

NUMISMATIC NOTE: The coinage of Philippopolis appears to be limited to the reign of Philip I. For this reason it can be presumed that it was a relatively insignificant place, and that despite the lavish honors it briefly received from its emperor-benefactor, it remained so. The most interesting issues of the city are the two denominations struck for Julius Marinus, as coins with his name or image were produced nowhere else. The obverses commemorate his apotheosis not only by means of the appropriate inscription, but also by showing his bust resting upon an eagle with spread wings. The reverse types depict Roma standing or seated.

SILBANNACUS c. A.D. 248(?)

Marcus Silbannacus, d. A.D. 248(?). This man is unknown from any source but a single coin bearing his name, which is in the cabinet of the British Museum. During the final year or two of the reign of Philip I, Silbannacus seems to have led a revolt in the West (perhaps on the Rhine); his coin was found in Lorraine. The reverse type is unusual in that it depicts Mercury holding not only his traditional caduceus, but also a small figure of Victory.

SPONSIANUS c. A.D. 248(?)

Sponsianus, lifespan unknown. Sponsianus may be the most mysterious of all "issuers" of coins in Roman history. His aurei — described in RIC as "strange and barbarous" — are placed at the end of the reign of Philip I, when at least two other revolts occurred. Based on their find sites in Transylvania, they may be associated with a revolt on the Danube, if they are to be linked to any revolt at all. Equally as vexing as the barbarous die engraving is the choice of reverse type, which seems to be copied from a Republican denarius struck in 135 B.C. (Cr. 242/1).

PACATIAN c. A.D. 248–249(?)

Tiberius (or Titus) Claudius Marinus Pacatianus, d. A.D. 248. The revolt of Pacatian on the Danube in the spring or early summer of 248 proved to be the beginning of the end for Philip I, who had been emperor for nearly four years. The commander Pacatian — either by design or unwillingly — was hailed emperor by Danubian legions who apparently had tired of Philip. Opinions on the length of his reign vary considerably among historians, with estimates ranging from a few weeks to a few months. In any case, his revolt seems to have been crushed by Decius, who had been sent to the region by Philip to take command in place of his own incompetent in-law, Severianus. As the result of Decius' arrival, Pacatian was assassinated by his soldiers sometime between the spring of 248 and early 249.

NUMISMATIC NOTE: This usurper's coins appear to have been struck in Moesia. The mint of Viminacium is often suggested, though it is worth noting that if this was his mint, it seems odd no provincial issues were struck there in his name, unless the production demands for his double-denarii were so great that the provincial coinage had to be abandoned. Pacatian's most interesting issue bears the reverse inscription ROMAE AETER(nae) AN(no) MILL(esimo) ET PRIMO, which translates to "the thousand and first year of eternal Rome."

JOTAPIAN c. A.D. 248–249(?)

Marcus Fulvius Rufus Jotapianus, d. A.D. 248. When Philip I appointed his brother Gaius Julius Priscus governor of Mesopotamia, with general authority over the Roman East, he no doubt hoped his brother would rule competently in the family's best interest. However, such a great amount of authority, which included the unorthodox title "praetorian prefect and ruler of the East," seems to have turned Priscus into an autocrat whose ruthless tax collections stirred the locals into revolt in the summer of 248.

In response, the army commander Jotapian was proclaimed emperor by his soldiers. He apparently controlled a vast area, including Northern Syria and Cappadocia, but was assassinated by his soldiers after a reign of no more than a year. Much like the revolt of Pacatian on the Danube, the length of Jotapian's reign is disputed. Though it may have lasted only a few weeks, it more likely endured several months, lasting into early or mid-249. Jotapian's claim to be a relative of Severus Alexander may well have been fictional. Alternatively, he may have been descended from the old rulers of Commagene, as Jotape was a name associated with that dynasty.

TRAJAN DECIUS A.D. 249–251

AUGUSTUS: A.D. 249–251
(A.D. 249–251: SOLE REIGN)
(A.D. 251: WITH HERENNIUS ETRUSCUS AND HOSTILIAN)

HUSBAND OF HERENNIA ETRUSCILLA
FATHER OF HERENNIUS ETRUSCUS AND HOSTILIAN

Gaius Messius Quintus Traianus Decius (*earlier* Gaius Messius Quintus Decius), c. A.D. 190/201–251. Born at Budalia, near Sirmium, Decius was one of the few Danubians of his era who rose to high rank in Rome. Though he hailed from a family of standing, he owed his success no less to his own skills than to his marriage to Herennia Etruscilla, who was descended from a noble Etruscan family.

Quite early in his career Decius gained senatorial rank, and later held important administrative posts, including the governorships of Nearer Spain and Lower Moesia. Toward the end of the reign of Philip I, Decius was the prefect of Rome. His encouragement to the emperor not to abdicate earned him the dubious honor of being sent to the Danubian front to put an end to the revolt of Pacatian and to rid the region of the Goths, Germans and Dacian Carpi who had flooded in during the crisis.

It could hardly have come as a surprise when in July the legions hailed Decius as Augustus, and compelled him to march against Philip. Indeed, Sosimus tells us that Decius warned Philip in advance that this was the inevitable conclusion, but that Philip asked him to go anyway. The veracity of this is doubtful; although Decius made overtures to Philip after the fact, it was clear that the two men could not rule jointly, and so the opposing armies met at Verona (or possibly at Beroea in Macedon) in September or October of 249.

In the resulting battle, Decius was victorious over the larger forces of Philip, who perished. The political chaos that had plagued Philip at the end of his reign was now silenced, and Decius — the first in a long line of emperors to hail from the Balkans — was master of the collapsing Roman world. He entered Rome in October, and his colleagues in the senate confirmed his rank and heaped him with honors. Most interesting of these was the bestowal of the surname Trajan, after the famous 2nd Century emperor who not only had an excellent relationship with the senate, but who also defeated the Dacian king Decebalus, and annexed Dacia as a province of the Empire.

Decius' main social agenda involved the ancient traditions of Rome, most especially the worship of previous emperors and the observation of traditional pagan ritual. This did not bode well for the few Christians in the Empire, who were compelled to honor the pagan rituals or face death. One victim of Decius' reform was Pope Fabian, who was martyred in 250. However dedicated Decius was to his social causes, the problems on the frontier took precedence, as the withdrawal of Decius' forces had made the Danubian frontier vulnerable to yet another barbarian invasion.

The Goths and the Carpi invaded Roman territory simultaneously, crossing the frozen waters of the Danube early in 250. Two future emperors became involved in affairs at this point: Trebonianus Gallus, then governor of Upper and Lower Moesia, and Valerian I, for whom Decius invented an office that gave him overall authority in Rome during the emperor's absence.

It was also in 250 that Decius raised his eldest son, Herennius Etruscus, to the rank of Caesar. Though only a teenager, the new Caesar was sent to the front that summer at the head of an army while Decius settled matters in Rome. However, it was not long before Decius too arrived, winning some important engagements against the Goths and the Carpi. He was able to save Nicopolis ad Istrum by inflicting heavy losses on the Gothic chieftain Kniva, who consequently abandoned his siege. Decius was also successful in driving the Carpi out of Dacia.

But after he had suffered a small defeat at Beroe Augusta Trajana, Decius learned that a local governor, Titus Julius Priscus (who had been besieged in Philippopolis for several months), had hailed himself emperor and defected to the Goths. Although Priscus was soon killed, Decius was unable to prevent the ravage of Thrace that resulted. He led his army to the Danube, where he linked up with the legions under the command of Trebonianus Gallus. Together they hoped to defeat the booty-laden Goths as they returned to their homeland. While awaiting the Goths, Decius learned of a rebellion in the city of Rome led by a certain Julius Valens Licinianus (by March this was suppressed by Valerian).

Meanwhile, the opportunity Decius and Gallus had been awaiting on the Gothic front arrived in the spring of 251. The initial engagement was a great success, prompting Decius to raise his eldest son to the rank of Augustus, and his youngest son, Hostilian (who was still in Rome), to the rank of Caesar (alternatively, this may already have occurred in 250). Riding the tide of good fortune, Decius sought a decisive victory over the

Goths — but the opposite occured. Under the leadership of the chieftain Kniva, the Goths ambushed the Romans in the marshes at Abrittus in June, or possibly July, of 251. There, the Goths delivered one of the great defeats in Imperial history, killing the 50- or 60-year-old Decius, his teenage son, Herennius Etruscus, and most of their army.

Unless we take as fact Shapur I's account of Gordian III dying in battle at Misikhe, Decius and Etruscus were the first Roman emperors to fall against a foreign enemy. It remains uncertain whether his defeat was due to the treachery of Trebonianus Gallus, who failed to rescue them with his reserve force, and who was subsequently hailed emperor. In any event, the ambush bears an uncanny resemblance to the even more serious defeat of the emperor Valens by the Goths near Adrianople in 378.

Numismatic Note: Decius produced one of the more interesting coinages of the 3rd Century, with his monetary policy seemingly being determined by runaway inflation. Not only did he introduce an entirely new denomination, the double-sestertius, but he also struck a small æ coin usually called a semis by numismatists. Rather than a semis (a low value coin abandoned more than a century before, and one which was of uncertain function even when it was in regular production), the small coin more likely was an as, though greatly reduced in weight. Supporting this theory is the significant reduction in weight which can be observed in the other æs denominations struck by Decius. It is worth noting that if the double-sestertius and the reduced as/semis were intended as remedies for inflation, the measures quickly failed, for they were not adopted by his immediate successors. He also struck a series of double-denarii honoring eleven of his deified Imperial predecessors (which are described in a separate listing following the regular coins of Decius). Many of Decius' coins celebrate Dacia, Pannonia and Illyricum, all provinces in the region from which he hailed. His double-denarii from Antioch differ from those of Rome not only in the style of artistry, but also by the presence of pellets or numerals either below the bust or in the exergue on the reverse. These pellets and numerals indicate the *officina* in which the coin was struck — a system adopted for some later coinages of Antioch.

HERENNIA ETRUSCILLA

AUGUSTA, A.D. 249–253(?)

WIFE OF TRAJAN DECIUS
MOTHER OF HERENNIUS ETRUSCUS AND HOSTILIAN

Herennia Cupressenia Etruscilla, lifespan unknown. Despite the commonness of Herennia Etruscilla's coins, the life of this noble Etruscan lady reads like a blank page. Had an inscription not confirmed that she was the wife of Decius, we would have to rely entirely on the numismatic evidence, which in this case is quite strong. There exist a handful of "hybrid" coins on which her obverse dies are paired with reverse dies intended for Trajan Decius and Herennius Etruscus. There is a strong possibility that coinage in her name continued to be struck under Trebonianus Gallus, as Gallus' wife was never hailed Augusta.

HERENNIUS ETRUSCUS

A.D. 251

CAESAR: A.D. 250–251
(UNDER TRAJAN DECIUS, AND
WITH HOSTILIAN(?))
AUGUSTUS: A.D. 251 (WITH TRAJAN DECIUS)

SON OF TRAJAN DECIUS AND HERENNIA ETRUSCILLA
BROTHER OF HOSTILIAN

Quintus Herennius Etruscus Messius Decius, d. A.D. 251. As the eldest son of Trajan Decius, Herennius Etruscus was destined to become involved in the Imperial duties of his father, who had been hailed emperor by his soldiers on the Danubian frontier and, after defeating the armies of Philip I in October of 249, gained the approval of the senate.

Though his father had pacified the Danubian front before leaving to confront Philip I, his battle preparations had deprived the region of the legions that defended it. Thus, the Goths and Carpi exploited this weakness by crossing the Danube again early in 250. As Decius prepared to lead a campaign to reclaim the region, one of the measures he took was to appoint Herennius Etruscus to the rank of Caesar.

Since matters were not yet settled in Rome, Decius placed Etruscus in command of the army, which the teenage Caesar then led to the Danubian front in the summer of 250. Decius joined him on the front soon thereafter, but the problems they faced were manifold, and Decius discovered that he could do little to prevent the Goths from ravaging Roman territory. Instead, the Romans waited to defeat the Goths when they attempted to cross back over the Danube. In the meantime, Decius and Etruscus joined their legions with those of the future emperor Trebonianus Gallus, who was then a governor in Moesia.

When the Goths returned in the spring of 251, Decius and son made their move. The initial engagement was a success, and in May or June of 251 Decius raised Etruscus to the rank of Augustus. At the same time he may also have raised his younger son, Hostilian, then residing in Rome, to the rank of Caesar (if this had not already occurred in 250).

Decius hoped to inflict a great defeat on the Goths. The opposite occurred, however, when the legions under joint command of Decius and Etruscus were ambushed by the Goths in June or July of 251. The teenage Etruscus and his middle-aged father were slaughtered along with the preponderance of their army. Thus, Etruscus and his father are known to history principally as the first Roman emperors to fall in battle against a foreign enemy. Trebonianus Gallus, who was in charge of the reserve force, failed to rescue Decius and his army, and it remains uncertain whether his inaction was treacherous or merely unfortunate.

HOSTILIAN A.D. 251

CAESAR: A.D. 250(?)–251
(VARIOUSLY UNDER TRAJAN DECIUS, HERENNIUS ETRUCUS(?) AND TREBONIANUS GALLUS(?))
AUGUSTUS: A.D. 251
(WITH TREBONIANUS GALLUS)

SON OF TRAJAN DECIUS AND HERENNIA ETRUSCILLA
BROTHER OF HERENNIUS ETRUSCUS
ADOPTIVE SON OF TREBONIANUS GALLUS

Gaius Valens Hostilianus Messius Quintus, d. A.D. 251. The reign of Hostilian is one of the sketchiest of the 3rd Century. Not only was his era extremely chaotic, but it is poorly documented by historians. Furthermore, his largely ceremonial status has to be judged in terms of the four Augusti with whom he was associated (and their individual chronologies are far from certain). It is most helpful first to discuss the progression of events, and then to discuss how they may have affected Hostilian.

As the son of Trajan Decius and the younger brother of Herennius Etruscus, Hostilian assumed the junior role in the family power structure, which also included his mother, Herennia Etruscilla, a noblewoman who held the rank of Augusta. Young Hostilian (then perhaps in his early teens) stayed in Rome with his mother while his father and older brother went to the Danube to fight the Goths in the summer of 250. Even at Rome the true power was not in the hands of Hostilian and his mother, for Decius had created a special post for Valerian (the future emperor) that accorded him great authority. This appointment was one of Decius' more prudent moves. In the early months of 251 Valerian crushed a serious rebellion at Rome that had been staged by a certain Julius Valens Licinianus.

In the course of waging war on the Danubian front, Decius and Etruscus (both of whom then held the rank of Augustus) were killed in an ambush in June or July of 251. Hostilian — safe in Rome — was the only surviving male of the ruling family, and he seems to have held only the rank of Caesar at the time of that tragedy.

Immediately after Decius and Etruscus were killed, the Danubian legions hailed their own commander, Trebonianus Gallus, as the new emperor. Gallus rapidly arranged an unfavorable peace with the Goths, and then marched to Rome to receive the confirmation of the senate. Sometime after his arrival, Gallus agreed to share the rank of Augustus with Hostilian. The subordinate rank of Caesar was given to Gallus' own son, Volusian, who also was betrothed to Hostilian's sister.

Though Hostilian had lost his father and brother to the Goths, he still had his mother and sister, and may have found comfort in having a new adoptive father and brother-in-law. But this tidy arrangement ended when Hostilian died of the plague, which at that time was a raging epidemic in the capital as well as through most of the Empire. Despite the lofty titles Hostilian briefly possessed, and the quantity of coins that were struck in his name, he accomplished little or nothing.

Chronological Note: Though most authorities ascribe Hostilian's reign exclusively to 251 (beginning in the spring, when his older brother Herennius Etruscus was hailed Augustus), others suggest he was hailed Caesar in mid- or late 250. All seem to be in agreement, however, that his brief tenure as Augustus belongs to 251, after Gallus arrived in Rome and negotiated their joint-rulership. This can most likely be dated to late June or July of 251. There is some numismatic evidence that during a very brief period after Gallus' arrival in Rome, Gallus was Augustus, Hostilian was Caesar and Volusian had not yet been given a title. But that initial arrangement probably lasted less than a month before Hostilian was made co-Augustus, and Volusian was hailed Caesar. The date of Hostilian's death is equally uncertain, with estimates ranging from August to November of 251.

NUMISMATIC NOTE: A coin type struck by his adoptive father, Trebonianus Gallus (APOLL[O] SALVTARI, Apollo standing, holding a branch and a lyre) invokes Apollo Salutaris ("the health-bringing Apollo"), to deliver the Romans from the plague. Though Gallus could not have known his young colleague would eventually die of the plague, his unusual type demonstrates just how serious the epidemic had become. A similar type was struck by Valerian I, into whose reign the plague persisted.

TREBONIANUS GALLUS
A.D. 251–253

AUGUSTUS: A.D. 251–253
(A.D. 251: WITH HOSTILIAN)
(A.D. 251–253: WITH VOLUSIAN)

FATHER OF VOLUSIAN
ADOPTIVE FATHER OF HOSTILIAN

Gaius Vibius Afinius Trebonianus Gallus, c. A.D. 204/6–253. Except that he hailed from an old Etruscan family in Perugia, little is known about the early life of Trebonianus Gallus. He was married to Afinia Gemina Baebiana, by whom he fathered Volusian. It comes as no surprise that Baebiana was not hailed Augusta, for the widow of Decius, Herennia Etruscilla, was still alive at the time Gallus was emperor.

Gallus' political career was distinguished, for he was a leading senator who had held the consulship in 245. But the event that enrolled him in the annals of history was his appointment in 250 as governor of Upper and Lower Moesia, a highly unstable but important province that had come under a fresh invasion by the Goths and the Carpi about the time he arrived. Gallus did his best to repel the Goths, but to little effect. The emperor Trajan Decius and his eldest son, Herennius Etruscus, soon arrived at the front, and even their efforts failed when a local governor named Priscus defected to the Goths.

However, what occurred in June or July of the following year (251) was worse than could have been imagined: Decius and Etruscus were ambushed and killed (along with most of their army) by the Goths near Abrittus. It was one of the great defeats in Roman history, and it is still uncertain whether Gallus (who was in charge of the reserve force) treacherously failed to warn Decius of the ambush. In any event, Gallus was promptly hailed emperor by his soldiers.

His first act was to negotiate peace with the Goths, and in so doing he promised an annual tribute of gold and allowed them to keep all of their booty and prisoners. The terms were disgraceful, but considering the success of the Gothic ambush on Decius, they were probably the best he could attain. But the worst was yet to come. Gallus now headed for Rome and prepared for a reign which a 19th Century historian aptly described as "a succession of miseries, devastations and horrors."

When he arrived at Rome, Gallus discovered that the city was suffering from an epidemic of the plague that was to cripple the Empire for at least another 15 years. The new emperor secured his position by sharing his authority with Hostilian, the teenage son of Trajan Decius, who had remained in Rome with his mother. Though the boy had held the rank of Caesar under his father, Gallus raised him to Augustus, while at the same time he gave his own son, Volusian, the subordinate rank of Caesar.

This careful arrangement was shattered sometime between August and November of 251, when Hostilian died of the plague. While Gallus raised his own son to the now-vacant office of junior Augustus, his time in the capital was far from pleasant. Not only was the plague causing great harm, but the Goths launched yet another invasion. It was not until the following year (252) that the governor of Lower Moesia, the future emperor Aemilian, crossed the Danube and defeated the Goths.

In that same year — as if the Romans were not already suffering enough — the Sasanian king, Shapur I, invaded and captured Armenia. In 252/3 Shapur invaded the wealthy Roman province of Syria, and was so successful that he even sacked Antioch, the third most important city in the Empire. Much like the plague, the armies of Shapur would prove to be a devastating force in the Empire for the next decade. But the destruction in Asia Minor was not limited to Sasanian offensives, for the Goths and other Germanic peoples also raided Asia Minor, probably because they had already stripped the Balkan region of most of its portable wealth.

Although the Goths had no intention of remaining in Asia, their raids were devastating and penetrated as far south as Ephesus. It seems that Gallus found a scapegoat for the ill-fortune of the Empire in the Christians. He renewed the persecutions of Trajan Decius, in which Pope Fabian had been martyred. With all of this chaos, Gallus' one area of success was on the Danubian frontier, where Aemilian was victorious. This may have been good news for the frontier legions, but it did not bode well for Gallus. The victorious Aemilian gave a large bonus to his legions, who then hailed him emperor and urged him to march on Rome.

Gallus had the senate declare Aemilian a public enemy and sent for help from another of his generals, the future emperor Valerian, who was recruiting troops on the Rhine. But the advance of Aemilian that spring (or summer) was too swift, and Valerian was unable to react in time. The small army that Gallus was able to muster was no match for Aemilian's seasoned and bribed legions. Both Gallus and his son, Volusian, were murdered by their own soldiers, who were unwilling to face certain defeat against Aemilian.

We know that these executions were carried out some 20 to 50 miles north of Rome, in rural Umbria, but authorities are divided as to whether they occurred in April or August of 253. Despite the magnitude of the ill-fortune Gallus faced, it is difficult to respect his feeble efforts at salvaging the Empire. Unlike more energetic emperors of the 3rd Century (such as Gallienus, Aurelian or Probus), Gallus seems to have been so overwhelmed that he was paralyzed into inaction.

His reign bears a striking parallel to that of Philip the Arab, as both men began by hastily negotiating peace treaties and making a quick dash to Rome. Later in their reigns, both men took refuge in the capital, hoping that their frontier generals would not only save the Empire but expect nothing in return. The final comparison, of course, is drawn in their manner of death, for both perished when their armies refused to support them in the moment of battle against the next contender.

NUMISMATIC NOTE: Seemingly in an attempt to combat runaway inflation, Gallus introduced a 'radiate' gold coin, which he struck alongside the traditional 'laureate' piece. The radiate crown normally indicated a double denomination, and Gallus' laureate gold coin may have been intended as a double aureus (a 'binio') even though it was only about 50% or 60% heavier than the laureate piece. In this respect it offers a ready parallel to the silver double-denarius of Caracalla. Both of Gallus' gold coins were considerably underweight, with the radiate pieces typically weighing about 5.8 grams, and the laureate coins only about 3.6 grams.

VOLUSIAN A.D. 251–253

CAESAR: A.D. 251
(UNDER TREBONIANUS GALLUS AND HOSTILIAN)
AUGUSTUS: A.D. 251–253
(WITH TREBONIANUS GALLUS)

SON OF TREBONIANUS GALLUS

Gaius Vibius Afinius Gallus Vendumnianus Volusianus, d. A.D. 253. Despite the volume of his coinage that survives, Volusian achieved very little in his approximately two years of rule, first as Caesar, then as Augustus. Volusian came to power when his father was hailed emperor by his soldiers following the ambush the Gothic king Kniva sprang on Trajan Decius at Abrittus in June or July of 251.

Shortly after Gallus returned to Rome, he was confirmed by the senate and arranged to share the title of Augustus with Hostilian, the son of Trajan Decius who had remained in Rome. Even though Volusian was older than Hostilian, he was given the subordinate rank of Caesar. Ties between Hostilian's family and his own were strengthened by Volusian's betrothal to Hostilian's sister. Furthermore, Gallus did not assign to his own wife (Afinia Gemina Baebiana) the title Augusta, for Herennia Etruscilla, the widow of Decius and mother of Hostilian, was alive and in possession of that title.

But this arrangement unraveled sometime between August and November of 251 when young Hostilian died of the plague that was ravaging not only Rome, but most of the Empire. With this turn of events, Volusian filled the now-vacant office of junior Augustus. No doubt news of terrible aggressions by the Goths and the Sasanians poured into Rome, further dampening the spirit of a population beset with critical problems of their own.

Instead of combating the invasions themselves, father and son remained at Rome, hoping the crises would resolve themselves. When Aemilian, the governor of Lower Moesia, began to have success against the Goths, his frontier legions hailed him emperor. Gallus and Volusian tried to secure aid from the general (and future emperor) Valerian, who was recruiting soldiers on the Rhine, but Aemilian marched to Italy at a furious pace and Valerian came too late to help.

Gallus and Volusian gathered what few soldiers they could muster that spring or summer of 253 and left Rome to face Aemilian. The two emperors didn't get more than about two days march from the capital before they were murdered by their own soldiers, who had no desire to engage the larger and more seasoned army led by Aemilian. We cannot be certain of Volusian's age, but his coin portraits indicate he was a young man, perhaps in his 20s or early 30s.

AEMILIAN A.D. 253

HUSBAND OF CORNELIA SUPERA

Marcus Aemilius Aemilianus, c. A.D. 207/8–253. Of this ephemeral emperor we know very little, except that he hailed from an obscure Mauretanian family which perhaps lived on the island of Jerba. A man of considerable talent, Aemilian rose to the high office of consul. During the reign of Trebonianus Gallus and Volusian, the Empire was besieged on all fronts and it was on this stage that Aemilian made his entry into history.

Troubles were numerous: the Sasanians were raiding Roman territory in the East, the plague was ravaging all parts of the Empire, and the Goths had launched yet another offensive across the Danube and made destructive sorties into Asia Minor. In 252, Aemilian, then governor of Lower Moesia (having in 251 taken over the post vacated by Trebonianus Gallus), executed the Goths who remained in Roman territory and crossed the Danube to inflict an important defeat on the remaining tribesman. While Aemilian's success was triumphant for the beleaguered frontier legions, it did not bode well for Gallus and Volusian, who remained in Rome as the frontiers unraveled.

Aemilian was energetic and ambitious, and was not bashful about his desire to become emperor, for he gave to his soldiers the money that was intended to subsidize a peace agreement with the Goths. In a virtual repeat of recent history, Aemilian's frontier legions hailed him emperor in the spring or summer of 253, and urged him to march on Rome. Gallus declared Aemilian a public enemy and sought the support of another of his generals, the future emperor Valerian, who was then raising troops in Germany and Gaul.

But the advance of Aemilian from Moesia to just outside Rome was too swift, and Valerian's efforts were in vain. Gallus was able to gather from the environs of Rome only a small army which, both in size and capability, was no match for Aemilian's seasoned legions. The inferior army of Gallus was not anxious to engage Aemilian, and so they mutinied and murdered Gallus and Volusian at Interamna in rural Umbria.

Being only a day or two from Rome, Aemilian proceeded there at the head of his enlarged army and gained the approval of the senate, which only weeks before had declared him a public enemy. Despite his immediate success, Aemilian would soon meet a similar fate, for the legions that Valerian had gathered from Raetia and Noricum were marching on Italy. Alerted to the advance of the challenger, Aemilian may have sought a compromise, but in any case led his army from Rome.

The armies met at a bridge near Spoleto in Umbria, and Aemilian was killed by his own soldiers. Though the fighting was inconsequential, there must have been an engagement, for thereafter the site came to be known as *Pons Sanguinarius*, "the bloody bridge." The hasty demise of Aemilian was perhaps a tragedy; he seemed to have the makings of an excellent frontier emperor.

Though authorities agree that Aemilian reigned for about three months, the exact timing is debated. Estimates cover the entire period of April through October. The two best possibilities are April through July, or August through October. The historical record seems to favor the former, whereas the numismatic record may support the latter, as his tetradrachms at Alexandria are dated only to "year two," suggesting that news of his accession reached Egypt sometime after the Egyptian New Year on August 29.

CORNELIA SUPERA

AUGUSTA, A.D. 253

WIFE OF AEMILIAN

Gaia Cornelia Supera, lifespan unknown. This empress is unknown to history except for her appearance on coinage. Indeed, it is exclusively on the strength of the numismatic evidence that she is identified as the wife of Aemilian. Authorities in the 19th Century and earlier had speculated she was possibly the consort of Trebonianus Gallus or the wife of Valerian II.

NUMISMATIC NOTE: Cornelia Supera's Latin issues are limited to double-denarii, which have only two reverse types, Vesta and Juno. Her provincial coinage, though also limited in scale, is more abundant, and includes issues struck at Parium in Mysia, Julia in Phrygia and Aegae in Cilicia.

URANIUS ANTONINUS

A.D. 253–254

Lucius Julius Aurelius Sulpicius Uranius Antoninus (*also* Sampsigeramus), d. A.D. 254(?). The chaos of the Roman Empire in the early 250s was viewed as an opportunity by the Sasanian king Shapur I, who occupied Roman Armenia in 252 and in 252/3 invaded the wealthy Roman province of Syria. The Persian armies made great advances and soon divided to attack simultaneously the cities of Antioch and Emesa.

Though Antioch was taken by treachery in the summer of 253 and suffered a terrible fate, Emesa offered tough resistance. Charged with the defense of Emesa was a certain Sampsigeramus, who is almost certainly Uranius Antoninus, a hereditary priest of Aphrodite and the sun-god El-gabal. This was the same office the emperor Elagabalus (from whom Uranius certainly was descended) had held before he became emperor in 218.

Not only did the Emesans defend their city, but they went on the offensive, driving the Sasanians out of their vicinity. It is believed that

Uranius Antoninus was urged to assume power based on this achievement. The Roman relief of Syria was understandably slow in coming. Not only was the plague paralyzing much of the Empire, but there was constant invasion across the Danube, and as if matters were not difficult enough, there were three different regimes in 253.

Though temporarily paralyzed, Rome was far from powerless, and the new emperor Valerian I was prepared for action. His first important deed was to nominate his eldest son, Gallienus, co-emperor. Leaving Gallienus in charge of the European theater, Valerian was free to campaign in Asia Minor. Either late in 253 or early in 254, Valerian was able to recover the capital city of Antioch, probably because it had been so completely depleted that the Sasanians simply abandoned it. What happened thereafter at Emesa is not certainly known, except that Uranius Antoninus either abdicated or was forcibly removed from power. It is also unknown whether Uranius Antoninus survived his brief tenure as ruler of Emesa, but the prospect seems unlikely.

Historical Note: Until very recently the circumstances of Uranius Antoninus' revolt was not understood; three usurpers of similar context are reported by ancient historians. A Uranius *and* an Antoninus are reported by Zosimius (writing c. A.D. 500), and a certain Taurinus is reported by the mid-4th Century historian Victor. Scholars of the 19th Century placed his revolt during the reign of Severus Alexander (222–235), and even until quite recently it was dated to c. 248–253/4 (for it was thought to have been sparked by the harsh taxations of Gaius Julius Priscus, the brother of Philip the Arab). Prompting this view was an aureus with the reverse type SAECVLARES AVGG and depicting a low column inscribed COS I. While this coin seemingly indicates a date *no earlier* than 248, when Philip I celebrated the millennium of Rome's foundation, it need not be associated with that date, as unrelated festivals bearing that name were also held by other emperors in the 3rd Century. Offering the most reliable evidence is a copper coin of his revolt bearing the date ΕΞΦ (year 565 of the Seleucid Era = A.D. 253/4), which certainly places him in power at that time.

Numismatic Note: Since this usurper does not claim the titles of Augustus or Imperator in his obverse inscriptions, he seems not to have taken those titles. The fact that the reverse inscriptions on his aurei end with AVG or AVGG need not alter that conclusion, for they undoubtedly were copied from the reverse inscriptions of regular Roman coins. All of Uranius Antoninus' coinage appears to have been struck at Emesa in 253 and 254. His aurei have Latin inscriptions, whereas his silver, billon and copper coinages have Greek inscriptions. His tetradrachms come in two distinctive types: high silver content pieces struck on thin, broad planchets, and billon pieces struck on thick planchets typical of the era. This usurper employed many different reverse types. References are to H.R. Baldus, Uranius Antoninus, Münzpragüng und Geschicte, Antiquitas 3 (1971).

VALERIAN I A.D. 253–260

AUGUSTUS: A.D. 253–260 (WITH GALLIENUS)

HUSBAND OF MARINIANA
FATHER OF GALLIENUS
GRANDFATHER OF VALERIAN II AND SALONINUS

Publius Licinius Valerianus, c. A.D. 193/195–260+. Little is known about Valerian's life before about the year 250, although he hailed from the distinguished Licinia family of Etruria, had served as consul during the reign of Severus Alexander, and had supported the revolt of the Gordiani in 238. His mark on history, however, was made at the end of his own tragic reign in 260, when he became the first Roman emperor to be captured alive by an enemy.

While a senator, Valerian came into a position of great power in 250, when the emperor Trajan Decius created a special post for him in Rome, providing him with virtually unlimited authority to maintain the peace during the emperor's absence. He used this authority to crush a rebellion in Rome led by a certain Julius Valens Licinianus in the early months of 251.

The succeeding emperor, Trebonianus Gallus (251–253), sent Valerian to the Rhine front to recruit soldiers, but his duties were cut short when Gallus urgently requested he lead an army to defend Italy from the advancing legions of the usurper Aemilian. Valerian's response was not fast enough to intercept Aemilian, whose freshly bribed legions marched at a rapid pace. Gallus could only muster a small army, and he was executed by his own soldiers at Interamna, not far outside of Rome. In the meantime, Aemilian extorted the approval of the senate for his own regime.

The news of Gallus' execution arrived while Valerian was en route, and it prompted his soldiers to hail him emperor in opposition to Aemilian. The large armies of the rivals met near Spoleto in Umbria (not far from where Gallus had been executed only three months before), and Aemilian was killed by his own soldiers, seemingly after a minor battle. Exactly when this occurred is debated, but most likely it was in July or October of 253. As these events unfolded, the eldest son of Valerian, Gallienus, was in Rome. An anxious senate seems to have hailed him Caesar before his victorious father arrived, though no coinage was struck reflecting this occurrence.

Valerian gained senate approval for his own regime (in September?), and hailed Gallienus co-Augustus.

Though we know in hindsight that the reigns of Valerian and Gallienus — greatly troubled though they were — would last many years, there was no indication at the time that this rapid succession of emperors would end with Valerian. To make matters worse, the frontiers were subjected to a fresh wave of assaults as Rome's legions were occupied with yet another civil war. Very early in their joint-reign, Valerian and Gallienus formally divided their responsibilities geographically, with the father taking command in Asia Minor and the son defending the borders in Europe. This was the greatest crisis the Empire had yet known, and had there not been two emperors, the history of the Romans might have been considerably different.

Valerian arrived in the East early in 254 on a mission to expel the Sasanians who under Shapur I had launched a damaging invasion in the previous year. Valerian first recovered Antioch, which had been so completely sacked that the Sasanians seem to have abandoned it before he arrived. He next turned his efforts to Emesa, which was held by the usurper Uranius Antoninus, who was soon expelled.

About this time the Goths were adding a new weapon to their arsenal, a naval fleet, which they seem to have obtained from the Bosporan kings. The pioneering venture, an assault on the town of Pityus in 256 by the Borani, failed miserably. But subsequent attacks with a new fleet in 257 resulted in the burning of Trapezus and the pillaging of Panticapaeum. The Goths quickly took to seafaring, which not only provided another dimension to their attacks, but also allowed them to launch lightning-fast assaults far and wide. Subsequent attacks by sea and land, caused Nicaea, Nicomedia and other important cities to be razed to the ground.

Although Valerian would have had his hands full with the Goths in Bithynia, two more threats emerged at the same time. The first was Shapur, who renewed hostilities for a third time within a generation; the second was an unseen foe, the plague. With three formidable enemies, Valerian was destined to struggle against all hope to save the beleaguered Roman East, while his son Gallienus could offer no help, for he faced similarly desperate conditions in Europe.

As troublesome as the Gothic and Scythian raiders were, the Sasanians were a more serious threat, and so Valerian focused on expelling Shapur, who seems to have been principally interested in looting and destroying rather than in occupying. The king's invasion was a great success, for he captured 37 cities throughout Mesopotamia, Armenia, Cappadocia and Syria, which included (yet again) Antioch, where Shapur may have installed a short-lived usurper named Cyriades or Mariades (though during which of Shapur's invasions is uncertain).

Seemingly by 258 the Sasanians had withdrawn and relative peace returned to Asia Minor, though any prosperity had been carted away by the Sasanians and Goths. A true recovery was not to take place, though, for in 259 Shapur invaded once again — his fourth such invasion in a generation. Valerian won a battle near Edessa, but the effects of the plague within his ranks forced him to withdraw to that city, where he was besieged. Seeing no good option, Valerian tried his hand at negotiation in April, May or June of 260 (accounts vary). Accompanied by only a small retinue of his top officials, Valerian was taken prisoner by Shapur, who evidently had no intention of negotiating.

We cannot be certain when Valerian died, for he was used by Shapur as a living trophy of his triumph over the Romans. Shapur is said to have mutilated the elderly emperor, and used his back as a stepping-stool when mounting his horse. When not being humiliated by such acts, Valerian was supposedly kept huddled in a small cage. After he died, we are told his skin was removed, dyed, stuffed and preserved so it could be displayed for a very long time in the royal palace.

Like his son Gallienus, Valerian has been unfairly maligned by later, revisionist historians of Christendom. Sparking this contempt was Valerian's persecution of Christians, whom he used as scapegoats for the monumental ills which Rome faced. His personal touch was to target Christians from the upper echelons in his Empire, against whom he introduced edicts in 257 and 258. Though these laws, reversed by Gallienus, seem indefensible, it is equally unjust to condemn all of Valerian's actions on the basis of this one policy.

NUMISMATIC NOTE: In addition to coinage in his own name, Valerian also struck for his family members. The coinage of Valerian and Gallienus is remarkably complex, and was struck at several mints, with the locations of some being uncertain. Among their most productive mints were Rome, Milan, Trier, Siscia, Sirmium, Cyzicus(?) and Antioch. It is of some interest that Valerian celebrated victories of Gallienus against the Germans, perhaps to increase morale among his own soldiers. His types sometimes refer rather optimistically to his exploits in the East. After his initial success against the Sasanians in 253/4, he issued types declaring him to be the "restorer of the Orient' (RESTITVT ORIENTIS) and even "restorer of the human race" (RESTITVT GENER HVMANI). Another type, APOLL SALVTARI, invokes "the health-bringing Apollo" to deliver the army and the people from the very plague which forced him into the fateful negotiations with Shapur.

MARINIANA

WIFE OF VALERIAN I
MOTHER OF GALLIENUS
GRANDMOTHER OF VALERIAN II AND SALONINUS

Egnatia Mariniana, died c. A.D. 253(?). Little is known of Mariniana, although she is suspected to have been the daughter of a governor of Moesia named Egnatius Marinianus. It is presumed that she died before her husband became emperor because all of her coinage is commemorative. She may have been the mother of both of Valerian I's children, though some sources suggest she was the mother only of the younger child, and that she was Valerian's second wife. In any case, her coinage is inextricably tied to the reign of Valerian and she almost certainly was his wife. Though Valerian and Mariniana's eldest son, Gallienus, is well-known to students of Roman history, their younger child, Publius Licinius Valerianus, does not make an appearance on coinage and apparently remained in Rome, where he was killed in 268 during the purge of Gallienus' adherents.

GALLIENUS A.D. 253–268

AUGUSTUS: A.D. 253–268
(A.D. 253–260: WITH VALERIAN I)
(A.D. 260: WITH VALERIAN I AND SALONINUS)
(A.D. 260–268: SOLE REIGN)

SON OF VALERIAN I AND MARINIANA
HUSBAND OF SALONINA
FATHER OF VALERIAN II AND SALONINUS

Publius Licinius Egnatius Gallienus, c. A.D. 213/8–268. The lengthy and chaotic reign of Gallienus is especially difficult to evaluate. Many historians (including ancient historians) have blamed him for the virtual collapse of the Empire, suggesting he was more interested in luxuriating than problem solving. The *Historia Augusta* scornfully reports that he wasted his time ". . . in sensual pleasures, visiting taverns, and growing old in the arms of a foreign woman."

However, Gallienus' vigorous actions and level-headed reform of the army make such criticism unjustified. Indeed, he was a remarkably effective emperor whose accomplishments were limited only by the chaos of the age. Gallienus may also be credited with reversing the edicts that his father had introduced in 257 and 258 to persecute Christians, resulting in nearly four decades of tolerance toward Christianity in the Empire.

Not only did Gallienus suffer great personal loss due to the destruction of his family, but his valiant efforts required that he campaign tirelessly throughout his 15-year reign, only to be struck down by an assassin. Indeed, the external difficulties which descended upon Rome during his principate can hardly be ascribed to his incompetence, for they derived from the failed policies of the past, and the whim of fate. No doubt, even Augustus or Trajan would not have found themselves better able to deal with the multitude of problems that Gallienus faced with such courage, fortitude and resilience.

Gallienus hailed from a distinguished Etruscan family and, like his wife, Salonina (whom he made Augusta upon his accession), was fond of art, literature and philosophy. Gallienus was an accomplished poet, and counted the Neoplatonic philosopher Plotinus among his close friends. He was also an advocate of the sculptural trend which glorified the achievements of the Greeks, and the Romans of the Augustan age.

In marked contrast to this cultured man was the grave task he faced. After his father, Valerian I, became emperor in July or October of 253, Gallienus entered into a partnership to deliver the Empire from certain destruction. He seems to have been hailed Caesar by the senate before his father's "victory" over Aemilian at Spoleto; he was quickly invested with the purple along with his father, and the joint-Augusti divided the Empire, with Gallienus taking command in Europe and his father marching to Asia Minor. Little could they have known that when they parted they would never see each other again.

The first five years of Gallienus' reign were primarily spent fighting Germans on the Rhine and Danube, for which he was hailed *Germanicus Maximus* five times between 255 and 258. In previous reigns, Gothic invasion of the Danube had been the most persistent threat, but with the Goths turning much of their attention to seafaring and raiding cities along the Black Sea, their threat to the European provinces was lessened. Instead, Germanic invasions became more frequent, especially after Valerian had withdrawn troops from the Rhine to check the invasion of Italy by Aemilian. By early 258 the Danube frontier had been invaded again, obliging the emperor (who since 256 had been assisted by his eldest son, the Caesar Valerian II) to lead the campaign in person. Not long after father and son arrived, young Valerian II died, the result either of warfare or natural causes. This was the first in a series of personal losses Gallienus would suffer.

Later in 258, Gallienus abandoned the Danubian campaign that had cost his eldest son's life so he could repel an invasion of Italy launched over the Rhine by the Alemanni (specifically, the Juthungi). Their advance was so swift that they nearly reached Rome before they were forced to retreat. When they did, they found Gallienus awaiting them near Milan, where he defeated them severely. About this time, Gallienus invested his younger son, Saloninus, with the rank of Caesar to replace Valerian II. Saloninus was then sent to Cologne to establish his court and see to the defense of the western provinces.

Fast approaching was 260 — the worst year the Romans would ever know. Catastrophes occurred almost simultaneously throughout the Empire. The *Historia Augusta* exaggerates the chaos of Gallienus' reign by suggesting there were more than 30 men who challenged his authority. In reality, there were perhaps seven serious revolts, but each took its toll on the disintegrating Empire.

In the East, Gallienus' father, Valerian I, was leading an army debilitated by the plague, and thus took refuge at Edessa. The Sasanian king Shapur I besieged him there, and seeing no good option, the elderly emperor tried to negotiate a truce with Shapur. However, the treacherous Persian king took the emperor and the distinguished members of his delegation prisoner, never to be released. Such a catastrophe had never before occurred in the history of the Empire, and Asia Minor was now in a state of chaos. The void was filled by the praetorian prefect Callistus ("Ballista") and the quartermaster-general Macrianus Senior. After conspiring to revolt, they installed at Antioch the latter man's two sons, Macrianus and Quietus, as rival emperors to Gallienus.

At about the same time the Rhine defenses were breached by the Alemanni, who invaded Gaul, and by the Franks, who advanced as far south as Spain. Amid this great invasion, the governor of Lower Germany, Postumus, staged his own revolt and besieged Gallienus' son, Saloninus, at Cologne. Postumus soon took the city, executing the teenager and his advisers. As a result, Rome lost its western provinces to a succession of independent rulers for the next 14 years.

Meanwhile, revolts erupted elsewhere in the Empire. There were revolts not resulting in coinage: in Byzantium (in response to the Gothic raids), in Egypt by one Aemilianus (in 262 or 263, thus not the emperor of 253), and in Pannonia and Moesia by Ingenuus. Although all three revolts were crushed, the one by Ingenuus was quickly resurrected by another usurper, Regalianus, whom Gallienus defeated by late 260 or early 261.

At this point one can appreciate the multitude of problems that afflicted Gallienus. Indeed, he could hardly be expected to simultaneously end revolts in the Propontis, Syria, Egypt, the Balkans and Gaul. Other less-spirited emperors before him (notably Philip I and Trebonianus Gallus) lost their nerve during times like this, whereas Gallienus simply continued to fight.

Gallienus had given his general Aureolus (who earlier had defeated Ingenuus) the task of ending the six-month-old revolt of Macrianus and Quietus, based in Antioch. Fortunately, Macrianus Senior and his eldest son, Macrianus, had brought their own army into Illyricum to overthrow Gallienus. There, in the spring of 261 they were defeated by one of Aureolus' commanders, Domitianus (who has been identified by some as the Gallic Domitianus listed in chapter 8). The remaining son, Quietus, held out for eight more months in the East before he was deposed by Odaenathus of Palmyra, who was acting as Gallienus' vice regent in Asia Minor .

Even in these victories, Gallienus found no peace, for his trusted general Aureolus staged his own revolt, seemingly in 262. However, the two men came to terms, and Aureolus was subsequently given command of Gallienus' new cavalry corp. Having restored order throughout most of the Empire, Gallienus returned to Rome in 263 to celebrate his *decennalia* with great pomp and circumstance.

During the ceremonies, Gallienus was no doubt dressed similarly to the manner described in the *Historia Augusta*: "He went out in public adorned with the radiate crown, and at Rome — where emperors always appeared in the toga — he appeared in a purple cloak with jeweled and golden clasps." Gallienus' style of dress bears a striking resemblance to that of the equally courageous Julius Caesar.

The ever-changing military situation forced Gallienus to make three important changes in military policy, the first being to exclude senators from command posts. Next, he made Milan his military hub, as it was central to the Danube and Rhine and served as a ready deterrent to an invasion of Italy. He also created a field army and a new cavalry corps (a mobile striking force sometimes called his "Dalmatian cavalry"). Though both were expensive additions, they were essential in fighting enemies who tended to coordinate the timing of their invasions, and who in recent years had made more effective use of heavy cavalry.

Reinvigorated, Gallienus and his cavalry commander, Aureolus, set out to recover the provinces lost to Postumus in the West. When the campaign began is uncertain; estimates range from late 263 to early 265. The emperor's progress against Postumus was impressive. He had trapped Postumus in a city in 265, but in the siege that followed Gallienus was injured by an arrow. This was his second such injury in the last few years, and it brought the offensive to a grinding halt.

Gallienus turned command over to Aureolus, who was unable to make further headway and who may justly be suspected of treachery for allowing Postumus to escape a siege which no doubt would have resulted in his death. With the offensive stalled, it would appear as though Gallienus came to some kind of non-aggression pact with Postumus, after which

Aureolus was, perhaps, sent to Raetia to raise more troops and then take up a defensive command in Milan.

Asia Minor had been enjoying relative stability under the Palmyrene leader Odaenathus, who had forced the Sasanians to sue for peace in 264. In 266 Odaenathus took the offensive against Shapur I, with some historians suggesting that he advanced so far into Mesopotamia that he sacked Ctesiphon. The growing power of Palmyra was a double-edged sword for Gallienus, who feared Odaenathus might change from ally to aggressor. In any case, Odaenathus and his eldest son were murdered in 267, either in a family squabble or the result of a conspiracy by Gallienus. Odaenathus's place was taken by his wife, Zenobia, and the royal couple's son, Vabalathus. A seemingly minor effort by the praetorian prefect Heraclianus to dislodge the two new regents failed, and served only to alert the Palmyrenes to Rome's hostility.

In 267, the Goths and the Heruli made preparations to invade Asia Minor and Illyricum in their destructive recent fashion — jointly by land and by sea. The assault, which began in late 267 or early 268, was particularly fierce, and is said to have involved some 2,000 ships and 320,000 soldiers. So thorough was the invasion that even the islands of Rhodes and Crete were attacked, and the Goths sailed to within sight of Italy before they were compelled by circumstance to return. However, the most intense pillaging was in Thrace, Macedon, Thessaly and central Greece.

After most of the damage had been inflicted and the Goths were returning with the spoils of war, the greatly outnumbered armies of Gallienus delivered to them a monumental defeat at Naïssus, where it is said some 30,000 to 50,000 Goths perished in a single day. There still exists confusion as to whether this victory belongs to Gallienus or to the next emperor, Claudius II, but the evidence strongly favors Gallienus despite the views of some later Christian writers, who favored Claudius II because their "Christian" hero Constantine the Great, claimed to be a descendant of his.

Unfortunately for the fate of Rome, Gallienus was not able to follow-up on his victory at Naïssus. Early in 268 (about when he had left for the Balkans), Aureolus revolted again, this time openly defecting to Postumus. Gallienus abandoned the Gothic war and arrived at Milan in September, after Aureolus seems already to have been besieged by the commander of the Dalmatian Cavalry, Claudius II. No doubt wanting to finish off Aureolus himself, Gallienus took over command of the siege and placed Claudius II in command of the reserve forces about 20 miles away at Ticinum.

After an exhausting reign of 15 years, Gallienus, then in his 50s, was murdered within a couple of weeks of his arrival at Milan. He was lured, unprotected, outside his command tent by a false alarm that a counter-offensive had been launched. Historians are certain that Claudius II either delivered the fatal stab or was at the very least a leader of the conspiracy. The other men implicated were also of Danubian origin: the prefect Heraclianus (who had failed to oust Zenobia and Vabalathus), Marcianus (who had helped defeat the Goths at Naïssus), and Aurelianus, who was destined himself to become emperor in 270. After a liberal bribe to the soldiers, Claudius II was hailed emperor in Gallienus' place. He concluded the siege of Milan, executed Aureolus, and then joined the senate — spiteful about Gallienus' policy of precluding them from commands in his army — in a massacre of Gallienus' family and adherents in Rome.

NUMISMATIC NOTE: The "silver" coinage of the Empire reached its absolute low point during the reigns of Gallienus, Claudius II and Aurelian (pre-reform). The double-denarii are of simple artistry, crudely struck on small, ragged planchets, and often appear to be merely copper (although they typically contain perhaps 2 percent silver). Among the most interesting double-denarii struck by Gallienus are those honoring the legions under his command, and those that portray animals sacred to the deities which the reverse inscriptions invoke to preserve the emperor. The SP in the reverse field of some of Gallienus' double-denarii may stand for *Secunda Pannonia*, the province in which the mint city Sirmium was located. For listings of the ceremonial 'entry' bronzes struck under Gallienus, see *The So-Called Interregnum Bronzes*, that follows the values listings of Severina.

Also of note is a coin bearing the obverse inscription DIVO CAES Q GALLIENO and the radiate bust of a boy (and the standard reverse type CONSECRATIO/flaming altar). This may represent another son of Gallienus named Quintus. Although doubts have been expressed about the authenticity of the coin, some researchers consider it to be an issue of Valerian II or Saloninus, in which case the Q might represent *quondam* (meaning "formerly") rather than the name Quintus.

SALONINA

AUGUSTA, A.D. 254–268

WIFE OF GALLIENUS
MOTHER OF VALERIAN II AND SALONINUS
DAUGHTER-IN-LAW OF VALERIAN I AND MARINIANA

Julia Cornelia Salonina Crysogone, d. A.D. 268. Despite the vast quantity of coinage struck in her name, we know very little about Salonina, who was a Greek, perhaps of Bithynian extraction. She married Gallienus in about 240 and was hailed

Augusta and *Mater Castrorum* ("mother of the camps") in 254, about a year after her husband became emperor.

It seems that Salonina was an ideal empress, for she had the temperament to endure the privations of war, yet was cultured despite the trials she faced. On many occasions her intervention proved vital to the accomplishments of her husband, and to the loyalty of the army. She had an interest in philosophy, and on that level was compatible with her husband, who was also fond of the arts (himself being an accomplished poet). Both husband and wife were in the circle of Plotinus, the famous Neoplatonic philosopher of the mid-3rd Century.

Salonina was not the only woman in Gallienus' life, however, for he had taken on as a concubine a woman named Pipa, who was the daughter of Attalus, king of the Marcommani. Officially, this was part of a negotiated agreement between the Romans and the Marcommani in which military assistance was given in exchange for land grants. Salonina appears not to have been a Christian, as has been sometimes supposed.

She had three children by Gallienus, two of whom (Valerian II and Saloninus) predeceased their parents during their short, tragic careers in government. The rest of the family was no more fortunate, seeming to have perished in September of 268 or shortly thereafter. Salonina and Gallienus died at Milan, whereas Gallienus' brother and his youngest child, Marinianus (who was consul in 268), perished at Rome during the purge of Gallienus' adherents that followed. Their youngest child, who according to different sources was a 3-year-old son named Licinius Egnatius Marinianus or a daughter named Licinia Galliena, had no coins issued in his or her name.

NUMISMATIC NOTE: Salonina featured prominently in the coinage of Gallienus. The most unusual type of her reign bears the inscription AVGVSTA IN PACE. In the past, this has been taken incorrectly as evidence of her being a Christian. The three children of Salonina are shown as small figures on the reverse of many of her coins and medallions with the inscription PIETAS AVGG (SC).

VALERIAN II

CAESAR: A.D. 256–258
(UNDER VALERIAN I AND GALLIENUS)

SON OF GALLIENUS AND SALONINA
BROTHER OF SALONINUS
GRANDSON OF VALERIAN I AND MARINIANA

Publius Licinius Cornelius Valerianus, d. A.D. 258. As the eldest son of Gallienus and Salonina, Valerian II was brought into the Imperial succession early in 256, when he was hailed Caesar. Later he joined his father on the Rhine frontier, where they had considerable success. In 258, however, they began to fight on the Danubian front, where Valerian II died in Illyricum early in the year of natural causes or in battle. This was a terrible blow to Gallienus, who had invested much hope in his eldest son for perpetuating his fledgling dynasty. Gallienus soon raised his next-oldest son, Saloninus, to the rank of Caesar in place of Valerian II. But this ended in tragedy when the young man was killed by the rebel Postumus in 260.

NUMISMATIC NOTE: Valerian II's lifetime coinage represents the continuation of the father-and-son dynasty originally formed by Valerian I and Gallienus. The most obvious allusion to this is the reverse type IOVI CRESCENTI ("the growing Jupiter"), which depicts Valerian II as the infant Jupiter riding on the back of the goat Amalthea. His posthumous coinage was considerable, and no doubt accurately reflects the amount of grief suffered by his family. Some researchers have speculated about more subtle indications of Valerian II's coinage, such as a long lock of hair that often falls behind the boy's ear, which may have been intended to equate him with the Egyptian god Horus, and thus with the renewal of time.

SALONINUS A.D. 260

CAESAR: A.D. 258–260
(UNDER VALERIAN I AND GALLIENUS)
AUGUSTUS: A.D. 260 (WITH GALLIENUS)

SON OF GALLIENUS AND SALONINA
BROTHER OF VALERIAN II
GRANDSON OF VALERIAN I AND MARINIANA

Publius Licinius Cornelius Saloninus Valerianus, c. A.D. 242–260. Following the unexpected death of Valerian II in 258, Gallienus invested his next-oldest son, Saloninus, with the rank of Caesar late in that year, almost certainly in concert with his efforts to repel the invasion of Italy by the Alemanni. He then sent Saloninus to Cologne to establish a court from which he could oversee affairs in the western provinces. Aiding his teenage son were the praetorian prefect Silvanus, and Postumus, the governor of Upper or Lower Germany.

The summer of 260 was especially troubled; not only was Saloninus' grandfather captured by the Sasanians, but, in his own part of the world, Germans had invaded Gaul and Spain. Amid all this chaos, the governor Postumus was hailed emperor by his soldiers. From the start, Saloninus and Silvanus were on the defensive, as Postumus laid siege to them in the court-city of Cologne. This dire development (either in June or in the fall of 260) necessitated raising Valerian II from Caesar to Augustus. But the acquisition of a new rank did not stave off the armies of Postumus, which soon took the city. After holding the rank of Augustus for only a few weeks, or at most three or four months, the unfortunate Saloninus, then at approximately age 17, was executed with Silvanus by Postumus, who then constructed a triumphal arch in memory of his victory.

NUMISMATIC NOTE: Saloninus' coinage as Augustus is extremely rare, with perhaps fewer than 20 specimens known. The mint must have been Cologne, the city in which he was besieged when his coinage as Augustus was struck. For a specialized study see N. Shiel, *The Coinage of Saloninus as Augustus*, ANSMN 24 (1979). The posthumous coinage for Saloninus was extremely small in comparison with that struck for his brother, Valerian II. Indeed, with a single emission from Lugdunum, it almost seems to be an afterthought or an oversight, especially since normal obverse dies (not ones specially inscribed DIVO) were employed. Perhaps Gallienus thought it was in the best interest of the Empire not to issue coins that advertised the crises which had befallen the family in 260, for his father had been captured and Saloninus had been executed under shameful circumstance.

MACRIANUS A.D. 260–261
(CO-EMPEROR WITH QUIETUS)

SON OF MACRIANUS SENIOR
BROTHER OF QUIETUS

Titus Fulvius Junius Macrianus, d. A.D. 261. Like many of the usurpers of the 3rd Century, Macrianus and Quietus assumed the title of Augustus under desperate circumstances. In their case, the Sasanian king Shapur I had captured the emperor Valerian I alive, and had led his army on an invasion of Syria. Antioch was sacked so severely that the destruction was more complete than had occurred seven years before, when Uranius Antoninus had revolted.

Since the Roman legions in the East were now leaderless, the commander Macrianus Senior filled the void, and hailed his two sons, Macrianus and Quietus, joint-emperors. The rebels made Antioch their headquarters and their revolt, which began in the fall or winter of 260, soon won approval throughout Asia Minor, Syria and Egypt. The true leaders of the revolt, the young men's father, Titus Fulvius Macrianus Senior and the praetorian prefect Callistus ("Ballista"), seem not to have appeared on coinage.

The Macriani went on the offensive, presumably to overthrow Gallienus, by leading their army to Illyricum. However, their Syrian legions were defeated by Domitianus, a subordinate of Gallienus' commander Aureolus. Some have speculated that this Domitianus is the one who issued the unique Gallic-style double-denarius (see his entry in chapter 8). Meanwhile, the remaining son, Quietus, and the prefect Callistus held out for eight more months in the East before they were deposed by Odaenathus, the leader of Palmyra, who was then acting as Gallienus' vice-regent in Asia.

NUMISMATIC NOTE: Macrianus' Imperial coinage is limited to aurei and billon double-denarii.

QUIETUS A.D. 260–261
(Co-Emperor with Macrianus)

Son of Macrianus Senior
Brother of Macrianus

Titus Fulvius Junius Quietus, d. A.D. 261. As related in the biography of Macrianus above, Quietus joined his elder brother as co-emperor in the chaos that followed the capture of Valerian I by the Sasanians in 260. Instigating the rebellion was Macrianus Senior, the father of both young men, and the praetorian prefect Callistus. When Quietus' brother and father (collectively known as the Macriani) led their army to the Balkans, where they were defeated by Imperial armies, Quietus remained in the East with Callistus (nicknamed Ballista, meaning "catapult") to maintain the revolt. They managed to hold out for about another eight months, and eventually took refuge at Emesa, where the locals murdered them when Odaenathus of Palmyra laid siege to the city on behalf of Gallienus.

Numismatic Note: Quietus' Imperial coinage is limited to aurei, billon double-denarii and asses.

REGALIANUS A.D. 260

Husband of Dryantilla

Cornelius Publius Gaius Regalianus, d. A.D. 260/261. In the same chaotic year that sparked the usurpations of Postumus in Gaul, and Macrianus and Quietus in Syria, a revolt occurred in the Balkans under the leadership of Ingenuus, the governor of Pannonia. Ingenuus was hailed emperor by his army at Sirmium in the summer of 260, but his hastily organized revolt did not long survive. He committed suicide shortly after being defeated in battle at Mursa by Gallienus' general, Aureolus.

Though Ingenuus was defeated, the cause of the revolt had not been extinguished, and the dissatisfied soldiers sought a new leader for their cause. In the fall of that same year they chose a commander named Regalianus, who may originally have fought alongside Aureolus to defeat Ingenuus. Though Regalianus led a quick campaign against the Sarmatians (in which he was victorious at Scupi, in Northern Macedonia), he met defeat at the hands of Gallienus within a few weeks, and was killed by his own soldiers late in 260 or early in 261. Little is known of Regalianus except that he was from Dacia, and that he claimed descent from the famous king Decebalus, who had been defeated by Trajan more than 150 years before.

Numismatic Note: The double-denarii of Regalianus were produced with dies of extremely poor workmanship, and were crudely overstruck on earlier double-denarii and denarii drawn from circulation. Since his coins are found in the vicinity of Carnuntum, it is assumed that his revolt was based there, and that his coins were struck in that region, possibly in the city itself.

DRYANTILLA

Augusta, A.D. 260

Wife of Regalianus

Sulpicia Dryantilla, d. A.D. 260/261(?). Little is known of Dryantilla except that she was the daughter of Claudia Ammiana Dryantilla and Sulpicius Pollio, an important senator and officer under Caracalla. There is no reason to doubt she was the wife of Regalianus, though it has been suggested she was his mother.

Numismatic Note: Dryantilla's double-denarii are of similarly crude manufacture to that of her husband.

CHAPTER EIGHT

Recovery of Empire
A.D. 268–285

CLAUDIUS II 'GOTHICUS'
A.D. 268–270

Brother of Quintillus

Marcus Aurelius Valerius Claudius, A.D. 214/5–270. A native of Dardania, Claudius II was the first in a long line of emperors who hailed from Illyricum, a region that had long been the Empire's strongest area for recruiting soldiers. Though an ambitious and energetic emperor, he is praised too highly by later Christian historians, who intensely disliked his predecessor, Gallienus, and who admired Claudius as a supposed relative of Constantine the Great.

Claudius had served vigorously under Gallienus, apparently helping to defeat the usurper Ingenuus in the summer of 260, and participating in the failed campaign against Postumus in 263/265. In the course of his service, Claudius II came to lead Gallienus' cavalry, and may have been the first man to engage Aureolus, the rebellious general who sided with Postumus and based his revolt at Milan. Once Gallienus had secured victory against the Goths, he returned to Milan and took over the siege, placing Claudius in command of the reserve forces at nearby Ticinum.

This must have upset Claudius, for he conspired with at least three other commanders (one of whom was the future emperor Aurelian) to murder Gallienus in September of 268. The army was angered by this, and it required a very liberal bribe of 20 aurei per man to restore their support, after which Claudius was hailed emperor in Gallienus' place. Claudius next completed the siege of Milan and executed Aureolus (whom he apparently lured out with a false promise to spare his life).

Meanwhile in Rome, the senate was overjoyed at the death of Gallienus, and engaged in a bloody purge of Gallienus' family and adherents. Because this was unpopular with the soldiers in the north of Italy, Claudius beseeched the senate to stop the purge. But the amount of attention Claudius could pay to Rome was limited; the Alemanni had crossed the Rhône in large numbers due to the garrisons of Raetia being weakened by the activities of Aureolus.

Claudius led his army east to check the Alemannian invasion at Lake Benacus. He did so with such success that half of the invading army was lost, earning him the title *Germanicus maximus*. During this campaign, the future emperor Aurelian was given command of the cavalry — the post the emperor himself had once held. Claudius wintered in Rome, where he was able to develop a strong relationship with the senate. Consequently, he was able to lobby them to deify Gallienus (a task they did not support) so as to shore up his own support in the army.

Early in the next year, Claudius seems to have received a request from Spain, beseeching deliverance from the separatist Empire of Postumus. At the same time there occurred a short–lived revolt by the Spanish nobleman Laelianus at Trier, in February or June of 269. Encouraged, Claudius sent an expeditionary force to southern Gaul and Spain under the leadership of Julius Placidianus, who easily restored Spain and the Gallic territories east of the Rhône to the Central Empire.

At the same time as the attack against Postumus' separatist Empire, Claudius returned to the Gothic front in the Balkans, where the general Marcianus was continuing to harass the Goths, and from where Claudius intended to drive them out for good. Despite some Goths returning from across the Danube to offer help to their besieged comrades, the tribes suffered terribly from hunger, the plague and from the legions of Claudius. Roman victories were substantial (though they seem not to include the *famous* battle at Naïssus, which is better attributed to Gallienus), and earned Claudius the surname *Gothicus maximus*.

As the Goths were beaten and dispersed, Claudius found a variety of new tasks at hand. Many barbarians who had escaped by means of the Herulian ships began to make piratic raids in the Aegean, but the cities themselves and the Roman fleet were able to defend suitably. Many of the Goths were either taken into the ranks of the Roman army or were settled in Roman territories; there seemed little else that could be done with so many refugees.

Then, in a virtual repeat of history, the upper Rhine was breached once again (this time by the Juthungi near Raetia) and the Vandals were preparing to invade Pannonia. These new emergencies required the emperor to leave the Gothic front before he was able to conclude the campaign. Thus, his campaign was placed in the able hands of his eventual successor, Aurelian, the general who seems to have been the other principal candidate considered as a replacement to Gallienus.

While in Pannonia, apparently on his mission against the Vandals, Claudius II died of the plague at Sirmium in August or September of 270 (though this, in error, is often placed quite early in 270). In the aftermath, Rome was plunged into yet another civil war as the senate and the Italian legions (through a donative) supported the claim of Claudius' brother, Quintillus, and the Illyrian legions then engaged on the Gothic front supported their own commander, Aurelian.

Claudius II enjoyed great military success during his brief reign but, because of the difficulties he faced in Europe, he was unable to oppose the expansion of Palmyra, which during his reign forcibly occupied most of Asia Minor, all of Syria and the Levant, and even the prize province Egypt. This unopposed conquest of the East must be taken into consideration before Claudius' European successes are too loudly applauded.

None-the-less, Claudius was renowned in his day (as evidenced by his vast commemorative coinage), and rightly so, for, as historians such as Edward Gibbon have noted, Claudius' brief reign was the beginning of the Empire's recovery from the chaos of the era of Gallienus.

NUMISMATIC NOTE: Excepting the initial donative of 268, Claudius' coinage continued the pitiful decline from the reign of Gallienus (though the massive *divo* coinage struck in his memory only serves to confirm that by the end of his reign, Claudius II was beloved by both senate and the army). It is noteworthy that his epithet *Gothicus* is included in the inscription on certain of his posthumous coins. He is further commemorated on coinage by Constantine the Great, who claimed to be the grandson of Claudius' daughter or niece. The extremely rare reduced sestertii (usually called asses) of Claudius II lack the traditional SC on the reverse.

QUINTILLUS A.D. 270

BROTHER OF CLAUDIUS II

Marcus Aurelius Claudius Quintillus (*earlier* Marcus Aurelius Quintillus), A.D. 229(?)–270. The younger brother of Claudius II, Quintillus had been placed in command at Aquileia to secure the West while Claudius personally led the offensive against the Goths. After news reached Italy of Claudius' death from the plague in August or September of 270, Quintillus paid a donative to the army, curried the support of the senate, and was thus hailed emperor.

Perhaps his first official acts were to have the senate consecrate his brother — something they were only too willing to do — and to add the name Claudius to his own. But his hope that the Illyrian armies would support him proved illusory, as they had in the meantime proclaimed for another Illyrian named Aurelian, who was Claudius' cavalry commander and who had taken over the Gothic campaign in the Balkans.

Aurelian continued to oversee the return of the Goths to their side of the Danube, and in the process spared cities *en route* the destruction they otherwise were certain to suffer. These important accomplishments caused his own soldiers and the legions in Pannonia to hail him emperor at Sirmium in opposition to the "legitimate" emperor, Quintillus. Recognizing that Quintillus faced certain defeat, his own soldiers abandoned his cause within days.

After a legitimate but brief reign, Quintillus committed suicide in November (or perhaps October) of 270, presumably at Aquileia, where he spent most of his reign. Though Zonoras and Eutropius erroneously place his reign at only 17 days, it clearly was longer, and in all likelihood was two or nearly three months. The names and fates of his wife and two children are unknown.

Chronological Note: Though it is the consensus of most scholars that the death of Claudius II, the reign of Quintillus and the accession of Aurelian occurred later in 270 (rather than earlier as was traditionally supposed), it is worth noting that Michael Grant, in *The Roman Emperors*, cites a papyrus dated "25 May" that indicates the defeat of Quintillus was by then known in Egypt. If the translation is reliable, then a return to the earlier chronology is warranted.

Numismatic Note: The aurei of Quintillus are extremely rare, with all known specimens being struck with the same artful obverse die. In addition to coins bearing his own image, Quintillus caused a great many coins to be struck in honor of his deceased brother, not only to honor him personally, but also in the hope it would generate support for himself as the legitimate successor. However, these posthumous coins, as well as a small issue he struck specifically honoring Pannonia, failed to have their intended effect.

AURELIAN A.D. 270–275

Husband of Severina

Lucius Domitius Aurelianus, c. A.D. 207/14 – 275. Like most of the emperors of his era, Aurelian was of extremely humble origins, though he had an outstanding career in the army. He became a cavalry commander under Gallienus (in whose murder he seems to have participated), and kept the same position under Gallienus' successor, Claudius II.

Although Aurelian was the second-most-likely successor to Gallienus, he had to wait another two years before his opportunity arose. Indeed, it came not long after Claudius II died of the plague in August or September of 270 (though possibly earlier, see the *Chronological Note* for Quintillus above), after which the deceased emperor's brother, Quintillus, ascended the throne with the support of the senate and the legions in Italy.

In the meantime, Aurelian was stationed in northern Greece and the Balkans, where he had been placed in charge of finishing operations against the now-humiliated Goths and Heruli. His success in this capacity was so impressive that the legions under his command and those in Pannonia hailed him emperor in opposition to Quintillus. His usurpation — for that is exactly what it was — gained widespread support, causing the legions of Italy to withdraw their support for Quintillus in October or November of 270 (if not much earlier), after which the luckless emperor committed suicide.

Aurelian was now the uncontested emperor of Rome, and though he enjoyed the confidence of the army, the senate was none too pleased that their "friendly" candidate had been lawlessly usurped. Aurelian's first task was to repel an invasion by the Vandals and Sarmatians on the Danube. This he did with such efficiency that they sued for peace.

Next, Aurelian responded to an invasion of Italy by the Marcomanni and Juthungi. Though initially routed, Aurelian was able to eject the invaders. Because the invasions of the latter two had penetrated Italy and threatened Rome itself, Aurelian began to construct a defensive circuit wall around the capital (which was completed by his successor, Probus). Perhaps as no other event of the 3rd Century, this was a clear indication of the decline of the ancient capital.

Aurelian next marched to the Balkans, where it seems three ephemeral revolts had occurred (by Septimius, Urbanus and a Domitianus, who may be the same man as the one who revolted in Alexandria 25 years later). About this time, Aurelian abandoned Dacia, a frontier province on the opposite side of the Danube that had proven too difficult to maintain. After one last campaign against the Goths in mid-271, all affairs were settled in central Europe, and Aurelian determined to recover the many provinces that had been lost to Palmyra in the East and the Gallo-Romans in the West.

His first task was the recovery of Asia and Egypt, which had been seized by Zenobia and Vabalathus largely during the reign of Claudius II. Very early in his reign, Aurelian had granted the Palmyrene queen and king the titles they desired, and even had struck coinage jointly with Vabalathus at Antioch and Alexandria. But now Aurelian was ready to wage war, and so he led his army into Asia late in 271 or, more likely, in the spring of 272. Aurelian liberated one city after another in Asia Minor and, near Antioch and Emesa, routed the armies of Palmyra. Vabalathus, Zenobia and the remaining armies took refuge in their capital city of Palmyra, where they surrendered in 272 after a brief siege. Meanwhile, the future emperor Probus recovered Egypt.

Aurelian then marched back to Europe with his two royal captives and battled the Carpi in a decisive campaign. The Asiatic troubles had not ended, however, for another revolt had sparked in Palmyra under the leadership of Antiochus, who was probably a descendant of Odaenathus. Aurelian returned to crush the new revolt, after which the Romans leveled the Palmyrenes' capital (which never recovered its former glory), and ousted their supporter in Alexandria, Firmius.

After returning Asia and Egypt to the Roman yoke, Aurelian's next task was to achieve the same in Gaul, Britain and the two Germanies, which formed the separatist Romano-Gallic Empire. Since its foundation in 260 by Postumus, the fortunes of this Empire had fallen greatly, and it seems that Aurelian was not only able to arrange the surrender of its two Augusti, Tetricus I and Tetricus II, in advance, but was actually invited to invade and "liberate" them.

Thus, instead of fighting an Empire that was at its peak of power (as had been the case with Palmyra), Aurelian was prepared for an easy conquest. However, a battle was still required — at least to achieve the illusion that there was a struggle for independence. The Roman and Gallo-Roman armies met not far from Paris, at Châlons-sur-Marne, in the spring of 274. Though the battle was harder-fought than Aurelian may have anticipated, he was victorious in the end, and captured the Tetrici for use in his triumph.

Aurelian could now rightly claim to be the most successful emperor since Trajan more than 150 years before, and he was not modest about taking credit where it was due. Later that year he returned to Rome and celebrated his grand triumph, at which he hailed his wife, Severina, Augusta, paraded his royal captives, and styled himself the "restorer of the world" (*restitutor orbis*). But much of his success had gone to his head, for he declared himself "god and lord" (*deus et dominus*), reflected in the unusual coin inscription DEO ET DOMINO NATO AVRELIANO AVG, which meant Aurelian was "born God and Master."

Late in 274, Aurelian set out to repel the Juthungi in Raetia, and in the summer of 275 marched east toward his next most desired campaign, the conquest of Persia. But he fell victim to his own strict discipline when he reprimanded his secretary, Eros, who, in fear of punishment, convinced some high-ranking officers that Aurelian intended to put them to death. Naturally, they struck first, and Aurelian was murdered in October or November of 275 at Caenophrurium (near Perinthus) while making ready to cross into Asia. Much beloved by his soldiers, Aurelian was deified by the senate, which is said to have resented his harsh authority. But few men in Roman history so richly deserved the high honors Aurelian received. In five energetic years he restored the integrity and the vast territories of the Empire.

Not all of the crises Aurelian faced were in the Balkans or in far-flung provinces. One "revolt" of special interest to numismatists occurred in Rome itself. This abortive rebellion was sparked by disgruntled mint workers who, under the leadership of a certain Felicissimus and with soldiers of their own, took up a defensive position on the Caelian hill. In the bitter fighting that ensued, the leadership of Aurelian himself was required, and as many as 7,000 soldiers died. Historians have attributed the revolt to either 271 or 274. In the former case it would probably have resulted from an effort to prevent profiteering from excessive debasement, whereas in the latter case it no doubt would have been in response to his coinage reforms, which were so closely regulated that very little opportunity remained for profiteering.

In addition to his reform of the coinage (which is discussed below), Aurelian also tried to regulate prices and assure delivery and affordability of staple products. In this respect he was much like Diocletian, who applied similar ideas on a larger scale. He also went to great lengths to formalize the worship of the sun, and its chief deity, Sol. In so doing, he built a grand temple to Sol in Rome and laid a foundation for pagan solar worship and Mithraism, which Constantine the Great would so effectively "fuse" with early Christianity about four decades later.

NUMISMATIC NOTE: Aurelian initiated a major reform of the Empire's coinage in the spring of 274 (at which point he also began to issue coins in the name of his wife, Severina). His reform was important enough so that even two centuries later it was praised by the historian Zosimus. At sensibly reduced weights and purities he reintroduced denarii, double-sestertii and sestertii (the latter two are usually called sestertii and asses, see the section on denominations), all three of which had been largely abandoned by his predecessors. Curiously, though (considering all of his reintroduced denominations), Aurelian seems to have abandoned the billon quinarius, an obscure ceremonial denomination.

Aurelian's most important contribution by far was the reform of the ailing double-denarius, which had become a negligible item under Gallienus, Claudius II and Quintillus. No doubt the recovery of the East, and thus its revenues, allowed Aurelian to revamp his "silver" coinage. Many scholars refer to his reformed double-denarius as an *aurelianianus*. The name change truly is necessary because, though it maintained most familiar aspects of the double-denarius, it was indeed a different coin from the double-denarius that it replaced. The aurelianianus was an improvement in every way: weight was increased, the planchet was made broader and round in shape, and the silver content was increased to 4.5 to 5 percent. Even the die-cutting was greatly improved.

The meaning of the marks XXI or KA (20:1 in Latin and Greek, respectively) that appear on the reverse of the aurelianianus has been much-debated among scholars. One explanation is that it means a 1/20th part (5 percent), and thus the ratio of silver to base metal. Other explanations have been offered (such as the evaluation of the aurelianianus at 20 reduced sestertii), but the former seems most convincing because of its sheer simplicity and apparent accuracy. Aurelian struck his aurelianiani in immense quantities in an effort to replace the heavily debased double-denarii that he concurrently was withdrawing from circulation. Regrettably, Aurelian's life was cut short not long after his reform began. His new aurelianianus was maintained (in appearance, at least) until the reign of Diocletian, but his other "reintroduced" denominations failed to effectively take hold under his successors.

Provincial coinage was struck with much less frequency after the reign of Gallienus. Even so, it did not escape Aurelian's attention and, in the opinion of some, it actually ceased to be struck on a large scale due to the proliferation of low-value double-denarii and aurelianiani, which eliminated the need. It is worth noting that certain bronzes of southeastern Asia Minor already in circulation were revaluated with countermarks, indicating in *assaria* their new denomination.

As was so often the case, the productive mint at Alexandria proved to be an exception to the rule. The potin tetradrachm of Alexandria remained a staple in Egypt for the next two decades, and Aurelian "reformed" it by reducing its weight by between 15% and 20%, and by withdrawing the earlier, heavier pieces from circulation. In this case, Aurelian pursued exactly the opposite theory that he applied to the Imperial coinage (in which he made the new coins more valuable, and withdrew the lesser-value pieces from circulation). It is also of note that Aurelian uses seven regnal years at Alexandria, but he only ruled for six calendar years. Thus, it has been suggested by W. Metcalf ("Aurelian's reform at Alexandria" in *Studies in Greek Numismatics in Memory of Martin Jessop Price*) that Aurelian 'compressed' his regnal years around the time the coinage was jointly being produced for Vabalathus. Seemingly, Aurelian's coins dated years 2 (B) and 3 (Γ) both fall within the regnal year that began on August 29, 271 and ended that same time in 272. Alternatively, both year 1 and year 2 tetradrachms would belong to 270 if the Egyptian papyrus cited by Grant (see the *Chronological Note* for Quintillus) can be taken as evidence of Aurelian ascending the throne *before* August 29, 270, when regnal years in Egypt began.

SEVERINA

AUGUSTA, A.D. 274–275

WIFE OF AURELIAN

Ulpia Severina, lifespan unknown. Regrettably little is known of Severina, a lady who is abundantly represented on coinage. Her family history is uncertain, but she may have been the daughter of Ulpius Crinitus, a renowned general who served under Valerian and who is said to have adopted Aurelian (in which case he may have betrothed his daughter to Aurelian).

In any event, her name indicates that she belonged to the Spanish family from which Trajan hailed, and thus was presumably related in some manner to Laelianus, the usurper who seems to have conspired with Claudius II in an attempt to overthrow Postumus in 269. Severina was hailed Augusta in 274 on the occasion of her husband's glorious triumph in Rome. Historians have long believed that she and the senate maintained the government for a period of up to six-months following the murder of Aurelian, but this does not appear to be based in historical fact. The numismatic evidence indicates that Severina issued coins at some mints after the issues for her husband had ceased, but it is not likely that the 'interregnum' between the murder of Aurelian and the accession of Tacitus lasted more than a few weeks. Of the subsequent fate of Severina and her daughter (whose name is not preserved) nothing is known.

NUMISMATIC NOTE: Imperial coinage in the name of Severina was struck only after she was hailed Augusta in 274. With the exception of Antioch (where her coins may have been struck as early as April, 274), her coins were not minted until the fall of 274 at the earliest. Similarly, at Alexandria her provincial coinage bears only the regnal years 6 and 7 — the reform years of Aurelian's coinage there. The authors of RIC note that Severina's final issues at Rome, Ticinum and Antioch are struck at all officinae of those mints, whereas the prior output had been shared by husband and wife. The bulk of Severina's final aureliani depict Concordia standing, holding two military standards; the symbolism of the type is significant if indeed she was at the helm alone. At Alexandria, Severina's tetradrachms dated year 7 (the final year of issue) are at least twice as common as those of the same date struck in her husband's name. Metcalf ("Aurelian's reform at Alexandria" in *Studies in Greek Numismatics in Memory of Martin Jessop Price*) notes that almost the entire difference in the population of year 7 Alexandrian tetradrachms is accounted for by a single reverse type for

Severina: an eagle standing left — which, not inconsequentially, is a type which Aurelian himself did not strike in year 7.

TACITUS A.D. 275–276

HALF-BROTHER OF FLORIAN

Marcus Claudius Tacitus, c. A.D. 200(?)–276. One of several emperors of the 3rd Century who claimed to have had important ancestors, Marcus Tacitus is said to have been a descendant of the most famous of all Roman historians, Cornelius Tacitus, who wrote his histories principally during the reigns of Trajan and Hadrian. But like much of the history recorded for the late 3rd Century, this story must be read with due skepticism.

The fiction begins with the idea that the murder of Aurelian so reviled the army that they begged the senate to select the new emperor on their behalf. The fiction continues that during an interregnum of perhaps as long as six months, the senate eventually selected a 75-year-old senator named Tacitus, who hailed from a noble Umbrian family and possessed a personal fortune of some 280 million sestertii. Having already been consul twice, and being a consul designate for 276, Tacitus accepted the burden of supreme power with great reluctance due to his advanced age.

In point of fact, the story reads like pure fiction. Recent revisions of the chronology of Aurelian's final year indicate that there was little or no time for an interregnum (for he seems to have been killed in October or November, not in April as was formerly believed). Indeed, it is far more likely that Tacitus was simply another Illyrian soldier whom the army lured out of retirement. Some historians even find the idea that Tacitus was so elderly untenable, and they believe rather that he was probably in his fifties. On the lighter side, we are told that he was fond of marbles, exotic glassware, and that he ate lettuce in large quantities, preferring it to other vegetables.

Once Tacitus assumed power in October or November of 275, he had Aurelian deified and is said to have enacted a number of beneficial laws and imposed capital punishment on all of the murderers of Aurelian who could be identified. Of his wife and several sons, we know nothing. However, he did make his half-brother, Florian, his praetorian prefect, and despite serious incursions along the Rhine and Danube by the Franks, Longiones and the Alemanni, the brothers marched east to the Balkans, where they gathered the army which Aurelian had already outfitted for a campaign in Asia.

Instead of marching against the Sasanians, however, they faced the more urgent task of repelling the Heruli and other piratic Goths, who had once again raided Asia Minor. The tribes entered in Pontus and Cappadocia, and advanced as far south as Cilicia before Tacitus and Florian could begin to combat them. The most distressing aspect of this invasion was the fact that Aurelian had mustered these barbarians as allies for his anticipated war on Persia, and in the meantime they had turned to piracy.

After some considerable success (including an important victory in Cilicia), Tacitus died at Tyana in Cappadocia in June or July 276. Accounts vary concerning the cause of his death. Indeed, he may have died of fever, fallen victim to murderers of Aurelian who had escaped persecution, or perished in a mutiny instigated by unfair taxes levied by a relative of his named Maximinus whom he had appointed governor of Syria (and who himself was murdered).

NUMISMATIC NOTE: Tacitus was the last emperor to issue provincial coinage outside of the Egyptian mint of Alexandria, which continued to strike for another two decades. Some of his aurelianiani may have reached 10% silver content, for they bear in their exergue the markings XI or IA (meaning 10:1 in Latin and Greek, respectively).

FLORIAN A.D. 276

HALF-BROTHER OF TACITUS

Marcus Annius Florianus, d. A.D. 276. The three-month reign of Florian was truly insignificant. The 4th Century historian Eutropius best summed it up by declaring Florian as an emperor ". . . who did nothing worth remembering." By far the most interesting aspect of his reign is how its circumstances almost exactly parallel those of Quintillus, who reigned for a similarly brief period in 270.

When Florian's maternal half-brother, Tacitus, was hailed emperor in 275, Florian was chosen as praetorian prefect, and together they led an expedition into Asia Minor to expel the Goths who were making piratic raids into Ponus, Cappadocia and Cilicia. When Tacitus died in June or July 276, of uncertain cause at Tyana, Florian was hailed emperor by the soldiers in his place. Afterward, the senate in Rome and most of the provinces confirmed his appointment. Florian next seems to have engaged the Goths one last time. However, more serious troubles to the South soon claimed his attention. The Syrian and Egyptian armies did not approve of Florian, and had hailed instead their own general, Probus (another soldier of Illyrian origin), as rival emperor. Florian marched south through the Cilician Gates to Tarsus, where he awaited the legions of Probus then advancing north. Although Florian's army was larger, it was in poor health due to the extreme climate, whereas Probus' smaller army was local and thus was accustomed to the heat.

After engaging in a skirmish, Probus wisely avoided a pitched battle and waited for the heat to take its toll on the Balkan legions led by Florian. With the passage of time, Florian's legions were persuaded by the enemy to avoid a senseless civil war by deposing their own candidate. Finding wisdom in the proposal, the very soldiers who had hailed Florian emperor less than three months before murdered him. Though his death seems to have occurred in August or September of 276, some historians prefer a slightly earlier date.

PROBUS A.D. 276–282

Marcus Aurelius Probus, A.D. 232–282. Much like his Illyrian predecessor Aurelian, Probus was hailed emperor by his own legions — in his case only a couple of weeks after the legitimate emperor, Florian, had been confirmed. The times were unstable, and in the previous few months three other emperors had perished, making Probus the fourth man within a single year to don the purple.

Civil war had cost Rome its security beginning in the 240s, and even now threatened to erase the impressive gains made by Aurelian. Vigorous action was required to rescue the Empire from another perilous slide, and Rome was fortunate that Probus had come into power. Probus was one of Aurelian's most effective generals, and it was he who recovered Egypt from Palmyrene control in 272 (though another man named Tenagino Probus had failed to liberate Egypt two or three years earlier). Subsequently, Probus gained command of Roman armies in the East, and it was from this position of power, in Syria and Egypt, that he staked his claim against Florian in the summer of 276.

From the very outset of the civil war, Probus demonstrated the military genius that would make his reign a success. Although he engaged in a skirmish with the larger forces of Florian, Probus avoided a pitched battle, relying instead on the summer heat and the seeds of discontent to win the battle. The strategy paid off, and in August or September of 276, Florian was murdered by his own troops, leaving Probus in full command. The senate, none too pleased at the turn of events, soon gave its approval.

That bloodshed was avoided was fortunate for Probus, since he would need every soldier the Empire had during the next six years. The first half of Probus' reign was spent defending the Empire against external invasion, whereas the second half was largely devoted to suppressing revolts from within. The first problem he faced was a massive invasion of Gaul and neighboring provinces by the Franks and other Germanic tribes, such as the Burgundians, Alemanni and Senones.

Some of these invasions had begun about the time Aurelian was murdered, but were ignored by the new emperor, Tacitus, who instead led an expedition against Gothic pirates in Asia Minor. The incursions across the Rhine and Upper Danube had now become critical, especially in Gaul, where they were no longer the typical border raids that that province experienced with some regularity, but the most severe destruction that had occurred there in about three centuries. Thus, Probus was forced to make the long and arduous journey from Cilicia to Gaul.

He wintered in Siscia *en route*. There he defeated the Goths and did much to restore the Balkan region before he continued his westward trek, visiting Rome along the way. He arrived in Gaul in the spring of 277 and spent two years pacifying the border provinces at great expense. In the process he recovered Raetia and defeated the Vandals in Illyricum. Throughout these campaigns Probus was always outnumbered by the invaders. The magnitude of his achievement cannot be underestimated. Next, he marched east to the Lower Danube where, in 279, he defeated the Getae and then visited Siscia and, in an Aurelianic fashion, declared himself "restorer of the world and of the army."

Just when he had settled affairs in Europe, Probus hastened to Asia Minor, where he fought a particularly brutal campaign against Lydius the Isaurian, who was leading his band of robbers on piratic raids in Pisidia, Pamphylia and Lycia. Meanwhile further east, two revolts erupted which, it seems, were handled by Probus' subordinates. The first of these occurred in Syria under Julius Saturninus, who seems to have been the local governor, and the second was brought about in Upper Egypt by a Nubian people called the Blemmyae. Probus then wintered in Antioch, and while in Asia perhaps signed a treaty with the Sasanian king Varhran II (276–293), resulting in the emperor's assumption of the title *Persicus maximus*.

Having visited most of his great Empire by 280 (he had gone from the Syrian border to Gaul and back again), Probus had achieved peace on the same grand scale as Aurelian. However, new troubles arose in the far west, and in a virtual repeat of when he was hailed emperor four years before, Probus traveled all the way back to Gaul. Along the way, he paused to settle about 100,000 Scythians within Roman territories.

The most serious of the western revolts was staged at Cologne by the generals Bonosus and Proculus, while a less destructive one was led by the governor of Britain, who was speedily suppressed by an officer named Victorinus. Putting down the revolt of Bonosus and Proculus was a very difficult task, but after several months of bitter warfare, Probus emerged victorious.

After a great many accomplishments rivaling those of Aurelian, Probus entered Rome late in 281 and celebrated his hard-earned triumphs. He sponsored lavish games in which thousands of exotic animals, captives and gladiators perished to the delight of the Roman spectators. After the festivities ended, Probus departed Rome and prepared to lead his army on the conquest of Persia that Aurelian had been ready to launch before his own unexpected murder.

But just as Probus was ready to depart Illyricum, a rebellion led by Marcus Aurelius Carus, his praetorian prefect, broke out in Raetia and Noricum. Underestimating the seriousness of the uprising, Probus sent an army led by subordinates to crush the revolt, only to learn that they had defected to the enemy's cause. Upon hearing this, the remaining soldiers in Illyria, having tired of iron discipline and civilian projects, murdered Probus in September of 282 in a look-out tower outside Sirmium, only a few miles from where historians tell us he had been born a half century before.

Probus had many accomplishments beyond the realm of war, for he devoted a great amount of effort to restoring the prosperity of regions that had been ravaged since the reign of Gallienus, principally Gaul and the Balkans. Although his most visible achievement was the completion of the circuit wall around Rome that was begun by Aurelian, he also drained marshes on the Danube and Nile, and introduced viticulture in Gaul and the Danubian region. To accomplish these ambitious projects, Probus put his soldiers to civilian work when they were not occupied by war. Although this was of great benefit to the people, the army found it exhausting and degrading.

The parallels between the reigns of Probus and Aurelian are as remarkable as those between the ephemeral reigns of Quintillus and Florian. Both men reigned for about the same duration, traveled tirelessly throughout their Empire, after which they both celebrated a grand triumph in Rome. And just when each prepared to embark on his most ambitious conquest yet — that of Persia — both of these great men were cut down in the Balkans by their own soldiers, the result of their harsh brand of discipline.

Numismatic Note: Though historians tell us Probus was born in Sirmium, his unusual coinage commemorating Siscia has invited speculation that this city (some 170 miles to the west of Sirmium) is his true place of birth. Of all coinages of the Roman emperors, that of Probus offers the greatest variety of obverse types, including unusual inscriptions and elaborate busts. Indeed, coinage types that would be considered unusually ornate during other reigns are absolutely commonplace. The mint marks are also complex, creating thousands of varieties. Because of the military nature of his reign, Probus' coins offer heavily armored obverse types and warlike reverse types. Additionally, since he traveled so widely, he has an unusually large number of *Adventus* types.

SATURNINUS A.D. 280

(Gaius(?) or Sextus (?)) Julius Saturninus, d. A.D. 280. Among the generals who rebelled against Probus, Saturninus provides us with perhaps the greatest mystery. A man reputedly of Moorish extraction, he should not be confused with the Publius Sempronius Saturninus who is said to have revolted in the East during the reign of Gallienus.

Sources often place his revolt in Egypt, where it may well have started (and as a result, it perhaps sparked the contemporary revolt of the Blemmyae on the Upper Nile). But considering he was either the governor of Syria or simply a general operating in that region, the location more likely was Antioch. We can be relatively certain that Saturninus revolted at the behest of his soldiers, for the numismatic evidence shows that he sought the approval of Probus, who then was in Pisidia waging war against the pirate Lydius the Isaurian. After a very brief reign that ended in a siege by armies loyal to Probus, Saturninus was killed by his own soldiers.

NUMISMATIC NOTE: In addition to the aurei Saturninus struck in his own name, he appears also to have struck aurei in the name of Probus with the reverse inscription ending in AVGG, a wishful gesture in the hope that he and Probus could reconcile.

PROCULUS, C. A.D. 280–281

Titus Aelius(?) Proculus, died c. A.D. 281. Perhaps the most serious revolt during the reign of Probus occurred in Gaul in 280. Though Probus had pacified Gaul in 277 and 278, the destruction was considerable and the region was far from recovered by the time the emperor marched east to pacify the Danubian district. Indeed, Gaul had only been reclaimed from the separatist Romano-Gallic emperors since 274.

Thus, for all the progress made by Aurelian and Probus, there was still ample cause for revolt among a population which had suffered almost endless revolution and invasion in the last two decades. While Probus was on the opposite side of the Roman world (near the border of Syria), the Gauls rebelled, hailing two generals, Titus Aelius Proculus and Quintus Bonosus, as joint emperors at Cologne. It is not certain whether their revolts began jointly, but there is little doubt that they soon joined forces.

Bonosus is said to have been of British descent, though his mother was Gaulish. As commander of the Rhine fleet at Cologne, he apparently lost a squadron to the Germans through his own carelessness and revolted out of fear of the punishment awaiting him. During the earliest stages of the revolt (when Proculus may have gained the allegiance of Lugdunum), it appeared as though their support would not waiver, but shortly after Probus arrived in person it lost momentum.

Probus eventually defeated the two rebels in separate engagements near Cologne, after which Bonosus is believed to have committed suicide. The circumstances of Proculus' death are less certain, for he either perished in battle or fled to the Franks (with whom he either sought or had already obtained some kind of alliance), who promptly delivered him to Probus for execution. A rebellion by the governor of Britain appears to have also fired up at the same time, but it was quickly suppressed by one of Probus' commanders named Victorinus.

NUMISMATIC NOTE: The coinages associated with this revolt have long been a source of debate. The double-denarii attributed to Bonosus are now generally dismissed as altered or misdescribed "barbarous radiates." However, the case for Proculus — whose coinage was unknown until very recently — is perhaps stronger. His coinage seems to be represented by a single specimen which many authorities accept as genuine: a silver-washed double-denarius of a crude style reminiscent of the later products of the Romano-Gallic Empire.

CARUS A.D. 282–283

AUGUSTUS: A.D. 282–283
(A.D. 282–283: SOLE REIGN)
(A.D. 283: WITH CARINUS AND NUMERIAN)

FATHER OF CARINUS AND NUMERIAN
FATHER-IN-LAW OF MAGNIA URBICA
GRANDFATHER OF NIGRINIAN

Marcus Aurelius Carus (or Numerius(?)), c. A.D. 224/230–283. Little is known of the early career of Carus, whom the emperor Probus made his praetorian prefect in 276. Although some ancient historians suggest Carus was born in Illyricum, others, more reliably, tell us he was born at Narbo, a quiet town on the southern coast of Gaul. As such, his short-lived dynasty represents a temporary break in the Illyrian line of emperors. The name of his wife is not known, though he did have a daughter, named Aurelia Paulina, and two sons, Carinus and Numerian, both of whom were associated with his principate.

Early in September of 282, just as Probus had restored order in the Roman world and was preparing to invade Persia, Carus was hailed emperor by legions in Raetia and Noricum, two neighboring provinces that spanned the Alps and the Upper Danube. Carus came to power with remarkable ease, for the Empire's soldiers had tired of the strict discipline and civilian work details enforced by Probus. Thus the armies Probus had sent to overthrow Carus joined his cause, and Probus was consequently murdered outside Sirmium later that month.

Historians disagree about whether Carus was in the Alpine provinces or was near Sirmium at the time of his accession, and further dispute whether he visited Rome before marching east. Carus' first orders of business were to demand the approval of the senate and to establish his dynasty by giving the rank of Caesar to his eldest son, Carinus, in October, and to his youngest son, Numerian, shortly thereafter — seemingly in November or December.

The duties of government were formally divided among family members. The eldest son, Carinus, was to rule in the West while his father and younger brother prepared to invade Persia. The latter two campaigned in Pannonia, where that winter they defeated the Quadi and the Sarmatians before departing to Asia. They had reached Antioch (their last stop before invading Persian territory) by February or March of 283, where it seems both Carinus and Numerian were raised from Caesars to Augusti.

The much-anticipated Persian campaign that followed was a great success in which Seleucia and the capital Ctesiphon were taken. The campaign was not necessary, for the Sasanians had not been a threat to Rome since the death of Shapur I in 272. Indeed, it seems to have been an expedition of glory and revenge, for Shapur had mercilessly ravaged the Roman East for three decades. Its success was due largely to the incompetence of the king, Varhran II (274/6–293), whose position was further weakened by civil war with his brother, Hormazd. In any case, both Aurelian and Probus had been prevented from conquering Persia by their sudden murders, and at long last, Carus and Numerian were able to claim the honor that had eluded those two great soldiers.

With the campaign being won so easily, the Romans planned to march well past the capital, deep into Sasanian territory. But the armies halted near Ctesiphon when the supreme commander, Carus, was discovered dead, some say in his command tent, along the banks of the Tigris. Carus died, we are told, of a lightning strike, but most historians attribute his death to the treachery of the praetorian prefect Aper, the man who also seems to have killed Numerian on the return journey. Though Carus probably died in July of 283 (after a 10-month reign), many historians prefer a later date, such as August or November.

NUMISMATIC NOTE: Though Carus earned the title *Parthicus* for his leading role in the Persian campaign, this title only appeares on coins struck for him posthumously, for his death (whatever the cause) was sudden. Occasionally his name is spelled in the Greek form KARVS instead of the Latin CARVS.

CARINUS A.D. 283–285

CAESAR: A.D. 282–283
(UNDER CARUS, WITH NUMERIAN)
AUGUSTUS: A.D. 283–285
(A.D. 283: WITH CARUS AND NUMERIAN)
(A.D. 283–284: WITH NUMERIAN)
(A.D. 284–285: SOLE REIGN, IN OPPOSITION TO DIOCLETIAN)

SON OF CARUS
BROTHER OF NUMERIAN
HUSBAND OF MAGNIA URBICA
FATHER OF NIGRINIAN

Marcus Aurelius Carinus, c. A.D. 250–285. In Carinus we find one of the most maligned of all emperors, for the ancient historians have nothing positive to say about him. To a large degree this can be attributed to the fact that he was succeeded by Diocletian, a man who assumed his power unlawfully as a usurper, and subsequently held power for more than two decades. Be that as it may, in so damning a character appraisal there may exist a core of truth.

Carinus is accused of many forms of treacherous and debauched behavior, but the most scathing reviews are of his rampant bisexuality. He is condemned as a corrupter of youth, who filled his courts with harlots, actors and pimps. In the realm of marital relations, the reviews are no better, for he is said to have had nine wives in all, abandoning some of them while with child. Not surprisingly, he is said to have been an insatiable adulterer — a vice that proved to be the motivation for his assassination in the heat of battle.

As the eldest son of the newly declared emperor Carus, Carinus was given command of the western half of the Empire so his father and younger brother, Numerian, could launch an offensive against Persia. Carinus was hailed Caesar in October 282 and was designated to hold the consulship of 283 with his father. Late in 282, Carus and Numerian led a campaign against the Quadi and the Sarmatians, after which they crossed into Asia, never to see Carinus again.

Carinus was soon occupied with a war in Gaul, where he repelled an invasion by Germans on the Rhine early in 283. He then returned to Rome, where he was hailed Augustus (as his younger brother had been at Antioch), and seems to have married Magnia Urbica, who was hailed Augusta. His next task was to repel an invasion of the Quadi along the Danube, after which he held his second consulate, this time with his brother, Numerian, for their father, Carus, had died sometime between July and November of 283.

Meanwhile in 284, Numerian was leading his victorious armies west in anticipation of a meeting with Carinus at Cyzicus. About this time, Carinus was conducting a war in Britain, for which he earned the title *Britannicus maximus*. But the unfortunate Numerian died *en route* in October or November, only a week's march from the location of the brothers' would-be summit meeting. Numerian's death was blamed on his praetorian prefect and father-in-law, Aper, who was executed by the commander of the guard, Diocletian. Since the soldiers apparently disliked Carinus, they hailed Diocletian emperor in opposition to him.

What no doubt would have been a productive meeting between brothers was now replaced by a perilous situation in which Carinus gained a formidable rival at the head of a large, hostile army. Throwing his lot into the middle of this chaos was another rival, named Julian, the governor of Venetia (Venice) who had been hailed emperor by the armies of Pannonia late in 284.

The two western rivals met near Verona in northern Italy early in 285, where Carinus defeated Julian, thus ending his two- or three-month usurpation. Carinus was now ready for the next contender, Diocletian, who had advanced into Moesia shortly after Julian perished. The battle occurred at Margum (not far from modern Belgrade) sometime between the early spring and late summer of 285. Though Carinus may actually have been on the verge of defeating Diocletian, he was assassinated in the midst of the battle by one of his own officers, whose wife he had reputedly seduced.

The death of Carinus brought an end to a short-lived dynasty, and ushered in a new, formidable era in Roman politics, spearheaded by Diocletian. In imitation of his predecessor, Diocletian soon shared his authority so as to make the defense of his vast Empire practicable.

NUMISMATIC NOTE: Carinus — evil though he seems to have been — went to great lengths to honor his family, for he not only issued coins in the name of his wife, Magnia Urbica, but also struck coins posthumously in honor of his father and brother, and for a boy, Nigrinian, who was presumably his son.

MAGNIA URBICA

AUGUSTA, A.D. 283–285

WIFE OF CARINUS
MOTHER(?) OF NIGRINIAN
DAUGHTER-IN-LAW OF CARUS
SISTER-IN-LAW OF NUMERIAN

Magnia Urbica, d. A.D. 285(?). Magnia Urbica is not mentioned by any ancient author, and is known only from her coinage and a few inscriptions. As such, nothing of substance is known of her, except that she was the wife of Carinus. She seems to have been married to Carinus in mid-283, upon which she was also hailed Augusta. At least one historian suggests she died in 285, when her husband was defeated and the memory of the short-lived dynasty was condemned.

The authors of the *Historia Augusta* almost certainly exaggerate when they report that Carinus had married nine women, for they are especially hostile toward this aspect of his life. One passage reads: "Carinus was the most polluted of men, an adulterer and constant corrupter of youth . . . and even made evil use of the enjoyment of his own sex. . . . By marrying and divorcing he took nine wives in all, and he put away some while they were still pregnant." Regardless of the quantities involved, it seems that Magnia Urbica was his last wife.

NUMISMATIC NOTE: Some of Magnia Urbica's coin inscriptions occur in the honorary dative case rather than the customary nominative case, and thus indicate that the coins are "dedicated to" the empress. Her coins are limited to later issues of European mints, some of which were struck concurrently with the Divo Numerian issues at Rome. Helping to prove her association with Carinus are a quinarius and a gold medallion that depict both of their busts. Her denarii and quinarii are very rare.

NIGRINIAN

SON OF CARINUS AND(?) MAGNIA URBICA
GRANDSON OF CARUS
NEPHEW OF NUMERIAN

Nigrinian, d. before A.D. 283. Like Magnia Urbica, who seems to have been his mother, Nigrinian is not mentioned in ancient literature. However, an inscription reveals that he was the grandson of Carus, and the numismatic evidence assures us that he was the son of Carinus, for it was very late in that emperor's reign that coins were struck for the deified boy. If the child was born to Magnia Urbica (Carinus' final wife), he must have died in infancy.

NUMISMATIC NOTE: Nigrinian's coins are of considerable rarity, and appear to have been struck only at Rome. On certain of his aurelianiani, he is shown bare-chested in a heroic pose. Deceptive 20th Century forgeries (commonly known by the name 'The Geneva Forgeries') exist of the coinage of Nigrinian and four other issuers. Many of the known examples are illustrated and described by R. A. G. Carson in the 1958 *Numismatic Chronicle*, pp. 47–58, pls. V–VI. An offprint of the article was published in 1977.

NUMERIAN A.D. 283–284

CAESAR: A.D. 282–283
(UNDER CARUS, WITH CARINUS)
AUGUSTUS: A.D. 283–284
(A.D. 283: WITH CARUS AND CARINUS)
(A.D. 283–284: WITH CARINUS)

SON OF CARUS
BROTHER OF CARINUS
UNCLE OF NIGRINIAN

Marcus Aurelius Numerius Numerianus, c. A.D. 253/4–284. As the youngest son of the Gallic-born Carus, Numerian was destined to share command in the Empire after his father overthrew the emperor Probus in September, 282. Ancient historians are unanimous in their appraisal of Numerian as a man unsuited to war, but remarkably accomplished in poetry and oratory.

After Carus' accession was ratified by the senate late in 282, he established his dynasty by giving the rank of Caesar in October to his eldest son, Carinus, whom he left in command of the West. Meanwhile, Carus and Numerian repelled an invasion of Pannonia led by the Quadi and the Sarmatians, in which it is said 16,000 barbarians perished. It was either during or at the end of this campaign that Numerian was also hailed Caesar, seemingly in November or December.

Carus and Numerian departed to Asia in December, 282 or early in 283, and reached Antioch in February or March of 283. At this time both Carinus and Numerian were raised to the rank of Augustus. Since Carinus was safeguarding Europe, his father and brother could embark on the Persian campaign knowing that they would not have to abandon their offensive midway to settle disturbances there.

The heyday of Persian military might had long passed, and the current king, Varhran II, was not only an ineffective ruler, but also was distracted by a dynastic contender, his brother Hormazd. Not surprisingly, the Roman campaign was a great success, and the capital Ctesiphon was sacked. However, before further advances could be made, the supreme commander, Carus, died not far from Ctesiphon, sometime between July and November of 283.

Ancient historians tell us he died from a lightning strike, but modern historians have rightfully suspected assassination, despite there being no evidence for it. The prime suspect is the praetorian prefect Aper, who was also the father-in-law of Numerian. Command of the army was now taken up by the approximately 30-year-old Numerian, who then shared the Empire with his brother Carinus.

Disheartened and not suited to the rigors of war, Numerian soon negotiated peace with Varhran II, who was only too willing to agree to an unfavorable treaty. It is uncertain whether Numerian spent the winter of 283/4 campaigning in Sasanian territory or led his armies back to Syria. In either case, his desire to leave Persia was motivated not only by his own temperament but also by his father's death and the fact that the campaign had already come to a successful conclusion.

Early in 284 the army embarked on the slow, arduous trek back toward Europe, where Numerian intended to meet with his brother. But this was not to be, for Numerian died *en route* in October or November of 284 near Nicomedia, only about 125 miles' march from Cyzicus, where the reunion was to take place. Indeed, Numerian had been dead for several days before the stench of his corpse revealed his fate to the columns of soldiers who followed his closed litter.

The natural suspect was Aper, who in recent days had claimed the emperor purposely remained hidden in his covered litter for the health of his eyes, which were afflicted by a debilitating infection. It is not certain whether Numerian died of natural causes or was murdered. In any case, his death was blamed on Aper, who was swiftly executed by the commander of the bodyguard, Diocles (Diocletian), who was subsequently hailed emperor in Numerian's place. Diocletian, who may have participated in Numerian's murder, thus emerged as a rival to Carinus, whom the soldiers disliked.

NUMISMATIC NOTE: Even though Carinus struck coins posthumously honoring Numerian, the overture did not win the support of the eastern armies, who had declared their support for Diocletian.

JULIAN OF PANNONIA
A.D. 284–285

Marcus Aurelius Sabinus Julianus, d. A.D. 285. When Numerian died in the East in the fall of 284, the Empire was split between the rival factions of his elder brother, Carinus, in the West, and the prefect Diocletian, who had been hailed in place of Numerian in the East. Thrown into the middle of this rivalry was Julian, the governor of Venetia (Venice) in north-eastern Italy, whose own revolt formed in Pannonia.

Since Julian's revolt took shape in the region surrounding Siscia, it was Carinus who had inherited the problem. The two western rivals confronted each other near Verona, where Julian was defeated early in 285.

Though some sources place the battle in Illyricum, and others suggest it occurred in December of 284, we can be certain that Julian's revolt occupied two or three months, and that it most likely lasted from November, 284 through early February, 285. After the battle, Carinus absorbed into his own army Julian's soldiers whom he desperately needed for the upcoming war with Diocletian, who already had crossed over from Asia.

Numismatic Note: Like many short-lived usurpers, no provincial coins were struck for Julian, whose coinage is limited to aurei and aureliani ani of the Siscia mint, which he controlled during his usurpation. It would seem that perhaps 30 of his aurei are known. The coinage of Julian was counterfeited by the maker of 'The Geneva Forgeries.' See the note for the coinage of Nigrinian for details.

CHAPTER NINE

The Separatist Empires

The Romano-Gallic Empire
c. A.D. 260–274

The Roman Empire was in a state of chaos in the year 260. Italy was recovering from a shocking invasion by the Juthungi, who had swept down from the Rhine only a few months before, and the senior emperor, Valerian I, had been captured by the Sasanians. Since Gallienus (the son of Valerian I) was then occupied on the Danube frontier, the western provinces were left in the hands of commanders who were to defend against Germanic invasion.

One of the men in charge of the Rhine defense was Postumus, the governor of Upper or Lower Germany, who rebelled against Gallienus in 260. Postumus was able to create his own separatist Empire by seizing western provinces that had been under Roman control for centuries. Indeed, this was no simple revolt, for it resulted in a new government, complete with a senate modeled after the one in Rome.

Throughout Postumus' reign, border wars along the Rhine and Danube kept both the Romans and the Gallo-Romans occupied enough so that they battled each other in only one serious campaign — and that ended in a stalemate. The core of Postumus' Romano-Gallic Empire was the three provinces of Gaul (Lugdunensis, Aquitania and Narbonensis), the two Germanys (Upper and Lower), and the island of Britain. Initially Postumus' Empire also included Raetia, but that was lost to Gallienus in 263.

The whole of Spain and the Gallic territories east of the Rhône were also part of the separatist Empire until the emperor Claudius II reclaimed them beginning in late 268 or early 269. Indeed, it was probably in 269 that Postumus was murdered. It seems that the founder of the separatist Empire had fallen victim to a conspiracy between the Spanish nobility (represented by the usurper Laelianus) and the new emperor, Claudius II.

After the murder of Postumus, the separatist Empire spun in decline for the next five years, being ruled by two members of noble Gallic families, Victorinus and Tetricus I (who associated his son with his reign). The significantly biased *Historia Augusta* declares of the Romano-Gallic emperors: ". . . they were all sent from heaven to prevent the Germans being afforded the opportunity of making themselves masters of Roman territory, while that monster Gallienus was entangled in a net of unheard of profligacy." Thus, we must take the scant, often contradictory information about this separatist Empire with a grain of salt.

The Romano-Gallic Empire ended when Tetricus I surrendered to the emperor Aurelian in the spring of 274 after a hard-fought battle at Châlons-sur-Marne (not far from Paris), which itself may have been a mere formality. Historians have rightly pointed out that a secret guarantee of surrender had probably been made in advance. With the vast size of the Roman Empire, the western provinces would prove equally hard to manage in the remainder of Roman history, and they were the base of revolts by many usurpers in the next two centuries.

NOTE: Much is still uncertain about the Romano-Gallic Empire, with two hotly debated subjects being chronology of the reigns and mint locations. The former is especially volatile. The beginning of Postumus' reign is placed in 259 or 260 (or seldom in 258), and its ending either in 268 or 269. The latter date affects the reigns of Laelianus and Marius, as well as the beginning of the reign of Victorinus (which belongs to 268 or 269). The dates of the reign of Tetricus I are inconsistently reported as beginning either in 270 or 271, and ending in 273, 274 or 275. The reign of Tetricus II offers different chronological challenges that are only made more difficult by the uncertainty of the framework to which it belongs. The chronology adopted here is by no means certain, though it does take into account current scholarship and opinions from outside the realm of numismatics. Romano-Gallic coins were struck in considerable quantities, with by far the largest outputs coming from Postumus and the Tetrici. They are found principally in France, but also in England, Belgium, Luxembourg, Holland, Germany and Switzerland, and perhaps elsewhere.

POSTUMUS A.D. 260–269

Marcus Cassianius Latinius Postumus, d. A.D. 269. The year 260 was catastrophic throughout the Roman Empire. In Asia Minor, the co-emperor Valerian I was captured alive by the Sasanians, the Juthungi had invaded Italy itself, and revolts were flaring up in the Propontis, Syria, Egypt, the Balkans and Gaul.

Gallienus, the son of the captured Valerian I, now had to manage the entire Empire himself, so he set out for the Balkans to quell the revolt led there by Ingenuus (and reactivated by Regalianus). In the meantime, he left the Rhine defense to his teenage son, Saloninus, and to subordinate military commanders, one of whom was Postumus, then the governor of

Upper or Lower Germany. The anticipated invasions occurred as the Alemanni poured over the Rhine and invaded Gaul, and the Franks cut as far south as Spain.

Amid this chaos, Postumus was hailed emperor by his legions in the summer or fall of 260, possibly at Deuso (modern Diessen in Holland), as this otherwise obscure village is commemorated on his coinage. (Alternatively, Deuso may be where Postumus was born, for he is said to have hailed from a village.) Postumus' first action was to besiege Cologne, where Saloninus and his praetorian prefect, Silvanus, had established their court.

Postumus had formerly co-directed Roman policy in Gaul with Silvanus, but the two men had quarreled, and now were enemies. Silvanus remained loyal to Saloninus and at some point while besieged probably suggested that the boy be raised from Caesar to Augustus. However, the prestige associated with the rise in rank did not protect Cologne from Postumus' legions. Both Saloninus and Silvanus were executed after the walls were breached shortly after the siege began, after which Postumus erected a triumphal arch to commemorate his victory at Cologne.

The renegade emperor established his headquarters at Trier, and went about creating a smaller version of the Roman Empire, complete with its own senate, consuls and praetorian guards. Postumus himself held the consulship on five occasions. Although he had the upper-hand on Gallienus now, Postumus had no intention of threatening Rome, and made that point clear to Gallienus, reporting that his express purpose was to protect the western provinces.

Postumus spent the next two years fighting the Germans, over whom he won a major victory at Magosa in 261. He appears to have visited Britain to secure the loyalty of that island province, and then returned to Gaul where he fought the Germans once again in 263. He had pacified his own rebel Empire — by now extending from the Rhine to the south of Spain — and he would now face the wrath of Gallienus.

Not only had Gallienus lost his eldest son in 258 and his father in 260, but he had lost his younger son, Saloninus, to the treachery of Postumus in 260. Inevitably, Gallienus invaded Postumus' territory with great ferocity sometime between late 263 and early 265. After trapping Postumus in "a town in Gaul," Gallienus began the siege, but was injured by an arrow and had to withdraw. He was obliged to pass the leading role onto his cavalry commander, Aureolus, who was unable to capitalize on the impressive gains made by Gallienus. The offensive turned into a stalemate, as Postumus wisely avoided fighting a pitched battle. The escape of Postumus from certain death in the siege invites speculation that Aureolus allowed him to escape because they had become allies (as was shown to be true a few years later).

From this point onward Gallienus was so occupied with crises in the rest of the Empire that he never again took the field against Postumus. Indeed, the historical and numismatic evidence would lead one to believe they had entered into a non-aggression pact. To be sure, however, Gallienus had Aureolus make preparations for taking up a defensive position at Milan, so as to discourage an invasion of Italy from Gaul.

Much to the disappointment of Gallienus, Aureolus revolted late in 267 or early in 268, clearly in alliance with Postumus, for he struck coins with Postumus' name and invited him to invade Italy. Whether Postumus feared a trap, decided to honor a pre-existing agreement with Gallienus or found the venture impractical is not certain. Traditional thinking has held that the uprising of Laelianus prevented Postumus' acceptance of Aureolus' invitation, but the revised chronology makes that impossible. In any case, he did not invade — a decision that either directly or indirectly caused the murder of all men concerned.

After having just defeated the Goths at Naïssus, Gallienus returned to Italy to wage war against his turncoat commander Aureolus, who by then seems to have already established himself in Milan. Both Gallienus and Aureolus perished at the siege late in 268, the emperor by assassination, the usurper by execution. The next emperor of Rome, Claudius II "Gothicus," was probably responsible for Gallienus' death, and certainly was the one who executed Aureolus.

Several months later, Postumus faced an identical crisis in his own realm, when one of his governors in Germany, a Spaniard named Laelianus, staged a revolt in Mainz sometime between February and June of 269. There is every reason to believe Laelianus' revolt occurred in concert with an invasion of the South by the new emperor, Claudius II. Not surprisingly, the first territory to fall to Claudius was Spain, a region in which Laelianus no doubt could assure the support of local nobility.

The Roman success in the South did little to distract Postumus from taking revenge on Laelianus, whose revolt he crushed in two months or less (probably ending in the spring of 269). Laelianus' death set into motion a series of violent overthrows, with the next victim being Postumus himself, for he was murdered in the aftermath sometime between April and August 269.

The founder of the separatist Empire was killed by his own soldiers, either for refusing to let them sack Mainz, or because there were men among them who secretly supported the apparent conspiracy of Laelianus and the Romans. Alternatively, he could have been killed by those who attributed their current predicament to Postumus' hesitation to invade Italy in the previous year.

NUMISMATIC NOTE: Postumus' first issue of double-denarii contained about 20 percent silver, and were complimented with uncommonly heavy aurei and a massive issue of sestertii and double-sestertii. All of these were far more impressive than the degenerate coins then being produced by Gallienus, and no doubt helped Postumus win support in his region. By the end of Postumus' reign, the purity of his double-denarii had dropped by more than half, to about 8 percent, a purity that still was three or four times higher than the issues of Gallienus or Claudius II. Coins bearing the letters CA or CCAA on the reverse were struck at Cologne (Colonia Claudia Agrippina Augusta).

In general, it can be said that Postumus was quite imaginative with his coinage, and that he no doubt must have taken a personal interest in determining its types. That Postumus associated himself with Hercules is clearly demonstrated by the coinage. On a level equal to Maximian (286–310), he identifies himself with the Graeco-Roman hero, initially on the localized level with Hercules of Deuso (and those of Lugdunum — MAGVSANO and PACIFERO), but later in a more general sense. Sometimes he is shown donning a club and the Nemean lion's hyde. On much rarer occasions his bust occurs jugate with Hercules. Postumus' reverse types depicting either Hercules or his attributes (club, bow, quiver, etc.) formed a regular part of his coinage, while a much rarer component depicts the labors of Hercules.

On other reverse types, Postumus — rightfully so — styles himself as "restorer" of the Gauls and as victor over the Germans. But later he extends these legitimate claims to the illusory by taking credit for the salvation of the Roman world (RESTITVTOR ORBIS and PACATOR ORBIS) and Rome's provinces in general (SALVS PROVINCIARVM). Whether these types reflect a quiet alliance between Gallienus and Postumus or are nothing more than simple braggadocio remains uncertain.

AUREOLUS A.D. 267(?)–268

ALLY OF POSTUMUS

Marcus (or Manius) Acilius Aureolus, d. A.D. 268. Aureolus rose from his obscure origins as a Dacian shepherd to become one of the Empire's most decorated generals. He was serving as Gallienus' governor of Illyricum when, in 260, he stamped out the rebellion of Ingenuus in Pannonia and Moesia, and sent his deputy commander, Domitianus, to defeat the Syrian legions of the Macriani that had invaded Illyricum.

Although both engagements were successful for Aureolus, the revolt of the Macriani persisted in Syria for another eight months, and Ingenuus' rebellion was renewed later in 260 by Regalianus, a rebel whom Gallienus himself eliminated. After these laudable successes, Aureolus revolted in 262, only to later reconcile with Gallienus. But this was not to be the last time Aureolus would rebel against his benefactor.

In recent years the Sasanians, the Sarmatians and others had employed heavy cavalry to great effect against the Roman legions, so Gallienus created a new cavalry corp, and chose Aureolus as a commander. The new (and very expensive) cavalry proved immediately effective in the war against Postumus that Gallienus and Aureolus waged sometime between late 263 and early 265. Indeed, Postumus was besieged in a town in Gaul, and his end seemed near. However, Gallienus was wounded by an arrow and was forced to leave the campaign in the hands of Aureolus, who was either incapable or treacherously unwilling to capitalize on Gallienus' gains, and thus the campaign was ended.

Although Postumus had not shown designs beyond his own borders previously, Gallienus was wary, and so enlisted Aureolus to take a defensive position. Though the details of his task are far from certain, it seems Aureolus was first sent to Raetia to recruit soldiers, which he was to then lead south to Milan, where they could safeguard Italy from possible invasion. But to the faithless Aureolus, this was just another opportunity to betray Gallienus, who was then occupied by a war in Greece against the Goths and Heruli.

From here out the story of Aureolus takes two different paths that historians cannot seem to reconcile, so they will be presented separately. In the first scenario Aureolus revolted while in Raetia or while already *en route* to Italy, and was intercepted by Gallienus (or one of his officers) at Pontirolo, where his army was routed and Aureolus was wounded. The usurper then occupied Milan, where he endured a siege by both Claudius II and Gallienus, or possibly just the latter.

Alternatively, Aureolus had already installed himself at Milan before he declared for Postumus, and Gallienus hurried back from northern Greece upon learning of his revolt. Aureolus may have briefly left Milan to intercept an army led by Gallienus or one of his subordinates, only to be wounded and return to Milan. This defeat may have been at the hands of the future emperor Claudius II, who seems to have begun the siege of Milan before Gallienus arrived. After Gallienus arrived, he took over the siege and placed Claudius II in command of the reserve forces at nearby Ticinum.

The two versions of this story conjoin at the point where Gallienus has taken over the siege of Milan (which no doubt was a bitter, personal affair). During the course of this siege, Gallienus was treacherously murdered in September of 268, almost certainly at the instigation of Claudius II, who was hailed the new emperor. Aureolus is said to have attempted to bribe Claudius II to save his own life and seems to have come to terms, for he surrendered. But any such deal that was made was not honored by Claudius II, for Aureolus was executed shortly after leaving the walls of Milan.

Most noteworthy about Aureolus' revolt, however, is its link to Postumus. Not only did he invite Postumus to invade Italy, but the numismatic record shows that Aureolus struck coins with the name and effigy of Postumus at Milan. It is possible that Aureolus was hoping to win Postumus' support through such overtures, but more than likely he had come to an agreement with him in advance. In either case, the alliance did not work out, for Postumus refused Aureolus' offer to invade. In the end, Postumus' refusal proved to be the doom of both Aureolus and Gallienus, and quite possibly contributed to his own downfall less than a year later.

NUMISMATIC NOTE: The aurei bearing the name of Aureolus are believed to be forgeries. However, while at Milan — a city never controlled by Postumus — Aureolus struck aurei and double-denarii in the name of Postumus. The coins struck by Aureolus are distinguished from Postumus' regular issues of Lugdunum and Cologne by their 'compact' die engraving and their thick, short planchets. Also distinguishing them is the frequent appearance of a P, S or a T in the exergue to indicate the three officinae in use at Milan (*Prima*, *Secunda* and *Tertiae*). This feature is unique to Milan for coins struck in the name of Postumus (though rarely a P or a V will occur in the left field on the reverse of double-denarii of Cologne). However, the best diagnostic for coins issued by Aureolus is the reverse inscription, for most often it ends with AEQVIT, EQVIT or EQVITVM (a reference to the Equites ('horsemen'), the special cavalry corp which Aureolus commanded). The only coins without reverse inscriptions ending with one of the three versions of (A)EQVITVM which are still attributed to Milan are those which have an officina marker in the exerge.

LAELIANUS A.D. 269

Ulpius Cornelius Laelianus, d. A.D. 269. Postumus was at his capital city of Trier when he learned that one of his governors in Germany, Laelianus (sometimes called "Lollianus" in the *Historia Augusta*), had staged a rebellion at Mainz. The date of the revolt is debated, but it probably began either in February or June of 269 and lasted only a month or two.

Postumus was in a dangerous position, for Laelianus had two legions of his own. This was equal to the number of soldiers Postumus could muster on short notice. To make matters worse, Postumus' territories to the South were concurrently under attack by the emperor Claudius II. This arrangement is so coincidental that it has led many researchers to read between the historical lines, and arrive at the conclusion that Laelianus' revolt was coordinated with the Roman offensive.

Whatever hopes Laelianus may have entertained, his revolt quickly failed. Postumus moved in rapidly and besieged him at Mainz, and after a few weeks, Laelianus was executed by his soldiers because, as the *Historia Augusta* reports, ". . . he tasked them too severely." Whatever the cause of his demise, his death seems to have occurred sometime between April and July of 269.

The siege of Mainz also proved fatal for Postumus, however, who was murdered by his own troops in the aftermath. The reason for Postumus' murder is open to speculation, although the traditional explanation is that he refused to allow his soldiers to sack the city.

We know little of Laelianus except that he apparently was a brave man of Spanish extraction and was a member of the noble family (the *Ulpii*) from whom the emperor Trajan (98–117) hailed. A blatant allusion to Spain occurs on an aureus that depicts Hispania reclining with a rabbit at her side. This coin type, taken as evidence in addition to his respectable Spanish *nomen*, shows that he probably enjoyed support among the nobility of Spain. Thus, his association with the invasion of Claudius II is made all the more likely, for in late 268 or early 269, Spain switched allegiance from Postumus to Claudius II, seemingly without a fight.

Numismatic Note: It must be presumed that Laelianus' coinage was struck at Mainz, for not only was that the base of his revolt, but several of his reverse dies were used by the subsequent usurper, Marius, in the production of his own coinage at Mainz. Though Laelianus has a few different reverse types for his aurei, his double-denarii employ only Victory and Pax as reverse types.

MARIUS A.D. 269

Marcus Aurelius Marius, d. A.D. 269. During the chaos that followed the murders of Laelianus and Postumus, the soldiers proclaimed one of their own, an enormously strong soldier and blacksmith named Marius, as their new emperor. Eutropius states that ". . . a workman of the lowest class, grasped the purple and was slain on the second day," and Marius Pollio suggests he "was only emperor for three days." But the extreme brevity of his reign can be dismissed on the numismatic evidence alone, which suggests his reign almost certainly lasted several months.

The circumstances of his death in the summer or fall of 269 are equally uncertain. Though he is said to have been killed with a sword of his own manufacture, by a soldier he had treated poorly at the forge where they had worked previously, it is equally likely that he was strangled to death as the result of a private quarrel.

Numismatic Note: With the exception of a small coinage produced at Trier(?), all of Marius' coinage seems to have been struck at Mainz. His own coinage shares reverse die links with the final issues of Laelianus. It is also of interest that some double-denarii of his successor, Victorinus, have portraits with the slightly modified portrait of Marius. Not only are these pieces quite rare, but they are also one of the best examples of "portrait fusion" on Roman coinage. Marius expanded the use of reverse types considerably over that of Laelianus. This, combined with the far greater commonness of his coins, suggests his reign was at least twice as long as that of his predecessor.

DOMITIANUS c. A.D. 269(?) or 271(?)

Domitianus, lifespan unknown. This issuer is unknown to history, but based on the style and fabric of the unique coin bearing his name and image (which some authorities question), his bid for the purple can securely be placed in the era of Victorinus (269–271). What follows is a description of the coin's occurrence and likely place in history as told in part 2 of volume 5 of *The Roman Imperial Coinage.*

"In 1900 a hoard of 1300 coins, from Gordian III to Aurelian, was discovered at Cleóns, Loire Inférieure, and fortunately fell into the competent hands of Colonel Allotte de la Fuÿe. The bulk of the hoard consisted mostly of coins of the Gallic Empire: there was one fine piece of Macrian the younger, and one coin of Gallic fabric in good preservation which bore the obverse inscription IMP C DOMITIANVS PF AVG., with a radiate, draped and cuirassed bust to right. The portrait is that of a large-featured, heavily bearded man, distinguishable from those of Victorinus and Tetricus I, though the style of the coin is similar to their regular coinage. . . . Though we have no historical record of any western usurper named Domitian, there seems no reason to doubt the genuineness of the coin, or to reject the attribution of it favoured by Colonel de la Fuÿe to Domitianus, '*dux Aureoli fortissimus et vehementissimus*,' who actually achieved the victory over the Macriani. We may fairly surmise that he made a momentary grasp at power either during the troubles which preceded, or those which followed, the reign of Victorinus, for the style of the coin suggests that his rebellion had place in a mint-city in Gaul. . . ."

The authors suggest in a footnote that the coin might also represent an attempt to rally the defeated Gallic army after the battle at Châlons-sur-Marne (where the Tetrici were defeated by Aurelian in the spring of 274), but based on the style and fabric of the coin, this seems far less likely than the original proposal of associating it with the reign of Victorinus. Indeed, it is not impossible, or even unlikely, that Domitianus was a usurper during the reign of Victorinus, rather than a contender at the beginning or ending of his reign.

VICTORINUS A.D. 269–271

SON OF VICTORIA
UNCLE OR FATHER(?) OF TETRICUS
GREAT-UNCLE OR GRANDFATHER(?) OF TETRICUS II

Marcus Piavvonius Victorinus, d. A.D. 271. The descendant of a noble Gallic family, Victorinus was proclaimed emperor by the soldiers after a two-day interregnum that followed the murder of Marius. It appears that sometime between summer and the month of November in 269, Victorinus opposed Marius' revolt, and that he was perhaps inspired to action by his mother, Victoria.

A wealthy noblewoman, Victoria (or Victorina or Vitruvia, for she is called by all three names in the dubious passages of the *Historia Augusta*), may have been instrumental in the downfall of Postumus, for she appears to have secured the throne for both Victorinus and Tetricus I. But in any event, Victorinus was one of the Gallic army's top men, having served as consul in the Romano-Gallic senate in 265 or 267, and being the tribune of the guards at Trier at the time of his elevation.

Although Victorinus may have been the natural successor to Postumus, he failed to earn recognition from Spain, which seems to have defected to the Romans during the brief usurpation of Laelianus. Victorinus' fortunes suffered an additional blow when the new emperor Claudius II gained the support of the Aedui and incited them to revolt in Central Gaul. In the process, Victorinus lost his territories east of the Rhône to Claudius II, and only after a protracted siege of Autun in the fall of 270 did he regain control of the heart of his Empire.

But in the end it was not military uprisings or Roman advances that brought down the regime of this brave and talented soldier, but rather his lust for the wives of his colleagues. His relentless pursuit of married women earned him powerful enemies who resented his transgressions, and Victorinus was killed after he propositioned one too many wives of his officers. His murder occurred at Cologne sometime in 271 (with accounts varying from the spring to early winter), ending a promising reign and forecasting the inevitable downfall of the Romano-Gallic Empire.

NUMISMATIC NOTE: Victorinus is unique among the Roman-Gallic emperors in that he was deified by his successor, Tetricus I, who struck memorial coins in his honor with the reverse inscriptions CONSECRATIO and CONSACRATIO, the latter being a Gallic peculiarity. Victorinus' coinage — which seems to have been struck at only one mint (perhaps Lugdunum) — records that he held two consulships and, more importantly, that his tribunician power was renewed three times (suggesting his reign exceeded two calendar years). Some 19th Century scholars suggested that the bust of Victory he sometimes used as a reverse type was meant to personify his mother, Victoria, thus named in the inscription VICTORIA AVG. Though the possibility exists, it is impossible to prove. The most imaginative of Victorinus' coins were his aurei, which commemorate more than a dozen Roman legions (and which some scholars consider to be more likely small medallions than coins). Though some of the legions were based in Britain and the Upper and Lower Rhine, most were stationed in the rest of the Roman world, as far afield as Egypt, Phoenicia, Judaea, Pannonia, Dacia and Moesia. Some scholars have suggested that the non-local legions named represent detachments or *vexillations* of these legions which served under Victorinus rather than the legions themselves.

TETRICUS I A.D. 271–274

AUGUSTUS: A.D. 271–274
(A.D. 271–274: SOLE REIGN)
(A.D. 274: BRIEFLY WITH TETRICUS II(?))

NEPHEW OR SON(?) OF VICTORINUS
FATHER OF TETRICUS II
GRANDSON OF VICTORIA

Gaius Pius Esuvius Tetricus, lifespan unknown. The uncertainty that followed the apparently spontaneous murder of Victorinus was resolved by the mother of the deceased, Victoria. If we are to believe the *Historia Augusta,* she used her wealth to secure the elevation of Tetricus, the governor of Aquitania who probably was her grandson, and at the very least a close relative.

Tetricus was hailed emperor at Bordeaux in 271 (accounts vary from spring to fall), and then established his court at Trier, from which he could deal more effectively with an anticipated invasion from Germany. He made a formal entry at Cologne and in the opening year of his reign fought the Germans. But the problems that had plagued Victorinus only grew under Tetricus, who was to be the last of the Romano-Gallic emperors.

At some point during his reign, Tetricus I raised his son, Tetricus II, to the rank of Caesar, and (it appears) to the rank of junior Augustus not long before their abdication. Tetricus I must have realized that his days were numbered, and that his greatly reduced Empire would soon fall to the new emperor, Aurelian, who returned to Europe late in 272 after crushing the more formidable separatist Empire of Palmyra. Though Aurelian may have begun his conquest as early as the summer of 273, Tetricus' Gallic army was defeated by Aurelian's legions in a hard-fought battle at Châlons-sur-Marne in the spring of 274. There, Tetricus and son surrendered to Aurelian. At long last, the Roman Empire was whole.

The battle at Châlons-sur-Marne may have been a mere formality, since there is ample circumstantial evidence to suggest that Tetricus had secretly agreed to surrender before the armies clashed. Indeed, Tetricus may have invited Aurelian to invade, and to thus to rescue him from the difficulties he faced. Although paraded as trophies in Aurelian's triumph, Tetricus and his son were honored and taken into Aurelian's administration. When the family's senatorial status was restored, the father was appointed governor of Lucania (in southern Italy) and is said to have lived to a greatly advanced age.

NUMISMATIC NOTE: The days when a separatist Empire seemed a good idea had long passed by the time Tetricus I assumed command. Gaul had now become a net importer of Roman coins, which were now of higher value than their Gallic counterparts. The double-denarii of Tetricus was greatly reduced in weight and purity, and had only 6% to 8% of the intrinsic value of Postumus' first issues. Furthermore, the planchets and method of striking had degenerated so greatly (even from the preceding reign of Victorinus) that differentiating the worst of the official coinages from the best of the "unofficial mint" issues is often impossible.

TETRICUS II A.D. 274(?)

CAESAR: A.D. 273–274 (UNDER TETRICUS I)
AUGUSTUS(?): A.D. 274 (WITH TETRICUS I)

SON OF TETRICUS I
GRAND-NEPHEW OR GRANDSON(?) OF VICTORINUS
GREAT-GRANDSON OF VICTORIA

Gaius Pius Esuvius Tetricus (II), lifespan unknown. Bearing the same name as his father, Tetricus II was raised to the rank of Caesar either in the spring or summer of 273 (though some scholars prefer 271), and shared the consulate with his father in 274. Along with his father, young Tetricus *filius* abdicated, and surrendered to Aurelian following the defeat of their army at Châlons-sur-Marne in the spring of 274. Though the young man was paraded through the streets of Rome in Aurelian's triumph, he was subsequently restored to senatorial status. He is said to have been very intelligent, and though we know little of his actual accomplishments, his career as a senator in Rome was stellar, for we are told that in his lifetime, no other senator was so highly esteemed.

NUMISMATIC NOTE: The nature of the titles accorded Tetricus II, and their chronology, has been contested among scholars for more than a century. There is ample numismatic evidence to suggest Tetricus II achieved the rank of Augustus, although coins indicating this are often suspected of being barbarous or outright counterfeits. Not to be dismissed are the coins with reverse inscriptions ending in AVGG, some of which are not rare and are of undoubted authenticity. The coins that actually name Tetricus II as Augustus on the obverse are so rare that, if genuine, they must fall within the final weeks of the reign of the Tetrici as they prepared for the invasion of Aurelian. The confusion of Tetricus II's reign is largely due to the unreliable literary sources of the period. For a closer study of the evidence, see "An Unpublished Coin in the Name of Tetricus II," by C. H. V. Sutherland in the ANSMN 11 (1964).

The Kingdom of Palmyra
c. A.D. 260–272

The stability of the Roman East was shattered in 260 when Valerian I was captured by the Sasanian king Shapur I. The eastern legions no longer had a leader, and so a revolt was sparked in Antioch by the praetorian prefect Callistus ("Ballista") and the quartermaster-general, Macrianus Senior. Though neither assumed the purple himself, they hailed Macrianus' two sons, Macrianus and Quietus, as emperors in opposition to Gallienus.

These developments had a similar effect in the European provinces, where revolts and invasions demanded the full attention of Gallienus. Unable to march into Asia himself, Gallienus had to rely on Septimius Odaenathus (a leading citizen of Palmyra whose family seemed to have been of recent importance, and who was only called "king of kings" posthumously) to restore order in Asia Minor. This meant not only suppressing revolts, but also keeping the Sasanians in check.

Palmyra (the "city of palms," also called Tadmor), a desert oasis located between Mesopotamia and Syria, long had served as a buffer state between Roman and Parthian territories. The region first caught the attention of Rome under Marc Antony in the mid-30s B.C., and was incorporated into the Roman province of Syria during the travels of Germanicus in the east in A.D. 18. Palmyra's affluence derived from its ideal location as a staging point for caravans bound for the Euphrates and the Persian Gulf, and thus to the sea-routes to India.

For seven years Odaenathus served the Romans admirably — first in 260, in the aftermath of Valerian's capture. The Sasanian army was defeated in Cilicia by the prefect Callistus (where even the harem of Shapur was captured), and on its retreat, Odaenathus delivered a second defeat, which drove the Persians out of Roman territory. In the process, Odaenathus reclaimed Mesopotamia for Rome. In 261 he turned his attention from the Sasanians to the Roman rebels, causing the murder of Queitus when he besieged Emesa. For these services, Gallienus gave Odaenathus the title "Ruler of the Romans" and "Governor of the East."

Although peace had already been established with the Sasanians, hostilities occurred again in 266, when Odaenathus defeated Shapur in a pitched battle near Ctesiphon. In the following year, 267, he led his army north to repel another invasion of Asia Minor by the Goths. The height of his achievement, in the fall of 267, Odaenathus and his eldest son were killed while returning from this campaign. The traditional explanation for his murder is a domestic squabble, but historians have not overlooked the possibility that it was committed by agents of Gallienus, who no doubt feared the growing power of his eastern viceroy.

The throne of Palmyra was inherited by Odaenathus' second wife, Zenobia, and her son, Vabalathus (also called Athenodorus). An unsteady peace now existed between Palmyra and Rome, and shortly before his own death in 268, Gallienus sent a general named Heraclianus on a campaign against Palmyra. The venture was a failure, and achieved the opposite of its intended result, for now Zenobia and Vabalathus were aware of Rome's hostility toward them. Neither Gallienus nor his successor, Claudius II, would grant Vabalathus the titles that his father had earned from years of valiant service.

Gallienus and Claudius II were so occupied with wars in Europe that they could pay no attention to the East, and so relations worsened between Palmyra and Rome. The Palmyrenes' great expansion occurred during the otherwise successful reign of Claudius II, when in 269 the queen and her son conquered lands as far west as Ancyra. In late 269 or early 270, during the last few months of the reign of Claudius II, they invaded and occupied the important province of Egypt, jeopardizing the grain supply to Rome.

Shortly after his accession, the new emperor, Aurelian, granted (either at the end of 270 or early in 271) the royal titles to Vabalathus and Zenobia which they had long demanded. Aurelian hoped this overture would placate them while he dealt with the local threat of the Vandals, Juthungi and Marcomanni. Though it probably had some mild effect, his gesture did not prevent the Palmyrenes from continuing to strengthen their authority throughout Asia, nor did it dissuade Zenobia from hailing herself Augusta, and Vabalathus from claiming the title Augustus. Egyptian papyri confirm that Vabalathus' revolt in 272 began after April 17 and had been suppressed by June 24.

When Aurelian had sufficiently stabilized Europe to focus on recovering his lost provinces in the East and West, he led his army past the walls of Byzantium and cut a path directly across Anatolia, recovering city after city. Finally, he engaged the Palmyrene armies at Immae, about a day's march from Antioch, where his cavalry was victorious over the Palmyrene commander, Zabdas. He next routed the enemy at Emesa, giving Zenobia no choice but to take refuge in her capital city of Palmyra.

The legendary siege skills of the Romans paid off yet again, for Zenobia and Vabalathus were captured later that year, narrowly escaping the prospect of the Sasanians being drawn into the conflict. In the meantime, the future emperor Probus had recovered Egypt. Although he spared the city destruction, Aurelian executed Cassius Longinus, the chief adviser of Zenobia (she blamed him for the revolt) and returned to Europe with his two royal captives so they could be displayed in his triumph at Rome.

After returning to Europe to fend off a new invasion by the Carpi, however, Aurelian learned that the 600 Roman archers stationed at

Palmyra under the command of Marcellinus and Sandarion had been slaughtered. A new revolt had been ignited, this time led by a certain Septimius Apsaeus under the titular figurehead Antiochus, a descendant of Odaenathus. We are told that the Palmyrenes had gained nominal support in Egypt from a certain Firmius, a man of whom the *Historia Augusta* gives a colorful, but certainly fictional account, and who may be the same man who, papyri indicate, assumed the title *epanorthotes* or corrector.

Aurelian made the arduous journey to the desert oasis for a second time, with Zenobia and Vabalathus still in chains, and crushed the rebellion in Palmyra. Next, he marched on Alexandria, where he caused Firmius to commit suicide. Once bitten, twice shy: Aurelian leveled Palmyra before he left. The city never recovered its former glory, although Diocletian did construct some baths there from 293 to 303 for his soldiers.

ZENOBIA A.D. 267–272

QUEEN: A.D. 267–270/1
AUGUSTA: A.D. 270/1–272

WIFE OF ODAENATHUS
MOTHER OF VABALATHUS
DAUGHTER OF JULIUS AURELIUS ZENOBIUS

Septimia Zenobia (Bat-Zabbai), born c. A.D. 241(?). As the queen of Palmyra, Zenobia gained authority through her husband and retained it through her son, Vabalathus. Zenobia herself claimed descent from the Macedonian rulers of Syria and Egypt, though her name indicates she was of Semitic heritage.

Thus, when Odaenathus was murdered in 267, the throne was passed onto the rightful heir, Vabalathus. The circumstances of Odaenathus' murder are still uncertain, but the fact that his eldest son Hairanes (by an earlier wife) perished with him leads one to conclude that it was a dynastic purge rather than a mere "domestic squabble" as we are often told. Whether it was Gallienus or Zenobia who caused the murders is unknown.

In any case, Zenobia and Vabalathus, her son by Odaenathus, inherited an Empire that was now all-powerful in the East thanks to the fierce leadership of Odaenathus. He had taken command on behalf of Rome, and had defeated the armies of Shapur I on several occasions. The result was that Zenobia and her son were in a unique position to threaten Roman supremacy in the East.

Bearing that in mind, it seems a foolhardy move for Gallienus to have sent an expedition against Zenobia in 268. Not only would the expedition's failure spell certain doom (for there would be no longer any doubt as to Rome's hostility), but even if successful, Gallienus was in no position to protect the east. So it comes as no surprise that Zenobia viewed Rome as an enemy, and that she took strong measures to consolidate her power as Rome went through another three emperors in as many years.

Gallienus, Claudius II and Quintillus all refused to give her son, Vabalathus, the same titles and honors won by his deceased father, and so the hostilities grew. During the reign of Claudius II (268–270), Zenobia led the campaigns by which Palmyra claimed Asia Minor and the Levant. Next, either late in the reign of Claudius II or early in the reign of Aurelian, she seized Egypt, a notoriously difficult land to conquer. Egypt was dear to the Romans both as the emperor's personal province and as one of the main sources of grain for Rome.

Having little choice in the matter, the new emperor, Aurelian, granted Vabalathus and Zenobia the titles they demanded, hoping it would buy him the time he needed to settle affairs in Europe. In the end of 271 or the spring of 272, Aurelian was ready to exact his revenge, and led his army across Anatolia, liberating the Greek cities and defeating the Palmyrene armies at Antioch, Emesa and finally at Palmyra, where Zenobia and her army eventually took refuge.

Supplies ran short in Palmyra, and Zenobia's Armenian allies defected to the Roman side. Zenobia then decided to appeal to the Sasanians for help. She made a dash toward the Euphrates on a camel, but was overtaken by the Roman horseman, after which the city fell. Late in 272 Aurelian returned to Europe with the Palmyrene royalty with the intention of featuring them in his triumph, bound with golden chains, while all along the arduous journey they attracted the curious spectator. The royal captives did not arrive in Rome until 273, after both the Danubian front and the second revolt in Palmyra and Alexandria were settled.

Two versions exist of Zenobia's fate: subsequent to Aurelian's triumph in Rome, she was beheaded by Aurelian or was allowed to retire to a villa near Tibur, where she married a senator and later died peacefully. The latter version seems more likely, for Eutropius says her descendants enjoyed good reputation, and the *Historia Augusta* tells us that during the reign of Valentinian I (364–375), her descendants were reckoned among the nobility in Rome.

Zenobia was said to be dark complexioned and exceptionally beautiful, with black eyes that were "powerful beyond the usual wont . . ." In inscriptions she is called Bat-Zabbai, daughter of La-Zabba, meaning the "one with beautiful long hair." Beyond her physical beauty, she was a shrewd stateswoman and proved to be a capable general in the field. The historians tell us that although chaste, she was not adverse to hunting and drinking with her generals or with visiting dignitaries.

NUMISMATIC NOTE: The coinage of Zenobia consists of billon double-denarii struck at Antioch and/or Emesa, and potin tetradrachms struck at Alexandria. Though her son had been issuing coins jointly with Aurelian since the emperor's accession late in 270, Zenobia does not appear on coinage until late spring of 272, when war was declared. Her striking seems not to have lasted more than about two months (perhaps considerably less), and consequently her coins are very rare. Like the sole issues of her son that were struck concurrently, her Alexandrian issues are dated year 5 (E), and thus are back-dated to 267, when her husband, Odaenathus, died (rather than to late 270, when their titles were recognized by Aurelian).

VABALATHUS A.D. 267–272

KING: A.D. 267–270/1
AUGUSTUS: A.D. 270/1–272

SON OF ODAENATHUS AND ZENOBIA
HALF-BROTHER OF HAIRANES (HERODES)

Lucius Julius Aurelius Septimius Vabalathus Athenodorus (also Wahballat), born c. A.D. 256/7(?). Much like his father, Odaenathus, Vabalathus owed his royal position to the bloodlines of his mother, Zenobia. After the murder of his father and step-brother in 267, Vabalathus and his mother assumed control of Palmyra, which at that time was the dominant force in Asia Minor.

Initially during the co-regency of Zenobia and Vabalathus, there was an unsteady peace between Palmyra and Rome, which was shattered by the failed expedition sent against Palmyra in 268 by Gallienus. The succeeding emperors, Claudius II and Quintillus, both refused to grant Vabalathus and his mother the titles they demanded. But in 269 and 270, during the reign of Claudius II, the Palmyrenes seized most of Asia Minor, from the heart of Anatolia to the border of Cyrene, including Egypt.

Late in 270 or early in 271, the new emperor Aurelian (270–275) thought it wise to grant Vabalathus the titles of his deceased father. Later still, most likely in 271, Vabalathus and his mother took further initiative against Rome, and Vabalathus boldly claimed the title of Augustus.

However, Rome was now in capable hands. By late 271 or the spring of 272, Aurelian began to direct his efforts to recovering the lost provinces in the East and West. In the resulting war, both Vabalathus and Zenobia were captured during the course of the siege of Palmyra, which fell later in 272. The king and his mother were then led away as captives for display in Aurelian's anticipated triumph at Rome.

NUMISMATIC NOTE: The coinage of Vabalathus consists of double-denarii struck at Antioch and potin tetradrachms (and one rare issue of Æ drachms) struck at Alexandria. Both main coinages were struck in two phases, the first being when he shared honors with Aurelian (late 270 through late 271 or spring 272), and the second being after he and his mother had declared themselves independent from Rome (after which Vabalathus was Augustus). The Imperial double-denarii Vabalathus struck jointly with Aurelian at Antioch have his own laureate portrait on the obverse and Aurelian's radiate bust on the reverse. (It is worth noting that scholars have disagreed as to which side is the obverse.) Equally challenging is Vabalathus' inscription, which adds VCRIMDR to his name. The likely interpretation is *Vir Clarissimus Rex* (or *Romanorum*) *Imperator Dux Romanorum* (with the first portion translating to 'most noble man, king' or 'most noble Roman man'). At the provincial mint of Alexandria, Vabalathus uses his own regnal years 4 (Δ) and 5 (E) to Aurelian's 1(A) and 2 (B), thus 'back dating' his accession to 267, when his father died.

THE ROMANO-BRITISH EMPIRE
C. A.D. 286/7–296/7

The island of Britain had always been a source of trouble for the Romans, as it offered the unenviable combination of being poor in natural resources and difficult to control. The Romans first took a serious interest in Britain after hearing reports of its mineral wealth, which only later were proven to be greatly exaggerated.

Although Julius Caesar campaigned there in 55–54 B.C., it was not until the reign of Claudius (41–54) that serious efforts at annexation were made. The next half century saw many tragedies in Britain, including the immensely destructive revolt of Boudicca in 60, in which some 70,000 Romans are said to have perished and London was burned to the ground. The Roman reprisals were equally ruthless. Not long after this, the governor Agricola (78–85) also campaigned with success.

Still later the emperors Hadrian and Antoninus Pius erected long walls to help defend Britain from the Picts and Scots in the north. The insurrections and border wars in Britain are almost too numerous to recall, and in hindsight, the Romans probably would have chosen to leave the island alone. But once they had staked their claim, the Romans were unwilling to suffer the loss of pride associated with abandoning it. Even the emperors Septimius Severus and Constantius I were to die at the frontier city of Eburacum (York), while preparing for campaigns in the north.

For a period of about 15 years (260–274), the island was incorporated into the Romano-Gallic Empire founded by Postumus. In this first separation from Rome, Britain did not play an important role, and indeed was drawn away from Rome largely by virtue of its geographic location. Britain had subsequently returned to Roman possession for only a dozen years before it once again fell into the hands of a separatist emperor. But this time Britain was the heart of the rebellion, not merely an adjunct.

Leading the revolt was a man of humble origins, the Roman naval commander-turned-pirate, Mausaeus Carausius. Later he added some coastal regions of northern Gaul to his Empire, and throughout was able to defy attempts of the emperor Maximian to unseat him. However, after about six years of independence, Carausius suffered a major defeat at Gesoriacum (Boulogne) at the hands of the new Caesar Constantius I, and was assassinated by his chief minister, Allectus, upon returning to Britain. Allectus took command in his place, but did little over the next three years except brace himself for the inevitable attack.

When it came in 296, the Roman invasion was swift and decisive, and Constantius returned Britain to the Roman world. The island rarely experienced a moment's peace thereafter, and was the source of numerous revolts, including those of Magnus Maximus (383–388) and Constantine III (407–411), both of which resulted in coinage. A general deterioration in the west caused the Romans to strip the island of its garrisons until it was abandoned for good in the 5th Century. Thereafter, Britain lost most of the wealth and prestige it once enjoyed, and reverted to a virtual barter economy. It subsequently came to be occupied by Angles, Saxons and Jutes, all people who earlier had frequently raided its coastal cities.

CARAUSIUS A.D. 286/7–293

Marcus Aurelius Valerius Carausius (*earlier* Mausaeus Carausius), d. A.D. 293. Carausius was a man of humble origins from Menapia, a seafaring region between the Waal and the Scheldt rivers. Carausius came to prominence in the Roman army, and by 285 had risen to a high position in the Channel Fleet, at which point he came into the service of the newly appointed Caesar Maximian.

At that time a band of oppressed Gaulish peasants, united under the name "the Bagaudae," had turned to marauding, and had elected two of their own, Amandus and Aelianus, as their emperors. Carausius' naval actions proved to be of great value to Maximian, who was able to crush the Bagaudae. After the operation was finished, it seems, Carausius was appointed as commander of the Channel fleet, though this may have happened earlier. Maximian entrusted his new, gifted commander with the task of ridding the western coasts of Frankish and Saxon pirates.

But it seems Carausius adopted the policy of attacking the pirates after they returned from their raids so that he could claim a portion of the booty for himself. On no level was this in Rome's best interest, so Maximian (who was busy fighting the Alemanni and Burgundians on the Rhine) sentenced him to death on the charge of embezzlement late in 286 or early in 287 (accounts vary). Carausius was forewarned of the charge and, having no other option, sailed his fleet around to the western shores of Britain, landing about 50 miles south of Hadrian's Wall.

There he met with the Scots and Picts, arranging a treaty of resistance to Rome, and defeated the army assembled by the Roman governor, Quintus Bassianus, who was stationed at nearby York. After absorbing many of the Roman soldiers into his own ranks, Carausius marched the nearly 200 miles to London, and assumed control. To the great advantage of Carausius, many new fortresses had been built on the Saxon shore of Britain, and Maximian himself was then occupied with Germans on the Rhine.

It was not until 288 or 289 that Maximian could launch an offensive against the rebel, but that attempt (which required the construction of a new fleet) was a disaster, and immediate plans of ousting Carausius were abandoned. In the truce that resulted, it is possible that Carausius negotiated rights to some territories in northeastern Gaul, though if not, he forcibly annexed them by 290.

Carausius was able to maintain his position while the Romans were sufficiently distracted, and as a result was able to organize his own Empire by copying the best aspects of Rome. Much like Postumus before him, he held consulships and he even assumed the titles *pontifex maximus* and *pater patriae*. Additionally, he struck coins honoring the legions, held Saecular Games — in short, he was building a Roman Empire in miniature.

He trumpeted such themes, especially the concept of a Roman renewal, on his coins. Not only does he use the inscription ROMANO RENOVA paired with the she-wolf suckling Romulus and Remus, but he frequently uses the curious letters R S R. A new translation for these letters is put forward by G. de la Bedoyere in the 1998 *Numismatic Chronicle*: instead of meaning *rationalis summae rei* (chief finance minister), as has long been thought, it almost certainly abbreviates *redeunt saturnia regna* ('the golden age returns'). These famous words appear in the second half of a line from Vergil's Fourth Eclogue, which are followed in the next sentence with *Iam nova progenies caelo demittitur alto* ('now a new generation is sent down from heaven above'), which no doubt represents the unusual inscription I N P C D A, which occurs on a medallion of Carausius. With this remarkable discovery, not only can we praise the suprisingly refined and subtle propaganda of this mere provincial, but we can avoid finding in the letters R S R a representation of the title Allectus is suspected as having held in Carausius' regime.

In hope that Diocletian and Maximian would recognize him as a partner rather than an enemy, Carausius appealed to the joint Augusti throughout his reign, even to the point of adopting their names, Aurelius and Valerius. Though abundantly reflected in the coinage, this "fraternal" policy was ineffective. The end for Carausius came about shortly after Diocletian and Maximian each adopted a Caesar in 293. The western Augustus, Maximian, chose Constantius I, who in the summer of 293 dislodged Carausius from his possessions in Gaul — including the important naval base of Gesoriacum (Boulogne). The latter feat was accomplished by a siege that starved the inhabitants and kept Carausius' navy at bay with a flimsy but effective palisade that Constantius I built across the harbor mouth (and which is said to have broken the day after the Carausians capitulated).

The new Caesar attacked Carausius' Frankish allies, clearing them from their island and mainland strongholds in Batavia. This setback weakened Carausius' authority, and effectively reduced his kingdom to the island of Britain. Through being cut off from the continent, Carausius' options were limited; he could no longer receive the supplies and military support that had made his reign tenable. Indeed, it was this critical loss that led to his assassination in 293 by his chief minister, Allectus, who then assumed the title of Augustus in his place.

NUMISMATIC NOTE: Carausius' coinage is remarkably varied in design content, with many elaborate obverse busts and a wide array of imaginative reverse types. Equally fascinating is the variety of issue marks that appear on the reverses. It is noteworthy that he produced denarii of good silver years in advance Diocletian's introduction of the argenteus (in 294). In doing so, Carausius may have been following in the footsteps of Postumus, who in 260 helped secure his own reign by producing coinage more valuable than that of the Romans. The aurei of Carausius are very rare, with perhaps 20 pieces known.

Of great interest are his overtures for recognition from Diocletian and Maximian, whom he styled as his colleagues on some of his coinage. Best known are his double-denarii that bear the jugate busts of Carausius, Diocletian and Maximian, declaring the three men as joint-Augusti both on the reverse (with the inscription ending AVGGG) and on the obverse, with the inscription CARAVSIVS ET FRATRES SVI (Carausius and his brothers). Other coins Carausius struck were entirely in the name of either Diocletian or Maximian, with no mention of himself except in the reverse inscriptions, which end AVGGG (and as such also refer to him). These coins may be distinguished from the regular products of Diocletian and Maximian by the peculiarities of their manufacture and the reverse inscription. Carausius' coinage has much in common — relatively speaking — with that of the Romano-Gallic emperors, including the unusual facing bust, also struck by Postumus.

ALLECTUS A.D. 293–296/7

MINISTER OF CARAUSIUS

Allectus, d. A.D. 296/7. Allectus was in a position of great authority in the regime of Carausius at the time of the latter's murder. His title and responsibilities are not certainly known (for he is variously called first minister, and even henchman and companion). Another possibility is that he was the chief finance minister (*rationalis summae rei*), though that long-held view has suffered a setback with the new reading of R S R as *redeunt saturnia regna* ('the golden age returns'). In essence, almost nothing is known about this shadowy figure, including his full name or his ancestry. Indeed, he may even have been sent by the emperors to undermine Carausius, as some of the ancient chroniclers intimate.

Speculation aside, we may be certain that Allectus had Carausius assassinated upon his return to Britain in the summer of 293, after he had lost the important naval base at Gesoriacum (Boulogne) to the new Caesar Constantius I. Though it would be unfair to blame Allectus for the collapse of his Empire (for the wheels had already been set in motion), it would be equally unfair to suggest he was a competent ruler, for we are told by the chroniclers that he "miserably oppressed the Britons and afflicted them with manifold disasters."

Now in possession of the hollow title of Augustus, Allectus managed affairs in Britain while Constantius eliminated the last of Carausius' former allies on the continent. In the meantime, the Romans also enlarged their fleet (Constantius at Boulogne and his praetorian prefect Asclepiodotus about 100 miles south at Rouen) for the anticipated invasion, which probably occurred in 296, though some scholars suggest 297. The attack was made simultaneously at two locations — by Constantius along the coast of Kent, and by Asclepiodotus in Hampshire.

The navy commanded by Asclepiodotus may have been launched on a rumor that Constantius had already sailed, and thus arrived sooner, narrowly missing the separatist fleet in the fog off the Isle of Wight. Upon disembarking near Clausentum, the Roman army burned its fleet and marched directly on London. *En route* they met the armies of Allectus while still in Hampshire. Allectus was killed in the ensuing battle, and the badly battered soldiers of Allectus retreated to London, which they intended to pillage, but they were prevented from doing so by the timely arrival of Constantius, who had led his fleet up the Thames. We are told that the Britons were overjoyed at the island's liberation by the Romans.

In retrospect, it is odd that the Tetrarchs chose this moment to invade Britain, for at the same time wars were raging elsewhere in the Empire. Diocletian had just begun to besiege Domitius Domitianus in Alexandria, Maximian was guarding the Rhine front in place of Constantius I, and Galerius was battling the Sasanians on the eastern frontier. If this troubled era demonstrated anything, it was that the Tetrarchic system of shared authority was incredibly effective in dealing with the crises of a vast Empire.

NUMISMATIC NOTE: Allectus initially followed in the numismatic footsteps of Carausius, but soon faltered. He produced a more limited range of reverse types, struck very few denarii (and these were merely billon) and eventually reduced the size and weight of the double-denarius. The fact that the reduced coinage has its own reverse type (war galley) and a QL or QC in its exerge has misled some researchers to conclude that it is a 'quinarius.'

The recovery of Britain from Allectus was commemorated on various gold coins and medallions issued by the Tetrarchs, including some struck at a specially opened mint at Iantinum. The most famous of these is the 10-aureus piece struck by Constantius I at Trier , which survived as part of the famous Arras Hoard. Its reverse is inscribed REDDITOR LVCIS AETERNAE (loosely translating to "returner of the eternal light") and depicts Constantius, holding a spear, riding horseback toward the city walls of London; beneath him is a galley along the bank of the Thames, and before him the kneeling figure of Britannia (or London) welcoming him with open arms. There is no mistake about the identification of the walled city, as the inscription LON appears beneath the scene.

CHAPTER TEN

The Tetrarchy
c. A.D. 284–313

The Tetrarchy is comparable in many ways to the Age of Augustus three centuries before. In both cases, a leader of rare talent salvaged Rome from a shameful state of affairs and set it on a path of reform. Though this involved restrictions of freedom, higher taxes and bigger government, its results were significant: borders were safeguarded, legal and administrative reforms were enacted, and a level of dignity was restored to the greatest power the Mediterranean world had ever known.

When we speak of the Tetrarchy, we speak of its founder, Diocletian. The true Tetrarchy only occupied 12 of Diocletian's 21 years on the throne, for prior to his expansion to four rulers there were only two, and for a very brief period in the beginning, there was only Diocletian himself. Although he shared power with his colleagues, he retained the right to legislate and to veto, and in that sense he was the sole architect of his unique brand of government. His greatest moment, however, occurred at the end of his career, when he voluntarily abdicated his throne — an act that had not occurred in Rome since the warlord Sulla did so in 79 B.C.

The form of government and the society created by Diocletian made a great impact on the future of Europe and the Near East. Indeed, the very foundations of Feudalism and of the serfdom of the peasant class can be traced directly to his social and economic reforms. It comes as no surprise that Diocletian (even more so than the Christian emperor Constantine the Great) represents the ideal king of Dark Age and Medieval Europe.

Diocletian went to great lengths to dignify the office of Augustus, for it had been severely debased in the previous decades by frequent usurpations. He wore richly woven robes and required anyone who approached him to perform *adoratio* by kneeling at his feet and kissing the hem of his robe. These measures also affected the future of the Empire, for subsequent emperors (including Constantine the Great, who abandoned the laurel wreath in favor of a Greek-style diadem) retained in their courts the dignity that Diocletian had re-established.

Diocletian also demonstrated, with great clarity, the need for division between East and West. He was not the first emperor to recognize this fact (Valerian I and Gallienus had also made it their policy), but he was the first to formalize it. No longer was it a matter of temporary convenience or of military necessity, but rather an organizational principle that came to be recognized as fact. After his reign, only the greediest of emperors who coveted the whole Empire for themselves could ignore Diocletian's model.

Throughout his more than two decades as Augustus, Diocletian attempted to unify all aspects of the Empire: political, military, administrative, economic, legal and religious. Indeed, with an Empire so large and diverse as his, this was a task worthy of men who chose Jupiter and Hercules as their patron deities. Diocletian's most important reforms were in the realms of politics and war. Only a few months after taking office, he shared his supreme authority with his comrade-in-arms Maximian. This allowed them to deal with invasions on the Rhine and the Danube, which not only happened with astonishing regularity, but quite often simultaneously. A few years later, in 293, they each adopted a Caesar with whom they shared their burden. This brought the number of rulers to four — hence the reason historians have applied the name the Tetrarchy (rule of four) to Diocletian's great creation.

The best effect of this expansion from two members to four was the new-found freedom it gave Diolcetian and Maximian. With few exceptions, the Caesars attended to the seemingly endless requirements of defending the Rhine and the Danube, and the Augusti applied themselves to larger tasks, such as administration, reform and raising the money necessary to support the government and the army.

The second effect was military flexibility. On some occasions all four of the Tetrarchs were required to wage war. The best example of this occurred in the years 297 and 298, when all four members were either stamping out rebellions or repelling invasions.

Much like the Adoptive Emperors of the 2nd Century, we may presume that if Diocletian had had suitable heirs, he would have preferred to share his authority with them rather than with army colleagues. But this natural tendency hardly detracts from the genius of Diocletian's willingness to share authority, for he no doubt would have demanded the same degree of loyalty and competence from his heirs that he did of his colleagues.

Indeed, it was a stroke of good fortune that he chose such a friend as Maximian with whom to share the burden of supreme power. If he had shared his authority with a more ambitious or less loyal man, his grand design would have quickly degenerated into yet another civil war. Trust and loyalty proved to be the cornerstones of their uncommon form of government.

Diocletian was the most thorough organizer since Augustus. He divided the Empire into four administrative units that were further subdivided into 12 dioceses and finally into 101 provinces. Though authorities have often disputed the details, the number of dioceses seems eventually to have increased to 14, and the number of provinces to 117.

The four administrative units defined the regions for which the Caesars and Augusti had primary responsibility. The dioceses were administered by "vicars" who answered directly to the four praetorian prefects who were attached to the Caesars and the Augusti. The governments of individual provinces were run by governors, who collectively were responsible to the vicar of their diocese.

The dioceses initially were: Britanniae (south of Hadrian's Wall), Galliae (northern Gaul), Viennensis (southern Gaul), Hispaniae (Spain and the westernmost part of North Africa), Italia (Italy and the trans-Alpine regions of Raetia and Noricum), Africa (central portion of North Africa, including Carthage), Pannoniae (the Pannonias and Dalmatia), Moesiae (the Moesias, what remained of Dacia and all of Greece), Thraciae (all of Thrace), Asiana (western part of *mod.* Turkey, including Lycia, Pamphylia and Galatia), Pontica (most of the southern Black Sea coast and Cappadocia) and Oriens (the vast territory from Cilicia due east to Mesopotamia, as well as Syria, the Levant, Egypt and Cyrenaica).

Diocletian purposely segregated the authority for civil and military matters. In so doing, he could have administrators do what they did best and have military men ply their trade. Furthermore, since governors and vicars had no military authority, the likelihood of their sparking a revolt was greatly reduced. Even the military commanders were unlikely to be able to gain enough support for a revolution, for their areas of responsibility often overlapped into different provinces.

The arrangement was cunning, as it eliminated most of the circumstances that had made it possible — even likely — that frontier commanders would revolt against the emperor. The losers in this arrangement, undoubtedly, were those of the senatorial class. Not only were they forbidden to hold military offices (a policy that Gallienus had initiated), but soon they were prevented from holding provincial governorships except in the regions traditionally allocated to them since the reign of Augustus.

The other great casualties were Italy and the city of Rome. Diocletian was a practical man who was unmoved by sentimental attachment. Though Italy and Rome may once have been the center of the Empire, Diocletian and his Illyrian colleagues saw them for what they were at that point in history. Italy was reduced to a diocese in the course of Diocletian's reorganization and became subject to taxation to which it traditionally had been immune (indeed, this was one of the main catalysts for the revolt of Maxentius in 306).

The focus of government and the army shifted from Rome to more conveniently located cities. In the West, Trier and Milan were the court cities, and in the East, Thessalonica, Nicomedia, and at a later stage, Antioch, all became court cities. The most important of these was the

Bithynian city of Nicomedia. Strategically located between the Danube and Syria, it became Diocletian's "second Rome" and was the precursor to Constantine's monumental decision to found Constantinople on the European shore only 50 miles to the west.

The invasions across the Rhine and Danube that had become epidemic in the 3rd Century required that the army be nearly doubled in size and undergo an extensive reorganization. The Empire now supported perhaps as many as 75 legions. The expansionist emperor Trajan had required only 30 legions, and Caracalla had only 33 legions at the height of his power. Furthermore, the naval fleets were strengthened and the land armies were reinforced with heavily armored cavalry.

Costly though it was, so large an army was necessary to combat the increased pressures on the frontiers and the greater sophistication of the arsenals employed by Rome's enemies. The army was reorganized into two main components: the *limitanei* (or *ripariensis*), which were stationed at fortifications permanently based along the borders, and the *comitatenses* ("soldiers of the retinue"), which were the mobile strike forces. The *comitatenses* were particularly strong in cavalry and were brought into action wherever the need arose.

Though estimates vary widely, a conservative view of the number of soldiers on the payroll would be about half a million, and there may well have been as many as 900,000. With so large an army to support, tax revenues became more important than ever before. Although Diocletian always managed to raise the money necessary, he had a sincere desire to limit the suffering of the citizens, so he introduced economic reforms by which he hoped to alleviate tax burdens and combat inflation. His two main tactics were a coinage reform in 294 and the establishment of maximum prices for goods and services in 301. Both failed miserably, for the economy was too complex to be controlled by laws.

Legal reform was equally far-reaching, and much more effective, as the Tetrarchs established a large bureaucracy to administer and enforce their revised laws. These reforms removed many of the incentives associated with a more liberal society and most citizens became trapped into their socio-economic roles. In this respect, Diocletian can rightly be considered the "father of Feudalism," a system by which the poor became virtual slaves to landowners in the Dark Ages and the Medieval world.

At the heart of the matter were Diocletian's efforts to stabilize agricultural production and streamline the manner in which the practical arts were passed from one generation to the next. Indeed, farm hands were legally tied to the farms they worked, and required the permission of the landlords to leave and seek work elsewhere. Those with skills in a given field were virtually forced to pass their occupations onto their offspring.

While these measures may have increased the efficiency of the economy in the short term, they critically reduced personal freedom.

The worship of the pagan gods was encouraged by Diocletian, who had adopted Jupiter as his personal patron deity. Since his colleague Maximian had similarly adopted Hercules, two "houses" or "dynasties" were founded within the Tetrarchic system: the Jovian (of Jupiter) and the Herculian (of Hercules). The two Augusti went so far as to declare themselves the sons of these deities, naming July 21, 287, as their divine birthdays. It is also significant that the solar worship promoted by previous emperors (notably Aurelian and Probus) was abandoned by Diocletian for a more traditional form of paganism. It was only after Diocletian's retirement that the worship of the sun-god Sol was once again popularized by Constantine the Great, who used that pagan solar deity to ease the conversion to Christianity within the ranks of his army.

Most especially affected by the religious fervor of Diocletian and his colleagues were the Christians, whose faith did not permit their worship of other gods, even if it was only a symbolic gesture. In 297 or 298 Diocletian required all soldiers and administrators to make sacrifices to the pagan gods; those who refused were expelled. A few years later, the Tetrarchs initiated a severe persecution of the Christians with the intent of destroying the religion.

Late in February of 303 Diocletian issued an edict calling for the destruction of churches and scriptures throughout the Empire, and later in the year, issued orders to imprison the entire Christian clergy. In April of 304 this was extended to all those professing the Christian faith, with death being the penalty. Constantius I in the West did not enforce many of the anti-Christian edicts, though Maximian did so with some vigor, seemingly out of loyalty to the wishes of Diocletian. In the East, however, it was pursued with great fervor by Diocletian; Galerius; his wife, Galeria Valeria; and their nephew, Maximinus Daia.

Diocletian must have been sorely disappointed when the Tetrarchy he had so carefully built collapsed. After all, the fail-safe of his system was its promise of smooth succession through the Caesars, who were destined to replace the Augusti. Soon enough this system was torn apart by dissatisfaction among heirs and potential heirs: obvious candidates were passed up for promotion while others were chosen because of their family ties or private agendas. If anything, this shows that it was Diocletian and the unquestioning loyalty he inspired in his colleagues that supported the system. Had the course of succession been determined with greater wisdom, the Tetrarchic system no doubt would have endured far longer. It was Galerius who succeeded Diocletian with the greatest authority, and he attempted to retain the facade of the Tetrarchy while maintaining absolute power. A similar effort had been made by Augustus, who was successful in his goal of consolidating his authority within a transparent framework of Republican government. Regrettably for the Empire, Galerius failed where Augustus and Diocletian had succeeded.

The Tetrarchic system collapsed entirely in 311, when the last of the original four, Galerius, died. Four men claiming the title of Augustus remained, but they were enemies of each other, entering into fair-weather alliances to prevent their own demise. By 312 the four were reduced to three, and by the summer of 313 only two remained — Constantine the Great in the West and Licinius I in the East. It is at this point that most historians agree the Constantinian Era begins.

Abbreviations of Titles

a	Augustus	c	Caesar
sa	Senior Augustus	sc	Senior Caesar
ja	Junior Augustus	jc	Junior Caesar
s-pa	Self-Proclaimed Augustus	pc	Princeps and Caesar
fa	*Filius Augustorum*	us:	Usurper

Note: The geographic divisions are only approximate, as members of the Tetrarchy often operated in areas in which they did not have primary authority. The region of Thrace, though located in Europe, was often considered part of the Asiatic realm. For the purposes of this table, Thrace is not strictly considered to be in either the European or Asiatic categories. The western and central portions of North Africa were usually considered part of the territories allocated along with Italy, whereas the eastern portions (including Egypt) belonged to the Asiatic portion.

JOINT-RULE OF DIOCLETIAN AND MAXIMIAN
(July 1, 285 to March 1, 293)

Date	West	East
285–286	Maximian (c) *us:* Amandus	Diocletian (a)
286–293	Maximian (ja) *us:* Carausius	Diocletian (sa)

FIRST TETRARCHY
(March 1, 293 to May 1, 305)

Date	Western Europe	Central/Eastern Europe	Asia
293–305	Constantius I (sc) *us:* Allectus	Maximian (ja) Galerius (jc)	Diocletian (sa) *us:* Domit. Domitianus

SECOND TETRARCHY
(May 1, 305 to July 25, 306)

Date	Western Europe	Central/Eastern Europe	Asia
305–306	Constantius I (sa)	Severus II (sc)	Galerius (ja) Maximinus Daia (jc)

THIRD TETRARCHY
(July 25, or later, 306 to Spring, 307)

Date	Western Europe	Central Europe	Asia
306– Feb. 307	Constantine I (jc)	Severus II (ja) *us:* Maxentius (pc)	Galerius (sa) Maximinus Daia (sc)
307 (Feb– Spring)	Constantine I (jc)	Severus II (ja) *us:* Maxentius (sa) *us:* Maximian (ja)	Galerius (sa) Maximinus Daia (sc)

PERIOD OF DISPUTE
(Summer, 307 to November 11, 308)

Date	Western Europe	Central Europe	Eastern Europe/Asia
307	Constantine I (jc,s-pa)	*us:* Maxentius (sa) *us:* Maximian (ja)	Galerius (sa) Maximinus Daia (sc)
308	Constantine I (jc,s-pa) *us:* Alexander	*us:* Maxentius (sa) *us:* Maximian (ja) (after April — in Gaul)	Galerius (sa) Maximinus Daia (sc)

FIRST REVISED TETRARCHY
(November 11, 308 to mid-310)

Date	Western Europe	Central/Eastern Europe	Asia
308	Constantine I (jc,s-pa) *us:* Alexander	Licinius I (ja) *us:* Maxentius (a)	Galerius (sa) Maximinus Daia (sc)
309	Constantine I (jc then fa; throughout s-pa) *us:* Alexander	Licinius I (ja) *us:* Maxentius (a)	Galerius (sa) Maximinus Daia (sc, then fa)
310	Constantine I (fa,s-pa) *us:* Maximian (a) *us:* Alexander	Licinius I (ja) *us:* Maxentius (a)	Galerius (sa) Maximinus Daia (fa)

SECOND REVISED TETRARCHY
(mid-310 to April, 313)

Date	Western Europe	Central /Eastern Europe	Asia
310 – May 311	Constantine I (ja) *us:* Alexander (-310)	Licinius I (ja) *us:* Maxentius (a)	Galerius (sa) Maximinus Daia (ja)
May 311– Oct. 312	Constantine I (ja)	Licinius I (ja) *us:* Maxentius (a)	Maximinus Daia (sa)
Oct. 312– 313	Constantine I (sa)	Licinius I (ja) shared w/ Constantine I (sa)	Maximinus Daia (ja)

DIOCLETIAN A.D. 284–305

AUGUSTUS: A.D. 284–285
(IN OPPOSITION TO NUMERIAN)
A.D. 285–286 (SOLE REIGN;
MAXIMIAN AS CAESAR)
A.D. 286–305 (WITH MAXIMIAN)

FATHER OF GALERIA VALERIA
FATHER-IN-LAW OF GALERIUS

Gaius Aurelius Valerius Diocletianus (*earlier* Diocles), c. A.D. 240/5–311/2(?). Of all the emperors of Rome, Diocletian stands second only to Augustus as a reformer and organizer. Indeed, he took command of an Empire shattered by revolution and invasion and introduced stability, as well as the novel concept that power could be willingly and loyally shared. He reorganized every aspect of Roman life — the provinces, the army, taxation, the economy and much more — in hope that his grand scheme would salvage his decaying Empire.

As if all that were not enough, when much of his dream was achieved and his health would no longer permit him to carry the burden of duty, he voluntarily retired from office. Ever conscientious, he forced his co-emperor, Maximian, to abdicate as well, and oversaw the orderly transfer of power to junior members of his command staff. Once he had accomplished all that, he believed he could retire to his palace along the shores of the Adriatic and tend his vegetable gardens knowing he had served his Empire well.

But it was not long before Diocletian's utopian arrangement was shattered, and it is this simple fact that forces historians to realize that Diocletian's achievement was unique, and perhaps could have been achieved by none other than himself. Immediately there were strife, jealousy and selfish power struggles that had not occurred since Diocletian assumed control more than two decades before.

Diocletian was born sometime between 236 and 245 to a humble family from Dalmatia, perhaps near Spalato, where he eventually retired. Although his father may have been a freedman (a former slave), Diocletian rose from his obscure origins to become emperor. He fought in the armies of Aurelian and Probus and served as a commander in Moesia in the 270s. During the great Persian campaign originally mounted by Carus in 283, he was appointed commander of the *protectores domestici* by Numerian, the son who replaced Carus as emperor in the East upon his father's unexpected death.

Upon the murder of Numerian late in 284, the soldiers chose Diocletian as the most suitable replacement. He may have been hailed for no reason other than the sincere hatred the soldiers harbored for Numerian's older brother, Carinus, who still retained the title of Augustus in the West. Diocletian's first act was to execute Aper, the praetorian prefect who was considered responsible for the murders of both Carus and Numerian. Though it is not inconceivable that Diocletian had a hand in their murders, the ancient historians do not indicate this and there is no reason to suspect it.

Diocletian was installed at Nicomedia on November 20, 284, as a rival to Carinus. Civil war was now inevitable. Diocletian marched west into the Balkans and confronted his opponent's armies near Verona (or Margum) in the spring or summer of 285. It appeared as though the larger army of Carinus had gained the upper hand in this pitched battle when the hated Carinus was struck down by one of his own embittered officers, leaving Diocletian the fortunate victor.

Diocletian now commanded the entire Roman army and was sole Emperor from Britain to Mesopotamia. Despite the chaotic method of his accession, Diocletian soon brought stability to the Empire. He quickly realized the gravity of his responsibilities and he determined that he must share his burden if he was to succeed. Initially he shared power with only one colleague, his comrade-in-arms Maximian, upon whom he bestowed the rank of Caesar in July of 285.

Maximian was immediately sent to Gaul to settle the revolt of the Bagaudae, which had hailed two of their own men, Amandus and Aelianus, as emperors. Upon successfully concluding that campaign, Maximian was invested with the rank of Augustus on April 1, 286. This made Maximian equal in almost every respect, except that only Diocletian retained sole authority to legislate and held veto power. More importantly, there existed a tacit understanding that Diocletian was the senior Augustus.

Perhaps on July 21, 287, the two Augusti formally declared themselves the sons of the deities to whom they professed loyalty. Diocletian chose Jupiter (Jove), the supreme deity of the Roman pantheon, whereas Maximian chose Hercules, the mythological hero who was Jupiter's instrument in ridding the world of evil. A further separation of duty and devotion occurred on the geographic level, for Maximian was to operate in the western portion of the Empire (Italy and all points west), while Diocletian was to oversee the Balkans, Asia and Egypt.

Diocletian spent the first eight years of his reign pacifying his eastern portion of the Empire. Initially he fought on the Danubian front against the Sarmatians and others, earning the title *Germanicus maximus*. In 287, however, he went to Asia Minor, where he reorganized the Syrian frontier and installed Tiridates III as king of Armenia. This had practical application, but also was a show of force for the Sasanians and proved to be a diplomatic victory.

From 288 to 289 he returned to the European theater and in the first year combined forces with his Imperial colleague to attack the Alemanni — Maximian crossing the Rhine and Diocletian crossing the Danube. In the following year, Diocletian renewed his campaign against the Sarmatians. At the same time, Maximian failed badly in his attempt to win back the isle of Britain, which in 286 or 287 had been lost to a piratic naval commander named Carausius. As a result, Carausius was able to seize the coastal regions of northern Gaul. For the moment, the two legitimate emperors had no choice but to suffer this territorial loss.

The year 290 is historically uncertain, for Diocletian may have remained in Europe, but more than likely he campaigned against the Saracens — an Arab tribe of the Sinai who had invaded Syria. By the following year he had met with his colleague at Milan and had resumed residence at Sirmium, seemingly taking on the Sarmatians once again in 292 and devoting the greater part of 293 to settling the Danubian front.

By this time, when Diocletian was preparing to celebrate his tenth anniversary (decennalia), the co-Augusti realized that they needed help. Thus, on March 1, 293, they expanded their system of shared authority to include two new members, who would hold the rank of Caesars and would each be subordinate to one of the Augusti. Perhaps the most immediate need for this expansion was the attack they planned against Carausius and his separatist British Empire. To make administration easier, the Empire had been partitioned into 12 dioceses, with each Augustus and Caesar assuming responsibility for a specific geographic region.

As his Caesar Diocletian chose Galerius, a man who seems to have been his praetorian prefect. Galerius was installed at Diocletian's eastern capital of Nicomedia, and to seal the pact, divorced his first wife to marry Galeria Valeria, the only daughter of Diocletian. At the same time in Milan, Maximian installed as his Caesar his praetorian prefect and son-in-law, Constantius I. The new Caesar of the West was immediately sent to dislodge Carausius from his naval bases on the Continent, which he did with great success by the summer of 293.

With the new formula providing greater flexibility to handle military threats in the far corners of the Empire, Diocletian was able once again to battle the Sarmatians in 294, perhaps with his new Caesar at his side. To numismatists this was an important year, for Diocletian implemented a significant coinage reform (see the *Numismatic Note* below), almost exactly two decades after Aurelian's great reform of 274.

Although the details are not clear (for some historians suggest Diocletian continued to fight on the Danube) it appears as though Diocletian returned to Syria in 295 and 296. The Sasanians were under the leadership of a new, fierce king, Narses, who perhaps was the cause of a revolt in Egypt. The Tetrarchs were stretched to the limit during the next three years, fighting on all fronts simultaneously. Indeed, this was the moment of glory for Diocletian, for his system of rule shared among four proved to be of great value.

Diocletian was immediately occupied with restoring Egypt, which had revolted under the leadership of Domitius Domitianus, and, presumably, a shadowy usurper named Achilleus. The chronology is far from certain, although it seems Diocletian was fully occupied toward the end of 296, through 297 and possibly into 298. He had taken Alexandria by 297, when Domitius Domitianus was probably executed.

In the meantime, Constantius I had recovered Britain from Allectus in 296 (or possibly 297), and subsequently had defeated the Alemanni. Maximian had defeated the Carpi and subsequently the Quinquegentiani, a Berber confederation that had revolted in Numidia. In the East, Galerius had initially faltered against the Sasanian king Narses, but by 298 had won an astounding victory, recovering Armenia, sacking the capital of Ctesiphon and claiming much of Mesopotamia for the Romans.

The remaining years of Diocletian's reign were relatively peaceful and he devoted himself to domestic reform. His first task, in 299, was to reorganize the eastern provinces, which had been the site of revolt and invasion in the preceding years. Meanwhile, the two Caesars were continuing to defend the Rhine and the Danube from a perpetual series of invasions by the Marcomanni, the Carpi, the Sarmatians, the Alemanni and other Germanic and nomadic invaders.

In 301, while still in the East at his headquarters in Antioch, Diocletian issued his ambitious Edict of Prices, which sought to restore stability to the economy. Maximum prices were set for a variety of goods and services in the hope that this would curb the ill effects of runaway inflation. Time proved, however, that this Edict was ineffective, as the economic forces at work could not be controlled even under the penalty of law.

In 302, Diocletian traveled throughout Asia Minor, and wintered in Nicomedia with his Caesar Galerius, who most historians believe was the motivating force behind the Edict of Persecution that Diocletian issued late in February, 303. This document called for the burning of Scriptures, the demolition of churches and the banning of meetings for worship. Later in the year, he issued edicts that went one step further by causing the imprisonment of clergymen.

During this same year, Diocletian traveled to Rome where he joined Maximian in a celebration of their *vicennalia* (20th anniversary in power) and their collective triumphs, which included the victory of Galerius against the Sasanians. This was the only time Diocletian visited Rome (which was now somewhat remote from the serious concerns of the Empire) during his tenure as Augustus.

Either late in 303 or early in 304, Diocletian took yet another of the many bold steps that characterized his principate, for he compelled his colleague Maximian to take an oath that they would retire from office simultaneously. Maximian was not pleased with the prospect of forfeiting his power, but he reluctantly agreed.

In mid-December, 303, Diocletian departed for Ravenna, and *en route* became so ill that he had to be carried in a litter. Despite his ill health, in 304 Diocletian joined Galerius on the Danubian front to inspect the fortifications. Perhaps once again under the influence of Galerius, he issued his final anti-Christian edict in April, after which he returned to Nicomedia. By year's end his illness had become so severe as to nearly prove fatal.

The aged emperor announced that on March 1 he and Maximian would jointly abdicate the throne and would be succeeded as Augusti by their Caesars, Constantius I and Galerius. Diocletian did so at his Imperial residence at Nicomedia and Maximian did likewise at his own headquarters in Milan. Though Diocletian's unprecedented gesture is viewed as an admirable act, we can assume with some certainty that if his health had not been so poor he would not have been so eager to retire. Nevertheless, his health improved in the spring.

An arrangement identical to that created by Diocletian followed in suit. Two new Caesars, Severus II and Maximinus Daia, were raised in place of the newly promoted Augusti. Controlling this transfer of power was Galerius, who was able to convince Diocletian to elect Caesars who were loyal to himself rather than to Constantius I, whose health was failing. In the process, the two most qualified candidates, Maxentius (the son of Maximian) and Constantine I (the son of Constantius I) were passed up for promotion.

Greatly anticipating retirement, Diocletian went to the magnificent palace he had built on the Adriatic coast at Salonae (Split) to tend to his gardens. Maximian reluctantly retired to Lucania in Southern Italy. However, the selfish designs of Galerius bred discontent, and by the following year both Constantine I and Maxentius had staked their own claims.

Even Diocletian was not excluded, for Maximian attempted to lure him out of early retirement so that they could jointly return to restore order. Diocletian refused, but Maximian ended up joining the revolt his son had sparked in Rome. Sharing power with his own son was no easy task, and Maximian tried unsuccessfully to overthrow him in 308, after which he sought asylum with his son-in-law and cautious ally, Constantine the Great (against whom he revolted in 310).

Since the Empire was in a state of Chaos, Galerius also appealed to Diocletian by hailing him consul for the tenth time and by asking him to preside at a conference at Carnuntum in November, 308. At the conference, Diocletian refused to emerge from retirement, but backed a new arrangement that was as transparent as the one of 305. Galerius remained the most powerful man in the Empire and Diocletian returned to retirement, probably living into his 70s and dying of natural causes. The date of his death, probably 311, 312 or 316, is disputed among the ancient sources.

NUMISMATIC NOTE: With the exception of some impressive issues of gold medallions, little of interest occured in the realm of numismatics prior to 293 in the reign of Diocletian. However, as part of his ambitious attempt to reform the economy, Diocletian completely overhauled the coinage system, which had continued to degenerate since the reform of Aurelian in 274. Diocletian's reform had long been attributed to the year 296, but more recently it has been convincingly placed c. 293/4.

Diocletian reformed the gold aureus by standardizing its purity and weight: initially, aurei were struck at 70 to the pound (about 4.6 grams), but two years later he struck them at 60 to the pound, increasing their weight to about 5.25 grams. Perhaps surprisingly, the reform of gold was not universal, as some of his mints struck aurei of varying weights. Further, in the *Maximal Edict* he specified that a Roman pound (c. 327 grams) of gold should not cost more than 50,000 *denarii communes* (a 'denomination' seemingly represented by the post-reform laureate).

He also re-introduced high-purity silver in the form of the argenteus, a coin which approximated the denarius issued by Nero more than two centuries before. However, this attempt failed as his argentei — the first coins of good silver to have been struck Empire-wide in about 4 decades — were quickly removed from the marketplace. Scholars have long suggested that they were exported in trade with the East and recoined into the Sasanian dirhems which are so common today.

Diocletian also reformed the bronze coinages by introducing massive 'laureate' bronze coins which often weighed more than 10 grams (and which contained 2–3% silver). This coin is known to collectors incorrectly as a 'follis,' but is better termed an *argentiferous nummus*, or simply a *nummus*, as is done in this catalog. Two smaller bronzes were also introduced: a 'radiate' of about 3.0 grams with less than 1% silver content (usually called a 'post-reform radiate'), and a still-smaller 'laureate' piece of half that weight and seemingly with no silver content which may have represented the *denarius communis*. Other small pieces, such as nummus fractions of uncertain value and the antiquated quinarius (now billon), were also struck for ceremonial purposes. But Diocletian's reforms went well beyond the weight and purity of his coins. He engaged in a massive recall of earlier coins (including stray provincial pieces), which were melted down. Furthermore, he nearly doubled the number of mints (from 8 to 14), and ceased the production of provincial coinage at Alexandria entirely.

MAXIMIAN A.D. 286–C. 310

CAESAR: A.D. 285–286 (UNDER DIOCLETIAN)
AUGUSTUS, 1ST REIGN: A.D. 286–305
(WITH DIOCLETIAN)
2ND REIGN: A.D. 307–308
(WITH MAXENTIUS & CONSTANTINE I)
3RD REIGN: C. A.D. 310 (INDEPENDENT)

SON-IN-LAW OF DIOCLETIAN
FATHER OF MAXENTIUS AND FAUSTA
STEP-FATHER OF THEODORA
GRANDFATHER OF ROMULUS

Marcus Aurelius Valerius Maximianus ('Maximian Herculius'), c. A.D. 240/50–c. 310. The first man to benefit from the rise of Diocletian was his comrade-in-arms Maximian. Like Diocletian, Maximian was of peasant Illyrian origin — the son of a shopkeeper near Sirmium — who had risen through the ranks of the army during the reigns of Aurelian, Probus and Carus. He seems to have been about five years younger than Diocletian, who not only had a healthy respect for Maximian's skills in the art of war, but must also have trusted him implicitly.

Maximian had two distinctly different careers as emperor — the first being a noble affair, the second being tragic and disgraceful. During the 20 years he served as Augustus with Diocletian, he had assumed power legitimately, and was loyal and efficient. But his forced retirement in 305 caused this healthy and ambitious man to seek any possible route back to power. At first he tried to persuade Diocletian to return with him, then he joined the rebellion of his son, Maxentius; later, he allied himself with Constantine the Great; and finally, in 310, he stole an Imperial treasury to finance his final, brief career as a renegade.

Maximian's rise to power came quickly. Not only was Diocletian unexpectedly hailed emperor, but he took the bold step of offering to share his supreme power with Maximian. Diocletian always remained the senior Augustus, with veto power and the exclusive right to legislate, yet he entrusted Maximian with a great deal of responsibility and gave him considerable freedom of action.

About three months after Diocletian had defeated Carinus, he accorded Maximian the rank of Caesar. Most historians agree this occurred on July 21, 285, though some suggest it occurred in November. Indeed, since there are no coins known of Maximian as Caesar, some historians question whether he ever held that rank. From the very outset, the two men divided their responsibilities geographically, with Diocletian in the East and Maximian operating in Italy and all points West.

Maximian's first task was to quell a revolt staged by the Bagaudae, a band of oppressed peasantry in Gaul, who had named two of their own, Amandus and Aelianus, as Augusti. With the help of a naval commander named Carausius, Maximian crushed the rebellion easily, after which Maximian repelled an invasion by the Alemanni and Burgundians along the Rhine. Maximian was rewarded with the rank of Augustus on April 1, 286, and in the following year declared himself the son of Hercules, his choice for a celestial patron, just as Diocletian had done with Jupiter.

The next few years provided enough localized crises to keep Maximian in the West. After the victory over the Bagaudae, Maximian entrusted Carausius with command of the Channel fleet so he could rid the western coasts of Frankish and Saxon pirates. But this confident gesture backfired, for Carausius himself turned to piracy and, upon becoming aware that he was slated for execution, staged a sea-borne rebellion by which he was able to take control of the island of Britain. Since Maximian was beset by successive invasions of Alemanni and Burgundians, he could do little to oppose the pirate ruler. His sole attempt to oust Carausius probably occurred in 289, and ended in disaster. So badly was he beaten that Carausius was able to take control of ports along the northern coast of Gaul either by seizing them outright or by gaining them in negotiation.

By 291 Maximian was able to take leave of Gaul and go to Milan for a conference with Diocletian, who in the meantime had been occupied on the Danubian and Persian frontiers. They no doubt discussed strategies for making their government and frontier defenses more effective, and for reclaiming the territories lost to Carausius. The course of action they eventually adopted was adding two junior members, Caesars, to the Imperial fold.

Maximian adopted his son-in-law, Constantius I, and Diocletian chose his praetorian prefect, Galerius. The ceremonies took place concurrently on March 1, 293, with Constantius I being installed at Milan and Galerius receiving his title at Nicomedia. In the West, Maximian retained control of Italy, Sicily and North Africa, and handed over control of the troublesome province of Gaul to Constantius I, who established his court at Trier.

One of the urgent purposes of this Imperial expansion was to defeat Carausius. Constantius I attacked Carausius' bases along the northern coast of Gaul, besieging and capturing Gesoriacum (Boulogne) in the summer, and soon thereafter seizing the remainder of Carausius' coastal possessions from his Frankish allies in Batavia. Utterly defeated on the Continent, Carausius returned to Britain that summer only to be assassinated by his chief minister, Allectus. Constantius embarked on three years of careful preparations for the anticipated invasion of Britain.

In 294 and 295 the West was relatively peaceful, whereas Diocletian and Galerius were fully occupied on the Danubian front and in Asia Minor. By 296, however, trouble erupted in all quarters of the Empire, and each of the four leaders was simultaneously occupied with war: Diocletian in Egypt, Galerius on the Danube and in Asia Minor, and Constantius I in Gaul and Britain. While Constantius was directing the invasion of Britain, Maximian kept the peace in the rest of the western part of the Empire. He began by reinforcing the defenses on the Rhine and by repelling an invasion of the Carpi on the Danube.

In that same year, 296, after defending the Rhine and the Danube, Maximian advanced south into Spain, where he seems to have campaigned briefly before crossing over either late in that year or in 297, to Numidia, where he suppressed an uprising by a Berber confederation known as the Quinquegentiani. By 298 all the dust had settled and the victories were impressive. The Sasanians had been roundly defeated, the rebellion of Domitius Domitianus and Achileus in Egypt had been crushed and Britain had been recovered.

Maximian had singlehandedly restored peace to North Africa, establishing a mint in Carthage, bringing an end to the Berber and Numidian raiding parties, and strengthening frontier defenses from Mauretania to Libya. For this he held a triumph in Carthage either late in 297 or on March 10 of 298 (sources differ), and held a formal Triumph when he reached Rome in 299.

During the remainder of the joint-reign of Diocletian and Maximian, most of the frontier warfare was conducted by the two Caesars. Diocletian devoted most of his effort to re-organizing and legislating in the East, with Maximian most often administering affairs in the West from his headquarters in Milan.

The year 303 was eventful, for not only did the Great Persecution of the Christians begin, but Diocletian and Maximian traveled to Rome, where in November they celebrated their *vicennalia* (20th anniversary) and multiple triumphs for victories in Britain, North Africa, Persia and Egypt. However, Diocletian's health was worsening, and when he left Rome for Ravenna in mid-December, he was so ill that he had to be carried in a litter. Either prior to leaving Rome in 303 or at Ravenna early in

304, Diocletian persuaded Maximian to swear an oath jointly to abdicate at some unspecified time in the near future.

During the remainder of 304, Dioceltian struggled with his illness, and spent most of his time with Galerius, who was lobbying for his two main agendas — the persecution of Christians and making certain that the next Tetrarchic arrangement would favor him exclusively. By the end of the year, Diocletian's illness was nearly fatal and he did not recover until the spring of 305. Having determined the time was right, he announced that on March 1, he and Maximian would abdicate and pass the titles of Augustus onto their Caesars, Galerius and Constantius I, who would in turn elect their own Caesars.

This was an especially difficult event for Maximian, who was not yet ready to abdicate, but felt obliged to keep his oath. To make matters worse, Galerius arranged affairs such that Maximian's own son, Maxentius, was passed over for promotion in favor of Galerius' nephew, Maximinus Daia, and a comrade-in-arms, Severus II. Maximian had no choice but to retire humbly to a villa in southern Italy, perhaps in Lucania.

The death of the new senior Augustus, Constantius I, in July of 306 brought about a new turn of events, for his son, Constantine I, seized power in the West. Galerius once again passed up Maxentius by acknowledging Constantine I as Caesar and promoting Severus II from Caesar to Augustus. This second insult to Maxentius, combined with Galerius' intention to eliminate the Praetorian camp in Rome and to impose new taxation on the city, caused a rebellion in the ancient capital. On October 28, 306, the citizens and the praetorian guards hailed Maxentius their leader, and he assumed the titles Princeps and Caesar. Joining Rome was all of southern Italy, the islands of Sicily, Sardinia and Corsica, and the important diocese of Africa.

Maxentius soon asked his father to join the revolt, which he did immediately, especially since his earlier efforts to lure Diocletian out of retirement had failed. He began by marshaling forces in Rome to oppose the expected invasion by Severus II, who was headquartered at Milan. Maximian and Maxentius abandoned any pretense of cooperation with Galerius and Severus II, and in February of 307 (or in April, at the latest) both assumed the title of Augustus. Despite his greater reputation, Maximian was considered the junior of the two, for the rebellion had been sparked by his son.

When Severus brought his armies to the walls of Rome in the spring of 307, Maximian put his decades of military experience to good use. Through both bribery and heartfelt appeals (he had formerly commanded the men in Severus' legions), he caused most of Severus' army to defect.

Severus retreated north, being pursued the whole while by Maximian, who eventually besieged him at Ravenna. Severus was coaxed into surrendering and abdicating on the condition that his life would be spared.

Realizing his victory was only temporary, Maximian traveled to Gaul to form an alliance with Constantine I, whom Galerius had grudgingly hailed Caesar in the West. Both men realized that Galerius was their enemy in common, and so Constantine married Maximian's daughter, Fausta, and made a half-hearted pact. Furthermore, Constantine proclaimed himself Augustus, even though his official rank remained Caesar.

Galerius invaded Italy later in 307. Maxentius acted first by executing the captive Severus II and then by employing his father's tactic of bribery, which caused another mass defection of troops to his cause. Not wanting to suffer the same fate as his ill-fated colleague, Galerius quickly withdrew to Illyria before Constantine had the opportunity to advance on his rear.

Maximian returned to Rome early in 308 to join his son, whom he promptly attempted to overthrow at a meeting (probably) on April 20. He failed in this endeavor and fled Italy to seek asylum with his new son-in-law, Constantine I. In the meantime, Constantine had stirred the vicar of North Africa, Lucius Domitius Alexander, to revolt against Maxentius. Whether Alexander did this based on a secret pact with Maximian before he returned to Italy is uncertain. In any event, it was a master stroke that contributed much to Maxentius' eventual downfall by starving Rome of most of its grain supply.

By now the Empire was in chaos, and Galerius was at a loss for a solution. So he called a conference at Carnuntum on November 11, 308, at which he hoped his opponents would be willing to make compromises. Galerius' first hope was to lure Diocletian out of retirement, but instead he only managed to gain his attendance and his approval for a new arrangement sometimes called the First Revised Tetarchy.

In the new arrangement, Constantine was confirmed as Caesar (though he still openly claimed the title Augustus), Maximian was stripped of his self-proclaimed title of Augustus, and Maxentius remained a public enemy. Meanwhile, Galerius retained his nephew, Maximinus Daia, as Caesar, and raised another of his comrades, Licinius I, to the post of Augustus which had been vacated by Severus II. In the end, nothing had really changed and further unrest became unavoidable.

Maximian returned to Gaul in defeat, and could do little more than serve as an adviser to Constantine. But after more than a year in that capacity, he grew unsatisfied. In a fit of desperation, in the spring of 310, Maximian revolted against Constantine, who was battling the Franks on the Rhine. He seized the Imperial treasure in Arles, declared himself emperor and, upon learning of Constantine's unexpectedly fast pursuit, fled south.

The purpose of his rebellion remains uncertain. It may have been an abortive attempt to overthrow Constantine in Gaul or, from the south of Gaul, he may have hoped to launch a naval expedition against his son in Italy or, even more likely, to come to the defense of Alexander in Carthage.

But Maximian's third reign (which some historians, citing Lactantius' *De Mortibus Persecutorum*, believe occured in 309) lasted only a few weeks. Indeed, his plans were foiled by his own daughter, Fausta, who betrayed his designs to her husband, Constantine. Constantine's fast pursuit from the Rhine ended in a siege of Massalia, where Maximian had taken refuge. By June or July of 310 (though some historians prefer 311), Constantine had executed his father-in-law or had allowed him to commit suicide.

The senate in Rome proclaimed Maximian *divus*, and Maxentius used this to the fullest political advantage, for not only did it stir up enmity against his sworn enemy Constantine, but it was well received by the army. Maximian's status changed late in 312 when Constantine took control of Rome and subjected him to *damnatio memoriae*. In an effort to rehabilitate Maximian's memory, his wife, Eutropia, later swore that he had not sired Maxentius.

NUMISMATIC NOTE: On the whole, Maximian's coinage follows the patterns established by Diocletian, and during the course of more than two decades as Augustus many interesting reverse types were created. Since Maximian's 'house' was devoted to Hercules, that hero makes frequent appearances on his coins. Sometimes Maximian appears in the guise of Hercules, donning a lion's skin and club about his shoulders (on aureliani-ani), or wearing the lion's scalp on his head (on post-reform gold medallions and aurei).

Coins were struck for Maximian during every stage of his Imperial career except the first and the last. Though ancient literary sources inform us that Maximian began his career with the subordinate rank of Caesar (from 285 to 286), the title does not appear on any of his coins; likewise, we can be certain that no coins are attributable to Maximian's ephemeral third reign as Augustus. Between these, however, coins were struck for Maximian during his first reign and for his first abdication (both with Diocletian), during his second reign (by Maxentius and Constantine the Great), and after his second abdication. After his death he was honored with commemorative coinages struck by his estranged son Maxentius, his spurned son-in-law Constantine the Great and his comrade-in-arms and beneficiary Licinius I.

AMANDUS C. A.D. 285–286

Gnaeus Silvius Amandus, d. A.D. 286. Of Amandus we know virtually nothing except that he was a leader of the Bagaudae (Bacaudae), a group of oppressed Gaulish peasants and army deserters who banded together and turned to marauding while Carinus and Diocletian were occupied with their own struggle in the Balkans. The name Bagaudae is of Celtic origin and appears to have meant "the warriors."

While this group was terrorizing Gaul, they apparently hailed two of their chieftains, Amandus and Aelianus, as emperors. Upon consolidating his own authority, Diocletian invested Maximian with the rank of Caesar and sent him west to end the marauding. Upon arrival, Maximian enlisted the assistance of the naval commander Carausius and was able swiftly to crush the revolt. Though some historians suggest the revolt was quelled late in 285, more likely it was not stamped out until the spring of 286.

As a consequence of this campaign, Maximian was raised to the rank of Augustus, and entrusted Carausius with supreme command of the Channel Fleet and the task of ridding the western coasts of Frankish and British pirates. As is related in his individual biography, Carausius soon carved out his own separatist Empire in Britain and coastal Gaul.

NUMISMATIC NOTE: No coins are known of Aelianus, and of Amandus the authors of RIC list three.

DOMITIUS DOMITIANUS C. A.D. 296–297/8

Lucius Domitius Domitianus, d. A.D. 297/8(?). Virtually nothing substantial is known of Domitius Domitianus, whose career as an Imperial thorn may have begun c. 271–272, when a man of that name challenged the emperor Aurelian in the Balkans. However, the revolt for which he is best known — and for which he struck coinage — occurred a quarter century later at Alexandria.

The years 296 and 297 were particularly troubled for the Tetrarchs, with wars developing simultaneously on several fronts. Constantius I was reclaiming Britain from the usurper Allectus, Maximian was fighting the Quinquegentiani in North Africa, Galerius was struggling against the Sasanians (whom he would later defeat), and Diocletian had personally devoted himself to stamping out the revolt which had been ignited in Egypt.

Revolts in Egypt were especially dangerous, for not only was that province a steady source of monetary revenue, but it was also one of the Empire's three main sources of grain. During this time period, revolts had broken out simultaneously in two of these primary sources, Africa and Egypt, and the Tetrarchs were rightly concerned about securing them.

The chronology and circumstances of Domitianus' revolt are far from certain. Some scholars place its beginning in 295 and its ending as late as 298. Estimates of its duration range from only a few months to perhaps two years. Adding to the confusion is the uncertain interplay between Domitius Domitianus and Aurelius Achilleus, a man with whom Domitianus is often confused. Though Achilleus may have been the true source of Domitianus' power, no coins are known that bear his name or likeness. It is possible that these two men revolted simultaneously, with Domitianus in Lower Egypt and Achilleus in Upper Egypt.

Unfortunately, the ancient sources are scanty, misleading or contradictory. Historians tend to link the Egyptian uprising to activities of the Sasanian king Narses, who in 296 attacked Armenia and even threatened Syria. Diocletian summoned Galerius from the Danubian front to launch a counteroffensive, which he did with disastrous results in 297. He acted rashly and was severely defeated by Narses at a battle that occurred between Callinicum and Carrhae.

However, Galerius received reinforcements from the Danubian front and launched a surprise offensive, recovering Armenia (from which the puppet king Tiridates had been expelled), moving freely along the Tigris and Euphrates, and even sacking the capital of Ctesiphon. In 298 Narses was forced to agree to a humiliating treaty that gave Rome new territory along the Upper Tigris and considerable war booty. So severe was the defeat that the terms of the agreement remained largely intact for four decades.

Since the ancient sources are not consistent in accounting for Diocletian's whereabouts during the earlier part of this period, it is difficult to determine exactly when and why the Egyptian revolt began. It could have begun in 296 as the result of Sasanian aggressions, or in 297 in response to Galerius' defeat. Some historians suggest that the Egyptian revolt occurred first (in 295 or 296) and thus provided Narses with the opportunity to attack Armenia and Syria.

In all probability, Domtianus' reign lasted about 18 months and occurred during the years 296 and 297. Most historians believe he was murdered either in the spring or the final weeks of 297, perhaps at the hand of Achilleus, who may no longer have considered him useful. Domitianus' death, however, seems not to have ended the revolt in Alexandria.

It may have been continued well into 298 with Diocletian besieging Achilleus for perhaps eight months.

NUMISMATIC NOTE: All of Domitius Domitianus' coinage was struck at Alexandria. It consists of six denominations — three each of Imperial and provincial coinage. The Imperial denominations are aurei, nummi and half-nummi, and provincial are octodrachms (or hexadrachms), tetradrachms and didrachms. With the latter pieces Domitianus earned the distinction of being the last man to strike Roman provincial coinage. Though all of his provincial coins are dated 'year two,' this fact alone yields no important information about the date or even necessarily about the duration of his revolt. The largest of his provincial coins depicts him with a radiate crown, whereas the two smaller ones show him laureate. Each denomination has only one reverse type: the largest portrays Serapis advancing, the next features the bust of Serapis, and the smallest shows Nike advancing.

GALERIUS A.D. 305–311

CAESAR: A.D. 293–305 (UNDER DIOCLETIAN)
AUGUSTUS: A.D. 305–306
(WITH CONSTANTIUS I)
A.D. 306–311 (VARIOUS ARRANGEMENTS)

SON-IN-LAW OF DIOCLETIAN
HUSBAND OF GALERIA VALERIA
FATHER OF MAXIMILLA (*w.* OF MAXENTIUS)
FATHER-IN-LAW OF MAXENTIUS
UNCLE OF MAXIMINUS DAIA

Gaius Galerius Valerius Maximianus (*originally* Maximinus, *sometimes called* Armentarius), c. A.D. 250/60–311. Of the early life of Galerius little is known, except that he was a peasant herdsman from a village on the banks of the Danube, not far from Serdica, in Dacia Ripensis (Upper Moesia). We are told that Galerius later renamed this village Romulianum in honor of his mother, Romula, who had emigrated from the far side of the Danube.

His personal life is a mystery, except that we are informed he had a daughter, Valeria Maximillia, by his first wife (whose name is not known), and a son, Candidianus, by a concubine. Like the other members of the First Tetrarchy, Galerius made his way up the ranks in the Army under Aurelian and Probus, and seems to have risen to become Diocletian's praetorian prefect.

Galerius came to power at the Imperial palace in Nicomedia on March 1, 293, when Diocletian appointed him as his Caesar in the eastern portion of the Empire. Concurrently, at a ceremony in Milan, Diocletian's colleague, Maximian, installed his own Caesar, Constantius I. With the addition of the two Caesars, the Tetrarchy was formed.

To strengthen his ties to Diocletian, Galerius was compelled to marry Diocletian's daughter, Galeria Valeria, shortly after his investiture — perhaps in June of 293. Galerius established his court at Thessalonica, for the territories under his care were Illyria, the Balkans and seemingly parts of western Asia Minor. Sources disagree about where the new Caesar spent his first three years in office, though most likely it was the Danubian front, keeping the Goths, Sarmatians, Marcomanni and Carpi in check while overseeing fort construction and civilian projects.

In 296 trouble erupted in two places in Asia: the Sasanian king Narses invaded Armenia and ousted the Roman puppet king Tiridates, and a revolt was sparked in Egypt under the usurper Domitius Domtianus. Diocletian devoted his attention to the Egyptian revolt and summoned Galerius to abandon his campaign against the Carpi and Sarmatians along the Danubian and instead to prevent Narses from advancing into the wealthy Roman province of Syria.

Galerius' first encounter with the Sasanian army was a disaster, for he attacked with an inferior force, and was severely defeated at a battle between Callinicum and Carrhae. By early in the following year Galerius had recovered and replenished his army with units from the Danubian front. He launched a surprise offensive into Armenia and recovered that region. Next he marched into Mesopotamia and even captured the capital city of Ctesiphon. Thoroughly beaten, Narses sued for peace, and agreed to unfavorable terms which not only ceded much of northern Mesopotamia to the Romans, but which initiated a peace that remained more or less intact for 40 years.

After so impressive a victory, Galerius proceeded to Antioch, whose citizens no doubt received him warmly as the man who had prevented Narses from sacking their city. He was joined there late in 298 by Diocletian, who had quelled the rebellion in Egypt with great difficulty after a long siege. Together, they celebrated a triumph apparently wintered in the capital city. From this point onward, Diocletian devoted himself principally to re-organizing Asia, while Galerius seems to have returned to the Danubian front, where he gained more victories against the Marcomanni, the Carpi and the Sarmatians.

Over these years, Galerius' impact upon Diocletian grew immensely, and he is believed to be the principal inspiration for Edicts that Diocletian issued in 303 and 304 calling for the persecution of Christians and the destruction of their temples and Scriptures. His influence over the senior

Augustus, however, only came to its full realization on March 1, 305, when Diocletian abdicated his throne, taking with him his reluctant colleague, Maximian. The selection of the two Caesars approved by Diocletian was made strongly in favor of Galerius, who now had his comrade, Severus II, and his nephew, Maximinus Daia, as junior colleagues. His unfortunate co-Augustus, Constantius I (the senior member of this Second Tetrarchy) was not only in ill health but had been politically outmaneuvered.

One of the better-qualified candidates who had been passed over was Constantine I, the eldest son of Constantius I. Ever since 293 the young man had served as an officer in the East. While he gained valuable experience, he was also something of a political hostage to help ensure the loyalty of Constantius I in Gaul. Also neglected for promotion was Maxentius, the son of Maximian. Both of these young men would prove troublesome to Galerius in the near future as they pursued, with force of arms, what they considered to be their rightful inheritances.

Now the most powerful man in the Roman government, Galerius moved his court from Thessalonica to Nicomedia and took command of Asia Minor as well as the Danubian provinces. His nephew, Maximinus Daia, was given command of Syria and Egypt, and Severus II was given Italy and North Africa. However, Galerius' house of cards began to collapse about 17 months later, when the senior emperor, Constantius I, died on July 25, 306, during a campaign against the Picts. Constantius' son, Constantine I, who had been released earlier that year by Galerius, had earned the affection of the soldiers and was hailed Augustus in his father's place. Since the young man held no rank at all, his assumption of the purple was a usurpation. He and Galerius finally agreed upon his assuming the title of Caesar, at which time Galerius raised Severus II from Caesar to the vacated title of Augustus.

Galerius was not particularly happy with this arrangement, even though at least it prevented an open war between East and West. But trouble was brewing elsewhere — this time in Rome itself. The greatly expanded army and bureaucracy created by Diocletian was effective, but costly. In order to raise revenue, new taxes were being imposed on Italy and on the city of Rome. This imposition combined with the intention of eliminating the praetorian guards in the capital, sparked a revolt. On October 28, 306, the Romans installed as their leader Maxentius, the son of Maximian, whom Galerius had passed up for promotion in 305.

Maxentius had only a small army, but he called his father out of retirement and together they assumed the titles of Augusti early in 307. They repelled the invasion of Severus II, who himself was captured and later executed. Galerius invaded later in 307, while Maximian was in Gaul seeking an alliance with Constantine I. But Galerius' luck was no better, and he quickly withdrew to Illyria to avoid capture. In the meantime,

Constantine I had appointed himself Augustus, and a new revolt arose in North Africa under the leadership of Lucius Domitius Alexander.

The Empire was in civil war, and Galerius invited Diocletian to emerge from retirement, which he refused to do. Instead, Diocletian agreed to attend a conference that Galerius held on November 11, 308, at Carnuntum, where he hoped to resolve the disputes. The results, however, were unsatisfactory. Nothing of substance changed except that the title of Augustus, vacated by Severus II upon his surrender at Ravenna in the spring of 307, was filled by another of Galerius' comrades, Licinius I.

Constantine remained officially only a Caesar, though he still proclaimed himself to be Augustus. Maximian was forced to abdicate and retire, while Maxentius was confirmed as a public enemy. Indeed, Galerius not only failed to make amends with these three men, but he also infuriated his nephew, Maximinus Daia, who was passed over for what he must have assumed would be a guaranteed promotion from Caesar to Augustus.

The conference was a failure, and the struggle continued Empire-wide. Galerius had little choice but to give Maximinus Daia and Constantine I each the title *Filius Augustorum* ("son of the Augusti") in 309 and Augustus in 310. Two other claimants, Maximian and Alexander of Carthage, perished in 310, but now Galerius' power was eroding and his health was failing. Indeed, by the summer of 310 Galerius had succumbed to an illness that would plague him for the year that remained of his life.

Galerius' final act was to issue an edict of religious toleration. He promulgated this on April 30, 311, at Serdica, just five days before he died. After his death, the Balkan territories were quickly occupied by Licinius I and Galerius' territories in Asia Minor were claimed by Maximinus Daia. Four men were now left to govern the Roman Empire — but this was no Tetrarchy as Diocletian had envisioned, for each man held the title of Augustus and each coveted the possessions of his rivals.

The death of Galerius was recorded in excruciating detail by the Christian writer Eusebius, and it remains one of the literary highlights of the era: "Without warning, suppurative inflammation broke out round the middle of his genitals, then a deep-seated fistular ulcer: these ate their way incurably into his inmost bowels. From them came a teeming indescribable mass of worms, and a sickening smell was given off; for the whole of his hulking body, thanks to over-eating, had been transformed even before his illness into a huge lump of flabby fat, which then decomposed and presented to those who came near with a revolting and horrifying sight."

Numismatic Note: In addition to his regular Imperial coinage, Galerius authorized a series of 'autonomous' coins at Antioch, Nicomedia and Alexandria as part of his persecution of Christians. These are listed in a separate section entitled *Pagan Coinage of The Great Persecution*, which follows the catalog entry of Maximinus Daia. After a most painful death, Galerius was consecrated and was honored by Maximinus Daia and Licinius I. Though these two Augusti would be expected to honor him (for they were his beneficiaries), Galerius was also honored by his nephew and bitter enemy Maxentius, who was willing to put aside his personal hatred to reap the benefits of associating his own outlawed regime with that of his deceased uncle.

GALERIA VALERIA

AUGUSTA, A.D. 293(?)–311

WIFE OF GALERIUS
DAUGHTER OF DIOCLETIAN

Galeria Valeria, d. A.D. 315. Galeria Valeria, the daughter of Diocletian and his wife Prisca, led an interesting life, though precious few details survive. Her life as Augusta was no doubt a comfortable existence in the Imperial courts of Thessalonica and Nicomedia, but good fortune abandoned her when her husband fell ill and died in 311.

She married Galerius either in 292 or in June of 293 (or perhaps around the time he was installed as Caesar on March 1, 293). Early in his reign, Galerius honored his wife by assigning the name Valeria to a new province that had been carved from Lower Pannonia. Valeria had no children of her own, so she adopted her husband's bastard son, Candidianus, whom he had sired with a concubine. The royal couple seems to have been compatible, for she supported Galerius in his endeavors, especially the persecution of Christians. There is ample reason to believe Valeria was equally as instrumental as her husband (if not more so) in influencing Diocletian on the matters that benefited Galerius' interests.

On his deathbed, Galerius asked Licinius I to ensure the welfare of his wife and his son, but Valeria feared for her safety, and fled to the court of Maximinus Daia, the nephew of her former husband. Regrettably, that arrangement did not work out either, for Maximinus Daia proposed marriage to her in 312. When she refused, he confiscated her estates and banished her and her mother to Syria, despite the protestations of her father, Diocletian. When Maximinus Daia neared death, Valeria and her mother escaped and wandered for many months in Syria until they were discovered (in Thessalonica, by some accounts) in 315. Mother and daughter were beheaded by Licinius I, who earlier had executed Candidianus along with the sons of Severus II and Maximinus Daia.

CONSTANTIUS I 'CHLORUS'

A.D. 305–306

CAESAR: A.D. 293–305 (UNDER MAXIMIAN)
AUGUSTUS: A.D. 305–306 (WITH GALERIUS)

HUSBAND OF HELENA AND THEODORA
FATHER OF CONSTANTINE THE GREAT (BY HELENA) AND CONSTANTIA (*w.* OF LICINIUS I; BY THEODORA)
SON-IN-LAW OF MAXIMIAN
GRANDFATHER OF CRISPUS, CONSTANTINE II, CONSTANTIUS II, CONSTANS, CONSTANTIUS GALLUS, JULIAN II, DELMATIUS, HANNIBALLIANUS, LICINIUS II AND NEPOTIAN

Flavius Valerius (or Julius) Constantius, c. A.D. 250–306. The shortest-lived of the original Tetrarchs, Constantius I was of humble Danubian origin and rose through the ranks of the army to become governor of Damiatia, and seemingly the praetorian prefect of the emperor Maximian. Constantius' nickname Chlorus ("the pale") was applied posthumously, not before the 6th Century, and his supposed Dardanian nobility and kinship to the emperor Claudius II "Gothicus" are a later invention of his eldest son.

In addition to his military and political career, Constantius (who was reputedly generous and capable) had a rich family life. One of his earliest associations was with a barmaid named Helena, whose father owned the tavern in Naïssus at which she worked. Although it is disputed whether he and Helena ever married, she did bear him a son, who later came to be known as Constantine the Great.

Constantius severed his relations with Helena sometime in the 280s so he could marry Theodora, the step-daughter of the emperor Maximian, under whom he was serving. He and Theodora were presumably a happy couple, for they had six children together. Though none of these children attained imperial rank, the second generation proved to be both prominent and ill-fated in that respect.

On March 1, 293, Constantius was promoted to the rank of Caesar by Maximian. After his investiture at Milan, he immediately departed for Trier, where he established his court. He had been allocated the province of Gaul, which at the time was not an enviable assignment, for Britain and parts of coastal Gaul were in the possession of the usurper Carausius, and Germans frequently launched invasions across the Rhine. Indeed, Constantius spent almost all of his career as Caesar and Augustus fighting on the Rhine and in Britain.

Constantius' first task was to expel Carausius from his land bases in Gaul so he would be confined to the island of Britain. In the summer of

293, fresh from his investiture, Constantius besieged Gesoriacum (Boulogne) in a risky campaign. After a siege that caused starvation, the city was captured. A palisade that Constantius had built across the mouth of the harbor prevented Carausius' navy from interfering with the siege.

The remaining portions of coastal Gaul held by Carausius were reclaimed from his Frankish allies in Batavia. Roundly defeated, Carausius returned to his island kingdom only to be assassinated by one of his ministers, Allectus, upon landing. Constantius next turned his attention to the Rhine frontier while the shipyards at Gesoriacum and Rotomagus (Rouen) began constructing vessels for an invasion of Britain.

By 296 (though some scholars suggest 297) the navy was ready and the long-anticipated invasion commenced. Constantius led his fleet from Gesoriacum to the coast of Kent, and his praetorian prefect, Asclepiodotus, sailed from Rotomagus to the southern shores of Hampshire, where he narrowly missed Allectus' fleet in the fog near the Isle of Wight.

Asclepiodotus disembarked his army and set his vessels ablaze before he led his legions on the nearly 100-mile journey to London. The Romans were met en route by Allectus' army, and in the ensuing battle the Romans were not only victorious, but killed Allectus as well. The remaining soldiers fled back to London, but were prevented from sacking the city by the timely arrival of Constantius' fleet, which could be seen sailing up the Thames at the very moment. The invasion was a resounding success, but Constantius did not have the luxury of time, for hostilities had renewed on the Rhine. The other members of the Tetrarchy were occupied with wars elsewhere (Maximian in Africa, Diocletian in Egypt and Galerius in Persia). But all these had had been concluded successfully by 298.

Constantius, however, faced a fresh invasion by the Alemanni, who had been forced across the Rhine by the Burgundians. This was a difficult year's-end campaign in which he was wounded, but he eventually gained the upper hand before a new wave of various Germans swept across the frozen Rhine early in 299. In 302 Constantius defeated the Alemanni at Langres in the most spectacular victory he had earned since expelling Carausius from Gaul and reclaiming Britain from Allectus.

Constantius' health began to deteriorate in the succeeding years, and by the time Diocletian and Maximian abdicated in May of 305 (which made Constantius the Senior Augustus), his health was quite poor. In the arrangements made for the succession, the two new Caesars, Severus II and Maximinus Daia, were both allies of Galerius, who consequently was the most powerful man in the Empire. The Caesar appointed to Constantius in the West was Severus II, who was given what seemed to be the safer command in Italy.

Shockingly passed over for promotion were the capable sons of the two western members of the Tetrarchy: Maximian's son, Maxentius, and

Constantius' own son, Constantine I. During the dozen years his father had commanded in the West, Constantine I had served as an officer for Diocletian. Though he was educated and trained in the art of war, he was also a "hostage" by which Diocletian could assure that Constantius would remain loyal.

After his promotion to Augustus, Constantius requested that Constantine I be sent west so they could be united. Constantius' health was now seriously faltering and the request seemed legitimate. None-the-less, when Constantine departed Nicomedia, he traveled as quickly and quietly as possible, for he suspected Galerius or Severus II might attempt to murder him *en route*. After journeying from the Propontis to Boulogne, young Constantine was finally reunited with his father in 306.

Father and son jointly campaigned against the Picts with such success that Constantius earned the title "Britannicus Maximus," and his son earned the admiration and affection of the soldiers under his father's command. However, this new arrangement ended on July 25, 306, when Constantius died of natural causes at Eburacum (York) after having served his Empire for a dozen years as Caesar and less than 15 months as Augustus.

Constantius' deathbed act was the transferal of *imperium* to his son, an event witnessed by the soldiers, we are told. Initially, Constantine took the title Augustus, but after some consideration he settled for the rank of Caesar, which Galerius was willing to grant him under the circumstances. In his father's place as Augustus in the west, Galerius promoted Severus II from his previous rank of Caesar.

NUMISMATIC NOTE: Coinage was struck in the name of Constantius I for a dozen years as Caesar, and for about 15 months as Senior Augustus. With the exception of some spectacular gold medallions, these issues are virtually identical to the issues of the other Tetrarchs. However, he was honored with large posthumous coinages struck by the rebel Maxentius and by his eldest son, Constantine the Great. Maxentius' most interesting commemoratives refer to Constantius I as a cousin or blood relative with the inscriptions COGN and ADFINI. This claim was a stretch, but was essentially true, for Constantius had married Maxentius' step-sister, Theodora.

On some of the coins struck by his own son, Constantius is praised as reposing with the greatest honor (REQVIES OPTIMORVM MERITORVM). These issues, struck c. 317–318, not only honor Constantius, but also two other deceased emperors: Constantine's father-in-law, Maximian, and Claudius II (268–270). The latter was an important part of Constantine's propaganda, in which he claimed descent from that beloved emperor based on a fictional kinship between Claudius II and his own father.

HELENA

AUGUSTA, A.D. 324–328/30

FIRST WIFE OF CONSTANTIUS I
MOTHER OF CONSTANTINE THE GREAT
STEP-MOTHER OF CONSTANTIA AND LICINIUS I
GRANDMOTHER OF CRISPUS, CONSTANTINE II, CONSTANTIUS II, CONSTANS, CONSTANTINA (W. OF HANNIBALLIANUS & CONSTANTIUS GALLUS) AND HELENA THE YOUNGER
GREAT GRANDMOTHER OF CONSTANTIA (W. OF GRATIAN)

Flavia Julia Helena (Saint Helena), c. A.D. 248/50–c. 328/330. Helena figures into the early life of the emperor Constantius I, whom she met while working at her father's tavern in Naïssus. She was a Bithynian by birth, and the city in which she was born was later renamed Helenopolis in her honor. Her life was most extraordinary, for not only was she the mother of Constantine the Great, but she began life as a barmaid and ended it as a Christian saint.

The details of her relationship with Constantius I are not certain. At the very least she was his mistress, but more than likely she was his wife, for they seem to have been married in about 270. This discrepancy may have been invented by the opponents of Constantine the Great, who wished to portray him as a bastard son by suggesting Helena was nothing more than a concubine.

Whether it was a legitimate marriage or something less formal, Helena's association with Constantius I ended in the 280s, when she was put aside so he could advance his career by marrying Theodora, the stepdaughter of the emperor Maximian. The exact date of the separation is unknown, though sometime between 287 and 289 seems likely.

Thereafter Helena remained somewhat anonymous, working behind the scenes to suppress the larger branch of the family that resulted from Constantius' subsequent marriage to Theodora. Considering her less-than-exalted behavior as a barmaid and her vicious behavior toward her stepchildren, her suitability for sainthood seems dubious at best. Both she and her daughter-in-law, Fausta, were given the title *Nobilissima Femina*, perhaps around 317, and were jointly hailed Augustae on November 8, 324.

By the time she was hailed Augusta, Helena had converted to Christianity. About two years later, perhaps in an effort to distance herself from the tragic deaths of Crispus and Fausta in 326, Helena embarked on a Christian pilgrimage to Holy Places, upon which she gathered numerous holy relics (the True Cross said to be among them) and constructed churches in Bethlehem and Jerusalem. Sources differ on the date of her death, which seems to have occurred when she was about 80 years old, sometime between 328 and 330 while *en route* to Rome.

NUMISMATIC NOTE: Helena's lifetime issues as *Nobilissima Femina* and Augusta parallel those struck by Constantine the Great for his wife Fausta, whereas her posthumous coinage was struck simultaneously with the issue honoring Theodora, the woman who in the late 280s replaced her as the wife of Constantius I.

As late as the 19th Century, many numismatists believed that each of the three coin types bearing the name Helena were struck for a different royal lady. They alloted the coinage as follows: those inscribed SECVRITAS REIPVBLICE were attributed to the wife of Constantius I, those struck with the title *Nobilissima Femina* were given to the wife of Crispus (however, these coins predate Crispus' wedding in 321), and the type inscribed PAX PVBLICA was given to the wife of Julian II 'the Apostate.' Such views have long since been abandoned based on hoard evidence and other indications which establish the dating criteria.

THEODORA

AUGUSTA, POSTHUMOUSLY(?)

SECOND WIFE OF CONSTANTIUS I
STEP-DAUGHTER OF MAXIMIAN
STEP-SISTER OF MAXENTIUS AND FAUSTA
MOTHER OF CONSTANTIA (W. OF LICINIUS I)
GRANDMOTHER OF DELMATIUS, HANNIBALLIANUS, CONSTANTIUS GALLUS, JULIAN II, LICINIUS II AND NEPOTIAN

Flavia Maximiana Theodora, lifespan unknown. Theodora was the daughter of Afranius Hanniballianus (the consul of 292 and praetorian prefect of Diocletian) and Eutropia, a lady who married the emperor Maximian, seemingly after Theodora was born. Sometime in the 280s (perhaps in 288) she entered into a dynastic marriage with Constantius I, a soldier who may have been her step-father's praetorian prefect. However, to marry her, Constantius I had to sever his ties to his former wife (or companion), Helena. A few years after they married, Constantius was raised to the rank of Caesar by his father-in-law.

Unlike most dynastic marriages, theirs flourished and in the process produced three daughters and three sons. Although none of these six children attained Imperial rank, Theodora's grandchildren figured prominently in the history of the Empire as the hapless victims of a dynastic cleansing in 337 which nearly made her branch of the family extinct.

Coinage was struck for six of her grandchildren, all but one of whom died under unpleasant circumstances. Delmatius and Hanniballianus were given prominent places in Constantine the Great's plan of succession, only to be promptly slaughtered by the grandchildren of Helena; Nepotian sparked a revolt in Rome which lasted only a month; and the three-year rule of Constantius Gallus is remembered only for his astonishing cruelty. Indeed, Julian II, "the Apostate," was the only one of her grandsons who served the Empire with distinction.

NUMISMATIC NOTE: Restricted to a single type of the smallest bronzes struck at Trier, Rome and Constantinople, Theodora's posthumous coinage was struck side-by-side with the posthumous commemoratives of Helena, the woman with whom Constantius I severed relations so he could marry Theodora. The very existence of Theodora's coinage is somewhat ironic, for it was struck by her step-grandchildren Constantine II, Constans and Constantius II, the three emperors who were responsible for the virtual extinction of Theodora's branch of the family in 337. Her title Augusta is unattested during her lifetime, and may have been awarded posthumously.

SEVERUS II, A.D. 306–307

CAESAR: A.D. 305–306 (UNDER GALERIUS)
AUGUSTUS: A.D. 306–307 (WITH GALERIUS)

Flavius Valerius Severus, d. A.D. 307. Although of humble Illyrian origin and not related to any of the Tetrarchs, Severus II was a close friend of Galerius, who hailed him Caesar upon his own promotion to Augustus when Diocletian and Maximian retired on May 1, 305. Of all the men who legitimately held titles in the Tetrarchy, Severus had the shortest and certainly the most unfortunate career.

Severus was installed as the Caesar for the western portion of the Empire, and technically served under the western Augustus, Constantius I. Since Constantius I was the Senior Augustus, Severus was senior in status to the other new Caesar, Maximinus Daia, who was the nephew of Galerius.

The new arrangement was stacked against Constantius I, for not only was his health failing, but both of the new Caesars were loyal to Galerius in the East. Theoretically, Severus should have been loyal to Constantius I, for not only was he the Senior Augustus, but he also was the Augustus under whom Severus (a Herculian) had been assigned to serve.

But Severus owed his position to his friend Galerius, so that is where his loyalty rested. The fact that Galerius willingly gave Severus Pannonia to add to his realm (which at that point was limited to Italy and North Africa) demonstrates that he was quite trusting of his comrade-in-arms.

On July 25 of 306, some 15 months after Severus had been hailed Caesar, Constantius I died at York while campaigning against the Picts. On his deathbed, he bequeathed his throne to his eldest son, Constantine I, who recently had joined him on the British front. Constantine and Galerius compromised, and finally agreed that the young man would be hailed Caesar in the West. Since that was Severus' job description, he was duly promoted to western Augustus.

However, this fortuitous turn of events brought no good luck to Severus, who was required about this time to enforce Galerius' new policies in southern Italy. Since this region had become less important with the passage of time, Galerius now intended to tax all of south Italy (including Rome), a region that had been exempt for centuries. He also intended to eliminate Rome's praetorian guard, which had already been reduced to a city garrison, and which he believed was an unnecessary expense.

Not surprisingly, the policy was immensely unpopular, and it was Severus who suffered the consequences. The citizens and soldiers in Rome favored revolt to submission. The praetorian guards spearheaded this movement, for they were slated for extinction. They chose as their leader Maxentius, the son of Maximian, the emperor who had been forced to retire in 305. Maxentius was also unhappy with the tide of events, for he had been passed over for promotion twice and was eager to stake his claim.

On November 28, 306, the rebellion became official, as Maxentius illegally assumed the titles Caesar and Princeps. He controlled Rome and all of southern Italy, and managed to gain the allegiance of Sicily, Sardinia, Corsica and North Africa, and later still, Spain. Over the winter, Maxentius had lured his father out of retirement and asked him to organize the defense of Rome, which had relatively few soldiers.

It seems as though Maxentius and Maximian had assumed the titles of Augustus by February 307, which left Severus with no option but to lead an army from his headquarters in Milan to Rome and crush the revolt. He set out late in February or early in March and arrived at the walls of Rome early in the spring (though some authorities prefer the fall of 307).

Since most of the soldiers under Severus' command had formerly served under Maximian, Severus was at a great disadvantage. There was a mass defection among Severus' soldiers when they heard the old emperor's pleas and were sufficiently tempted by his bribes. Severus was now on the defensive, and his retreat up the Italian peninsula was not swift enough to avoid being forced to take refuge at Ravenna.

In a matter of days Severus had abdicated his throne and surrendered (March or April) on the condition that his life be spared. Severus was escorted back to Rome and Maximian immediately set out for Gaul, where he hoped to make an alliance with Constantine the Great.

Galerius was furious at the turn of events and launched his own invasion of Italy, probably in April. This caused Maxentius to execute Severus sometime during the summer of 307. Not surprisingly, Galerius' soldiers began to defect in large numbers, for they were just as easily enticed by the liberal bribes of Maxentius. Not wishing to meet the same fate as his old friend Severus, Galerius quickly retreated to Illyria, burning everything in his path so as to prevent Maxentius from pursuing him.

MAXIMINUS II DAIA

A.D. 310–313

CAESAR: A.D. 305–309 (UNDER GALERIUS)
FILIUS AUGUSTORUM: A.D. 309–310 (UNDER GALERIUS)
AUGUSTUS: A.D. 310–313 (VARIOUS ARRANGEMENTS)

NEPHEW OF GALERIUS

Gaius Galerius Valerius Maximinus (earlier "Daia"), c. A.D. 270 (or 284?)–313. Maximinus Daia was born in Illyria, probably in 270, though some authorities suggest he was born on November 20, 284, the same day Diocletian was hailed emperor. He was the son of a sister of Galerius, and thus found rapid promotion in the army until he became a member of the Imperial bodyguard.

Pagan historians found little grounds upon which to fault Daia's character, except that he was of rustic origin and upbringing, and was "rather greedy for wine." However, Christian historians saw him as a force of evil equal to his uncle Galerius.

When the two founders of the Tetrarchy, Diocletian and Maximian, abdicated on May 1, 305, the previous two Caesars, Constantius I and Galerius, were promoted to Augusti. Though Galerius technically was the junior of the two new Augusti, he held sway over Diocletian and was able to secure appointments of two Caesars who were loyal to him. These new Caesars were Maximinus Daia, his nephew, and an old comrade-in-arms, Severus II. In one fell swoop, Galerius had effectively gained control of all but the westernmost territories that were governed by Constantius I. Clearly, Galerius aimed to replace Diocletian in every respect.

On the occasion of his appointment, Maximinus Daia was adopted by Galerius. To further cement their ties, Maximinus' own daughter (who may have just been born) was betrothed to his uncle's son, Candidianus. But what began as an ideal relationship soon turned into a bitter disappointment for Maximinus Daia, for he was twice overlooked for promotion by his uncle Galerius.

Maximinus Daia immediately departed for his provinces of Syria and Egypt, and made his headquarters at Antioch. Though extremely important, Syria and Egypt were remote from Europe, which proved to be the main theater of action during the post-abdication period. There, in 306, power was seized in the West by Constantine I and in Italy by Maxentius. Thrown into the mix were Maximian (who joined his son's revolt in Italy, later took refuge with Constantine in Gaul and eventually rebelled on his own account), and Alexander of Carthage, the vicar in the western part of North Africa who revolted against the rebel Maxentius.

Daia suffered his first disappointment late in the summer of 306, when he learned that the Senior Augustus Constantius I had died on campaign in Britain. His death left vacant the position of Junior Augustus (as Galerius thus became Senior Augustus), which Galerius chose to fill with Severus II rather than his nephew. The fact that Severus II was already established in Europe (for in the process his territory did not change) must have entered into the decision, but that did little to soothe Daia's bruised ego. Even so, Daia did move up in rank, for he was now the Senior Caesar, with Constantine I becoming Junior Caesar.

His second disappointment occurred in the spring of 307, when Severus II was captured and subsequently killed by the rebels Maxentius and Maximian. Instead of promoting his nephew from Caesar to the now-vacant post of Junior Augustus, Galerius did nothing at all for about 20 months, at which point he held a conference at Carnuntum on November 11, 308. Only one thing of substance was accomplished there: Galerius appointed another of his comrade-in-arms, Licinius I, to the post vacated by Severus II.

Maximinus Daia was understandably upset. Not only had the office remained vacant for nearly two years, but when his uncle did fill it, he chose one of his friends — a man who had never even held the office of Caesar. Maximinus Daia had probably just assumed the promotion would be his and that someone new would be appointed Caesar in his place. When Galerius gave the position to Licinius, it must have come as a far greater shock to Daia than when he was overlooked earlier on account of Severus II.

Galerius' actions proved to be foolhardy for disappointment was not limited to his nephew, but spread to the legions he commanded. The Empire was in a state of chaos, and the last thing Galerius could risk was a rebellion in Syria or Egypt. Thus, later in 309, he raised both Maximinus Daia and Constantine I from Caesar to *Filius Augustorum* ("son of the Augusti"), a "promotion" that both young men realized was meaningless. By mid-310, the soldiers of Maximinus Daia hailed him Augustus; they had grown tired of waiting for Galerius (who was now terribly ill) to do this voluntarily. Upon being informed of this development, Galerius conferred the rank of Augustus on his nephew on May 1, 310, and reluctantly did the same for Constantine, who demanded equal billing.

When Galerius finally succumbed to his terminal disease in May, 311, his territories were seemingly bequeathed to Licinius, but effectively were up for grabs. The two Augusti in a position to seize them were Licinius I and Maximinus Daia, both of whom aggressively staked their claims. Licinius was only able to claim Thrace, for Maximinus Daia had reacted more quickly, and was able to claim all of Asia. The two men encountered each other at the Propontis and narrowly averted battle by negotiation.

Maximinus Daia wintered in Nicomedia and abolished the edict of religious toleration (Edict of Serdica) that Galerius had put into effect less than a week before he died. With great personal conviction, Maximinus Daia stepped up his anti-Christian activities in the east, determined to destroy Christianity and to establish a pagan church with the organizational efficiency which the Christians had created. To support his goals, Daia falsified petitions from cities and forged documents, such as the Acts (or Memoirs) of Pilate.

The Roman world was once again in a state of chaos, as four hostile Augusti ruled over a divided Empire. Maximinus Daia was seemingly in a position of strength, occupying all of the wealthy East and possessing a large, loyal army. Since all four Augusti were concerned about potential aggressions by their neighbors, pacts were made early in 312. The first to unite were Constantine I and Licinius I, which caused Maximinus Daia and Maxentius to follow suit. In the aftermath, Daia declared war on Constantine.

Before Galerius died, he not only bequeathed his territories to his old friend Licinius I, but also requested that he care for his wife, Galeria Valeria, and his son, Candidianus. Licinius may have been willing in this respect, but Valeria was not, and so she fled to the court of her nephew, Maximinus Daia. But there Valeria found trouble, for Daia (who, we are told by Christian writers, had always fancied his aunt), insisted on marrying her. When she refused, Daia treated her poorly, confiscating her estates and banishing her to Syria. Not even the protestations of Valeria's father, Diocletian, prevented the outrage.

In the end, the alliance between Constantine I and Licinius I proved the stronger of the two, for it is they who survived the civil war that followed. Late in 312, Constantine invaded Italy and defeated Maxentius at the Battle of the Milvian Bridge. This victory brought all of the Western

Empire under his command. Now only three Augusti remained, with Constantine having been named Senior Augustus by the senate. Maximinus Daia had little choice but to recognize Constantine's leading role, revoke his declaration of war and reluctantly to obey his demand that Christian persecutions in the East must end.

Daia ceded so much to Constantine out of necessity, for in that same year, 312, much of his own territory suffered from a poor harvest, and thus famine. This caused widespread civil unrest and increased brigandage and piracy, especially in Armenia, where there was violent opposition to Maximinus Daia's insistence on the worship of the pagan gods.

Daia's problems were not limited to his own realm, however, as his co-Augusti met for a conference in Milan in the beginning of 313. Determined to oppose any stronger alliance between Constantine and Licinius than already existed, Maximinus Daia led his army on a long march from Syria to Thrace. With the cruelty of a taskmaster, he drove his armies at great speed across Asia Minor during the height of winter. What had so alarmed Maximinus Daia was the planned marriage of Constantine's half-sister, Constantia, to Licinius I. Furthermore, the two European Augusti shared support of the edict of religious toleration known as the Edict of Milan. Though the marriage occurred on schedule in February, the conference was interrupted by Daia's surprise invasion of Thrace, the easternmost territory belonging to Licinius I. Daia crossed the Hellespont late in March and laid siege to Byzantium (which he may or may not have captured), after which he seems to have captured Heraclea.

Constantine returned to his capital of Trier as Licinius sped east to confront Maximinus Daia. This could hardly have been better news for Constantine, who, bent on sole domination of the Empire, figured this conflict would eliminate one of his two rivals. The numerical advantage was with Maximinus Daia, whose 70,000 soldiers more than doubled the 30,000 men Licinius could muster to oppose him. However, Daia's soldiers were exhausted and were frustrated by their forced march from Syria.

The opposing armies met late in April in south-eastern Thrace, and the demoralized armies of Maximinus Daia were easily defeated by Licinius, who proved himself the more capable general. Historians disagree not only on the date, but also on the location of this watershed battle. It most likely occurred on April 30, 313, at Tzirallum (near Heraclea). Alternatively, it may have taken place on May 1 at Tzirallum, or nearby Byzantium, or even further inland at Adrianople.

Though later history shows that Licinius was no convert to Christianity, at this stage in time he was a supporter of the religion based on his new alliance with Constantine. Thus, the battle was not merely one of East against West, but one of Christianity against paganism. Just as had occurred with Constantine's Christian armies against Maxentius' pagan armies a few months earlier in Italy, Licinius' outnumbered "Christian" armies were victorious.

During the course of the battle, Maximinus Daia escaped and, dressed as a slave, fled toward the Propontis and the city of Nicomedia, after which he headed due south to Cilicia. He survived some three to six months thereafter, eventually being discovered and besieged, sometime between July and September, in Tarsus, where he either died of natural causes or committed suicide.

His death was probably a quick and practical affair, albeit Christian writers of the day described it in the most horrific of terms. He is said to have become blind and reduced to a virtual skeleton, and to have taken a poison which, unbeknownst to him, required four excruciating days to prove fatal. Of the poison's effects we are told: ". . . amid groans which he uttered as if he were being burnt, he breathed out his guilty spirit in a death of detestable horror." All of this is certainly fiction, for it bears too convenient a parallel to the excruciating death of his uncle Galerius, who was his equal in Christian persecutions.

NUMISMATIC NOTE: Coinage for Maximinus Daia was struck in all three phases of his reign, as Caesar, as *Filius Augustorum* and as Augustus. His issues as Caesar and as *Filius Augustorum* largely follow the pattern established by his uncle Galerius, with coins of the latter category not only being quite rare, but limited to nummi of Siscia and Thessalonica. His issues as Augustus — although not as interesting as those of Maxentius or Constantine — did include noteworthy types. As a Jovian (the "house" founded by Diocletian), he frequently depicted Jupiter. As a devout eastern pagan, he favored the sun-god Sol, showing him in a facing quadriga on billon argentei, and on his reduced nummi standing, holding either a globe or the head of the Greco-Egyptian god Serapis.

MAXENTIUS A.D. 307–312

PRINCEPS AND CAESAR: A.D. 306–307
AUGUSTUS: A.D. 307–308 (WITH MAXIMIAN AND CONSTANTINE I)
A.D. 308–312 (SOLE REIGN)

SON OF MAXIMIAN AND EUTROPIA
BROTHER OF FAUSTA
HUSBAND OF VALERIA MAXIMILLA
FATHER OF ROMULUS
SON-IN-LAW OF GALERIUS AND GALERIA VALERIA
BROTHER-IN-LAW OF CONSTANTINE THE GREAT
STEP-BROTHER-IN-LAW OF CONSTANTIUS I
STEP-BROTHER OF THEODORA
UNCLE OF CONSTANTINE II, CONSTANTIUS II AND CONSTANS

Marcus Aurelius Valerius Maxentius, c. A.D. 279 or 283–312. Maxentius was probably born in Syria in about 283, seemingly while his father was participating in the Persian campaign under Carus and Numerian. Alternatively, he could have been born four years earlier, in 279. He had a wife, Valeria Maximilla, who bore him two sons, the name of only one of whom, Romulus, is known.

In genealogical terms, he was better qualified for promotion than anyone else in the Empire, for he was the only son of Maximian (who had abdicated with Diocletian) and was the son-in-law of Galerius (who had just been promoted to Augustus in Diocletian's place). Despite these relations, Maxentius had not been given any serious responsibilities, such as military commands or consulships.

When Diocletian and Maximian retired in 305, and two new Caesars were added to the Tetrarchy, it must have come as a shock to Maxentius that he was passed up for promotion. This occurred again in August of 306, when the western Augustus, Constantius I, died. Instead of pushing hard to have his son-in-law promoted, Galerius acquiesced to the demands of young Constantine I by hailing him Caesar.

Fewer than a hundred days later, the new emperor Severus II announced that South Italy and the city of Rome would be subjected to certain taxes to which they had been immune since time immemorial. Furthermore, he announced that the praetorian guard in Rome (which by then was little more than a city garrison) was to be eliminated altogether. To the citizens this was an outrage and to the guards it spelled doom, so a rebellion was formed. As their leader the Romans chose Maxentius, who was then living on the outskirts of Rome.

It was a desperate move, for Rome had only a small civic army in the praetorian guards, whereas Severus II had a large force stationed at Milan, in the north of Italy. But at least one important aspect was considered before the revolt began: the compliance of North Africa was assured. This meant the Romans and South Italians would have an abundance of grain during their struggle. Furthermore, Sicily had also joined their revolt, providing a much smaller but important source of food.

On October 28, 306, Maxentius assumed the titles of Caesar and Princeps. At this stage he was proceeding cautiously and respectfully, hoping that his father-in-law would formally recognize not only the plight of the Romans, but also his desire to be included in the Imperial power structure. But Maxentius did not get the response for which he had hoped; instead, Galerius had his junior colleague, Severus II, prepare for war.

Maxentius did likewise over the winter of 306/7 by luring his father, Maximian, out of his unwanted retirement in Southern Italy. Initially, his inclusion in the revolt was perhaps the only thing that saved it from instant failure. Maximian hurriedly organized the army and the city's defense, and marshaled the funds necessary to wage war. Though the circumstances were hardly ideal, he was eager to emerge from a dull, forced retirement.

By February of 307 (though some authorities suggest April), Maxentius and Maximian had assumed the titles of Augustus, and braced themselves for invasion by Severus II, whom the rebels had deprived of the vast majority of the territory allotted to him. The only areas still under Severus' authority were Northern Italy and Pannonia; he intended to recover Southern Italy, Sicily, Corsica, Sardinia and the diocese of Africa.

Late in February or early in March, Severus II led his army the 300 miles from Milan to Rome, where he confronted the rebels. But even before he reached the walls of Rome (which had been built by Aurelian and Probus some three decades ago), his campaign was faltering. Maximian undermined the loyalty of Severus' soldiers by offering generous bribes and by appealing to their former loyalties, since they had previously been under his command.

One of the first to take up the cause of the rebels was Severus' own praetorian prefect, Anullinus, who publicized the bribes in Severus' camp. The combination of sentimentality and gold proved too powerful, and most of Severus' army defected to the cause of the rebels in Rome. Severus was now on the defensive, and he decided to withdraw before his losses increased.

But events were happening too rapidly. Maximian struck while the circumstances weighed in his favor. He immediately pursued Severus up the Italian peninsula, nearly overtaking him before he obtained refuge within the walls of Ravenna, some 180 miles north of Rome. Within a matter of days Severus was compelled to abdicate his throne and surrender in exchange for his life.

Maximian and his son had won the first contest, but they knew the stakes would now be raised, so Severus II was delivered back to Rome (in the summer of 307) while Maximian headed to Gaul, where he hoped to make a pact with Constantine I, the Caesar in the West. In the meantime, Galerius — now the only man in the Empire to legitimately hold the title Augustus — prepared to exact his revenge. By April 1, 307, the rebels no longer were recognizing his authority.

When Galerius invaded, Severus II was either executed or forced to commit suicide. Galerius' attempt to unseat Maxentius was no more successful than his predecessor's, and he soon retreated before his own entire army defected. Recalling the fate of Severus, Galerius burned the land as he traveled so that any pursuit would be hindered. He managed to leave Italy and take up a defensive position in Illyria.

Meanwhile, Maximian had been successful in Gaul, for he had made a defensive pact with Constantine, which was sealed by the marriage of his own daughter Fausta and Constantine. No longer content with the title of Caesar, by July 25, 307, Constantine felt confident enough to assume unlawfully the title of Augustus. Maximian supported the self-promotion, as both he and his son Maxentius had taken that same step about six months earlier.

This arrangement among the Augusti surely was no more than a fair-weather pact. Not only did Constantine resist Maximian's request that he cut off Galerius' departure from Italy, but later in 307, it would seem, Spain pledged its allegiance to Maxentius. Constantine could hardly view this as anything other than a betrayal, since it probably was instigated by agents of Maxentius. Thereafter, the pact between Constantine and Maxentius rapidly deteriorated. Maximian returned to Rome later in that year to join his son, who, despite his relative youth and inexperience, was considered the senior of the two Italian Augusti.

The first ten months of 308 were relatively uneventful in the East, but much happened in the West, where fortune abandoned the Italian rebels. The basis of their failure was their inability to share authority. At a meeting of military officers in Rome, probably on April 20, Maximian attempted to overthrow his son but failed to gain support, and fled to Gaul, where he sought asylum with his new son-in-law, Constantine.

This shift was to have a devastating effect on Maxentius' regime. Later in the year (though possibly in 309) his father, with the support of Constantine, convinced Lucius Domitius Alexander, the vicar of the diocese of Africa, to abandon Maxentius. Not only had Alexander probably been appointed to his post by Maximian, when he was a legitimate emperor, but Maximian was considered something of a hero in the region, where a decade before he had led the campaign that quelled the revolt of the Quinquegentiani.

Maximian knew only too well that without grain from this fertile region, Rome would soon be in the grips of famine, and that his son's regime would be endangered. Perhaps then he would consider sharing power with his father. Maxentius seems to have been at a loss for what to do; he did not retaliate against Alexander, Maximian or Constantine for at least one year.

With so many contenders for authority, Galerius was equally concerned about the future, and later in 308, on November 11, he hosted a conference at Carnuntum, a legionary camp and city on the Danube in Upper Pannonia. At the conference, nothing was truly resolved. Diocletian refused to emerge from retirement, Maximian was formally stripped of all titles, Maxentius was declared a public enemy and Constantine I was confirmed as Caesar in the West, but the only actual change was the appointment of Licinius I, a comrade-in-arms of Galerius, to replace the recently slain Severus II.

But this insubstantial change was to have a negative consequence: it enraged Galerius' nephew, Maximinus Daia, who inexplicably had been "leap-frogged" and remained at the rank of Caesar. Galerius would pay for this in the near future, as both Maximinus Daia and Constantine demanded greater titles. In 309 he officially raised both of them from Caesar to the meaningless rank of *Filius Augustorum* ("son of the Augusti"), and in 310 to the rank of Augusti.

The year 309 was remarkably bad for Maxentius. On the personal level, he was still stinging from his father's attempt to overthrow him, his sister was residing in Gaul with his enemy Constantine and the vicar Alexander had betrayed his trust. To this, he could add the tragic death of his young son Romulus, who in 309 had been made consul for the second time. Maxentius honored his son with consecration, temples and a coinage. In terms of his domain, it was also a difficult year for Maxentius. Not only had he lost the diocese of Africa in the previous year, but in the present year he seems to have lost Spain (which was reclaimed by Constantine I). To make matters worse, much of Northern Italy was lost to Licinius I, the new Augustus whom Galerius had stationed in Pannonia.

Amid this dissension, the Romans were rioting, for they were suffering from a great famine without the African grain. Maxentius was wise enough to feed his praetorian guards and soldiers well, and used them to crush the riots without mercy. We are told some 6,000 citizens died as a result. Ancient historians also inform us that Maxentius' harsh financial exactions and tireless pursuit of other men's wives also caused dissent.

Maxentius realized that without the grain it was simply a matter of time before his regime toppled. Thus, by the end of 309 (or equally likely, early in 310), he sent his praetorian prefect, Rufius Volusianus, on an expedition to Carthage. The campaign was incredibly destructive and effective. The rebellious vicar Alexander was forced to hang himself (probably late in the summer or in the fall of 310) and the diocese of Africa was restored to Maxentius.

Constantine remained silent throughout the whole affair. He had purposely distanced himself from Italian affairs, hoping that Maxentius would be overthrown in the natural course of events. Back in 307 Constantine had not cut off Galerius' retreat from Italy, and now, in 310/11, he did not come to the aid of Carthage, even though he was an ally and he stood to suffer if Maxentius recovered that important diocese.

Maximian was in the most difficult position of all, for he had grown tired of simply being an adviser to Constantine, without a title and without serious responsibilities. Constantine, who was busy fighting the Franks on the Rhine, did not want Maximian to interfere, so he insisted that Maximian remain in Arles, far from harm's way.

In a move that must have surprised everyone, Maximian staged a revolt of his own, seemingly in the spring of 310. He seized the Imperial treasury at Arles, hailed himself Augustus and fled south to Massalia. However, Constantine was in very close pursuit. His father-in-law's plan had been betrayed by his daughter, Fausta (Constantine's wife). Maximian was captured within weeks of his betrayal and was either forced to commit suicide or was executed. The reason for his ill-fated revolt is open to speculation. One strong possibility is that he intended to sail for Carthage and help Alexander resist the invasion of Maxentius' prefect.

Thus in 310 the horizons were brightening considerably for Maxentius: Rome was no longer in famine and, for better or for worse, his father was out of the picture. Maxentius immediately had the senate consecrate his father, perhaps out of familial devotion but certainly for the political advantage it offered in celebrating the memory of a man who had been killed by Constantine.

While all these major developments were occurring in the western portion of the Empire, trouble was quietly brewing in the East. Galerius, the senior Augustus, was critically ill and died early in May 311 of a disease that had been plaguing him for a year. A mad scramble ensued, as his territories were consumed by Licinius I and Maximinus Daia — the former gaining Thrace and the latter the remainder of Asia Minor. War was averted through negotiation when the rivals met at the crossroads of Europe and Asia.

The Roman world was now divided into four geographic regions, each ruled by a hostile Augustus. Constantine had the western provinces, Maxentius occupied Italy and Africa, Licinius had all of the Balkans, Pannonia and Illyria, and Maximinus Daia controlled all of Asia and Egypt. With all four men feeling threatened by their neighbors, two alliances resulted: Licinius I joined Constantine I and Maxentius joined Maximinus Daia.

With civil war inevitable, and after six years of residency in Gaul (principally fighting on the Rhine), Constantine led an army of approximately 40,000 men to the north of Italy, where he invaded the territories of Maxentius. All the while, he kept an uneasy eye on Illyria, where his new ally Licinius I commanded a large army. This was a risky venture for the traditionally cautious Constantine, for we are told that he was outnumbered greatly by Maxentius, who had 150,000 or more men stationed in northern Italy.

But numerical superiority did not prevent Constantine from invading, nor did it prevent him from succeeding, for Maxentius' legions were undisciplined. Constantine captured Segusio, Turin, Milan and Verona, near which Maxentius' prefect, Rufius Volusianus, perished. After capturing Brescia and Aquileia, Constantine had secured the north; in the meantime, his partisans were hard at work undermining Maxentius' sagging popularity in Rome.

As Constantine's armies camped outside Rome on the eve of the pitched battle that would take place at the Milvian Bridge, Constantine (who thus far had been under the exclusive protection of Sol-Apollo) is alleged to have had a vision and a dream that caused him to convert to Christianity. He instructed his men to paint a cross or a Christogram (a monogram of Christ's name) on their shields, and to go into battle in the morning under the protection of the Christian god.

That next morning, October 28, 312, precisely six years after he had illegally assumed power there, Maxentius led his army outside Rome to engage Constantine. Maxentius dared not risk a prolonged siege, for he was already unpopular in the city and the likelihood of a palace coup increased with each passing day. The armies met in a skirmish on the Via Flaminia, after which Maxentius forced a pitched battle at the Milvian Bridge. In the course of the fight, Maxentius' army was thrown into retreat and the bridge of boats over which the men were retreating collapsed. Maxentius drowned along with thousands of his men in the waters of the Tiber.

Constantine was victorious, and assuming he could trust Licinius not to attack, he had become master of the entire Western Empire. The citizens of Rome received him well and the senate declared him the Senior Augustus in the Empire (*titulus primi ordinis*). Much to the joy of the citizens, he disbanded the praetorian guard. Maxentius' body was fished out of the Tiber, his head severed and placed on a pike and, after sufficient display in Rome, was sent to Carthage as proof of his demise.

NUMISMATIC NOTE: Perhaps the most impressive coinage of the Tetrarchic period was produced by Maxentius at five cities in Italy and at Carthage. Though his silver coins are extremely rare, he struck many types of gold aurei and medallions and a large quantity of æs coinage. His nummi are especially diverse in their designs (both obverse and reverse), and they are supplemented with regular issues of fractional pieces. In these two respects, his æs issues are quite unlike other coinages of the period.

The overriding theme on Maxentius' coinage is patriotism. He went to great lengths to show that he was the only leader who would champion Rome's old privileges and customs. One of his most telling types bears the inscription CONSERVATOR VRBIS SVAE, meaning "protector of his city." Maxentius' desire to show family links (which he believed entitled him to hold power legitimately) resulted in his striking honorary coinages for his father Maximian and for his in-laws, Constantius I and Galerius.

His gold is unusually impressive, for it includes a series of medallions typically of 2-, 4- and 8-aurei weight. Most examples of these medallions are from a single cache (known as the "Parthenico Hoard") reportedly recovered from a Mediterranean shipwreck. His gold medallions were almost certainly struck to pay army officers, including those who had defected from the defeated armies of Severus II and Galerius.

In terms of his regular gold, the most significant issues are aurei from Ostia which depict on their obverses the emperor's full-facing head. This form of portraiture was later used by Licinius and Constantine, but was abandoned until it was reintroduced on a large scale by Constantius II (337–361) in a militant form commonly known as three-quarter facing. By the 5th Century this style of bust (depicting the emperor wearing a helmet and armor, and holding a shield and spear) assumed popularity once again, and subsequently was the standard design for gold solidi in the Byzantine Empire.

ROMULUS

Son of Maxentius
Grandson of Maximian and Galerius
Nephew of Fausta

Marcus Valerius (*or* Marcus Aurelius) Romulus, c. A.D. 294 (or 306)–309. Named after the legendary eponymous founder and first king of Rome, Romulus was one of two sons born to the rebel Maxentius and his wife Maximilla (the daughter of Galerius, who does not appear on coinage). The name of his brother is not known. Romulus held the unusual distinction of being the grandson of two emperors.

Romulus never held the rank of Caesar, but was appointed consul in 308 and in 309. His extreme youth rendered the appointments purely ceremonial. In the year of his second consulship Romulus died, dashing Maxentius' hope of having an heir to the Empire he was attempting to build. The boy was consecrated and was honored with buildings and an impressive coinage. Estimates of the boy's age vary considerably: some historians suggest he was about 15 years old, and others only about 3 years old.

The death of Romulus was a severe blow to Maxentius, just when the last thing he needed was more bad news. In 309, Rome was in the grips of a famine, with shipments from Carthage withheld by the rebellious vicar Alexander. The starving population frequently rioted, and Maxentius' efforts to suppress them resulted in the deaths of 6,000 citizens. Making the famine even worse was the fact that Alexander had been coaxed to rebellion by Maxentius' own father, Maximian, who had failed in an attempt to overthrow him in the previous year. With his father in exile, his son dead, and his sister married to Constantine I, Maxentius had only his wife left as a close family member.

NUMISMATIC NOTE: All of Romulus' coins were struck at Rome or Ostia by his father after the boy died. Maxentius introduced some of the more interesting inscriptions to ever appear on Roman coins, and those he struck for his deified son are no exception. The NV represents *Nobilissimus Vir* ("most noble man") and BIS CONS indicates that he was twice consul.

The standard reverse type for Romulus' coins is architectural, with two structures of similar form being represented. Both are circular, have a domed roof surmounted by an eagle and have two ornamented doors, one of which is shown ajar. The fact that the building is sometimes shown with an unadorned brick exterior, and other times with four or six columns adorning the facade, indicates they are meant to represent two different structures (see Hill, *The Monuments of Ancient Rome as Coin Types*, pp. 13–15).

The unadorned building is considered to be the Sepulchre of Divus Romulus, originally located on the Appian Way but since destroyed, and the one bearing four or six Corinthian columns represents the Temple of Divus Romulus. Maxentius began to construct the latter building in honor of his son and in the name of Romulus, the legendary founder of Rome, but he died before it was completed. Constantine the Great completed its construction, and most of the original structure is still intact and can be seen in the Forum.

ALEXANDER OF CARTHAGE
A.D. 308–310

Lucius Domitius Alexander (Valerius Alexander), d. A.D. 310. Sources differ on the origin of Alexander, but he seems to have come from peasant stock either in Phrygia or Pannonia. The chronology of his rebellion is also debatable, with some scholars preferring c. 308–309, and others 308–310 or 308–311. Although elderly and timid, Alexander had served as governor of the diocese of Africa since 303, no doubt as an appointee of the western Augustus, Maximian.

When Maxentius revolted against Galerius and Severus II late in 306, an important part of his "Empire" was the province of Africa, whose vicar Alexander had sworn allegiance to Maxentius' cause. However, by the summer or fall of 308 (most likely in June or July), Alexander had declared himself Augustus at the encouragement of Constantine I and Maximian.

Constantine had established his rule in Gaul as a self-proclaimed Augustus and an officially recognized Caesar. At his side was his father-in-law, Maximian, who had been stripped of all titles and had sought asylum with Constantine after he failed to overthrow his son, Maxentius, in April of 308. By this point in time, both Constantine and Maximian considered Maxentius an enemy, not only because of his treatment of Maximian, but also because in 307 he had seized Spain, a region which Constantine regarded as being within his own realm. Thus it comes as no surprise that Constantine and Maximian encouraged Alexander to revolt against Maxentius.

Alexander and the citizens of North Africa were quite willing to support the designs of Maximian. A decade earlier he (as a legitimate emperor) had freed that region from the scourge of piratic raids made by Numidian outlaws and the members of a Berber confederation known as the Quinquegentiani.

While there from c. 296/7 to 297/8, Maximian had established a mint in Carthage, strengthened frontier defenses from Mauretiania to Libya, and had held a Triumph in Carthage either late in 297 or in the spring of 298. More recently, the anti-Christian elements thought highly of Maximian for his enforcement of Diocletian's Edict of 303, which was upheld with particular severity in North Africa.

Because he was based in Carthage, Alexander controlled one of the three sources of grain most important to Europe and to Rome. Since Maxentius could not feed his people with grain from Egypt (then securely in the hands of Maximinus Daia, the nephew of the emperor Galerius), the harvests from western North Africa were essential to his survival. Without grain from Carthage, it was only a matter of time before the Romans overthrew Maxentius. Indeed, Rome's citizens succumbed to near-starvation in 309, resulting in terrible riots that Maxentius had to crush without mercy, causing the deaths of some 6,000 citizens. Either late in 309 or early in 310, Maxentius sent his praetorian prefect, Rufius Volusianus, on an expedition to recover North Africa and to overthrow Alexander. The operation was a great success, and after a reign of perhaps 18 months, Alexander was strangled to death, seemingly late in the summer or in the fall of 310. Some scholars, citing Zosimus' *Nea Historia* (penned c. 500), suggest Alexander remained in power until 311, but this idea has been abandoned by most scholars.

The expedition had severe consequences for the people of North Africa because Constantine the Great and Maximian (the two men who had prompted Alexander to revolt) did not come to come to their defense. The campaign was so destructive that Constantine later devoted many years to rehabilitating the region.

At this point an interesting, but purely speculative possibility arises. If Volusianus' expedition against Carthage was launched early in 310 (as many historians believe), Maximian may have revolted against Constantine with the intention of aiding Alexander (and, in the process, establishing his own regime at Carthage). After all, Maximian headed directly for Massalia after he seized the treasury at Arles, and this port city was an ideal staging point for such an expedition. We cannot be certain, however, that that was his purpose for taking refuge there. He was being pursued by Constantine and may have entered that city for lack of any better options.

NUMISMATIC NOTE: Alexander issued aurei and nummi from the mint at Carthage, which Maximian had established in 296 or 297. Not surprisingly, the reverse types of his coinage largely celebrate the city of Carthage and his province of Africa, and allude to his desire for recognition from the legitimate authorities of the Empire. His coins are among the noted rarities in the Imperial series, and excellent forgeries of his æs (of the type commonly called 'The Geneva Forgeries') exist. Many of the known examples are illustrated and described by R. A. G. Carson in the 1958 *Numismatic Chronicle*, pp. 47–58, pls. V–VI. The article was also published in 1977 as an offprint.

CHAPTER ELEVEN

The Constantinian Era
c. A.D. 313–364

Named after Constantine the Great, this era was the most important in late Roman history. During the half century from 313 to 363, the foundations of the post-pagan world were laid by Constantine and his descendants. Within the Imperial government, Christianity found its first and greatest supporter in Constantine, who transformed a once-persecuted, fringe religion into the crown jewel of Western civilization.

More so than at any other point in Roman history, here western civilization took a turn from its past. For that reason, the Constantinian Era represents a watershed moment in the world of Late Antiquity. In this 50-year period, a new civilization was born as pagan Rome forfeited its storied past to the post-Classical world. So monumental a change, however, was not immediate, and in some respects is barely recognizable without careful study.

Though there were many causes for discord within the Empire, three emerge as the principal sources of strife in the Constantinian Era. First, the ruling family founded by Constantius I (Caesar, 293–305; Augustus, 305–306) was divided into two rival branches formed by the offspring of two different women — Fausta and Theodora, the former branch being in power and the latter being persecuted. Second, the long-standing rivalry between East and West was given focus by the fact that there were now two capitals, Rome and Constantinople. Third, the Christian faith came to be divided principally along the lines of Arianism (strongly supported in the East) and Orthodox Catholicism (promoted mainly in the West).

The history of this era is intricate, tedious and in many ways unfulfilling to the student more in tune with the old ways of paganism. No longer are horrific acts motivated purely by the age-old faults in human nature, but instead are often tied to religion. Initially this war was waged between paganism and Christianity, but soon thereafter it came to be fought by the various factions of Christianity. Energetic theologians and bishops offered differing interpretations of the religion they shared in common, causing the fragmentation of church and society.

The religious life of pagan Rome was far from passionate. Satisfaction was derived from ritual and tradition rather than from the spirituality of blind faith. Christianity inspired passionate debate — this is the aspect of the Constantinian Era that is often difficult to appreciate. Few in the modern western world can imagine going to war over the schism between Orthodoxy and Arianism, but the fact remains that this was sufficient cause for war, or at the very least, civil strife.

The fact that Constantine founded a city to defend his Christian state was of paramount importance to the history of the western world. Constantinople was built on the site of the Greek colony Byzantium, and its location (on the European shore of the narrows that divided Europe from Asia) was hand-picked for its strategic importance. We learn something of Constantine's reformist nature in his decision not to further develop Diocletian's capital of Nicomedia (slightly more than 50 miles away on the Asiatic shore), nor to stay in his earlier Thracian capitals of Sirmium and Serdica (which he had called "my Rome").

In two very important respects Byzantium was hardly an ideal site for a city: it was deficient in drinking water and was prone to attack from its hinterland. But Constantine and his successors overcame these disadvantages by building defensive walls (first by Constantine, and subsequently by Anthemius, the prefect of Theodosius II) and aqueducts.

Overall, Constantinople's advantages far outweighed its disadvantages. Constantine became impressed with the strategic importance of the "golden horn" when in this vicinity he defeated his rival Licinius I in September, 324. Its location and magnificent harbor gave it ready access to grain shipments from Egypt and the Cimmerian Bosporus. It was also an ideal staging point for naval expeditions, or for land armies destined for the Danube or the Euphrates.

Seemingly from about 326, when it was inaugurated, Constantinople was styled as the "New Rome," or *altera Roma* ("second Rome"). Eventually, like Rome, it was divided into 14 regions (though with limited space one was located outside its wall and another on the Asian side of the strait). That Constantine named the city in his own honor ("city of Constantine") comes as no surprise, for much like Romulus, the legendary eponymous founder of Rome, Constantine believed he was founding a capital for a new Empire of his own design.

Like Constantine's other visionary projects, however, the importance of Constantinople was not immediately felt. It has been estimated that a dozen years after construction had begun, no more than about 50,000 people lived there (and even they were lured in by incentives, such as free grain distributions). But within a few generations the city of Constantine changed the world. It was formally dedicated in 330, and from the name of the Greek city upon which it had been built the term Byzantine was derived 14 centuries later to refer to the new cultural milieu.

Despite the potency of his vision, and the success of his many plans, Constantine was no model man. He was suspicious, envious, murderous, hypocritical, treacherous and a war-monger. His crimes against humanity were manifold, and his actions rarely fell into a category that would be embraced by the Christian faith he so staunchly defended.

His transgressions were often of the most sinister kind — such as his hasty decisions to execute his wife and eldest son on charges he later came to doubt. Constantine was a typical Roman emperor: cruel out of necessity. For this reason many historians believe he did not morally convert to Christianity until he was on his deathbed, for he knew better than any other that as long as he reigned, he would have to be ready and willing to commit mortal sins.

It is justifiable to say that most of the Constantine's successes — with the notable exception of embracing Christianity — were built upon the achievements of Diocletian. Like that of the Tetrarchy, the Constantinian government was based on a rigid framework by which political and military stability could be achieved, no matter how bad the infighting or how serious the threat of invasion. The Empire weathered a great many problems, including the shameful fratricidal wars propagated by Constantine's sons.

The foundation of the Constantinian Era may, with good reason, be assigned to the year 313. In this year two men — Constantine the Great and Licinius I — emerged victorious from the collapse of the Tetrarchy. At first neither man was strong enough to dislodge the other, so they were forced to share the Empire. The fact that they were in-laws had no bearing on their desire to rid themselves of one another. The Empire was divided politically, religiously and geographically: Christian Constantine in the West, and pagan Licinius in the East. The break was too severe, and the rival emperors fought two costly civil wars between 313 and 324 in which Constantine overcame Licinius and emerged as sole ruler of a Roman Empire that had not been united for 40 years. Such civil wars were costly, not only in terms of life and currency, but also in less tangible ways.

Threats to Imperial security, however, were not strictly internal. The most formidable opponents of the Romans were located on the far sides of the Rhine, the Danube and on the eastern frontier. On the Rhine, the Romans were in constant warfare with the Germanic federation known as the Alemanni; on the Danube they fought back invasions by the Quadi and the Goths; and on their eastern frontier, they frequently came into conflict with the Sasanians. In subsequent years, after the Empire was formally divided, a host of new nomadic and semi-nomadic enemies, such as Huns, Vandals and Suevi arrived on the borders.

Not surprisingly, the Roman army grew alarmingly during this era, by some estimates reaching 75 legions under Constantine (a slight increase over Diocletian's 67 or more legions). Tiberius had had only 25 legions, Trajan conquered vast territories with 30 and Caracalla had only 33.

Though many of Constantine's field army legions only contained 1,000 men, and others were below the traditional strength of about 5,400 men, it becomes clear how severe a burden the military had become during Constantine's age.

Furthermore, Constantine's legions were aided by field armies, Palatine and non-Palatine auxiliaries, light and heavy cavalry, the personal guardians of the emperor (numbering perhaps 15,000 alone) and the mercenaries among the *foederati* — the immediate neighbors of the Romans who contracted to help protect the Empire's borders. All told, Constantine may have employed and outfitted about 900,000 soldiers during peak periods — a force considerably larger than the typical level of 300,000 to 550,000 maintained from the time of the Julio-Claudians to the fall of the West.

Beyond the costs of maintaining a large army, Constantine also had to pay for a formidable Imperial bureaucracy, yet another institution he had adopted directly from Diocletian. Revenue was critical and the collection of the taxes necessary to support these costly institutions was efficient and relentless. Penalties for illegal activities were far more severe during the Late Roman period than in previous ages. Indeed, life was regimented and costly, but the reward was a greater level of security from brigands and barbarians.

In adopting Christianity, Constantine initially saw political advantage in his struggle to defeat his opponents in the Tetrarchy. Later it became a more consuming passion as Constantine saw it as a tool for unifying and controlling his subjects. However, his desire to use Christianity as a rallying point, through which his subjects would become loyal citizens and taxpayers, failed.

The fragmentation of the Christian church was the greatest threat to Constantine's carefully laid plans, and he devoted an enormous amount of his energy trying to rectify ideological differences. The most important of the early Christian heretics was Arius, the Presbyter of Alexandria. His teachings were condemned by Constantine at the Council of Nicaea in 325, but then rehabilitated in about 335, due in large part to lobbying by the moderate theologian Eusebius of Nicomedia (the bishop by whom Constantine was later baptized).

Arius' rehabilitation only worsened matters in the long term, for the Empire came to be sharply divided between Orthordoxy and Arianism during the reigns of Constantine's sons and beyond. Especially recalcitrant was Bishop Athanasius of Alexandria, whose political wrangling nearly caused a civil war in 346 between his Orthodox Catholic supporter Constans, in the West, and his heretic Arian opponent Constantius II, in the East. The pre-existing rivalry between East and West was only intensified by divisions within the Christian Church. By the time Constantius II came to power, most westerners had become Orthodox Catholics, and most easterners had come to support the teachings of the heretic Arian.

The main rift was as follows: the Alexandrian priest Arius (c. 250–336) preached the separateness of God and Christ, whereas Orthodox Catholics (led by the Bishop Athanasius) believed that Christ was part of God, only lesser. To Arians, Christ was a separate being who served as God's representative in the physical universe. This view allowed Christianity to be truly monotheistic, unlike the polytheism of Graeco-Roman paganism.

Though Constantine was successful in defeating his opponents on the battlefield and in administering his Empire, he failed to secure a peace beyond his own lifetime. Historians have long been vexed by his decision to divide the Empire he had fought so hard to unite. In 335 he named five heirs to his throne — three being his own sons by Fausta, and two others being half-nephews from the branch of the family descended from his stepmother, Theodora.

It is impossible to believe that a deeply suspicious and warlike man such as Constantine could have thought this arrangement would work. In a sense, it was a return to Diocletian's Tetrarchy: the three sons and one half-nephew, Delmatius, were given the titles Caesar and responsibilities for territories that did not overlap. However, it also was quite different: there was no clear-cut order of seniority such as had been arranged by Diocletian (two Augusti and two Caesars, one being senior in each case). Additionally, Constantine added to Diocletian's formula a half-nephew, Hanniballianus, who was given the un-Roman title *Rex* and stationed on the eastern border. Clearly, his role as "king" was to provoke the Sasanians and then to defend his territories against them.

Not only was the Empire now divided among five young men who essentially held equal rank, but collectively they represented two rival branches of the family, which was a guarantee of infighting. The only possible explanation is that Constantine viewed this as temporary, and that he planned on altering the arrangement later — perhaps after he could observe how his potential heirs handled their responsibilities. If that was Constantine's plan, he did not live long enough to see it through. Just as he was setting out on his much-anticipated Persian campaign in the early summer of 337 (the enemy had been sufficiently provoked to break the peace treaty of 40 years), he died in the outskirts of Nicomedia. Before he passed away, Constantine was baptized and cleansed of a lifetime of sin.

What followed could hardly have surprised Constantine, for his offspring had inherited his instinct for survival. Within a couple of months his three sons had arranged the murders of their half-cousins along with other descendants of Theodora and their partisans. Only the three sons of Constantine remained in power, each assuming the title of Augustus and claiming his share of the Empire.

According to Julian II, who wrote retrospectively as a survivor of the brothers' murderous purge in 337, the names of those specifically responsible were kept a well-guarded secret (though historians tend to credit Constantius II as being the ring-leader). Some two decades after Julian II's death, the murders were defended by St. Gregory of Nazianzus, who briefly served as Bishop of Constantinople in 381. Gregory — a quarrelsome man who disliked Julian II — explained that the army would have supported only the true sons of Constantine as their leaders, and that the murders were a preemptive strike against a revolt that would have resulted. Though the barbarity of the act can hardly be defended, it did come to pass that the three grandsons of Theodora who were spared on account of their youth or frail health later haunted the sons of Constantine: two staged rebellions and one behaved savagely when given authority.

With events such as these clouding Constantine's legacy, it is difficult to call his reign or "dynasty" a resounding success in its own time. It is best, perhaps, to view him as a visionary, for he acted decisively upon his belief in the decline of the West and of paganism. His foundation of Constantinople (shifting of the Imperial focus eastward) and his adoption of Christianity proved over the slow course of time to have been landmark decisions. Historians have not overstepped their bounds by crediting him with saving Western civilization from the Moslem horde.

With the exception of Procopius (usurper, 365–366) and Anthemius (467–472), both of whom claimed a distant kinship to the Constantinian line, the last reigning member of the family was Julian II, a half-nephew from Theodora's side of the family. Considering that Julian II was a devout pagan, he provides an ironic conclusion to the Empire's first Christian dynasty.

After briefly being ruled by the former *comes domesticorum* (count, or companion of the household body guards) Jovian (363–364), the Empire had its unity shattered permanently by discord within the army. From February, 364, the two capitals, Rome and Constantinople, would manage their affairs separately. On the rare occasion when they had reason to interact, it was in hostility as often as it was in cooperation. The fact that their emperors were often of the same families seemed not to have affected matters decisively in one direction or the other.

Forcing the division of the Empire were the armies of Gaul (which were loyal to the memory of Julian II) and the eastern armies that had formerly served under Constantius II. Their cultural and political differences were so insurmountable that they decided civil war was avoidable only if two emperors reigned — one in Rome and one in Constantinople. The brothers Valentinian I and Valens took command, and except for two very brief periods after the deaths of Gratian (378/9) and Theodosius I (394/5), and a few later periods (which were as brief as they were inconsequential), East and West were never without separate emperors again.

For the reasons detailed above, after this chapter (which ends with the death of Jovian in 364) the biographies and value listings are divided between the Eastern Roman Empire and the Western Roman Empire.

Aug. = Augustus
Caes. = Caesar
us: = Usurper
beg. = beginning

The Constantinian Era

Period	West	East
	The Licinian Wars	
313–324	Constantine I (Aug., beg. 307) Crispus (Caes., beg. 316) Constantine II (Caes., beg. 316)	Licinius I (Aug., beg. 308) Val. Valens (co-Aug., 316–317) Licinius II (Caes., 317–324) Martinian (co-Aug., 324)
	Constantine as Sole-Augustus	
324–335	Constantine I (Aug.) Crispus (Caes., d. 326) Constantine II (Caes.) Constans (Caes., beg. 333)	Constantine I (Aug.) Constantius II (Caes.)
335–337	Constantine I (Aug.) Constantine II (Caes.) Constans (Caes.) Delmatius (Caes.)	Constantine I (Aug.) Constantius II (Caes.) Hanniballianus (Rex Regum)
	The Sons of Constantine	
337–340	Constantine II (Aug.) Constans (Aug.)	Constantius II (Aug.)
340–350	Constans (Aug.)	Constantius II (Aug.)
	Civil War and Decline	
350–360	Constantius II (Aug.) *us:* Magnentius (Aug., 350–353) *us:* Decentius (Caes., 350–353) Vetranio (co-Aug., 350) *us:* Nepotian (Aug., 350) Julian II (Caes., 355–360)	Constantius II (Aug.) Const. Gallus (Caes., 351–354)
360–361	*us:* Julian II (Aug.)	Constantius II (Aug.)
361–363	Julian II (Aug.)	
363–364	Jovian (Aug.)	

LICINIUS I A.D. 308–324

HUSBAND OF CONSTANTIA
FATHER OF LICINIUS II
SON-IN-LAW OF THEODORA AND (POSTHUMOUSLY) CONSTANTIUS I
UNCLE OF DELMATIUS, HANNIBALLIANUS, CONSTANTIUS GALLUS, JULIAN II AND NEPOTIAN
HALF-BROTHER-IN-LAW OF CONSTANTINE THE GREAT

Gaius Valerius Licinianus Licinius, c. A.D. 250 or c. 263/5–325. Making the fastest rise in the Tetrarchy was Licinius I, a soldier who was hailed Augustus by his comrade Galerius even though he had not previously held the rank of Caesar. Licinius survived the turmoil of the age to become sole rival to Constantine the Great, against whom he waged and lost two costly civil wars.

Little is known of Licinius' origins except that he was born of peasant stock in Dacia Ripensis (Upper Moesia) sometime around 250 or in the early 260s. Early in his career in the army, Licinius came to know Galerius, the man whom Diocletian made his Caesar in 293 and eventually, in 305, chose as his replacement as Augustus.

As an officer in the army, Licinius served with distinction on Galerius' campaign against the Sasanians in 297 and 298. This was one of the great Roman successes of the age, and no doubt established Licinius' credibility. Thereafter, he took up a command in the Danube and was a lieutenant on Galerius' failed expedition into Italy in 307.

Because of this association with Galerius (who was Diocletian's Caesar), Licinius was adopted by Diocletian. After having proved his competence and loyalty several times over, Licinius was promoted to the rank of Junior Augustus at the Conference of Carnuntum on November 11, 308. While Galerius no doubt viewed Licinius as the best man for the job, his choice infuriated other claimants, such as Constantine I, who at the same conference was reduced from self-proclaimed Augustus to Caesar. Equally upset was Galerius' own nephew, Maximinus Daia, was had been "leap-frogged" and remained a Caesar.

Licinius settled into his headquarters in Pannonia, and instead of trying to oust his various enemies (Maxentius in Italy, Alexander in Carthage or Constantine I in Gaul), he took on a defensive posture. When Galerius died of illness in 311, a contest began between Licinius and Maximinus Daia (whose soldiers had already proclaimed him Augustus in 310). The bitter rivals quickly partitioned Galerius' former territories, with Maximinus Daia getting all of the Asiatic territories and Licinius having to settle for the smaller European portion.

The two men narrowly avoided a war when they confronted each other at the Bosporus. They declared a truce, but each prepared for the war they knew was inevitable. Licinius' first preparation was to make an alliance with Constantine I in early in 312 — a measure countered by Maximinus Daia, who entered into an alliance with the rebel Maxentius. Battle lines had been formally drawn.

Within the year Constantine himself invaded Italy and deposed Maxentius, leaving the Empire with only three emperors: Constantine the Great, Licinius I and Maximinus Daia. The former two met at Milan in 313, where their alliance was formalized with Licinius' marriage to Constantine's half-sister, Constantia, and the joint issuance the Edict of Milan, which established religious tolerance in the Empire.

Meanwhile, all was not well with Maximinus Daia in the East. His realm was suffering from a famine induced by bad harvests, he had lost his ally Maxentius, and he had grown concerned over the alliance of Licinius and Constantine. Therefore, while his two opponents were occupied with their meeting in Milan, Daia took the initiative and invaded Thrace, the easternmost portion of Licinius' territory. Licinius hastily departed Milan before all issues had been settled and marched east to defend his territories.

The armies of Licinius and Maximinus Daia clashed late in April, 313, near Adrianople, where Daia's larger force (which was exhausted and demoralized by its fast march across Anatolia in winter) was roundly defeated. During the battle, Maximinus Daia managed to escape in disguise and flee back to Asia, where he died in the fall of that same year at Tarsus. Licinius wasted no time in executing a great many of Daia's supporters and in taking command of all Asia and Egypt, which he happily added to his Balkan holdings. The remainder of the Empire in the West belonged to his ally and in-law, Constantine the Great.

For the first time since the foundation of the Tetrarchy, only two men ruled. In the beginning the two Augusti tried to cooperate. Licinius enforced the Edict of Milan in his eastern realm, for Christians had suffered greatly under the successive regimes of Galerius and Maximinus Daia. Licinius insisted that all property confiscated from Christians during the earlier "Great Persecution" should be restored.

This and other actions (such as claiming to be a descendant of Philip I, who was thought of by some to be the first Christian emperor), led writers of the day to conclude that Licinius was a Christian. But his later actions against Christians proved that he was no convert from paganism.

The alliance of Constantine and Licinius I soon proved to be merely one of convenience, and the men inevitably came into conflict. It was clear to all that the Empire was divided by rivals in the East and West. During the next 11 years, Constantine and Licinius brought their children into the Imperial fold and engaged in two costly civil wars.

In an effort to prevent conflict, the two emperors installed a man named Bassianus as a quasi-independent ruler in Rhaetia and Pannonia, regions that together formed a "buffer state" along the northern and eastern borders of Italy. Bassianus was related by marriage to both men: he was Constantine's half-brother-in-law and he was the husband of the sister of Licinius' wife. Theoretically, he would have no greater loyalty to either of the emperors.

However, Licinius convinced Bassianus to revolt in his favor. Constantine learned of the treachery late in July, 315, and rushed from the Rhine front to Italy. However, he did not consider it prudent to act immediately. Tensions escalated over the next year and the so-called First Licinian War erupted in August or September of 316. Licinius quickly lost ground to Constantine, who advanced into the Balkans and defeated him in two battles, first on October 8 at Cibalae (about 50 miles west of Sirmium), and then further south-east at Campus Adriensis.

During the course of these battles, Licinius officially deposed Constantine for what he considered to be unlawful aggressions. In place of the now "illegal" emperor Constantine, Licinius raised his frontier commander Valerius Valens to the rank of Augustus in the West.

Though in military terms the defeats were not complete, Licinius and Valerius Valens decided to sue for peace, which they gained through negotiations held very early in 317. In the settlement, Constantine gained the title of Senior Augustus (formerly held by Licinius I), took control of all Balkan territories except Thrace and half of Moesia, and had Valerius Valens deposed. Licinius agreed to all of these terms and also executed Valerius Valens as an added measure of security.

The reconciliation resulted in more territory for Constantine, who controlled most of the western portion of the Empire. The acquisition of the Balkans was especially important because it was a prime region for recruiting soldiers. On March 1, 317, not long after their agreement had been forged, the sons of both emperors were formally raised to the rank of Caesar: Licinius II by his father and the half-brothers Crispus and Constantine II by their father.

Several years passed in which the rival emperors tolerated each other, but Licinius realized that Constantine would not be content until he had conquered the whole Empire. Licinius suspected that Christians in Asia Minor were conspiring against him on behalf of Constantine, and so he expelled all Christian officers from his army and began to persecute them in 320 and 321. For Constantine, who had adopted Christianity about a decade earlier, this was not only an affront to his own agenda, but it also constituted a breach of the Edict of Milan, to which both men had agreed in 313.

Hostilities between East and West continued to escalate, and in the summer of 322 (or possibly in 323) Constantine entered Licinius' territory of Thrace on the pretext that he was protecting the region from encroachment by the Goths. Technically, this was a legal act, but Licinius perceived it (perhaps rightly so) as an unwarranted aggression. By mid-324 the Second Licinian War had begun. This time, however, the results would not be as indecisive as they had been in the first contest.

Constantine won an important battle against Licinius at Adrianople on July 3, 324. By now Constantine's eldest son, Crispus, was old enough to participate, and he was entrusted with the fleet. In a brilliant maneuver, Crispus captured the fleet of Licinius, which was considerably larger than his own.

Facing defeat on land and at sea, Licinius retreated to Byzantium, where he was besieged and was forced to return to Asian soil. At some point during his retreat — in a virtual replay of the final days of the First Licinian War — Licinius hailed his *magister officiorum* Martinian as emperor of the West in place of Constantine. Martinian's task was to get reinforcements from Asia and organize what remained of their fleet so as to prevent Constantine from crossing over from Europe. Regrettably for Licinius and for himself, he was not successful.

In this second war the stakes were high, and Constantine would settle for nothing less than total victory. The combined forces of East and West exceeded 250,000 men and 500 ships. Not surprisingly, the casualties (which may have exceeded 60,000 in Licinius' army alone) were substantial.

After crossing over to Asian soil, the Licinians were routed at Chrysopolis on September 18, 324. Licinius abandoned his plan to establish himself at Calchedon and instead led the remainder of his army about 45 miles east to Nicomedia, where he prepared to make a last stand. His ranks once had numbered about 150,000, but by this stage they were reduced to one-fifth that amount by casualties and defections.

Clearly this "last stand" could have no good outcome for Licinius. But a final battle was avoided when Constantia, the wife of Licinius and half-sister of Constantine, negotiated terms of surrender in which the lives of Licinius I and Martinian were to be spared. Constantine had now gained control over the whole Roman Empire, and he placed Licinius and Martinian under house arrest — the former at Thessalonica and the latter in Cappadocia.

The men, however, did not long survive. Constantine failed to keep his promise and executed both former emperors, presumably in the spring of 325. In defense of Constantine's act, two Christian historians inform us that Licinius earned his death through his treacherous behavior. The 5th Century historian and lawyer Scholasticus records that Licinius secretly conspired with the Goths to overthrow Constantine. The 12th Century historian Zonaras offers a slightly different version, in which Licinius actually escaped to the Carpathian mountains, where his would-be allies, the Visigoths, executed him.

CONSTANTIA

Augusta, A.D. 313–324

Wife of Licinius I
Mother(?) of Licinius II
Daughter of Constantius I and Theodora
Half-sister of Constantine the Great
Stepdaughter of Helena
Aunt of Delmatius, Hanniballianus, Constantius Gallus, Julian II and Nepotian

Flavia Julia Constantia, c. A.D. 295(?)–c. 330. Constantia was one of two daughters of the emperor Constantius I and his second wife, Theodora. As such, she was a half-sister of Constantine the Great, who had been born to Constantius I's first wife (or concubine), Helena. Constantia led a tragic life — initially because her branch of the family was persecuted as rivals to Constantine the Great and later because of her arranged marriage to Constantine's rival, Licinius I.

Constantia came to the political forefront in 313, when she entered into a political marriage with Constantine's co-emperor, Licinius I, to whom she had been betrothed in 310 or 312. The wedding took place in February, 313 at Milan, where Constantine and Licinius had met to formalize their alliance and issue the famous Edict of Milan.

Though Constantine and Licinius I began their careers as comrades in arms under Galerius and grew to become luke-warm allies after they had achieved Imperial rank, they came to be bitter enemies. This development placed Constantia in a difficult position. A parallel may be drawn with Fausta, the second wife of Constantine the Great, whose loyalty was likewise tested between her husband and her father, Maximian.

In 313 Constantia was hailed Augusta, and within the next two years gave birth to a son. Whether this son was the one raised to the rank of Caesar in 317 is not entirely certain (see the biography of Licinius II for details). Family bliss, however, was interrupted late in 316 when her husband and Constantine went to war. The so-called First Licinian War ended in stalemate and a new truce that favored Constantine.

The Second Licinian War erupted in 324 and came to a more conclusive end than had the first. Constantia's husband was roundly defeated in a quick campaign and had it not been for her intervention, Licinius I no doubt would have been killed in a "last stand" he was preparing to take at Nicomedia. However, in a single night at the palace in Nicomedia, Constantia convinced her husband to surrender to Constantine. The next day she negotiated terms of surrender on her husband's behalf, which included a promise that the lives of Licinius I and his son, the Caesar, would be spared. That same evening the three dined together, after which Licinius was taken to Thessalonica under house arrest. The fact that Constantine went back on his promise a few months later and executed Licinius I is hardly a discredit to Constantia.

Constantia retained favorable status with her half-brother. However, because her husband had been deposed, Constantia was demoted in 324 from Augusta to *Nobilissima Femina.* At the same time, Constantine raised both his mother, Helena, and his wife, Fausta, to the rank of Augusta. Constantia spent the remainder of her life in Constantine's court, involving herself in the heated debates of Christian dogma that raged at the time. In particular, she seems to have devoted herself to restoring the Christian heretic Arius, who had been condemned at the Council of Nicaea in 325.

NUMISMATIC NOTE: It is curious that Licinius I did not strike coins for Constantia when she was hailed Augusta, especially since she soon gave birth to a son. Coins were struck in her name only after her demotion from Augusta. On these excessively rare bronzes, Constantia is styled as both *Nobilissima Femina* and the sister of Constantine (SOROR CONSTANTINI AVG).

LICINIUS II

CAESAR, A.D. 317–324

SON OF LICINIUS I AND(?) CONSTANTIA
GRANDSON OF CONSTANTIUS I AND THEODORA
COUSIN OF DELMATIUS, HANNIBALLIANUS, CONSTANTIUS GALLUS, JULIAN II AND NEPOTIAN
HALF-NEPHEW OF CONSTANTINE THE GREAT
HALF-COUSIN OF CRISPUS, CONSTANTINE II, CONSTANTIUS II, CONSTANS, CONSTANTINA (W. OF HANNIBALLIANUS & CONSTANTIUS GALLUS) AND HELENA THE YOUNGER (W. OF JULIAN II)

Flavius Valerius Constantinus Licinianus Licinius ("Licinius Junior"), c. A.D. 313/4 or c. 315–326. As a son of Licinius I, the Augustus in the East from 313 to 324, Licinius II was destined to inherit his father's Empire. To that effect, he was raised to the rank of Caesar on March 1,

317, while still a small child. His investiture occurred at Serdica in a formal ceremony shared with Crispus and Constantine II, the two eldest sons of his father's rival, Constantine the Great.

We know little of Licinius II other than the circumstances of his achieving that rank, and the fact that he was deposed in 324 and executed in 326. Beyond this, the sources become muddied, for Licinius I had two sons: one who was born to his wife, Constantia, and another who was born a bastard to his Syrian concubine, Mamertina. Determining which of these two boys was the one hailed Caesar (and depicted on coins) may not be done with absolute certainty; therefore, their fates are discussed separately below.

As was called for in the surrender treaty of 324, the Caesar Licinius II was stripped of his rank and exiled with his father to Thessalonica, only to witness the latter's execution early in 325. Licinius II was eventually moved from Thessalonica to Pola, where in 326 (perhaps around the same time Constantine executed his son, Crispus, and his wife, Fausta) he too was executed.

The other young man, an illegitimate half-brother of Licinius II, had his status restored by rescript after the war and was given high rank. However, he was later implicated in the Cypriot revolt staged by Calocaerus in 334 (which was thwarted by the future Caesar Dematius), and as punishment was either executed or condemned to slavery at an Imperial weaving-mill in Carthage in 336.

NUMISMATIC NOTE: Licinius II is perhaps more properly named Licinius Junior, as his name on coinage often appears as LICINIVS IVN (or IVNIOR on a medallion of Nicomedia). By far his most interesting issues are his facing-head solidi and the reduced nummi which show his bust confronted either with the bust of his father or of Constantine II. Other nummi of interest are those which show that Licinius I bestowed upon his own son the additional name Constantine as a show of good faith in the agreement made at Serdica on March 1, 317. The inscriptions occur at Nicomedia in the form VA CO LICINIVS NOB (or N) CS, at Heraclea as D N VAL CONST LICINIVS NOB C, and at Alexandria in the expanded form VAL CONSTANTINVS LICINIVS N CAES. The goodwill did not last long, however, for the coins are very rare and were probably restricted to 317.

VALERIUS VALENS A.D. 316–317

Gaius Aurelius Valerius Valens, d. A.D. 317. During the First Licinian War, when Licinius I was losing ground in the Balkans to Constantine I, he officially deposed Constantine for his unlawful aggressions. He then optimistically replaced Constantine with Valerius Valens, one of his own frontier generals (*dux limitatis*) who was destined to hold the title of Augustus for only three months before being executed.

Like most details of the period, exactly when Valerius Valens was hailed Augustus is not certain. It may have occurred at the battle at Cibalae on October 8, 316, or shortly thereafter when the Licinian armies were conducting a fighting retreat. In response to his being hailed co-Augustus, Constantine seems to have raised his two eldest sons, Crispus and the infant Constantine II, to the rank of Caesar (though they were not formally installed until the spring of 317).

In either case, Licinius and Valerius Valens were on the defensive and shortly into the New Year sued for peace. Constantine assumed the title of Senior Augustus, took control of all Balkan territories except Thrace (and half of Moesia) and demanded that Valerius Valens be deposed. Licinius agreed to the terms and went one step further by executing Valerius Valens, probably in January (perhaps on the 8th) of 317. The execution was not merely an act of good faith toward Constantine, but also removed a potential rival within Licinius' own realm.

NUMISMATIC NOTE: Deceptive 20th Century forgeries (commonly known by the name "The Geneva Forgeries") exist of the nummi of Valerius Valens and of four other issuers. Many of the known examples are illustrated and described by R. A. G. Carson in the 1958 *Numismatic Chronicle*, pp. 47–58, pls. V–VI. An offprint of Carson's article was published in 1977.

MARTINIAN A.D. 324

Sextus Marcius(?) Martinianus, d. A.D. 325. The fate of Martinian was virtually identical to that of Valerius Valens — both men briefly served as the co-emperor of Licinius I in the final months of his civil wars with Constantine the Great. Martinian did not reign as long (about two months) as Valerius Valens, but he survived a few months longer after being deposed, for he was not executed until the following year.

During the final stage of the Second Licinian War, Licinius officially deposed Constantine for his military aggressions into Thrace, which along with half of Moesia was Licinius' only European possession. In Constantine's place, Licinius made his Master of Offices (*magister officiorum*), Martinian, emperor of the West. Martinian was the second-highest-ranking officer in Licinius' administration and though the Imperial bodyguards were under his command, the *magister officiorum* was not a military post.

The First Licinian War (316–317) had been relatively nondestructive in comparison with the second. This time the combined land forces exceeded 250,000 men and some 500 ships. With such large armies and navies, it is not surprising that the casualties and defections were enormous.

By mid-324 the war had begun, and Licinius immediately began to lose ground to Constantine. He engaged in a fighting retreat toward the Bosporus and late in July he instructed Martinian to muster whatever soldiers and vessels he could to prevent Constantine from crossing onto Asian soil. Martinian, however, was unable to prevent the enemy's advance, for Constantine's eldest son, Crispus, made a flotilla of light transport ships, and Constantine's legions entered Asia Minor virtually unopposed.

Licinius was routed yet again at Chrysopolis on September 18, 323, by which point the deaths in his army exceeded 60,000 and defections numbered 50,000 or more. The Licinian army (now reduced from 150,000 to about 30,000) abandoned its defensive position at Calchedon and retreated further east to Nicomedia, where they hoped to make one last stand. However, the lives of the two emperors and their army were spared by Constantia, the wife of Licinius I and a half-sister of Constantine, who intervened and negotiated an honorable surrender in late September or early October.

In exchange for their abdications, Constantine promised to spare the lives of Licinius, his son Licinius II, and the co-emperor, Martinian. The royal captives were placed under house arrest: Licinius I and Licinius II at Thessalonica, and Martinian in Cappadocia. True to form, Constantine soon went back on his word and executed both former emperors in the spring of 325, followed by the execution of Licinius II in 326.

Numismatic Note: Counterfeits of the nummi of Martinian were produced by the same forger who produced certain coins of Valerius Valens (for details see the note for the latter's coinage).

CONSTANTINE I 'THE GREAT'

A.D. 307–337

CAESAR (RECOGNIZED): A.D. 306–309
FILIUS AUGUSTORUM (RECOGNIZED):
A.D. 309–310
AUGUSTUS (SELF-PROCLAIMED): A.D. 307–310
AUGUSTUS (RECOGNIZED): A.D. 310–337

SON OF CONSTANTIUS I AND HELENA
HUSBAND OF MINERVINA AND FAUSTA
FATHER (BY MINERVINA) OF CRISPUS AND (BY FAUSTA) OF CONSTANTINE II, CONSTANTIUS II, CONSTANS, CONSTANTINA (*w.* OF HANNIBALLIANUS & CONSTANTIUS GALLUS) AND HELENA THE YOUNGER (*w.* OF JULIAN II)
SON-IN-LAW OF MAXIMIAN AND EUTROPIA
BROTHER-IN-LAW OF MAXENTIUS
HALF-BROTHER OF CONSTANTIA (*w.* OF LICINIUS I)
HALF-UNCLE OF DELMATIUS, HANNIBALLIANUS, CONSTANTIUS GALLUS, JULIAN II, LICINIUS II AND NEPOTIAN
GRANDFATHER OF CONSTANTIA (*w.* OF GRATIAN)

Flavius Valerius Constantinus, c. A.D. 272/3, 274 (*alternately,* early 280s)–337. The importance of Constantine the Great to western history cannot be underestimated. Only two other Roman emperors — Augustus and Diocletian — had so great an impact on the future of his world. For Constantine is inextricably tied to the emergence of Christianity as the chief religion of the Western world, and thus with the introduction of Europe into the post-Classical world.

Constantine was born at Naïssus to Helena, a Bithynian barmaid, and Constantius I, a Danubian soldier whose origins were humble but who achieved the ranks of Caesar and Augustus in the course of his duty. It is not known if Constantine's parents were married, but we can be certain that Constantine was not ashamed about his origins, for he extensively honored his parents in coinage and on other media. Historians sharply disagree on the subject of Constantine's birth year, though most favor sometime between 272 and 274. Some of his panegyrists suggest he was born in the early 280s, but these almost certainly are attempts to falsify his youth.

By all accounts Constantine was a violent, suspicious, temperamental and intimidating man. The historian Eusebius reports that as a young man Constantine was tall, graceful, and so completely surpassed "his contemporaries in personal strength that he struck terror into them." Indeed, this man (who later in life gained the nickname "bull neck") must have been a frightening adversary, either in armor on the battlefield or in jewel-encrusted robes in the royal court.

Throughout his lifetime, Constantine's behavior was opportunistic and inconsistent, for he followed policies that served his immediate needs.

Foremost was his adoption of Christianity, the teachings of which he failed to embrace. His impious personal behavior and his retention of the pagan title *Pontifex Maximus* until his death demonstrate his hypocrisy on a policy that was the cornerstone of his reign.

When Constantine's father began to rise to the highest levels of the government, he was forced to end his association with Constantine's mother, Helena, so he could marry Theodora, the step-daughter of the emperor Maximian. Constantius I and Theodora subsequently had several children, thus creating a separate branch of the "Constantinian" family. Because the first generation of this rival branch was persecuted by Helena and Fausta, its members were fairly innocuous. However, the second generation figured tragically into the Imperial politics of Constantine and his three surviving sons.

The story of the first Christian emperor is especially complex because his treatment by Christian writers of the Late Roman and Byzantine eras is excessively flattering. At the same time they praise Constantine, these same historians unfairly vilify his many opponents. For scholars, this is a task not unlike trying to determine the point of view of the Germans or Sasanians through histories written by Romans.

In truth, Constantine was an enigma. On the one hand he was a self-assured emissary of God, and on the other he was an utterly ruthless murderer and a single-minded aggressor who would go to any length to become sole emperor. This balance of qualities, seemingly in opposition, did not prevent kings of the Middle Ages from viewing him as the archetype of the European Christian king.

His major failures were few, but important. For example, it is hard to imagine that a man of his worldly character would have believed that his three sons and two half-nephews would share the Empire cooperatively after he died. But whatever his failings, the achievements of Constantine were numerous. He was a brilliant general, administrator and statesman who not only led Europe's conversion from paganism to Christianity, but began construction of Constantinople (a "new Rome") on the Golden Horn, an act that proved to be Europe's salvation for a millennium after his death.

He chose the location of his new city for the strategic importance it played in the two wars he waged against Licinius I. Indeed, the foundation of Constantinople (on a Greek settlement named Byzantium) ranks as one of the great events of late antiquity. For this and other important reasons, many historians consider him to be the first of the so-called Byzantine emperors.

Because Constantine's father was Caesar in the West, the Eastern Augustus Diocletian retained Constantine as a "hostage" in his court at

Nicomedia to ensure the good behavior of the boy's father. While serving in Diocletian's court, Constantine came to know his eventual rival, Licinius I, for both of them served with distinction in Galerius' campaign against the Sasanians from 297 to 298.

By the time Diocletian and Maximian abdicated in May of 305, the health of Constantius I had begun to fail, so he petitioned that his son, Constantine, should be released to join him in the West. The new Augustus in the East, Galerius, granted the request, and in 306 Constantine embarked on the long journey from Nicomedia to Boulogne, where he met his father. Wary of possible assassination by Galerius or the Caesar Severus II, Constantine traveled swiftly and discreetly.

Both Constantine and his father were in dangerous positions, for even though Constantius I was technically the Senior Augustus, he had been politically outmaneuvered by Galerius, who had been Diocletian's confidant. Indeed, Galerius was so intent on installing his own candidates Severus II and Maximinus Daia in the vacant offices of Caesar that he bypassed two prime candidates: Constantine (who was the son of the current Senior Augustus) and Maxentius, the son of the retired emperor Maximian.

In that same year (306) Constantine and his father sailed to Britain, where they shared command in the war against the Picts. In the process Constantine came to be admired by the soldiers under his father's command, and they supported his cause when Constantius I transferred his *imperium* to Constantine while on his deathbed at York on July 25, 306. The event is said to have been witnessed by soldiers, and in one swift action, Constantine commandeered authority in Gaul, Britain and Spain.

Initially, Constantine took the title Augustus, for he was determined to be a direct replacement for his deceased father. Upon further reflection, however, he changed his mind. Not only was it an "illegal" act (for the title of Augustus would naturally go to one of the two men who already held the rank of Caesar), but Galerius grudgingly offered him the legitimate title of Caesar. Constantine accepted, and Galerius promoted the Caesar Severus II to Augustus.

Constantine cautiously remained in the West during this early part of his reign, devoting himself to defending the Rhine. He waged war on the Franks from 306 to 307, and made sorties into the territory of the Bructeri. In 308 he even bridged the Rhine near Cologne to lead a punitive expedition. With few breaks from frontier warfare, he remained more or less occupied with the Rhine until he left Gaul in 312.

Because Constantine had essentially forced Galerius to hail him Caesar in 306, Maxentius (the son of Maximian, who had no rank) viewed Constantine as the man who had robbed him of the new opening in the

Tetrarchy created by the death of Constantius I. As a result, Constantine and Maxentius would never see eye-to-eye, and this was just the beginning of their personal conflict.

Believing he never would be offered a legitimate chance for authority, Maxentius rebelled in Rome on October 28, 306, claiming the titles Princeps and Caesar. Maxentius soon added to his renegade government his own father, Maximian, who had unwillingly retired in 305 with Diocletian.

The father and son rebels proclaimed themselves Augusti early in 307 as they braced in the spring for an invasion of Italy led by the newly appointed Augustus, Severus II. The invasion was easily repelled by Maximian, who bribed the invader's soldiers. Severus II was captured and forced to abdicate, and by the summer had been executed. The Tetrarchy now numbered only three — an insufficiency that was not remedied until November, 308.

Immediately after the victory over Severus II, Maximian left his son, Maxentius, in Italy and traveled to Gaul to see Constantine. The two men — seeing Galerius as their enemy-in-common — made a pact that was sealed on March 31 with Constantine's marriage to Fausta, the daughter of Maximian and sister of Maxentius. Now fully committed to opposing Galerius, Constantine did not hesitate to accept the title of Augustus that Maximian offered him in July, 307 (though he remained a Caesar in the mind of Galerius).

As these events were occurring in Gaul, Italy was invaded a second time, later in 307. This incursion was led by Galerius himself, but it proved no more successful than the effort led earlier by Severus II. Forewarned by the fate of his predecessor, Galerius hastily withdrew to Illyria before his retreat could be cut off, either by Maxentius or by his Gallic ally Constantine. About this time, perhaps, Spain switched its allegiance from Constantine to Maxentius — an event that Constantine no doubt attributed to treachery on the part of Maxentius.

Having achieved his mission in Gaul, Maximian returned to Rome early in 308 to join his son, only to discover that they were unable to share authority. Maximian tried to overthrow his son in April of 308 but failed and fled to Gaul to take refuge with his new son-in-law, Constantine. Together, in the summer or fall of 308, they convinced the vicar of North Africa, Lucius Domitius Alexander, to revolt against Maxentius.

By denying Rome most of its grain supply, Domitius Alexander had the potential to starve the Romans, and thus to topple Maxentius' regime (presumably so that his benefactor Maximian could step in and take command). Short food supplies caused civil unrest in Rome, and Maxentius used his well-fed Praetorian guardsmen to quell civilian riots in which some 6,000 died.

Realizing his peril, either late in 309 or early in 310 Maxentius outfitted an expedition against Carthage that was extraordinarily destructive, but which restored North Africa to his domain and caused the death of Alexander. Though some historians (following Zosimus' *Nea Historia*) suggest the African revolt ended in 311, it more likely ended late in the summer or in the fall of 310.

Since the Empire now had six claimants (one legitimate Augustus, two legitimate Caesars and three rebels), Galerius held a conference at Carnuntum on November 11, 308. At this meeting he hoped to find a solution to the problems the Empire faced — one that would still work in his own favor. However, Galerius' inflexibility assured that nothing was resolved, and though a new member was added to round out the Tetrarchy, none of the parties (save Galerius and the new member, Licinius I) emerged satisfied.

Installed at Carnuntum as the replacement for the slain Severus II was Galerius' comrade Licinius I, who was appointed Junior Augustus even though he had not previously held the rank of Caesar. As for the other participants: Maximinus Daia remained Caesar and was enraged for being "leapfrogged" by Licinius I; Constantine was confirmed as Caesar (though he still claimed to be Augustus); Maximian was forced to abdicate a second time; and Maxentius and Alexander remained condemned as public enemies.

The civil war reached a new level of crisis in 309 when the Syrian and Egyptian soldiers of Galerius' nephew, Maximinus Daia, threatened to declare him Augustus. This concerned Galerius, who had thus far counted on the cooperation of his nephew. Fearing the consequences of inaction, Galerius gave to both Daia and Constantine the nebulous title *Filius Augustorum* ("Son of the Augusti") so as to keep the rivals satisfied. However, both recipients realized it was an empty promotion that had no more authority than did their old rank of Caesar.

Constantine did not attend the conference at Carnuntum in person, but rather sent his father-in-law, Maximian, as his representative. Thus, when Maximian returned to Gaul without a title, he was allowed to serve as an adviser to Constantine. But that arrangement did not last long, and in a fit of desperation in the spring of 310 (though this date is debated among scholars), Maximian revolted while Constantine was waging war on the Rhine.

Maximian's "third reign" was not only ephemeral, but its purpose is unknown. Maximian was hotly pursued by Constantine, who abandoned his campaign on the Rhine and chased Maximian to Marseilles, where the downtrodden ex-emperor either committed suicide or was executed. It is about this time that Constantine adopted into his propaganda the emperor Claudius II (268–270), a hero whom he claimed was a relative of his father, Constantius I. Though Constantine invented the claim in 310, he did not promote it on coinage until 316, during the First Licinian War.

Meanwhile, in 310, events in the East took a fortuitous turn for Constantine: Maximinus Daia was hailed Augustus by his own soldiers, leaving Galerius no choice but to ratify the promotion. Since Constantine had received promotions in-step with Daia, Galerius likewise raised him from *Filius Augustorum* to Augustus to avoid similar problems in the West. At long last, Constantine was officially an emperor. Moreover, he seems to have regained possession of Spain from Maxentius.

Early in May, 311, the scenario was simplified when the Senior Augustus Galerius died of disease. His territories were quickly claimed by Licinius I (in Europe) and Maximinus Daia (in Asia), who drew their territorial line at the Bosporus. Now only four claimants remained — though it was no Tetrarchy, for the Empire was ruled by four *de facto* emperors: Maximinus Daia, Licinius I, Maxentius and Constantine — each of whom was a rival to the other.

Each of the participants was insecure about his position, and so two alliances emerged. Constantine and Licinius I made a pact of mutual defense and sealed it with the marriage of Constantine's half-sister, Constantia, to Licinius I. In response, Maximinus Daia and Maxentius subsequently joined forces, though theirs quickly proved to be the weaker of the two alliances.

After six years spent defending his own borders in Gaul, Constantine went on the offensive in the fall of 312 and invaded Italy to oust his rival Maxentius. Surprisingly, Constantine launched his campaign with considerably fewer soldiers than his opponent, but that did not prevent a series of victories in Northern Italy that led to the final confrontation just outside Rome.

This was perhaps the pivotal event in the reign of Constantine. It branded him an aggressor, and it proved to be the moment at which he shed his patronage of Apollo and Sol, and instead embraced the Christian faith. On the eve of the battle, while camped in the outskirts of Rome, Constantine is said to have dreamed and to have experienced a celestial vision, causing him to convert to Christianity. As a result of his transformation, Constantine instructed his men to paint a cross or a Christogram (a monogram of Christ's name) upon their shields prior to the battle on October 28, 312. The civil war between Maxentius and Constantine had now taken on a religious dimension: paganism vs. Christianity.

After six years of less-than-competent rule in Italy, Maxentius had become so unpopular in Rome that he decided to force a pitched battle before his support eroded any further. The two armies initially engaged one another on the Via Flaminia, and finally at the Milvian Bridge. Despite his numerical superiority and urgency, Maxentius did not fare well, and his army was thrown into retreat. Thousands of Maxentius' soldiers, along with Maxentius himself, died in the waters of the Tiber as they hurriedly tried to cross to the river on a bridge of boats that collapsed.

Constantine was now the uncontested emperor in most of Europe. He was welcomed by the senate, which unhesitatingly declared him the Senior Augustus in the Empire (*titulus primi ordinis*). Constantine dismantled the long-lived institution of the praetorian guards and introduced new top military offices known collectively as *magistri militum*. The two main officers were now the *magister peditum*, who was in charge of the infantry or foot soldiers, and the *magister equitum*, who led the cavalry. The title of the overall military commander in the later Empire came to be known as the *magister militum* ("Master of Soldiers").

Now only three men ruled the Empire, and Maximinus Daia (who occupied all of Asia and Egypt) clearly was the odd man out. Thus when Constantine and Licinius I met at Milan in February, 313, to formalize their alliance, Daia sensed that he must strike swiftly if he was to survive. As his two enemies were conducting the marriage of Licinius I and Constantia and were issuing the Edict of Milan (which established tolerance for all religions), Daia led his soldiers from Syria to Thrace on a winter march.

Early in the spring, Daia invaded Licinius' European territory of Thrace. Daia's journey was so swift that Licinius I had to leave Milan before all of his business had been concluded so he could repel the invasion. Constantine no doubt savored the moment, for one of his two competitors would certainly perish in this campaign.

Daia's army was larger than Licinius', but his soldiers were exhausted and demoralized. Not surprisingly, they fought poorly and were defeated late in April, 313, seemingly near Heraclea. Though Daia himself escaped dressed as a slave, he died as a fugitive before the year was out. Licinius' victory was quite profitable; not only did he rid himself of a dangerous foe, but he also took possession of all Asiatic territories. In the meantime (by late May), Constantine had returned to his traditional capital of Trier.

The Empire was now ruled by only two men, Constantine and Licinius I, who were linked by a dynastic marriage and a political alliance. Theoretically, this was an ideal point at which a new Tetrarchy could be established, with each Augustus adopting a Caesar. But that was not to be, for the two men inherently distrusted one other, and each ultimately desired supreme power. The peace they shared was uneasy from the start — so much so that they installed a man named Bassianus in Rhaetia and Pannona, two provinces that together constituted a "buffer state" along the Italian border. Since Bassianus was related to both men by marriage (he was Constantine's half-brother-in-law, and was the husband of Licinius' wife's sister), he might have been able to carry out his duties with impartiality. However, while Constantine was occupied with problems associated with the Donatist schism in North Africa, Bassianus seems to have been enticed by Licinius to revolt on his behalf.

Late in July of 315, Constantine responded to the treachery of Bassianus by rushing to Italy to prevent any westward spread of the rebellion. Tensions rose over the course of the next year, and the First Licinian War began in August or September of 316.

Constantine acted swiftly and Licinius retreated eastward, suffering defeats on October 8 at Cibalae and subsequently at Campus Adriensis. Licinius officially "deposed" Constantine for his aggressions, and replaced him as emperor in the West with his own frontier commander Valerius Valens. The addition of Valerius Valens did not change the outcome for Licinius, who sued for peace very early in 317.

The spoils of Constantine's victory (luke-warm though it was) included the undisputed title of Senior Augustus, the execution of Valerius Valens and control of most of the Balkan territories (except Thrace and half of Moesia). On March 1, 317, both emperors held formal ceremonies at which their sons (Crispus, Constantine II and Licinius II) were raised to the rank of Caesar.

During the next six years, Constantine remained in the Balkans to keep an eye on Licinius. His family also began to grow: already born were Constantine II (at Arles, in 316) and Constantius II (in Illyria, in 317) and soon to follow was Constans (at Constantinople, in 320 or 323). In addition, Constantine's eldest son, Crispus, who was born to the wife (or consort) of his youth, Minervina, was fast maturing.

Constantine and Licinius remained cautious allies until Constantine entered Thrace at the head of an army in the summer of 322 (or possibly 323) on the pretext that he was defending the region from encroachment by Goths. Though this was a legal act, Licinius saw it for what it was — an unwarranted aggression into his own sovereign territory. Just as in the previous war, the hostilities escalated until, by mid-324, the Second Licinian War had begun.

Constantine achieved an important victory against Licinius at Adrianople on July 3, 324, and Licinius' navy was captured by Constantine's eldest son, Crispus (who did so with a much smaller fleet). Licinius retreated to Byzantium, where he was besieged and opted to cross over to Asia. In a virtual repeat of his actions in the First Licinian War, Licinius hailed his *magister officiorum* Martinian as emperor in place of Constantine. Martinian and Licinius, however, were defeated badly at Chrysopolis on September 18, 324 and soon prepared to make a last stand at Calchedon.

Licinius' original army of about 150,000 men had been reduced by casualty and desertion to only about 30,000. Neither side desired a final battle, for it would be Roman against Roman. The surrender of Licinius and Martinian was arranged by Constantia, the wife of Licinius and half-sister of Constantine. Both Licinius and Martinian were deposed, though Constantia arranged that their lives should be spared, and they should be allowed to live in exile.

Licinius was placed under house arrest in Thessalonica together with his young son, Licinius II, and Martinian was sent to Cappadocia. Contrary to the promises he had made at the time of surrender, Constantine ordered the executions of the men in the spring of the following year (325), ostensibly because they had conspired to overthrow his regime, but more likely because they represented a potential threat.

A round of promotions within Constantine's family followed the victory: on November 8, 324, the day he founded the city of Constantinople (his "New Rome" on the Bosporus), both his mother, Helena, and wife, Fausta, were promoted from Nobilissima Femina ("most noble woman") to Augusta, and Constantius II, his middle son by Fausta, was formally hailed Caesar.

After nearly two decades of warfare from Gaul to the Bosporus, Constantine had taken command of the whole Empire. At this point Constantine began the projects that would shape the future of the western world. Chief among these was his greatest architectural accomplishment, Constantinople, but also included were many other religious and secular buildings throughout his Empire.

Constantine also worked tirelessly to unify the factions of the Christian church. His most significant act (since failing to solve the Donatist schism at Arles in 314) was the Council of Nicaea, which he hosted in 325. Here, Christian orthodoxy was defined in the Creed, and an illusory victory was won over Arianism (which was condemned as heresy). Constantine also developed a framework by which he could bequeath the Empire to family members, and planned extensively for the conquest of Persia, which was cut short by his own death.

By far the darkest year of Constantine's reign was 326, for within a short span he ordered the execution of his eldest son, Crispus, his wife, Fausta, and his exiled half-nephew Licinius II. Not only did these tragic murders damage his legacy among pagans and Christians alike, but they caused some of his leading advisers and theologians (as well as his mother, Helena, who conveniently embarked on a pilgrimage to the Holy Land) to leave his court, apparently in protest of his behavior.

Constantine's family was large and complex. Both he and his father had sired children with two different women, thus creating three branches to the Constantinian family. Most remote to Constantine was the step-family created by his father, and most immediate were the two branches of direct descendants he had sired. Needless to say, this created hostile rivalries.

Constantine's step-family was persecuted by his own mother, Helena, and his wife, Fausta. His eldest son, Crispus, was also targeted by Fausta, who saw him as a rival to her own three sons by Constantine. The rivalry between Fausta and Crispus came to a head in 326, when Fausta leveled charges of an uncertain nature against Crispus. So serious and convincing were these charges that Constantine executed his eldest son in August or September, 326.

Crispus was the emperor's only son by Minervina, the woman with whom he had had a long-term relationship prior to his political marriage to Fausta. (Though Constantine most likely was married to Minervina, hostile Christian historians — who attempted to contrast the 'pagan' and 'Christian' phases of his life — considered her to be nothing more than a concubine.) Because of his impressive naval victory against Licinius I in 324, Crispus had achieved a hero status among the Romans. Indeed, his rise and fall is comparable to that of the equally heroic Germanicus, who had fallen victim to a family plot orchestrated by Tiberius some three centuries earlier.

One can hardly condemn Fausta's motives (she was either concerned for the welfare of her children or was smarting from rejection, as it was rumored that Crispus refused her amorous advances), but her actions constituted treachery of the highest order. Constantine believed the charges made by Fausta and seems to have behaved rashly by ordering the execution of Crispus; he soon regretted this decision so greatly that he tried to clear his conscience by ordering the execution of Fausta a month or two later. In a state of mourning, Constantine erected a golden statue in honor of the martyred Crispus, the son whom he had "unjustly condemned."

Perhaps lending credence to the rumors that amorous rejection caused the fiasco is the punitive legislation Constantine drafted. Constantine's most severe laws concerned sexual behavior: rapists and girls who eloped with their lovers were to be burned alive; nurses who assisted eloping girls were to have molten lead poured down their throats; parents were deported if they concealed a seduction of their daughter; and girls who were raped while far from home were punished for having wandered so far astray. Considering that Constantine's paranoia was equaled only by his prudery, his reasons for this legislation must remain a mystery.

The round of murders in 326 greatly simplified the Constantinian family structure: Helena, Constantine's elderly mother, had taken leave; his wife, Fausta, was dead, as was his eldest and most promising son, Crispus. He did, however, have three sons and two daughters (by Fausta) as well as the members of his step-family (who were able to emerge from their exile now that both Helena and Fausta were removed from the political scene).

The next great event in the reign of Constantine occurred in the summer of 330, when he officially dedicated his eponymous eastern capital on May 11. This grand event was followed two weeks later with a celebration of his 25th anniversary in power. Clearly, he had emerged from the tragic executions of 326 by focusing his efforts on the substantive affairs of church and state.

In 328 he had campaigned against the Alemanni on the Rhine with his young son Constantine II at his side. Later still, in 332, he began a major campaign against the Goths, which he continued in 334 against the Sarmatians. Constantine II, at that time about 16 years old, left Trier to join his father for the Gothic campaign. Together they won great victories, including one against the Visigothic king Alaric I, who suffered nearly 100,000 deaths among his followers.

In the succeeding years, Constantine's other heirs were given greater responsibilities: in 333 his middle son, Constantius II, was installed at Antioch, and his youngest son, Constans (who was then either 9 or 12 years old), was hailed Caesar on Christmas day. Toward the end of 335, Constantine formalized his plan for succession by dividing the Empire among his three sons (who already were Caesars) and two of his half-nephews (who were brothers).

Though there were five heirs, only four were confirmed as Caesars (the fifth, Hanniballianus, had a non-Roman title and peripheral duties). Constantine had created his own junior Tetrarchy that was loosely based on the one Diocletian had created more than four decades before. Throughout the two years that remained of his life, however, Constantine never relinquished sole proprietorship of the title of Augustus.

Since Constantine II was most familiar with the western provinces, he was allotted Gaul, Britain and Spain (and seemingly the westernmost part of North Africa, either as part of the original allotment or as a later addition). The rest of the Empire was divided between the four other heirs: Constantius II received Asia Minor; Constans received Italy and Illyria (and eventually the lower Danubian provinces and North Africa); the half-cousin Delmatius received the lower Danubian provinces (and seemingly the city of Constantinople); and the other half-cousin, Hanniballianus, inherited the Pontus and Armenia (with the title "King of Kings").

By 336, Constantine (then probably in his early 60s) had recaptured much of the Dacian lands that Trajan had conquered but which long ago had fallen back into barbarian hands. Now he was able to focus on his last important goal: conquering Persia. He had purposely installed Hanniballianus on the Persian frontier with the boastful title "King of Kings" to antagonize the Sasanian king Shapur II. His presumptions were correct, and Shapur II invaded Armenia — breaking the treaty the Sasanians had agreed to under Diocletian, and thus giving Constantine an ideal opportunity to retaliate.

In the very midst of preparations — indeed, while he was *en route* to the eastern front — Constantine died on May 22, 337. While on his deathbed at Achyrona (an Imperial residence outside Nicomedia) Eusebius, the Arian bishop of Nicimedia, baptized Constantine, cleansing him of a lifetime of mortal sins.

Soon thereafter, Constantius II, Constantine's 20-year-old son, presided over his funeral in Constantinople. The ceremony was held at the Church of the Twelve Apostles, where the emperor was proclaimed the 13th Apostle. Later still, he was declared a Christian saint, just as had been done for his mother, Helena.

Following Constantine's death, there was an interregnum of 110 days during which his heirs kept the titles they had been given, and Constantine's idealistic formula (in which power was shared by the two branches of the family) was put to the test. It failed immediately and miserably. In less than three months many of Constantine's half-brothers and half-nephews (including Delmatius and Hanniballianus) were murdered, virtually exterminating the rival branch of the Constantinian family. The path for the three sons of Fausta finally had been cleared of immediate obstacles.

The three brothers absorbed the territories once ruled by Delmatius and Hanniballianus and hailed themselves Augusti on September 9, 337. Religious and territorial squabbles began among the three brothers even before the half-cousins were murdered. This was a tragic beginning to a fratricidal contest in which only one of the three surviving heirs would die a natural death.

CHRONOLOGICAL NOTE: Much is disputed about the chronology of Constantine's reign. The Theodosian Code, which records the travels of the emperor by listing the date and place of Imperial constitutions, is our most complete source, but its accuracy has been challenged. Of particular importance is the date of Constantine's victory over Maxentius at the Milvian Bridge. Though traditionally given to the year 312, Patrick Bruun, in his *Studies in Constantinian Chronology* (ANS NNM 146, 1961), citing numismatic and historical evidence, suggests it occurred exactly one year earlier, in 311. Though his view may be correct, it has not been adopted in standard references.

NUMISMATIC NOTE: Like Diocletian, Constantine was an avid reformer of coinage in all metals. Thus, his coinage is complex and diverse, incorporating many denominations and a considerable variety of reverse types. At different stages in his reign Constantine abandoned Diocletian's denominations, and thus established a path for coinage which would survive the remainder of the Roman Empire and serve as the foundation for the succeeding "Byzantine" series.

In gold Constantine replaced the reformed Tetrarchic gold aureus (struck at 60 to the pound) with the lighter solidus, which was struck at 72 to the pound. The transition began in 309, but overlapped through 324, after which gold coins of aureus weight make only occasional appearances as ceremonial pieces. Constantine complimented his new *solidus* with two half-denominations: a semissis *or* semis (struck at 144 to the pound) and the 1-1/2 scripulum *or* nine-siliqua piece (typically c. 1.6–1.7 grams). Both seem to have begun as ceremonial coins, with the former becoming part of the regular system of the Byzantine Empire, and the latter being phased out and replaced by the smaller, more practical gold tremissis (one-third solidus) introduced in the 380s and struck at 216 to the pound.

Silver coin production in the form of the Tetrarchic argenteus (of high purity, 96 to the pound) had ceased by c. 312, though this denomination briefly re-emerged in billon form (perhaps 25% silver). Constantine resurrected silver coinage in two entirely new forms of high purity silver: the *miliarensis* and the *siliqua*. The first was probably a ceremonial piece and was struck in two varieties: at 60 and 72 to the pound (imitating the gold standards, respectively, of the aureus and the solidus). The so-called *siliqua* (which was probably called an argenteus) was introduced in 324 and was struck at 96 to the pound. Intrinsically this was an exact duplication of Diocletian's argenteus, but its thin, broad fabric and low relief gave it a markedly different appearance. Principally for this reason, the term siliqua is used to describe this coin in this catalog, even though it is probably incorrect. Late in the reign of Constantius II (337–361), Constantine's longest-surviving son, the siliqua was reduced to 144 to the pound, thus giving rise to the concept of heavy and light siliquae (though "pre-reform" and "post-reform" are, perhaps, more accurate designations).

Base metal and billon coinage also underwent considerable change during the three decades of Constantine's reign. From a large nummus of about 27–31mm (which Constantine struck as Caesar), the denomination was continually reduced in size and weight. The first drop occured c. 307/8 and and the second c. 311/3; the nummus was eventually reduced in size to what numismatists call an Æ3 (c. 17–22mm). In 335/6 this once-impressive coin was further reduced to a size category most often called Æ3/4 (15–18mm), and finally, around the time of Constantine's death, it was reduced again to the Æ4 module (10–12mm). The nummus continued to be reduced in weight, purity (the small traces of silver being replaced with lead) and value, eventually becoming what was called a *nummus minimus*. Constantine struck various 'fractional' nummi denominations in the base metal and billon series, most of which are not understood fully, but seemingly are half- or quarter-nummi, or are late examples of the antiquated quinarius.

The development of Constantine's bust types is also of interest. These began with a relatively crude image with laurel wreath and short-cropped hair (in the 'pagan' phase of his reign). Gradually his effigy was transformed into a less-militant image with longer hair, curling at the nape of the neck. The portrait on some of Constantine's final issues is 'upward gazing,' which, when combined with the royal diadem (in place of the laurel wreath), is remniscent of the ancient Greek portraiture of six centuries before. In terms of their general treatment, Constantine's portraits are uniformly youthful, harking back to the Augustan ideal.

Also noteworthy is the shift in emphasis of reverse types from pagan to Christian. Constantine's earliest issues primarily honor the sun-god Sol, and Jupiter, the chief pagan deity. Later, these two deities were abandoned in favor of personifications (and deities-turned-personifications, such as Victory).

Constantine made the best use of his coins for propaganda, paying careful attention to the historical events of his reign. Although most of his commemorative types bear portraits of himself or his sons on the obverse, there was a rather large series of coins and medallions which featured the busts of 'Roma' and 'Constantinopolis' — the personifications of the Empire's two capitals. These issues were so popular that they were perpetuated under Constantine's sons, and in the case of the small silver pieces (c. 1.0g.), even into the 5th and 6th Centuries.

Unfortunately, the remarkable variety of reverse types largely ended with Constantine's reign. Although his sons issued coins of some iconographic interest and variety, there was a homogenization of design which would only increase with the passage of time. The once-vibrant Roman coinage fast became standardized in appearance and lost most of its artistic merit — setbacks from which it never recovered.

The commemorative coins struck after Constantine's death are limited to the smallest and least-valuable denomination, the reduced nummus of the Æ4 module. As a perfect reflection of his institutionalization of Christianity through a gradual transition from paganism, the most common piece shows Constantine driving a quadriga of horses (in the manner of the sun-god Sol) skyward toward the hand of God (the *manus Dei*), which emerges from clouds to receive him into heaven.

FAUSTA

Augusta, a.d. 324–326

Second wife of Constantine the Great
Mother of Constantine II, Constantius II, Constans, Constantina (*w.* of Hannibalianus & Constantius Gallus) and Helena the Younger (*w.* of Julian II)
Daughter of Maximian and Eutropia
Sister of Maxentius
Stepmother of Crispus
Daughter-in-law of Helena and (posthumously) of Constantius I
Aunt of Romulus

Flavia Maxima Fausta, d. A.D. 326. Fausta was wed to Constantine the Great on March 31, 307, perhaps at Arles or Lugdunum. The union cemented a political alliance that had just been established between the rebel governments of Constantine in Gaul, and Maxentius and Maximian in Italy. Constantine's marital status prior to his marriage with Fausta is uncertain, but whether or not he was married to Minervina (the woman by whom earlier he had sired Crispus), he ceased having relations with her.

The father and son rebels in Italy, Maximian and Maxentius, began on friendly terms, sharing their authority. After Maximian had returned to Italy from Gaul (where he made the alliance with Constantine), he had a falling out with his son in April, 308, and fled back to Gaul as a fugitive. There he took refuge with his daughter and new son-in-law, Constantine. Determined to oust Maxentius from Italy, Constantine and Maximian instigated the North African vicar Alexander to rebel against Maxentius.

Maximian, who still held the outlaw title of Augustus, represented Constantine at the Conference of Carnuntum in November 308, where he was stripped of his self-proclaimed title and returned to Gaul in despair. Thereafter he took on an advisory role in his son-in-law's Gallic government. This turn of events allowed Fausta to spend more time with her father while her husband was fighting Germans on the Rhine.

This situation was unsatisfactory for Maximian, who grew restless. Either late in 309 or in the spring of 310, he declared himself emperor and seized the treasury at Arles. Unfortunately for Maximian, Fausta betrayed him to Constantine, who departed hastily from the German front and pursued his father-in-law, who fled south and was eventually captured and killed.

Clearly, Fausta had to choose sides once she became privy to her father's plot. The fact that she chose to betray her father and inform Constantine perhaps indicates that her relationship with her father was poor. In the succeeding years the marriage of Fausta and Constantine produced five children, each of whom was destined to play an important role in state affairs. The births of three sons demonstrate the extent of Fausta's travels, for Constantine II was born at Arles in 316, Constantius II in Illyria in 317 and Constans at Constantinople in 320 or 323. Her two daughters each married half-cousins: the eldest, Constantina, married the short-lived heirs Hanniballianus and Constantius Gallus; Helena the Younger married Julian II, the last emperor of the Constantinian dynasty.

Beginning with her betrayal of her own father and later with her treacherous efforts to ensure the succession of her three sons, Fausta proved her loyalty. She earned in parallel with her mother-in-law, Helena, the titles *Nobilissima Femina* ("most noble woman"), presumably in 317, and Augusta on November 8, 324, after the conclusion of the Second Licinian War. Though Fausta was the wife of Rome's first Christian emperor, she remained a pagan throughout her life.

The one act for which she will forever be known is the framing of her stepson, Crispus, in mid-326. The charges she leveled against him are not certainly known, but they were compelling enough that Constantine ordered his own son's execution. Most historians agree that Fausta falsified the charges in an effort to clear the path of succession for her own three sons.

But in this act of treachery, Fausta sealed her own fate. In the fall of that same year, perhaps in September or October, Fausta was condemned by her husband in what seems to have been the reaction of a father whose guilty conscience had gotten the better of him. She was suffocated to death in a hot bath either at Trier or in Rome (opinions vary). However, it was also rumored that Fausta was executed for having an adulterous affair with a palace official — a slave, or perhaps even the stepson whom she had betrayed. In any case, the deaths of Crispus and Fausta are inextricably linked, either by fact or by effect.

NUMISMATIC NOTE: Coins issued in the name of Fausta (as Augusta) were struck in parallel with those of her mother-in-law Helena, except that Fausta's ended with her death in 326 and those of Helena continued to be struck at some mints.

CRISPUS

CAESAR, A.D. 316–326

SON OF CONSTANTINE THE GREAT AND MINERVINA
STEPSON OF FAUSTA
HALF-BROTHER OF CONSTANTINE II, CONSTANTIUS II, CONSTANS, CONSTANTINA (W. OF HANNIBALLIANUS & CONSTANTIUS GALLUS) AND HELENA THE YOUNGER (W. OF JULIAN II)
HALF-COUSIN OF DELMATIUS, HANNIBALLIANUS, CONSTANTIUS GALLUS, JULIAN II, LICINIUS II AND NEPOTIAN
GRANDSON OF CONSTANTIUS I AND HELENA

Flavius Julius (*or* Valerius) Crispus, c. A.D. 300 or 303/5–326. The eldest son of Constantine the Great, Crispus was born while his father was a political hostage in the courts of Diocletian and Galerius. He was the only child born of his father's union with Minervina, a woman who more than likely was his first wife, but who may have been a concubine. Later in his life, detractors rumored that Crispus was a bastard child, and had no blood connection to Constantine. However, this is best regarded as hostile propaganda spread by his stepmother, Fausta.

Crispus was awarded the rank of Caesar along with his infant half-brother Constantine II late in 316, perhaps on October 8. The investiture was probably informal, for it seems to have been a response to the raising of the general Valerius Valens to the rank of Augustus by Constantine's rival in the East, Licinius I. The First Licinian War, which occasioned these appointments, was concluded by treaty on February 17, 317, greatly to the advantage of Constantine, who gained much of the Balkans as a result.

Less than two weeks after the truce, Constantine and Licinius I confirmed their agreement on March 1, at Serdica. There, a ceremony was held at which Crispus, Constantine II and Licinius' son, Licinius II, were formally hailed Caesar. Thereafter, Crispus (then a young teenager) was sent to Trier to hone his skills in war and administration. Among his educators was Lactantius, author of *De Mortibus Persecutorum*.

In 320 Crispus served with distinction in campaigns against the Alemmani and Franks, making it plain that he possessed talent in the art of war. Family life was also good for Crispus: he enjoyed the full confidence of his father, had been adopted by his stepmother, and on March 1, 321, had married a woman named Helena (not Helena the Younger, wife of Julian II). Though Helena bore him a son in 322, no coins were struck for her or her child.

Crispus' greatest hour came late in 324 during the Second Licinian War. The young Caesar was placed in charge of the Constantinian fleet and during the course of his maneuvers he captured the considerably larger fleet of Licinius. Not long after, he used the transport vessels under his command to make a flotilla, over which his father's soldiers marched onto Asian soil to complete their victory. As a consequence of these actions, Crispus achieved hero status, for his naval victory was compared to that achieved off Salamis 630 years earlier by the Macedonian king Demetrius Poliorcetes. Christian historians, such as Eusebius, were not shy about heaping praise upon him and comparing him to his father.

But Crispus' glory was short-lived, perhaps because his achievements were too impressive. Crispus accompanied his father and stepmother, Fausta, to Italy, where he soon was accused of potentially treasonous charges, the exact nature of which are not known. The approximately 21-year-old Crispus was convicted and executed at Pola, seemingly in August or September of 326.

The episode of Crispus' downfall remains a mystery to historians. Some suspect the charges were treason and that they stemmed from Crispus' rumored request that his father abdicate on the 20th anniversary of his reign (which occurred in that very year, or in 327, depending on how it is reckoned). A more fanciful rumor then in circulation was that Fausta had fallen in love with him and that she came to detest him when he rebuffed her amorous advances.

The overwhelming likelihood is that Fausta implicated her son-in-law and that regardless of the nature of the charges, her aim was to remove him as a rival to her own three sons (who were then quite young, and no competition for the hero Crispus). Constantine soon realized the magnitude of his error and commemorated his promising son with a golden statue in honor of "the son whom I unjustly condemned." The grief-stricken emperor soon executed Fausta on charges that most historians believe were linked to the death of Crispus.

NUMISMATIC NOTE: The date traditionally cited for Crispus' being hailed Caesar, March 1, 317, seems only to have been the formal date of investiture. Coins dated to late 316 were struck in Crispus' name at Trier, Arles and Ticinum.

DELMATIUS

Caesar, A.D. 335–337

Grandson of Constantius I and Theodora
Brother of Hanniballianus
Brother-in-law and half-cousin of Constantina (w. of Hanniballianus & Constantius Gallus)
Nephew of Licinius I and Constantia
Cousin of Constantius Gallus, Julian II, Licinius II and Nepotian
Half-nephew of Constantine the Great
Half-cousin of Crispus, Constantine II, Constantius II, Constans and Helena the Younger (w. of Julian II)

Flavius Julius Delmatius (or Dalmatius), c. A.D. 313 (or c. 315?)–337. Perhaps the most tragic tale of the Constantinian Era is that of the descendants of Theodora and the emperor Constantius I, for their branch of the family was at odds with Constantine the Great and his sons. As one of several grandchildren of Theodora, Delmatius was persecuted throughout his childhood and eventually was murdered because his bloodlines established him as a rival to the throne.

Delmatius spent his early years in quiet exile, studying in Toulouse with his brother, Hanniballianus, who was a year or two his junior. As Delmatius matured, Constantine the Great must have considered his half-nephew a capable leader, for in 334 he appears to have entrusted him with the task of suppressing the revolt of Calocaerus in Cyprus (some historians, perhaps rightly, attribute this action to his homonymous father, however).

Delmatius (be he the half-nephew or half-brother of Constantine) not only stamped out the revolt, but also burned the usurper alive as punishment. Furthermore, he gathered sufficient evidence of the involvement of Licinius I's bastard son (who had survived his father's downfall and held high rank) so that he too was killed, or at the very least was condemned to slavery.

When Constantine the Great announced his plan of succession on September 18, 335, he included Delmatius. The honors fell upon Constantine's three remaining sons (Constantine II, Constantius II and Constans) and his two eldest half-nephews from Theodora's branch of the family, the brothers Delmatius and Hanniballianus.

Hanniballianus was installed on the Persian border with the un-Roman titles *Rex regum et Pontiacarum gentium*, so there were in essence only four members of the regular rulership (all of whom were Caesars). As such, Delmatius may have been added to the mix so that a new Tetrarchy (hereditary though it was) would be created.

Delmatius was given the lower Danube territories (the eastern and southern Balkans), consisting of Thrace, Macedon and Achaea. This region at the time was peaceful, but it included the Danube frontier (sometimes called the "Gothic bank") and was a prime region for recruiting soldiers. His territory did not extend into Illyria (Pannonia), which we are told was occupied by Constans. Historians have rightly suspected that Constantine the Great purposely gave Delmatius the city of Constantinople (in Thrace) in hopes that the capital would not become a focus for dispute among his three sons.

Following Constantine's death on May 22, 337, there was an interregnum of 110 days during which each of the successors retained their titles and theoretically ruled in the name of the deceased Constantine. However, sometime during this period the brothers Delmatius and Hannibalianus were executed along with their father and other members of their lineage, thus leaving Constantine's three sons to carve up the Empire. Spared in the purge because of their youth or sickliness were three of Delmatius' cousins: Nepotian, Constantius Gallus and Julian II, each of whom would later play a role in Imperial politics.

NUMISMATIC NOTE: The amount of coinage struck for Delmatius is considerably larger than that for his brother Hanniballianus. He coined at nine Imperial mints from Gaul to the Bosporus whereas his brother struck only at Constantinople. Just as with his brother, Delmatius' name is not spelled consistently, sometimes occuring as Dalmatius (both on coins and in literary sources), though on coinage this variant occurs most often on issues of Thessalonica and Nicimedia.

HANNIBALLIANUS

REX REGUM, A.D. 335–337

GRANDSON OF CONSTANTIUS I AND THEODORA
BROTHER OF DELMATIUS
HUSBAND AND HALF-COUSIN OF CONSTANTINA (FUTURE W. OF CONSTANTIUS GALLUS)
NEPHEW OF LICINIUS I AND CONSTANTIA
COUSIN OF CONSTANTIUS GALLUS, JULIAN II, LICINIUS II AND NEPOTIAN
HALF-NEPHEW OF CONSTANTINE THE GREAT
HALF-COUSIN OF CRISPUS, CONSTANTINE II, CONSTANTIUS II, CONSTANS AND HELENA THE YOUNGER (W. OF JULIAN II)

Flavius Claudius Hanniballianus (or Hannibalianus) c. A.D. 314/5(?)–337. Hanniballianus was the younger son of Flavius Delmatius, son of Constantius I (emperor, 305–306) and his second wife, Theodora. Although the elder Dematius never achieved office higher than consul (in

333), his sons Delmatius and Hanniballianus shared in the plan of succession enacted by his half-brother, Constantine the Great, in 335.

Since Constantine the Great was born to Constantius I's first companion, Helena, the descendants of that emperor's subsequent wife, Theodora, were considered rivals to a throne that was jealously guarded by Constantine, his mother Helena, and his wife Fausta. Thus, the descendants of Theodora, including Hanniballianus, lived in semi-exile until about 326, when Fausta was executed and Helena embarked on her pilgrimage to the Holy Land.

Hanniballianus was later styled *Nobilissimus* ("most noble") by Constantine, and in November of 335, when he was perhaps 20 years old, he was brought into the Imperial fold. Constantine gave him titular control over the massive region of Pontus and the buffer-state Armenia. Instead of the rank of Caesar (which was accorded to the other four heirs), he was given the extra-Imperial title *Rex regum et Pontiacarum gentium* ("King of kings and of the Pontic peoples").

In addition to governing responsibilities, Constantine further honored Hanniballianus by arranging that his eldest daughter, Constantina, become his wife. Even though this marriage of half-cousins linked the rival family branches of Helena and Theodora, it failed to prevent inter-family warfare (as Constantine, no doubt, had hoped it might).

By giving Hanniballianus the boastful title "King of Kings" (*Rex regum*), Constantine not only established the nature of his authority in Armenia, but also made it clear that one day he was to take the place of Shapur II (309–379) within his own kingdom. Further antagonizing the Sasanians was Hanniballianus' coin type, which features the river-god Euphrates reclining.

Hanniballianus made his headquarters at Caesarea in Cappadocia, which was an important military hub in the Roman East but was not particularly central to his appointed territories. Because of this, many historians have come to view his role in the administration as overseer of the eastern front rather than strictly as governor of Armenia and Pontus.

Armenia was particularly troubled at this point in time. The Sasanians invaded it sometime in 335 or 336, and in so doing broke a treaty which had stood for nearly 40 years. The surprise attack was provoked by Constantine's military buildup on the frontier, and though the Armenians were able to oust Shapur's armies with Roman help, they appear to have lost their Christian king Tigranes in the process.

The Persian campaign was now Constantine's driving ambition and he could justify his mission by the fact that Shapur II had broken their peace treaty. Indeed, leading his armies beyond Rome's eastern border was perhaps the only important goal Constantine had not yet achieved. But the emperor of 30 years died just as he was embarking on his monumental invasion, and within three months of that tragic event Hanniballianus himself was murdered along with his brother Delmatius and many of his family members and partisans.

The murders occurred sometime between May 22 and September 9, 337, and were engineered by the three sons of Constantine, who had no desire to share their inheritance with descendants of Theodora. Hanniballianus' widow, Constantina (herself the eldest sister of the murderers), disappeared from the political scene after the purge, only to re-emerge powerfully in 350, when she supported the Pannonian Master of the Infantry Vetranio, and later still, in 351, when she was married to another of her half-cousins, Constantius Gallus.

NUMISMATIC NOTE: All of Hanniballianus' coins were struck at Constantinople. The first issue in silver is extremely rare and is dated by scholars to 335. His second was in base metal and is dated to 336–7, and is part of the GLORIA EXERCITVS issues struck for the other members of Constantine's family after the module had been reduced yet again (making them what are usually called Æ4's). Both issues have a similar reverse scene of the river-god Euphrates reclining (on silver) or seated (on æs), with the former being inscribed FELICITAS PVBLICA and the latter SECVRITAS PVBLICA. His name is spelled Annibalianus on the silver coins and on some of his base metal issue.

CONSTANTINE II A.D. 337–340

CAESAR, A.D. 316–337

SON OF CONSTANTINE THE GREAT AND FAUSTA
BROTHER OF CONSTANTIUS II, CONSTANS, CONSTANTINA (W. OF HANNIBALLIANUS & CONSTANTIUS GALLUS) AND HELENA THE YOUNGER (W. OF JULIAN II)
HALF-BROTHER OF CRISPUS
HALF-COUSIN OF DELMATIUS, HANNIBALLIANUS, CONSTANTIUS GALLUS, JULIAN II, LICINIUS II AND NEPOTIAN
GRANDSON OF CONSTANTIUS I, HELENA, MAXIMIAN AND EUTROPIA
UNCLE OF CONSTANTIA (W. OF GRATIAN)

Flavius Claudius (or Julius) Constantinus ("Constantine Junior"), c. A.D. 316–340. Surprisingly little is known about Constantine II, the eldest son of Constantine the Great and Fausta. His personality is largely a mystery except that we know he was so fanatical about Orthodox Christianity that he threatened civil war in defense of his faith. Of his two wives, nothing of substance is known, not even their names.

Although his parentage was questioned in ancient times, we may be certain that Constantine the Great was his father, and that Fausta — not a concubine — was his mother. He was born at Arles, a city in southern Gaul about 20 miles from the Mediterranean coast, and spent most of his life in the western provinces.

Sometime late in 316, before he had reached his first year, Constantine II was given the extraordinary rank of Caesar alongside his much older half-brother, Crispus. About half a year later (after the First Licinian War had ended), Constantine II and Crispus were formally invested with that rank together with the child Licinius II, who was the heir of Constantine the Great's rival, Licinius I. The ceremony was held on March 1, 317, at Serdica. Constantine II was elected consul four times (320, 321, 324 and 329) during the two decades he held the rank of Caesar.

Constantine II's formative years were eventful. In 323, though only about 7 years old, he accompanied his half-brother, Crispus, on campaign in Germany and in the following year, 324, the Empire came entirely under the control of their father, Constantine I. In September of that year Constantine I deposed Licinius I. In 326, Constantine II lost two close relatives: his mother, Fausta, and his beloved half-brother, Crispus. Both were executed on orders of his father in a confused atmosphere of suspected treason and infidelity.

The round of family executions certainly made it clear to Constantine II that no one was indispensable in his father's regime and that being a family member in and of itself offered no protection. Constantine II, though motherless and only about 10 years old, was now the senior heir in the Roman Empire. Consequently, he was sent to Trier to take over Crispus' Gallic command.

Perhaps to acknowledge this important promotion, in 328 Constantine II's birthplace, Arles, was renamed Constantina in his honor. The young heir wasted no time in taking military action, and is credited with defeating the Alemanni about this time, though he was merely at his father's side. In 332, he temporarily left the Rhine frontier and joined his father's campaign against the Goths and Sarmatians in Thrace and Moesia. Their campaign was so successful was that they reportedly caused one of their opponents, the Visigothic king Alaric I, to sustain nearly 100,000 deaths among his followers. Constantine II subsequently returned to Trier.

Toward the end of 335, Constantine the Great announced a plan for succession. The Empire was divided among his three sons, who already were Caesars, and two half-nephews (themselves brothers), who were brought into the Imperial fold. Since Constantine II was so familiar with the western provinces, he was allotted Gaul, Britain and Spain, and seemingly the westernmost part of North Africa (south of Spain), either as part of the original allotment or as a later addition.

The rest of the Empire was divided between the four other relatives: Constantius II, Constantine II's younger brother, received Asia Minor; his youngest brother, Constans, received Italy and Illyria (and eventually the lower Danubian provinces and North Africa); a half-cousin, Hannibal-lianus, inherited Pontus and Armenia; and another half-cousin, Delmatius, received the lower Danubian provinces and (seemingly) Constantinople.

This arrangement survived the nearly two years left in the life of Constantine the Great, who throughout retained supreme power as Augustus. However, when Constantine died on May 22, 337, his idealistic allotment (in which power was shared by two branches of the family) was put to the test.

Constantine II wasted no time in exerting his 'seniority' over his two brothers and two half-cousins, for on June 17, 337 (only 26 days after his father had died. Indeed, perhaps immediately after the news had traveled the 1,200 miles from Nicomedia to Trier), he issued a document which released Bishop Athanasius from his exile in Trier. This involved a particularly thorny religious matter, and one which would haunt Constantine's legacy.

The anti-Arian Bishop Athanasius had been exiled from his see in Alexandria, and had sought refuge with Constantine II at Trier. Now that Constantine II was attempting to test his authority, he ordered that Athanasius be allowed to return safely to Alexandria, even though that city was not within his own realm. This infuriated Constantius II, a fanatical Arian, who took exception to this proposal both politically and religiously. However, with more than enough on his own agenda, Constantius II tolerated Athanasius' return on November 23, 337.

Sometime during the 110 days after Constantine's death, the three sons of Constantine conspired to murder Delmatius and Hanniballianus together with most of their family members and partisans. That Constantius II took the lead in this purge is acknowledged by most historians. The brothers then carved up the territories once occupied by their half-cousins, and on September 9, 337, each assumed the title of Augustus.

As the Senior Augustus, Constantine II was theoretically in the position of greatest responsibility, but he was the loser in the aftermath. His alloted territories in the West were remote, troubled and impoverished compared with those given to his two younger brothers. Furthermore, he was the only one who did not benefit from the murder of his half-cousins, because he was geographically isolated from the territories which came up for grabs. Angered by all of this, Constantine II antagonized his nearest neighbor, Constans, by demanding that he forfeit Italy and North Africa. The demand was refused.

Tensions among the brothers rose, and in June of 338, only nine months into their independent reigns, they met in the Balkans (perhaps at

Viminacium) to settle their territorial disputes. If anything, this made matters worse for Constantine II, for all of his demands were refused by his two younger brothers, who themselves had formed a loose alliance of mutual protection from Constantine II.

Having gained no satisfaction from negotiation, Constantine II turned to force of arms. In the spring of 340 he launched a surprise offensive against his youngest brother, leading a large land and naval force into Italy while Constans was away in the Balkans. If he assumed there would be an element of surprise, he was sorely disappointed when a large army that Constans had left behind ambushed him near Aquileia. The war was over almost as soon as it had begun, for in March or April of 340, the 24-year-old Constantine II was killed in a pitched battle. His corpse was thrown into the Alsa river by Constans' soldiers, but later was salvaged and sent to Constantinople for an honorable burial.

NUMISMATIC NOTE: On many of Constantine II's coins, his name appears in the form CONSTANTINVS IVN., with the abbreviation IVN being expanded to IVNIOR on a gold medallion from Thessalonica. The date traditionally cited for Constantine II being hailed Caesar (March 1, 317) must be considered only as the formal date, for his earliest coinage at Trier, Arles and Ticinum demonstrates he achieved the rank late in 316.

CONSTANS A.D. 337–350

CAESAR, A.D. 333–337

SON OF CONSTANTINE THE GREAT AND FAUSTA
BROTHER OF CONSTANTINE II, CONSTANTIUS II, CONSTANTINA (W. OF HANNIBALLIANUS & CONSTANTIUS GALLUS) AND HELENA THE YOUNGER (W. OF JULIAN II)
HALF-BROTHER OF CRISPUS
HALF-COUSIN OF DELMATIUS, HANNIBALLIANUS, CONSTANTIUS GALLUS, JULIAN II, LICINIUS II AND NEPOTIAN
GRANDSON OF CONSTANTIUS I, HELENA, MAXIMIAN AND EUTROPIA
UNCLE OF CONSTANTIA (W. OF GRATIAN)

Flavius Julius Constans, A.D. 320 or 323–350. The youngest son of Constantine the Great, Constans was born into the opulent court of Constantinople, where he studied under Christian tutors and was prepared for a leading role in state affairs. Though none of the three sons of Constantine and Fausta receive good reviews from the ancient historians, Constans' may be the worst. Indeed, in his case it was his caustic personality that proved to be his undoing.

Historians are sharply divided on his date of birth, but Constans was either 9 or 12 years old when he was hailed Caesar on Christmas day, 333. An arranged marriage to the daughter of the Cretan minister Ablabius was planned for him, but it did not materialize, and his would-be bride later married the Sasanian king Shapur II.

Nearly two years later, late in 335, Constans was installed in Italy as the ruling Caesar. Though his father remained the only Augustus, he had divided the Empire among five heirs, two being Constans' brothers (Constantine II in the western provinces, and Constantius II in Asia Minor), and two being his half-cousins (Delmatius in the lower Balkans, and Hanniballianus on the Persian front).

When Constantine I died in May, 337, Constans was baptized and soon thereafter conspired with his brothers to murder their half-cousins, Delmatius and Hanniballianus. The purge complete, the three brothers absorbed the now-vacant territories and hailed themselves Augusti on September 9, 337.

Because of his relative youth, Constans reigned with the help of advisers and was technically subordinate to his eldest brother, Constantine II, who had established his own court at Trier. Within months a conflict emerged, for despite his seniority, Constantine II ruled the relatively unrewarding provinces of Gaul, Britain and Spain. To make matters worse, his geographic isolation prevented him from benefiting from the "land rush" that followed the murder of the half-cousins.

Constans and Constantius II benefited enormously from the purge: the former nominally took control of the Balkan territories once ruled by Delmatius, and Constantius II gained Hanniballianus' former territories of Pontus and Armenia. Constantine II was understandably jealous, for his seniority was not reflected in the division of spoils, and he demanded of Constans that he forfeit Italy and North Africa. But the request was roundly rejected.

With the specter of war looming, the brothers held a conference in June of 338 in the Balkans, perhaps at the military hub of Viminacium. Here, no doubt, Constantine II hoped to acquire more territory and assert himself over his younger brothers. But nothing of the sort occurred. In fact, the exact opposite transpired, for Constans and Constantius II entered into an informal alliance, each confirming the others' territories. Young Constans now had an impressive realm that stretched from Constantinople in the East to the borders of Italy and North Africa in the West

Later in 338 and into 339 tensions continued to mount, and Constans became increasingly concerned that he and his elder brother would go to war. The alliance between the two younger brothers strengthened, and Constans proved his sincerity by offering to recruit an army to help Constantius II fight the Sasanians. In 339, he may also have given the city of Constantinople and its Thracian hinterland to his brother. It seems he also assuaged another of Constantius II's concerns by accepting into Rome the Alexandrian Bishop Anathasius, whom the Arian Constantius II had exiled as a trouble-maker.

Meanwhile, Constantine II was still dissatisfied, and no doubt feared the consequences of his younger brothers becoming too closely allied. War could no longer be avoided and in the spring of 340 Constantine II invaded Italy, only to die in an ambush outside Aquileia. Constans, who was at the time in the Balkans recruiting soldiers for Constantius II, gained total victory without even being present for the battle.

The political environment had changed a great deal in three short years: of the original six rulers, only two remained, and the Empire was divided between Europe and Asia. Domination of the Balkans remained yet uncertain, for in the settlement that followed the death of Constantine II, Constans may have forfeited all or part of the Lower Balkans to Constantius II (who already had Constantinople).

Nearly a decade remained of the reign of Constans, then a young man of 17 or 20. He does not receive good reviews from historians such as Aurelius Victor and Eutropius, who berate him for his avarice, meanness, contempt, depravity and flagrant homosexuality. Constans can hardly be credited with much common sense either, for he behaved contemptuously toward his soldiers, who came to despise him. He is known to have waged war against the Franks in the latter half of 341, successfully concluding this campaign in the spring of 342. Either later in that year, or in the early part of 343, Constans sailed to Britain, for which voyage he gained the historical distinction of being the last legitimate emperor to visit that island. We know virtually nothing of his operations there, except that they occurred in the vicinity of Hadrian's Wall.

In the realm of religion Constans was something of a hero to many in the West, for he crusaded fanatically on behalf of Catholic Orthodoxy and strongly opposed the Arianism espoused by eastern "heretics" (such as his brother Constantius II). Religious infighting was only enflamed at the Council of Serdica and almost came to blows in 346, when Constans threatened war against Constantius II if the Bishop Athanasius (a defender of the Nicene faith against Arianism) was not allowed to return to his see at Alexandria on October 21, 346. Constans was also hailed for his persecutions of non-Catholic Donatists in Africa in 347.

The 12-year reign of Constans ended swiftly and by surprise on January 18, 350, at Augustodunum, where he was deposed by his own field commander (*comes rei militaris*) Magnentius. The coup took place at a party hosted by Constans' finance minister, Marcellinus, and from there, news spread to the army, which wasted little time in supporting Magnentius. Constans fled toward the Spanish border but was overtaken by soldiers near the Pyrenees and killed by Gaiso, one of Magnentius' officers.

CONSTANTIUS II A.D. 337–361

CAESAR, A.D. 324–337

SON OF CONSTANTINE THE GREAT AND FAUSTA
BROTHER OF CONSTANTINE II, CONSTANS, CONSTANTINA (*w.* OF HANNIBALLIANUS & CONSTANTIUS GALLUS) AND HELENA THE YOUNGER (*w.* OF JULIAN II)
HALF-BROTHER OF CRISPUS
HALF-COUSIN OF DELMATIUS, HANNIBALLIANUS, CONSTANTIUS GALLUS, JULIAN II, LICINIUS II AND NEPOTIAN
GRANDSON OF CONSTANTIUS I, HELENA, MAXIMIAN AND EUTROPIA
FATHER OF CONSTANTIA (*w.* OF GRATIAN)

Flavius Julius Valerius Constantius, A.D. 317–361. The middle son of Constantine the Great and Fausta, Constantius II was destined to be the longest-surviving of Constantine's heirs, and the one who would most convincingly promote the policies of his father. But his 34 years on the throne were not glorious and peaceful. Constantius II was tormented by religious conflict, rebellion, fratricidal warfare, civil strife and fearsome invasions across the Rhine, Danube and Euphrates.

Constantius II proved very much to be his father's son. He was cautious, strategic, suspicious and prone to cruelty. He was also brave in the face of danger, and seemed never to shy away from the unenviable tasks that faced men who held his office. Some of his contemporaries considered him stupid, dull-witted and unduly influenced by palace eunuchs. Despite these handicaps, on most occasions Constantius II found the most efficient solutions to his many problems.

Constantius II was born in Illyria, perhaps at the provincial capital of Sirmium, in 317, only a few months after his father had won a luke-warm victory in the First Licinian War. Some six years later, just after his father defeated Licinius I at Adrianople (the first important battle of the Second Licinian War), Constantius II was nominated Caesar in July or August of 324. He was officially invested on November 8, 324, seemingly at the ceremony where his mother, Fausta, and grandmother Helena were hailed Augustae.

By defeating Licinius I for the second time, Constantine had taken control of the entire Roman world. However, tragedy struck late in 326, when Constantine executed both his eldest son, Crispus, and his wife,

Fausta. Since Crispus had formerly been situated in Gaul, Constantius II was sent there to take command in his place. However, he was soon relieved by his older brother, Constantine II, and was able to return to the East.

In 333, a decade after he was hailed Caesar (then about age 16), Constantius II was installed at Antioch to take on serious responsibilities. In 335, Constantine's plan for succession was formalized, and he divided the Empire among his three sons (Constantine II, Constantius II and Constans) and his two eldest half-nephews (Delmatius and Hanniballianus).

In 336, Constantius II journeyed to Constantinople, where in July he celebrated his father's *tricennalia* (30th year in power) and his own marriage to a half-cousin whose name is not recorded, but who was the sister of Julian II.

Constantius II had been allotted the wealthy East, to which he had become acclimated over the previous nine years. His domain stretched from the Bosporus to Cyrenaica, and included the important regions of Syria and Egypt. The eastern front (technically Armenia and Pontus), however, was given to his half-cousin Hanniballianus, to whom Constantine had accorded the title "King of Kings" (*Rex regum*).

For most of his reign Constantius II used Antioch as his base of operations. Not only was it more affluent than Constantinople (which, newly founded, had not yet come to prominence), but it was ideally located for responding to the frequent Sasanian invasions of Northern Mesopotamia.

Constantine had left his children two grave problems: he had stirred up the Sasanians into a warlike state, and he had divided his Empire among five heirs who were unlikely to share. Of Constantine the Great's three sons, Constantius II proved the most capable in dealing with these problems, not merely because he was perhaps the most competent, but also because he was based in Asia Minor, the region most immediately and directly affected. When his father died in May, 337, Constantius II presided over the funeral in Constantinople, and at age 20 wasted no time in recruiting the army to execute the leading members and partisans of the rival family branch founded two generations earlier by the emperor Constantius I and his wife, Theodora. Among those to fall were the Caesar Delmatius and the *Rex regum* Hanniballianus, the two half-cousins with whom the sons of Constantine shared their inheritance.

Though Delmatius and Hanniballianus shared the same grandfather as the sons of Constantine, that is where their similarities ended. Even though Constantius II was not the eldest of the three sons of Constantine, historians rightly have surmised that he took the leading role in the purge. Though Constans was nearby, he was perhaps too young to be of much assistance, and his eldest brother, Constantine II, at Trier, was too far away.

The purge was quick and efficient, but not entirely ruthless, for the brothers spared the three youngest and sickliest of their half-cousins.

These were Constantius Gallus, Nepotian and Julian II, each of whom later proved to be a thorn in the side of Constantius II (who no doubt regretted that he had shown any mercy at all). Many saw the murders as a necessary evil, for seldom (if ever) had two rival branches of a family ruled together peacefully.

Once the murders had occurred, the three sons of Constantine each assumed the title of Augustus on September 9, 337, 110 days after their father had died. Each ruled in his appointed provinces, but the least satisfied of the heirs was the eldest son, Constantine II, who had been given the remote and relatively impoverished western provinces of Gaul, Spain and Britain (and seemingly the westernmost part of North Africa).

Trouble began to brew almost immediately — first on the religious front, and then on the territorial front. Less than a month after their father's death — even before the half-cousins were murdered, and fully 12 weeks before the brothers hailed themselves Augusti — Constantine II (a devout Orthodox Catholic) antagonized Constantius II (an Arian) by releasing the controversial bishop Athanasius from his exile at Trier and restoring him to his see in Alexandria.

Since Athanasius' Orthodox views opposed those held by Constantius II, in whose realm Alexandria was situated, this became a major diplomatic conflict. However, Constantius II found it expedient to appease his elder brother. Only in 339 did he grow so incensed at the activities of Athanasius that he exiled him to Rome, where the bishop was offered refuge by Constantius II's younger brother, Constans (who was not only an Orthodox Catholic but who, by this time, was a staunch ally of Constantius II).

After the three became Augusti, Constantine II flexed his illusory authority as Senior Augustus over the youngest brother, Constans, by demanding that he forfeit Italy and the remainder of North Africa, and thus make the land distribution more equitable. Though the demand seems fair (Constans had all of the Balkans, which at that point in time included Constantinople, and Constantius II had all of Asia, the Holy Land and Egypt), it was rejected.

In June, 338, the three brothers held a conference in the Balkans, probably at Viminacium, to find a solution. But the results did not favor Constantine II, whose territorial demands were again refused. The two younger siblings banded together: they confirmed each others' territorial acquisitions from Delmatius and Hanniballianus, and agreed to support each other in the event Constantine II became aggressive. After the conference, Constantius II hurried back to Antioch, whence he led a counter-offensive against the Sasanian king Shapur II (309–379), who had invaded Roman territory in the meantime.

In many ways the conference of June, 338 was a repeat of the one hosted at Carnuntum 30 years earlier by Galerius, then the Senior Augustus of the revised Tetrarchy. Galerius invited all claimants to participate in negotiations, but in the end he forced his own agenda. All of Galerius' rivals left the Balkans dissatisfied and prepared for the civil war that would follow.

With nothing resolved, trouble continued to brew between the brothers Constantine II and Constans. Constantius II, however, remained aloof because of the wars he fought against the Sasanians each and every summer from 338 to 350. In the spring of 340, less than two years after the failed conference, Constantine II invaded Italy in an attempt to take it from his brother forcibly. However, he died in the process, leaving only two emperors to rule: Constans in Europe and Constantius II in Asia.

During the tense period between the conference of June, 338 and the invasion of Italy in the spring of 340, Constans seems to have given Constantius II control of Constantinople and its Thracian hinterland. Though found on European soil, Constantinople was already "eastern" in character. Its inclusion in the Asian territories of Constantius II only made this aspect of its culture all the more prevalent.

Constantius II and Constans co-existed for the next decade (340 to 350), but were never on particularly good terms. The fact that Constantius II was usually occupied with Sasanian invasions of Northern Mesopotamia no doubt improved relations between the brothers, for there was less idle time for controversies to emerge. Constans had fewer problems in the West. This was perhaps fortunate, for he seemed less competent to deal with them.

The Orthodox Catholic Constans, however, was fully occupied by religion, which was the only cause for a serious conflict between him and Constantius II. Their inherent opposition as supporters of Orthodoxy and Arianism was intensified at the Council of Serdica, and in 345 their differences were brought to the forefront with the death of Bishop Gregory of Alexandria (who had replaced the exiled Athanasius).

In 346, Constans threatened war against his older brother if he did not allow Athanasius to reclaim his now-vacant see at Alexandria. It was an uncanny return to the conflict Constantius II had earlier experienced with his older brother Constantine II, for the restoration of Athanasius — the champion of the anti-Arian Nicene doctrine — to Alexandria was the focus of debate.

The problem was resolved when Constantius II conceded, and allowed Athanasius to return to Alexandria in October 346. Constantius II no doubt viewed the compromise as a matter of the utmost practicality, for in the spring of that year the Sasanians had besieged the city of Nisibis on Rome's eastern frontier. Indeed, amid all the religious controversy, Constantius II was preparing for a campaign (against Shapur II), which he led personally in 347.

In January of 350, the western emperor Constans fell victim to a coup led by his field commander Magnentius. The Gallic armies, who despised Constans, immediately supported the coup, and hailed Magnentius as their new emperor. In some respects this was a fortunate development for Constantius II, for he now had an entirely legitimate reason to wage war in the West, and to take command of the whole of the Empire, just as his father had done a quarter century before. For the meantime, however, he was still too occupied with Shapur II to visit the Balkans in person.

Instead, he was fortunate to have his eldest sister, Constantina, in Pannonia (Illyria). She prevented the spread of Magnentius' revolt beyond the borders of Italy by convincing Vetranio, the Pannonian Master of the Infantry (*magister peditum*), to side with Constantius II (for his loyalty was wavering). With her blessings (and perhaps at her insistence), Vetranio was hailed emperor at Sirmium on March 1, 350.

Vetranio held the Balkans for Constantius II, allowing him to finish his war with the Sasanians. In the meantime, Magnentius lost Cologne to the Frankish turncoat Silvanus, and suffered a usurpation in Rome in June, 350 by Nepotian, one of Constantius II's three surviving half-cousins. While Nepotian's revolt alarmed Magnentius, it ended within a month.

The real threat to Magnentius' immediate safety was posed by Germans along the Rhine, whom Constantius II had stirred up to harass Magnentius' rear. In response, Magnentius raised his relative Decentius to the rank of Caesar in July or August, 350 and left him in Gaul to defend the Rhine. Though both Constantius II and Magnentius now each had two fronts to concern them, the problems in Mesopotamia were coming temporarily to an end, and Constantius II was able to travel to Europe to deal with Magnentius in person.

Constantius II departed Antioch at the head of an army and crossed onto European soil late in the fall of 350. He had traveled barely more than 50 miles in Thrace when, at Heraclea, he was met by embassies from both Vetranio and Magnentius — the former to assure loyalty, the latter to discuss options to war. The eastern emperor continued his westward trek for more than 350 miles until he arrived at Naïssus (*mod.* Nis), and oversaw the abdication of Vetranio on Christmas day, 350.

While wintering in the Balkans, Constantius II awaited his chance to confront Magnentius in the spring. When additional diplomatic efforts failed early in 351, Constantius II realized he was going to be in Europe for the foreseeable future, and enlisted the help of one of his two remaining half-cousins, Constantius Gallus, whom he raised to the rank of Caesar on March 15.

In addition to receiving rank, Gallus was also married to Constantina (the emperor's sister, who had earlier supported Vetranio), and was sent to Antioch with a praetorian prefect, Thalassius, to rule Asia in the emperor's name. Gallus' task seemed relatively easy, for Shapur II was behaving peacefully.

Now feeling confident in the security of Asia, Constantius II invaded Italy in the summer of 351. His army was smaller than that commanded by Magnentius, who defeated him at Atrans. Now uncertain as to how he would fare in the war, Constantius II offered to make peace with the rebel, but Magnentius refused, and instead invaded Pannonia that same summer.

Constantius II back-pedaled as Magnentius advanced more than 75 miles into Pannonia and captured the capital Siscia. The rebel pushed more than 150 miles further, to the vicinity of Sirmium (which was beyond Constantius II's rear), and then doubled back to the northwest another 70 miles or so, where he established himself at Mursa (*mod.* Osijek). It was at this village, about 10 miles from the Danube, that the two armies met on September 28, 351, in one of the bloodiest battles of the century.

Though the enormous casualties (about 55,000) were suffered almost equally, Constantius II won the day with his cavalry and archers, who picked apart Magnentius' infantry. The victory of cavalry over infantry was a watershed moment in military history, and greatly influenced the future composition of the Imperial armies. It was now Magnentius' turn to retreat, which he did slowly back to Aquileia in Italy. Both armies had suffered so terribly that neither was anxious to confront the other.

However, by the summer of 352, Constantius II was in a position to launch a second invasion of Italy, only to discover upon arrival that his opponent had fled and taken refuge in Gaul. Thus, Italy and Sicily were taken almost without a fight, as were North Africa and Spain (both of which appear to have sided with Constantius II about this time). In one fell swoop Magnentius had lost the greater part of his rebel Empire, which was now reduced principally to Gaul. Constantius II pursued his enemy, and in August of 353, both Magnentius and his relative, the Caesar Decentius, committed suicide.

Now that he had gained control over the whole Empire, Constantius II was destined to face new and equally menacing tasks. The first was to remove his cruel and unpopular half-cousin Gallus from his Caesarship in Antioch. Gallus had been ruling viciously and incompetently ever since he had been installed. Until this point, Constantius II could do little to remedy the situation, for he could hardly confront a usurpation in Asia Minor before he had resolved his problems in the West.

Constantius II recalled Gallus to Milan in 354, certain he would not resist, for he seems to have misled his young colleague into believing he would be re-assigned in the West. However, when Gallus arrived at Istra (not far from the Italian border) in the winter of 354, he was arrested, tried and beheaded.

Now Constantius II ruled the whole Empire alone. He was far too suspicious a man to elect a colleague who was not a family member (as Diocletian had done), yet he had no children of his own. There was only one eligible relative: his half-cousin Julian II. Considering the poor experiences he had had with his brothers and other half-cousins, Constantius II no doubt would have brought Julian into power only when he decided it was absolutely necessary.

Developments in the West, however, did not afford Constantius II a moment's rest. Both in the summer of 354 and in the spring of 355, he campaigned in Raetia against the Alemanni. Just as these campaigns finished, he was faced with a revolt at Cologne by Silvanus, the Frankish Master of Infantry (*magister peditum*) who had defected to Constantius II early in the campaign against Magnentius. Silvanus was hailed Augustus by his soldiers on August 11, just four days after he had distributed their long-overdue pay.

Silvanus' revolt was symptomatic of the overly suspicious nature of Constantius II, for he usurped out of fear he would be executed for treason based on documents that were forged by his rivals (and that since had been proven false). Silvanus, however, was murdered on September 7 by the emperor's Master of Cavalry (*magister equitum*), Ursicinus. The rebellion had ended, but Cologne paid the price, for in the aftermath it was sacked by Germans who had opportunistically crossed the Rhine.

This event, as well as other threats on the Rhine and Danube, convinced Constantius II that he could not rule his vast Empire alone. He thus called upon his only remaining young relative, Julian II (who was the half-brother of the recently executed Gallus). Although Julian had been summoned shortly after Gallus' death and charitably excused to resume his studies in Athens, this time the emperor was certain he needed Julian.

Then a young man in his early 20s, Julian was hailed Caesar at Milan on November 6, 355. Just as Constantius II had done with Gallus, he gave Julian one of his sisters (this time his youngest sister, Helena the Younger) as a bride on the occasion of his investiture. The emperor and the Caesar were destined to share the consulship three times, in 356, 357 and 360, but were eventually to become rivals.

The eastern front was peaceful at this time, seemingly because Shapur II's own eastern borders were threatened by nomadic Chionites, presumably the first Hunnic peoples to arrive in the Middle East. This was fortunate for the Romans, for throughout the next five years there was continual trouble on both the Rhine and the Danube. Constantius II gave Julian the task of defending Gaul from the Germans, while he himself mainly saw to defending the Danube.

Julian's task was made more difficult by Constantius II, who did not offer him the support he required. Not only did Julian have a minuscule army but, to make matters worse he was given no money to pay his soldiers for at least the first three years he reigned as Caesar. Through all these hardships, Julian proved to be a strong leader and a capable administrator who greatly reduced the local tax burdens. Not surprisingly, over the course of five years he earned the undying loyalty of his men.

Constantius II had his hands full in the meantime. In 356 he fought the Alemanni in concert with Julian, and in April and May of 357 took a well-earned break to visit Rome to celebrate his 35th anniversary in power (though he had been Caesar only since 324). The procession and ceremony that accompanied his triumphal entry into Rome is recorded in detail by the historian Ammianus.

At the end of May, Constantius II left Rome and headed for Pannonia (Illyria), where in the spring of 358 he waged a quick and successful campaign against the Sarmatians and Quadi, and entered Sirmium in triumph. The war against the Sarmatians, Quadi and Suevi was waged successfully into the spring of 359, after which Constantius II learned that Shapur II had invaded Northern Mesopotamia after protracted negotiations had failed. Constantius II closed out his affairs in the Balkans and left for Constantinople, where he wintered.

He learned of the first loss before he even reached Constantinople: the fortress-city Amida (on the Tigris) had fallen in October despite 73 days of stubborn resistance by Ursicinus, the officer who had murdered the usurper Silvanus in 355 and who was now the emperor's Master of Infantry (*magister peditum*).

Early in 360, while journeying through Cappadocia, the emperor demanded of Julian II that a large portion of his Gallic army be sent to participate in the Persian war. The Gallic armies refused to obey Constantius II's command and instead mutinied in February, bestowing the rank of Augustus on Julian II at Paris. Constantius II was so concerned with Shapur II's invasion that he did not immediately oppose his rival half-cousin. Instead, during the summer, fall and winter of 360 he traveled extensively in Cappadocia, Northern Mesopotamia and Syria. The Sasanians made impressive gains in the war, and the emperor's presence did not prevent the Mesopotamian cities of Singara and Bezabde from falling into enemy hands. After the campaigning season ended, Constantius II returned to winter at his old capital of Antioch, which he had not visited since he had departed in the spring of 349.

Constantius II contemplated how he would deal simultaneously with the Sasanians and the Roman armies in Gaul, for he could not be in both places at the same time. In the meantime, Julian had fought hard in 360 to pacify the Rhine front so as to free himself to head east early in 361.

Much to the surprise of Constantius II, all was quiet on the Persian front when he visited it in the summer of 361. Shapur II had sustained such heavy losses in his campaigns of the previous year that he had ceased hostilities. This gave Constantius II the opportunity to turn his attention to Julian, who had by then advanced into Italy and Pannonia. In the fall of 361, Constantius II left Antioch to march on Europe, but less than 100 miles into his journey he fell ill and died on November 3 at Mopsuestia in Cilicia.

Constantius II was baptized on his deathbed by Euzoius, the Arian Bishop of Antioch, and is said to have named Julian II his successor at the same time. The latter act prevented the civil war that no doubt would have erupted between Constantius' own eastern legions and the Gallic army commanded by Julian, who reached Constantinople early in December, 361 and entered Antioch by June, 362.

The transfer of power was peaceful, but it did not prevent rivalry within the army, which was united by Julian for a campaign against the Sasanians. Less than 28 months later, after the deaths of Julian II and his successor, Jovian, the army would cause the Empire to be permanently divided between East and West.

Though few ancient or modern historians consider Constantius II a dynamic leader, his achievements must not be underestimated. Not only did he keep the Empire whole on the occasions when it could have more seriously disintegrated, but he also supported the two important institutions his father had built: Christianity and the city of Constantinople. Indeed, it was his loyalty to his father's legacy that assured that the pagan Julian II did not unduly disturb Imperial Christendom.

Constantius II was intensely interested in religion, and assumed a high role in church affairs as a "bishop extraordinary." Unlike his two brothers, he opted for the conservative route offered by the Alexandrian priest Arius (c. 250–336), who preached the separateness of God and Christ. Arius represented one side of a major schism in the church, with his main rival being Bishop Athanasius (his superior at the see of Alexandria), who insisted that Christ was part of God, only lesser.

Arius followed the teachings of the Christian Apologists of the previous generation who espoused that Christ was not only younger and inferior to God, but was a separate entity. By professing that God was of one essence, was whole and was transcendent, Arius believed Christ was merely God's manifestation in the physical universe who acted as his intermediary in the earthly world.

To divide the essence of God between himself and Christ, Arius suggested, was to take a dangerous step toward polytheism. After all, the "victory" of Christianity over paganism was seen by many as one of monotheism over polytheism; if God shared his essence with Christ, Christianity was little more than a polytheistic faith. But the opposition led by Athanasius had many supporters, especially among the monks of Egypt and the Christian population in the Latin West.

Athanasius' Orthodox Catholicism was at odds with the majority of Christians in the Greek East, who did not enjoy being subservient to the Papacy and who were suspicious of Athanasius' new piety. This religious conflict dovetailed with the existing political and social differences between East and West, which were so easily defined along geographical lines. Despite Constantius II's intentions, Arianism did not long survive him as the view taken by the government, suffering defeat only a generation after he died.

Of the emperor's personal life we know a considerable amount from the frank writings of the eye-witness historian Ammianus. All told, Constantius took three wives, the first of whom was a step-cousin whose name is unknown. The second was named Eusebia, and the third Faustina. It was only the latter by whom Constantius II sired a child, a daughter named Constantia who was born soon after her father died, and who at age 16 married the emperor Gratian (in 378).

Constantius II was extraordinarily reserved, a poor public speaker and was considered dim-witted. For this reason, he relied heavily on his grand chamberlain, the Arian eunuch Eusebius. This influential courtier became all-powerful in the East and caused the downfall of Constantius Gallus in 354. Though Eusebius oversaw affairs in the East while Constantius II was fighting in Europe, his "reign" ended in 361 when he fell victim to Julian II at the Calchedon Tribunal.

In the realm of athleticism, Ammianus tells us Constantius II was more accomplished than he was in mental pursuits. His short, bowed legs seem to have made him a good runner and jumper. Constantly campaigning, and not without natural talent, the emperor became highly skilled in all arts of war, such as riding, javelin-throwing and, especially, archery.

The paranoia for which Constantius II became notorious is revealed in two passage from Ammianus: ". . . if he discovered any ground, however false or slight, for suspecting an attempt upon the throne he showed . . . a cruelty which easily surpassed that of Caligula (Gaius) and Domitian and Commodus." He continues: "He enclosed the little building in which he used to sleep with a deep ditch crossed by a collapsible bridge; when he went to bed he dismantled the planks and pins, which he reassembled when he was going out at daybreak."

Numismatic Note: In addition to the coins Constantius II struck on his own account, issues bearing his name were also minted by Constantine the

Great, Magnentius, Vetranio, Nepotian and by the citizens of Trier, who revolted in his favor against Magnentius and Decentius.

Two important numismatic developments occurred in his reign: In 355/6 he reduced by one-third the weight of the silver siliqua (the successor of Diocletian's argenteus), and c. 348 he introduced two new base metal denominations, seemingly in conjunction with the 1,100th anniversary of the foundation of Rome.

Much confusion has surrounded the latter two coins, and various names have been applied, with the most common one being *centenionalis*. Though the name *centenionalis* occurs in ancient inscriptions and refers to coins, one of the two recorded citations considerably post-dates the era of these denominations. The most recognizable feature of the new æs coins is the reverse inscription FEL TEMP REPARATIO (loosely translated: "happy days are here again"). The larger of the two coins (called a Billon Æ2 in this catalog), is most often called a *centenionalis*, and the smaller (called a Billon Æ3 in this catalog) a *half-centenionalis*. Circulating alongside these two new denominations was the Æ4, which was a further-reduced descendant of Diocletian's argentiferous nummus.

The reign of Constantius II is also notable for the frequent use of ornate busts, especially on gold. Though some of the facing busts produced by Constantius II qualify as fully frontal, most are oriented slightly to the right (a style commonly called "three-quarter facing"). Constantius II had a particular liking for this portrait type and he adorned his bust in a militant fashion, with cuirass, decorated shield, helmet and spear. This presentation became commonplace a generation or two later, and was the standard format used by most of the early Byzantine emperors.

MAGNENTIUS A.D. 350–353

BROTHER OR COUSIN OF DECENTIUS
HUSBAND OF JUSTINA (FUTURE W. OF VALENTINIAN I)

Flavius Magnus Magnentius, c. A.D. 303–353. Probably born in 303 at Amiens (Ambianum) to a Frankish mother and British father, Magnentius seems originally to have been a slave of the emperor Constantine the Great. He pursued a career in the Roman army, at first in a barbarian contingent but later in the army of Constans, becoming a field commander (*comes rei militaris*) in charge of the senior palatine units of the western army, called the Herculiani and Joviani.

Constans, the Augustus in the West, was hated by his soldiers who, after suffering under him for a decade, eagerly supported Magnentius' coup.

Magnentius' rebellion did not begin on the battlefield or the Imperial palace, but rather at a birthday party held on January 18, 350, at Augustodunum (*mod.* Autun) by the emperor's finance minister, Marcellinus. Into this festive occasion walked Magnentius, donning the purple. The soldiers rapidly pledged allegiance to Magnentius, and Constans fled to the south, only to be overtaken and executed near the Pyrenees.

The revolt was a quick success and Magnentius had become sole emperor in the west. However, his easternmost territories, such as Italy and Illyria, were as yet out of reach, and in truth he only controlled Gaul, to which he soon added Britain and Spain. Not long thereafter, however, Italy and North Africa also pledged their allegiance to Magnentius. But the revolt did not spread further east, as the Pannonian Master of Infantry (*magister peditum*) Vetranio, who initially was wavering in his loyalty, remained loyal to the house of Constantine — then represented only by Constantius II, who was battling the Sasanians in the East. In the absence of a rightful emperor in the Balkans, Vetranio was hailed emperor on March 1, on the insistence of the emperor's eldest sister, Constantina.

Not long after Vetranio sided with Constantius II, Magnentius also suffered a setback in Rome, where Nepotian, a half-nephew of Constantine the Great, staged a counter revolution on June 3. In the process, most of Magnentius' supporters in the western capital were killed, including the prefect Anicius. Nepotian's revolt, however, was quelled within the month.

All the while, Magnentius was trying to make peace with Constantius II, with whom he was quite willing to share the Empire. In one of his more creative strategies, he tried to marry the emperor's sister, Constantina. But this, too, failed. In the meantime, Constantius II had stirred up the Germans along the Rhine so they would create a distraction at Magnentius' rear. This sinister development, as well as the revolt of Nepotian in Rome, convinced Magnentius that he needed help in his struggle. In the summer of 350 he raised his relative Decentius to the rank of Caesar and left him in Gaul to defend it from invasion across the Rhine.

When Constantius II arrived in the Balkans, Magnentius realized that war was inevitable. In a last-ditch effort to achieve a peaceful outcome, Magnentius sent an embassy to meet Constantius II at Heraclea late in the fall of 350, but the rivals could not come to terms. On Christmas day, 350, Constantius II oversaw the abdication of Vetranio and determined to finish off Magnentius himself.

Diplomatic efforts in 351 failed miserably, largely due to the tribulations of the envoys, all of whom were taken captive by the opposition. The rival emperors were in difficult positions: each realized this struggle would end no time soon, and yet they both had to keep their eyes on two fronts. Magnentius had given rank to Decentius so he could defend the Rhine, and now, in the spring of 351, Constantius II raised his own half-cousin, Constantius Gallus, to the rank of Caesar to manage affairs in Asia.

The war between Magnentius and Constantius II could now begin. The first attack was launched by Constantius II, whose smaller armies were defeated on the border of Italy at Atrans in the summer of 351. Encouraged by this, Magnentius refused an offer from Constantius II to settle and went on the offensive, leading his armies from Aquileia into Illyria in the summer of 351. The usurper quickly gained the upper-hand, took Siscia and advanced as far as Sirmium beyond which he slipped past Constantius II's rear and established himself at Mursa (*mod.* Osijek).

Not long thereafter, on September 28, 351, the two armies clashed at Mursa for one of the costliest battles of the entire 4th Century. Constantius II had superior cavalry and archers, but Magnentius commanded a much stronger infantry, composed of both legionaries and German and Frankish auxiliaries. The auxiliary infantrymen were unarmored, however, and they proved easy targets for the eastern archers. Eventually, Magnentius' auxiliaries had suffered so greatly that Constantius II's cavalry and lancemen were able to force the Gallic legions to break formation.

About 55,000 men died that day, and though the casualties were fairly evenly distributed, the battle proved ruinous for Magnentius, who was clearly the loser. It was a particularly costly battle that weakened Roman military power in the West at a time when this could least be afforded. The Germans whom Constantius II had aroused along the Rhine were raiding deep into Roman territory.

Magnentius made a slow retreat to Italy, taking refuge at Aquileia, where he continued to make religious concessions to the pagan senatorial aristocracy. This policy served him well at this critical stage, for his supporters were numerous in Italy. Those who openly opposed his regime escaped across the Adriatic to join the cause of Constantius II.

By the summer of 352, Constantius II was poised for an invasion of Italy. Aware of his own vulnerability, Magnentius decided to flee to Gaul, allowing his rival to take possession of Italy and Sicily in the fall of 352 without a struggle. North Africa and Spain seem also to have declared against Magnentius about this time, thus reducing the rebel's territory to Gaul and, perhaps, Britain.

It seemed only a matter of time before Magnentius would have to offer battle to Constantius II. However, even this opportunity was not afforded the rebel. In the summer of 353, Magnentius became separated from his army and was forced to take refuge at Lugdunum, while at the same time his relative Decentius was faring badly in Germany. Germanic raids were taking their toll and the city of Trier had revolted in favor of Constantius II. Though the two had planned to join their forces, it was not possible.

Each of the rebels met separate fates: Magnentius committed suicide at Lugdunum on August 10, 353, rather than surrendering, and Decentius committed suicide eight days later while encamped near Sens. Though Magnentius also forced suicide on his own mother and youngest brother, he was survived by his wife, Justina, who some 15 years later married the western emperor Valentinian I. After a long struggle, Constantinian rule was restored in the West, and for the first time in 16 years the Empire was under the command of one emperor.

NUMISMATIC NOTE: In addition to striking coins in his own name, Magnentius also struck for Constantius II (early in his rebellion, when he still hoped to reconcile), and for his relative Decentius, whom he later associated with his regime. Magnentius' coinage is quite complex and is treated in detail by Pierre Bastien in his *Le Monnayage de Magnence* (350–353), first published in 1964 and revised in 1983. Magnentius' coinage policy varied depending on the mint. At Rome, for example, he sometimes divided production equally among the six officinae: coins in the name of Constantius II were struck at the first three officinae (P, B and T), and those in the name of Magnentius himself were struck at the latter three (Q, E and S).

His most remarkable reverse type shows the Christogram (Chi-Rho) flanked by A and w (Alpha being the first letter of the Greek alphabet, and Omega the last). This issue shows that Magnentius was a policy opportunist, for it was intended to incite the Orthodox Catholics of the West against the invading eastern emperor Constantius II, who was a devout Arian. The type, which bears the inscriptions SALVS AVG NOSTRI or SALVS DD NN AVG ET CAES, occurs either unadorned or within a wreath.

DECENTIUS

CAESAR, A.D. 350–353

BROTHER OR COUSIN OF MAGNENTIUS

Flavius Magnus Decentius, d. A.D. 353. Little is known of Decentius, other than that he was a close relative of the western usurper Magnentius, variously regarded as his brother or cousin. Decentius was hailed Caesar by Magnentius while the latter was preparing to oppose the invasion of the eastern emperor, Constantius II.

Magnentius had good reason to elevate Decentius, for Constantius II had stirred up Germans along the Rhine, who began to invade Roman territory. Since Magnentius was occupied on the eastern border of Italy awaiting Constantius II, he was particularly vulnerable on the Rhine front.

Researchers disagree about when Decentius achieved his rank. Though most suggest it occurred sometime between March and July of 351 (seemingly in response to Constantius Gallus' being hailed Caesar by Constantius II), it likely occurred in July or August of 350, shortly after Nepotian was deposed in Rome and the Germans along the Rhine became active. This opinion seems more in line with the numismatic evidence.

After being hailed Caesar, Decentius was given a small army and instructed to defend Gaul while Magnentius remained in Italy to confront Constantius II, who was encamped in Pannonia. With such scanty resources, however, Decentius could do little more than scramble from one emergency to another.

Early in their struggle (prior to the Battle of Mursa) the usurpers lost the important city of Cologne to a Frankish officer named Silvanus, who defected to Constantius II. (Silvanus was rewarded in 352/3 with the office of Master of Infantry [*magister peditum*] in Gaul, but in 355 he rebelled against his benefactor upon being confronted with false charges of treason.) The rebels' collective fate suffered greatly in the summer of 352 when Magnentius was forced to abandon Italy and he lost the allegiance of Spain and North Africa.

Meanwhile, Decentius had come into conflict with hostile Germans, including Chnodomarius, a leader of the Alemanni. Indeed, it may have been his lack of success against Chnodomarius that caused the city of Trier (then under the leadership of a certain Poemenius) to defect to the cause of Constantius II. Exactly when the revolt at Trier occurred is uncertain, though 353 is probable. Equally uncertain is whether the city was recaptured by Decentius. This seems unlikely, however, since the historian Ammianus tells us Poemenius was still alive in 355, some two years after the death of Decentius.

As Magnentius continued his westward retreat, the Gallic kinsmen planned to unite their armies in Gaul and offer battle to Constantius II. Before they could meet, however, Magnentius became separated from his army and took refuge at Lugdunum, where he was besieged and soon took his own life. Eight days elapsed before news of Magnentius' suicide reached Decentius, who was encamped almost 200 miles away, near Sens. Certain that his fate also was sealed, Decentius killed himself on August 18, 353.

NUMISMATIC NOTE: The regular coinage of Decentius follows the pattern of his senior partner, Magnentius. When Poemenius closed Trier's gates to Decentius, his counter-revolutionary government struck gold solidi and base-metal Æ2's in the name of Constantius II, the emperor to whom they had defected. Each denomination seemingly had only one reverse design, and each was curious in a surprisingly different way: the solidi are unusually heavy for that period in the West, and the Æ2's are underweight, crudely produced, and show no palpable silver content. The Æ2's bear the reverse type of the Christogram flanked by A and w, a design originated by Magnentius as anti-Arian propaganda against Constantius II. The fact that the people of Trier chose this familiar type is not only ironic, but seems to show that Magnentius' propaganda failed to have the necessary impact. For descriptions of these emergency issues from Trier, see the listings of Constantius II.

VETRANIO A.D. 350

Vetranio, died c. A.D. 356. An elderly soldier who had served under Constantine the Great, Vetranio had achieved the rank of Master of Infantry (*magister peditum*) in Pannonia when Magnentius overthrew the legitimate western emperor, Constans, early in 350. Vetranio's loyalty wavered initially, but within two months he chose to oppose Magnentius, who was then advancing eastward.

Vetranio was hailed emperor by his troops at Mursa on March 1, 350, seemingly because there was a need for an emperor on-site, and Constantius II was then unable to leave the Persian front. This bold maneuver probably was not Vetranio's idea, but rather that of Constantina, the eldest daughter of Constantine the Great and a sister of Constantius II. It is generally accepted that Vetranio had no personal designs on the throne and that he agreed to assume the title of Augustus out of necessity.

Having failed to recruit Vetranio, Magnentius tried another route to undermining Constantius II's authority in the Balkans: he sought the hand of Constantina in marriage. But in this he failed as well, and Constantina remained unmarried for another year until her brother arranged a marriage for her with a half-cousin named Constantius Gallus.

Another setback for Magnentius occurred early in June, when another of Constantius II's half-cousins, Nepotian, revolted against Magnentius in Rome. Fortunately for Magnentius, the rebellion ended in 27 days, and he was able to take command once again in the western capital (this was probably the occasion upon which Magnentius named his relative Decentius as his Caesar).

Vetranio's 10 months as Augustus were relatively uneventful, for he seems to have done little more than maintain a defensive position and sustain the loyalty of the Balkan legions until Constantius II arrived late in the fall of 350. Just after crossing onto European soil, Constantius II met at Heraclea with embassies sent by Magnentius and Vetranio, after which he traveled more than 350 miles to meet personally with Vetranio at Naïssus (*mod.* Nis). He praised Vetranio's loyalty, and on Christmas day he formally accepted his abdication and provided him with an opulent estate at Prusa in Bithynia, where he retired and eventually died c. 356.

NUMISMATIC NOTE: Vetranio struck coins at Siscia and Thessalonica both in his own name and in that of Constantius II, the emperor to whom he pledged his loyalty. His most interesting reverse type bears the inscription HOC SIGNO VICTOR ERIS (loosely translated: "by this sign you shall conquer") and depicts an emperor being crowned by Victory and holding a labarum (a banner inscribed with the monogram of Christ). The type refers to the vision experienced by Constantine the Great prior to the Battle of the Milvian Bridge on October 28, 312, and for this reason some researchers believe it is Constantine himself who is being crowned, not Vetranio as might otherwise be assumed. Vetranio uses the identical scene on solidi inscribed SALVATOR REIPVBLICAE ("savior of the state"), a combination which may allude to Constantine the Great having been the savior of the Empire.

NEPOTIAN A.D. 350

GRANDSON OF CONSTANTIUS I AND THEODORA
NEPHEW OF LICINIUS I AND CONSTANTIA
COUSIN OF DELMATIUS, HANNIBALLIANUS, CONSTANTIUS GALLUS, JULIAN II AND LICINIUS II
HALF-NEPHEW OF CONSTANTINE THE GREAT
HALF-COUSIN OF CRISPUS, CONSTANTINE II, CONSTANTIUS II, CONSTANS, CONSTANTINA (W. OF HANNIBALLIANUS & CONSTANTIUS GALLUS) AND HELENA THE YOUNGER (W. OF JULIAN II)

Constantinus Flavius Popilius Nepotianus, d. A.D. 350. Nepotioan was one of the ill-fated grandchildren of Theodora who survived (on account of his youth) the dynastic purge by the sons of Constantine the Great in the summer of 337. Like his two surviving cousins, Constantius Gallus and Julian II, Nepotian lived in semi-exile in his youth, but emerged after the execution of Fausta in 326.

Though Nepotian served as consul in 336, we hear little else of him until June 3, 350, when, in the heat of the moment, he was hailed emperor in Rome by a mob. The rebel government of Magnentius had assumed control in Rome nearly 20 weeks earlier, after having overthrown the regime of the legitimate emperor Constans. Nepotian and his ruffians confronted and killed Anicius, Magnentius' praetorian prefect of Italy. A more thorough purge of Magnentius' partisans occurred in the days that followed.

It is impossible to determine whether Nepotian revolted on his own behalf or on behalf of his half-cousin, Constantius II (for whom he issued coins). No doubt time would have made this clear, but his regime ended so quickly that we are forced to speculate on that point. Perhaps Nepotian should have devoted less time to his meticulous coinage and more to securing his counter-revolutionary regime, for all that which good fortune delivered to him was taken away on the 30th day of the same month.

Leading the counter-counter-revolution in Rome was Marcellinus, the man at whose party Magnentius had been hailed emperor (and who had since become his *magister officiorum*, or chief administrator). Predictably, a vengeful purge followed, one in which Nepotian, his mother and his ringleaders were killed.

Numismatic Note: Nepotian's coinage was struck only at Rome, and was limited to two denominations (solidi and Billon Æ2's) and to two basic reverse types. His production mode was virtually identical to that which Magnentius had established at Rome, for he too struck coins in the name of Constantius II. On his billon coinage of the GLORIA ROMANORVM type, Nepotian follows Magnentius' formula by dividing production equally among the six officinae at Rome. However, Nepotian may have used all six officinae at Rome to coin the gold and billon issues in his own name with the reverse inscription VRBS ROMA. There is no satisfactory explanation for Nepotian's curious use of three different obverse inscriptions, one of which was used exclusively for gold and the other two for billon.

When Rome was recovered by Magnentius, he may have celebrated the event by raising his kinsman Decentius to the rank of Caesar and certainly did so by striking coins at Rome with the inscriptions BIS RESTITVTA LIBERTAS and RENOBATIO VRBIS ROME. The former inscription denotes that Rome was "twice liberated" by Magnentius (first from Constans, then from Nepotian), and the second (more properly RENOVATIO VRBIS ROMAE) is more generic in application. Though the first type was struck only in the name of Magnentius, the second was struck in the names of both Magnentius and Decentius.

CONSTANTIUS GALLUS

CAESAR, A.D. 351–354

GRANDSON OF CONSTANTIUS I AND THEODORA
HALF-BROTHER OF JULIAN II
HUSBAND AND COUSIN OF CONSTANTINA (FORMER W. OF HANNIBALLIANUS)
NEPHEW OF LICINIUS I AND CONSTANTIA
COUSIN OF DELMATIUS, HANNIBALLIANUS, LICINIUS II AND NEPOTIAN
HALF-NEPHEW OF CONSTANTINE THE GREAT
HALF-COUSIN OF CRISPUS, CONSTANTINE II, CONSTANTIUS II, CONSTANS, AND HELENA THE YOUNGER (W. OF JULIAN II)

Flavius Claudius Constantius Gallus (earlier Flavius Claudius Gallus), c. A.D. 325/6–354. Born at the obscure city of Massa Veternensis in Etruria, Constantius Gallus was one of the three grandsons of Theodora who survived extermination by the grandsons of Helena in 337. Though Gallus' father and brother were killed in the family massacre, Gallus was permitted to live because he was sickly and was expected to die. Also surviving the purge was his younger half-brother, Julian II, with whom he shared the same father, Julius Constantius. The two boys spent six years of their childhood together at the fortress of Macellum in Cappadocia, where they received a strict Christian education.

Little else is known of Gallus until he came to power in 351. It was a time of extreme crisis, for the East was under threat of invasion by the Sasanians and the West had recently fallen to the usurper Magnentius. The only legitimate emperor remaining was Constantius II, who up until this point had ruled in Asia Minor, while his brothers (both now dead) had ruled in Europe. However, Constantius II was anticipating an extended stay in Europe to defeat Magnentius and recover the western provinces. So he decided to share his Imperial burden with his eldest half-cousin, Gallus, who was then in his mid-20s.

Gallus was hailed Caesar at Sirmium on March 15, 351, at which point he added Constantius to his given name and married his emperor's sister, Constantina (who had formerly been married to Gallus' cousin Hanniballianus). To aid Gallus as his praetorian prefect, Constantius II appointed the officer Thalassius. Constantius II remained in the Balkans as Gallus and Thalassius traveled hastily to Antioch, where they established their court by mid-May.

The Asiatic provinces of the Empire were relatively peaceful at the time, but Gallus overreacted to the few problems that arose, including several conspiracies — real and imagined — which he brutally suppressed. He also quelled a rebellion in Isauria, and crushed with great ferocity a revolt in Syria Palestina in 352 and a civilian riot at Antioch late in 353. His cruel and cavalier behavior made him unpopular with the public, the army and the palace eunuchs who had long held sway in the courts of the East.

Inspiring him to behave so irresponsibly, we are told, was his wife, Constantina, whom the historian Ammianus describes as a "mortal fury." Regrettably, no coins were struck in her name. After about two years of abuse, a plot was launched by the chamberlain Eusebius, who had flooded Constantius II with complaints of his half-cousin's behavior. The emperor responded by sending the prefect Domitianus and the quaestor Montius to divine the truth of the matter. During the course of the investigation, however, Gallus so incensed the soldiers and the populace against the intrusion that the two men were lynched.

Constantius II was now in a difficult position, for if forced into a corner, Gallus might rebel — and Constantius II already had his hands full with the Gallic revolt. Thus he recalled Gallus to Milan in 354, seemingly under the pretense that he was to be re-assigned in the West. During the course of the arduous journey from Antioch, Gallus suffered the loss of his wife, Constantina, who died in Bithynia. Gallus was arrested late in 354 not far from the Italian border, at Istra, and was tried for various crimes against the state. Found guilty, the 29-year-old Caesar was beheaded on the Emperor's orders.

JULIAN II 'THE APOSTATE'
A.D. 360–363

CAESAR: A.D. 355–360
(UNDER CONSTANTIUS II)
AUGUSTUS: A.D. 360–361
(RIVAL OF CONSTANTIUS II)
A.D. 361–363 (SOLE REIGN)

GRANDSON OF CONSTANTIUS I AND THEODORA
HALF-BROTHER OF CONSTANTIUS GALLUS
HUSBAND AND HALF-COUSIN OF HELENA THE YOUNGER
NEPHEW OF LICINIUS I AND CONSTANTIA
COUSIN OF DELMATIUS, HANNIBALLIANUS, LICINIUS II AND NEPOTIAN
HALF-NEPHEW OF CONSTANTINE THE GREAT
HALF-COUSIN OF CRISPUS, CONSTANTINE II, CONSTANTIUS II, CONSTANS AND CONSTANTINA (W. OF HANNIBALLIANUS & CONSTANTIUS GALLUS)

Flavius Claudius Julianus, A.D. 331/2–363. Few 4th century emperors are as well known as Julian II, a remarkably talented man whose attempt to restore pagan worship not only earned him the appellation "the Apostate," but also made his reign an uncanny conclusion to the Constantinian legacy. By anyone's reckoning, Julian's reign was an anachronism; his effort to revive paganism proved too little and too late to withstand the rushing tide of Christendom.

Julian's religious policy as emperor was rooted in his childhood experience, of which the defining moment had been his narrow escape from the massacre of his branch of the family in 337. We are told Julian was spared because of his extreme youth (as were his cousin Nepotian, and his half-brother, Constantius Gallus, who was sickly). The murderous behavior of the three sons of Constantine proved beyond a doubt to Julian that Christians often did not practice what they preached.

Because his branch of the Constantinian family was out of favor, young Julian and his half-brother maintained a low profile. Julian was educated in Constantinople, where at an early age he was introduced to Classical learning. After the death of his tutor Bishop Eusebius of Nicomdia in 341, Julian and Gallus were sent to the remote fortress of Macellum in Cappadocia. There they spent six years in quiet isolation and received a formal Christian education. Julian was a scholarly child whose interest in Classical learning was not eliminated by his Christian indoctrination.

By about 347 Julian and Gallus were able to emerge from their exile, and in 351 Gallus was given the rank of Caesar by his half-cousin, the emperor Constantius II. While Constantius waged war in Europe, Gallus reigned in the east. During Gallus' three years of cruel and poor administration, Julian renewed his studies of Classical subjects at Ephesus, Pergamum and other centers of learning. Under the tutelage of leading Neoplatonist philosophers, such as Maximus of Ephesus, Julian quietly converted to paganism.

In 354 Gallus was stripped of his title and executed, leaving Constantius II and Julian as the only surviving males of the Constantinian line. As a consequence, Julian, then in his early 20s, had to abandon his studies in Athens so he could join his Imperial relatives in Milan. While there he found an ally in Constantius II's wife, Eusebia, who not only protected him from mortal danger on more than one occasion, but also arranged for him to return to Athens and resume his studies. However, the emperor's problems were too great to allow Julian the luxury of being a student, and he was ordered to return to Milan, where, on November 6, 355, he was appointed Caesar. As routinely transpired, a dynastic marriage complemented the giving of rank, and Julian was wed to one of the emperor's sisters, Helena the Younger.

Although the usurpers Magnentius and Decentius had been defeated in August of 353, Constantius II was forced to stay in Europe because of the problems on the Rhine. Therefore, he passed on to Julian the unenviable task of defending Gaul from Germanic invasion, which freed the emperor to attend to the troubled Danube. Julian spent most of the next five years campaigning on the Danubian front, and afterward returned to Asia to repel a Sasanian invasion.

Julian quickly proved that his talents transcended scholarship. The fact that he was a skilled soldier and administrator came as an unwelcome surprise to Constantius II, who had hoped he would perform adequately enough to defend Gaul, but not so well as to win the undying loyalty of his soldiers. To thwart Julian's success, Constantius II ordered his own commander stationed in modern Switzerland to deny Julian the help he desperately needed.

As a relative newcomer to the art of war, Julian's first years were especially difficult. Not only were the Franks and Alemanni a perennial threat, but just three months prior to his investiture in 355 the armies stationed north of the Seine rebelled at Cologne under Master of the Infantry *(magister peditum)* Silvanus. The rebellion ended within a month, but Silvanus' armies (which had just been paid), were still in a rebellious frame of mind.

In 356 Julian drove marauding Germans out of Gaul (seemingly in concert with Constantius II), but paid a heavy price when he lost two legions to an ambush. Though he subsequently pushed northward and recovered the important city of Cologne, he was unable to keep it and was forced to retreated to Sens, where he was besieged during the winter by the Alemanni.

In the succeeding years, from 357 to 359, Julian faced a great many challenges, not the least of which was the treachery of Constantius' commanders who, under orders, failed to help him in his campaigns. Julian's army often was remarkably small, perhaps 13,000 men. Even so, he had the courage to use his men offensively against barbarian armies of three times his strength.

On some occasions (even though Julian preferred caution over aggression) he had to give in to his army's desire to attack. In one such case, at Strasbourg in 357, his army demanded that they be allowed to launch a risky evening offensive. The results were impressive: 6,000 enemy fell on the battlefield and thousands more drowned in their attempt to escape across the Rhine. The Romans lost only 243 soldiers and four officers.

Not only did Julian campaign with success against the Franks and the Alemanni, but he also reformed the taxation system, cutting out waste and corruption, and as a result reducing the tax burden in Gaul by more than two-thirds. His task was especially difficult because his soldiers had not been paid or been given bonuses since before he had arrived. Somehow, though, Julian managed to quell rebellions, retain the loyalty of the soldiers and earn their patience on the fiscal front.

Constantius II — then marching into Asia Minor to repel an invasion by Shapur II — was alarmed by the enormous popularity of his junior colleague, who in 359 was proving his bravado by crossing the Rhine and ravaging the lands occupied by the Alemanni. Constantius II tried to reduce Julian's authority by ordering him to send a large part of his army for the campaign against the Sasanians. But the western armies saw through the ruse and refused to obey. In a rebellious spirit, the soldiers promoted the reluctant Julian to the rank of Augustus at Paris in February, 360. Once again the Empire was divided, with rival Augusti ruling in the East and West. Though Julian tried to gain the approval of Constantius II through diplomacy, his efforts failed, for his rise was understandably viewed as a usurpation.

Julian campaigned in Gaul during the remainder of 360, suffering the death of his wife, Helena, who expired childless. The new emperor headed east early in 361 to confront Constantius II, by now openly accusing the emperor of being the leading conspirator in the purge of Julian's family nearly a quarter-century before. In the meantime, Constantius II was finishing his Persian campaign and preparing to deal with his rebellious half-cousin.

A decade earlier, when Magnentius had similarly revolted, Constantius successfully distracted his rival by stirring up the Germans along the Rhine. It comes as no surprise, then, that he followed the same strategy in his campaign against Julian. But his attempt to arouse Vadomar, a king of the Alemanni, failed. Having pacified the Rhine front in advance, Julian was able to make his journey to the Balkans unhindered. He arrived by the summer of 361 and had nearly crossed over to Asian soil when Constantius II fell fatally ill. On his deathbed, Constantius II named Julian as his successor, and it was he who inherited the whole Empire upon the death of his half-cousin on November 3, 361.

Fortunately for both armies, the expected battle never occurred, but the East versus West rhetoric with which the rival emperors had inspired their armies was fresh in their minds. As sole emperor, Julian had to oversee the integration of his loyal Gallic legions and the hostile eastern legions who had formerly served under Constantius II and who, only a few weeks earlier, had been intent on killing him. On December 11, 361, Julian entered Constantinople, the city in which he had been born and baptized nearly three decades before.

Julian inaugurated his reign in poor fashion, for only a few days after arriving at Constantinople he set up a court in which adherents to his former rival (most notably the grand chamberlain Eusebius) were prosecuted in what is known as the Calchedon tribunal. After wintering in Constantinople, Julian departed in mid-May 362, crossing over to Asia.

He made his way across the heart of Anatolia and arrived in Antioch by June, where he established his court in the palace formerly occupied by Constantius II. Within weeks of his arrival, Julian made public his intentions to restore observance of the pagan cults throughout the Empire; this could hardly have come as a surprise, for Julian had declared his loyalty to paganism months earlier while encamped at Naïssus. However, Antioch proved to be the city which most vehemently opposed his attempt to restore paganism.

The end of 362 was quite eventful, for late in October the famous Temple of Apollo at Daphne (on the outskirts of Antioch) was destroyed by fire. This was shortly after Julian had failed to observe the festival of Apollo traditionally held there (this rite had pagan origins, but had since become largely Christian). He devoted the first part of 363 to preparing for a Persian campaign that he intended to lead personally. Like so many emperors before, Julian was seeking glory, hoping perhaps to duplicate the achievements of Trajan or Alexander the Great.

At this stage the conflicts between the Gallic commanders and the eastern commanders were becoming more serious. At about 65,000 men, the expedition was perhaps the largest ever mounted against the Persians, but a division within the command could only have disastrous results. Nonetheless, Julian set out from Antioch on March 5, and by the 18th he had reached Carrhae, an outpost which often changed hands during conflicts between the Romans and Sasanians. From Carrhae Julian led his armies south to the Euphrates and advanced deep into enemy territory, defeating the Sasanian armies at every engagement during the next three months.

Riding the tide of victory, Julian next besieged the capital of Ctesiphon. This proved an impossible task for his armies, however, and Julian decided to abandon his siege and return to Roman territory along the Tigris river. Only 10 days later, the 31-year-old emperor was killed during a skirmish in the heart of Mesopotamia, near a place named Phrygia. The details of the event are uncertain: it most likely occurred on June 26 (though some historians suggest July), and it is not certain whether he was killed by the enemy or, as was rumored, by of one of the Christian soldiers under his command.

Upon Julian's death, the two factions of the army finally agreed to hail Jovian, the *comes domesticorum*, as the new emperor. To spare his starving army from certain defeat, the new emperor agreed to a disgraceful treaty and returned to Antioch, where he immediately revoked Julian's pro-pagan legislation. Thus ended Julian's anachronistic attempt to restore pagan worship in the Empire.

Julian reformed many aspects of his Empire, proving that his earlier efforts in Gaul were not merely populist, but were a reflection of his desire to improve the conditions of his subjects. Julian was especially opposed to bureaucratic waste and was a great patron of literature. In addition to founding a library in the Basilica in Constantinople (which came to house some 120,000 volumes), Julian himself was a prolific and gifted writer. Indeed, more of his writings survive than do those of any other emperor, including Marcus Aurelius. His compositions run the literary gamut from spiritual investigations to biting satire.

Though Julian's religious policy certainly was pro-pagan, it was not necessarily repressive of other religions. With characteristic clarity, Julian realized that Christianity was a threat to paganism primarily because it was supported by the government. Thus, he starved Christianity of the government subsidies it had come to enjoy under previous regimes. In implementing his "affirmative action" policy toward paganism, Julian prohibited many pro-Christian activities, excluded Christians from certain teaching posts and supported the struggling faith of Judaism (and seemingly planned to rebuild the Temple in Jerusalem).

For these actions and especially his personal conversion to paganism, Julian came to be known as "the Apostate." Unlike ardent persecutors such as Galerius and Maximinus Daia, Julian did not attempt the wholesale destruction of Christianity, but rather tried to discourage it subtly by repealing its favored status and ridiculing it. Had he reigned a few decades, Julian's light-handed approach might have been far more dangerous to the survival of Christianity than were any of the horrific persecutions of the Tetrarchs.

NUMISMATIC NOTE: Julian struck coinage both as Caesar and as Augustus. His portraits are among the most interesting in the Late Roman Empire because significantly different styles of engraving can be observed. His beard must have been a refreshing change for die cutters, as no heavily bearded effigies had appeared on Roman coins for more than 125 years. Much like that of the emperor Macrinus (217–218), Julian's beard is shown both short and long.

Julian's most intriguing reverse type occurs on his billon Æ1's struck as Augustus. A humped bull is shown beneath two stars and the inscription SECVRITAS REIPVBLICAE ("the safety of the state"). Not only is the type unusual and enigmatic, but it is discussed in surviving ancient literature. In his own writings, Julian berates the people of Antioch for mocking his coinage, and though Julian does not provide the specifics, the historian Socrates Scholasticus in his *Historia Ecclesiastica* tells us that Julian was referring to his coinage with the bull. The type was struck throughout the Empire, with a particularly large output in Antioch itself.

Differing views exist of the meaning of Julian's bull. The idea most widely accepted among scholars is that it is a symbol of his leadership or guardianship of the people, and that as such it has no pagan connotation. Others suggest it represents a sacrificial animal, or that the bull offers proof that Julian's natal sign was Taurus (his birthdate is not recorded in ancient texts). Still others suggest it represents an actual object — a statue of the Egyptian Apis bull that was unearthed in Egypt late in 362 and was later delivered to the emperor in Antioch. If the latter provides the explanation, the bull would symbolize the re-emergence of paganism; but many scholars reject this enticing theory. It may be of some consequence that of the 13 mints that struck æs for Julian, only Rome and Alexandria — perhaps the two most likely centers for production of a "pagan" issue — did not strike the type.

JOVIAN A.D. 363–364

Flavius Jovianus, c. A.D. 330/1–364. The son of the general Varronianus, who commanded the officers corps as *comes domesticorum* for Constantius II, Jovian was born at Singidunum (*mod.* Belgrade) late in the reign of Constantine the Great. By 363 Jovian had filled his father's shoes and was commanding that élite corps for Julian II during that emperor's ill-fated expedition against Persia.

The historian Ammianus tells us Jovian was uncommonly tall — so much so that ". . . for some time no royal robe could be found to fit him." Of his qualifications for office, Ammianus offers terse disapproval by speaking of his moderate education and his greed, and of the excessive time he spent "jesting in public" and pursuing wine and women. On the positive side, he acknowledges that Jovian made his appointments with great care.

One day after Julian's death in June 363, the soldiers offered the emperorship to the praetorian prefect Saturninius Secundus Salutius, who declined on account of his advanced age. The soldiers' next choice was Jovian, one of the few qualified men who was satisfactory to the commanders of both rival factions in the army — those from the eastern army formerly commanded by Constantius II and the Gauls who had accompanied Julian II on his trek to the East. Since the rivalry was not only cultural but political, the opposing officers had a difficult time agreeing on candidates. In the meantime, the Roman army (which had penetrated deeply into enemy territory) was facing starvation and was suffering increasingly hostile attacks by the Sasanians. Jovian had little choice but to sign an unfavorable treaty with the Sasanian king Shapur II.

The Romans forfeited all territory east of the Tigris, parts of Armenia (which was essentially abandoned by the Romans) and the cities of Nisibis and Singara, both of which were west of the Tigris. The loss was grave, for these lands had been acquired by the Romans during the campaigns of

Galerius, in 298 to 299, and of Septimius Severus a century before that. In exchange, Jovian was permitted to withdraw his demoralized army unhindered.

The emperor led his soldiers on an exhausting march back to Antioch, where on October 22 he restored the anti-pagan laws that his predecessor, Julian II, had abolished. The new emperor stayed only briefly at his capital before embarking on a long journey to Illyria (Pannonia). He struck northward to Tarsus, where he visited Julian II's temporary tomb, and from there journeyed north to Ancyra, the ancient capital of Phrygia, where he arrived a few days before the end of 363.

While residing at Ancyra, Jovian assumed the consulate in 364 with his son, Varronianus, on January 1. We are told that Varronianus (who was named after his grandfather) was very young and cried loudly when being placed on the curule chair. Understandably, this was taken as an ill-omen. Jovian soon was back on the road, heading toward Constantinople. However, on the evening of February 17, 364, while sleeping at Dadastana (on the border of Galatia and Bithynia), the 33-year-old emperor died.

We are told by ancient sources that his death was accidental, most likely caused by fumes emanating from a brazier in his sleeping quarters, although the noxious smell of fresh plaster in his quarters or indigestion are also mentioned as possibilities by Ammianus. Following Jovian's death, the two factions in the army clashed once again, causing the Empire to be divided between East and West — an action that may have been motivated by recent unrest within the army then stationed in Gaul.

NUMISMATIC NOTE: Jovian had neither the time nor the inclination to change the Imperial coinage. He was the last emperor to strike significant quantities of the Æ1, a large coin that was phased out by his successors. Jovian abandoned the "bull" design Julian II had chosen for the Æ1; whether pagan or not, it had been in any case a highly personalized selection, and it comes as no surprise that Jovian changed it to the more generic type of a standing emperor holding a *labarum* and a Victory on globe. The portrait of Jovian — clean-shaven and youthful — harkens back to the Constantinian model which the pagan Julian II had temporarily abandoned.

A Brief Introduction to the Divided Empire

Along the banks of the river Tigris in 363, Julian II "the Apostate," the last legitimate heir of Constantine the Great, met an ignominious end. Julian was replaced by Jovian, a soldier who maintained a unified Empire for almost two years before his own death, which was not in the heat of battle, but from the fumes of a brazier. Shortly after Jovian's death, the chemistry of the Empire changed forever, as its two capitals were destined for permanent separation.

Forcing this separation were the armies of Gaul (which had supported the usurpation of Julian II) and the Eastern armies (which had formerly served under Constantius II). They were forced to cooperate by Julian II during his reign as Augustus (361–363), but after his death could not agree on viable candidates for the throne. Initially, they settled on Jovian as a man who was inoffensive to either party, but after his death in 364, they decided that two emperors must reign — one in the East, and one in the West. When the two armies came to this arrangement with Valentinian I and Valens, civil war was narrowily averted. Except for two half-year periods at the end of the lives of Gratian (378/9) and of Theodosius I (394/5) and a few later periods (which were as brief as they were inconsequential), the East and West were never without separate emperors again.

The cities of Rome and Milan served as the capital of the Western Roman Empire, and the wealthy new city of Constantinople became the capital of the Eastern Roman Empire. The split formally occurred in 364, but became more severe in 395, when the brothers Honorius and Arcadius inherited their father's temporarily united Empire. No longer was one of the emperors senior to the other, instead they were completely equal and independent. Even though the two emperors continued to strike coins in each others' names, and laws were supposed to be applied universally in the East and West, the sharpness of the division increased with the passage of time. Though both Roman, the two Empires acted with increasing autonomy, and occasional hostility. Indeed, their relations were so poor that war was narrowly avoided on several occasions. After the deaths of Honorius and Arcadius, a more congenial relationship was achieved.

In this era the historian must make a critical choice. Should the last 112 years of the Empire be discussed principally in terms of the East-West division, or in terms of ruling houses of Valentinian, Theodosius and Leo? The latter route has been chosen by most historians, as it offers a comfortable transition from the Tetrarchic and Constantinian eras. But the former

The Divided Empire

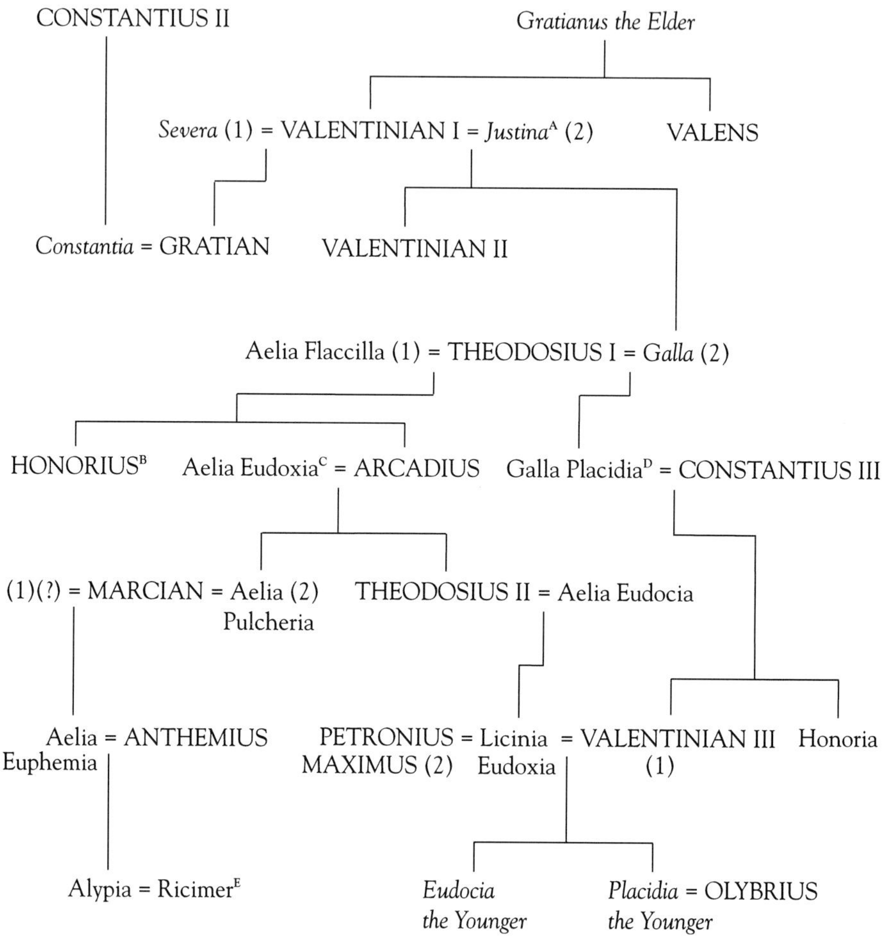

A. Formerly the wife of the usurper Magnentius
B. Husband of Maria & Thermantia the Younger (daughters of the Master of Soldiers Stilicho)
C. Daughter of Bauto the Frank
D. Formerly the wife of Athaulf the Visigoth
E. Uncle of the Master of Soldiers Gundobad

Note: Names in CAPITALS are of emperors; names in *italics* are of people not found on coinage.

is undoubtedly more appropriate. Not only does it offer a true picture of the post-Constantinian world, but also it avoids the chronological chaos of the overlapping reigns in Rome and Constantinople.

We must remember that although the political interplay between East and West was significant, the life of an average citizen of Constantinople — even in the most critical of times — was scarcely affected by current events in Rome. Even so, presentation as a "divided" Empire need not be at the expense of understanding the dynastic ties that linked East and West. It is hoped that the accompanying chart and table will be of value in clarifying the historical framework.

WESTERN EMPIRE	EASTERN EMPIRE
c. A.D. 364–395	
Valentinian I, 364–375 Gratian, 367–383 Valentinian II, 375–392 *usurper*: Magnus Maximus, 383–388 *usurper*: Flavius Victor, 387–388 *usurper*: Eugenius, 392–394	Valens, 364–378 *usurper*: Procopius, 365–366 Theodosius I, 379–395 *wife*: Aelia Flaccilla
c. A.D. 395–457	
Honorius, 393–423 *usurper*: Constantine III, 407–411 *usurper*: Constans II, 409/10–411 *usurper*: Maximus, 409–411 *puppet*: Priscus Attalus (1st), 409–410 *usurper*: Jovinus, 411–413 *usurper*: Sebastianus, 412–413 *puppet*: Priscus Attalus (2nd), 415–416 Constantius III, 421 *wife*: Galla Placidia *usurper*: Johannes, 423–425 Valentinian III, 425–455 *sister*: Honoria *wife*: Licinia Eudoxia *usurper*: Petronius Maximus, 455 Avitus, 455–456	Arcadius, 383–408 *wife*: Aelia Eudoxia Theodosius II, 402–450 *sister*: Aelia Pulcheria (*w.* of Marcian) *wife*: Aelia Eudocia Marcian, 450–457
c. A.D. 457–476+	
Majorian, 457–461 Libius Severus (Severus III), 461–465 Anthemius, 467–472 *wife*: Aelia Euphemia *daughter*: Alypia (*w.* of Ricimer) *usurper*: Olybrius, 472 *usurper*: Glycerius, 473–474 Julius Nepos, 474–475/480 *usurper*: Romulus Augustus, 475–476	Leo I, 457–474 *wife*: Aelia Verina Patricius, 470–471 (as Caesar) Leo II, 474 Zeno, 474–475 & 476–491 *wife*: Aelia Ariadne *usurper*: Basiliscus, 475–476 *wife*: Aelia Zenonis *usurper*: Marcus, 475–476 Leo Caesar, 476–477 (as Caesar)

The concept of dividing the Empire between two Augusti was nothing new to the Romans. It made its debut more than two centuries before the death of Jovian, when Marcus Aurelius and Lucius Verus inherited supreme power from Antoninus Pius. But their experiment was little more than a solution for a specific crisis, and it was abandoned as soon as Verus concluded his Parthian campaign (after which the two emperors campaigned together in the West).

A terrifying prospect of a divided Empire emerged after the death of Septimius Severus, for his two sons could not tolerate each other. Though a division along geographic lines would have separated the quarrelsome siblings, it undoubtedly would have resulted in a civil war. For this reason, the division of the Empire was prevented by their mother, Julia Domna. The first *bona fide* division was achieved by Valerian I and his son, Gallienus, who acted with great autonomy — the father in Asia, and the son in Europe. When Valerian I was captured by the Sasanians in 260, Gallienus realized the magnitude of his loss as he desperately tried to control his vast Empire alone.

The next division of consequence occurred during the Tetrarchy. Initially it included two members (Diocletian in the East, and Maximian in the West), but in 293 it was expanded to include four members, each of whom was responsible for a specific geographic region. With the last vestiges of the Tetrarchy disappearing in 313, the Empire came to be divided between the two survivors of the system — Constantine the Great and Licinius I. After nearly a decade of hostility and mistrust, Constantine overcame Licinius and ruled the whole Empire for the next 13 years.

Upon Constantine's death in 337, the Empire was carved up among his three sons. This division was formalized with geographic boundaries, and was revised several times between 337 and 361, with different combinations of brothers and cousins sharing authority. After the last son of Constantine the Great died in 361, the Empire was inherited intact by one of Constantine's nephews, Julian II (361–363). Julian ruled the Empire single-handedly for three years until his own death, at which point authority passed to the soldier Jovian (363–364), whose brief rule brought the Constantinian Era to a close.

Thus, the end of Jovian's reign in 364 is the ideal point at which to change the arrangement of this catalog. The format is still chronological, except that the two Empires are discussed separately. Though it would have been virtually as practical to separate East from West beginning with the Tetrarchs some 80 years before, the consequences would have been too great. Not only would it have detracted from the historical element of the Tetrarchic and Constantinian eras, but it would have been fundamentally misleading, for the Empire was not yet divided, only partitioned.

The West

The story of the last century is one of deterioration in the West, and prosperity in the East. Over time the western provinces fell one by one: Spain to the Visigoths ('wise Goths') and the Suevi, Gaul to the Franks, Burgundians and Visigoths, North Africa to the Vandals, and eventually Britain to the Saxons, Angles and Jutes. Other European lands once possessed by the Romans were occupied by the Alemanni and Lombards, and by nomadic invaders such as the Gepids, Avars and Bulgars. The most crippling losses, however, were Illyria and Italy, both of which fell to the Ostrogoths ('bright Goths').

Leading up to the fall of Italy were a series of Germanic and Hunnic invasions, during which Rome was sacked by Visigoths in 410, narrowly escaped destruction by Attila the Hun in 452, and was sacked again in 455, this time by the Vandals. In a great stroke of historical irony, this last desecration of Rome was launched from Carthage — the city which had been the great nemesis of Rome during the ancient Republic. Though the Romans had thoroughly defeated the Punic colonists of Carthage more than six centuries before, the old site was re-occupied in 439 by fair-haired Germans migrating from Spain.

During the last century that Italy was under Roman sovereignty, it was essentially ruled by generals who held the title Master of Soldiers (*Magister Militum*). With names like Arbogast, Ricimer, Orestes and Stilicho, these men were usually of full or partial barbarian parentage. The more famous leaders among the barbarians (such as Geiseric, Odovacar, Alaric and Athaulf) were also influential in western Roman politics. In some cases they married into the royal families or forced the senate in Rome to hail as emperor a candidate of their choosing.

Though the various Germanic nations were enemies of Rome, they were also enemies of each other. The survival of the Romans was due in large part to the skillful exploitation of national rivalries, which caused the "barbarians" to fight among themselves. Their other principal tool of survival was gold. It was a long-standing policy of the Romans to buy peace with their enemies by annual or occasional payments of tribute. Indeed, it was a confusing time, for the political environment was ever-changing, based on who was migrating where.

Amid all of this chaos, there existed a curious bond between Roman and most Germanic barbarians, for they had a mutual interest in preserving Christianity and Roman civilization (including all of its spiritual, material and cultural aspects). As such, there existed a fine balance of enmity and unity, resulting in a cultural assimilation during the 4th and 5th Centuries.

Roman rule in Italy ended in August of 476, when the German soldier Odovacar ousted Romulus Augustus. Constitutionally, Roman rule continued until 480, when Julius Nepos (the last legitimate emperor, who since 476 had been in exile in Dalmatia) was murdered. The final blow to Italy, however, did not occur until 489, when the Ostrogothic king, Theodoric, executed Odovocar and took possession of the peninsula in the name of his own people. (For more information on the fall of the Western Roman Empire, see the discussion that follows the biography of Romulus Augustus.)

The East

Meanwhile, the Eastern Roman Empire remained on a relatively steady course that laid the foundation for what is commonly known as the Byzantine Empire. The East was wealthier, and was built upon Greek and Asiatic cultures far older than Rome itself. Based in Constantinople, the Byzantine Empire survived a thousand years after Rome fell, though the Romans of the East had their share of problems along the way.

The main enemy of the Eastern Roman Empire was Persia, which was then under the rule of the Sasanian kings. The Sasanians were fire-worshippers who under their king Shapur I had overthrown the previous rulers, the Parthians, in 224/6. This revolution was considered to be a revival of true Achaemenid rule, which had first been toppled by Alexander the Great and later was usurped by the nomadic Parthians.

Though mortal enemies, the Sasanians and the Romans often cooperated to stem the tide of nomadic invasions from the Asiatic steppes. Just as the western Romans shared a loose cultural bond with the Germanic peoples, so did the Eastern Romans with the Sasanians. But their bond was not built on the similarities of their civilizations, but rather on the fact that both *had* civilizations. An influx of uncultivated people from the steppes of Asia would serve the interests of neither Roman nor Sasanian.

The Sasanians eventually forfeited their dominion over the non-Roman East to the Arabs, who arose as a united force early in the 7th Century. By the middle of that century their Arabic invasion had ousted the last of the Sasanian kings. But that event, which was succeeded by complex and interesting encounters with Arabs, Venitians and Crusaders, lies well beyond the scope of this work. (For more information on the Eastern Roman Empire, see the introduction to chapter twelve.)

CHAPTER TWELVE

The Western Roman Empire A.D. 364–480

VALENTINIAN I A.D. 364–375

A.D. 364–367: Sole reign
A.D. 367–375: Senior Augustus
(with Gratian)

Ruling in the East:
Valens (364–378) and *Procopius* (365–366)

Brother of Valens
Husband of Severa and Justina
Father (by Severa) of Gratian and (by Justina) of Valentinian II and Galla
Father-in-law of Theodosius I and Constantia (*d.* of Constantius II)
Grandfather of Galla Placidia
Great-grandfather of Valentinian III and Honoria

Flavius Valentinianus, A.D. 321–375. Valentinian I was hailed emperor at Nicaea on February 26, 364, just ten days after the accidental death of Jovian, in whose army he was a commander of a division of spearmen. His elevation came only after long discussion, and much like the elevation of his predecessor, seems to have been arrived at for a lack of better options. Valentinian hailed from peasant stock in Pannonia, though his father had become a general in the army, and thus he was able to receive a good education. He had many enviable talents, which were not limited to administration and soldiering, but apparently included painting and sculpting. His temperament was rigid, and he was not lenient when it came to pronouncing punishment or seeking revenge. But on balance the bad qualities he had were few, and in any case were well-suited to survival as emperor.

Valentinian spent much of his youth in Africa, and later in his career served in Mesopotamia under Constantius II. He was dismissed from a similar position by Julian II, who banished him to Egypt for his Christian beliefs. However, Valentinian was recalled from his exile by the next emperor, Jovian, who sent him to Gaul to help restore order in the West. His success in that task earned him yet another commander position in the army. Instead of continuing the failed policy of ruling the Empire alone, Valentinian soon made his younger brother Valens co-emperor and split the Empire, with his brother ruling in the East and Valentinian ruling in the West. He chose the West because it was in greater need of attention than the East, and so he decided to take on the task himself. Although the concept of dividing the Empire between East and West was nothing new, in this case the policy endured virtually undisturbed until the collapse of the West in 476.

As emperor of the West, Valentinian made his capital at Milan, but did not have the luxury to reside there, as he devoted himself almost exclusively to frontier defense. With the exception of delivering relief to Britain in 367 (which had been overrun by Saxons), Valentinian focused on stabilizing the German nations. Indeed, he spent seven consecutive years in Germany constructing fortifications and doing his best to keep the existing rivalries between Germanic nations alive and active. As if this were not enough to occupy him, the Eastern part of Europe became a problem, for in 374 Germans and Sarmatians crossed the Danube and invaded Raetia. Valentinian once again moved his headquarters, this time to Sirmium so he could launch offensives across the Danube himself.

To pay for his peaked military demands, taxes were raised in the Empire. Perhaps because he and his family had risen from humble origins, Valentinian was especially moderate on the underprivileged and took care to keep the tax burden from affecting the poor too severely. Further, he created a political apparatus through which the poor could seek justice through officers known as Defenders of the People. The wealthy class must not have enjoyed the consequences of Valentinian's regime, but at least his energetic frontier warfare spared them invasion and the like.

Valentinian was married throughout his reign, initially to Marina Severa, by whom he sired Gratian. He divorced Severa in 368 and married Justina (the widow of Magnentius), with whom he had yet another son, Valentinian II. These step-brothers were destined to become emperors, and indeed they shared leadership of the West for eight years. Aware of a decline in his own health, Valentinian in 367 had appointed his eldest son Gratian (then 8 years old) as co-emperor in the West. He did this with great pomp and circumstance, and purposely tied his dynasty to the army, in hopes that when he passed, the army would support his legacy. Indeed, the "dynasty" he established (often called the House of Valentinian) lasted nearly a century. Though Valentinian himself reigned less than 12 years, his was perhaps the last successful principate in the West. He died at his military headquarters at Bregetio on November 17, 375, from a rage-induced stroke while receiving a delegation sent by the Quadi.

NUMISMATIC NOTE: Valentinian and Valens took a hard line on the devaluation of the solidus and the silver coinage when in 366/7 they introduced a law to reduce the problem of taxes being paid in underweight, impure or false solidi. In its most extreme circumstances, this law required the coins used for payment to be melted down into bars of pure gold. This effort stabilized the solidus at a very high purity and weight (72 to the Roman pound), for in some cases it had fallen below 95 percent pure, and was being struck at lower weights. This proved to be a wise venture, for it made Roman coinage the high standard by which all other currencies were judged, and gave Romans more bargaining power with their enemies, federates and army.

GRATIAN A.D. 367–383

A.D. 367–375: JUNIOR AUGUSTUS (WITH VALENTINIAN I)
A.D. 375–383: SENIOR AUGUSTUS (WITH VALENTINIAN II)

Ruling in the East:
VALENS (364–378), THEODOSIUS I (379–395) AND ARCADIUS (383–408)

SON OF VALENTINIAN I (AND SEVERA)
HUSBAND OF CONSTANTIA (*d.* OF CONSTANTIUS II)
NEPHEW OF VALENS
HALF-BROTHER OF VALENTINIAN II AND GALLA (*w.* OF THEODOSIUS I)

Flavius Gratianus, A.D. 359–383. Gratian, the eldest son of Valentinian I and Marina Severa, was born at Sirmium five years before his father became emperor, and later in life was well known for his preference for barbarian clothing and his passion for hunting. His other strong devotion was to Christianity, in the name of which he was an avid persecutor of pagans.

While aged only 7, Gratian was named consul — an appointment which was merely symbolic, and to those who still held the senate in high esteem, must have been insulting. But more was to come, because Gratian's father, whose health was failing, proclaimed him junior Augustus on August 24, 367, at a lavish ceremony at Ambiani. Father and eldest son had jointly held the titles of Augustus in the West for more than eight years when Valentinian I died suddenly on the Danubian frontier in 375. Thus the Western Roman Empire fell into the hands of 16-year-old Gratian as would be expected. But only five days later the army hailed Gratian's 4-year-old half-brother, Valentinian II, as co-emperor of the West. A brief power struggle involving several important military men ensued, but with little serious consequence, peace was restored. It is much to the credit of Gratian that civil war was averted, for he behaved charitably and suggested his young brother establish his court in Illyria while he set out to manage affairs in the less-stable western provinces.

Because of his youth, Gratian was strongly influenced by his former tutor, the poet Ausonius, and his Master of Infantry, Merobaudes. Ausonius worked hard to restore good relations with the senate, which had been alienated by the harsh policies of Gratian's father. Gratian established his court at Trier, from which he was able to direct campaigns against the Alemanni from 376 to 378. In the latter year he married Constantia, the 16-year-old daughter who was born posthumously to Constantius II and his third wife, Faustina. Constantia (in whose name no coins were struck) died in 383, and was able to produce only one son, who died in childhood.

But in 378 — the year of Gratian's marriage — the Romans suffered perhaps their greatest defeat in history. The Visigoths had been making overtures of war in the East (for the province of Thrace, though European, belonged to the East), and the emperor Valens had led an army to deal with this tense situation. In August Valens apparently grew tired of waiting for Gratian's army to arrive, or was eager to defeat them single-handedly, and so launched an offensive before Gratian's reinforcements arrived. Indeed, we are told that Gratian arrived at Adrianople only in time to witness the aftermath of the virtual destruction of the Eastern army, and the death of his uncle, Valens.

Gratian had now inherited the whole Empire, which he theoretically shared with his 7-year-old half-brother. Even though Valentinian II would have ruled only in name for at least the first decade, it would have been simple enough for the brothers to divide the Empire between themselves. But instead of pursuing that disastrous option, or taking on more than he could handle, Gratian eventually decided to appoint a cousin of his by marriage as the replacement of his slain uncle. After the Eastern throne had remained vacant for about six months, the general Theodosius (who recently had been recalled from Spain to take charge of the Danubian frontier) was hailed Augustus in the East in January of 379.

Together Gratian and Theodosius I kept the Goths and the Alans in check, but in 383 Gratian's attention was required in Britain, where a commander named Magnus Maximus had revolted, and subsequently crossed the channel. When Gratian neared Paris his army deserted for lack of monetary incentive, and left the 24-year-old emperor to flee for his life. Gratian was overtaken near Lugdunum and was executed there on August 25, 383, exactly 16 years and one day after he had ascended the throne.

NUMISMATIC NOTE: Gratian was the first emperor to drop *pontifex maximus* from his titulature, for he perceived it to be a relic of the pagan age.

VALENTINIAN II A.D. 375–392

A.D. 375–383: JUNIOR AUGUSTUS (WITH GRATIAN)
A.D. 383–392: SOLE REIGN

Ruling in the East:
VALENS (364–378), THEODOSIUS I (379–395) AND ARCADIUS (383–408)

SON OF VALENTINIAN I (AND JUSTINA)
BROTHER OF GALLA (*w.* OF THEODOSIUS I)
HALF-BROTHER OF GRATIAN
NEPHEW OF VALENS
BROTHER-IN-LAW OF THEODOSIUS I
UNCLE OF GALLA PLACIDIA

Flavius Valentinianus, A.D. 371–392. Five days after the sudden death of his father, the 4-year-old Valentinian II was hailed co-emperor (November 22, 375) with his older half-brother, Gratian, who had nominally held that title with their father for more than eight years. This symbolic act was engineered by Valentinian's mother, Justina (a devout Arian who formerly was the wife of the usurper Magnentius), the Frankish Master of Infantry Merobaudes, and the Danubian commander Equitius. Both Justina and Merobaudes took advantage of dissatisfaction among the Danubian soldiers, who had tired of the Germans making the important decisions.

Power was now shared in the West by Gratian and the adults who represented the child Valentinian II. The division of the West was formal, with the court of Valentinian II having authority in Italy, western Illyria and Africa. That Gratian did not respond to this lawless elevation with force, and indeed that he did not resent his sibling, is much to his credit. When Gratian was killed by Magnus Maximus in 383, Valentinian's court moved from Illyria to Milan. A temporary peace was arranged between Valentinian II and the usurper, which lasted for nearly four years.

While at Milan, the influence of the emperor's mother was greatly diminished because of her loss of a religious dispute with St. Ambrose. But more serious matters were at hand, for Magnus Maximus was still in control of the westernmost provinces, and in 387 he launched an invasion of Italy. In fear of his life, Valentinian II (now about 16 years old) and his mother fled Milan and sought refuge in Thessalonica. Indeed, it was through his mother's efforts that the Eastern emperor Theodosius I agreed to invade Italy and to restore her son's rule. Regrettably, she was unable to enjoy the fruits of her labor, for she died in 388.

Having taken part in the campaign against Magnus Maximus, Valentinian II was able to maintain his principate. However, his authority in the

West was greatly diminished, for Theodosius I remained in Italy for nearly four years thereafter. Throughout this period, young Valentinian was at odds with the Frankish Master of Infantry Arbogast, whom Theodosius had endowed with great authority in the West. At one point Valentinian tried to oust the Frankish soldier, but found that when Arbogast refused to resign, he could not forcibly retire him.

Their tense joint-rulership ended on May 15, 392, when the 21-year-old Valentinian (held against his will at Vienna in southern Gaul) died, either by his own hand or by strangulation on the orders of Arbogast. This treacherous act brought about the extinction of the luckless House of Valentinian. Three months later Arbogast installed the usurper Eugenius on the throne in Rome, and through him ruled in the West for the next two years.

MAGNUS MAXIMUS
A.D. 383–388

A.D. 383–387: SOLE REIGN
A.D. 387–388: SENIOR AUGUSTUS (WITH FLAVIUS VICTOR)

Ruling in the East:
THEODOSIUS I (379–395) AND ARCADIUS (383–408)

FATHER OF FLAVIUS VICTOR

Flavius Magnus Clemens Maximus, d. A.D. 388. The Spaniard Magnus Maximus was a distant relative and comrade-in-arms of Count Theodosius, the illustrious father of Theodosius I, the emperor in the East at the time of Maximus' revolt.

Maximus earlier had served in North Africa, and had become the commander of the Roman army in Britain, where he was fighting the Picts and the Scots when his soldiers hailed him emperor in July of 383. He quickly moved into Gaul and also claimed Spain for himself. The rightful emperor of the West, Gratian, traveled west to crush Maximus' rebellion, but when he reached Gaul his troops abandoned him and the 24-year-old emperor fled, only to be overtaken and killed at Lugdunum on August 25. Theodosius I (struggling with the Sasanians in the East) and Valentinian II (helpless in Milan) were not able to combat Maximus' insurrection.

The usurper was able to extend his territories, and to enlist the help of the infantry commander Merobaudes. In the summer of 384 Theodosius I met with envoys of Maximus and there found it practical to recognize

Maximus as a *de facto* emperor (co-regent of the West), thus dividing the Empire into three distinct portions. In 387 Maximus took advantage of the undefended Alpine passes and invaded Italy in May of 387. The 16-year-old Valentinian II escaped with his mother to Thessalonica, where they sought the protection of the Eastern emperor Theodosius I.

Maximus' unlawful cause found some ardent supporters in Italy, including the renowned orator and consul Quintus Aurelius Symmachus. At this time Maximus raised his young son, Flavius Victor, as his junior co-emperor. In the following year, however, Theodosius patched up a peace with the Sasanians and then led his army of Romans, Huns and Visigoths on a fast march through the Balkans. Maximus stayed in Aquileia and sent an army toward the Balkans to combat Theodosius, but his legions were defeated several times, and Theodosius marched into Italy, where he found Maximus at Aquileia. Despite his pleas for mercy, the usurper was finally defeated and then beheaded in July or August, 388.

His son, Flavius Victor (who may have been with him or remained in Gaul), was captured and executed by the Frankish Master of Infantry Arbogast. Having gone to great expense to restore peace in the West, Theodosius remained in Italy for more than three years and placed young Valentinian II under the tutelage of Arbogast. A fanatical Orthodox Christian, Maximus was quite active in his religious persecutions, and even found a place in Welsh legend. Indeed, it would have been an interesting Empire had Maximus succeeded in ruling the West, as the entire Empire would have been ruled by Spaniards, who no doubt would have created a Spanish dynasty with their sons.

FLAVIUS VICTOR A.D. 387–388

JUNIOR AUGUSTUS (WITH MAGNUS MAXIMUS)

Ruling in the East:
THEODOSIUS I (379–395) AND
ARCADIUS (383–408)

SON OF MAGNUS MAXIMUS

Flavius Victor, d. A.D. 388. The young son of Magnus Maximus, Flavius Victor was proclaimed co-emperor by his father sometime in the middle of 387, when the latter was wresting Italy from Valentinian II. The coinage is careful to show his youth and small stature, indicating he was subordinate to his father.

Flavius Victor, whose age is not known (indeed he may have been only an infant), was emperor for only about a year before he was executed after his father's defeat by Theodosius I. It is not entirely certain whether he was left in Gaul while his father occupied Italy, or if he accompanied him, though the former seems likely. In any case, his death came in August of 388 at the hands of the general Arbogast, either with his father or shortly thereafter.

NUMISMATIC NOTE: Flavius Victor's coins were struck at Trier and the newly captured Italian mints of Milan and Aquileia. The reverse inscription on his rare solidus BONO REIPVBLICE NATI, meaning "born for the good of the state," is among the most charming in the Imperial series.

EUGENIUS A.D. 392–394

Ruling in the East:
THEODOSIUS I (379–395) AND
ARCADIUS (383–408)

Flavius Eugenius, d. A.D. 394. History records very little of Eugenius, who on August 22, 392, was chosen to replace Valentinian II more than three months after the latter had been murdered. Making this choice was Arbogast, a Frankish general whom the Eastern emperor Theodosius I had named co-regent with Valentinian II. Eugenius was well-suited for the job because he was only a middle-ranking court official who had formerly been a professor of rhetoric and Latin.

Eugenius was the ideal puppet emperor, for he was not likely to defy the authority of the court officials and military commanders who had installed him. Although a Christian himself, Eugenius was bearded and tolerated a brief revival of paganism in Rome in an effort to gain support against Theodosius I. After all, it was Theodosius' relentless persecution of pagans and heretics that provided a spark for revolution. By the spring of 393 Eugenius had moved East to occupy Italy, and it must have angered Theodosius that he had to lead an army to defend Italy for a second time in just a few years. Arbogast continued to rule the Western Roman Empire through Eugenius until Theodosius I routed their army near Aquileia (or along the Frigidus river in Pannonia) on September 5–6, 394. After their defeat, Eugenius was captured and executed and Arbogast fled, only to take his own life a few days later.

HONORIUS A.D. 393–423

SOLE REIGN
(EXCEPT 421, WITH CONSTANTIUS III)

Ruling in the East:
THEODOSIUS I (379–395), ARCADIUS (383–408) AND THEODOSIUS II (408–450)

SON OF THEODOSIUS I AND AELIA FLACCILLA
BROTHER OF ARCADIUS
BROTHER-IN-LAW OF AELIA EUDOXIA
UNCLE OF THEODOSIUS II AND AELIA PULCHERIA
HALF-BROTHER OF GALLA PLACIDIA

Flavius Honorius, A.D. 383/4–423. Born at Constantinople, Honorius was the younger son of the reigning emperor Theodosius I and his first wife, Aelia Flacilla. Honorius' reign was one of the most tragic and mismanaged in all Roman history. Honorius was hailed emperor in January, 393, which raised the number of emperors in the East to three: Theodosius I (age 46 or 47), Arcadius (age 16), and Honorius (age 8). However promising this might have seemed, it soon became apparent that Honorius and his brother had inherited none of their father's talent, and that both were destined to be ruled by their generals.

Honorius' reign began in the midst of a tragedy, for at that time the West was in the hands of the usurper Eugenius (392–394). The last legitimate emperor of the West, Valentinian II, had been killed eight months earlier, and so the task of restoring order in the West fell squarely on the shoulders of Theodosius I. Thus, when Theodosius left Constantinople in 394 to oust Eugenius from Italy, he left his eldest son, Arcadius, in the East to oversee matters during his absence.

Though Theodosius was successful in defeating Euguenius and his supporters, the great emperor himself died in 395, leaving the 18-year-old Arcadius emperor in the East, and the 12-year-old Honorius emperor in the West. Both boys had ambitious generals as their advisers, the one appointed to Honorius being the half-Vandal Master of Soldiers Flavius Stilicho. His position was secure, for not only had he been appointed by Theodosius I, but he was married to a niece of Theodosius, and had wed both of his own daughters (first Maria then, after her death, Thermantia the Younger) to Honorius.

The death of Theodosius was particularly damaging to relations between East and West, as the generals Stilicho (regent in the West) and Rufinus (regent in the East) fought for control of Illyria, an important province which provided a steady supply of army recruits. Their private quarrel caused an uprising by the Visigoths under their chieftain Alaric.

Though the Goths ravaged much of the Balkans and Greece from 395 to 397, the two generals were more concerned with their own struggle than with sparing Greece from destruction. The conflict ended in treachery when Stilicho (in what seemed to be a peaceful gesture) had Rufinus assassinated. When Stilicho refused to cooperate in the war against Alaric, he was declared a public enemy in 397 by Arcadius, and tensions between East and West rose to a new height.

A revolt in North Africa proved equally dangerous, for the leader of the rebellion sought to ally himself with Arcadius in the East. Fortunately the crisis ended, and disaster was narrowly averted. But the woes of the Western Roman Empire were just beginning, and the remainder of Honorius' reign is a virtual laundry list of catastrophe. The close proximity of the Goths convinced Honorius that his current capital at Milan was vulnerable to fast invasion, and so in 404 he moved his court further south to Ravenna, a city with easy access to the sea and natural protection afforded by its marshy environs. The measure proved wise, because in 405 a confederate army led by the Ostrogoths invaded Italy, and was repelled by Stilicho.

Riding the tide of this recent victory, the ambitious Stilicho planned for his invasion of Illyria, and tried to gain the cooperation of the Visigoth Alaric in his enterprise. But he was foiled when a Germanic invasion was launched across the Rhine in 406. Even though Germany, Gaul and Britain were laid waste to on an almost inconceivable scale, Stilicho was still preoccupied with his desire to recapture Illyria, and offered no substantive help to the depleted legions in the far West. Thus, the legions supported a rebellion that began in Britain and spread into Gaul and Spain. Though the first two leaders of this revolt were quickly murdered and replaced by their own soldiers, it signaled the beginning of nearly a decade of chaos in the westernmost provinces, which continued virtually unabated from 406 to 415.

During this period, the Roman armies were divided among loyalists and usurpers, and thus were ineffective against the Germans, who poured across the Rhine to settle in Gaul and Spain. The details are sketchy and intricate, and are presented in the biographies of Constantine III (407–411), Constans II (410–411), Maximus (409–411), Jovinus (411–413), Sebastianus (412–413) and Priscus Attalus (second reign, 414–415). In the meantime, Italy and eastern Europe were equally chaotic, for Alaric and his Visigoths were being kept at bay only through the payment of huge sums of gold.

The year 408 was especially important, for Honorius' older brother Arcadius, emperor in the East, died on May 1. He was replaced by his 7-year-old son, Theodosius II, who had been hailed Junior Augustus in 402. But Stilicho's ambition was unbounded, and he claimed the right of regency over East as well as West, only to be arrested on August 22 by his own mutinous soldiers, who had been told he was planning to overthrow Honorius and install his own son, Eucherius, on the throne. The short-sighted senate was fed up with German generals, and drove a great many German soldiers out of Italy. But this purge (which kept another German from holding such a position for the next half-century) was a Pyrrhic victory, for most of the Germans joined the Visigoths.

With the loss of Stilicho and the western provinces in open revolt, Alaric, in October, led his Visigoths on a second invasion of Italy — and this one proved effective. Alaric blockaded Rome from 408–410, and their siege was so effective that they avoided sacking it in the first year only because they were paid a vast sum of gold by the senate. But in 409 they renewed their pressure, captured Rome's port, and forced the senate to declare a candidate of their own, Priscus Attalus, as emperor in place of Honorius. But Alaric soon tired of his arrangement with Priscus Attalus and arranged to meet with Honorius near his court in Ravenna. During the process, however, his delegation was attacked by a hated compatriot, Sarus. Alaric suspected it was no coincidence, and that Honorius had arranged it. So Alaric broke off negotiations and engaged in some treachery of his own, through which the gates opened for him.

The Visigoths poured into Rome in August of 410 and sacked the Eternal City for about three days. In addition to booty, the invaders took captives, including the emperor's beloved half-sister, Galla Placidia. This event shocked the Roman world, but the news was not immediately understood by the dull-witted Honorius, who was then residing at his court in Ravenna. The historian Procopius informs us that when he was told that "Rome had fallen," he first thought that his pet cock — named Roma — had died. His perplexed response, ". . . and I was only just feeding him," reveals his simplistic nature. The sack of Rome also did little for the Visigoths, whose leader died later that year during his southward trek, from which he had hoped to invade North Africa. Their subsequent fate in Spain and southern Gaul was luckless, after which they decided to return to central Gaul and settle.

Though Rome had not been sacked in almost eight centuries, the Western Roman Empire's misfortunes did not end there. The next five years were plagued with continued rebellion in the westernmost provinces. Some good luck, however, did come to Honorius in the form of a valiant general named Constantius (better known as Constantius III), who was able to quell revolts in the West, defeat the Visigoths, and recover Honorius' half-sister, Galla Placidia, whom he made his reluctant wife in 417. Since Honorius was ever-reliant on his generals, he must have felt good about this new arrangement with Constantius III. However, in February of 421, he hailed his prize general as his co-emperor, a decision which seemed to please neither Honorius or his nephew, Theodosius II (who refused to recognize the elevation). As unwilling as Honorius was to share his office, he no doubt was saddened when a few months later (September, 421) Constantius III died of what seemingly were natural causes.

The childless Honorius was thus robbed of an immediate heir, but in turn received a future one, for Constantius III and Placidia had had two children, one of whom was the future emperor Valentinian III. Ancient historians tell us of another part of Honorius' personality, for he was unnaturally fond of his half-sister. His public expressions of this love, which appeared blatantly incestuous to those observing, caused riots between various political factions in the streets of Ravenna. However, their love became strained and turned sour, causing Honorius to banish Galla Placidia and her children in 422 or 423. After an exhausting and luckless reign of more than 30 years, Honorius — then aged 39 — died of natural causes shortly thereafter on August 25, 423. His death incited yet another revolt, in which power was seized by a faction backing a usurper named Johannes, who ruled for 18 months until he was deposed in 425 by an army sent from Constantinople. In his place, the rightful emperor, the 6-year-old Valentinian III, was installed.

NUMISMATIC NOTE: There are imitations of Honorius' solidi, tremisses, siliquae and half-siliquae attributed to the Visigoths (see RIC X, pp. 451–2); of his solidi and siliquae attributed to the Suevi (see RIC X, p. 465); and of his siliquae, half-siliquae and Æ4's attributed to the Vandals and N. Africa in general (see RIC X, p. 467ff.).

CONSTANTINE III A.D. 407–411

A.D. 407–408: SOLE REIGN
A.D. 408–409/410: AUGUSTUS (WITH CONSTANS II, AS CAESAR)
A.D. 409/410–411: SENIOR AUGUSTUS (WITH CONSTANS II)

Ruling in the East:
ARCADIUS (383–408) AND THEODOSIUS II (408–450)

FATHER OF CONSTANS II

Flavius Claudius Constantinus, d. A.D. 411. During the early 5th Century, Britain was slowly denuded of its legions because of more pressing needs on the continent. The general Stilicho withdrew most Roman troops from Britain and Gaul to repel an Ostrogothic army led by

Radagaisus that penetrated northern Italy late in 405. (Stilicho defeated the Ostrogoths, but only with the aid of the Huns and by keeping Alaric's Visigoths in line with large sums of gold.)

Though disaster was averted in Italy, the provinces of Britain and Gaul were unprotected. A great invasion of Gaul was launched across the frozen Rhine by Burgundians, Vandals, Alans, Alemanni, Franks and Suevi, which not only devastated Germany and Gaul, but also incited the Picts to ravage Britain. This led to chaos and disaffection within the army, which was not impressed with the feeble efforts of Stilicho, and so in 406 took matters into its own hands by raising three men in quick succession as emperor: Marcus, Gratian and Constantine III. The first two were rapidly deposed by their own soldiers, and of them we have no coins.

Constantine III was a common soldier, and in 407 he wrote to Honorius explaining his hesitance, but none-the-less he asked for confirmation. He mobilized his depleted army and quickly moved into Gaul, where he established his court at Arles. In 408 he raised his eldest son, Constans II, to the rank of Caesar, and his youngest son, Julian, to *Nobilissimus* ("most noble"). Regrettably, no coins were struck in the name of Julian. However, we do have coins in the name of Constans II, whose principal task was to conquer the north of Spain, which he did briefly.

In 409 the Visigoth Alaric launched his invasion of Italy, and as a result Constantine III was able to gain temporary recognition from Honorius, with whom he held the consulship in that year. This did not please Theodosius II in Constantinople, who did not agree to the pact, which in part involved Constantine III providing help to Honorius in repelling the Visogoths. However, in the same year treacherous actions by his own general Gerontius cost Constantine III his recently acquired territories in northern Spain.

Instead of coming under the protection of the Roman armies, Spain was now being ravaged by Vandals and other Germans with whom Gerontius seems to have made a pact. Then in 409 the rebellious general raised a man named Maximus (perhaps his own son), as emperor in Spain. Thus, at the very peak of its nominal achievement, the Empire of Constantine III began to collapse. He recalled his son, Constans II, from Spain in 410 and hailed him co-emperor, perhaps in preparation for an invasion of Italy (in 410) that never materialized. Early in 411, Constans II was besieged and executed by Gerontius at Vienne, and later in the same year Constantine III himself was besieged by Gerontius at Arles. With him, and sharing his fate, was his youngest son, Julian. But his turncoat general had to abandon his venture because an army led by Honorius' general, Constantius (the emperor of 421, later called Constantius III), was fast approaching.

Thus Gerontius fled and Constantius III renewed the siege of Arles. In September, Constantine III was captured just after he had taken the vows of priesthood. But this act was futile, and did not spare his life as he had hoped. Constantine III was executed on orders of Honorius while being transported to Ravenna. Though his rebellion (and the offshoot rebellion of Maximus in Spain) were crushed, a new Gallic revolt led by Jovinus was sparked in the same year.

NUMISMATIC NOTE: This rebel's most interesting coins — inscribed VICTORIA AAAVGGGG — were struck only at Lugdunum. Though once believed to represent Honorius, Theodosius II, Constantine III and Constans II, hoard evidence has shown that they were struck before Constans II was hailed co-emperor; therefore, they are dated to 407–408, and must refer to Honorius, Arcadius, Theodosius II and Constantine III.

CONSTANS II A.D. 409/10–411

A.D. 408–409/10: CAESAR
(UNDER CONSTANTINE III)
A.D. 409/410–411: JUNIOR AUGUSTUS
(WITH CONSTANTINE III)

Ruling in the East:
ARCADIUS (383–408) AND
THEODOSIUS II (408–450)

SON OF CONSTANTINE III

Constans, d. A.D. 411. As might be expected, the historical information on Constans II — who we are told was a monk before being hailed Caesar — is incomplete, and in some cases contradictory. We do know he was associated with his father's revolt during its second year, but probably with the rank of Caesar. One source, Olympiodorus, tells us Constans was first made Caesar, and was elevated to the rank of Augustus in 409 (or later) when he was recalled from Spain by his father. More than likely he was given the rank of Augustus in 410, either because of a host of new problems which his father faced, or because of a planned invasion of Italy.

The first task entrusted to Constans II was to add Spain to his father's fugitive kingdom. This goal he achieved in 408 and 409 with the help of the general Gerontius. However, the territorial gain was short-lived as the Spanish soldiers guarding the pass at the Pyrenees revolted, allowing the Vandals and other Germanic migrants to flow directly from Gaul into Spain. Unable to control the situation he had been sent to remedy, Constans II fled back to Gaul, leaving the Roman citizens with no choice but to take refuge within the walled cities of Spain.

Historians tell us that a severe famine forced many of them to resort to cannibalism. Constantine III blamed Gerontius for the treachery of the Spanish soldiers, and thus the general made a pact with the Vandals in hopes it would preserve his life. As part of the pact, Gerontius declared Maximus (who perhaps was his own son) as emperor of Spain.

From all this chaos in Spain, Constans II was recalled to Gaul by his father, where he was hailed co-emperor. But Gerontius proved to be a fatal thorn in the side of young Constans II, for early in 411 he besieged him at Vienne and soon executed him. Only a few months later, Gerontius proceeded to besiege the boy's father Constantine III at Arles. Constans II had a younger brother named Julian (for whom no coins were struck) who was hailed *Nobilissimus* ("most noble") when Constans II was made Caesar.

NUMISMATIC NOTE: Constans II is most often referred to only as "Constans," but in this catalog he is designated "Constans II" to easily distinguish him from the earlier emperor of the same name who reigned from 337–350. His extremely rare coinage (of which there are Cigoi forgeries) seems to be limited to silver siliquae of Trier with the standard Roma-seated reverse, all bearing the mint marks KONT or SMTR.

MAXIMUS A.D. 409–411

Ruling in the East:
THEODOSIUS II (408–450)

SON OF GERONTIUS(?)

Maximus, d. A.D. 422(?). The rebellion of Constantine III occurred out of desperation, for Germans were pouring across the Rhine in numbers not thought possible. The legions stationed in the West were receiving no help from the emperor Honorius, who had his hands full keeping the Visigoths out of Italy.

The leading general in this rebellion was Gerontius, who was as versatile as he was talented. In 408 he and Constantine III's son, Constans II, conquered northern Spain. However, the gain was short-lived as Germans poured through Gaul and directly into Spain. Historians suspect Gerontius spared his own interests by coming to secret arrangements with the invaders. While this may have been a sensible course of action, it did not please Constantine III, who recalled his son after he learned that Gerontius had appointed a certain Maximus as emperor in Spain.

The identification of Maximus has been a point of considerable debate. Some suggest he was Gerontius' son, but perhaps more likely he was his senior household officer (*domesticus*). Maximus' reign lasted into 410, a year when six men claimed the title Augustus in the Roman Empire (the other five being Honorius, Theodosius II, Priscus Attalus, Constantine III and Constans II).

In 411, however, the western provinces were being reclaimed by Honorius. In that year not only had Constantine III and Constans II been killed, but Maximus' supporter Gerontius had been forced to commit suicide. Maximus had apparently been with Gerontius at the siege of Arles, and also had fled when he learned that Honorius' general Constantius III was fast approaching. But instead of choosing suicide, Maximus sought protection among his barbarian allies in Spain, at which point his reign of about two years ended. Maximus was officially deposed by Honorius and allowed to retire to an obscure, private life in Spain. It is possible (but not certain) that he is the same *Maximus tryannus* who rebelled in Spain in about 420, only to be captured. That particular Maximus was paraded in the streets of Ravenna in 422 during Honorius' *tricennalia*, and subsequently executed.

NUMISMATIC NOTE: The coins struck by Maximus designate only three Augusti, which presumably are meant to be Honorius, Theodosius II and himself, thus denying recognition of the Visigothic puppet emperor Priscus Attalus and of the Gallic usurpers Constantine III and Constans II, with whom he was at odds. All of his coins were struck at Barcelona, and all bear the mint mark SMBA. Though Maximus' coin portraits are always bearded, Cigoi forgeries exist on which he is unbearded.

PRISCUS ATTALUS
FIRST REIGN A.D. 409–410

Ruling in the East:
THEODOSIUS II (408–450)

Priscus Attalus, d. after A.D. 417. A Roman senator of Ionian Greek origin, and a pagan follower of Symmachus, Priscus Attalus came into the political limelight in 408, when he took a leading role as representative of the senate in negotiations with Alaric the Visigoth, who had begun a siege of Rome. In January, 409, Attalus was named count of the sacred largess, and later in the year was named consul. When the Visigoths captured the city's granaries in 409 and threatened to starve the Romans out, the senate bowed to the Gothic demands by appointing Priscus Attalus emperor in opposition to Honorius (who was currently reigning at Ravenna).

As part of his installation, Attalus had to be baptized, and so he was, by an Arian bishop. The western emperor Honorius was probably regretting the execution of his best general Stilicho only a year before. Despite Stilicho's lust for power, he had managed to keep the Visigoths in check. But all that had changed, and the Visigoths, led by their chieftain, Alaric, had gained the upper hand in Italy.

Attalus served as Alaric's agent in Rome until the Visigoths failed to take Ravenna in 410, when fresh armies arrived from Theodosius II in the East. Thus, Alaric renewed his focus on Rome, where in June he deposed Attalus, who received a pardon from Honorius. When the Visigoths entered Rome in August (24th through the 26th) of 410, it was the first time the city had been sacked in eight centuries. Attalus was immediately taken hostage by Alaric, and subsequently led away as a prisoner when the Visigoths left. The coins Priscus Attalus struck prior to this traumatic event are the height of irony, for their inscription INVICTA ROMA AETERNA ("the unconquerable, eternal Rome") could not have been further from the mark. This seemingly permanent reversal, however, is only half of Attalus' story, for he reigned yet a second time at the behest of the Goths, from 414 to 415. For details of the second reign, refer to that separate biographical entry.

NUMISMATIC NOTE: The coins struck by Priscus Attalus during his first reign at Rome are well known and indicate an issuance of respectable size. More controversial, however, are his non-Rome-mint issues, which offer a host of possiblilities for both mint location and reign (first or second). Especially thorny is an issue of siliquae of greatly inferior style and weight (c. 1.00 grams) which almost certainly are of Gallic origin. They bear the same types as the RESTITVTIO REIP issue attributed to Attalus' second reign, except that the inscription is VICTORIA AAVGG (or AVGGG) and the mint mark is PSRV. Based on the mint mark, some authorities assign this issue to Ravenna (a city which Attallus besieged, but never controlled) during the first reign, but the authors of RIC consider these coins to be non-Imperial issues of the Visigoths (see RIC X, p. 450), listed under the heading of "Pseudo-Ravenna/Arles coinage."

JOVINUS A.D. 411–413

A.D. 411–412: SOLE REIGN
A.D. 412–413: SENIOR AUGUSTUS (WITH SEBASTIANUS)

Ruling in the East:
THEODOSIUS II (408–450)

BROTHER OF SEBASTIANUS

Jovinus, d. A.D. 413. Just at the point when the Western Roman Empire appeared to be recovering from its ill fortunes of 407–411 (during which Rome was sacked by the Visigoths and the westernmost provinces fell to the usurpers Constantine III, Constans II and Maximus), a new revolt was sparked against Honorius. This time it was supported by the Germans along the Rhine, and led by Jovinus, the most powerful nobleman in Gaul.

Jovinus was proclaimed emperor in 411 either at Mainz or Mundiacum (Muntzen) by the Alan king, Goar, and the Burgundian king, Gundahar (Guntiarus). Soon after the revolt had formed, the Visigothic king, Athaulf, was persuaded by Priscus Attalus (the Gothic puppet emperor in Rome from 409–410) to join in the cause of Jovinus.

All seemed to be moving in the right direction for Jovinus, until he curried the support of Sarus (who was disliked by Athaulf) and then in 412 appointed his brother, Sebastianus, as co-emperor — a move which caused Athaulf to withdraw his support. Athaulf secretly began negotiating with Honorius, offering to betray Jovinus. With the help of Honorius' Gallic prefect Dardanus, Athaulf defeated Sebastianus and beheaded him. Next they besieged Valentia, the Gallic city to which Jovinus had fled for refuge. After a confused reign of about two years, Jovinus surrendered to Athaulf and Dardanus. But soon after Jovinus had been transferred to the Romans, he was executed at Narbonne by Dardanus, after which his head was delivered to Honorius at Ravenna on August 30.

NUMISMATIC NOTE: Jovinus struck at Trier, Lugdunum and Arles. Cigoi forgeries of Jovinus' siliquae exist.

SEBASTIANUS A.D. 412–413

Junior Augustus (with Jovinus)

Ruling in the East:
Theodosius II (408–450)

Brother of Jovinus

Sebastianus, d. A.D. 413. Very little is known of this ephemeral emperor. Sebastianus was made co-emperor by his brother, Jovinus, about a year after the latter had been declared emperor by the Alans and Burgundians. But his inclusion in the revolt proved to be its undoing, for Jovinus' ally, the Visigothic king Athaulf, did not approve of Sebastianus' appointment. After a reign which probably lasted less than one year, Sebastianus was betrayed and executed by Athaulf, who had conspired with the legitimate Western emperor Honorius and his Gallic prefect Dardanus. Sebastianus' severed head was then delivered to Honorius as proof of Athaulf's loyalty. Jovinus' death at the hands of Athaulf and Honorius came shortly thereafter (see the preceding biography).

Numismatic Note: Sebastianus' coins are of the greatest rarity, and indeed no hoard evidence has come to light to support their authenticity, as the provenances of the extant specimens are not known. There are perhaps fewer than a dozen specimens recorded, most of which, it seems, are of dubious authenticity. The reported specimens all are siliquae of a single emission from Arles.

PRISCUS ATTALUS

SECOND REIGN, A.D. 414–415

Ruling in the East:
Theodosius II (408–450)

Priscus Attalus, d. after A.D. 417. Though this shadowy character had earlier proven ineffective as a puppet emperor of the Visigoths in 410 (see his earlier biographical entry), he had been taken as a prisoner by King Alaric. Much like the royal lady Galla Placidia, Attalus remained in Visigothic hands under Alaric's successor, Athaulf, who brought him to Gaul in January of 414. There he composed verses to honor his king's marriage to Placidia at Narbonne, and in the following year, 415, was hailed for yet a second time as emperor in opposition to Honorius (with whom Athaulf had cooperated — without satisfaction — to defeat the rebels Jovinus and Sebastianus).

Attalus' second reign was a virtual repeat of his first, for he proved virtually useless as an ally, and his ill-gotten principate was short-lived (and was terminated in the same year that his sponsoring Gothic king died). However, this time his benefactor did not die of natural causes, but at the hands of the Roman commander (and future emperor), Constantius III.

After an embarrassing career as puppet king to the Goths, Attalus was captured by Honorius' soldiers in April or May of 416 (though he may have been deposed by Athaulf in 415) and taken to Rome, where he was paraded through the streets. Since his execution might have enraged the senate, the usurper was instead banished to the Lipari islands where he lived out the rest of his days. But before he left Rome, Honorius cut off one of Attalus' thumbs and forefingers so he could never again draw a bow, and thus could never lead a revolt. The fall of Attalus' regime signaled the end of nearly a decade of war between Germans, Romans and usurpers of every extraction. Although far from stable, the westernmost provinces finally returned to a state of relative peace.

Numismatic Note: The possibility that Priscus Attalus struck coins during his second reign, in Gaul, has been acknowledged by many authorities. The candidates, however, are excessively rare and at present do not offer incontrovertible proof that such a coinage existed. The most likely issue is a solidus with the mint mark COMOB below NB (certainly = Narbonne). Regrettably, this coin is cited by Banduri as being in the French royal collection, and cannot be confirmed. The other likely candidate is a siliqua with the (perhaps) incomplete mint mark SV which is of lighter weight than those struck at Italian mints (see the *note* to Attalus' first reign for siliquae with the mint mark PSRV, which have led some to "expand" this coin's mint mark to PSRV, and thus to speculate that it too belongs to Attalus' first reign). Interestingly, both the solidus and siliqua discussed above bear the reverse inscription RESTITVTIO REIP, an inscription that does not occur on Attalus' earlier coins of Rome, and one which is particularly appropriate for a "second reign" coinage.

CONSTANTIUS III A.D. 421

JUNIOR AUGUSTUS (WITH HONORIUS)

Ruling in the East:
THEODOSIUS II (408–450)

SECOND HUSBAND OF GALLA PLACIDIA

FATHER OF VALENTINIAN III AND HONORIA
HALF-BROTHER-IN-LAW OF HONORIUS AND ARCADIUS
FATHER-IN-LAW OF LICINIA EUDOXIA
GRANDFATHER OF PLACIDIA THE YOUNGER (W. OF OLYBRIUS)

Flavius Constantius (III), d. A.D. 421. A soldier of exceptional skill, Constantius III came into the limelight in 411, when he suppressed the Gallic revolt of Constantine III and his son, Constans II. His efficiency and skill earned him the office of *Magister utriusque militae* (Master of Both Branches of Soldiery) by that same year. He held that post for a decade under Honorius, and exerted great authority in Imperial affairs.

Constantius' most important campaign was his vigorous naval blockade of Spain and Gaul in 415, which resulted in the murder of the Visigothic king Athaulf. In the process Constantius III was able to negotiate the return of the emperor's half-sister, Galla Placidia, who had been forcibly married to Athaulf. As a result of his actions, Constantius III earned her hand in a forced-marriage consummated on January 1, 417, upon which his second consulship began. This political union transformed the Danubian military commander into a member of the Theodosian royal family. The strength of his position was increased with the birth of their first child, Honoria, and in 419 with the birth of their only son, the future emperor Valentinian III.

Constantius III took another step toward the principate in 420, when he was appointed consul together with the eastern emperor Theodosius II. Though his brother-in-law Honorius may have been senior Augustus, he was also incompetent and childless. So on February 8, 421, Honorius reluctantly declared his brother-in-law Constantius III as his co-emperor, and in effect adopted his son Valentinian III as heir. The elevation of Constantius was well-received in the West where his achievements were known, but it was not acknowledged by the eastern emperor Theodosius II. This created the possibility of civil war, about which Constantius III was already bellowing.

It seems that becoming emperor did not suit his personality, for Constantius III did not take well to the formal atmosphere of the court in Ravenna, and perhaps as a consequence became avaricious (which he apparently was not before his elevation). We are told he was an affable host at dinner, but was extremely conscious of the dignity of his appearance before his soldiers and the public.

However, the new emperor's health did not long hold out. After a reign of less than seven months, the promising leader died, probably of natural causes, at Ravenna on September 2, 421. Though not accepted by Theodosius II during his lifetime, he was posthumously recognized as a legitimate emperor by Theodosius in 425, the year that he restored the western throne in the name of Constantius' son, Valentinian III.

In the last years of his life it must have been apparent to Constantius that his wife's affection for her half-brother Honorius was bordering on incest. As such, some contemporary sources suggest that Constantius' death was not the result of illness, but rather of murder. Honorius, after all, had much to gain from Constantius' death: avoiding a civil war with his nephew, Theodosius II, freeing the hand of his beloved Galla Placidia, and "inheriting" his son, Valentinian III, as an heir to the throne. Indeed, young Valentinian III proved to be the legacy of Constantius III's brief reign, for the boy had the only legitimate claim to the western throne after the death of Honorius.

Numismatic Note: The coinage of Constantius III is limited to gold solidi (rev. VICTORIA AVGGG, emperor standing, foot on captive, holding standard and globe topped with Victory) and gold tremisses (rev. VICTORIA AVGVSTORVM, Victory advancing right, holding wreath and globus cruciger). Both issues were struck at Ravenna, which is identified by the RV in the reverse field. Scholars dismiss variant issues (sometimes with the reverse type of a votive in wreath, or the obverse inscription D N CONSTANTIVS AVG or CONSTANTIVS AVG) as Germanic imitations. Seventeenth century forgeries of a fictional half-siliqua with the reverse type Victory advancing left (and with the mint mark SMN = Nicomedia) are known.

GALLA PLACIDIA

Augusta, A.D. 421–450

Daughter of Theodosius I (and Galla)
Wife of Athaulf (the Visigoth) and Constantius III
Mother (by Constantius III) of Valentinian III and Honoria
Half-sister of Arcadius and Honorius
Mother-in-law of Licinia Eudoxia
Granddaughter of Valentinian I (and Justina)

(Aelia) Galla Placidia, A.D. 388/90–450. Few Roman ladies had lives more eventful than that of Galla Placidia. She endured many tragedies that individually would have been sufficient to ensure her place in history.

Her first role of note was as a hostage, for she was captured when the Visigoths sacked Rome in 410. Although captured by their king, Alaric, she remained a hostage under his successor, Athaulf, who married her in an attempt to unite the fortunes of the Goths and the Romans. Hardly a better choice existed, for she was the daughter of Theodosius I and the half-sister of the reigning western emperor, Honorius. The wedding occurred in 414 at Narbonne, and Placidia was soon with child. But the union failed to have its intended effect, for Athaulf was blockaded by the Roman commander Constantius III, and in 414/5 was murdered along with his infant son Theodosius by a rival chieftain at Barcelona. Fully aware of the value of this royal lady, the Visigoths ransomed her to the Romans for the princely sum of 600,000 measures of grain and the right to return (from coastal Spain and Gaul) to central Gaul with federal status.

Now freed from captivity at great expense, Placidia was forced by her half-brother Honorius to marry his prize general, Constantius III, on January 1, 417. It was not a happy union, but it produced two children: a daughter named Honoria in 417/8, and the future emperor Valentinian III in 419. Four years later, in 421, Constantius III became co-emperor with Honorius, and Placidia was hailed Augusta (a title that was not recognized in the East until 423, and which she apparently held until her death 29 years later). Her unfortunate husband, however, died within the year.

After this tragic event, Placidia's already warm relationship with her half-brother grew to become incest. His public expressions of affection (which we are told were blatantly incestuous to the observer), enraged court officials and caused riots between various political factions in the streets of Ravenna. Foremost in opposition to Galla was the Master of Soldiers Castinus. What began as love between Honorius and Placidia soon turned into hatred, and the emperor banished her in 423. She fled with her two children to Constantinople, where she received asylum in the court of her nephew, Theodosius II. But her absence from the West was not lengthy. Honorius had been replaced by a rebel named Johannes, who in about 18 months was ousted by an army sent from Constantinople.

Placidia returned to Italy to have her son, Valentinian III, crowned emperor of the West. For the first dozen years of her child's reign, Placidia was the dominant influence in the courts, and in essence ran the government of the West (incompetently, according to Cassiodorus). But as her son grew, so did the authority of the general Aëtius, whom Placidia herself had appointed Master of Soldiers in 429. Placidia's attempt in 430 to replace Aëtius with Boniface failed, and from that point onward her influence over her son was greatly reduced. In her declining years Placidia devoted herself to civic projects. After having survived many ordeals, Placidia died in Rome on November 27, 450, less than five years before her son fell victim to assassins and Rome was sacked for a second time.

Numismatic Note: Galla Placidia's coinage can be divided into two phases: 421–422 (struck at Ravenna in association with her husband, Constantius III, who died in 421) and 424–450 (which includes both Italian and Constantinopolitan coinage). The coins with the inscriptions AEL PLACIDIA AVG and GALLA PLACIDIA AVG were struck exclusively at Constantinople under Theodosius II, whereas those with D N GALLA PLACIDIA P F AVG (by far the most common variety) were struck at western mints under Honorius, Theodosius II and Valentinian III.

JOHANNES A.D. 423–425

Ruling in the East:
Theodosius II (408–450)

Johannes (John), c. A.D. 380–425. Little is known of Johannes, except that he may have been of Gothic origin, and that he had risen in Honorius' court to become a high-ranking civil servant, the *primicerius notariorum* (senior notary).

The last of the western usurpers associated with the reign of Honorius, Johannes was installed in September or November 423, shortly after the unexpected death of Honorius (whose only legitimate heir, Valentinian III, was living in exile with his mother, Galla Placidia, in Constantinople). Providing Johannes' support was the Master of Soldiers Castinus, who had been instrumental in the banishment of Galla Placidia and her son. Johannes ruled in Castinus' name for more than a year before the eastern emperor Theodosius II sent an army West. In the meantime, Johannes had tried to gain approval from Theodosius II, who would not even allow his embassy to plead his case.

Although Theodosius II had objected to the elevation of the child's father, Constantius III earlier in 421, he supported the claim of his grandchild, Valentinian III, no doubt because he believed restoring him and his mother would give him greater control over events in the West.

Early in 425 Theodosius II sent an army by sea to end the rebellion of Johannes. In the meantime Johannes had sent one of his generals, Aëtius (the future Master of Soldiers), to raise an army among the Huns. But his mission did not materialize, and indeed, its failure was the cause of Johannes' downfall. Even when the Constantinopolitan fleet was partially ruined off the coast of Italy (with one of its two commanders, Ardaburius the elder, being taken hostage after he washed ashore near Ravenna) Johannes did not act decisively because the Hunnic reinforcements had not arrived. Meanwhile, the other commander, Ardaburius' son, Aspar, landed and managed to enter Ravenna unopposed early in May or in June of 425. Aspar's journey through the marshes and easy entry to Ravenna were attributed by some contemporaries to the guidance of an Angel. After a reign of only 18 months, Johannes was promptly arrested and condemned to death by Galla Placidia. Johannes was reportedly taken to Aquileia where before he was executed he was mutilated and paraded around the circus on the back of a donkey before cheering crowds.

Numismatic Note: The portraits of Johannes are perhaps the most extraordinary on coinage of late antiquity. Unlike the clean-shaven portraits of his contemporaries, Johannes' image recalls the glorious aspects of art more akin to Phidias' work in 5th Century B.C. Johannes also issued gold coins at Ravenna in the name of the eastern emperor Theodosius II in hopes of gaining his recognition. In his own name, Johannes struck gold at Ravenna and Milan, silver at Ravenna, and Æ4's at Rome (principally) and Arles.

VALENTINIAN III A.D. 425–455

A.D. 424–425: CAESAR
(UNDER THEODOSIUS II)
A.D. 425–455: SOLE REIGN

Ruling in the East:
THEODOSIUS II (408–450) AND
MARCIAN (450–457)

SON OF CONSTANTIUS III AND GALLA PLACIDIA
FIRST HUSBAND OF LICINIA EUDOXIA
FATHER OF EUDOCIA THE YOUNGER AND PLACIDIA THE YOUNGER (*w.* OF OLYBRIUS)
BROTHER OF HONORIA
SON-IN-LAW OF THEODOSIUS II AND AELIA EUDOCIA
HALF-COUSIN OF THEODOSIUS II AND AELIA PULCHERIA
BROTHER OF HONORIA
HALF-NEPHEW OF HONORIUS AND ARCADIUS
GRANDSON OF THEODOSIUS I (AND GALLA)
GREAT-GRANDSON OF VALENTINIAN I

Flavius Placidus Valentinianus, A.D. 419–455. As the only son of Constantius III and Galla Placidia, young Valentinian belonged to the Theodosian family by virtue of his mother. Though his political legacy lie in the West, he spent his early years in exile in Constantinople with his mother.

The revolt of Johannes in 423 launched Valentinian's career at an early age, as he and his mother were sent west in 424 so they could be in Italy when Johannes was overthrown. *En route*, Valentinian III was hailed Caesar at Thessalonica on October 23, 424. When the eastern fleet ousted Johannes early in May or in June of 425, the path was cleared for the 6-year-old Valentinian, who sailed with his family to Italy, where he was hailed emperor of the West on the one-year anniversary of his being hailed Caesar. This occurred with the full approval of the eastern emperor, his future father-in-law, Theodosius II. At long last, order was restored in the West.

In 437, when Valentinian III had reached his 18th year, he married the beautiful Licinia Eudoxia, presumably at the urging of his mother, who still wielded great authority. Although his reign was devoid of usurpers, many disheartening events occurred during his three decades on the western throne. Of great concern was the unchecked growth in the power of the Visigoths in southwestern Gaul.

Equally disturbing, if not more so, was the emigration of the Vandals to North Africa. In 429 (the year that Aëtius was promoted to Master of Soldiers) the Vandals, under the leadership of Gaiseric, crossed from Spain into North Africa and continued to move east. By 439 they had taken Carthage, and three years later had forced Valentinian III to recognize their possession of the wealthiest portion of North Africa. This complicated the importation of grain (grown locally) and gold from the trans-Saharan caravans. Furthermore, it proved to be the staging ground for the invasion of Italy and the sack of Rome that followed Valentinian's death in 455.

Also of grave concern was Attila the Hun, whose mounted warriors had unraveled Roman security in both the East and West. Early in Valentinian's reign, his top general, Aëtius, used the Huns to combat the Visigoths and Burgundians. But this policy was reversed when Attila later made aggressions of his own. Indeed, it was a confederation of Roman and Visigothic armies led by Aëtius that in June, 451, routed Attila at the Battle of the Catalaunian Plains (in the heart of modern France). Although the Visigothic king Theoderic I died in the battle, Attila was driven across the Rhine.

Attila was not easily deterred, though, and he returned to the center of Europe in 452, sacking many cities, including Aquileia, which he leveled completely. The Hunnic chieftain stopped short of sacking Rome itself, not for a lack of strength, but out of fear that the victory would bring him bad fortune, as it had done 42 years earlier to Alaric's Visigoths. Fortunately for Romans both in the West and the East, Attila died of natural causes in 453.

Even in the Eastern Roman Empire Valentinian found trouble. When his cousin Theodosius II died in 450 without an heir, the right to appoint the new emperor belonged to Valentinian. However, Theodosius II's widow and the Master of Soldiers Aspar took matters into their own hands, and appointed a soldier named Marcian. Although this was hardly constitutional, there was nothing Valentinian III could do to oppose it.

Just when Valentinian had rid himself of Attila and had grudgingly acknowledged Marcian, another foe emerged from within his ranks. It seems his Master of Soldiers Aëtius had grown all-powerful, and had threatened the lives of the emperor and his chamberlain Petronius Maximus. Thus, on September 21, 454, Valentinian III mustered his courage and personally murdered his prize general with the thrust of a dagger. This act was viewed in dim light by his contemporaries, one of whom told the emperor "with your left hand you have cut off your right hand."

Less than a year later, on March 16, 455, the 36-year-old Valentinian III was assassinated by two former bodyguards of Aëtius, who were motivated by Petronius Maximus to avenge their general's death. The pair of senseless acts cleared the path of succession for Petronius Maximus, who either arranged, or at the very least encouraged both murders. Valentinian's reign was yet another signpost in the decline of the Western Roman Empire, and constituted the extinction of the Theodosian line in the West.

Historians tell us that Valentinian was a skilled archer and horseman, and that he was a good sprinter. However, we are also told that he was effeminate, superstitious, kept company with astrologers and magicians, and was a rampant adulterer. No doubt, these character flaws were instrumental in his downfall. His hedonistic and aloof demeanor cost Rome its claims to Gaul, Spain and North Africa, and immediately after his death, led to the sack of Rome itself. Furthermore, had superstition and an untimely death not conspired against Attila the Hun, Valentinian almost certainly would have lost what remained of his diminished Empire.

NUMISMATIC NOTE: The weight of copper nummi (Æ4s, which often are called *nummi minimi*), which had been modest but attractive coins under Arcadius, was reduced by 25 percent in 425. The result was a pitiful coin that was tariffed at the rate of 25 pounds of coined nummi to the gold solidus. Twenty years later a government edict was required to stabilize the nummus at 7,000/7,200 to the gold solidus in Rome. There are imitations of Valentinian's solidi, semisses, tremisses and siliquae attributed to the Visigoths (see RIC X, pp. 453–6). Some of his solidi and tremisses are attributed to the Burgundians or Franks (see RIC X, pp. 463–4), and some of his tremisses are attributed to the Suevi (see RIC X, p. 466).

HONORIA

AUGUSTA, A.D. 426(?)–450(?)

SISTER OF VALENTINIAN III
DAUGHTER OF CONSTANTIUS III AND GALLA PLACIDIA
HALF-NIECE OF HONORIUS AND ARCADIUS
HALF-COUSIN OF THEODOSIUS II AND PULCHERIA
SISTER-IN-LAW OF LICINIA EUDOXIA
AUNT OF EUDOCIA THE YOUNGER AND
PLACIDIA THE YOUNGER (*w.* OF OLYBRIUS)
GRANDDAUGHTER OF THEODOSIUS I (AND GALLA)

Justa Grata Honoria, A.D. 417/8–454. Though Honoria was born in the West, her early years were spent in exile in Constantinople with her mother and brother. By 425 she had returned to the West, for her brother had been installed as the new emperor in Ravenna. Honoria's life is largely a mystery: not only is she scarcely mentioned, but even when she is, the information is often contradictory. We cannot be certain when she was hailed Augusta, though one inscription suggests it was shortly after she arrived in Italy, and thus 425 or 426 are possibilities. Some researchers, however, suggest she was not hailed until she was age 13 or 16.

Little is known of how Honoria and her younger brother, the emperor, got along early in their lives, but their relationship collapsed when Valentinian discovered that his sister was with child as a result of an adulterous affair. Her enraged brother perhaps suspected a plot was at hand, and executed the man responsible (a court official named Eugenius, who managed her estates). Not surprisingly, the sources disagree on the date of this event, which may have occurred in 434 or 449, though the latter seems far more likely. Honoria did not escape punishment. We are told that Valentinian also arranged her marriage to a certain Herculanus Bassus, a man of consular rank and of good character.

Honoria was so enraged at her brother's actions that in 450 she messengered a secret appeal to Attila the Hun, who construed it as a marriage proposal, and who in June of that year demanded half of the Empire as a dowry. The eastern emperor Theodosius II (who died only a few weeks later) advised Valentinian to hand his impudent sister over to Attila, but Valentinian did not follow his cousin's advice, perhaps out of fear it would legitimize Attila's fraudulent claim to half of the Empire. Attila proceeded to invade the western Roman provinces to take by force that which he was denied, but he was repelled in 451 at the Battle of the Catalaunian Plains. Honoria was nearly executed for her treachery, was stripped of her title Augusta (either at the time of her disgrace in 449 or certainly by the time of the crisis of Attila) and may have been exiled as well. She seems to have been forcibly married to Herculanus and to have died before 455.

NUMISMATIC NOTE: All of Honoria's coins were struck by her brother Valentinian III at Ravenna and Rome.

LICINIA EUDOXIA

AUGUSTA, A.D. 439–C. 490

WIFE OF VALENTINIAN III AND PETRONIUS MAXIMUS
DAUGHTER OF THEODOSIUS II AND AELIA EUDOCIA
MOTHER OF EUDOCIA THE YOUNGER AND PLACIDIA THE YOUNGER (*w.* OF OLYBRIUS)
DAUGHTER-IN-LAW OF CONSTANTIUS III AND GALLA PLACIDIA
SISTER-IN-LAW OF HONORIA
NIECE OF AELIA PULCHERIA
GRANDDAUGHTER OF ARCADIUS AND AELIA EUDOXIA

Licinia Eudoxia, A.D. 422/3–c. 490. Yet another late Roman lady who was celebrated for her great beauty was Licinia Eudoxia, the daughter of Aelia Eudocia and Theodosius II, the ineffective but long-reigning emperor of the East. In 424, while still an infant, she was betrothed to the 5-year-old Valentinian III, who was then living in exile in Constantinople. On October 29, 437, when Licinia Eudoxia had reached her 15th year, she was wed to her betrothed, who was now an effeminate 18-year-old and emperor in the West.

The union was ideal, as it literally wed the fortunes of East and West. Valentinian traveled to Constantinople for the royal wedding, which occurred on October 29, 437. The newlyweds wintered in Thessalonica, and then made a ceremonial entry into their capital of Ravenna early in 438. On August 6 of the following year (seemingly after the birth of her first daughter) Licinia Eudoxia was proclaimed Augusta, a title she retained for the remainder of her tumultuous life. Though Valentinian III reportedly engaged in open, adulterous affairs, their union endured. Together they produced two daughters, neither of whom are represented on coinage. The first was Eudocia the younger, in 438 or 439, and the second, Placidia the younger (the future wife of Olybrius), sometime before 443. No coins were struck in the names of her children.

Upon the murder of Valentinian III in March of 455, the widowed Eudoxia favored Majorian (who later was installed by Ricimer) as her husband's replacement. But instead she was forcibly married to Petronius Maximus, the man who had engineered the downfalls of Aëtius and Valentinian, and in the process had claimed the throne for himself. But it was Licinia Eudoxia who had the final revenge against her unwanted husband, for it is believed that she summoned the Vandal king Gaiseric to her aid. Not only was this course of action sure to get results, but Eudoxia's daughter, Eudocia the younger, had been engaged to Gaiseric's son Huneric. (Even this had been stolen by Petronius Maximus, who forced her to be betrothed instead to his own son, Palladius, who had been raised to Caesar.)

Though the advance of the Vandal army did cause the murder of her unwanted husband, it also resulted in the sack of Rome itself in June of 455. Licinia Eudoxia paid a high personal price for her act, for she and her two daughters were subsequently taken to Carthage as captives of Gaiseric. They remained captive for seven years until, in 462, her release was secured by the eastern emperor, Leo I. Though one account suggests she returned to Rome, the overwhelming evidence suggests she went to Constantinople, where she spent the remainder of her life. The date of her death is not recorded, though it probably was in the very early 490s.

NUMISMATIC NOTE: Licinia Eudoxia's coins were struck by her husband Valentinian III, her father Theodosius II, and his successor Marcian. They may be divided into three further categories based on the obverse inscriptions. Used only at Italian mints were D N ELIA EVDOXIA P F AVG (exclusively on tremisses and half-siliquae) and LICINIA EVDOXIA P F AVG (almost exclusively on the facing-head solidi). Her more common inscription, AEL EVDOXIA AVG (used only on gold of Constantinople), however, is a source of confusion because it is the same one that was used by her grandmother, Aelia Eudoxia (in fact, it was the only inscription used by Aelia Eudoxia). Fortunately, this inscription is shared only on certain solidi and tremisses, each of which may be distinguished by aspects of their reverses. On the solidi it is the actual design that provides the diagnostic, for the grandmother Aelia Eudoxia exclusively used a seated Victory (and Licinia Eudoxia did not use that design at all). On the tremisses, however, both women employ identical types, so we must rely on the mint mark: Aelia Eudoxia used CON, and Licinia Eudoxia used CONOB*.

PETRONIUS MAXIMUS A.D. 455

Ruling in the East:
MARCIAN (450–457)

SECOND HUSBAND OF LICINIA EUDOXIA
SON-IN-LAW OF THEODOSIUS II AND AELIA EUDOCIA

Flavius Anicius Petronius Maximus, c. A.D. 396–455. Hailing from what apparently was an important family, Petronius Maximus became one of the most renowned senators in Rome during the reigns of Honorius and Valentinian III, and amassed a great personal fortune in the process. In addition to other high posts, such as consul, he was on at least two occasions prefect of Italy and city prefect of Rome. But his lust for power, history shows, greatly outstripped his ability to maintain it.

In essence, Petronius Maximus custom-designed a plot to replace Valentinian III, who is said to have seduced his wife. First, he so greatly poisoned Valentinian's relationship with his prize general, Aëtius, that in 454 Valentinian III murdered the very man who had preserved his throne. In turn, it seems, Petronius Maximus encouraged two of Aëtius' former bodyguards to exact revenge by murdering their emperor. Then, in an act of supreme impudence, Petronius Maximus not only claimed the office of emperor for himself, but also forced Valentinian's widow, Licinia Eudoxia, to marry him. In addition, he forced Eudoxia's eldest daughter, Eudocia the younger, to marry his own son, Palladius, who had been given the rank of Caesar (but for whom no coins were struck).

The degree of plotting is almost inconceivable, yet Petronius Maximus achieved it with great precision, as he was even able to out-maneuver Majorian, a high-ranking soldier who was a more desirable candidate (and who would rule two years later). Petronius Maximus usurped the throne of the Western Roman Empire on March 17, 455, but his reign was destined to decline quickly, for it lasted a mere 76 days. All of his underhanded plotting had so enraged his unwilling bride, Licinia Eudoxia, that she called upon Gaiseric, the king of the Vandals in Carthage, to intervene.

News of Gaiseric's acceptance of her invitation reached Rome early in May, and instead of organizing a defense, Petronius Maximus readied himself for escape. While on his horse and attempting to flee the doomed city on May 31, 455, he was killed by a mob of angry Romans who pelted him with stones. As was customary for rogue emperors in Rome, his body was mutilated and tossed into the Tiber. On June 1, Gaiseric's Vandals entered Rome and sacked it, until the 16th, removing most every portable item of value. Among the loot was Licinia Eudoxia and her two daughters, Placidia the younger and Eudocia the younger, who became honored captives. When they reached Carthage, Eudocia the younger married Gaiseric's son, Huneric, as had been arranged before the usurpation of Petronius Maximus.

NUMISMATIC NOTE: Only solidi are known for Petronius Maximus. Indeed, the first issues of his brief reign were created from existing dies of Valentinian III on which the obverse inscription was re-engraved. Only one reverse type, depicting the emperor placing his foot on a human-headed serpent, was employed. He did strike at Ravenna (with the mint mark RV above COMOB), but the majority of his production was at Rome (RM above COMOB). Forgeries by Cigoi are easily distinguished by the obverse inscription, which is unbroken as compared to the genuine issues, upon which MAXIMVS is broken either after the first M or the A.

AVITUS A.D. 455–456

Ruling in the East:
MARCIAN (450–457)

Marcus Maecilius Flavius Eparchius Avitus, d. A.D. 456. The sack of Rome by Gaiseric's Vandals was far more complete than that of the Visigoths in 410, as most every portable item of value was removed. After an interregnum of about 40 days, the Visigothic king Theoderic II appointed his old friend Avitus, a native of southern Gaul, to the vacant office of emperor in the West.

Avitus hailed from a senatorial family from the Auvergne and had held most of the important governmental posts in Gaul. Among his close friends was Theoderic I, the Visigothic king who died in battle against Attila the Hun in 451. Indeed, just before he was hailed, he was serving as Petronius Maximus' personal envoy to the Visigoths, and he only learned of the latter's murder when he was in Gaul. His elevation to emperor occurred at Toulouse on July 9 or 10, 455, at the behest of Theoderic II, the new king of the Visigoths, and was ratified by an assembly of Gallo-Roman nobleman in August.

Later that year Avitus made his way back to Italy, after which his elevation was acknowledged by Marcian in Constantinople. The two emperors joined forces to curb the pirating of the Vandals, which at first was ineffective, but in 456 resulted in a victory off the coast of Corsica by a commander named Ricimer, who Avitus promptly named his new Master of Soldiers. The son of a Suevian father and a Visigothic mother (daughter of the Visigothic king Wallia), Ricimer would prove to be the most important man in the West for nearly a generation. He was to hold absolute power in Rome for the next 16 years, making and deposing the long list of emperors that followed Avitus.

Life in Italy was especially treacherous for Avitus, who was unpopular among the local aristocracy and the senate because of his provincial origins and his personal indulgences. Complicating his plight was a severe famine in Rome, about which there was little he could do. With all of these strikes against him, Avitus also suffered from a loss of support by his Visigothic allies, who had committed their military might to a war against the Suevi and were ravaging what remained of Roman Spain.

Avitus was soon forced to dismiss his Gallic advisers and his Gothic bodyguards, which made him an easy target for the team of Majorian and Ricimer. In order to pay off his Gallic and Gothic compatriots, Avitus was forced to sell quite a few bronze statues, which did not endear him to Romans who were familiar with the works of art. With the popularity of Avitus at an all-time low, he was vulnerable to Ricimer, who was being hailed as the Deliverer of Italy because of his naval victory over the Vandals.

After Avitus had reigned only about 15 months, Majorian and Ricimer openly rebelled, and deposed him on October 17, 456. He fled Rome in hope of surviving the rebellion, but was overtaken by Ricimer, who defeated him in battle and made him bishop of Piacenza. Avitus died shortly thereafter *en route* to Gaul, either while on a pilgrimage or while in flight after learning that the senate desired his execution. The supremacy of Ricimer thus began with the deposition of Avitus.

NUMISMATIC NOTE: The vast majority of Avitus' coinage was solidi struck at the re-opened Gallic mint of Arles. His rare tremisses may belong to Arles, though most attribute them to Milan. There are imitations of Avitus' solidi and tremisses attributed to the Visigoths (see RIC X, p. 457).

MAJORIAN A.D. 457–461

Ruling in the East:
LEO I (457–474)

Flavius Julius Valerius Majorianus, d. A.D. 461. After Avitus was deposed, there was a tense interregnum of more than five months during which the eastern emperor Marcian died and power was peacefully transferred to Leo I. Meanwhile, matters in the West were being attended to by the Master of Soldiers Ricimer, who had selected Majorian as his first candidate for the throne.

Majorian hailed from an accomplished military family. His maternal grandfather (after whom he was named) had been Master of Soldiers in Illyria under Theodosius I, and his father was a top financial minister in Gaul for the general Aëtius. Indeed, when the emperor Valentinian III was murdered in 455, his widow, Licinia Eudoxia, had favored Majorian as his replacement. But she and Majorian were outmaneuvered by Petronius Maximus, who not only seized the throne, but also forced marriage upon Licinia Eudoxia.

During the brief reign of Avitus (455–456), Majorian allied himself with Ricimer, the Master of Soldiers who was by then calling the shots in the Western Roman Empire. Together they openly rebelled and ousted the unpopular Avitus. Not surprisingly, Majorian was Ricimer's choice as the new emperor, and they lobbied Constantinople for approval. The man of letters Sidonius Apollinaris reported that the interregnum occurred because Majorian was reluctant to take the high office that he was offered. However, the concerns Majorian may have had were put aside when news reached Italy that the eastern emperor, Marcian, had died. Majorian was hailed emperor of the West on April 1, 457, and was installed officially on December 28.

Although some historians assert that Majorian's appointment was approved in Constantinople, the evidence on this point is not clear. In any event, Majorian established his court at Ravenna, and at the end of 458 shifted to Gaul so he could deal with the Visigoths and Burgundians. He was there for the remainder of 458 and 459, where, despite his military successes, he was not as popular as he was in Italy.

His next task was to free his Empire of the Vandal threat, which had been a cause of terror for a generation or more. His first encounter with the Vandals was in Campania, where a raiding party had landed and begun to pillage. Majorian caught them by surprise and drove them back to sea without their booty, and without the Gaiseric's brother-in-law, who was one of the many casualties. By 460 he had assembled a fleet of about 300 warships in Spain with which he hoped to attack the Vandals. However, through treachery on the part of some Romans, the entire fleet was captured by the Vandals while in port, before it could even be launched. Now without a fleet, the Romans had to agree to humiliating terms to maintain the peace.

Majorian returned to Italy in 461, where his popularity had greatly eroded and his benefactor Ricimer had turned against him. After a reign of more than four years he abdicated his throne after he was captured in Northern Italy on August 2. Five days later, on August 7, Majorian was executed (or allowed to commit suicide) at Tortona, though some sources report that dysentery was the cause of death. The Western Roman Empire then entered a second interregnum, this time of slightly more than three months, while Ricimer lined up his next candidate.

Majorian's principate was a great success until an episode of treachery caused the destruction of his fleet. The ancient sources tell us that Majorian was a man of exceptional talent, and his record proves that he was determined to restore the glory of Rome in the West. No doubt these virtues constituted a threat to Ricimer, who only too eagerly pounced upon Majorian during his moment of vulnerability so that he could install a less ambitious candidate.

NUMISMATIC NOTE: With very rare exception, the solidi of Majorian are of an ornate obverse type showing his helmeted and cuirassed bust facing right, holding a spear and a shield inscribed with a Chi-Rho. This type originated with a rare issue of Honorius from Ravenna, but was produced in quantity only by Majorian, whose successor abandoned it. He struck prodigious issues of gold tremisses and nummi (Æ4's), the latter of which are unusually heavy for the period; most (if not all) of his silver was struck in Gaul. There are imitations of Majorian's solidi and tremisses attributed to the Visigoths (see RIC X, pp. 458–9).

LIBIUS SEVERUS (SEVERUS III) A.D. 461–465

Ruling in the East:
LEO I (457–474)

Libius (or Livius) Severus (also called Severus III), d. A.D. 465. The western throne remained vacant for more than three months after the abdication and death of Majorian. Though the Master of Soldiers Ricimer had seized the opportunity to overthrow Majorian, he apparently had not yet lined up his next candidate. Eventually he decided upon a shadowy character named Libius Severus, whom he installed on November 19, 461.

Severus hailed from Lucania in south-western Italy, a region that was especially vulnerable to Vandal raiders. Though he reigned for almost exactly four years, he remains a historical blank page, and clearly was no more than a puppet emperor.

The Western Roman Empire was firmly in the hands of Ricimer, who managed every aspect of its finances, foreign relations and defense while Severus was in office. It should come as no surprise that historians disagree about whether Libius Severus ever gained the approval of Leo I in Constantinople. The traditional historical view (based largely on the writings of Jordanes) is that he did not. However, he struck many coins in the name of Leo I at Italian mints, and there are inscriptions that suggest he did gain approval in the East. Thus, there is ample reason to reconsider the traditional view.

Severus' reign was far from peaceful, and Ricimer had his hands full defending his Empire. In addition to a campaign he led against the Alans, Ricimer had to contend with Roman generals and the Vandal king Gaiseric. The Vandals routinely raided the Italian coast and used their king's captive-bride, Licinia Eudoxia, as leverage in destabilizing Italian politics.

Indeed, the Romans were fortunate that they did not suffer invasion during Severus' reign, for the Vandals were conspiring with Aegidius (Majorian's Master of Soldiers in Gaul who had recently accepted the title of King of the Franks) to overthrow Ricimer. Had domestic problems with the Visigoths not kept Aegidius occupied in Gaul, Italy most likely would have been simultaneously invaded from the sea by Vandals and across the Alps by Aegidius. Libius Severus died on November 14, 465. His death is usually attributed to natural causes, but it is more likely (as was rumored by Cassiodorus) that he was poisoned by Ricimer, who by now had found him to be more of a liability than an asset.

NUMISMATIC NOTE: Unlike his two immediate predecessors, Libius Severus struck coins only in Italy, for the mint at Arles was in the hands of Aegidius, who had broken with Ricimer and established his own Romano-Frankish enclave. Of special interest is the gold semissis denomination (which was revived by Severus), and the Æ4's, which bear the monogram of Ricimer and are listed separately under his name. There are imitations of Severus' solidi and tremisses attributed to the Visigoths (see RIC X, pp. 459–60).

RICIMER

Master of Soldiers, A.D. 456–472

Son-in-law of Anthemius and Aelia Euphemia
Husband of Alypia
Uncle of Gundobad

Flavius Ricimer, d. A.D. 472. Just like Sejanus and Gundobad, Ricimer finds a valid place in a book on Roman numismatics. Not only was he instrumental in the high affairs of state, but he makes an appearance on coinage itself. Ricimer was a soldier of Visigothic and Suevian parentage. He was the grandson of a Visigothic king and had family ties to royalty among the Suevi and Burgundians. Although debarred from the throne because of his barbarian birth, Ricimer's military successes made him the most powerful man in Rome soon after he was made Master of Soldiers (*Magister Militum*) by the emperor Avitus.

For 16 years he was the main force behind the raising and deposing of western emperors, who served as his puppets. His one moment of concession was during the reign of Anthemius, who had been sent at the head of an army by the eastern emperor Leo I. But even so, Anthemius knew that his own survival depended on the support of Ricimer, and thus he offered the hand of his daughter, Alypia, to Ricimer, and they were wed in the fall of 467. It is worth noting that Ricimer played no part in leading the Roman armada against the Vandals in 468, although he certainly had to deal with the consequences of its unfathomable failure. Nothing here will be said of his extraordinary actions, for they may be gleaned from the biographies of the emperors whom he controlled. Only six weeks after appointing Olybrius to the throne, Ricimer died on August 18, 472, presumably of natural causes.

Numismatic Note: Ricimer's record on coinage is controversial to some scholars, but too likely to be excluded. The small bronzes in question depict on their obverse Libius Severus and bear his appropriate inscriptions (on the rare occasion that they are visible). However, the wreath on the reverse contains a monogram that is not that of Severus. Since the monogram usually is composed of the letters R M I C E, it is rightly believed to be that of Ricimer. The inclusion in some instances of an "A" within the monogram is a stumbling block to some authorities, but with no other feasible candidate to be found, they must still belong to Ricimer, who, after all, was the source of Severus' power. Though these nummi seem to have originated late in the reign of Libius Severus, they were perhaps largely struck during the 17-month interregnum that followed the latter's death.

Most if not all of these nummi were struck at Rome; some heavier specimens of poor workmanship appear to be contemporary imitations.

ANTHEMIUS A.D. 467–472

Ruling in the East:
Leo I (457–474)

Husband of Aelia Euphemia
Father of Alypia
Father-in-law of Ricimer
Son-in-law of Marcian

Procopius Anthemius, d. A.D. 472. After the death of Libius Severus the Western Roman Empire endured more than a year and a half without an emperor. Finally, Ricimer — who was in control throughout — chose to cooperate with the eastern emperor Leo I in hopes of getting military support in his war against the Vandals. Early in 467 the Vandals moved their piratic operations from Italy and Sicily and raided the Greek Peloponnese. While this proved fruitful for Gaiseric, it might have been counterproductive in the long run, for Leo I realized he could no longer ignore affairs in the West.

Thus, Leo I appointed a high-ranking Constantinopolitan named Procopius Anthemius as Caesar for the West. Anthemius held numerous Imperial ties in the East, for he was married to the daughter of the former eastern emperor Marcian, and as his chief general, had scored victories over the Goths and Huns. He was a possible successor to his father-in-law in 457, but was outmaneuvered by the Master of Soldiers Aspar, who installed Leo I instead.

Anthemius' ancestry was also illustrious. His maternal grandfather, named Procopius, served as the regent for the emperor Theodosius II (402–450) during his childhood. He also claimed to be a descendant of the Procopius who usurped the throne of Valens in 365 and 366 and was one of the last members of the House of Constantine the Great. However, all of these recommendations would not assure his survival in the West, for he needed to maintain good relations with the Master of Soldiers Ricimer, who was the most powerful man in Italy. To this effect, in advance of his journey, Anthemius had offered Ricimer the hand of his own daughter, Alypia, in marriage. The offer was accepted, and the road was paved for Western Roman Empire to have a new, legitimate emperor who was duly recognized in the East.

By April 12 of that same year Anthemius had reached the outskirts of Rome, where he was hailed Augustus by the senate. During his more than five years as emperor in the West, Anthemius was never popular, for he was a Greek of Galatian ancestry, and worse yet, he had been sent from the East. Thus, it is ironic that the defining event of his reign — a failed naval expedition against the Vandals — was one borne of his cooperation with Constantinople.

Through no fault of his own, the great 1,100-ship armada assembled by Leo I and captained by his brother-in-law Basiliscus, was destroyed by the Vandals in 468. This tragedy not only devastated the spirit of the Romans, but it virtually bankrupted the Eastern Roman Empire. Anthemius' thin support slipped with the passage of time, especially since he failed to deal with serious problems brewing in Gaul, where the Visigoths were planning to annex the whole country. Though the Romans resisted, the Visigoths scored important victories in which several Roman generals and Anthemius' son Anthemiolus perished.

Furthermore, Ricimer viewed Anthemius as a threat to his own supremacy, for he had every intention of furthering eastern authority in the West. Anthemius resided in Rome, whereas Ricimer based himself in the North at Milan. Though the two reconciled their differences in 470 with the help of the bishop of Ticinum, it was just a matter of time before a change occurred.

In the spring of 472 Ricimer arranged a coup, selecting as his next candidate a patrician from the East named Olybrius, who had been sent to Italy as an envoy of Leo I. Together they besieged Anthemius in Rome, who, with the support of a small Visigothic army headed by Bilimer, was able to hold out for about three months. In the aftermath Anthemius tried to escape dressed as a beggar, but was captured and beheaded on the orders of Ricimer's nephew, Gundobad. Historians disagree about when this occurred, which may have been in March or April, but more likely was on July 11, 472.

NUMISMATIC NOTE: There are imitations of Anthemius' tremisses attributed to the Visigoths (see RIC X, p. 460).

AELIA EUPHEMIA

AUGUSTA, A.D. 467–472(?)

WIFE OF ANTHEMIUS
DAUGHTER OF MARCIAN (BY HIS FIRST WIFE)
MOTHER OF ALYPIA
MOTHER-IN-LAW OF RICIMER

(Aelia) Marcia Euphemia, lifespan unknown. Regrettably, the ancient historians recorded very little of Aelia Euphemia, except that she bore Anthemius one daughter and four sons. Historians are not certain of her lifespan, nor when she lost the title of Augusta. Her only daughter, Alypia (who makes a single appearance on coinage), was wed to the Master of Soldiers Ricimer in hopes of uniting the 'emperor-making' general of the West and the appointee of Leo I in the East. This attempt failed, and Alypia's fate is unknown.

Of Euphemia's sons, more is known. All but the one who in 471 died in battle in Gaul played interesting roles in eastern politics during the reign of Zeno. The eldest, Marcian (named after his grandfather, the emperor) was destined for high political office, since he was married to Leontia, the youngest of the two daughters of the emperor Leo I and Verina. He took his chance in 479 when his mother-in-law, Verina, convinced him to overthrow Leo. However, the revolt failed immediately, leading to the banishment of Verina and the capture of Marcian. The latter was banished to Cappadocia, but soon escaped and raided Ancyra with a group of rustic bandits, after which he was again captured, and banished by his father-in-law to a fortress in Isauria. Marcian's younger brother, Procopius (named after his distant ancestor, the usurper Procopius, 365–366), was also involved in the failed revolt against Zeno, but immediately fled to the camp of Theodoric in Thrace. Of the youngest son, named Romulus, little is recorded.

NUMISMATIC NOTE: All of Aelia Euphemia's coins were struck by her husband, Anthemius. Only the solidus (in two types) was struck in sufficient quantity to be collectible, though a siliqua and a nummus (Æ4) are known, but each is apparently unique. Her sons are not known to have held the title of Caesar or Augustus, and do not seem to be represented on coinage. However, her daughter Alypia makes one brief appearance on coinage (see her biography below), and may also have been hailed Augusta.

ALYPIA

AUGUSTA(?), A.D. 467(?)–472(?)

WIFE OF RICIMER
DAUGHTER OF ANTHEMIUS AND AELIA EUPHEMIA
GRANDDAUGHTER OF MARCIAN

Alypia, lifespan unknown. As the only daughter of Anthemius and Aelia Euphemia, Alypia was destined for an interesting life. When her father had been nominated as the next emperor of the West by Leo I, it probably came as little surprise to Alypia that she would be a valuable diplomatic asset to her father's fledgling regime. Thus, in 467, the year in which all of these events occurred, Alypia was wed to the "emperor-making" general, Ricimer, who was still the most powerful man in Italy.

The gesture was intended not only to bind the fates of Anthemius and Ricimer, but also to strengthen the ties between East and West. The marriage was childless, and proved to be less than effective in binding the two parties. In April of 472 Ricimer sponsored a patrician named Olybrius as emperor in opposition to Anthemius. Though Anthemius and his family were able to hold out in Rome for about three months, their resistance ended on July 11, 472, when Anthemius was captured and beheaded.

Although ancient sources make no mention of it, the numismatic evidence suggests Alypia may have been hailed Augusta along with her mother. If indeed this occurred, it would have been similar to the earlier cases of Aelia Pulcheria and Honoria, both of whom were hailed Augusta even though they were only sisters of the emperor. The fate of both Alypia and her mother are unknown. Alypia had four brothers, whose lives are related in the biography of her mother.

NUMISMATIC NOTE: Offering evidence that Alypia may have been hailed Augusta with her mother is a coin in the cabinet at Dumbarton Oaks. The reverse of this unique solidus shows mother and daughter side-by-side. The figure representing Alypia is smaller than that of Euphemia, and from the viewer's eye appears on the right, which is the position of lesser honor. But this is the proper iconography for such an issue, and each is attired the same, and in the manner associated with women who held the rank of Augusta. Even though Alypia was childless and there is no literary evidence of her being hailed Augusta, her marriage to Ricimer was of such importance to Anthemius' imported regime that an exception may have been made.

OLYBRIUS A.D. 472

Ruling in the East:
LEO I (457–474)

HUSBAND OF PLACIDIA THE YOUNGER
SON-IN-LAW OF LICINIA EUDOXIA

Anicius Olybrius, d. A.D. 472. Descended from the powerful senatorial family the Anicii (which was notorious for its greed), Olybrius managed to escape from Rome just before it was sacked by the Vandals in 455. He settled into a luxurious life in Constantinople, and in 462 married Placidia the younger, the teen-age daughter of the former western emperor Valentinian III, who had just arrived in the eastern capital after spending seven years in Carthage as a captive of the Vandal king Gaiseric.

The eastern emperor, Leo I, had negotiated her release while he was warming relations with the Vandals, who had begun to extend their piratic raids into eastern territory. By marrying Placidia the younger (for whom no coins were struck), Olybrius became both a member of the House of Theodosius, an in-law of the Vandal Gaiseric, whose own son, Huneric, was married to Placidia's sister, Eudocia the younger. This latter relation proved fruitful for Olybrius, who became Gaiseric's candidate for the Western throne following the puppet-reign of Libius Severus (461–465). However, Gaiseric's plans did not materialize and the eastern emperor Leo I instead backed his own candidate, a nobleman named Anthemius.

In the meantime, Olybrius and Placidia the younger had a daughter named Ancia, who herself was destined for greatness in a later era. Throughout Olybrius' subsequent adventures, his wife remained in Constantinople, for she had experienced a lifetime's adventure before she had reached her 20th year. Although Olybrius had been passed up as western emperor the first time around, a new opportunity arose in 472, when he was sent to Rome by Leo I to resolve the conflict between Ricimer and his puppet emperor Anthemius.

What happened next — Ricimer selecting Olybrius as the new western emperor — is of some interest, for the circumstances of it are not entirely certain. Although Olybrius had been sent only on a diplomatic mission, his sojourn turned into an opportunity unparalleled. One ancient source, John Malalas, tells us that an urgent letter dispatched by Leo I accusing Olybrius of treason fell into the hands of Ricimer, who may have confronted Olybrius with the unwelcomed news. Additionally, Ricimer may have considered Olybrius' marriage ties to Gaiseric to be a windfall, for if he were emperor, peace might be achieved more easily with the

Vandals. That it would offend Leo I in the East was probably of no great concern, for Ricimer had long been at odds with the eastern monarch.

In any event, Olybrius was hailed emperor in opposition to Anthemius (apparently in April, 472), and the latter was promptly besieged in Rome. After a resistance of about three months, Anthemius tried to escape dressed as a beggar, but was captured. He was beheaded by Ricimer's nephew Gundobad, possibly in March or April, but more likely on July 11 of 472. However, the 'emperor-making' general Ricimer died on August 18 — only a few weeks after he had ousted Anthmius and installed Olybrius.

With this shocking turn of events, the new emperor Olybrius had to fend for himself, establishing a rapport with Gundobad, Ricimer's nephew and replacement as Master of Soldiers. After a reign of about six or seven months, Olybrius died of dropsy, perhaps on November 2, 472. With three powerful men perishing in the course of a few months, the throne was vacant for more than four months after Olybrius' death, during which Gundobad tried to maintain his new-found authority.

NUMISMATIC NOTE: The coins of Olybrius are great rarities, with perhaps fewer than 20 specimens known in total for all types of solidi and tremisses. He chose an interesting inscription, SALVS MVNDI ("savior of the world") for his solidi and tremisses of Rome; all of his gold has the reverse type of a plain or jewelled cross. Olybrius seemingly coined no silver or copper coins. Lead seals with the extraordinary SALVS MVNDI reverse type are known, and are paired with an obverse depicting the facing busts of two emperors (inscr. DD NN AVGG), and as such may be presumed to represent Olybrius and Leo I, the reigning monarchs in the West and the East.

GLYCERIUS A.D. 473–474

Ruling in the East:
LEO I (457–474), LEO II (474)
AND ZENO (474–475 & 476–491)

Flavius Glycerius, died c. A.D. 480. The year 472 proved to be a watershed, for not only had two emperors perished, but the all-powerful Ricimer had died as well. Though the eastern emperor Leo I now had the legal right to rule in the West, the true power was held by a Burgundian prince named Gundobad, who had succeeded his uncle, Ricimer, as Master of Soldiers.

Gundobad had emerged on the scene only recently, and had been given the rank of patrician by the former emperor, Olybrius, for his help in the overthrow of Anthemius. After an interregnum of more than four months, Gundobad named Glycerius, a man of no particular distinction, as the next emperor of the West. This elevation, which occurred on March 5, 473, was not recognized in Constantinople, for in the meantime Leo I had enlisted Julius Nepos, a Dalmatian nobleman, to restore order in Italy.

The puppet-king Glycerius had his hands full defending Italy from an invasion led by Widimir, king of a branch of the Ostrogoths. Glycerius chose to bribe Widimir rather than fight him, and was able to divert their armies to Gaul. But Glycerius' problems were just beginning, for he would lose the support of his army just as a conquering force arrived from the East. His Master of Soldiers, Gundobad, left Italy to become heir-apparent of the Burgundians upon learning that his brothers had been killed. Shortly thereafter, in June of 474, Julius Nepos landed his forces near the mouth of the Tiber and captured Glycerius without a fight.

On the 19th of June, Julius Nepos claimed the title of Augustus for himself, which was ratified by the senate on the 24th. Though there is no indication that Leo I had asked Julius Nepos to do anything more than depose Glycerius, the eastern emperor had died in the meantime, and Nepos seized the opportunity at hand. After a mismanaged reign of nearly 16 months, Glycerius was spared execution and was instead appointed bishop of Salona, a see comfortably within the territory ruled by Nepos' family. The vacated office of Master of Soldiers was initially filled by Ecdicius, and then by Orestes. Despite the mercy Nepos had shown toward Glycerius, many historians believe that Nepos was murdered in a plot hatched by Glycerius.

NUMISMATIC NOTE: The coins of Glycerius are quite rare, with apparently fewer than 50 specimens known. Most of his coins are solidi and tremisses; silver siliquae and half-siliquae are excessively rare, and no copper nummi seem to have been struck, despite their being listed by Cohen.

GUNDOBAD

MASTER OF SOLDIERS, A.D. 472–474

NEPHEW OF RICIMER

Gundobad (*or* Gundobald), lifespan unknown. The maternal son of the Burgundian king, Gundioc, Gundobad was himself Burgundian prince. He inherited the office of Master of Soldiers in 472 from his uncle Ricimer, who died in that year. His first notable act — for which he was granted patrician status — occurred in July of 472, when he beheaded emperor Anthemius on the orders of Ricimer, who subsequently installed Olybrius on the throne. However, both Ricimer and Olybrius died in 472, leaving Gundobad the new Master of Soldiers, and heir of the role of emperor-maker.

Like all barbarians of the Arian faith, Gundobad was debarred from the throne, and it does not seem that being emperor was an ambition of his. After a short interregnum following the death of Olybrius, Gundobad named Glycerius emperor of the West even though constitutionally the right to decide belonged to the eastern emperor Leo I. In due course, Leo I raised his own candidate, the Dalmatian Master of Soldiers, Julius Nepos, whom he sent to Italy with an army to oust Gundobad and his puppet emperor. But before Nepos arrived, Gundobad learned that his two brothers had died, perhaps by murder, which left him the sole heir to the Burgundian throne. As such, he abandoned his post as Master of Soldiers, which was filled, in turn, by Ecdicius and by Orestes, the former secretary to Attila the Hun. Gundobad returned across the Alps to the territories of the Burgundians, where he eventually succeeded his father as king of that nation.

NUMISMATIC NOTE: Coins ascribed to Gundobad bear on their reverse a monogram composed of the letters B N G A D. The fact that this monogram is paired with an obverse type of Zeno makes the attribution all the more likely. However, unlike the monogram coins of Ricimer (which were legitimate strikings of the Rome mint), the issue of Gundobad are best viewed as Burgundian imitations of Zeno's eastern coinage, and presumably were struck during his tenure as king of the Burgundians.

JULIUS NEPOS A.D. 474–475/480

Ruling in the East:
LEO II (474), ZENO (474–475 & 476–491), *Basiliscus* (475–476) AND *Marcus* (475–476)

Flavius Julius Nepos, d. A.D. 480. When Glycerius usurped the western throne in March of 473, the eastern emperor, Leo I, determined to recover authority in the West, which legally had passed to him when the throne became vacant by the death of Olybrius. Either in 473 or 474, Leo I enlisted the services of Julius Nepos, the Master of Soldiers in Dalmatia and a nephew by marriage of his wife.

Nepos had inherited command of Dalmatia, in which his family had established a hereditary monarchy. Though nominally under the aegis of the Eastern Roman Empire, Nepos reigned in Dalmatia with almost total autonomy. The request from Leo I seemed to be an even greater opportunity to Nepos, who proceeded to Constantinople, from where he launched his expedition to recover the Western Empire. He executed his task with great efficiency, landing his army near the mouth of the Tiber and capturing Glycerius without a fight on the 19th of June, 474. Glycerius was spared execution and instead was appointed bishop of Salona, a see within the territory ruled by Nepos' family.

Though it is not clear that Leo (who, in the meantime had died) had asked Nepos to do anything more than depose Glycerius, Nepos seized the opportunity before him. The fact that the Eastern Empire was embroiled in its own war of succession between Zeno and Basiliscus no doubt led Nepos to the conclusion that he must act decisively, even if that meant autonomously. His claim to the now-vacant title of Augustus in the West was confirmed by the senate on June 24.

Nepos had, however, leaped out of the frying pan and into the fire, for many forces were at work in the West. Of great concern were the Visigoths, who for nearly a decade had threatened to annex all of Gaul and to no longer be mere federates of the Romans. Under the leadership of their new king, Euric, they (like the Vandals in North Africa) created their own independent state. Nepos and the Romans in Gaul were unable to resist the warlike Visigoths, and by treaty in 475 Nepos agreed to their demands, which included most of Gaul and Spain.

Throughout his reign, Nepos was unable to gain the allegiance of the Italians and Germans, who did not want to be ruled by yet another emperor sent from the Greek east. Nepos appointed Ecdicius, the son of the former emperor Avitus, as his new Master of Soldiers. But Ecdicius proved wholly ineffective against the Visigoths, so Nepos replaced him with a Pannonian named Orestes, who had formerly been secretary to Attila the Hun.

But this proved — almost tiresomely so — to be a repeat of recent history in the West, for Orestes rebelled against his benefactor and raised a new candidate (in this case his own son, Romulus Augustus) as emperor. Orestes led an army out of Rome to besiege Nepos at Ravenna, but the fickle Nepos fled by sea on August 28, 475, before Orestes' army arrived. He proceeded to his native land of Dalmatia, where he resumed his duties as hereditary ruler.

While in exile Nepos remained the constitutional western emperor, though he had no opportunity to reclaim his throne without help from the

East. When Orestes and his son, Romulus Augustus, were overthrown in late August 476, power was seized by a German soldier, Odovacar. Though Nepos remained in Dalmatia during the nearly four years left of his life, the numismatic evidence shows that he was recognized as emperor-in-absentia by Odovacar (who similarly acknowledged Zeno's authority). Indeed, when Odovacar wrote to Zeno suggesting that a separate emperor was no longer necessary in the West, Zeno showed support for Nepos by replying that such correspondence should be delivered to the rightful western emperor, Nepos.

Regardless of the formalities observed by the three men, Odovacar was made a patrician by Leo and adopted the title of king while Nepos remained exiled in Dalmatia. Zeno, who had only just regained his throne from the usurpers Basiliscus and Marcus, was either unable or unwilling to meddle in western affairs. Julius Nepos was murdered near Salona on May 9, 480, by two of his retainers who may have been acting on behalf of Glycerius, the usurper whom almost six years earlier Nepos had replaced. As a fitting end to the tale of Nepos, his beloved Dalmatia was occupied by Odovacar in the following year.

Numismatic Note: Though it is customarily stated that the issues of Romulus Augustus are the "last" struck for an emperor in the West, in actuality that honor goes to Julius Nepos. Nepos struck coinage in his own name (as well as for Leo II and Zeno) while he was an emperor in residence in Italy (474–475), and had issues struck on his behalf subsequently while he was in exile in Dalmatia (476–480). Hoard evidence, reverse die links and stylistic factors confirm that Odovacar struck solidi in the name of both Julius Nepos and Zeno at Milan and Ravenna after Romulus Augustus had been deposed. These western issues in the name of Zeno are often collected in lieu of coins bearing Nepos' name, for they command a lesser price. Furthermore, some solidi were struck in Nepos' name at Constantinople by Zeno, who continued to recognize Nepos as his western colleague until his murder in 480. It remains uncertain whether or not Nepos coined at Salonae during his exile. During the first year of his reign, Nepos reintroduced the half-siliqua, and with it two original designs, some of which he struck in his own name, and some in the names of his eastern colleagues. There are imitations of Nepos' tremisses attributed to the Visigoths (see RIC X, p. 461).

ROMULUS AUGUSTUS
A.D. 475–476

Ruling in the East:
ZENO (474–475 & 476–491),
Basiliscus (475–476) AND *Marcus* (475–476)

SON OF ORESTES (MASTER OF SOLDIERS)

Romulus "Augustus," d. after A.D. 507. Romulus Augustus, who has traditionally been called the last emperor of the Western Roman Empire, was neither the last, nor even a legitimate emperor. Indeed, he was merely a figurehead for his father's army, and was deposed four years before the last rightful western emperor, Julius Nepos, died.

None-the-less, his story and his coinage (which was struck at three Italian mints) is of some interest. He was nicknamed Augustulus ("the little emperor") because of his youth; but even this aspect of his life is a mystery; estimates of his age range from that of an small child to a 16-year-old. The additional name Augustus, added to his first name, Romulus, may have derived from its being spelled out on his coinage rather than being abbreviated in the usual form (AVG). Alternatively, it may have been spelled out fully because it already was a formal part of his name.

Romulus was the son of Orestes, a Pannonian soldier who had formerly been secretary to Attila the Hun. Within a few months of his being installed as Master of Soldiers, Orestes revolted against his benefactor, Julius Nepos, who fled on August 28, 475, to his native Dalmatia. Though Nepos remained the constitutional emperor of the West, he was never able to return to Italy and reclaim the throne. Curiously, about two months passed before Orestes hailed his son emperor on October 31, 475. Perhaps forcing the decision was news from the East that Zeno had ended the usurpation of Basilicus and Marcus and regained his throne.

Even though Orestes and Romulus Augustus held the two highest offices in the Western Roman Empire, they were dependent on the German mercenaries for their base of power. It took about 10 months before the Germans became fed up with the Pannonian Master of Soldiers and staged a coup of their own. The leader of the revolt was the 43-year-old Flavius Odovacar (Odacer), a German soldier whose father had also served Attila the Hun in a diplomatic capacity.

Prompting the revolt was a desire by the Germans to be given one-third of the land in Italy, as had been done in other areas of the Empire to placate Germanic invaders. It is uncertain whether Orestes gained his power by making such a promise, or whether it was sprung upon him. Regardless, when he refused the request, the Germans determined to take it all by force of arms. Orestes fled toward Pavia and took refuge in Ticinum, but was captured and executed on August 28, 476.

The Germans entered Ravenna a few days later (September 4) to depose and execute the boy-emperor Romulus, but his youth and beauty caused Odovacar to act mercifully. Instead of executing the youth, who had reigned for about 10 months, he simply deposed him. Furthermore, he granted him a massive annual pension of 6,000 solidi and sent him to Campania, where he resided at a villa in the gulf of Naples for at least three more decades. Odovacar was now in control of Italy, though the fact that he nominally recognized the authority of Julius Nepos as western emperor and Zeno as emperor in the East is proven by the coins he struck in their names at mints under his control.

NUMISMATIC NOTE: Coinage in the name of Romulus Augustus is composed almost exclusively of solidi and tremisses. Some extremely rare silver half-siliquae of Ravenna (which borrow the interesting type introduced by Julius Nepos) are known, and until very recently no nummi were known.

COLLAPSE OF THE WEST

When the senate in Rome and Odovacar informed Zeno (who had only just recovered his own throne in Constantinople) that he was now master of both East and West, it must have come as a mixed blessing. Indeed, such a flattering offer had little value to Zeno, who knew that in practice he would have to acquiesce to Odavacar's claim to Italy. None-the-less, Zeno made an attempt to establish a good relationship with Odovacar. He first granted him the title of patrician, and then asked him to support the return of Julius Nepos, who was still the constitutional emperor of the West.

Though pleased with his new status as patrician, Odovacar apparently refused to restore Nepos, and elected instead to take the title of King of Italy. Having little choice in the matter, Zeno granted Odovacar all of Italy, just as in recent times the Romans had granted Gaul to the Visigoths and North Africa to the Vandals. When Julius Nepos was murdered in 480, there was no longer any hope that a Roman would rule in Rome, and Odovacar promptly expanded his kingdom to include Noricum, Raetia, Sicily and Dalmatia.

Although the regime of Odovacar might seem to have been a clean break from the traditional Roman rule, in reality it was little more than a change in semantics. Odovacar had simply chosen the title of King (*rex*) rather than Augustus. Zeno dealt with him in the same tentative fashion as eastern emperors had with the German generals who had effectively ruled the West for the last few generations.

But alas, in 489 Odovacar's rule was challenged by the Ostrogothic king Theodoric, whom Zeno had convinced to invade Italy. This was a master stroke by Zeno, for in one fell swoop Odovacar was ousted and the Eastern Roman Empire was rid of the ever-looming threat of Theodoric's Ostrogoths, who had now moved westward. Odovacar was able to maintain his status as King of Italy until 493, when Theodoric tricked him into surrendering, and unhesitatingly executed him.

CHAPTER THIRTEEN

The Eastern Roman Empire
A.D. 364–491

This final chapter chronicles the history of the Eastern half of the divided Roman Empire, from the accession of Valens in 364 through the reign of Zeno, which ended in 491. A general discussion of the divided Empire is presented at the beginning of chapter twelve, which includes material relevant to this chapter. Accompanying that discussion is a table that displays the reigns in East and West. Outside of a tabular format, this can be difficult to visualize because the reigns are usually overlapping. Both the introduction and the table should be of value in gaining a proper historical perspective on this final era of the Roman Empire.

One of the most heated debates about the Late Roman Empire concerns when it ended. Historians are at odds on this point, and each point of view has something to recommend it. Some would place the changeover from the Roman Empire to the Byzantine Empire during the Tetrarchy, which began with the accession of Diocletian in 284, for it was during this era that the Empire was divided between East and West with great deliberation.

Others cite the reign of Constantine the Great (307–337) as the turning point. Firstly, he founded Constantinople and made it the enduring capital of the East, and secondly, he institutionalized Christianity; and if one associates anything with the Byzantine Empire, it is Constantinople and Christendom.

A case can also be made for the year 364 (the point at which East and West are divided in this catalog), for the division was formalized. Perhaps equally valid is the year 395, when Theodosius the Great died and the Empire was split between his two sons, Honorius and Arcadius. After all, it was during this period that the last vestiges of paganism were stamped out, and the division of East and West actually became hostile (though relations later warmed again). However, the traditional point of transition is 476, the year that Italy and its venerable capital, Rome, passed into barbarian hands. Italy was no longer ruled by an emperor, but by a German named Odovacar who chose the title of king.

These viewpoints raise a number of valid questions. Most challenging of all is, perhaps, determining if any date before 476 is really acceptable. Did the various components of Roman society change at sufficiently different rates so that the search for a point other than 476 is futile? What becomes apparent is that the transition was not an "event,"' but rather a process. Despite the cultural differences between the citizens of Rome and Constantinople, both considered themselves to be Romans in every sense of the word. After all, what were the options? Certainly nothing was as noble and as civilized as being a Roman. This view persisted in the Eastern Empire for many centuries after Rome itself fell.

The word "Byzantine" was first used to describe the post-476 Eastern Empire by the French historian Montesquieu in the 18th Century. It was an invention of this historian, and was derived from Byzantium (Byzantion), the name of the old Greek colony upon which Constantinople was built. The term was totally unknown to the people of the age to which it applies. Ever since Montesquieu's time, the word "Byzantine" has had a negative connotation. Indeed, it is used to describe a degenerate society that is little more than a pale shadow of its former being. Such a sweeping generalization cannot fairly be made of the Byzantine Empire, for it alone was the savior of Western Christendom. For nearly a thousand years after Rome fell, the city of Constantinople served as the stalwart barrier that spared Western civilization from nomadic and Islamic invasion from the East.

VALENS A.D. 364–378

Ruling in the West:
VALENTINIAN I (364–375), GRATIAN (367–383) AND VALENTINIAN II (375–392)

BROTHER OF VALENTINIAN I
UNCLE OF GRATIAN, VALENTINIAN II AND GALLA (*w.* OF THEODOSIUS I)

Flavius Julius, c. A.D. 328–378. In 364, following the death of Jovian, the Empire fell into the hands of Valens' older brother, Valentinian I. On March 28, about one month after his elevation, Valentinian I proclaimed Valens co-emperor, and gave him responsibility for the Eastern Empire.

Like his older brother, Valens also had served in the armies of the emperors Julian II and Jovian. In both cases Valens was a member of the *protector domesticus*, or the household guards. Valens' principate began in crisis, for in 365 a rebellion was staged by the soldier Procopius. Though he had widespread support and immediately gained control of Constantinople, Valens was able to crush Procopius' rebellion in the following year. In the process of his revolt, Procopius had sought the assistance of the Visigoths, who were anxious for conquest even though the revolt had been crushed. Valens took matters into his own hands and crossed into Visigothic territory, where he ravaged their lands from 367 through 369.

Yet another usurpation — this time led by an official named Theodorus in Antioch — occurred from 371 to 372, but was also crushed. In the meantime his brother, Valentinian I, died of a rage-induced stroke in 375, leaving Valens as the senior Augustus. The West was now in the hands of Valens' 16-year-old nephew, Gratian, who was nominally joined by his 4-year-old half brother, Valentinian II. But the troubles of the now-separate West were not the immediate concern of Valens, who was renewing aggressions against the Sasanians. Although his campaign was a success, it was not stellar, and a luke-warm peace was negotiated in 376.

Indeed, the timing of this settlement may have been the result of a new threat on the western borders of Valens' Empire, for a new enemy, the Huns, were causing problems for the Romans. So fierce were these eastern mounted warriors that the Ostrogothic nation in the Ukraine was virtually destroyed, and the Visigoths of Romania had poured across the Danube and into Roman territory to escape the Mongol hordes. Though in reality the Romans may have had little choice in the matter, their allowance of the Goths to settle in Roman territory soon proved to be a fatal mistake. Dispossessed of their lands, the Visigoths soon became restless and resentful of their fate, and began to ravage the Balkans at the very same time that another wave of Germanic people crossed the Danube to flee the Huns.

Valens' swift attention was required, and so he left Persia to confront the Visigoths. Valens engaged the Visigoths in a pitched battle on August 9, 378, near Adrianople, at which the Roman army was so severely beaten that Valens is known to posterity almost exclusively for this defeat. Either out of necessity or poor judgment, Valens engaged the Visigoths on their own terms, and led his legions into a terrifying ambush. Boxed in by Visigothic charges, fully two-thirds of the eastern Roman army was butchered, most of those being infantry, which seems to have been totally annihilated.

The whole affair is hauntingly similar to the Gothic victory of 251 that not only cost the lives of the emperors Trajan Decius and Herennius Etruscus, but also resulted in the slaughter of their army. One of the casualties was the 50-year-old Valens, who either perished in battle or was burned alive in the nearby house of a peasant where he had taken refuge to dress his wounds.

Of great interest are the circumstances of the Battle of Adrianople, for Valens did not wait for the arrival of Gratian's western army, which was *en route*. Some historians suggest Gratian's arrival was deliberately delayed in the hope that he would, in essence, be coming to the rescue of his uncle, whereas others believe Valens did not wish to share the glory of victory with his nephew, and so engaged the Visigoths before Gratian arrived. Though the truth may never be known, it is worth acknowledging that both explanations could co-exist and still be truthful.

Although not as talented as his brother, Valentinian I, Valens shared much in common with him. Both tried to better the life of the common man, and at the same time punished those who unfairly took advantage of the government. Valens managed to rule the Eastern Empire competently, doing much in his 14 years to establish peace with the Goths, protect Armenia from Sasanian aggressions, and reduce taxes. By Christian historians he is principally remembered as an Arian who took singular delight in persecuting Catholics, pagans and philosophers.

PROCOPIUS A.D. 365–366

Ruling in the West:
VALENTINIAN I (364–375)

Procopius, c. A.D. 326–366. A native of Cilicia and a relative of Julian II, Procopius served the court of Constantius II and was a commander in the army which Julian II assembled for his invasion of Persia. Upon Julian's death, Procopius brought the emperor's corpse to Cilicia for burial, and allowed Jovian to assume the high office even though it was rumored that Procopius had been named his successor.

After Jovian died, the new emperor, Valentinian I, divided the Empire between East and West so it could be managed properly. He assumed responsibility for the more unstable West and installed his younger brother, Valens, in the East. Because of this sudden change of regime, Procopius was forced into hiding out of fear that he would be arrested or executed as a potential usurper. But when Valens was traveling to Syria in the year following his accession, Procopius re-emerged in Constantinople, where he staged a rebellion. It was an easy task, for there was much dissatisfaction with Valens' father-in-law, Petronius, an official who was despised for his greed and cruelty.

Procopius was hailed emperor by disaffected soldiers on September 28, 365, and sought help from the Visigoths in his bid to overthrow Valens. Though initially successful, Procopius soon began to lose his German generals, who were defecting with large numbers of soldiers to Valens. After a reign of eight months, Procopius was defeated in battle at Nacolea in Phrygia on May 27, 366, after which he was executed. The future western emperor Anthemius (467–472) claimed descent from Procopius.

NUMISMATIC NOTE: Procopius struck coins at four mints Heraclea, Constantinople, Cyzicus and Nicomedia, with Heraclea being the only one that produced only æs.

THEODOSIUS I A.D. 379–395

A.D. 379–383: SOLE REIGN
A.D. 383–395: SENIOR AUGUSTUS (WITH ARCADIUS)

Ruling in the West:
GRATIAN (367–383), VALENTINIAN II (375–392), *Magnus Maximus* (383–388), *Flavius Victor* (387–388), *Eugenius* (392–394) AND HONORIUS (393–423)

SON-IN-LAW OF VALENTINIAN I
BROTHER-IN-LAW OF VALENTINIAN II
HUSBAND OF AELIA FLACCILLA AND GALLA (*sister* OF VALENTINIAN II)
FATHER OF ARCADIUS AND HONORIUS (BY AELIA FLACCILLA), AND OF GALLA PLACIDIA (BY GALLA)
FATHER-IN-LAW OF CONSTANTIUS III AND AELIA EUDOXIA
GRANDFATHER OF HONORIA, VALENTINIAN III, AELIA PULCHERIA AND THEODOSIUS II
GREAT-GRANDFATHER OF LICINIA EUDOXIA

Flavius Theodosius, c. A.D. 346/7–395. One of the renowned leaders of the late Roman Empire, Theodosius I was born at Cauca in north-west Spain. He was the son of the renowned general Count Theodosius, who had crushed insurrections in Britain (against the Picts and Scots) and North Africa and had served as Valentinian I's commander-in-chief on the Rhine.

His son, the future emperor, had served with his father and had learned much about soldiering and leadership. But Count Theodosius was executed for high treason in 375/6, perhaps out of fear that he would stage his own revolution amid the confusion that existed after the death of Valentinian I. The Count's son then retired to Spain and married Aelia Flacilla, who bore him two sons, the future emperors Arcadius and Honorius. In a later marriage, he sired a daughter named Galla Placidia, who was destined to live an extraordinary life.

However, after the destruction of the eastern Roman armies in August of 378 at Adrianople by the Visigoths, Count Theodosius' son (a cousin of Gratian by marriage) was lured out of his early retirement in Spain to take command of the armies on the Danube as *magister equitum*. About six months later, the western emperor Gratian invested Theodosius I with supreme power in the East. The ceremony took place at Sirmium on January 19, 379. Though both men carried on the affairs of state with general success, they did not see eye-to-eye and were often at odds.

Theodosius' first challenge was to safeguard the Eastern Empire with his depleted and demoralized army. He did this by making compromises with the Visigoths and the Sasanians, both of which proved to be lasting if not ideal. Of special interest was the bargain he struck with the Visigoths, whom he was unable to hold back with his depleted armies. Theodosius allowed the Visigoths to cross the Danube and settle in Thrace, where they were given land as well as regular payments. Furthermore, they were allowed to maintain their own tribal governments and to live under their own laws. In return, the Visigoths were to provide standing armies for the Romans to protect their borders from invasion. It was far from an ideal solution, but it seems Theodosius had little choice in the matter.

This arrangement was also extended to other peoples, such as Huns, and over time evolved from a temporary solution to a permanent part of Roman life. But all of this required vast sums of money, and so Theodosius applied taxes to all owned property, leaving nothing exempt. Some of his related laws made virtual slaves of humble tenant farmers, who were forbidden to move without the permission of their masters. Even the tax collectors feared Theodosius, for they would be severely flogged if they did not collect all that was due.

The year 383 began on a high note when Theodosius raised his eldest son Arcadius to the rank of Junior Augustus, but turned to crisis when a Spanish kinsman named Magnus Maximus revolted in Britain and in August killed the senior western emperor Gratian. Again, having little choice in the matter, Theodosius acknowledged Maximus as *de facto* co-emperor with young Valentinian II. However, when in 387 Maximus invaded Italy, Theodosius patched up a peace with the Sasanians in Armenia and marched at great speed into Italy. There his army of Romans, Huns and Goths defeated the usurper at Aquileia, and nominally restored Valentinian II (who had fled) to his throne.

Theodosius I remained in Italy for more than three years, trying to settle the Danubian front, though in the process he had to abandon the westernmost portion. In 391 he returned to Constantinople, where he raised his youngest son, Honorius, to the rank of Junior Augustus. In doing so, Theodosius had left the Frankish soldier Arbogast as regent for the emperor Valentinian II, who was now 20 years old, but far from capable of running an Empire. This proved to be a foolish decision, for Arbogast soon caused the murder or suicide of Valentinian II and installed a court official named Eugenius as the new emperor of the West. For a second time, Theodosius I led an army into Italy, and this time he defeated the legions of Eugenius and Arbogast on September 5–6, 394.

Theodosius I had now assumed control of the entire Roman Empire, though he made no formal gestures to unite East and West. However, this new arrangement lasted only five months, for after a reign of nearly 16 years, the 49-year-old emperor died of natural causes at Milan on January 17, 395. Successful enough to be surnamed "the Great," Theodosius was renowned in his day as an ardent defender of Christianity, and it is little more than a footnote of the era that the last Olympic Games were probably held during his reign, as he banned all pagan cults. Like many emperors, the historians simultaneously offer praise and condemnation on his various personality traits, and as such he is a difficult person to size up. Since Theodosius' dynasty had been formed long before his death, the temporarily united Empire was divided between his two incompetent sons, Arcadius in the East and Honorius in the West.

AELIA FLACCILLA

Augusta, a.d. 379–386/8

Wife of Theodosius I
Mother of Arcadius and Honorius
Step-mother of Galla Placidia
Mother-in-law of Aelia Eudoxia
Grandmother of Aelia Pulcheria and Theodosius II

Aelia Flavia Flaccilla, d. A.D. 386/8. Little is known of Aelia Flaccilla except that she was renowned for her piety and generosity to the poor. Born to a good family in Spain, Flaccilla was the daughter of Antonius, who had attained the high post of prefect of Gaul. It may be assumed that her marriage to Theodosius I in about 376 was a wedding of fortunes, for the latter had retired to his ancestral estates in Spain at that time. Perhaps they had planned to spend the remainder of their lives as local nobility.

However, three years after they were wed, Theodosius was recalled by the western emperor Gratian, who first gave him command of the Danubian region and a few months later crowned him emperor in the East. Flaccilla bore him two children, Arcadius in 377 and Honorius in 383/4 — brothers who would share the Empire they inherited from their father. In 386 (or 388), after a decade or more of marriage to Theodosius, Aelia Flaccilla died in Thrace (by one account). Theodosius remarried in 388, this time to Galla, the sister of Valentinian II, for whom no coins were struck, but who gave birth to the ill-fated Galla Placidia.

Numismatic Note: Aelia Flacilla's coinage — the first such issue for an empress since the 330s — heralded a return to the time-honored Roman practice of striking coinage for the important women of the Empire. The fact that she assumed her first name, Aelia, as part of her title had a profound effect on future empresses, who adopted it as a title (rather than as a name). Though she struck æs at eight mints, tremisses and siliquae were struck only at Constantinople.

ARCADIUS A.D. 383–408

A.D. 383–395: JUNIOR AUGUSTUS (WITH THEODOSIUS I)
A.D. 395–402: SOLE REIGN
A.D. 402–408: SENIOR AUGUSTUS (WITH THEODOSIUS II)

Ruling in the West:
GRATIAN (367–383), VALENTINIAN II (375–392), *Magnus Maximus* (383–388), *Flavius Victor* (387–388), *Eugenius* (392–394), HONORIUS (393–423), *Constantine III* (407–411) AND *Constans II* (408–411)

SON OF THEODOSIUS I AND AELIA FLACCILLA
BROTHER OF HONORIUS
HUSBAND OF AELIA EUDOXIA
FATHER OF THEODOSIUS II AND AELIA PULCHERIA
HALF-BROTHER OF GALLA PLACIDIA
FATHER-IN-LAW OF MARCIAN AND AELIA EUDOCIA
GRANDFATHER OF LICINIA EUDOXIA

Flavius Arcadius, c. A.D. 377–408. Of all the late Roman emperors, Arcadius may have been the most fortunate, for despite the brevity of his life and his general lack of talent, his reign was remarkably placid.

The eldest son of Theodosius I and Aelia Flacilla, Arcadius was born in Spain in about 377 and was proclaimed co-emperor with his father, Theodosius I, on January 19, 383. He was only 6 years old at the time of his elevation, and was fortunate to enjoy a dozen years under the tutelage of his father. But even this potentially fine training could not compensate for Arcadius' lack of natural ability.

When Theodosius left Constantinople in 394 to oust Eugenius from Italy, he placed Arcadius in a position of great authority along with the praetorian prefect Flavius Rufinus. When his father died in 395, the 18-year-old Arcadius became sole emperor in the East, and his 12-year-old brother, Honorius, inherited the western throne. At the outset Rufinus was marginally in control of Arcadius, and tried to persuade him to join their fortunes through a marriage to his own daughter. But much like Sejanus to Tiberius, the prefect was of humble birth and no such match was made.

It was not long before Rufinus came into conflict with Stilicho, a German soldier who held similar sway over Honorius in the West. Their disagreement caused an uprising by the Visigoths under their chieftain

Alaric, who proceeded to ravage much of Greece. In response, Stilicho marched east not only to quell the uprising, but also to claim the province of Illyria (and thus the large number of soldiers it produced) for the West. The conflict ended in a bit of treachery on the part of Stilicho, who in the guise of peaceful surrender, instead had Rufinus assassinated.

Stilicho continued to be a thorn in Arcadius' side when in 397 he refused to cooperate in the war against Alaric's Visigoths, and so he was declared a public enemy, while at the same time Alaric was given the title of Master of Soldiers in the Balkans. These severe tensions between East and West were only exacerbated by a revolt in North Africa by a man named Gildo, who sought to ally himself with Arcadius in the East. Though the crisis soon ended satisfactorily, it could have been a formula for disaster.

In 395 Arcadius married Aelia Eudoxia, the daughter of the Frankish general Bauto, and promptly hailed her Augusta. The dullard Arcadius was more than willing to let his energetic and beautiful wife run the affairs of state almost single-handedly from 400 until her death in 404. Indeed, her first actions were to check the aggressions of Stilicho (who was still considered a fugitive by the rulers in Constantinople) by pitting him against the Visigothic prefect, Alaric. But the issue found no resolution due to invasions from Germany and an uprising in Britain. In 401 the royal couple had their only child, a son named Theodosius II, who at age 1 was hailed co-emperor with his father in the year 402. When Aelia Eudoxia died in childbirth in 404, the reins of power passed largely to the praetorian prefect Anthemius (not the future emperor of that name), who suppressed an uprising by the Isaurians in Anatolia.

After a reign of more than a quarter century, the 31-year-old Arcadius died of natural causes at Constantinople on May 1, 408. He was succeeded by his only son, Theodosius II — then only 7 years old — whom he had hailed co-Augustus six years earlier. What Arcadius left can hardly be called a legacy, for he was unimpressive in person, sluggish, dull, and apparently had no enviable skills. Indeed, he was not suited for the demands of the throne, and had no choice but to let more energetic men and women run the Empire in his name.

AELIA EUDOXIA

AUGUSTA, A.D. 400–404

WIFE OF ARCADIUS
DAUGHTER OF BAUTO THE FRANK
DAUGHTER-IN-LAW OF THEODOSIUS I (POSTHUMOUSLY) AND AELIA FLACCILLA
SISTER-IN-LAW OF HONORIUS
MOTHER OF THEODOSIUS II AND AELIA PULCHERIA
MOTHER-IN-LAW OF MARCIAN AND AELIA EUDOCIA
GRANDMOTHER OF LICINIA EUDOXIA

(Aelia) Eudoxia, d. A.D. 404. History records very little of this royal lady. Eudoxia was a daughter of Bauto the Frank, a general of Valentinian I who in 385 repelled a Sarmatian offensive and thus was presented the high office of consul. After her father died, she was raised in the household of his comrade-in-arms, Promotus, a general who defeated the Ostrogoths in 386 and who was instrumental in the suppression of Magnus Maximus.

When Promotus died in 391, she came under the care of the powerful eunuch Eutropius, who was lord chamberlain in the court of Theodosius I. Indeed, it was at his urging that Eudoxia married the emperor's son, Arcadius, on April 27, 395, some three months after his father died in Milan. This was no easy feat, for a rival named Rufinus, the praetorian prefect of the East, was lobbying for Arcadius to marry his own daughter. But Eudoxia emerged victorious, and as the wife of the legitimate emperor of the East, she inherited a position of great power.

In succeeding years she worked hard to undermine the influence of Eutropius in the Imperial court. She achieved this in 399 with the help of a certain Gainas, who she then undermined in the following year. After she had given birth to two daughters, Eudoxia received the title Augusta on January 9, 400, and for the four remaining years of her life she was virtual ruler of the Eastern Roman Empire. Although she possessed great beauty, she had a quick temper and a forceful personality — all qualities which permitted her to dominate her lackluster husband.

Eudoxia was also a pious Christian who frequently argued with high-ranking Christian officials (most notably St. John Chrysostom, the patriarch of Constantinople), and went to great lengths to destroy all the remnants of paganism. Some historians credit her with causing irreparable harm to the relationship between church and state for centuries to come. All told, she and Arcadius had five children, two of whom were the future emperor Theodosius II, and Pulcheria, the future wife of the emperor Marcian. It was Pulcheria who inherited her mother's strength of character, for she tirelessly managed her brother's affairs for decades. After nearly a decade of marriage and meddling in palace politics, Aelia Eudoxia died early in October, 404, the result of a miscarriage.

NUMISMATIC NOTE: All of Aelia Eudoxia's coins were struck by her husband Arcadius. Gold was struck in the three principal denominations, with the solidi being the most common. Eudoxia's silver is very rare, and the bronze quite common. For details about how to distinguish Aelia Eudoxia's coins with the obverse inscription AEL EVDOXIA AVG from coins of her granddaughter, Licinia Eudoxia, with the same inscription, see the notes accompanying the biography of Licinia Eudoxia and the coinage listings of both women.

THEODOSIUS II A.D. 402–450

A.D. 402–408: JUNIOR AUGUSTUS (WITH ARCADIUS)
A.D. 408–450: SOLE REIGN

Ruling in the West:
HONORIUS (393–423), *Constantine III* (407–411), *Constans II* (409/10–411), Maximus (409–411), Priscus Attalus (409–410) AND (415–416), *Jovinus* (411–413), *Sebastianus* (412–413), CONSTANTIUS III (421), *Johannes* (423–425) AND VALENTINIAN III (425–455)

SON OF ARCADIUS AND AELIA EUDOXIA
BROTHER OF AELIA PULCHERIA
HUSBAND OF AELIA EUDOCIA
FATHER OF LICINIA EUDOXIA
BROTHER-IN-LAW OF MARCIAN
FATHER-IN-LAW OF VALENTINIAN III AND PETRONIUS MAXIMUS
NEPHEW OF HONORIUS
HALF-COUSIN OF VALENTINIAN III AND HONORIA
GRANDSON OF THEODOSIUS I AND AELIA FLACCILLA

Flavius Theodosius, A.D. 401–450. As the only son of the emperor Arcadius and Aelia Eudoxia, Theodosius II was declared Augustus on January 10, 402, when he was exactly 9 months old. Though merely a formality, his elevation left no doubt that he was destined to inherit his father's Empire. In fact, we are led to believe that Arcadius appointed the Sasanian king Yezdegerd as the child's guardian.

Arcadius died a premature, natural death at age 31 in the year 408, which made the 7-year-old Theodosius II the new emperor of the East.

The early years of his reign were managed almost entirely by his regent and praetorian prefect Anthemius (*not* the emperor of the same name). Two serious crises — a grain shortage and an invasion of Moesia by the Huns — were both managed admirably by Anthemius, who in 413 (shortly after Rome was sacked by the Visigoths) also began construction of a massive circuit wall around Constantinople. Equally influential was Antiochus, and other palace eunuchs who had been firmly established in the eastern courts for more than half a century.

Beginning in 414, however, both Antiochus and Anthemius fade into obscurity, for that was the year Theodosius' regency was transferred to the boy's older sister, Aelia Pulcheria (who herself was only 15 years old). Not only did she take over as regent, but she forced Anthemius to resign as praetorian prefect. For the remaining 36 years of Theodosius' reign, Pulcheria would be her brother's strongest influence, often running the affairs of state single-handedly.

One of her arrangements was the marriage in 421 of her brother to Aelia Eudocia, a young lady formerly named Athenais who was the daughter of an Athenian sophist. But Pulcheria came to regret this choice, for the new empress soon began to supplant her authority, and within two years she had also been hailed Augusta. She and Pulcheria often clashed, which eventually caused Eudocia to be expelled.

The West once again erupted into chaos in 423. Within a couple of months the matriarch Galla Placidia had been banished and her half-brother, the emperor Honorius, had died. A usurper named Johannes assumed control and Theodosius II (who had given asylum to Galla Placidia and her children) now had to raise an army so order could be restored in the West. The latter was achieved in 425, and Galla Placidia's only son, Valentinian III (the cousin of Theodosius II), was installed as the western emperor. Since Theodosius II had been the force behind restoring Thodosian rule in the West, his relations with that half of the Empire were excellent. This was a welcome change from the open hostility of the regents of Honorius and Arcadius.

In 437 Theodosius betrothed his only daughter, Licinia Eudoxia, to his cousin, Valentinian III, who had been emperor in the West (in name) for a dozen years. His family woes continued in the East, and he did not have the strength of character to interfere with the rivalry between his sister and wife. Indeed, it became so intense that it broke up his marriage in 442 or 443, and forced Licinia Eudocia to retire to Jerusalem after the divorce.

Though the military threats that afflicted the East could hardly compare with the chaos in the West, three were especially serious: the Sasanians, though defeated in 421, rose later at inopportune moments; the Goths often ravaged Roman territory, as they had been doing since the reign of

Valens; and worse still were the Huns, a nomadic confederation that came to be led by the infamous Attila in 434. Theodosius bought peace with Attila through humiliating concessions averaging nearly 50,000 gold solidi annually from the years 422 to 450. But Theodosius' failure to pay what he had promised prompted the Huns to sack the Balkans from 441 to 447, during which they leveled several important cities. Attila then made another peace with Theodosius, after which he ravaged the western portion of the Empire (related in the biographies of Valentinian III and Marcian).

Less than a decade after he had divorced his wife, Theodosius II died of natural causes on July 28, 450, possibly from a fall off his horse. Because he was elevated at such a young age, he held the title of Augustus for nearly half a century, and thus was the longest-reigning of all Roman emperors. He even outstripped the great Augustus, who actually ruled longer — 56 years all together — but who only held the title of Augustus for 41 years.

However, this accomplishment could hardly have pleased Theodosius II, who hardly knew a moment of security in his half century of life. Theodosius was kind, generous, scholarly and peaceful — indeed he possessed all the wrong qualities to lead an Empire constantly under siege. He was a skilled calligrapher, and applied this talent to his all-consuming passion of religion by patiently copying old manuscripts into the late hours of the night. He apparently did not care much for the tedious details of running an Empire, and is said to have routinely signed official documents without inquiring into their contents. What most historians describe as weakness in his personality, might better be described as kindness.

But Theodosius' gentle nature cost Constantinople dearly, for he more often achieved peace with gold and concessions than he did with war. The two great accomplishments of Theodosius' reign were the walls around Constantinople and the *Theodosian Code*, a legal document which took eight years to compile and was finally published in 438. Not only were they useful in their own day, but both proved to be works of lasting value. The former protected the capital of Christendom from invaders of every description for more than 1,000 years, and the latter has continued to influence lawmakers into the modern age. It is also noteworthy that in his religious zeal (no doubt greatly influenced by Pulcheria), Theodosius II ordered the destruction of all pagan temples in the eastern Mediterranean.

NUMISMATIC NOTE: The gold tremissis was first struck in large quantity by Theodosius II. The weight of the copper nummus (Æ4), which had been a modest but attractive coin under Arcadius, was in 425 reduced by 25 percent. The result was a paltry coin that remained so until the reform of Anastasius I in 498, at which point it was trading at 14,000–16,800 to the gold solidus. Anastasius I introduced a massive copper piece valued at 40 nummi that was tariffed at 20 pounds of coined nummi to the gold solidus. With the exception of a brief hiatus from 420 to 422, a star appears on the reverse of the precious metal coins of Theodosius II. Not only is this the easiest way to distinguish his coins from those of Theodosius I, but it became a defining characteristic of most subsequent issues struck in the East. While Theodosius' coinage in the East is common, very little was struck in his name at western mints. The year 430 was of significance, for it marked the hundredth anniversary of the foundation of Constantinople. In commemoration of this event (which coincided with preparations for Theodosius' *tricennalia*), a new reverse type of Constantinopolis seated left was introduced on the solidus. There are imitations of Theodosius' solidi attributed to the Visigoths (see RIC X, p. 453).

AELIA PULCHERIA

AUGUSTA, A.D. 414–453

SISTER OF THEODOSIUS II
DAUGHTER OF ARCADIUS AND AELIA EUDOXIA
WIFE OF MARCIAN
SISTER-IN-LAW OF AELIA EUDOCIA
HALF-COUSIN OF VALENTINIAN III AND HONORIA
STEP-MOTHER OF AELIA EUPHEMIA (*w.* OF ANTHEMIUS)
GRANDDAUGHTER OF THEODOSIUS I AND AELIA FLACCILLA
NIECE OF HONORIUS
AUNT OF LICINIA EUDOXIA

(Aelia) Pulcheria, A.D. 399–453. Being older than her brother Theodosius II, Pulcheria acted as his regent throughout most of his reign, even after he had come of age. On July 4, 414, when she was aged 15, Pulcheria was hailed Augusta and supplanted the regent Anthemius as the decision-maker in the palace. She held the title of Augusta for the nearly 40 years that remained of her life, and found it easy (and indeed necessary) to dominate her weak-minded and indulgent brother.

However, she had to share her authority with others, most notably her sister-in-law, Aelia Eudocia. The two royal ladies did not get along very well, and they were frequently in conflict. Historians suggest Pulcheria was supplanted by Eudocia in the late 420s and 430s, but that she eventually defeated Eudocia, who was expelled from the courts by 443/4 and forced to retire to Jerusalem. Pulcheria appears to have been a woman of great character and generosity. She apparently was also chaste, and early in her life had taken a vow of celibacy along with her two sisters, Arcadia and Marina (for both of whom no coins were struck). This drastic measure no doubt stemmed from strong religious beliefs, but was undertaken mainly to avoid the prospect of outsiders marrying into the hierarchy and becoming rivals to their brother.

Indeed, Pulcheria did not marry until her 51st year, and even then it was not for love, but to legitimize the principate of Marcian, who she and the Master of Soldiers Aspar had chosen to succeed her deceased brother. The marriage was unconjugal, and Marcian was denied his rights as husband so that Pulcheria could remain chaste. Though Pulcheria's strong influence in secular policies can only be assumed, her importance in religious debate is a matter of record. Indeed, she was instrumental in both summoning and implementing the canons of the extremely important Fourth Ecumenical Council of the Church at Chalcedon in 451. Three years into her marriage to Marcian, Pulcheria died in July of 453 — the same year in which Attila the Hun died. Ever true to her pious and generous nature, Pulcheria left all of her earthly effects to the poor.

NUMISMATIC NOTE: All of Aelia Pulcheria's coins were struck at Constantinople by her brother, Theodosius II, and her husband, Marcian. They seem to have been struck at intervals throughout the entire period 414 to 453.

AELIA EUDOCIA

AUGUSTA, A.D. 423–460

WIFE OF THEODOSIUS II
DAUGHTER-IN-LAW OF ARCADIUS AND AELIA EUDOXIA
SISTER-IN-LAW OF AELIA PULCHERIA
MOTHER OF LICINIA EUDOXIA
MOTHER-IN-LAW OF VALENTINIAN III AND PETRONIUS MAXIMUS

(Aelia) Eudocia (*earlier* Athenais), d. A.D. 460. Aelia Eudocia first traveled to Constantinople in 420 or 421 to resolve a legal dispute with her brothers over their inheritance. Though still a pagan, her beauty and quick wit caught the attention of the empress Aelia Pulcheria, who thought her to be the ideal bride for her brother.

Under the influence of Pulcheria, Theodosius II married Athenais (who had been baptized with the name Eudocia) on June 7, 421. Aelia Eudocia must have been an unusual member of the Imperial court (which was virtually monastic during her lifetime), for although a Christian, she paid much attention to Classical learning. Her Athenian father, Leontius, was a man of letters, and she inherited his penchant for literature, for she wrote verse herself (some of which survives). One of her closest associates was the pagan poet Cyrus, who held several of the highest offices in Constantinople, but who was ruined because of his enormous popularity with the people.

Eudocia had only one daughter, Licinia Eudoxia, who was destined to be the wife of the emperor Valentinian III, and subsequently had a boy who died young. In consequence of her giving birth to Licinia Eudoxia, Eudocia was hailed Augusta on January 2, 423. Though she shared this lofty rank with her sister-in-law, Pulcheria, her status was subordinate. Nonetheless, the new empress wasted little time before she began to wield her authority in the Imperial court. Eudocia and her sister-in-law were of different temperaments, and though the two court matriarchs began on good terms, they later clashed. This proved harmful to both women.

In October 437, her daughter, Licinia Eudoxia, married the western emperor Valentinian III, and thus departed for Ravenna in the following year. It was at this time (and seemingly because of this event) that Eudocia left Constantinople on a pilgrimage to Jerusalem. After this, her position in the Imperial court began to disintegrate. Two of her foremost allies fell in 440 and 441, and Eudocia was eventually expelled on a serious charge, perhaps of adultery. She was excluded from court life by 443/4 (shortly after her marriage to Theodosius II failed) and so she once again traveled to Jerusalem, where she spent the rest of her life. There is ample evidence to suggest she retained her title of Augusta until her death there on October 20, 460. She was buried in the basilica of St. Stephen, the church that she herself had founded.

NUMISMATIC NOTE: All of Aelia Eudocia's coins were struck by her husband, Theodosius II.

MARCIAN A.D. 450–457

Ruling in the West:
VALENTINIAN III (425–455), *Petronius Maximus* (455) AND AVITUS (455–456)

HUSBAND OF AELIA PULCHERIA
FATHER OF AELIA EUPHEMIA
FATHER-IN-LAW OF ANTHEMIUS
SON-IN-LAW OF ARCADIUS AND AELIA EUDOXIA
BROTHER-IN-LAW OF THEODOSIUS II
GRANDFATHER OF ALYPIA

Flavius Valerius Marcianus, c. A.D. 391/2–457. Although not a blood relation to any previous emperor, Marcian was an accomplished soldier of Illyrian or Thracian origin who had risen to high office within the army. His career was eventful, and in the early 430s he was taken as a prisoner of war in North Africa by the Vandals while serving under Aspar, an Alan who was then a general of Theodosius II. At the time of his elevation he was *domesticus* to Aspar, who had since risen to become Master of Soldiers.

Marcian was of sufficiently good character to be chosen as the successor to Theodosius II, who had died of natural causes late in July 450 without an heir. Making this decision were Aspar and Pulcheria, the sister of Theodosius II, who had largely managed the affairs of state for her brother throughout his 48-year reign. But the decision may have been an easy one, for we are told that on his deathbed Theodosius II requested of Aspar that Marcian succeed him.

Upon his accession on August 25, 450, Marcian was married to Pulcheria — not for love, but for the good of the Empire. (Marcian himself was a widower and advanced in age.) Although Valentinian III in the West did not acknowledge his elevation until the spring of 452, Marcian immediately took a strong position against Attila the Hun by refusing to pay the annual indemnity of 2,100 pounds of gold that had been promised by his weakling predecessor. Marcian is quoted as having remarked "I have iron for Attila, but no gold."

Though it was a courageous act, it was seemingly a foolish one. Fortunately, the Eastern Romans were spared retribution when, in 453, Attila died on the last of his numerous wedding nights. The Hunnic nation then disintegrated after they were defeated in 454 by a Gothic confederation at the Battle of Nedao. Had Attila not died prematurely (or been occupied with his conquests in the West), the fate of the Eastern Empire might have been significantly different.

But his stand against Attila was uncharacteristic for his reign, which was introspective. Indeed, Marcian (on the advice of Aspar) did nothing to prevent the Vandals from sacking Rome, and he gave part of Pannonia to the Gepids. Neither of these acts served to warm relations between East and West, which had been harmed by the very fact that Marcian was hailed emperor without the constitutional consent of Valentinian III. Even in his own realm, Marcian was timid, for he dared not confront the Sasanians, who had become quite aggressive in the buffer state of Armenia. Clearly, in this case Marcian was wisely conserving his resources in the event the Huns declared war.

Marcian had a daughter from a previous marriage, Euphemia, who later married the western emperor Anthemius (467–472). If Marcian succeeded in any way, it was financially, for when his he died the treasury was laden with more than 100,000 pounds of gold — the equivalent of 7.2 million solidi. Regrettably, all of this and more was lost by his successor, who lost an 1,100-ship armada in an expedition against the Vandals in 468.

After a productive, peaceful, and fortunate reign of more than six years, the 65-year-old emperor died on January 27, 457, after suffering from an illness of about six months. With his death also came a conclusion to the Theodosian and Valentinian lines. Though most historians believe Marcian died of natural causes, some sources report that he was poisoned. Since his wife, Pulcheria, had died four years before and Marcian had no son, there was no successor-in-waiting. Thus, the choice for his replacement fell upon the army, which was led by Aspar.

LEO I A.D. 457–474

A.D. 457–470: SOLE REIGN
A.D. 470–471: AUGUSTUS
(WITH PATRICIUS, AS CAESAR)
A.D. 471–473: SOLE REIGN
A.D. 473–474: AUGUSTUS
(WITH LEO II, AS CAESAR)
A.D. 474: SENIOR AUGUSTUS (WITH LEO II)

Ruling in the West:
MAJORIAN (457–461), LIBIUS SEVERUS (461–465),
ANTHEMIUS (467–472), *Olybrius* (472) AND *Glycerius* (473–474)

HUSBAND OF AELIA VERINA
FATHER OF AELIA ARIADNE AND LEONTIA (W. OF PATRICIUS)
BROTHER-IN-LAW OF BASILISCUS
FATHER-IN-LAW OF PATRICIUS AND ZENO
GRANDFATHER OF LEO II

Flavius Valerius Leo (I), c. A.D. 401 or 411–474. A man of humble origins, apparently from the Bessi tribe in Thrace, Leo (who is sometimes called "the Great") rose from total obscurity to found a dynasty that would rule Constantinople until the end of what most historians consider to be the Eastern Roman Empire.

Leo owed his high career to the patronage of Aspar, the powerful Alan Master of Soldiers in the East. Since there was no designated successor to Marcian, the choice was made by the army, and Aspar proclaimed Leo emperor on February 7, 457. Aspar probably elected Leo so that the most legitimate candidate, former emperor's son-in-law Anthemius (who later was emperor in the West in 472), would not ascend the throne.

Despite the debt of gratitude that Leo owed Aspar, the new emperor went to great lengths to shed the influence of his benefactor. This internal war went in Leo's favor when in 466 he rapidly promoted Zeno, and it ended with the murder of Aspar in 471. Much to Leo's credit, he broke the power of the German soldiers led by Aspar, who had dominated his court and threatened the stability of the Empire. But to achieve this he had to replace them with equally fierce (and apparently less-well-mannered) Isaurians, led by a capable soldier named Taracsis, who is better known by his adopted name, Zeno.

Throughout this five-year conflict one of the principal issues was choosing a successor for Leo, who showed no signs of nearing death. However, his only son had died at five months old in 463, and he had only daughters. The first to advance was Zeno, who in 466 or 467 married Aelia Ariadne, Leo's eldest daughter. Soon after, Zeno went to Thrace to fight the Huns, leaving Aspar in Constantinople. The latter strengthened his own position in 470 when one of his sons, Patricius, was hailed Caesar and betrothed to Leo's younger daughter, Leontia. Now there were two qualified candidates for the succession, though neither of them were popular in Constantinople.

The rivalry ended, however, when Aspar tried to win over Zeno's Isaurian soldiers, but failed to do so before Zeno returned from Thrace and counteracted his efforts. Though Leo sympathized with Zeno, it seems that the order to execute Aspar in 471 came directly from Leo. Though Patricius survived the ambush, he was seriously wounded and was deprived of his rank and of the prospect of a royal marriage. Now only Zeno remained as a viable successor.

Although Leo was the emperor of the East, he took considerable interest in the ill-fortunes of the West. In 467 he appointed Anthemius as emperor in the West, and in 473/4 enlisted the services of Julius Nepos to oust the usurper Glycerius. But with the chaotic environment in Italy, both men were deposed in short order. Another of his interventions in the West occurred in 468, and it was such a catastrophe that it single-handedly has blackened his record. Ever since the Vandals had occupied Carthage in 439, the Western Roman Empire had suffered the consequences. Not only was their traditional grain supply jeopardized, but the sea-borne Vandals often turned to piracy in Sicily and Italy.

So Leo assembled an armada of more than 1,100 ships, which deployed about 100,000 men. The expense (estimated at 7.5 million to 9.5 million gold solidi) was extraordinary, and it bankrupted the Eastern treasury. However, it was anticipated that Leo's investment in the fleet would produce enough revenue in loot that the expense was justifiable. Leo entrusted this vital mission to his brother-in-law, the future usurper Basiliscus.

Through what must have been a stroke of good luck, Basiliscus won impressive naval engagements at the outset, sending 340 Vandal ships to the floor of the sea. However, the gross incompetence so natural to Basiliscus soon emerged as he naively fell victim to the Vandal's treachery. The great Roman armada was destroyed in its entirety, and with its destruction came dire consequences. The West was now demoralized and at risk, and the East was bankrupt. The failure of the armada was equally as tragic as the defeat suffered in 378 by the emperor Valens at Adrianople.

But after this great loss, Leo still had more than five years to reign, during which he was often occupied with finding a successor (as was related above). In October of 473, while in a declining state of health, Leo gave the title of Caesar to the young son of Zeno, who was also named Leo, and who is known to historians as Leo II. This seemed a more practical option than giving that rank to Zeno himself, for he would have been an unpopular choice. When Leo's health took a dramatic turn, he hailed Leo II Augustus, and the aged emperor died a few days later, either in late January or early February of 474.

AELIA VERINA

AUGUSTA, A.D. 457–484

WIFE OF LEO I
MOTHER OF AELIA ARIADNE AND LEONTIA (*w.* OF PATRICIUS)
SISTER OF BASILISCUS
MOTHER-IN-LAW OF PATRICIUS, ZENO AND ANASTASIUS I (EMPEROR, A.D. 491–518)
GRANDMOTHER OF LEO II
AUNT OF MARCUS

(Aelia) Verina, d. A.D. 484. A most remarkable woman, Verina married Leo I (who was her senior by decades) before he became emperor in 457, and thus she bore the title of Augusta from the outset of his reign. Though her rise to fame and power was relatively smooth, her later years were dangerous and eventful, as she ended her days as a perennial rebel against her son-in-law, Zeno.

Although Verina was influential during her husband's principate, she had a greater effect on the affairs of state after he died in 474. First, she oversaw his succession. The legal heir was her grandson, Leo II, who had been raised first to the rank of Caesar, then to Augustus just before her husband's death. However, Leo II was merely a child, and a sickly one at that. To prevent an inevitable crisis, she arranged for her son-in-law (the boy's father, Zeno) to be proclaimed co-emperor. The child Leo II soon died, leaving Zeno as sole emperor in the East. Thus her task of managing the succession was achieved.

But her son-in-law proved to be every bit as unpopular as was expected. Verina regretted her choice for many reasons, not the least of which being that she now was somewhat subordinate to her own daughter, who had also become Augusta with the elevation of Zeno. So Verina plotted Zeno's overthrow. Her ingenious solution was to inform Zeno that his life was in jeopardy, and thus trick him into fleeing Constantinople.

Though her plan worked perfectly, her subsequent machination quickly began to unravel. The senate hailed her brother, Basiliscus, as emperor, whereas Verina had hoped the honor would go to her lover, Patricius (the Master of Offices, not the Patricius who was Caesar from 470–471, the first husband of her youngest daughter). Very soon, Basiliscus and his sister's lover, Patricius, were at odds, and the latter was executed. This enraged Verina, who then diverted her energies to ousting her brother and restoring son-in-law Zeno, whom she had just overthrown. Such actions put her in great danger with Basiliscus.

Historians differ in their views on what happened next. Some suggest Verina was able to conceal her guilt from Zeno (and thus escape immediate punishment), whereas others believe she was imprisoned upon his return. The remainder of her life was equally tumultuous. She continued to be one of Zeno's most formidable enemies, constantly plotting against him and threatening the stability of his regime. Not surprisingly, she spent much of her life as a prisoner in barren fortresses in Isauria.

Verina had three children with her husband, Leo I: a son who died young in 463, and two daughters. The eldest daughter was Ariadne, the wife of the future emperor Zeno. The younger daughter (for whom no coins were struck) was Leontia, who twice was involved with men who aspired to the throne. Her first betrothal was to Patricius, a son of the Master of Soldiers Aspar. This young man was raised to the rank of Caesar in 470 by Leo I, but apparently the marriage never occurred, especially after his father was murdered in 471.

Leontia's second association (which this time resulted in marriage) was with Marcian, a young man who was named after his grandfather, the emperor of 450–457. In 479 this second Marcian joined forces with his mother-in-law, Verina, in an effort to overthrow Zeno. However, the revolt failed immediately, leading to the banishment of Verina and the capture of Marcian. The most notable act of her later life (well beyond the scope of this work) was staging the revolt of Leontius, which in the fall of 484 resulted in her own death later that year after she took refuge with rebels at the fortress of Cherris in Isauria.

NUMISMATIC NOTE: Most of Aelia Verina's coins were struck late in the reign of her husband Leo I, though hoard evidence indicates that some were struck earlier in Leo's reign. It is also possible that some were struck during the brief reigns of her brother Basiliscus, or of her grandson Leo II.

PATRICIUS

CAESAR, A.D. 470–471 (UNDER LEO I)

SON OF ASPAR (MASTER OF SOLDIERS)
HUSBAND OF LEONTIA (D. OF LEO I)
SON-IN-LAW OF LEO I AND AELIA VERINA
BROTHER-IN-LAW OF AELIA ARIADNE

Patricius, lifespan unknown. The elevation of Leo I in February 457 was due largely to the patronage of Aspar, the Master of Soldiers in the East who had served under the previous emperor, Marcian. But the debt of gratitude that Leo owed Aspar did not take hold, for the new emperor went to great lengths to free himself from the influence of his benefactor.

Leo targeted the German soldiers led by Aspar who held sway over his court, and replaced them with equally fierce Isaurians, who were led by a soldier who adopted the name Zeno and was destined to become emperor. Since Leo I had no living son to succeed him, the claims of succession would no doubt be determined by the marriages of his two daughters, Ariadne and Leontia. The first to take advantage of this prospect was the Isaurian Zeno, who in 466 or 467 married Leo's eldest daughter, Ariadne.

Later, in 470, Aspar strengthened his position while Zeno was away at war, for he managed to convince Leo I to raise to the rank of Caesar his eldest son Patricius (not to be confused with Patricius, the lover of Aelia Verina). This enraged the Constantinopolitans, for Patricius was an Arian, and consequently not suitable for the office. Aspar also requested that Patricius be wed to Leo I's younger daughter, Leontia, but it seems that the emperor did not agree to this. None-the-less, by hailing Patricius Caesar, Leo I made it clear that Aspar's son was his successor.

Even with this development, Zeno had not given up hope, and his rivalry with Aspar grew until in 471 Aspar tried to win over Zeno's Isaurian soldiers. But this last bit of treachery was his undoing, for Zeno hastened back from the Hunnic war to defend his interests. Historians seem to agree that it was Leo I who ordered the ambush in which Aspar and his youngest son perished. Even though Patricius survived the ambush, he was seriously wounded and was subsequently deprived of both his title and his prospect of a royal marriage. The murder of Aspar was not without consequence to the Romans, for an Ostrogothic chieftain named Theoderic Strabo ("squint-eye") began to ravage parts of Thrace, and was only persuaded to stop through bribery.

NUMISMATIC NOTE: No coins were struck in the name of Patricius, although a solidus in the name of Leo may portray him on the reverse. The inscription SALVS REIPVBLICAE is followed by a C, which many scholars believe indicates that the young man on the reverse is a Caesar. The standing figure is a young man, nimbate and wearing a diadem and crown, sometimes on a low dias. Since the obverse bears the name Leo and the title Augustus (D N LEO PERPET AVG), the issue must belong to Leo I or to his grandson, Leo II. The identification of the issuer is paramount in determining who is represented by the standing figure on the reverse.

If the coin was struck by Leo II (Caesar 473–474; Augustus in 474), the figure would most certainly be Leo II himself, for it would have to have been struck during his approximately two-week reign as sole Augustus. The authors of RIC put forth this view, with the crux of their argument being that the standing figure is diademed, and must be an Augustus (thus making Patricius, a Caesar, an unlikely candidate).

To this end a comparison may be drawn with certain solidi struck by Basiliscus while Marcus was his Caesar. The reverse depicts two figures enthroned — the junior figure is bare-headed whereas the senior figure is diademed (thus: Basiliscus Augustus and Marcus Caesar). As important as the diadem is to this issue (on which two people are simultaneously depicted), it alone is not strong enough to contradict the identification of the standing figure as Patricius. The comparison with the solidus of Basiliscus and Marcus, after all, need not be taken too literally, for that coinage was itself highly unorthodox as a joint-issue.

If the solidus was struck by Leo I (as is proposed by the authors of the Dumbarton Oaks catalogue, and as is followed in this catalogue), the figure on the reverse must either be Leo I or his Caesar Patricius. Because the figure is diademed, Leo I has been suggested, but the purposely youthful appearance of the figure makes this highly unlikely. Considering the reverse inscription ends with the otherwise inexplicable letter 'C' (most likely an abbreviation of 'Caesar'), Patricius seems not only to be a likely candidate, but the one to which the inscription refers.

LEO II A.D. 474

A.D. 473–474: CAESAR (UNDER LEO I)
A.D. 474: JUNIOR AUGUSTUS (WITH LEO I)
A.D. 474: SENIOR AUGUSTUS (SOLE REIGN, AND WITH ZENO)

Ruling in the West:
Glycerius (473–474) AND JULIUS NEPOS (474–475/480)

SON OF ZENO AND AELIA ARIADNE
GRANDSON OF LEO I AND AELIA VERINA
NEPHEW OF LEONTIA (*w.* OF PATRICIUS)

Leo (II), A.D. 467–474. One of the great concerns of the aging Leo I was finding a successor, for his only son had died in 463 while only five months old. He was determined to do this so that civil war would be prevented after his death. He made his first serious attempt in 470, when he raised the son of the German Master of Soldiers Aspar, a young man named Patricius, to the rank of Caesar. However, with the murder of Aspar in 471, the hopes of that family disintegrated.

Now the only viable successors belonged to the family of Zeno, an Isaurian soldier who had become the most important man in Leo's army, and several years earlier had married his eldest daughter, Aelia Ariadne. Together they had a son, also named Leo, who is known to historians as Leo II. When Leo I's health began to fail late in 473, he announced that his grandson, Leo II, was to be his heir. Leo I bypassed the boy's father, his son-in-law Zeno, because it would have been met with great protestation.

The boy Leo II was hailed Caesar in October, 473. When Leo I's health failed more dramatically in January, 474, he raised his grandson from Caesar to Augustus. His timing was right, for the aged emperor died a few days later, either in late January or early February of 474. The throne of the Eastern Empire now fell squarely into the hands of the 7-year-old Leo II, who in addition to being young, was also quite sickly.

Aware of the frailty of the situation, the boy's grandmother (Leo I's widow), Aelia Verina, arranged for her grandson to appoint his own father, Zeno, as his co-emperor. This occurred on February 9, 474, and proved to be prudent, for the Eastern Empire was now in the hands of both father and son. The sickly Leo II died of natural causes (though it was rumored Zeno had killed him) in November of the very same year, thus leaving his father, Zeno, as sole emperor. Although only an emperor in name, the brief reign of Leo II served as the conduit by which power was transferred from Leo I to Zeno.

NUMISMATIC NOTE: No coins were struck for Leo II as Caesar (from October, 473 to January, 474), as the pieces often ascribed to this period actually belong to the Leo Caesar associated with Zeno in the aftermath of the revolt of Basiliscus (for these, see the listing for Leo Caesar, 476–477). It is doubtful whether any coins were struck in the name of Leo II during his very brief joint reign with Leo I and his subsequent sole reign (collectively, from January to February 9, 474). Two possibilities, however, are a particular tremissis with a youthful bust (see D.O., p. 172), or the solidus described in the catalog entry for Patricius. Indeed, the coinage of Leo II seems to have been struck exclusively during his joint-reign with Zeno (from February 9 to November, 474). The numismatic evidence makes it quite clear that even though Leo II was merely a child, he held the "senior" position of Augustus as compared to his father Zeno. This is demonstrated by his name coming first in the obverse inscription, and by his smaller figure appearing at the more honorable position (on the left from the viewer's perspective) when the seated figures of Leo II and Zeno are shown on the reverse of those coins.

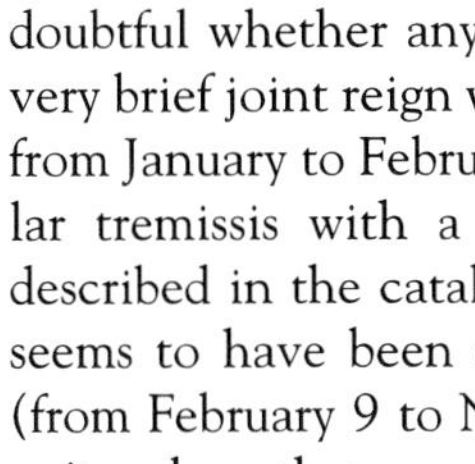

ZENO A.D. 474–475 & 476–491

A.D. 474: JUNIOR AUGUSTUS (WITH LEO II)
A.D. 474–475: FIRST SOLE REIGN
A.D. 475–476: DEPOSED
A.D. 476–477: AUGUSTUS
(WITH LEO CAESAR, AS CAESAR)
A.D. 477–491: SECOND SOLE REIGN

Ruling in the West:
Glycerius (473–474), JULIUS NEPOS (474–475/480),
Romulus Augustus (475–476) AND *Odovacar* (KING, 476–493)

HUSBAND OF AELIA ARIADNE
FATHER OF LEO II
SON-IN-LAW OF LEO I AND AELIA VERINA
BROTHER-IN-LAW OF LEONTIA (*w.* OF PATRICIUS)

Zeno (*earlier* Tarasis or Tarasicodissa), d. A.D. 491. Hailing from an illustrious family in Isauria (south-eastern Asia Minor), the future emperor Zeno came into the service of emperor Leo I, who was trying to rid his capital of the German soldiers led by the Master of Soldiers Aspar.

In 466 Leo began to promote Zeno, who was then going by his birth name Tarasis or Tarasicodissa. In 468 Leo arranged that he marry his eldest daughter, Aelia Ariadne, and appointed him Master of Soldiers in Thrace. For these important occasions, he divorced his wife, Arcadia, and changed his name to Zeno in honor of an Isaurian who had achieved high office in recent memory.

Over the next several years Zeno was in conflict with the general Aspar, who managed to have his own son, Patricius, hailed Caesar while Zeno was at war and away from Constantinople. A quick return by Zeno in 471 ended these threats, and resulted in the murder of Aspar and the deposition of Patricius. Shortly before emperor Leo I died in late January or February of 474, he'd hailed Zeno's son (his own grandson), Leo II, co-emperor, leaving no doubt who would succeed him. But the child was sickly, and so the widowed Aelia Verina had her son-in-law Zeno hailed co-emperor with her grandson Leo II on February 9, 474. Leo II died within months, and Zeno became sole emperor in November 474.

But Verina soon came to regret her decision to appoint her son-in-law emperor, and she hatched a plot to oust him. She did so by advising him that he must flee Constantinople immediately to avoid the assassin's blade. Believing his mother-in-law spoke truthfully, Zeno fled on January 9, 475, and crossed the Bosporus to Calchedon. Thus, his "first reign" was less than two months long.

With Zeno out of the capital, Verina ordered the slaughter of the Isaurians who remained in Constantinople. Even though the coup was a success due to the treachery of Verina, she was not justly rewarded: she wanted her lover Patricius to be crowned Augustus, but the men in power chose instead her brother, Basiliscus, who soon executed Patricius. Not surprisingly, this act caused Verina to despise her brother, and to turn against him. She then devoted herself to restoring Zeno, so that Basiliscus would pay for his actions.

Basiliscus handled his affairs so incompetently that he required no help to alienate the army, the Church and the people. After more than 19 months in exile, Zeno gained the allegiance of the generals Illus and Armatus, and was able to easily reclaim his throne from Basiliscus late in August of 476. Basiliscus and his family were exiled to Cappadocia and starved to death. According to some accounts, Verina was able to mask her guilt from Zeno, and was thus spared a similar fate because she had helped in the overthrow of Basiliscus.

Zeno was now firmly in control of the Eastern Empire again, and so he began to solve the myriad of problems he faced, not the least of which was a recently emptied treasury. Another problem was a bargain he had made with Armatus, the Master of Soldiers (and nephew) of Basiliscus whom he convinced to switch allegiance. Among the promises he made to

Armatus to secure his change of heart was that he would be appointed to a high office, and that his son (then named Basiliscus, though it was later changed to Leo) would be promoted to the rank of Caesar. Armatus was made a consul and given the post of Master of Soldiers of Thrace, and his son was made Caesar in 476.

However, sometime in 477(the year the Vandal Gaiseric died), Zeno decided he could endure no more of Armatus' outrageous behavior, and so he executed him and deposed his son. Another of Zeno's immediate concerns was the western portion of the Empire, which had fallen into a state of disrepair during his absence. The rightful emperor Julius Nepos had fled Italy, which was now in the hands of the German soldier Odovacar. Zeno could do little to restore Nepos, and was forced to abandon the Western Roman Empire. Zeno ceded Italy to Odovacar, who assumed the title of king. The remainder of Zeno's reign — which extends beyond the scope of this work — was turbulent and fraught with rebellion. After a disturbed reign of 17 years, Zeno died of natural causes on April 9, 491, and was succeeded by the first Byzantine emperor, Anastasius I.

NUMISMATIC NOTE: Coinage in the name of Zeno occured in several periods. The first coinage is from his joint-reign with Leo II from February 9 to November, 474 (which is covered in the listings of Leo II). His next coinage, belonging to Zeno's brief 'first reign' (from November, 474 to January 9, 475), is understandably rare. Since the diagnostics which distinguish these coins from the second reign issues are not consistent or entirely certain, they are not listed separately in this catalog. For discussions of the possible diagnostics, see RIC X, pages 111 and 215, and D.O. pages 174–5. For catalog listings, see RIC X, nos. 901–3 and 3605-6, and D.O. nos. 604–5.

During the next phase of Zeno's life, when he was deposed (from January 9, 475 to late August, 476), it appears as though some coinage was struck in his name at Antioch. When Basiliscus was ousted and Zeno's regime was restored ('second reign'), a new phase of coinage commenced. Initially Zeno struck coinage jointly with Leo Caesar (from August, 476 to sometime in 477), all of which are covered in the listings of Leo Caesar.

Not surprisingly, it is the coinage from his 'second reign' following the deposition of Leo Caesar (from 477 to 491) which accounts for the vast majority of Zeno's issues. At Western mints, some of these coins were struck concurrently with issues in the name of Julius Nepos, even though the latter had been in exile in Dalmatia since 476. Naturally, such coins are attributed to mint operations under Odovacar, and the issues in the name of Zeno, thus, are often collected in place of the much rarer issues which bear the western emperor's name. Furthermore, there are imitations of Zeno's solidi and tremisses attributed to the Visigoths (see RIC X, p.

462), and imitations of his nummi (Æ4's) bearing the monogram of the western Master of Soldiers Gundobad on the reverse which are attributed to the Burgundians (see, respectively, RIC X, p. 464, and the separate listing for Gundobad in this catalog).

Perhaps the most interesting issue in Zeno's name, however, is the rare copper 40-nummus piece (catalog nos. 3818-9), the denomination of which is identified by the XL (=40) on the reverse. It comes in two varieties, each of which appear to have been struck with only one pair of dies. It was struck at Rome for only a very brief time, apparently under Odovacar, and seemingly under the auspices of the senate. Though traditionally dated to the end of Zeno's reign (so as to place it as close as possible to the reform of Anastasius I in 498), it more likely belongs to c. 477. On one of the varieties the numeral IIII occurs under Zeno's bust. This could indicate a regnal year rather than an officina, and if so, would lead us exactly to 477/8. This matches well with the historical context, for this was the period in which Odovacar was appealing to Leo I to reign in both the East and West; to which Leo I responded that Julius Nepos was still emperor in the West. These events could easily explain both why the issue was initiated, and why it ceased so quickly.

It clearly was a revival coinage, celebrating the glories of the Roman past. It has a large planchet, individualized portrait, grandiose inscription, an acknowledgement of the senate, and it copies a Flavian reverse type. Undoubtedly it was inspired by a heavily worn asses of Vespasian which had been "recycled" for circulation (*see* the discussion in the Introduction) in the late 5th and early 6th centuries A.D.

AELIA ARIADNE

AUGUSTA, A.D. 474(?)–515

WIFE OF ZENO AND ANASTASIUS I
(EMPEROR, A.D. 491–518)
DAUGHTER OF LEO I AND AELIA VERINA
SISTER OF LEONTIA (W. OF PATRICIUS)
MOTHER OF LEO II
NIECE OF BASILISCUS
COUSIN OF MARCUS

(Aelia) Ariadne, d. A.D. 515. A royal lady who was destined to survive nearly six decades as a member of the Imperial family in Constantinople, Aelia Ariadne was the elder daughter of the emperor Leo I and the ever-scheming Aelia Verina. Her first marriage, in 466 or 467, was to the Isaurian soldier Zeno, by whom she had a son named Leo (called Leo II by historians) in 467.

When her father died in 474 the succession fell upon her child Leo II, who was so sickly that his father was proclaimed co-emperor. When the boy died later that same year, her husband, Zeno, became sole-emperor in the East. Throughout all this, Ariadne was hailed Augusta. It is uncertain exactly at which stage this occurred, but it certainly was sometime in 474. In receiving this title, Ariadne had eclipsed the authority of her mother, Verina, who had become accustomed to being the only Augusta in the palace. Thus, Verina's tenure as Augusta began with her being tricked by her own mother into fleeing Constantinople less than two months into her husband's reign.

When Zeno's reign was restored in the following year (476), she returned with him and replaced her mother as the matriarch of the palace. Regrettably, very little is recorded of her actions thereafter, though they must have been interesting, for her husband's reign was ever-in-jeopardy. Even though her mother had wronged her, Ariadne fought for her release from exile. Indeed, at one point she plotted against the general Illus because he would not permit her return. In this case Illus came out on the losing end, for he lost one of his ears in the process.

When Zeno died in 491 it fell upon Ariadne and leaders in the army to choose his successor. They decided upon Anastasius I (emperor 491–518), a man of considerable talent who not only became emperor, but on May 20, 491, also became Ariadne's second husband. Thus Ariadne had the distinct honor of being both the last empress of the "Roman Empire" and the first empress of the "Byzantine Empire." But since these are distinctions made only in the modern age, Verina, who died in 515, was none the wiser.

NUMISMATIC NOTE: Aelia Ariadne's solidi are somewhat unusual for they do not have the customary *Manus Dei* (hand of God) crowning her from above. This aspect had invited suspicion about the authenticity of all Ariadne's solidi, but the inclusion of one in a Scandanavian find has remedied such doubts. Though the authors of the Dumbarton Oaks catalog place her coins during the first sole reign of Zeno (474–475), the authors of RIC argue this is unlikely based on the style of the Victory and the absence of the *Manus Dei*, which was still present on the solidi of Aelia Zenonis. Instead, Ariadne's solidi more likely belong to the second sole reign of Zeno (477–491), with some possibly being struck by her second husband, Anastasius I (491–518). The explanation for the latter may be found in their being two distinct groups of her solidi and tremisses, one with a heavy bust, the other with a slight bust.

BASILISCUS A.D. 475–476

A.D. 475: SOLE REIGN
A.D. 475: AUGUSTUS
(WITH MARCUS, AS CAESAR)
A.D. 475–476: SENIOR AUGUSTUS
(WITH MARCUS)

Ruling in the West:
JULIUS NEPOS (474–475/480) AND *Romulus Augustus* (475–476)

BROTHER OF AELIA VERINA
HUSBAND OF AELIA ZENONIS
FATHER OF MARCUS
BROTHER-IN-LAW OF LEO I
UNCLE OF AELIA ARIADNE AND LEONTIA (*w.* OF PATRICIUS)

Basiliscus, d. A.D. 477. Although the succession of Zeno through his son, Leo II, was legitimate, the new emperor was unpopular. Furthermore, his mother-in-law, Aelia Verina (who had arranged his succession), wanted to be rid of him. The unpopularity of Zeno made a revolt imminent, and it was engineered by his mother-in-law, Aelia Verina, who tricked Zeno into fleeing Constantinople on January 9, 475.

Though her scheme worked perfectly, her follow-up plan failed. The senate was not supportive of her lover, Patricius (not the same Patricius as was Caesar from 470–471), and her brother, Basiliscus, seized the throne. Basiliscus and Patricius soon quarreled, and the latter was executed. Considering his sister had perhaps single-handedly created Basiliscus' career, and then supported him in the aftermath of his monumental loss of the Roman armada in 468, his selfish actions would appear unjustified.

This whole turn of events deeply angered Verina, who turned her fury against her brother. This was the last thing Basiliscus needed, for he was scarcely more popular than the emperor he had replaced. Adding to his woes was a terribly destructive fire in Constantinople that, among many other buildings, destroyed important repositories for manuscripts and ancient Greek sculptures. He managed to alienate the religious establishment by coming out in support of the Monophysites, who were very much out of favor in their belief that Christ had only a single nature. And, as if all this weren't enough, through some foolish decisions Basiliscus alienated his two leading generals, the Ostrogothic Master of Soldiers Theoderic Stabo, and the Isaurian Illus.

Amid all this, Aelia Verina began to lobby for Zeno's return, and as a result was forced into hiding to avoid the wrath of her brother. In due course Basiliscus associated his wife and son with his regime. His wife,

Aelia Zenonis, was presumably hailed Augusta upon his takeover in January, 475. His son, Marcus, was given the rank Caesar late in the summer of 475, and apparently within weeks was raised to the rank of co-Augustus (from late summer 475 to August 476). Having alienated his leading generals, his sister, the religious hierarchy (who, when the tide turned against him, he tried to lure back by making a retraction to his earlier comments), Basiliscus was without allies.

Zeno gained the allegiance of both Illus and Armatus and marched into Constantinople unopposed late in August 476. Thus ended Basiliscus' 20-month usurpation. As a consequence, Basiliscus, his son, Marcus, and the rest of his family were exiled to Cappadocia, where they were cruelly starved to death in the following year. When their surrender had been negotiated, Zeno had promised not to "shed their blood," and so he determined that through a bloodless death by starvation he could both keep his promise and kill them.

Numismatic Note: Basiliscus' coins were struck at mints under his control in the East, as well as at Italian mints during the usurpation of Romulus Augustus. His issues fall into three categories: his sole reign (January to late summer 475), his reign with Marcus as Caesar (late summer[?] 475), and his reign with Marcus as co-Augustus (late summer 475 to August 476). Issues of the latter two are cataloged under the listings for Marcus.

AELIA ZENONIS

Augusta, A.D. 475–476

Wife of Basiliscus
Sister-in-law of Leo I and Aelia Verina
Mother of Marcus

(Aelia) Zenonis, d. A.D. 477. Aelia Zenonis was the unfortunate bride of Basiliscus — a man who knew nothing but dishonor in the later years of his life. She apparently was hailed Augusta in January, 475 during the first days of her husband's revolt against Zeno.

The story of Zenonis is an interesting one, for during the revolt we are told that she fell in love with her husband's nephew, Armatus. Their suffering, as one contemporary historian reports, "was finally cured by the medicine of copulation." Wishing only success for her handsome young lover, Zenonis persuaded her husband to appoint him to the high offices of consul and Master of Soldiers of Thrace, which infuriated the other Master of Soldiers, the Ostrogoth Theoderic Strabo ("squint-eye").

By all contemporary accounts, Armatus was a megalomaniac who paraded in the streets on horseback, claimed to be descended from the Greek hero Achilles, and had earned the derogatory name Pyrrhus ("pink cheeks") from the populace. When Basiliscus sent Armatus to hunt down Zeno (who was in exile in Isauria), the latter's generous promises caused Armatus to switch his allegiance. Upon regaining his throne, Zeno initially kept his promises to Armatus, but soon realized his mistake and had him executed. As for Armatus' adulterous lover, Aelia Zenonis, she had already been exiled to Cappadocia where she starved to death with her husband and sons.

NUMISMATIC NOTE: All of Aelia Zenonis' coins — seemingly limited to gold solidi and copper nummi — are of great rarity, and were struck by her husband, Basiliscus.

MARCUS A.D. 475–476

A.D. 475: CAESAR (UNDER BASILISCUS)
A.D. 475–476: JUNIOR AUGUSTUS (WITH BASILISCUS)

Ruling in the West:
JULIUS NEPOS (474–475/480) AND *Romulus Augustus* (475–476)

SON OF BASILISCUS AND AELIA ZENONIS
NEPHEW OF LEO I AND AELIA VERINA
COUSIN OF AELIA ARIADNE AND LEONTIA (*w.* OF PATRICIUS)

Marcus, d. A.D. 477. Of Marcus we know very little. He was the eldest son of the usurper Basiliscus, and he had two younger brothers, whose names are not recorded, and who are sometimes mistakenly associated with the coinage that is properly attributed to Leo Caesar, who served under the emperor Zeno.

His father's revolt began opportunistically, for the original rebellion had been staged by his sister, Aelia Verina. But once this had occurred, Basiliscus seized the opportunity to become emperor, even though it was at the expense of his sister's desire to place her own candidate on the throne. Not only did Basiliscus have the exiled emperor Zeno as an enemy, but he also could count his enraged sister as a foe. Further still, Basiliscus was unpopular among the religious leadership, the people and the army. It seems a miracle his regime ever got off the ground.

One of his first steps was to hail his wife, Aelia Zenonis, as Augusta. Late in the summer of that same year, 475, Basiliscus raised his son, Marcus, to the rank of Caesar. This arrangement seems to have lasted for only a few weeks before the young man was raised to Augustus. Within days of

Basiliscus taking this step, Julius Nepos had taken flight in the West. Marcus held the rank of Augustus with his father into the next year, until they were deposed by Zeno late in August, 476. Along with the rest of his family, Marcus was exiled to Cappadocia, where he was starved to death in the following year.

Numismatic Note: Just as with the succeeding issues of Zeno and Leo Caesar, it was a highly unusual practice that joint-issue coins were struck. Typically, coins devoted to the Augustus and to the Caesar were struck separately. Coins were struck for Marcus both while he was Caesar in 475 and while he was Augustus from the late summer of 475 until August, 476. In the former case, the coins are solidi with C at the end of the obverse inscription (which draw a parallel, perhaps, to the solidi attributed in this volume to Patricius), and in the latter, the inscription ends with AVG. All gold for Marcus was struck at Constantinople, though the Æ4's that bear his combined monogram with Basiliscus were struck at three mints at the very least .

LEO CAESAR

Caesar, a.d. 476–477 (under Zeno)

Adopted Caesar of Zeno
Son of Armatus (*nephew* of the usurper Basiliscus)

Leo (*formerly* Basiliscus), d. a.d. 477(?). The fugitive emperor Zeno made many promises while raising the support necessary to regain his throne. Among these were two he made to gain the allegiance of Armatus, the Master of Soldiers and the nephew of the usurper Basiliscus. The first was that Armatus himself would be appointed to a high office, and the second was that his son (then named Basiliscus) would be raised to the rank of Caesar.

When the usurper Basiliscus was overthrown in August of 476, Zeno re-established himself as emperor in Constantinople. Zeno honored his promises to Armatus and his son, but soon realized his error and sometime in 477 executed his fair-weather friend, and deposed his son, the *Nobilissimus Caesar* ("most noble Caesar"). The execution, however, occurred several months after Armatus' son had been hailed Caesar. Since the child's original name, Basiliscus, was the same as the recently deposed usurper, it was necessary to change it. Thus, the child's name was changed to Leo, and it appears in that form on the rare coins attributed to his brief political career. There is no literary evidence to suggest the boy, Basiliscus, changed his name to Leo, but in this case the numismatic record seems to offer what the written histories do not.

NUMISMATIC NOTE: Just as with the virtually contemporary issues of Basiliscus and Marcus, it was uncommon that joint-issue coins were struck. In this and many other references, this particular Leo is given the added name *Nobilissimus Caesar* to readily distinguish him from the two previous emperors of that name.

These issues have long been controversial, and though several options for their attribution exist, only two have merit. The first is that Zeno and Leo are the two younger sons of the usurper Basiliscus (whose names, regrettably, are not preserved in the ancient sources). Though plausible, the evidence against this theory far outweighs any argument for it. The second option (first postulated in 1822 by the French numismatist Baron Marchant) is convincingly argued by the authors of the Dumbarton Oaks catalog, and is thus adopted here.

Of great interest to this series, and to the theory itself, is the identification of a die of Basiliscus and Marcus that mint workers re-cut with the inscription of Zeno and Leo Caesar. If Basiliscus had been producing coins for his two youngest sons, it seems unlikely that he would have re-cut one of his own functional dies rather than create a fresh one. Conversely, it is probable that Zeno would have re-cut and recycled dies of Basiliscus upon his return.

There are other compelling argument as well. Firstly, if both Zeno and Leo were Caesars, it would be unprecedented for the era that there would be no mention of Basiliscus on the coinage, for he was the reigning Augustus. Secondly, there is ample literary evidence of Basiliscus' son Marcus' being hailed Caesar, yet there is no mention of his two younger brothers holding that title. Finally, and most potently, the D N and the CAES in the obverse inscriptions refer to a single Augustus and a single Caesar, not to two Caesars.

Bibliography

This bibliography principally contains works on Roman history and coinage, though certain important references from related fields are included. When a reference is more readily located by its name or abbreviation than by the name of its author, it is listed in that manner.

The following list is far from comprehensive, and the reader should consult Dennis Kroh's *Ancient Coin Reference Reviews* (Florida, 1993) for evaluations of major works, and Elvira Clain-Stefanelli's *Numismatic Bibliography* (Munich, 1985) for a comprehensive listing of numismatic works published up through 1985.

Alföldi, Andreas. *A Festival of Isis in Rome Under the Christian Emperors of the IVth Century* (Budapest and Leipzig, 1937).

—. *Die constantinische Goldprägung. Untersuchung zu ihrer Bedeutung für Kaiserpolitik und Hofkunst* (Mainz, 1963).

—, and Elisabeth Alföldi and Curtis Clay. *Die Kontorniat Medallions* (2 vols., Berlin, 1976).

Amandry, Michel. *Le Monnayage des Duovirs Corinthiens* (Paris, 1988).

(Arras) *Le Tresor de Beaurains, dit d'Arras*, by Pierre Bastien and Catherine Metzger (Wetteren, 1977).

(Ashmolean) *Coins of the Roman Empire in the Ashmolean Museum*, by Colin M. Kraay and C.H.V. Sutherland (vol. 1, 1975).

(von Aulock) *Sylloge Nummorum Graecorum: The Collection Hans von Aulock* (18 vols., Berlin, 1957-86; 4-vol. reprint, 1987 with a separate index volume).

von Bahrfeldt, M. *Die romische Goldmünzprägung wahrend der Republik und unter Augustus* (Halle, 1923).

Baldus, H.R. *Uranius Antoninus, Münzprägung und Geschichte* (Bonn, 1971).

Banti, A. and L. Simonetti. *Corpus Nummorum Romanorum* (18 vols., Florence, 1972+).

Bastien, Pierre. *Le monnayage de bronze de Postume* (Wetteren, 1967).

—. *Le monnayage de l'atelier de Lyon, de la réouverture de l'atelier par Aurélien à la mort de Carin (fin 274-285)* (Wetteren, 1976).

—. *Le monnayage de l'atelier de Lyon, Dioclétien et ses corégents avant la réforme monétaire, 285-294* (Wetteren, 1972).

—. *Le monnayage de l'atelier de Lyon, De la réforme de Dioclétien à la fermeture temporaire de l'atelier en 316 (294-316)* (Wetteren, 1980).

—. *Le Monnayage de Magnence (350-353)* (2nd ed., Wetteren, 1983).
(Becker) *Becker the Counterfeiter*, by George F. Hill (two parts, London, 1924-5; reprints).
Bellinger, A. *The Syrian Tetradrachms of Caracalla and Macrinus* (New York, 1940).
Berk, Harlan. *Roman Gold Coins of the Medieval World, 383-1453 A.D.* (Chicago, 1986).
(BMC) *Catalogue of the Greek Coins in the British Museum*, various authors. (29 vols, London, 1873-1927).
(BMCRE) *Coins of the Roman Empire in the British Museum* by Harold Mattingly, et. al. (6 vols., London, 1923-1975).
(BMCRR) *Coins of the Roman Republic in the British Museum*, by H.A. Grueber (3 vols., London, 1910).
Brauer Jr., George C. *The Decadent Emperors: Power and Depravity in Third-Century Rome* (New York, 1995, reprint of 1967 original entitled *The Young Emperors: Rome, A.D. 193-244*).
Broughton, T.R.S. *The Magistrates of the Roman Republic* (2 vols., New York, 1951-2; supplement, New York, 1960).
Brown, Peter. *The World of late Antiquity, A.D. 150-750* (London, 1971).
Brunn, Patrick. *Studies in Constantinian Chronology* (ANS NNM 146, New York, 1961).
Burnett, Andrew. *Coinage in the Roman World* (London, 1987).
Burns, Thomas S. *Barbarians Within the Gates of Rome: A Study of Roman Military Policy and the Barbarians, ca. 375-425 A.D.* (Indiana, 1994).
Butcher, Kevin. *Roman Provincial Coins: An Introduction to the Greek Imperials* (London, 1988).
Buttrey Jr., Theodore V. *The Triumviral Portrait Gold of the Quattuorviri Monetales of 42 B.C.* (ANS NNM 137, New York, 1956).
Caesar, Julius. *The Battle for Gaul.* Anne and Peter Wiseman, trans. (Boston, 1980).
Carradice, Ian. *Coinage and Finances in the Reign of Domitian, A.D. 81-96* (Oxford, 1978).
Carson, R.A.G. *Principal Coins of the Romans* (3 vols., London, 1978-81).
—. *Coins of the Roman Empire* (London, 1989).
Christiansen, E. *Coins of Alexandria and the Nomes* (London, 1991).
Clarke, M.L. *The Noblest Roman: Marcus Brutus and His Reputation* (London, 1981).
Cohen, H. *Description historique des monnaies frappées sous l'empire roman* (8 vols., 2nd ed., Paris, 1880-1892).
(Copehagen) *Sylloge Nummorum Graecorum: The Danish National Museum, Copenhagen* (43 vols., 1942+; 8-vol. reprint, 1982+).
Cornell, T. and J. Matthews. *Atlas of the Roman World* (New York, 1982).

Crawford, Michael H. *Coinage and Money Under the Roman Republic: Italy and the Mediterranean Economy* (Berkley and Los Angeles, 1985).
—. *Roman Republican Coinage* (2 vols., Cambridge, 1974).
(Cunetio) *The Cunetio Treasure, Roman Coinage of the Third Century A.D.*, by Ed Besley and Roger Bland (London, 1983).
Curtis, Col. J. *The Tetradrachms of Roman Egypt* (Chicago, 1957).
Dattari, G. *Numi Augg. Alexandrini* (Cairo, 1901).
Depeyrot, Georges. *Les Monnaies d'Or de Diocletien A Constantin I (284-337)* (Wetteren, 1995).
(Dumbarton Oaks) *Catalog of Late Roman Coins in the Dumbarton Oaks Collection and in the Whittemore Collection*, by Philip Grierson and Melinda Mays (Washington D.C., 1992).
Foss, Clive. *Roman Historical Coins* (London, 1990).
Frolova, N.A. *The Coinage of the Kingdom of the Bosporus* (Oxford, 1979).
(Geneva) "The Geneva Forgeries," by R.A.G. Carson (1958 *Numismatic Chronicle*, pp. 47-58).
Geissen, A. *Katalog Alexandrinischer Kaisermünzen, Köln* (5 vols, Cologne, 1974-83).
(Getty) *Ancient Portraits in the J. Paul Getty Museum, Volume I* (Malibu, 1987).
Giacosa, G. *Women of the Caesars. Their Lives and Portraits on Coins* (Milan, 1977).
Gibbon, Edward. *The Decline and Fall of the Roman Empire* (originally published beginning in 1776; numerous reprints).
Gnecchi, F. *I medaglioni romani* (3 vols., Milan, 1912).
Göbl, R. *Die Münzprägung des kaisers Aurelianus* (Vienna, 1993).
—. *Regalianus und Dryantilla. Dokumentation, Münzen, Texte, Epigraphisches* (Vienna, 1970).
Gordon, C.D. *The Age of Attila* (New York, 1993, reprint of 1960).
Grant, Michael. *Aspects of the Principate Tiberius* (ANS NNM 116, New York, 1950).
—. *Art in the Roman Empire* (London and New York, 1995).
—. *From Imperium to Auctoritas, a Historical Study of the AES Coinage in the Roman Empire, 49 B.C.-A.D. 14* (Cambridge, 1946).
—. *History of Rome* (New York, 1978).
—. *Roman Anniversary Issues: An exploratory study of the numismatic and medallic commemoration of anniversary years 49 B.C.-A.D. 375* (Cambridge, 1950).
—. *Roman Imperial Money* (London, Edinburgh and New York, 1954).
—. *The Antonines: The Roman Empire in Transition* (New York and London, 1994).
—. *The Army of the Caesars* (New York, 1974).

—. *The Emperor Constantine* (London, 1993).
—. *The Fall of the Roman Empire* (Revised ed., New York, 1990).
—. *The Roman Emperors* (New York, 1985).
—. *The Six Main AES Coinages of Augustus* (Edinburgh, 1953).
Green, Peter. *Alexander to Actium: The Historical Evolution of the Hellenistic Age* (Berkeley and Los Angeles, 1990).
Hahn, W. *Moneta Imperii Romani/Byzantini: Die Ostprägung des Romischen Reiches im 5 Jahrhundert* (Vienna, 1989).
Harl, Kenneth W. *Coinage in the Roman Economy, 300 B.C. to A.D. 700* (Baltimore and London, 1996).
—. *Civic Coins and Civic Politics in the Roman East, A.D. 180-275* (Berkley and Los Angeles, 1987).
Harlan, Michael. *Roman Republican Moneyers and Their Coinage, 63 B.C.-49 B.C.* (London, 1995).
Head, Barclay V. *Historia Numorum* (2nd ed., London, 1911).
Hendin, David. *Guide to Biblical Coins* (3rd ed., New York, 1996).
Hewitt, K.V. "The Coinage of L. Clodius Macer (A.D. 68)" (1983 *Numismatic Chronicle*, pp. 64-80).
Hill, Philip V. *The Coinage of Septimius Severus and his Family of the Mint of Rome, A.D. 193-217* (London, 1977).
—. *The Dating and Arrangement of the Undated Coins of Rome, A.D. 98-148* (London, 1970).
—. *The Monuments of Ancient Rome as Coin Types* (London, 1989).
Howgego, C.J. *Greek Imperial Countermarks* (London, 1985).
(Hunter) *Roman Imperial Coins in the Hunter Coin Cabinet. University of Glasgow* (5 vols., by Anne Robertson, Oxford, 1962-82).
Imhoof-Blumer, F. and P. Gardner. *Ancient Coins Illustrating Lost Masterpieces of Greek Art* (reprint: Chicago, 1964).
Kadman, Leo. *The Coins of Akko Ptolemais* (Schocken, 1961).
—. *The Coins of Caesarea Maritima* (Jerusalem, 1957).
—. *The Coins of the Jewish War, 66-73 A.D.* (Jerusalem, 1960).
von Kaenel, Hans-Markus. *Münzprägung und Münzbildnis des Claudius* (Berlin, 1986).
Kent, J.P.C., M. Hirmer and A. Hirmer. *Roman Coins* (London, 1978).
Kindler, A. *The Coinage of Bostra* (Warminster, 1983).
Klawans, Zander H. *Imitations and Inventions of Roman Coins: Renaissance Medals of Julius Caesar and the Roman Empire* (Santa Monica, 1977).
—. *Reading and Dating Roman Imperial Coins* (1959, Racine, WI).
Kraay, C. M. *The Aes Coinage of Galba* (ANS NNM 133, New York, 1956).
Kraft, Konrad. *Das system der Kaiserzeitliche münzprägung in Kleinasien, materialien und Entwürfe* (Berlin, 1972).

Lacam, G. *La Fin de L'Empire Romain et Le Monnayage or en Italie, 455-493* (2 vols., Lucerne, 1983).

(Levante) *Sylloge Nummorum Graecorum Switzerland I: Levante-Cilicia* (with Supplement I), by Eduardo Levante (Berne, 1986; supplement, 1993).

Lindgren, H.C. *Ancient Greek Bronze Coins: European Mints* (California, 1989).

— and Frank Kovacs. *Ancient Bronze Coins of Asia Minor and the Levant from the Lindgren Collection* (California, 1985).

(LRBC) Late *Roman Bronze Coinage, A.D. 324-498* by R.A.G. Carson, Philip Hill and J.P.C. Kent (reprint: London, 1965).

MacDowall, David W. *The Western Coinages of Nero* (ANS NNM 161, New York, 1979).

Martin, Peter-Hugo. *Die anonymen Münzen des Jahres 68 nach Christus* (Mainz, 1974).

Mattingly, Harold. *Roman Coins From the Earliest Times to the Fall of the Western Empire* (London, 1928).

Mazzini, G. *Monete imperiale romane* (5 vols., Milan, 1957-8).

(MEC) *Medieval European Coinage, Volume I, The Early Middle Ages (5th-10th centuries)*, by Philip Grierson and Mark Blackburn (Cambridge, 1986).

Melville-Jones, John. *A Dictionary of Ancient Roman Coins* (London, 1990).

Meshorer, Ya'akov. *Ancient Jewish Coinage* (2 vols., New York, 1982).

—. *The Coinage of Aelia Capitolina* (Jerusalem, 1989).

Metcalf, William E. *The Cistophori of Hadrian* (ANS NS 15, New York, 1980).

—. *The Silver Coinage of Cappadocia, Vespasian-Commodus* (ANS NNM 166, New York, 1996).

Mildenberg, Leo. *The Coinage of the Bar Kokhba War* (Salzburg, 1984).

Millar, Fergus. *The Roman Near East, 31 B.C.-A.D. 337*(Cambridge and London, 1993).

Milne, J.G. *Catalogue of Alexandrian Coins* (London, 1971; reprint of 1933 with supplement).

Mionnet, Théodore-Edme. *Description des médailles antiques, greques et romaines* (7 vols., 9 supp. vols., 1806-37; 16-vol. Graz reprint 1972-3).

Oxford Classical Dictionary, The. Hornblower, S. and Spawforth, A., eds. (3rd ed., Oxford, 1996).

Oost, Stewart Irvin. *Galla Placidia Augusta: A Biographical Essay* (Chicago, 1968).

Paulys Real. *Encyclopädie der classischen Altertumswissenschaft* (multi-volume, Stuttgart, 1894 onward)

Penn, R.G. *Medicine on Ancient Greek and Roman Coins* (London, 1994).
Price, Martin J. and Bluma Trell. *Coins and Their Cities* (London, 1977).
(RIC) *The Roman Imperial Coinage*, various authors. (10 vols., 1923-1994, with reprints).
Richter, G.M.A. *The Portraits of the Greeks* (Ithica, 1984).
Ridgeway, W. *The Origin of Metallic Currency and Weight Standards* (New York, 1976; reprint of 1892).
Rosenberger, M. *The Rosenberger Israel Collection* (4 vols., Jerusalem, 1972-4).
(RPC) *Roman Provincial Coinage, Volume I* (with Supplement I), by Andrew Burnett, Michel Amandry and Pere Pau Ripollès. (London and Paris, 1992; reprinted 1998 with a supplement).
(RSC) *Roman Silver Coins*, various authors. (5 vols., 1952-1987 with reprints).
Sayles, Wayne G. *Ancient Coin Collecting*, (vols. 1,3 and 4, Iola, WI, 1996).
Scarre, Chris. *Chronicle of the Roman Emperors* (New York, 1995).
Schiel, N. *The Episode of Carausius and Allectus: the literary and numismatic evidence* (Oxford, 1977).
Sear, David R. *Greek Imperial Coins and Their Values: The Local Coinages of the Roman Empire* (London, 1982).
—. *The History and Coinage of the Roman Imperators, 49-27 B.C.* (London, 1998).
—. *Roman Coins and Their Values* (4th revised ed., London, 1988).
Seyffert, Oskar. *The Dictionary of Classical Mythology, Religion, Literature and Art* (New York, 1995, reprint of 1891 original entitled *The Dictionary of Classical Antiquities*).
Spaulding, O.L. and H. Nickerson. *Ancient and Medieval Warfare* (New York, 1993; originally entitled *Warfare*).
Spijkerman, A. *The Coins of the Decapolis and Provincia Arabia* (Jerusalem, 1978).
Stevenson, Seth W. *A Dictionary of Roman Coins: Republican and Imperial* (London, 1964; reprint of 1889 original).
Stoneman, Richard. *Palmyra and Its Empire: Zenobia's Revolt Against Rome* (Ann Arbor, 1994).
Stumpf, Gerd R. *Numismatische studien zur chronologie der Römischen statthalter in Kleinasien* (122v. Chr.-163 n.Chr.) (Saarbrücken, 1991).
Sutherland, C. H. V. *Coinage in Roman Imperial Policy, 31 B.C.-A.D. 68* (London, 1951).
—. *Roman Coins* (London and New York, 1974).
—. *Roman History and Coinage 44 B.C.-A.D. 69, Fifty Points of Relation from Julius Caesar to Vespasian* (Oxford, 1987).
— and N. Olçay and K.E. Merrington. *The Cistophori of Augustus* (London, 1970).

Sydenham, E. A. *The Coinage of Caesarea in Cappadocia* (New York, 1978; reprint of 1933 with supp.).
—. *The Coinage of the Roman Republic* (London, 1952).
—. *Historical references on coins of the Roman Empire from Augustus to Gallienus* (London, 1917).
Syme, R. *The Roman Revolution* (Oxford, 1939).
Szaivert, W. *Die Münzprägung der Kaiser Marcus Aurelius, Lucius Verus und Commodus* (Vienna, 1986).
Tonybee, Jocelyn M. C. *Roman Historical Portraits* (London, 1978).
—. *Roman Medallions* (ANS NS no. 5, New York, 1944).
(Traité) *Traité des monnaies grecques et romaines*, by Ernst Babelon. (9 vols., Paris, 1901-32).
Troxell, Hyla A. *The Coinage of the Lycian League* (ANS NNM 162, New York, 1982).
Ulrich-Bansa, Oscar, Jr. *Moneta Mediolanensis (352-498)* (Venice, 1949).
Voegtli, Hans. *Bilder der Heldenpenen in der Kaiserzeitlichen Griechischen münzprägung* (Basel, 1977).
Walker, D.R. *Metrology of the Roman Silver Coinage* (3 parts, Oxford, 1976-8).
Who Was Who in the Roman World. Bowder, Diana, ed. (Ithica, NY, 1980).
Wruck, W. *Die Syrische Provinzialprägung von Augustus bis Traian* (Stuttgart, 1931).

Other Sources:

Among the most important sources are *festschrifts*, which are collections of essays, usually in honor of a scholar. Examples include: *Scripta Nummaria Romana: Essays Presented to Humphrey Sutherland* (London, 1978), *Essays in Roman Coinage Presented to Harold Mattingly* (Oxford, 1956), *Studies in Greek Numismatics in Memory of Martin Jessop Price* (London, 1998).

Equally useful are journals, of which a great many exist, ranging from those intended mainly for the collector (such as the monthly magazine *The Celator*) to those containing scholarly articles (such as the *Numismatic Chronicle*, the *Swiss Numismatic Review*, the *American Numismatic Society Museum Notes* (continued as the *American Journal of Numismatics*), and others which offer both (such as the *Journal of the Society of Ancient Numismatics*).

Index of People and Sections (in alphabetical order)

(Volume I and Volume II)

Index of People and Sections (in order of presentation)